Essentials of Sociology
A DOWN-TO-EARTH APPROACH

seventh edition

James M. Henslin
Southern Illinois University, Edwardsville

PEARSON

Boston   New York   San Francisco

Mexico City   Montreal   Toronto   London   Madrid   Munich   Paris

Hong Kong   Singapore   Tokyo   Cape Town   Sydney

Senior Series Editor: Jeff Lasser
Development Editor: Jennifer Albanese
Associate Editor: Deb Hanlon
Series Editorial Assistant: Erikka Adams
Senior Marketing Manager: Kelly M. May
Composition Buyer: Linda Cox
Manufacturing Buyer: Megan Cochran
Electronic Composition and Editorial Production Service: Nesbitt Graphics, Inc. and Dusty Friedman
Interior Design: Carol Somberg
Foldout: Designed and produced by DK Education, a division of Dorling Kindersley Limited, London, England.
Photo Researcher: Kate Cook Cebik (interior), Laurie Frankenthaler (chapter openers)
Cover Administrator: Linda Knowles

For related titles and support materials, visit our online catalog at www.ablongman.com.

Between the time website information is gathered and then published, it is not unusual for some sites to have closed. Also, the transcription of URLs can result in typographical errors. The publisher would appreciate notification where these errors occur so that they may be corrected in subsequent editions.

Cataloging-in-Publication Data not available at time of publication.
ISBN 0-205-50440-X

Printed in the United States of America
10 9 8 7 6 5 4 3 2 1   VHP   10 09 08 07

Chapter Opener Art Credits

Chapter 1: *Rainy Day Crowd* by Diana Ong, 1999. Computer graphics. © Diana Ong/SuperStock.

Chapter 2: *Night Stories* by R. C. Gorman, 1994. Lithograph, 26 × 34". © R. C. Gorman/Navajo Gallery.

Chapter 3: *Orgullo de Familia (Family Pride)* by Simon Silva, 1997. Gouache. From *Gathering the Sun* by Alma Flor Alda, illustrated by Simon Silva. Illustrations copyright © 1997 by Simon Silva, www.simonsilva. com. Used with permission of the illustrator and BookStop Literary Agency, LLC. All rights reserved.

Chapter 4: *Street Scene (Boy with Kite)* by Jacob Lawrence, 1962. Egg tempera on hardboard, 23 7/8 × 30". Conservation Center of the Institute of Fine Arts, New York University, NY, USA. Photo © The Jacob and Gwendolyn Lawrence Foundation/Art Resource, NY. © 2006 The Jacob and Gwendolyn Lawrence Foundation, Seattle/Artists Rights Society (ARS), New York.

Chapter 5: *Human Pyramid of Businesspeople* by David Tillinghast, 1998. Acrylic. © David Tillinghast/Images.com.

Chapter 6: *Prisoners Exercising (After Gustave Dore's Print)* by Vincent van Gogh, 1890. Oil on canvas, 80 × 64 cm. Pushkin Museum of Fine Arts, Moscow. © Alinari Archives/CORBIS.

Chapter 7: *Farmers Work in Rice Paddies in Taiwan* by Franklin McMahon. © Franklin McMahon/CORBIS.

Chapter 8: *New Jersey* by Jacob Lawrence, 1946. Photo © Smithsonian American Art Museum, Washington, DC/Art Resource, NY. © 2006 The Jacob and Gwendolyn Lawrence Foundation, Seattle/Artists Rights Society (ARS), New York.

Chapter 9: *Filipina: A Racial Identity Crisis* by Pacita Abad, 1990. Acrylic, handwoven cloth, dyed yarn, beads, gold thread on stitched and padded canvas, 250 × 160 cm. © Pacita Abad Art.

Chapter 10: *Women in Burkah* by Pacita Abad, 1979. Oil on canvas, 125 × 88 cm. © Pacita Abad Art.

Chapter 11: *We The People* by Fred Otnes, 1978. Mixed media, collage, 24 × 20". © Fred Otnes/Images.com.

Chapter 12: *Circle of Love* by Michael Escoffery, 1996. Mixed media. Private Collection. Photo © Michael Escoffery/Art Resource, NY. © 2006 Michael Escoffery/Artists Rights Society (ARS), New York.

Chapter 13: *Students/Literacy* by Pascale Carrivaul. © Pascale Carrivaul/ Images.com.

Chapter 14: *Feast of San Gennaro* by Sharon Florin, 1998. Oil on canvas, 30 × 36". © 1998 Sharon Florin. Courtesy of the artist and Paintings DIRECT, Inc. (www.PaintingsDIRECT.com)

Chapter 15: *People With Globe and Computer* by Jose Ortega, 1998. Digital image. © Jose Ortega/Images.com.

Credits continue on PC1, which is a continuation of this copyright page.

To my fellow sociologists, who do such creative research on social life and who communicate the sociological imagination to generations of students.

With my sincere admiration and appreciation,

Jim Henslin

Brief Contents

PART I **The Sociological Perspective**

CHAPTER 1   The Sociological Perspective 2

CHAPTER 2   Culture 34

CHAPTER 3   Socialization 58

CHAPTER 4   Social Structure and Social Interaction 82

PART II **Social Groups and Social Control**

CHAPTER 5   Social Groups and Formal Organizations 112

CHAPTER 6   Deviance and Social Control 138

PART III **Social Inequality**

CHAPTER 7   Global Stratification 166

CHAPTER 8   Social Class in the United States 192

CHAPTER 9   Inequalities of Race and Ethnicity 220

CHAPTER 10   Inequalities of Gender and Age 254

PART IV **Social Institutions**

CHAPTER 11   Politics and the Economy 290

CHAPTER 12   Marriage and Family 322

CHAPTER 13   Education and Religion 352

PART V **Social Change**

CHAPTER 14   Population and Urbanization 382

CHAPTER 15   Social Change: Technology, Social Movements, and the Environment . . 414

Contents

To the Student from the Author   xxviii
To the Instructor from the Author   xxx

PART I   The Sociological Perspective

---

1 The Sociological Perspective   2

The Sociological Perspective   4
  Seeing the Broader Social Context   4

Origins of Sociology   5
  Tradition Versus Science   5
  Auguste Comte and Positivism   6
  Herbert Spencer and Social Darwinism   6
  Karl Marx and Class Conflict   7
  Emile Durkheim and Social Integration   7
  Max Weber and the Protestant Ethic   8

Sexism in Early Sociology   9
  Attitudes of the Time   9
  Harriet Martineau and Early Social Research   9

Sociology in North America   9
  Early History: The Tension Between Social Reform
    and Sociological Analysis   9
  Jane Addams and Social Reform   9
  ■ *Down-to-Earth Sociology:* Early North American
    Sociology: Du Bois and Race Relations   10
  W. E. B. Du Bois and Race Relations   10
  Talcott Parsons and C. Wright Mills: Theory Versus
    Reform   12
  The Continuing Tension and the Rise of Applied
    Sociology   12
  ■ *Down-to-Earth Sociology:* Careers in Sociology:
    What Applied Sociologists Do   13
  ■ *Down-to-Earth Sociology:* Capturing Saddam
    Hussein: A Surprising Example of Applied
    Sociology   14

Theoretical Perspectives in Sociology   14
  Symbolic Interactionism   14
  Functional Analysis   16
  Conflict Theory   18
  Levels of Analysis: Macro and Micro   18
  Putting the Theoretical Perspectives Together   19
  How Theory and Research Work Together   19

Doing Sociological Research   20
  A Research Model   20
  ■ *Down-to-Earth Sociology:* Enjoying a
    Sociology Quiz—Sociological Findings
    Versus Common Sense   21

Research Methods   22
  Surveys   24
  ■ *Down-to-Earth Sociology:* Loading the Dice: How
    Not to Do Research   26
  Participant Observation (Fieldwork)   26
  Secondary Analysis   28
  Documents   28
  Experiments   28
  Unobtrusive Measures   29

Ethics in Sociological Research   29
  Protecting the Subjects: The Brajuha
    Research   29
  Misleading the Subjects: The Humphreys
    Research   29
  Values in Sociological Research   30

Summary and Review   31

2 Culture 34

What Is Culture? 36
- Culture and Taken-for-Granted Orientations to Life 37
- Practicing Cultural Relativism 38
- ■ *Cultural Diversity around the World:* You Are What You Eat? An Exploration in Cultural Relativity 39

Components of Symbolic Culture 39
- Gestures 40
- Language 42
- ■ *Down-to-Earth Sociology:* Emoticons: "Written Gestures" for Expressing Yourself Online 43
- ■ *Cultural Diversity in the United States:* Miami— Language in a Changing City 44
- Language and Perception: The Sapir-Whorf Hypothesis 45
- ■ *Cultural Diversity in the United States:* Race and Language: Searching for Self-Labels 45
- Values, Norms, and Sanctions 46
- Folkways and Mores 46

Many Cultural Worlds 47
- Subcultures 47
- Countercultures 47

Values in U.S. Society 50
- An Overview of U.S. Values 50
- ■ *Mass Media in Social Life:* Why Do Native Americans Like Westerns? 52
- Value Clusters 52
- Value Contradictions and Social Change 52
- Emerging Values 52
- Culture Wars: When Values Clash 53
- Values as Blinders 53
- "Ideal" Versus "Real" Culture 54

Technology in the Global Village 54
- The New Technology 54
- Cultural Lag and Cultural Change 54
- Technology and Cultural Leveling 55

Summary and Review 56

3 Socialization 58

What Is Human Nature? 60
- Feral Children 60
- Isolated Children 60
- Institutionalized Children 60
- ■ *Down-to-Earth Sociology:* Heredity or Environment? The Case of Oskar and Jack, Identical Twins 61
- Deprived Animals 63

Socialization into the Self and Mind 63
- Cooley and the Looking-Glass Self 63
- Mead and Role-Taking 64
- Piaget and the Development of Reasoning 65
- Global Aspects of the Self and Reasoning 66

Learning Personality and Emotions 66
- Freud and the Development of Personality 66
- Socialization into Emotions 67
- ■ *Cultural Diversity around the World:* Do You See What I See?: Eastern and Western Ways of Perceiving and Thinking 68
- Society Within Us: The Self and Emotions as Social Control 69

Socialization into Gender 69
- Gender Messages in the Family 69
- Gender Messages from Peers 70
- Gender Messages in the Mass Media 70

Agents of Socialization 71
- The Family 71
- ■ *Mass Media in Social Life:* From Xena, Warrior Princess, to Lara Croft, Tomb Raider: Changing Images of Women in the Mass Media 72
- The Neighborhood 73
- Religion 73
- Day Care 73
- The School and Peer Groups 73
- ■ *Cultural Diversity in the United States:* Caught Between Two Worlds 74
- The Workplace 75

Resocialization 75
- Total Institutions 75
- ■ *Down-to-Earth Sociology:* Boot Camp as a Total Institution 76

Socialization Through the Life Course 77
    Childhood (From Birth to About Age 12) 77
    Adolescence (Ages 13–17) 78
    Transitional Adulthood (Ages 18–29) 79
    The Middle Years (Ages 30–65) 79
    The Older Years (About 65 on) 79

Are We Prisoners of Socialization? 80

Summary and Review 80

4 Social Structure and Social Interaction 82

Levels of Sociological Analysis 84
    Macrosociology and Microsociology 84

The Macrosociological Perspective: Social Structure 85
    ■ *Down-to-Earth Sociology:* College Football as Social Structure 86
    Culture 87
    Social Class 87
    Social Status 87
    Roles 88
    Groups 89
    Social Institutions 89
    Societies—and Their Transformations 89
    Biotech Society: Is a New Type of Society Emerging? 93
    ■ *Sociology and the New Technology:* "So, You Want to Be Yourself?" Cloning in the Coming Biotech Society 94
    What Holds Society Together? 95

■ *Cultural Diversity in the United States:* The Amish: *Gemeinschaft* Community in a *Gesellschaft* Society 96

The Microsociological Perspective: Social Interaction in Everyday Life 97
    Stereotypes in Everyday Life 97
    Personal Space 97
    ■ *Down-to-Earth Sociology:* Beauty May Be Only Skin Deep, But Its Effects Go On Forever: Stereotypes in Everyday Life 98
    Dramaturgy: The Presentation of Self in Everyday Life 98
    ■ *Mass Media in Social Life:* You Can't Be Thin Enough: Body Images and the Mass Media 102
    Ethnomethodology: Uncovering Background Assumptions 103
    The Social Construction of Reality 105
    Social Interaction on the Internet 106

The Need for Both Macrosociology and Microsociology 106
    ■ *Sociology and the New Technology:* When Worlds Collide: Virtual Reality and the Real World 107

THROUGH THE AUTHOR'S LENS

When a Tornado Strikes: Social Organization Following a Natural Disaster

When TV news announced that a tornado had ripped apart a town just hours from my own, not only destroying buildings but also taking lives, I wondered how the people were adjusting to their sudden loss. These photos, taken the next day, show a community in the process of rebuilding. (Page 108)

Summary and Review 110

5 **Social Groups and Formal Organizations**   112

Social Groups   114

Primary Groups   115

Secondary Groups   115

In-Groups and Out-Groups   117

Reference Groups   118

Social Networks   119

■ *Down-to-Earth Sociology:* Facebooking: The Lazy (But Efficient) Way to Meet Friends   120

A New Group: Electronic Communities   121

Bureaucracies   121

The Characteristics of Bureaucracies   121

■ *Cultural Diversity in the United States:* How Our Own Social Networks Perpetuate Social Inequality   122

The Perpetuation of Bureaucracies   123

The Rationalization of Society   124

Coping with Bureaucracies   124

■ *Down-to-Earth Sociology:* The McDonaldization of Society   125

Working for the Corporation   126

Stereotypes and the "Hidden" Corporate Culture   126

■ *Thinking Critically:* Managing Diversity in the Workplace   127

U.S. and Japanese Corporations   128

Group Dynamics   129

Effects of Group Size on Stability and Intimacy   129

Effects of Group Size on Attitudes and Behavior   130

Leadership   131

The Power of Peer Pressure: The Asch Experiment   132

The Power of Authority: The Milgram Experiment   133

■ *Thinking Critically:* If Hitler Asked You to Execute a Stranger, Would You? The Milgram Experiment   133

Global Consequences of Group Dynamics: Groupthink   135

Summary and Review   136

6 **Deviance and Social Control**   138

What Is Deviance?   140

■ *Cultural Diversity around the World:* Human Sexuality in Cross-Cultural Perspective   141

How Norms Make Social Life Possible   141

Sanctions   142

■ *Thinking Critically:* Is It Rape, or Is It Marriage? A Study in Culture Clash   142

Competing Explanations of Deviance: Sociobiology, Psychology, and Sociology   143

The Symbolic Interactionist Perspective   144

Differential Association Theory   144

Control Theory   145

Labeling Theory   146

The Functionalist Perspective   148

Can Deviance Really Be Functional for Society?   148

Strain Theory: How Social Values Produce Deviance   148

Illegitimate Opportunity Structures: Social Class and Crime   149

■ *Down-to-Earth Sociology:* Islands in the Street: Urban Gangs in the United States   150

The Conflict Perspective   152

    Class, Crime, and the Criminal Justice
      System   152

    Power and Inequality   152

    The Law as an Instrument of
      Oppression   153

Reactions to Deviance   154

    Street Crime and Prisons   154

   ■ *Thinking Critically:* "Three Strikes and You're
      Out!": Unintended Consequences of Well-
      Intended Laws   155

    The Decline in Crime   156

    Recidivism   156

    The Death Penalty and Bias   157

   ■ *Down-to-Earth Sociology:* The Killer Next Door:
      Serial Murderers in Our Midst   158

    Legal Change   160

   ■ *Thinking Critically: Changing Views: Making Hate a
      Crime*   160

    The Medicalization of Deviance: Mental
      Illness   161

    The Homeless Mentally Ill   162

    The Need for a More Humane
      Approach   163

Summary and Review   163

7 Global Stratification 166

Systems of Social Stratification 168

Slavery 168

■ *Mass Media in Social Life:* What Price Freedom? Slavery Today 170

Caste 171

Class 172

Global Stratification and the Status of Females 172

What Determines Social Class? 173

Karl Marx: The Means of Production 173

Max Weber: Property, Prestige, and Power 174

Why Is Social Stratification Universal? 175

The Functionalist Perspective: Motivating Qualified People 175

The Conflict Perspective: Class Conflict and Scarce Resources 176

Lenski's Synthesis 177

How Do Elites Maintain Stratification? 177

Ideology Versus Force 177

Comparative Social Stratification 178

Social Stratification in Great Britain 179

Social Stratification in the Former Soviet Union 179

Global Stratification: Three Worlds 180

The Most Industrialized Nations 180

The Industrializing Nations 180

■ *Thinking Critically:* Open Season: Children as Prey 181

The Least Industrialized Nations 181

THROUGH THE AUTHOR'S LENS

The Dump People: Working and Living and Playing in the City Dump of Phnom Penh, Cambodia

I could hardly believe my ears when I learned that people were living in the city dump of Phnom Penh, the capital of Cambodia. This photo essay reveals their life far better than words ever could. These men, women, and children are not only scavenging trash, but also they are participating in a community. (Page 184)

How Did the World's Nations Become Stratified?   186
  Colonialism   186
  World System Theory   186
  ■ *Thinking Critically:* When Globalization Comes Home: *Maquiladores* South of the Border   187
  Culture of Poverty   188
  Evaluating the Theories   188

Maintaining Global Stratification   188
  Neocolonialism   188
  Multinational Corporations   189
  Technology and Global Domination   189
  A Concluding Note   190

Summary and Review   190

8 Social Class in the United States   192

What Is Social Class?   194
  Property (Wealth)   194
  Power   197
  Prestige   197
  ■ *Down-to-Earth Sociology:* How the Super-Rich Live   198
  Status Inconsistency   200

Sociological Models of Social Class   200
  ■ *Down-to-Earth Sociology:* The Big Win: Life After the Lottery   201
  Updating Marx   202
  Updating Weber   202
  Social Class in the Automobile Industry   205

Consequences of Social Class   206
  Family Life   206
  Education   206
  Religion   206
  Politics   206
  Physical Health   207
  Mental Health   297

  ■ *Thinking Critically:* Mental Illness and Inequality in Health Care   208

Social Mobility   208
  Three Types of Social Mobility   208
  ■ *Cultural Diversity in the United States:* Social Class and the Upward Mobility of African Americans   209
  Women in Studies of Social Mobility   210
  The New Technology and Fears of the Future   210

Poverty   211
  Drawing the Poverty Line   211
  Who Are the Poor?   212
  ■ *Down-to-Earth Sociology:* Exploring Myths About the Poor   213
  Children of Poverty   214
  ■ *Thinking Critically:* The Nation's Shame: Children in Poverty   215
  The Dynamics of Poverty   215
  Welfare Reform   216
  Why Are People Poor?   216
  Where Is Horatio Alger? The Social Functions of a Myth   217

Summary and Review   217

9 Inequalities of Race and Ethnicity   220

Laying the Sociological Foundation   222

Race: Myth and Reality   222

Ethnic Groups   223

■ *Cultural Diversity in the United States:* Tiger Woods and the Emerging Multiracial Identity: Mapping New Ethnic Terrain   224

Minority and Dominant Groups   226

■ *Down-to-Earth Sociology:* Can a Plane Ride Change Your Race?   225

How People Construct Their Racial-Ethnic Identity   227

Learning Prejudice   227

Individual and Institutional Discrimination   229

Theories of Prejudice   230

Psychological Perspectives   230

Sociological Perspectives   231

Global Patterns of Intergroup Relations   232

Genocide   232

Population Transfer   233

Internal Colonialism   233

Segregation   234

Assimilation   234

Multiculturalism (Pluralism)   234

Race and Ethnic Relations in the United States   234

■ *Cultural Diversity in the United States and around the World:* "You Can Work for Us, But You Can't Live Near Us"   235

European Americans   235

Latinos   237

■ *Down-to-Earth Sociology:* Unpacking the Invisible Knapsack: Exploring Cultural Privilege   238

African Americans   240

■ *Thinking Critically:* Reparations for Slavery: Justice or Foolishness?   244

■ *Down-to-Earth Sociology:* Stealth Racism in the Rental Market: What You Reveal by Your Voice   245

Asian Americans   246

Native Americans   247

Looking Toward the Future   249

The Immigration Debate   249

■ *Cultural Diversity in the United States:* Glimpsing the Future: The Shifting U.S. Racial–Ethnic Mix   250

Affirmative Action   251

Toward a True Multicultural Society   251

Summary and Review   252

10 Inequalities of Gender and Age   254

Inequalities of Gender   256

Issues of Sex and Gender   256

Gender Differences in Behavior: Biology or Culture?   256

THROUGH THE AUTHOR'S LENS

Work and Gender: Women at Work in India

Like women in the West, women in India are not limited to the home. Their work roles, however, stand in sharp contrast with those of women in the West. This photo essay illustrates some of the amazing differences I saw. (Page 258)

Opening the Door to Biology   260

How Females Became a Minority Group   261

    The Origins of Patriarchy   262

■ *Cultural Diversity around the World:* "Psst. You Wanna Buy a Bride?" China in Transition   262

Gender Inequality in the United States   264

    Fighting Back: The Rise of Feminism   264

    Gender Inequality in Education   264

■ *Down-to-Earth Sociology:* The Gender Gap in Math and Science: A National Debate   266

Gender Inequality in Health Care   267

    Gender Inequality in the Workplace   268

■ *Down-to-Earth Sociology:* Cold-Hearted Surgeons and Their Women Victims   268

    Sexual Harassment—And Worse   272

    Gender and Violence   272

■ *Cultural Diversity around the World:* Female Circumcision   274

The Changing Face of Politics   274

    Glimpsing the Future—with Hope   275

Inequalities of Aging   276

Aging in Global Perspective   277

    The Social Construction of Aging   277

    Industrialization and the Graying of the Globe   278

    The Graying of America   278

The Symbolic Interactionist Perspective   281

    Ageism: The Concept   281

    Shifting Meanings of Growing Old   281

    The Influence of the Mass Media   281

■ *Mass Media in Social Life:* Shaping Our Perceptions of the Elderly   282

The Functionalist Perspective   282

    Disengagement Theory   282

    Activity Theory   283

    Continuity Theory   284

The Conflict Perspective   284

    Social Security Legislation   284

    Intergenerational Conflict   284

Looking Toward the Future   287

■ *Thinking Critically:* How Long Do You Want to Live? Approaching Methuselah   287

Summary and Review   288

PART IV Social Institutions

11 Politics and the Economy   290

Politics: Establishing Leadership   292

Power, Authority, and Violence   292

    Authority and Legitimate Violence   292

    Traditional Authority   293

    Rational-Legal Authority   293

    Charismatic Authority   293

    The Transfer of Authority   294

Types of Government   294

    Monarchies: The Rise of the State   295

    Democracies: Citizenship as a Revolutionary Idea   295

    Dictatorships and Oligarchies: The Seizure of Power   296

The U.S. Political System   296

    Political Parties and Elections   296

    Voting Patterns   297

    Lobbyists and Special-Interest Groups   299

Who Rules the United States?   300

    The Functionalist Perspective: Pluralism   300

    The Conflict Perspective: The Power Elite   301

    Which View Is Right?   302

War and Terrorism: Ways of Implementing Political Objectives   302

    War   302

    ■ *Down-to-Earth Sociology:* Prisoner Abuse at Abu Ghraib: A Normal Event   303

    Terrorism   304

    The Economy: Work in the Global Village   304

The Transformation of Economic Systems   305

    Preindustrial Societies: The Birth of Inequality   305

    Industrial Societies: The Birth of the Machine   305

    Postindustrial Societies: The Birth of the Information Age   305

    ■ *Down-to-Earth Sociology:* Is Big Brother Knocking on the Door? Civil Liberties and Homeland Security   306

    ■ *Down-to-Earth Sociology:* Your Author Is a Suspect!   307

    Biotech Societies: The Merger of Biology and Economics   308

    Implications for Your Life   308

    Ominous Trends in the United States   309

THROUGH THE AUTHOR'S LENS

Small Town USA: Struggling to Survive

All across the nation, small towns are struggling to survive. How can small towns contend with cutthroat global competition when workers in some countries are paid a couple of dollars a day? Many small towns are left in a time warp as history shifts around them. This photo essay tells the story. (Page 310)

World Economic Systems   312

Capitalism   312

Socialism   314

Ideologies of Capitalism and Socialism   315

Criticisms of Capitalism and Socialism   315

The Convergence of Capitalism and
   Socialism   315

Capitalism in a Global Economy   316

Corporate Capitalism   316

Multinational Corporations   317

A New World Order?   317

■ *Cultural Diversity around the World:* Doing
   Business in the Global Village   319

Summary and Review   320

12 Marriage and Family   322

**Marriage and Family in Global
Perspective**   324

What Is a Family?   324

Common Cultural Themes   324

**Marriage and Family in Theoretical
Perspective**   326

The Functionalist Perspective: Functions and
   Dysfunctions   326

The Conflict Perspective: Gender and Power   327

■ *Thinking Critically:* The Second Shift—Strains and
   Strategies   328

The Symbolic Interactionist Perspective: Gender
   and Housework   329

The Family Life Cycle   329

Love and Courtship in Global Perspective   329

■ *Cultural Diversity around the World:* East Is East
   and West Is West: Love and Arranged Marriage
   in India   330

Marriage   331

Childbirth and Child Rearing   332

Family Transitions in Later Life   334

Diversity in U.S. Families   334

African American Families   334

Latino Families   335

Asian American Families   336

Native American Families   336

Single-Parent Families   337

Families Without Children   337

Blended Families   338

Gay and Lesbian Families   338

Trends in U.S. Families   339

Postponing Marriage and Childbirth   339

Cohabitation   339

Unmarried Mothers   340

■ *Down-to-Earth Sociology:* "You Want Us to
   Live Together? What Do You Mean By
   That?"   341

Grandparents as Parents   342

The Sandwich Generation and Elder
   Care   342

Divorce and Remarriage   342

Problems in Measuring Divorce   343

Children of Divorce   344

■ *Down-to-Earth Sociology:* "What Are Your Chances
   of Getting Divorced?"   344

Grandchildren of Divorce   345

The Absent Father and Serial Fatherhood   346

The Ex-Spouses   346

Remarriage   346

Two Sides of Family Life   347

The Dark Side of Family Life: Battering, Child
   Abuse, and Incest   347

■ *Down-to-Earth Sociology:* "Why Doesn't She Just
   Leave?" The Dilemma of Abused Women   348

The Bright Side of Family Life: Successful
   Marriages   349

The Future of Marriage and Family   350

Summary and Review   350

13 Education and Religion 352

Education: Transferring Knowledge and Skills 354

Education in Global Perspective 354
Education and Industrialization 354
Education in the Most Industrialized Nations: Japan 354
■ *Down-to-Earth Sociology:* Community Colleges: Challenges Old and New 355
Education in the Industrializing Nations: Russia 356
Education in the Least Industrialized Nations: Egypt 357

The Functionalist Perspective: Providing Social Benefits 358
Teaching Knowledge and Skills 358
Cultural Transmission of Values 358
Social Integration 358
■ *Down-to-Earth Sociology:* Home Schooling: The Search for Quality and Values 359
Gatekeeping 360

The Conflict Perspective: Perpetuating Social Inequality 361
The Hidden Curriculum 361
Tilting the Tests: Discrimination by IQ 361
Stacking the Deck: Unequal Funding 362

The Symbolic Interactionist Perspective: Fulfilling Teacher Expectations 362
The Rist Research 362
How Do Teacher Expectations Work? 363

Problems in U.S. Education—And Their Solutions 363
Problems: Mediocrity and Violence 363
Solutions: Safety and Standards 365

■ *Thinking Critically:* Breaking Through the Barriers: Restructuring the Classroom 365

Religion: Establishing Meaning 366

What Is Religion? 366

The Functionalist Perspective 367
Functions of Religion 367
■ *Down-to-Earth Sociology:* Religion and Health: What We Know and Don't Know 368
Dysfunctions of Religion 369

The Symbolic Interactionist Perspective 369
Religious Symbols 369
■ *Down-to-Earth Sociology:* Terrorism and the Mind of God 370
Rituals and Beliefs 371
Religious Experience 371

The Conflict Perspective 372
Opium of the People 372
A Legitimation of Social Inequalities 372

Religion and the Spirit of Capitalism 372

Types of Religious Groups 373
Cult 373
Sect 374
Church 374
Ecclesia 374
Variations in Patterns 374

Religion in the United States 375
Characteristics of Members 375
Characteristics of Religious Groups 376
Secularization and the Splintering of U.S. Churches 377

The Future of Religion 379

Summary and Review 379

PART V Social Change

14 Population and Urbanization 382

POPULATION IN GLOBAL PERSPECTIVE 384

A Planet with No Space to Enjoy Life? 384

The New Malthusians 384

The Anti-Malthusians 385

Who Is Correct? 386

Why Are People Starving? 387

Population Growth 388

■ *Down-to-Earth Sociology:* How the Tsunami Can Help Us to Understand Population Growth 389

Why the Least Industrialized Nations Have So Many Children 390

Implications of Different Rates of Growth 391

The Three Demographic Variables 392

Problems in Forecasting Population Growth 394

■ *Cultural Diversity around the World:* Killing Little Girls: An Ancient and Thriving Practice 395

URBANIZATION 397

The Development of Cities 397

THROUGH THE AUTHOR'S LENS

A Walk Through El Tiro in Medellin, Colombia

One of the most significant changes in the world is the global rush of poor, rural people to the cities of the Least Industrialized Nations. Some of these settlements are dangerous. I was fortunate to be escorted by an insider through this section of Medellin, Colombia. (Page 398)

The Process of Urbanization 400

U.S. Urban Patterns 401

■ *Down-to-Earth Sociology:* Reclaiming Harlem: "It Feeds My Soul" 403

The Rural Rebound 404

Models of Urban Growth 404

City Life 406

Alienation and Community 406

Who Lives in the City? 407

Urban Sentiment: Finding a Familiar World 408

The Norm of Noninvolvement and the Diffusion of Responsibility 408

Urban Problems and Social Policy 408

Suburbanization 408

■ *Down-to-Earth Sociology:* Urban Fear and the Gated Fortress 409

Disinvestment and Deindustrialization 410

The Potential of Urban Revitalization 411

Summary and Review 412

15 Social Change: Technology, Social Movements, and the Environment 414

How Social Change Transforms Social Life 416

The Four Social Revolutions 416

From *Gemeinschaft* to *Gesellschaft* 416

Capitalism, Modernization, and Industrialization 416

Conflict, Power, and Global Politics 417

Theories and Processes of Social Change 419

Cultural Evolution 419

Natural Cycles 419

Conflict over Power 419

Ogburn's Theory 420

How Technology Changes Society 421

The Cutting Edge of Change: The Computer 422

Cyberspace and Social Inequality 422

Social Movements as a Source of Social Change 422

■ *Down-to-Earth Sociology:* The Coming Star Wars 425

Types of Social Movements 425

Propaganda and the Mass Media 426

The Stages of Social Movements 427

■ *Down-to-Earth Sociology:* "Tricks of the Trade"— Deception and Persuasion in Propaganda 428

■ *Thinking Critically:* Which Side of the Barricades? Prochoice and Prolife as a Social Movement 429

The Growth Machine Versus the Earth 430

Environmental Problems in the Most Industrialized Nations 430

■ *Down-to-Earth Sociology:* Corporations and Big Welfare Bucks: How to Get Paid to Pollute 431

Environmental Problems in the Industrializing and Least Industrialized Nations 432

The Environmental Movement 433

■ *Thinking Critically:* Ecosabotage 433

■ *Cultural Diversity around the World:* The Rain Forests: Lost Tribes, Lost Knowledge 434

Environmental Sociology 435

Summary and Review 436

Epilogue: Why Major in Sociology? 439

Glossary G-1

Suggested Readings SR-1

References R-1

Name Index NI-1

Subject Index SI-1

Boxed Features

Down-to-Earth Sociology

How the Super-Rich Live

IT'S GOOD TO SEE how other people live. It gives us a different perspective on life. Let's take a glimpse at the life of John Castle (his real name). After earning a degree in ... at MIT and an ... banking ...

Early North American Sociology: Du Bois and Race Relations, 10

Careers in Sociology: What Applied Sociologists Do, 13

Capturing Saddam Hussein: A Surprising Example of Applied Sociology, 14

Enjoying a Sociology Quiz—Sociological Findings Versus Common Sense, 21

Loading the Dice: How *Not* to Do Research, 26

Emoticons: "Written Gestures" for Expressing Yourself Online, 43

Heredity or Environment? The Case of Oskar and Jack, Identical Twins, 61

Boot Camp as a Total Institution, 76

College Football as Social Structure, 86

Beauty May Be Only Skin Deep, but Its Effects Go On Forever: Stereotypes in Everyday Life, 98

Facebooking: The Lazy (But Efficient) Way to Meet Friends, 120

The McDonaldization of Society, 125

Islands in the Street: Urban Gangs in the United States, 150

The Killer Next Door: Serial Murderers in Our Midst, 158

How the Super-Rich Live, 198

The Big Win: Life After the Lottery, 201

Exploring Myths About the Poor, 213

Can a Plane Ride Change Your Race?, 225

Unpacking the Invisible Knapsack: Exploring Cultural Privilege, 238

Stealth Racism in the Rental Market: What You Reveal by Your Voice, 245

The Gender Gap in Math and Science: A National Debate, 266

Cold-Hearted Surgeons and Their Women Victims, 268

Prisoner Abuse at Abu Ghraib: A Normal Event, 303

Is Big Brother Knocking on the Door? Civil Liberties and Homeland Security, 306

Your Author Is a Suspect!, 307

"You Want Us to Live Together? What Do You Mean By That?", 341

"What Are Your Chances of Getting Divorced?", 344

"Why Doesn't She Just Leave?" The Dilemma of Abused Women, 348

Community Colleges: Challenges Old and New, 355

Home Schooling: The Search for Quality and Values, 359

Religion and Health: What We Know and Don't Know, 368

Terrorism and the Mind of God, 370

How the Tsunami Can Help Us to Understand Population Growth, 389

Reclaiming Harlem: "It Feeds My Soul", 403

Urban Fear and the Gated Fortress, 409

The Coming Star Wars, 425

"Tricks of the Trade"—Deception and Persuasion in Propaganda, 428

Corporations and Big Welfare Bucks: How to Get Paid to Pollute, 431

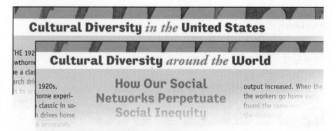

Cultural Diversity *in the* United States

Cultural Diversity *around the* World

How Our Social Networks Perpetuate Social Inequity

You Are What You Eat? An Exploration in Cultural Relativity, 39

Miami—Language in a Changing City, 44

Race and Language: Searching for Self Labels, 45

Do You See What I See?: Eastern and Western Ways of Perceiving and Thinking, 68

Caught Between Two Worlds, 74

The Amish: *Gemeinschaft* Community in a *Gesellschaft* Society, 96

How Our Own Social Networks Perpetuate Social Inequality, 122

Human Sexuality in Cross-Cultural Perspective, 141

Social Class and the Upward Mobility of African Americans, 209

Tiger Woods and the Emerging Multiracial Identity: Mapping New Ethnic Terrain, 224

"You Can Work for Us, But You Can't Live Near Us", 235

Glimpsing the Future: The Shifting U.S. Racial–Ethnic Mix, 250

"Pssst. You Wanna Buy a Bride?" China in Transition, 262

Female Circumcision, 274

Doing Business in the Global Village, 319

East Is East and West Is West . . . Love and Arranged Marriage in India, 330

Killing Little Girls: An Ancient and Thriving Practice, 395

The Rain Forests: Lost Tribes, Lost Knowledge, 434

mass Media in social life

Why Do Native Americans Like Westerns?, 51

From Xena, Warrior Princess, to Lara Croft, Tomb Raider: Changing Images of Women in the Mass Media, 72

You Can't Be Thin Enough: Body Images and the Mass Media, 102

What Price Freedom? Slavery Today, 170

Shaping Our Perceptions of the Elderly, 282

> SOCIOLOGY *and the* NEW TECHNOLOGY

freshments, output again went up.

How Our Social Network

"So, You Want to Be Yourself?" Cloning in the Coming Biotech Society, 94

When Worlds Collide: Virtual Reality and the Real World, 107

Thinking Critically

Managing Diversity in the Workplace, 127

If Hitler Asked You to Execute a Stranger, Would You? The Milgram Experiment, 133

Is It Rape, or Is It Marriage? A Study in Culture Clash, 142

"Three Strikes and You're Out!": Unintended Consequences of Well-Intended Laws, 155

Changing Views: Making Hate a Crime, 160

Open Season: Children as Prey, 181

When Globalization Comes Home: *Maquiladores* South of the Border, 187

Mental Illness and Inequality in Health Care, 208

The Nation's Shame: Children in Poverty, 215

Reparations for Slavery: Justice or Foolishness?, 244

How Long Do You Want to Live? Approaching Methuselah, 287

The Second Shift—Strains and Strategies, 328

Breaking Through the Barriers: Restructuring the Classroom, 365

Which Side of the Barricades? Prochoice and Prolife as a Social Movement, 429

Ecosabotage, 445

Special Fold-Out Section

Racial Categories in the U.S. Census

This colorful fold-out, which looks at United States Census forms over a span of more than two hundred years, illustrates one of the fundamental sociological truths about race—that races are arbitrary social constructions, not fixed biological categories, and that racial classifications change over time and from one society to another.

Guide *to* Social Maps

Social Maps illustrate the old Chinese saying, "A picture is worth ten thousand words." They allow you to see at a glance how social characteristics are distributed among the fifty United States or among the nations of the world. The U.S. Social Maps are a concise way of illustrating how our states compare on such factors as divorce, voting, poverty, or women in the work force. On a global level, these Social Maps show how the world's nations rank on such characteristics as income, the percentage of elderly, and the number of large cities.

These Social Maps are unique to this text. I have produced them for you from original data. At a glance, you can see how your state compares with your region and the other states—or you can see how the United States compares with other countries. I hope that you find these Social Maps informative. If you have any suggestions for other Social Maps that you would like to see in the next edition, please share them with me.

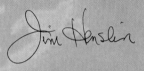

FIGURE 6.1   Some States Are Safer: Violent Crime in the United States 151

FIGURE 6.4   Executions in the United States 157

FIGURE 7.2   Global Stratification: Income of the World's Nations 182

FIGURE 8.6   Patterns of Poverty 212

FIGURE 9.5   The Distribution of Dominant and Minority Groups 237

FIGURE 10.4 Women in the Work Force 269

FIGURE 10.8 The Graying of the Globe 279

FIGURE 10.12 As Florida Goes, So Goes the Nation . . . 280

FIGURE 11.1 Which Political Party Dominates 297

FIGURE 11.6 The Globalization of Capitalism: U.S. Ownership in Other Countries 317

FIGURE 11.7 The Globalization of Capitalism: Foreign Ownership of U.S. Business . . . 318

FIGURE 12.10 The "Where" of U.S. Divorce 343

FIGURE 14.10 How Many Millions of People Live in the World's Largest Megacities? 413

FIGURE 14.11 How Urban Is Your State? The Rural-Urban Makeup of the United States 414

FIGURE 15.3 How Does Your State Rank? The Location of the Worst Hazardous Waste Sites 443

To the Student from the Author

WELCOME TO SOCIOLOGY! I've loved sociology since I was in my teens, and I hope you enjoy it, too. Sociology is fascinating because it holds the key to so much understanding of social life.

If you like to watch people and try to figure out why they do what they do, you will like sociology. Sociology pries open the doors of society so you can see what goes on behind them. *Essentials of Sociology: A Down-to-Earth Approach* stresses how profoundly our society and the groups to which we belong influence us. Social class, for example, sets us on a path in life. For some, that path leads to better health, more education, and higher income, but for others, it leads to poverty, dropping out of school, and even a higher risk of illness and disease. These paths blazed by social class are so significant that they affect our chances of reaching our first birthday, and even the likelihood of our getting in trouble with the police. They even influence how our marriage will work out, the number of children we will have—and whether we will read this book in the first place.

When I took my first course in sociology, I was hooked. Seeing how marvelously my life had been affected by these larger social influences opened my eyes to a new world, one that has been fascinating to explore. I hope that this will be your experience also.

From how people become homeless to how they become presidents, from why people commit suicide to why women are discriminated against in every society around the world—sociology spans all of these questions. This breadth of discovery, in fact, is what makes sociology so intriguing. We can place the sociological lens on broad features of society, such as social class, gender, and race-ethnicity, and then immediately turn our focus on some smaller corner of life. If we look at two people interacting—whether quarreling or kissing—we can see how these broad features of society are being played out in their lives.

We aren't born with instincts. Nor do we come into this world with preconceived notions of what life should be like. At birth, we have no ideas of race-ethnicity, gender, age, or social class. We have no idea, for example, that people "ought" to act in certain ways just because they are male or female. Yet we all learn such things as we grow up, as we come under the influence of family, friends, and the institutions of our society. Uncovering the "hows" and the "whys" of this process is also part of what makes sociology so fascinating.

One of sociology's many pleasures is that as we study life in groups (which can be taken as a definition of sociology), whether those groups are in some far-off part of the world or in some nearby corner of our own society, we constantly gain insights into ourselves. Observing how *their* customs affect *them* makes more visible the influences of our own society on ourselves.

This book, then, can be part of an intellectual adventure: It can lead you to a new way of looking at your social world—and, in the process, help you to better understand both society and yourself.

No matter what your major—whether it be nursing, teaching, physics, engineering, or whatever—sociology provides valuable insight into social relationships. Some people use these principles to help them get along with others. Some even use them to get raises and promotions at work. An individual I know began to apply sociological principles of how groups operate with such success that he moved from being an instructor at a college to the president of my own university. From there, he became the chancellor of a large university system. He told me that applying sociology was the basis of his success.

I wish you the very best in college—and in your career afterward. It is my sincere hope that *Essentials of Sociology: A Down-to-Earth Approach* will contribute to that success.

Jim Henslin

James M. Henslin, Professor Emeritus
Department of Sociology
Southern Illinois University, Edwardsville

P.S. I enjoy communicating with students, so feel free to comment on your experiences with this text. Because I travel a lot, it is best to reach me by e-mail: henslin@aol.com

To the Instructor from the Author

REMEMBER WHEN YOU FIRST GOT "HOOKED" on sociology, how the windows of perception opened as you began to see life in society through the sociological perspective? For most of us, this was an eye-opening experience. This text is designed to open those windows onto social life, so students can see clearly the vital effects of group membership on their lives. Although few students will develop what Peter Berger calls "the passion of sociology," at least we can provide them the opportunity.

To study sociology is to embark on a fascinating process of discovery. We can compare sociology to a huge jigsaw puzzle: Only gradually do we see how the intricate pieces fit together.

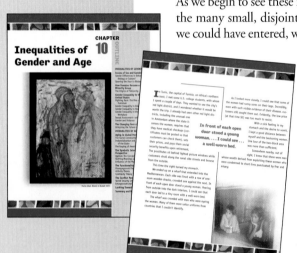

As we begin to see these interconnections, our perspective changes as we shift our eyes from the many small, disjointed pieces to the whole that is being formed. Of all the endeavors we could have entered, we chose sociology because of the ways in which it joins together the "pieces" of society and the challenges that it poses to "ordinary" thinking. It is our privilege to share with students this process of awareness and discovery called the sociological perspective.

As instructors of sociology, we have set ambitious goals for ourselves: to teach both social structure and social interaction and to introduce students to the sociological literature—both the classic theorists and contemporary research. And we would like to accomplish this in ways that enliven the classroom, encourage critical thinking, and stimulate our students' sociological imagination. Although formidable, these goals are attainable. This book, based on many years of frontline (classroom) experience, is designed to help you reach these goals. Its subtitle, *A Down-to-Earth Approach,* is not used lightly. My goal is to share the fascination of sociology with students and thereby make your teaching more rewarding.

Over the years, I have found the introductory course especially enjoyable. It is singularly satisfying to see students' faces light up as they begin to see how separate pieces of their world fit together. It is a pleasure to watch them gain insight into how their social experiences give shape to even their innermost desires. This is precisely what this text is designed to do: to stimulate your students' sociological imagination so that they can better perceive how the pieces of society fit together and begin to understand what this means for their own lives.

Filled with examples from around the world as well as from our own society, this text helps make today's multicultural, global society come alive for students. From learning how the international elite carves up global markets to studying the intimacy of friendship and marriage, students can see how sociology is the key to explaining contemporary life—and their own place in it.

In short, this text is designed to make your teaching easier. There simply is no justification for students to have to wade through cumbersome approaches to sociology. I am firmly convinced that the introduction to sociology should be enjoyable and that the introductory textbook can be an essential tool in sharing the discovery of sociology with students.

The Organization of this Text

 This text is laid out in five parts. Part I focuses on the sociological perspective, which is introduced in the first chapter. We then look at how culture influences us (Chapter 2), examine socialization (Chapter 3), and compare macrosociology and microsociology (Chapter 4).

Part II, which focuses on social groups and social control, adds to the students' understanding of how far-reaching society's influence is—how group membership penetrates even their thinking, attitudes, and orientations to life. We first examine the different types of groups that have such profound influences on us and then look at the fascinating area of group dynamics (Chapter 5). After this, we focus on how groups "keep us in line" and sanction those who violate their norms (Chapter 6).

In Part III, we turn our focus to social inequality. We examine how social inequality pervades society and how it has an impact on our own lives. Because social stratification is so significant, I have written two chapters on this topic. The first (Chapter 7), with its global focus, presents an overview of the principles of stratification. The second (Chapter 8), with its emphasis on social class, focuses on stratification in U.S. society. After establishing this broader context of social stratification, we examine inequalities of race and ethnicity (Chapter 9) and then those of gender and age (Chapter 10).

Part IV helps students become more aware of how social institutions encompass their lives. We first look at politics and the economy, our overarching social institutions (Chapter 11). We then turn our focus to the family (Chapter 12), education, and religion (Chapter 13). One of the emphases in this part of the book is how our social institutions are changing and how their changes, in turn, influence our orientations and decisions.

With its focus on broad social change, Part V provides an appropriate conclusion for the book. Here we examine why our world is changing so rapidly, as well as catch a glimpse of what is yet to come. We first analyze trends in population and urbanization, those sweeping forces that affect our lives so significantly but that ordinarily remain below our level of awareness (Chapter 14). We conclude the book with an analysis of technology, social movements, and the environment (Chapter 15), which takes us to the cutting edge of the vital changes that engulf us all.

Themes and Features

Six central themes run throughout this text: down-to-earth sociology, globalization, cultural diversity, critical thinking, the new technology, and the growing influence of the mass media on our lives. For each of these themes, I have written a series of boxes. These boxed features are one of my favorite components of the book. They are especially valuable in the way they introduce the controversial topics that make sociology such a lively activity.

Let's look at these six themes.

Down-to-Earth Sociology

As many years of teaching have shown me, all too often textbooks are written to appeal to the adopters of texts rather than to the students who must learn from them. Therefore, a central concern in writing this book has been to present sociology in a way that not only facilitates understanding but also shares its excitement. During the course of writing other texts, I often have been told that my explanations and writing style are "down-to-earth," or accessible and inviting to students—so much so that I chose this phrase as the book's subtitle. The term is also featured in my introductory reader, *Down-to-Earth Sociology: Introductory Readings,* 14th edition (New York: The Free Press, 2007).

This first theme is highlighted by a series of boxed features that explore sociological processes that underlie everyday life. The topics that we review in these ***Down-to-Earth Sociology*** boxes are highly diverse. In them, we analyze how sociology was used to capture Saddam Hussein (Chapter 1), the relationship between heredity and environment (Chapter 3), how football can help us understand social structure (Chapter 4), facebooking (Chapter 5), serial killers (Chapter 6), what life is like after hitting it big in the lottery (Chapter 8), the taken-for-granted privileges attached to being white (Chapter 9), the gender gap in math and science (Chapter 10), greedy surgeons and their women victims (Chapter 10), prisoner abuse at Abu Ghraib (Chapter 11), civil liberties and Big Brother's homeland security (Chapter 11), our chances of getting divorced (Chapter 12), why so many abused women don't leave their abusers (Chapter 12), religion and health (Chapter 13), terrorism in the name of God (Chapter 13), how the tsunami can help us to understand world population growth (Chapter 14), the gentrification of Harlem (Chapter 14), the coming Star Wars (Chapter 15), and corporate welfare (Chapter 15).

This first theme is actually a hallmark of the text, as my goal is to make sociology "down to earth." To help students grasp the fascination of sociology, I continuously stress sociology's relevance to their lives. To reinforce this theme, I avoid unnecessary jargon and use concise explanations and clear and simple (but not reductive) language. I often use student-relevant examples to illustrate key concepts, and I have based several of the chapters' opening vignettes on my own experiences in exploring social life. That this goal of sharing sociology's fascination is being reached is evident from the many comments I receive from instructors and students alike that the text helps make sociology "come alive."

Globalization

The second theme, *globalization,* explores the impact of global issues on our lives and on the lives of people around the world. As the new global economy increasingly intertwines the fates of nations, it vitally affects our own chances in life. The globalization of capitalism influences the kinds of skills and knowledge we need, the types of work available to us, the costs of the goods and services we consume, and even whether our country is at war or in a time of peace. In addition to the strong emphasis on global issues that runs throughout this text, I have written a separate chapter on global stratification. I have also featured global issues in the chapters on social institutions as well as in the final chapters on social change: technology, population, urbanization, social movements, and the environment.

What occurs in Russia, Japan, and China, as well as in much smaller nations such as Afghanistan and Iraq, has far-reaching consequences on our own lives. Consequently, in addition to the global focus that runs throughout the text, the next theme, cultural diversity, also has a strong global emphasis.

Cultural Diversity in the United States and around the World

The third theme, *cultural diversity,* has two primary emphases. The first is cultural diversity around the world. Gaining an understanding of how social life is "done" in other parts of the world often challenges our taken-for-granted assumptions of social life. At times, learning about other cultures gives us an appreciation for the life of other peoples; at other times, we may be shocked or even disgusted at some aspect of another group's way of life (such as female circumcision) and come away with a renewed appreciation of our own customs.

To highlight this subtheme, I have written a series of boxes called ***Cultural Diversity around the World.*** Among the topics in this subtheme are food customs that shock people from different cultures (Chapter 2), how Easterners and Westerners perceive the world differently (Chapter 3), human sexuality in Mexico and Kenya (Chapter 6), selling brides in China (Chapter 10), female circumcision in Africa

(Chapter 10), love and arranged marriage in India (Chapter 12), infanticide in China (Chapter 14), and the destruction of the rain forests and indigenous peoples of Brazil (Chapter 15).

The second emphasis is **Cultural Diversity in the United States.** In this subtheme, we examine groups that make up the fascinating array of people who comprise the U.S. population. The boxes that I have written with this subtheme review such topics as the controversy over Spanish and English (Chapter 2), the terms that people choose for their own racial-ethnic self-identification (Chapter 2), the resistance of social change by the Amish (Chapter 4), how our own social networks contribute to social inequality (Chapter 5), how Tiger Woods represents a significant change in racial-ethnic identification (Chapter 9), and discrimination against immigrants (Chapter 9).

Looking at cultural diversity—whether it be in the United States or in other regions of the world—often challenges our own orientations to life. Seeing that there are so many ways of "doing" social life highlights the arbitrariness of our own customs—and our taken-for-granted ways of thinking. These contrasts help students to develop their sociological imagination. They are better able to see connections among key sociological concepts such as culture, socialization, norms, race-ethnicity, gender, and social class. As your students' sociological imagination grows, they can attain a new perspective on their own experiences—and a better understanding of the social structure of U.S. society.

Critical Thinking

The fourth theme, *critical thinking,* focuses on controversial social issues and engages students in examining the various sides of those issues. In these sections, titled **Thinking Critically,** I present objective, fair portrayals of positions and do not take a side—although I occasionally play the "devil's advocate" in the questions that close each of the topics. Like the boxed features, these sections can enliven your classroom with a vibrant exchange of ideas. Among the issues addressed are our tendency to conform to evil authority, as uncovered by the Milgram experiments (Chapter 5), bounties paid to kill homeless children in Brazil (Chapter 7), *maquiladoras* on the Mexican-U.S. border (Chapter 7), social class inequality in the treatment of mental and physical illness (Chapter 8), reparations for slavery (Chapter 9), and ecosabotage (Chapter 15).

Because these *Thinking Critically* sections are based on controversial social issues that either affect the student's own life or are something in which students are vitally interested, they stimulate both critical thinking and lively class discussions. These sections also can be used as the basis for in-class debates and as topics for small discussion groups. (Using small discussion groups can enliven a class and be an effective way of presenting sociological ideas. I describe this teaching technique in the Instructor's Manual.)

Sociology and the New Technology

The fifth theme, *sociology and the new technology,* explores an aspect of social life that has come to be central to our lives. We welcome these new technological tools, for they help us to be more efficient at doing our tasks, from making a living to communicating with others—whether those people are nearby or on the other side of the globe. The significance of the new technology goes far beyond the tools and the ease and efficiency they bring to our tasks, however. The new technology is better envisioned as a social revolution that will leave few aspects of our lives untouched. It even penetrates our being, shapes our thinking, and leads to changed ways of viewing life.

This theme is introduced in Chapter 2, where technology is defined and presented as a major aspect of culture. The impact of technology is then discussed throughout the text. Examples include how technology is related to cultural change (Chapter 2), the implications of technology for maintaining global stratification (Chapter 7), how the consequences of technology differ by social class (Chapter 8),

and how technology led to social inequality in early human history and how it now may lead to world peace—and to Big Brother (Chapter 11). The final chapter (Chapter 15), "Social Change: Technology, Social Movements, and the Environment," concludes the book with a focus on this theme.

To highlight this theme, I have written a series of boxes titled **Sociology and the New Technology.** In these boxes, we explore how technology is changing society and affecting our lives. We examine, for example, the implications of cloning for our coming society (Chapter 4) and the seductiveness of virtual reality (Chapter 4).

The Mass Media and Social Life

In the sixth theme, we stress how the *mass media* affect our behavior and permeate our thinking. We consider how they penetrate our consciousness to such a degree that they even influence how we perceive our own bodies. As your students consider this theme, they may begin to see the mass media in a different light, which should further stimulate their sociological imagination.

To make this theme more prominent for students, I have written a series of boxed features called **Mass Media in Social Life.** Among these are an analysis of why Native Americans like Western novels and movies even though Indians are usually portrayed as losers (Chapter 2), the influence of computer games on images of gender (Chapter 3), the worship of thinness—and how this affects our own body images (Chapter 4), slavery in today's world (Chapter 7), and how the mass media shape our perceptions of the elderly (Chapter 10).

New Topics

Because sociology is about social life and we live in a changing global society, the topics of an introductory text must reflect the national and global changes that engulf us, as well as new sociological research. Among the many new topics in this edition are the new research technique, computer-assisted self-interviewing (Chapter 3); a study of orphanages in India that updates the classic *U.S. study of the effects of interaction on babies* (Chapter 3); an experiment on monkeys' masculine/feminine toy preferences (Chapter 3); the portrayal of women on televised sports (Chapter 3); facebooking (Chapter 5); torture by U.S. agents as an example of groupthink (Chapter 5); my research with a serial killer (Chapter 6); China and India entering the race for global domination (Chapter 7); data on U.S. income inequality by quintiles taken back to 1935 (Chapter 8); and social class and upward social mobility of African Americans (Chapter 8).

New, too, are the educational attainment of Latinos by country of origin (Chapter 9); doctorates awarded by race-ethnicity (Chapter 9); the civilians ("Minutemen") who have begun to patrol the U.S.-Mexico border (Chapter 9); the gender-height gap in pay (Chapter 10); the national debate on the gender gap in math and science (Chapter 10); the struggle of U.S. small towns to survive (Chapter 11); applying statistics to understand one's chances of getting divorced (Chapter 12); research that shows that both mothers and fathers are spending *more* time with their children than did parents in the 1970s and 1980s (Chapter 12); the first sociological study on the effects of divorce on grandchildren (Chapter 12); real-life experience of a sociologist who was a battered wife (Chapter 12); religion and health (Chapter 13); a comparison of education in the United States and China (Chapter 13); the *micropolis,* the latest government classification of urban areas (Chapter 14); and the coming Star Wars (Chapter 15).

Most of the tables and figures in this text are computed from original data and are available nowhere else. As I update them, I sometimes add new categories, such as the race-ethnicity of doctorates and the educational attainment of Latinos by country of origin to Table 9.3, and the data on U.S. income inequality by quintiles taken back to 1935 in Figure 8.3.

As is discussed in the next section, some of the most interesting—and even fascinating—new topics are presented in a visual form.

New and Expanded Features

Through the Author's Lens   Using this format, students are able to look over my shoulder as I experience other cultures or explore aspects of this one. These photo essays should expand your students' sociological imagination and open their minds to other ways of doing social life, as well as stimulate thought-provoking class discussion.

This edition has a new photo essay:

Small Town USA: Struggling to Survive   To take the photos for this essay, I went off the beaten path. On a road trip from California to Florida, instead of following the interstates, I followed those "little black lines" on the map. They took me to out-of-the-way places that the national transportation system has bypassed. Many of these little towns are putting on a valiant face as they struggle to survive, but, as the photos show, the struggle is apparent, and, in some cases, so are the scars (Chapter 11).

The last edition presented five photo essays in the series *Through the Author's Lens.* I have retained them in this edition.

When a Tornado Strikes: Social Organization Following a Natural Disaster   When a tornado hit a small town just hours from where I live, I drove there to see the aftermath of the disaster. The police let me in to view the neighborhood where the tornado had struck, destroying homes and killing several people. I was impressed by how quickly people were putting their lives back together, the topic of this photo essay (Chapter 4).

The Dump People of Phnom Penh, Cambodia   Among the culture shocks I experienced in Cambodia was not to discover that people scavenge at Phnom Penh's huge city dump—this I knew about—but that they also live there. With the aid of an interpreter, I was able to interview these people, as well as photograph them as they went about their everyday lives. An entire community lives in the city dump, complete with restaurants amidst the huge piles of garbage. This photo essay reveals not just these people's activities but also their social organization (Chapter 7).

Work and Gender: Women at Work in India   As I traveled in India, I took photos of women at work in public places. The more I traveled in this country and the more photos I took, the more insight I gained into gender relations. Despite the general submissiveness of women to men in India, women's worlds are far from limited to family and home. Women are found at work throughout the society. What is even more remarkable is how vastly different "women's work" is in India than it is in the United States. This, too, is an intellectually provocative photo essay (Chapter 10).

A Walk through El Tiro in Medellin, Colombia: One of the most significant social changes in the world is taking place in the Least Industrialized Nations. There, in the search for a better life, people are abandoning rural areas. Fleeing poverty, they are flocking to the cities, only to find even more poverty. Some of these settlements of the new urban poor are dangerous. I was fortunate to be escorted by an insider through a section of Medellin, Colombia (Chapter 14).

Photo Essay on Subcultures   To help students better understand subcultures, I have retained the photo essay in Chapter 2. Because this photo essay consists of photos taken by others, it is not a part of the series, *Through the Author's Lens.* The variety of subcultures featured in this photo essay, however, should be instructive to your students.

Photo Collages   Because sociology lends itself so well to photographic illustrations, this text also includes photo collages. In Chapter 2 (page 40), students can catch a glimpse of the fascinating variety that goes into the cultural relativity of beauty. The collage in Chapter 5 (page 116) illustrates categories, aggregates, and secondary groups, concepts that students sometimes wrestle to distinguish. In Chapter 10 (page 257), students can see how differently gender is portrayed in different cultures.

Other Photos by the Author   Sprinkled throughout this edition are photos that I took during travels to India and Cambodia. These photos illustrate sociological principles and topics better than photos available from commercial sources. As an example, the possibility of photographing and interviewing a feral child was one of the reasons that I went to Cambodia. While in the United States, I was told about a feral child who had been discovered living with monkeys and who had been taken to an orphanage in Cambodia. That particular photo is on page 60. Another of my favorites is on page 140.

Special Pedagogical Features

In addition to chapter summaries and reviews, key terms, and a comprehensive glossary, I have included several special features to aid students in learning sociology. **In Sum** sections help students review important points within the chapter before going on to new materials. I have also developed a series of **Social Maps,** which illustrate how social conditions vary by geography.

Chapter-Opening Vignettes   These accounts feature down-to-earth illustrations of a major aspect of each chapter's content. Some are based on my research with the homeless, the time I spent with them on the streets and slept in their shelters (Chapters 1 and 8). Others recount my travels in Africa (Chapters 2 and 10) and Mexico (Chapter 14). I also share my experiences when I spent a night with street people at Dupont Circle in Washington, D.C. (Chapter 4). For other vignettes, I use current and historical events (Chapters 9, 13, and 15), classic studies in the social sciences (Chapters 3 and 6), and even a scene from a novel (Chapter 11). Students have often told me that they find the vignettes compelling, that they stimulate interest in the chapter.

Thinking Critically About the Chapters   I close each chapter with three critical thinking questions. Each question focuses on a major feature of the chapter, asking students to reflect on and consider some issue. Many of the questions ask the students to apply sociological findings and principles to their own lives.

On Sources   Sociological data are found in an amazingly wide variety of sources, and this text reflects that variety. Cited throughout this text are standard journals such as the *American Journal of Sociology, Social Problems, American Sociological Review,* and *Journal of Marriage and the Family,* as well as more esoteric journals such as the *Bulletin of the History of Medicine, Chronobiology International,* and *Western Journal of Black Studies.* I have also drawn heavily from standard news sources, especially the *New York Times* and the *Wall Street Journal,* as well as more unusual sources such as *El País.* In addition, I cite unpublished papers by sociologists.

Acknowledgments

The gratifying response to earlier editions indicates that my efforts at making sociology down to earth have succeeded. The years that have gone into writing this text are a culmination of the many more years that preceded its writing—from graduate school to that equally demanding endeavor known as classroom teaching. No text, of course, comes solely from its author. Although I am responsible for the final words on the printed page, I have received excellent feedback from instructors who used the first six editions. I am especially grateful to

Reviewers

Sandra L. Albrecht, *The University of Kansas*

David Allen, *Georgia Southern University*

Angelo A. Alonzo, *Ohio State University*

Kenneth Ambrose, *Marshall University*

Alberto Arroyo, *Baldwin-Wallace College*

Karren Baird-Olsen, *Kansas State University*

Linda Barbera-Stein, *The University of Illinois*

Richard J. Biesanz, *Corning Community College*

Charles A. Brawner III, *Heartland Community College*

Shelly Breitenstein, *Western Wisconsin Technical College*

Richard D. Bucher, *Baltimore City Community College*

Richard D. Clark, *John Carroll University*

John K. Cochran, *The University of Oklahoma*

Matthew Crist, *Moberly Area Community College*

Russell L. Curtis, *University of Houston*

William Danaher, *College of Charleston*

John Darling, *University of Pittsburgh–Johnstown*

Ray Darville, *Stephen F. Austin State University*

Nanette J. Davis, *Portland State University*

Tom DeDen, *Foothill College*

Paul Devereux, *University of Nevada*

Lynda Dodgen, *North Harris Community College*

James W. Dorsey, *College of Lake County*

Helen R. Ebaugh, *University of Houston*

Obi N. Ebbe, *State University of New York–Brockport*

Margaret C. Figgins-Hill, *University of Massachusetts–Lowell*

Robin Franck, *Southwestern College*

David O. Friedrichs, *University of Scranton*

Richard A. Garnett, *Marshall University*

George W. Glann, Jr., *Fayetteville Technical Community College*

Norman Goodman, *State University of New York–Stony Brook*

Anne S. Graham, *Salt Lake Community College*

Donald W. Hastings, *The University of Tennessee–Knoxville*

Penelope E. Herideen, *Holyoke Community College*

Michael Hoover, *Missouri Western State College*

Hua-Lun Huang, *University of Louisiana*

Charles E. Hurst, *The College of Wooster*

Dick Jobst, *Pacific Lutheran University*

Mark Kassop, *Bergen Community College*

Alice Abel Kemp, *University of New Orleans*

Dianna Kendall, *Austin Community College*

Gary Kiger, *Utah State University*

Ross Koppel, *University of Pennsylvania*

Jenifer Kunz, *West Texas A&M University*

David Kyle, *University of California–Davis*

Patricia A. Larson, *Cleveland State University*

Abraham Levine, *El Camino Community College*

Mike Lindner, *Gloucester County College*

Fr. Jeremiah Lowney, *Carroll College*

Cecile Lycan, *Spokane Community College*

John J. Malarky, *Wilmington College*

Patricia Masters, *George Mason University*

Bonita Sessing Matcha, *Hudson Valley Community College*

Ron Matson, *Wichita State University*

Armaund L. Mauss, *Washington State University*

Roger McVannan, *Broome Community College*

Evelyn Mercer, *Southwest Baptist University*

Robert Meyer, *Arkansas State University*

Richard B. Miller, *Missouri Southern State College*

Beth Mintz, *University of Vermont–Burlington*

Meryl G. Nason, *University of Texas, Dallas*

Craig J. Nauman, *Madison Area Technical College*

W. Lawrence Neuman, *University of Wisconsin–Whitewater*

Charles Norman, *Indiana State University*

Laura O'Toole, *University of Delaware*

Mike Pate, *Western Oklahoma State College*

William Patterson, *Clemson University*

Phil Piket, *Joliet Junior College*

Annette Prosterman, *Our Lady of the Lake University*

Adrian Rapp, *North Harris Community College*

Donald D. Ricker, *Mott Community College*

Howard Robboy, *Trenton State College*

Terina Roberson, *Central Piedmont Community College*

Alden E. Roberts, *Texas Tech University*

Sybil Rosado, *Benedict College*

Kent Sandstrom, *University of Northern Iowa*

Don Shamblin, *Ohio University*

Walt Shirley, *Sinclair Community College*

Laura Siebuhr, *Centralia College*

Marc Silver, *Hofstra University*

Michael C. Smith, *Milwaukee Area Technical College*

Roberto E. Socas, *Essex County College*

Sherry Sperman, *Kansas State University*

Susan Sprecher, *Illinois State University*

Randolph G. Ston, *Oakland Community College*

Kathleen Tiemann, *University of North Dakota*

Tracy Tolbert, *California State University*

Suzanne Tuthill, *Delaware Technical Community College*

Lisa Waldner, *University of Houston–Downtown*

Larry Weiss, *University of Alaska*

Douglas White, *Henry Ford Community College*

Stephen R. Wilson, *Temple University*

Stuart Wright, *Lamar University*

Meifang Zhang, *Midlands Technical College*

I am also indebted to the fine staff of Allyn and Bacon, with whom it has been a pleasure to work. I want to thank Jeff Lasser, whose editorial direction continues to make an impact on the text; Judy Fiske, for constantly hovering over the many details—and supporting my many suggestions; Dusty Friedman, who always does an outstanding job of overseeing both the routine and the urgent; Jennifer Albanese, who has been so prompt in providing research assistance; Kathy Smith, for copyediting; Kate Cebik, for her tireless efforts in photo research—and such a great attitude to "keep on looking." I also want to thank Karen Hanson, who first saw the merits of this project and gave it strong support, and Hannah Rubenstein, who made vital contributions to earlier editions on which this text is based. It is difficult to heap too much praise on such capable people, whose efforts have coalesced with mine to produce this book. The students are the beneficiaries of our combined efforts, whom we constantly kept in mind as we prepared this edition.

Since this text is based on the contributions of many, I would count it a privilege if *you* would share with me your teaching experiences with this book, including suggestions for improving the text. Both positive and negative comments are welcome. It is in this way that I learn.

I wish you the very best in your teaching. It is my sincere desire that *Essentials of Sociology: A Down-to-Earth Approach* contributes to that success.

Jim Henslin

James M. Henslin, Professor Emeritus
Department of Sociology
Southern Illinois University, Edwardsville

I welcome your correspondence. E-mail is the best way to reach me: henslin@aol.com

A NOTE FROM THE PUBLISHER ON SUPPLEMENTS

 Instructor's Supplements

Instructor's Manual *Lori Ann Fowler, Tarrant County College*

For each chapter in the text, the Instructor's Manual provides At-a-Glance grids that link main concepts to key terms and theorists as well as to other supplements. Each chapter in the Instructor's Manual includes a list of key changes to the new edition, chapter summaries and outlines, learning objectives, key terms and people, classroom activities, discussion topics, recommended films, Web sites, and additional references. The Instructor's Manual also includes a section by James M. Henslin on using small in-class discussion groups. Adopters can request a print copy or download the electronic file by logging in to our Instructor Resource Center.

Test Bank *Anthony W. Zumpetta, West Chester University*

The test bank contains approximately 150 questions per chapter in multiple choice, true/false, short answer, essay, and open-book formats. There is also a set of questions based on the text's figures, tables, and maps. All questions are labeled and scaled according to Bloom's Taxonomy. Adopters can request a print copy or download the electronic file by logging in to our Instructor Resource Center.

Computerized Test Bank

The printed Test Bank is also available through Allyn and Bacon's computerized testing system, TestGen EQ. This fully networkable test generating software is available on a multiplatform CD-ROM for Windows and Macintosh. The user-friendly interface allows you to view, edit, and add questions, transfer questions to tests, and print tests in a variety of fonts. Search and sort features allow you to locate questions quickly and to arrange them in whatever order you prefer. Adopters can request a copy on CD or download the electronic file by logging in to our Instructor Resource Center.

PowerPoint™ Presentation *Dan Cavanaugh*

These PowerPoint slides feature lecture outlines for every chapter and corresponding artwork from the text. PowerPoint software is not required, as a PowerPoint viewer is included. Available on request at no additional cost to adopters. Available online from our Instructor Resource Center, and also on the Instructor's Resource CD-ROM.

Instructor's Resource CD with PowerPoint Presentation

This CD contains electronic versions of all of our Instructor Supplements in two formats: as PDF files, and word processing files (which can be edited). Includes the Instructor's Manual, Test Bank, Study Guide, Study Guide Plus, and Telecourse Faculty Guide. The CD also includes the PowerPoint Presentation for this edition, and all the tables, graphs, and figures from the text in an easily accessible electronic format.

The Sociology Digital Media Archive IV

This CD-ROM contains hundreds of graphs, charts, and maps that you can use to build PowerPoint slides to supplement your lectures and illustrate key sociological concepts. If you have full multimedia capability, you can use the DMA's video segments and links to sociology Web sites. Available on request to adopters.

Allyn and Bacon Transparencies for Henslin's Introductory Sociology

This package includes over 100 color acetates featuring illustrations from the Henslin texts. Available on request to adopters.

Allyn and Bacon/ABC News Sociology Videos

If you like to use news footage and documentary-style programs to illustrate sociological themes, this series of videos contain programs from *Nightline, World News Tonight,* and *20/20.* Each video has an accompanying User's Guide (available electronically). Available titles are *Poverty and Stratification, Race and Ethnicity, Gender, Deviance,* and *Aging.* Videocassettes are available on request to adopters.

The Video Professor: Applying Lessons in Sociology to Classic and Modern Films   *Anthony W. Zumpetta, West Chester University*

This manual describes hundreds of commercially available videos that represent nineteen of the most important topics in introductory sociology textbooks. Each topic lists a number of movies, along with specific assignments and suggestions for class use. Adopters can request a print copy or download the electronic file by logging in to our Instructor Resource Center.

Exploring Society Telecourse Faculty Guide

Allyn and Bacon provides special assistance for instructors who use the video series from Dallas TeleLearning, *Exploring Society.* This manual coordinates reading and video assignments, contains the entire content of the Telecourse Study Guide (see Student Supplements), and correlates all test questions in our Test Bank with twenty-two half-hour video programs. Adopters can download the electronic file by logging in to our Instructor Resource Center. For information about the *Exploring Society* Telecourse, contact Dallas TeleLearning directly (1-972–669–6650, http:/telelearning.dcccd.edu).

InterWrite PRS (Personal Response System)

Assess your students' progress with the Personal Response System—an easy-to-use wireless polling system that enables you to pose questions, record results, and display those results instantly in your classroom. Designed by teachers, for teachers, PRS is easy to integrate into your lectures:

- Each student uses a cell-phone-sized transmitter which they bring to class.

- You ask multiple-choice, numerical-answer, or matching questions during class; students simply click their answer into their transmitter.

- A classroom receiver (portable or mounted) connected to your computer tabulates all answers and displays them graphically in class.

- Results can be recorded for grading, attendance, or simply used as a discussion point.

Our partnership with PRS allows us to offer student rebate cards bundled with any Allyn and Bacon/Longman text. The rebate card is a direct value of $20.00 and can be redeemed with the purchase of a new PRS student transmitter. In addition, institutions that order 40 or more new textbook + rebate card bundles will receive the classroom receiver—a $250 value—software and support at no additional cost. Contact your Allyn and Bacon/Longman representative or visit **http://www.ablongman.com/prs** for more information.

Student Supplements

Study Guide Plus *Lori Ann Fowler,*
Tarrant County College

The Study Guide Plus includes successful study strategies, a glossary of words to know, chapter summaries, learning objectives, key terms and people, and student projects. Practice tests with 80 questions per chapter in multiple-choice, true-false, short answer, matching, and essay formats help students prepare for quizzes and exams. An answer key is provided for all questions.

Study Guide *Lori Ann Fowler, Tarrant County College*

The Study Guide includes exercises; key terms and key people, plus lecture outlines that correspond to the PowerPoint presentation for this text. Practice tests with 25 multiple choice questions per chapter help students prepare for quizzes and exams. Packaged on request at no additional cost with this text.

Study Card for Introduction to Sociology

Compact, efficient, and laminated for durability, the Allyn and Bacon Study Card for Introductory Sociology condenses course information down to the basics, helping students quickly master fundamental facts and concepts and prepare for an exam.

Exploring Social Life: Readings to Accompany *Essentials of Sociology: A Down-to-Earth Approach* *James M. Henslin*

This brief reader, revised for the Seventh Edition, contains one reading for each chapter of the text, chosen and introduced by James M. Henslin. The reader can be purchased separately at full price or packaged with this text for an additional $5 net to the bookstore. An Instructor's Manual for the reader is available electronically from our Instructor Resource Center.

Companion Web Site with Online Study Guide for Sociology: A Down-to-Earth Approach (www.ablongman.com/henslin)

This Web site features practice tests for each chapter including multiple-choice, true-false, and essay questions; annotated Web resources; interactive map activities; and *eThemes of the Times for Introductory Sociology,* the full text of thirty articles from the *New York Times* chosen to complement the various topics in this course. For native Spanish speakers, a second version of each practice test is available in Spanish.

VideoWorkshop for Introductory Sociology

VideoWorkshop is a supplement that brings sociological concepts to life with high quality video footage, on an easy-to-use CD-ROM. The VideoWorkshop CD-ROM contains two kinds of video—television news stories, and interviews with prominent sociologists, who discuss some of the important research studies and debates within their fields. Each video segment is paired with a set of observation questions and activities in the accompanying Student Guide. The Student Guide also includes assignments based on viewing popular films that illustrate sociological themes. The VideoWorkshop Student Guide with CD-ROM is packaged free on request with this text. The Instructor Guide with CD-ROM includes the complete contents of the Student Guide, plus an overview of each video segment, as well as teaching suggestions.

Exploring Society Telecourse Study Guide

The Telecourse Study Guide is designed to correlate *Essentials of Sociology* with the twenty-two video programs in the *Exploring Society* series from Dallas TeleLearning. Each section coordinates reading and video assignments and includes summaries, learning objectives, outlines, key terms and people, and student application projects. There is also a self-test section containing multiple-choice, true-false, fill-in-the-blank, matching, and essay questions.

Online Course Management

MySocLab—CourseCompass Version

MySocLab is a state-of-the-art interactive and instructive solution for introductory sociology, delivered within CourseCompass, Allyn and Bacon's course management system (powered by Blackboard and hosted nationally on our server). MySocLab is designed to be used as a supplement to a traditional lecture course, or to completely administer an online course. Customize your course or use the materials as presented. Built around a complete e-book version of the text, MySocLab enables students to explore important sociological concepts, by watching television news stories, listening to interviews with prominent researchers and social scientists, reading current newspaper articles, analyzing data from graphs and maps in the text, and performing other hands-on activities. Customize your course or use the materials as presented. Available at no additional cost to students when the text is packaged with a MySocLab CourseCompass Student Access Code Card.

MySocLab—Website Version

Provides virtually the same online content and interactivity as the CourseCompass MySocLab, without any of the course management features or requirements. Available at no additional cost to students when the text is packaged with a MySocLab Website Student Access Code.

WebCT and Blackboard Test Banks

For colleges and universities with **WebCT**™ and **Blackboard**™ licenses, we have converted the complete Test Bank into these popular course management platforms. Adopters can request a copy on CD or download the electronic file by logging in to our Instructor Resource Center.

Additional Supplements

Research Navigator™ (Access Code Required)

This online research database is available free to students when the text is packaged with a MySocLab Access Code Card, or the *ResearchNavigator.com Guide: Sociology* (see next page). Searchable by keyword, it gives your students access to thousands of full-text articles from scholarly social science journals and popular magazines and newspapers included in the *ContentSelect Research Database,* as well as a one-year archive of *New York Times* articles.

ResearchNavigator.com Guide: Sociology *Joseph E. Jacoby, Bowling Green State University*

This manual includes tips, resources, and URLs to aid students conducting research on Pearson Education's research website, **www.researchnavigator.com**. Each copy contains a student access code for the Research Navigator database, offering students free, unlimited access to a collection of more than 25,000 discipline specific articles from top-tier academic publications and peer-reviewed journals, as well as the *New York Times* and popular news publications. The Guide introduces students to the basics of the Internet and the World

Wide Web, and includes tips for searching for articles on the site, and a list of journals useful for research in their discipline. Also included are hundreds of Web resources for the discipline, as well as information on how to correctly cite research. Packaged on request at no additional cost with this text.

Building Bridges: The Allyn and Bacon Guide to Service Learning *Doris Hamner*

This manual offers practical advice for students who must complete a service-learning project as part of their required course work. Packaged on request at no additional cost with this text.

Careers in Sociology, Third Edition *W. Richard Stephens, Eastern Nazarene College*

This supplement explains how sociology can help students prepare for careers in such fields as law, gerontology, social work, business, and computers. It also examines how students of sociology enter the field. Packaged on request at no additional cost with this text.

College and Society: An Introduction to the Sociological Imagination *Stephen Sweet, Ithaca College*

This supplemental text uses examples from familiar surroundings—the patterns of interaction, social structures, and expectations of conduct on a typical college campus—to help students see the ways in which large society also operates. Available for purchase separately or packaged with this text at a special discount.

About the Author

JIM HENSLIN, who was born near the Canadian border in Minnesota, graduated from high school and junior college in California and from college in Indiana. Awarded scholarships, he earned his Master's and doctorate degrees in sociology at Washington University in St. Louis, Missouri. After this, he was awarded a postdoctoral fellowship from the National Institute of Mental Health, and spent a year studying how people adjust to the suicide of a family member. Jim's specialties in sociology span the micro and the macro—the sociology of everyday life, deviance, and international relations. Among his numerous books is *Down-to-Earth Sociology: Introductory Readings* (Free Press), now in its fourteenth edition. Jim has also published widely in sociology journals, including *Social Problems* and *American Journal of Sociology*.

While still a graduate student, Jim taught at the University of Missouri at St. Louis. After completing his doctorate, he joined the faculty at Southern Illinois University, Edwardsville, where he is Professor Emeritus of Sociology. Jim says, "I've always found the introductory course enjoyable to teach. I love to see students' faces light up when they first glimpse the sociological perspective and begin to see how society has become an essential part of how they view the world."

Jim enjoys reading and fishing. His two favorite activities are writing and traveling. Jim especially enjoys visiting and living in other cultures, for this brings him face to face with behaviors and ways of thinking that he cannot take for granted, experiences that "make sociological principles come alive." He is currently living in Latvia, where, among other activities, he is doing research on the survivors of Russian gulags.

The Sociological Perspective

Diana Ong, *Rainy Day Crowd*, 1999

The Sociological Perspective
Seeing the Broader Social Context

Origins of Sociology
Tradition Versus Science
Auguste Comte and Positivism
Herbert Spencer and Social
    Darwinism
Karl Marx and Class Conflict
Emile Durkheim and Social
    Integration
Max Weber and the Protestant Ethic

Sexism in Early Sociology
Attitudes of the Time
Harriet Martineau and Early Social
    Research

Sociology in North America
Early History: The Tension
    Between Social Reform and
    Sociological Analysis
Jane Addams and Social Reform
W. E. B. Du Bois and Race Relations
Talcott Parsons and C. Wright
    Mills: Theory Versus Reform
The Continuing Tension and the
    Rise of Applied Sociology

**Theoretical Perspectives in
Sociology**
Symbolic Interactionism
Functional Analysis
Conflict Theory
Levels of Analysis: Macro and Micro
Putting the Theoretical
    Perspectives Together
How Theory and Research Work
    Together

Doing Sociological Research
A Research Model

Research Methods
Surveys
Participant Observation
Secondary Analysis
Documents
Experiments
Unobtrusive Measures

Ethics in Sociological Research
Protecting the Subjects
Misleading the Subjects
Values in Sociological Research

Summary and Review

Even from the glow of the faded red-and-white exit sign, its faint light barely illuminating the upper bunk, I could see that the sheet was filthy. Resigned to another night of fitful sleep, I reluctantly crawled into bed.

The next morning, I joined the long line of disheveled men leaning against the chain-link fence. Their faces were as downcast as their clothes were dirty. Not a glimmer of hope among them.

No one spoke as the line slowly inched forward. When my turn came, I was handed a cup of coffee, a white plastic spoon, and a bowl of semiliquid that I couldn't identify. It didn't look like any food I had seen before. Nor did it taste like anything I had ever eaten.

My stomach fought the foul taste, every spoonful a battle. But I was determined. "I will experience what they experience," I kept telling myself. My stomach reluctantly gave in and accepted its morning nourishment.

The room was eerily silent. Hundreds of men were eating, each immersed in his own private hell, his head awash with disappointment, remorse, bitterness.

> **I was determined. "I will experience what they experience," I kept telling myself.**

As I stared at the Styrofoam cup that held my coffee, grateful for at least this small pleasure, I noticed what looked like tooth marks. I shrugged off the thought, telling myself that my long weeks as a sociological observer of the homeless were finally getting to me. "This must be some sort of crease from handling," I concluded.

I joined the silent ranks of men turning in their bowls and cups. When I saw the man behind the counter swishing out Styrofoam cups in a washtub of cloudy water, I began to feel sick to my stomach. I knew then that the jagged marks on my cup really had come from a previous mouth.

How much longer did this research have to last? I felt a deep longing to return to my family—to a welcome world of clean sheets, healthy food, and "normal" conversations.

The Sociological Perspective

Why were these men so silent? Why did they receive such despicable treatment? What was I doing in that homeless shelter? After all, I hold a respectable, professional position, and I have a home and family.

Sociology offers a perspective, a view of the world. The *sociological perspective* (or imagination) opens a window onto unfamiliar worlds and offers a fresh look at familiar worlds. In this text you will find yourself in the midst of Nazis in Germany, warriors in South America, and even the people I visited who live in a city dump in Cambodia. But you also will find yourself looking at your own world in a different light. As you view other worlds—or your own—the sociological perspective will enable you to gain a new vision of social life. In fact, this is what many find appealing about sociology.

The sociological perspective has been a motivating force in my own life. Ever since I took my introductory course in sociology, I have been enchanted by the perspective that sociology offers. I have thoroughly enjoyed both observing other groups and questioning my own assumptions about life. I sincerely hope the same happens to you.

Granted their deprivation, it is not surprising that the homeless are not brimming with optimism. This scene at the Atlanta Union Mission in Atlanta, Georgia, is typical of homeless shelters, reminiscent of the many meals I ate in soup kitchens with men like this.

Seeing the Broader Social Context

The **sociological perspective** stresses the social contexts in which people live. It examines how these contexts influence people's lives. At the center of the sociological perspective is the question of how groups influence people, especially how people are influenced by their **society**—a group of people who share a culture and a territory.

To find out why people do what they do, sociologists look at **social location,** the corners in life that people occupy because of where they are located in a society. Sociologists look at how jobs, income, education, gender, age, and race–ethnicity affect people's ideas and behavior. Consider, for example, how being identified with a group called *females* or with a group called *males* when we are growing up shapes our ideas of who we are and what we should attain in life. Growing up as a male or a female influences not only our goals in life but also how we feel about ourselves and the way we relate to others in dating and marriage and at work.

Sociologist C. Wright Mills (1959) put it this way: "The sociological imagination [or perspective] enables us to grasp the connection between history and biography." By *history*, Mills meant that each society is located in a broad stream of events. Because of this, each society has specific characteristics—such as its ideas about the proper roles of men and women. By *biography*, Mills referred to the individual's specific experiences. In short, people don't do what they do because of inherited internal mechanisms, such as instincts. Rather, *external* influences—our experiences—become part of our thinking and motivations. The society in which we grow up and our particular location in that society lie at the center of what we do and what we think.

Consider a newborn baby. If we were to take the baby away from its U.S. parents and place it with a Yanomamö Indian tribe in the jungles of South America, you know that when the child begins to speak, his or her words will not be in English. You also know that the child will not think like an American. He or she will not grow up wanting credit cards, for example, or designer jeans, a new car, and the latest video game. Equally, the child will unquestioningly take his or her place in Yanomamö society—perhaps as a food gatherer, a hunter, or a warrior—and he or she will not even know about the world left behind at birth. And whether male or female, the child will grow up assuming that it is natural to want many children, not debating whether to have one, two, or three children.

This brings us to *you*—to how *your* social groups have shaped *your* ideas and desires. Over and over in this text, you will see that the way you look at the world is the result of your exposure to human groups. I think you will enjoy the process of self-discovery that sociology offers.

Origins of Sociology

Tradition Versus Science

Just how did sociology begin? In some ways, it is difficult to answer this question. Even ancient peoples tried to figure out social life. They, too, asked questions about why war exists, why some people become more powerful than others, and why some are rich, but others are poor. However, they often based their answers on superstition, myth, or even the position of the stars and did not test their assumptions.

Science, in contrast, requires the development of theories that can be tested by research. Measured by this standard, sociology only recently appeared on the human scene. It emerged about the middle of the 1800s, when social observers began to use scientific methods to test their ideas.

Sociology grew out of social upheaval. The Industrial Revolution had just begun, and masses of people were moving to cities in search of work. Their ties to the land—and to a culture that had provided them with ready answers to life's difficult questions—were broken. The cities greeted them with horrible working conditions: low pay; long, exhausting hours; dangerous work. For families to survive, even children had to work in these conditions; some children were even chained to factory machines to make certain they could not run away. Life no longer looked the same, and tradition, which had provided the answers to social life, no longer could be counted on.

Tradition suffered further blows. The success of the American and French revolutions encouraged people to rethink social life. New ideas arose, including the conviction that individuals possess inalienable rights. As this new idea caught fire, many traditional Western monarchies gave way to more democratic forms of government. People found the ready answers of tradition inadequate.

About this same time, the *scientific method*—using objective, systematic observations to test theories—was being tried out in chemistry and physics. Many secrets that had been concealed in nature were being uncovered. With

This eighteenth-century painting (artist unknown) depicts women from Paris joining the French Army on its way to Versailles on October 5, 1789. The French Revolution of 1789 not only overthrew the aristocracy but also upset the entire social order. This extensive change removed the security of looking to the past as a sure guide to the present. The events of this period stimulated Auguste Comte to analyze how societies change. His writings are often considered the origin of sociology.

tradition no longer providing the answers to questions about social life, the logical step was to apply the scientific method to these questions. The result was the birth of sociology.

Auguste Comte and Positivism

This idea of applying the scientific method to the social world, known as **positivism,** apparently was first proposed by Auguste Comte (1798–1857). With the French Revolution still fresh in his mind, Comte left the small, conservative town in which he had grown up and moved to Paris. The changes he experienced in this move, combined with those France underwent in the revolution, led Comte to become interested in what holds society together. What creates social order, he wondered, instead of anarchy or chaos? And then, once society does become set on a particular course, what causes it to change?

As Comte considered these questions, he concluded that the right way to answer them was to apply the scientific method to social life. Just as this method had revealed the law of gravity, so, too, it would uncover the laws that underlie society. Comte called this new science **sociology,** "the study of society" (from the Greek *logos,* "study of," and the Latin *socius,* "companion" or "being with others"). Comte stressed that this new science not only would discover social principles but also would apply them to social reform. Sociologists would reform the entire society, making it a better place to live.

To Comte, however, applying the scientific method to social life meant practicing what we might call "armchair philosophy"—drawing conclusions from informal obser-vations of social life. He did not do what today's sociologists would call research, and his conclusions have been abandoned. Nevertheless, Comte's insistence that we must observe and classify human activities to uncover society's fundamental laws is well taken. Because he developed this idea and coined the term *sociology,* Comte often is credited with being the founder of sociology.

Herbert Spencer and Social Darwinism

Herbert Spencer (1820–1903), who grew up in England, is sometimes called the second founder of sociology. Spencer disagreed profoundly with Comte that sociology should guide social reform. He was convinced that no one should intervene in the evolution of society. Spencer thought that societies evolve from lower ("barbarian") to higher ("civilized") forms. As generations pass, the most capable and intelligent ("the fittest") members of the society survive, while the less capable die out. Thus, over time, societies improve. If you help the lower classes, you interfere with this natural process. The fittest members will produce a more advanced society—unless misguided do-gooders get in the way and help those who are less fit to survive.

Spencer called this principle "the survival of the fittest." Although Spencer coined this phrase, it usually is attributed to his contemporary, Charles Darwin, who proposed that organisms evolve over time as they adapt to their environment. Because of their similarity to Darwin's ideas, Spencer's views of the evolution of societies became known as *social Darwinism.*

Auguste Comte (1798–1857), who is credited as the founder of sociology, began to analyze the bases of the social order. Although he stressed that the scientific method should be applied to the study of society, he did not apply it himself.

Herbert Spencer (1820–1903), sometimes called the second founder of sociology, coined the term "survival of the fittest." Spencer thought that helping the poor was wrong, that this merely helped the "less fit" survive.

Like Comte, Spencer was more of a social philosopher than a sociologist. Also like Comte, Spencer did not conduct scientific studies. He simply developed ideas about society. After gaining a wide following in England and the United States, Spencer's ideas about social Darwinism were discarded.

Karl Marx and Class Conflict

The influence of Karl Marx (1818–1883) on world history has been so great that even the *Wall Street Journal,* that staunch advocate of capitalism, has called him one of the three greatest modern thinkers (the other two being Sigmund Freud and Albert Einstein).

Marx, who came to England after being exiled from his native Germany for proposing revolution, believed that the engine of human history is **class conflict.** He said that the *bourgeoisie* (boor-zhwa-ZEE) (the *capitalists,* those who own the means to produce wealth—capital, land, factories, and machines) are locked in conflict with the *proletariat* (the exploited class, the mass of workers who do not own the means of production). This bitter struggle can end only when the workers unite in revolution and throw off their chains of bondage. The result will be a classless society, one free of exploitation, in which people will work according to their abilities and receive according to their needs (Marx and Engels 1848/1967).

Marxism is not the same as communism. Although Marx supported revolution as the only way that the workers could gain control of society, he did not develop the political system called *communism.* This is a later application of his ideas. Indeed, Marx felt disgusted when he heard debates about his insights into social life. After listening to some of the positions attributed to him, he shook his head and said, "I am not a Marxist" (Dobriner 1969b:222; Gitlin 1997:89).

Emile Durkheim and Social Integration

The primary professional goal of Emile Durkheim (1858–1917), who grew up in France, was to get sociology recognized as a separate academic discipline (Coser 1977). Up to this time, sociology had been viewed as a part of the study of history and economics. Durkheim achieved this goal when he received the first academic appointment in sociology at the University of Bordeaux in 1887.

Durkheim also had another goal: to show how social forces affect people's behavior. To accomplish this, he conducted rigorous research. Comparing the suicide rates of several European countries, Durkheim (1897/1966) found that each country had a different suicide rate, and that these rates remained about the same year after year. He also found that different groups within a country had different suicide

Karl Marx (1818–1883) believed that the roots of human misery lie in class conflict, the exploitation of workers by those who own the means of production. Social change, in the form of the overthrow of the capitalists by the workers (proletariat), was inevitable from Marx's perspective. Although Marx did not consider himself a sociologist, his ideas have influenced many sociologists, particularly conflict theorists.

The French sociologist **Emile Durkheim** (1858–1917) contributed many important concepts to sociology. His comparison of the suicide rates of several countries revealed an underlying social factor: People are more likely to commit suicide if their ties to others in their communities are weak. Durkheim's identification of the key role of social integration in social life remains central to sociology today.

rates and that these, too, remained stable from year to year. For example, Protestants, males, and the unmarried killed themselves at a higher rate than did Catholics, Jews, females, and the married. From this, Durkheim drew the insightful conclusion that suicide is not simply a matter of individuals here and there deciding to take their lives for personal reasons. Rather, *social factors underlie suicide,* and this is what keeps a group's rates fairly constant year after year.

Durkheim identified **social integration,** the degree to which people are tied to their social group, as a key social factor in suicide. He concluded that people who have weaker social ties are more likely to commit suicide. This factor, he said, explained why Protestants, males, and the unmarried have higher suicide rates. It works this way, Durkheim argued: Protestantism encourages greater freedom of thought and action, males are more independent than females, and the unmarried lack the connections and responsibilities that come with marriage. In other words, because their social integration is weaker, members of these groups have fewer of the social ties that keep people from committing suicide.

Over a hundred years later, Durkheim's work is still quoted. His research was so thorough that the principle he uncovered still applies: People who are less socially integrated have higher rates of suicide. Even today, those same groups that Durkheim identified—Protestants, males, and the unmarried—are more likely to kill themselves.

From Durkheim's study of suicide, we see the principle that was central in his research: *Human behavior cannot be understood simply in individualistic terms; we must always examine the social forces that affect people's lives.* Suicide, for example, appears at first to be such an intensely individual act that psychologists should study it, not sociologists. Yet, as Durkheim illustrated, if we look at human behavior (such as suicide) only in individualistic terms, we miss its *social* basis.

Max Weber and the Protestant Ethic

Max Weber (Mahx VAY-ber) (1864–1920), a German sociologist and a contemporary of Durkheim, also held professorships in the new academic discipline of sociology. Like Durkheim and Marx, Weber is one of the most influential of all sociologists, and you will come across his writings and theories in the coming chapters. Let's consider an issue Weber raised that remains controversial today.

Religion and the Origin of Capitalism. Weber disagreed with Marx's claim that economics is the central force in social change. That role, he said, belongs to

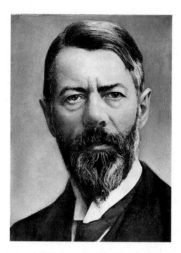

Max Weber (1864–1920) was another early sociologist who left a profound impression on sociology. He used cross-cultural and historical materials to trace the causes of social change and to determine how social groups affect people's orientations to life.

religion. Weber (1904/1958) theorized that the Roman Catholic belief system encouraged its followers to hold onto traditional ways of life, while the Protestant belief system encouraged its members to embrace change. Protestantism, he said, undermined people's spiritual security. Roman Catholics believed that they were on the road to heaven because they were baptized and were church members. Protestants, however, did not share this belief. Protestants of the Calvinist tradition were told that they wouldn't know if they were saved until Judgment Day. Uncomfortable with this, they began to look for "signs" that they were in God's will. Eventually, they concluded that financial success was the major sign that God was on their side. To bring about this "sign" and receive spiritual comfort, they began to live frugal lives, saving their money and investing the surplus in order to make even more. This, said Weber, brought about the birth of capitalism.

Weber called this self-denying approach to life the *Protestant ethic.* He termed the readiness to invest capital in order to make more money the *spirit of capitalism.* To test his theory, Weber compared the extent of capitalism in Roman Catholic and Protestant countries. In line with his theory, he found that capitalism was more likely to flourish in Protestant countries. Weber's conclusion that religion was the key factor in the rise of capitalism was controversial when he made it, and it continues to be debated today (Barro and McCleary 2003). We'll explore these ideas in more detail in Chapter 13.

Sexism in Early Sociology

Attitudes of the Time

As you may have noticed, we have discussed only male sociologists. In the 1800s, sex roles were rigidly defined, with women assigned the roles of wife and mother. In the classic German phrase, women were expected to devote themselves to the four K's: *Kirche, Küchen, Kinder, und Kleider* (church, cooking, children, and clothes). Women who tried to break out of this mold experienced severe social disapproval.

Few people, male or female, received any education beyond basic reading, writing, and a little math. Higher education, for the rare few who received it, was reserved for men. A handful of women from wealthy families, however, did pursue higher education. A few even managed to study sociology, although the sexism that was so deeply entrenched in the universities stopped them from obtaining advanced degrees or becoming professors. In line with the times, their research was almost entirely ignored.

Harriet Martineau and Early Social Research

A classic example is Harriet Martineau (1802–1876), who was born into a wealthy English family. When Martineau first began to analyze social life, she would hide her writing beneath her sewing when visitors arrived, for writing was considered "masculine" and sewing "feminine"

Interested in social reform, **Harriet Martineau** (1802–1876) turned to sociology, where she discovered the writings of Comte. She became an advocate for the abolition of slavery, traveled widely, and wrote extensive analyses of social life.

(Gilman 1911:88). Martineau persisted in her interests, however, and she eventually studied social life in both Great Britain and the United States. In 1837, two or three decades before Durkheim and Weber were born, Martineau published *Society in America,* in which she reported on this new nation's customs—family, race, gender, politics, and religion. Despite her insightful examination of U.S. life, which is still worth reading today, Martineau's research met the same fate as the work of other early women sociologists and, until recently, was ignored. Instead, she is known primarily for translating Comte's ideas into English.

Sociology in North America

Early History: The Tension Between Social Reform and Sociological Analysis

Transplanted to U.S. soil in the late nineteenth century, sociology first took root at the University of Kansas in 1890; at the University of Chicago in 1892; and at Atlanta University, then an all-black school, in 1897. It was not until 1922 that McGill University gave Canada its first department of sociology. Harvard University did not open a department of sociology until 1930, and the University of California at Berkeley didn't have one until the 1950s.

Initially, the department at the University of Chicago, which was founded by Albion Small (1854–1926), dominated sociology. (Small also founded the *American Journal of Sociology* and was its editor from 1895 to 1925.) Members of this early sociology department whose ideas continue to influence today's sociologists include Robert Park (1864–1944), Ernest Burgess (1886–1966), and George Herbert Mead (1863–1931). Mead developed the symbolic interactionist perspective, which we will examine later.

Jane Addams and Social Reform

Although many North American sociologists combined the role of sociologist with that of social reformer, none was as successful as Jane Addams (1860–1935). Like Harriet Martineau, Addams came from a background of wealth and privilege. She attended the Women's Medical College of Philadelphia, but dropped out because of illness (Addams 1910/1981). During one of her many trips to Europe, Addams observed and was impressed by the

Jane Addams, 1860–1935, a recipient of the Nobel Peace Prize, worked on behalf of poor immigrants. With Ellen G. Starr, she founded Hull-House, a center to help immigrants in Chicago. She was also a leader in women's rights (women suffrage), as well as the peace movement of World War I.

work being done on behalf of London's poor. From then on, she worked tirelessly for social justice.

In 1889, Addams cofounded Hull-House, located in Chicago's notorious slums. Hull-House was open to people who needed refuge—to immigrants, the sick, the aged, the poor. Sociologists from the nearby University of Chicago were frequent visitors at Hull-House. With her piercing insights into the ways in which workers were exploited and how immigrants adjusted to city life, Addams strived to bridge the gap between the powerful and the powerless. She worked with others to win the eight-hour work day and to pass laws against child labor. Her efforts at social reform were so outstanding that in 1931 she was a cowinner of the Nobel Prize for Peace, the only sociologist to win this coveted award.

W. E. B. Du Bois and Race Relations

Another sociologist who combined sociology and social reform is W. E. B. Du Bois (1868–1963), the first African American to earn a doctorate at Harvard. After completing his education at the University of Berlin, where he attended lectures by Max Weber, Du Bois taught Greek and Latin at Wilberforce University. He then went to Atlanta University in 1897, where he remained for most of his career.

Although Du Bois was invited to present a paper at the 1909 meetings of the American Sociological Society, he was too poor to attend. When he could afford to attend

subsequent meetings, discrimination was so prevalent in the United States that hotels and restaurants would not allow him to room or eat with the white sociologists. Later in life, when Du Bois had the money to travel, the U.S. State Department feared that he would criticize the United States and at the height of the Cold War refused to give him a passport (Du Bois 1968).

Du Bois' lifetime research interest was relations between whites and African Americans, and he published a book on this subject *each* year between 1896 and 1914. The Down-to-Earth Sociology box on the next page is taken from one of his books. Du Bois' insights into race relations were heightened by personal experiences. For example, he once saw the fingers of a lynching victim on display in a Georgia butcher shop (Aptheker 1990).

At first, Du Bois was content to collect and interpret objective data. Later, frustrated at the continuing exploitation of blacks, he turned to social action. Along with Jane Addams and others from Hull-House, Du Bois founded the National Association for the Advancement of Colored People (NAACP) (Deegan 1988). Continuing to battle racism both as a sociologist and as a journalist, he eventually embraced revolutionary Marxism. At age 93, dismayed that so little improvement had been made in race relations, he moved to Ghana, where he is buried (Stark 1989).

W(illiam) **E**(dward) **B**(urghardt) **Du Bois** (1868–1963) spent his lifetime studying relations between African Americans and whites. Like many early North American sociologists, Du Bois combined the role of academic sociologist with that of social reformer. He was also the editor of *Crisis*, an influential journal of the time.

Down-to-Earth Sociology

Early Sociology in North America: Du Bois and Race Relations

THE WRITINGS OF W. E. B. DU BOIS, who expressed sociological thought more like an accomplished novelist than a sociologist, have been neglected in sociology. To help remedy this omission, I reprint the following excerpts from pages 66–68 of *The Souls of Black Folk* (1903). In this book, Du Bois analyzes changes that occurred in the social and economic conditions of African Americans during the thirty years following the Civil War.

For two summers, while he was a student at Fisk, Du Bois taught in a segregated school housed in a log hut "way back in the hills" of rural Tennessee. The following excerpts help us understand conditions at that time.

In the 1800s, poverty was widespread in the United States. Most people were so poor that they expended their life energies on just getting enough food, fuel, and clothing to survive. Formal education beyond the first several grades was a luxury. This photo depicts the conditions of the people Du Bois worked with.

It was a hot morning late in July when the school opened. I trembled when I heard the patter of little feet down the dusty road, and saw the growing row of dark solemn faces and bright eager eyes facing me. . . . There they sat, nearly thirty of them, on the rough benches, their faces shading from a pale cream to deep brown, the little feet bare and swinging, the eyes full of expectation, with here and there a twinkle of mischief, and the hands grasping Webster's blue-black spelling-book. I loved my school, and the fine faith the children had in the wisdom of their teacher was truly marvelous. We read and spelled together, wrote a little, picked flowers, sang, and listened to stories of the world beyond the hill. . . .

On Friday nights I often went home with some of the children,—sometimes to Doc Burke's farm. He was a great, loud, thin Black, ever working, and trying to buy these seventy-five acres of hill and dale where he lived; but people said that he would surely fail and the "white folks would get it all." His wife was a magnificent Amazon, with saffron face and shiny hair, uncorseted and barefooted, and the children were strong and barefooted. They lived in a one-and-a-half-room cabin in the hollow of the farm near the spring. . . .

I liked to stay with the Dowells, for they had four rooms and plenty of good country fare. Uncle Bird had a small, rough farm, all woods and hills, miles from the big road; but he was full of tales,—he preached now and then,—and with his children, berries, horses, and wheat he was happy and prosperous. Often, to keep the peace, I must go where life was less lovely; for instance, 'Tildy's mother was incorrigibly dirty, Reuben's larder was limited seriously, and herds of untamed insects wandered over the Eddingses' beds. Best of all I loved to go to Josie's, and sit on the porch, eating peaches, while the mother bustled and talked: how Josie had bought the sewing-machine; how Josie worked at service in winter, but that four dollars a month was "mighty little" wages; how Josie longed to go away to school, but that it "looked liked" they never could get far enough ahead to let her; how the crops failed and the well was yet unfinished; and, finally, how mean some of the white folks were.

For two summers I lived in this little world. . . . I have called my tiny community a world, and so its isolation made it; and yet there was among us but a half-awakened common consciousness, sprung from common joy and grief, at burial, birth, or wedding; from common hardship in poverty, poor land, and low wages, and, above all, from the sight of the Veil* that hung between us and Opportunity. All this caused us to think some thoughts together; but these, when ripe for speech, were spoken in various languages. Those whose eyes twenty-five and more years before had seen "the glory of the coming of the Lord," saw in every present hindrance or help a dark fatalism bound to bring all things right in His own good time. The mass of those to whom slavery was a dim recollection of childhood found the world a puzzling thing: it asked little of them, and they answered with little, and yet it ridiculed their offering.

* "The Veil" is shorthand for the Veil of Race, referring to how race colors all human relations. Du Bois' hope was that "sometime, somewhere, men will judge men by their souls and not by their skins" (p. 261).

Talcott Parsons and C. Wright Mills: Theory Versus Reform

During the 1940s, the emphasis shifted from social reform to social theory. Talcott Parsons (1902–1979), for example, developed abstract models of society that greatly influenced a generation of sociologists. Parsons' models of how the parts of society work together harmoniously did nothing to stimulate social activism.

C. Wright Mills (1916–1962) deplored the theoretical abstractions of this period, and he urged sociologists to get back to social reform. He warned that an imminent threat to freedom was the coalescing of interests on the part of a group he called the *power elite*—the top leaders of business, politics, and the military. Shortly after Mills' death came the turbulent late 1960s and 1970s. This precedent-shaking era sparked interest in social activism, and Mills' ideas grew popular among a new generation of sociologists.

The Continuing Tension and the Rise of Applied Sociology

The apparent contradiction of these two aims—analyzing society versus working toward its reform—created a tension in sociology that is still with us today. Some sociologists believe that their proper role is to analyze some aspect of society and to publish their findings in sociology journals. This is called *basic (or pure) sociology*. Others say that basic sociology is not enough: Sociologists have an obligation to use their expertise to try to make society

C. Wright Mills was a controversial figure in sociology because of his analysis of the role of the power elite in U.S. society. Today, his analysis is taken for granted by many sociologists and members of the public.

a better place in which to live and to help bring justice to the poor.

Somewhere between these extremes lies **applied sociology,** which uses sociology to solve problems. (See Figure 1.1, which contrasts basic and applied sociology.) One of the first attempts at applied sociology—and one of the most successful—was one I just men- tioned: the founding of the National Association for the Advancement of Colored People. As illustrated in the Down-to-Earth Sociology box on the next page, today's applied sociologists work in a variety of settings. Some work for business firms to solve problems in the workplace.

Figure 1.1 **Comparing Basic and Applied Sociology**

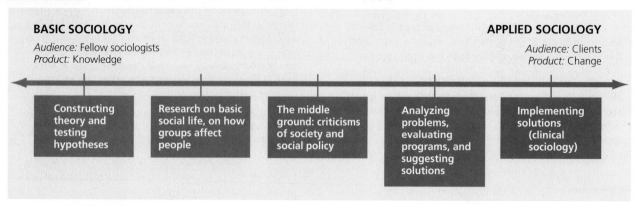

Source: By the author. Based on DeMartini 1982.

Others investigate social problems such as environmental pollution, the relationship between pornography and rape, or how AIDS spreads. A new specialty in applied sociology is determining ways to disrupt terrorist groups (Ebner 2005). The Down-to-Earth Sociology box on the next page presents a startling example of applied sociology.

Applied sociology is not the same as social reform. It is an application of sociology in some specific setting, not an attempt to rebuild society, as early sociologists envisioned.

Consequently, a new tension has emerged in sociology. Sociologists who want the emphasis to be on social reform say that applied sociology doesn't even come close to this. It is an application of sociology but not an attempt to change society. Others, who want the emphasis to remain on discovering knowledge, say that when sociology is applied, it is no longer sociology. If sociologists use sociological principles to help teenagers escape from pimps, for example, is it still sociology?

Down-to-Earth Sociology

Careers in Sociology: What Applied Sociologists Do

MOST SOCIOLOGISTS TEACH IN COLLEGES and universities, sharing sociological knowledge with college students, as your instructor is doing with you in this course. Applied sociologists, in contrast, work in a wide variety of areas—from counseling children to studying how diseases are transmitted. Some even make software more user-friendly. To give you an idea of this variety, let's look over the shoulders of four applied sociologists.

Leslie Green, who does marketing research at Vanderveer Group in Philadelphia, Pennsylvania, earned her bachelor's degree in sociology at Shippensburg University. She helps to develop strategies to get doctors to prescribe particular drugs. She sets up the meetings, locates moderators for the discussion groups, and arranges payments to the physicians who participate in the research. "My training in sociology," she says, "helps me in 'people skills.' It helps me to understand the needs of different groups, and to interact with them."

Stanley Capela, whose master's degree is from Fordham University, works as an applied sociologist at HeartShare Human Services in New York. He evaluates how children's programs—such as ones that focus on housing, AIDS, group homes, and preschool education—actually work, compared with how they are supposed to work. He spots problems and suggests solutions. One of his assignments was to find out why it was taking so long to get children adopted, even though there was a long list of eager adoptive parents. Capela pinpointed how the paperwork got bogged down as it was routed through the system and suggested ways to improve the flow to accelerate the process.

Laurie Banks, who received her master's degree in sociology from Fordham University, analyzes statistics for the New York City Health Department. As she examined death certificates, she noticed that a Polish neighborhood had a high rate of stomach cancer. She alerted the Centers for Disease Control, which conducted interviews in the neighborhood. They traced the cause to eating large amounts of sausage. In another case, Banks compared birth certificates with school records. She found that problems at birth—low birth weight, lack of prenatal care, and birth complications—were linked to low reading skills and behavior problems in school.

Joyce Miller Iutcovich, whose doctorate is from Kent State University, is president of Keystone University Research Corporation in Erie, Pennsylvania. She is also a past president of the Society for Applied Sociology. Iutcovich does research and consulting, primarily for government agencies. In one of her projects, she designed a training program for child care providers. She also did research on how well the caregivers did. Her research and program improved the quality of care given to children by the Pennsylvania Department of Public Welfare. Her organization also administers the Pennsylvania Substance Abuse and Health Information Clearinghouse, which distributes over 300,000 pieces of literature a month.

From just these few examples, you can catch a glimpse of the variety of work that applied sociologists do. Some work for corporations, some are employed by government and private agencies, and others run their own businesses. You can also see that you don't need a doctorate in order to work as an applied sociologist.

Down-to-Earth Sociology

Capturing Saddam Hussein: A Surprising Example of Applied Sociology

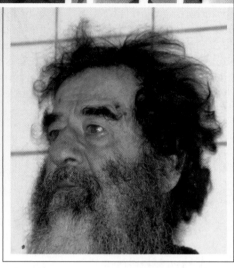

Applied sociology takes many twists and turns, but perhaps none as startling as assisting in the capture of Saddam Hussein. After U.S.-led forces took over Baghdad, Hussein disappeared. His capture became a pressing goal with two purposes. The first was symbolic: a sign of the coalition's triumph. The second was practical: to prevent Hussein from directing resistance to the occupation of Iraq.

But Hussein was nowhere to be found. Rumors placed him all over the map, from neighboring countries to safe houses in Baghdad. To find him, U.S. intelligence officers began to apply sociology, specifically, a form known as *network analysis*. Analysts drew up a "people map." On a color-coded map, they placed Hussein's photo in a yellow circle, like a bull's-eye. They then drew links to people who were connected to Hussein, placing their photos closer to or farther from Hussein's photo on the basis of their level of intimacy with Hussein (Schmitt 2003).

The photos placed closest to Hussein on this map of social relationships represented an intimate and loyal group.

These people were the most likely to know where Hussein was, but because of their close ties to him, they also were the least likely to reveal this information. Those who were pictured slightly farther away knew people in this more intimate group, so it was likely that some of them had information about Hussein's whereabouts. Because these individuals' social ties to Hussein were not as strong, they provided the weaker links to try to break.

The approach worked. Using software programs to sift through vast amounts of information gained from informants and electronic intercepts, the analysts drew an extensive people map that pictured these social relationships. Identifying and focusing on the weaker links led to the capture of Saddam Hussein.

As I write this, analysts are using applied sociology in a similar way to hunt down Osama bin Laden. They are mapping the links in bin Laden's tribal network to identify weaknesses that might reveal his whereabouts (KRT 2003).

Theoretical Perspectives in Sociology

Facts never interpret themselves. In everyday life, we interpret what we observe by using "common sense." We place our observations (our "facts") into a framework of more-or-less related ideas. Sociologists do this, too, but they place their observations in a conceptual framework called a *theory*. A **theory** is a general statement about how some parts of the world fit together and how they work. It is an explanation of how two or more "facts" are related to one another.

Sociologists use three major theories: symbolic interactionism, functional analysis, and conflict theory. Let's first examine the main elements of these theories. Then let's see how each theory helps us to understand why the divorce rate in the United States is so high. As we do so, you will see how each theory, or perspective, provides a distinctive interpretation of social life.

Symbolic Interactionism

We can trace the origins of **symbolic interactionism** to the Scottish moral philosophers of the eighteenth century, who noted that individuals evaluate their own conduct by comparing themselves with others (Stryker 1990). This perspective was brought to sociology by Charles Horton Cooley (1864–1929), William I. Thomas (1863–1947), and George Herbert Mead (1863–1931). Let's look at the main elements of this theory.

Symbols in Everyday Life.

Symbolic interactionists study how people use symbols to develop their views of the world and to communicate with one another. Without symbols, our social life would be no more sophisticated than that of animals. For example, without symbols we would have no aunts or uncles, employers or teachers—or even brothers and sisters. I know that this sounds strange, but it is symbols that define for us what relationships are. There would still be reproduction, of course, but no symbols to tell us how we are related to whom. We would not know to whom we owe respect and obligations or from whom we can expect privileges—the stuff that human relationships are made of.

Look at it like this: If you think of someone as your aunt or uncle, you behave in certain ways, but if you think of that person as a boyfriend or girlfriend, you behave quite differently. It is the symbol that tells you how you are related to others—and how you should act toward them.

To make this clearer

> Suppose that you are head-over-heels in love with someone and are going to marry this person tomorrow. The night before your marriage, your mother confides that she had a child before she married, a child that she gave up for adoption. She then adds that she has just discovered that the person you are going to marry is this child.
>
> You can see how the symbol will change overnight!—and your behavior, too!

Symbols allow the existence not only of relationships but also of society. Without symbols, we could not coordinate our actions with those of other people. We could not make plans for a future date, time, and place. Unable to specify times, materials, sizes, or goals, we could not build bridges and highways. Without symbols, there would be no movies or musical instruments. We would have no hospitals, no government, no religion. The class you are taking could not exist—nor could this book. On the positive side, there would be no war.

In short, symbolic interactionists analyze how our behaviors depend on the ways we define both ourselves and others. They study face-to-face interactions; they look at how people work out their relationships and how they make sense out of life and their place in it. Symbolic interactionists point out that even the self is a symbol, for it consists of the ideas we have about who we are. And the self is a changing symbol: As we interact with others, we constantly adjust our views of who we are based on how we interpret the reactions of others. We'll get more into this later.

Applying Symbolic Interactionism.

To explain the U.S. divorce rate (see Figure 1.2 on the next page), symbolic interactionists look at how people's ideas and behavior change as symbols change. They note that until the early 1900s, Americans thought of marriage as a sacred, lifelong commitment. Divorce was seen as an immoral, harmful action, a flagrant disregard for public opinion.

Then, slowly, the meaning of marriage began to change. In 1933, sociologist William Ogburn observed that personality was becoming more important in mate selection. In 1945, sociologists Ernest Burgess and Harvey Locke noted the growing importance of mutual affection, understanding, and compatibility in marriage. Gradually, people's views changed. No longer did they see marriage as a lifelong commitment based on duty and obligation. Instead, they began to view marriage as an arrangement, often temporary, that was based on feelings of intimacy. The meaning of divorce also changed. Formerly a symbol of failure, it became an indicator of freedom and new beginnings. Removing the stigma from divorce shattered a strong barrier that had prevented husbands and wives from breaking up.

Symbolic interactionists note that ideas about marital roles and parenthood also changed—and they point out that none of these changes strengthen marriage. For example, from tradition, newlyweds knew what they had a right to expect from each other. In contrast, with today's much vaguer guidelines, couples must figure out how to divide up responsibilities for work, home, and children. As they struggle to do so, many flounder. Although couples find it a relief not to have to conform to what they consider to be burdensome notions, those traditional expectations (or symbols) did provide a structure that made marriages last. When these symbols changed, the structure they had created was weakened, making marriage more fragile and divorce more common.

Similarly, ideas of parenthood and childhood used to be quite different. Parents had little responsibility for their children beyond providing food, clothing, shelter, and moral guidance. And this was only for a short time, for children began to contribute to the support of the family early in life. Among many people, parenthood is still like this. In Colombia, for example, children of the poor often are expected to support themselves by the age of 8 or 10. In advanced industrial societies, however, we assume that children are vulnerable beings who must depend on their parents for financial and emotional support for many years—often until they are well into their twenties. That this is not the case in many cultures often comes as a

Figure 1.2 **U.S. Marriage, U.S. Divorce**

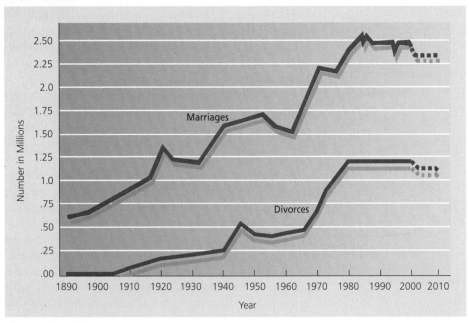

Sources: By the author. Based on *Statistical Abstract* 1998:Table 92; earlier editions for earlier years; "Population Today" 2006. The broken lines indicate the author's estimates.

surprise to Americans, who assume that their own situation is some sort of natural arrangement that is worldwide. The greater responsibilities that we assign to parenthood place heavy burdens on today's couples and, with them, more strain on marriage.

Symbolic interactionists, then, look at how changing ideas (or symbols) put pressure on married couples. No single change is *the* cause of our divorce rate, but, taken together, these changes provide a strong push toward divorce.

Functional Analysis

The central idea of **functional analysis** is that society is a whole unit; it is made up of interrelated parts that work together. Functional analysis, also known as *functionalism* and *structural functionalism,* is rooted in the origins of sociology. Auguste Comte and Herbert Spencer viewed society as a kind of living organism. Just as a person or animal has organs that function together, they wrote, so does society. Like an organism, if society is to function smoothly, its various parts must work together in harmony.

Emile Durkheim also viewed society as being composed of many parts, each with its own function. When all the parts of society fulfill their functions, society is in a "normal" state. If they do not fulfill their functions, society is in an "abnormal" or "pathological" state. To understand society, then,

functionalists say that we need to look at both *structure* (how the parts of a society fit together to make the whole) and *function* (what each part does, how it contributes to society).

Robert Merton and Functionalism. Robert Merton (1910–2003) dismissed the organic analogy, but he did maintain the essence of functionalism—the image of society as a whole composed of parts that work together. Merton used the term *functions* to refer to the beneficial consequences of people's actions: Functions help keep a group (society, social system) in equilibrium. In contrast, *dysfunctions* are consequences that harm society. They undermine a system's equilibrium.

Functions can be either manifest or latent. If an action is *intended* to help some part of a system, it is a *manifest function.* For example, suppose that the government becomes concerned about our low rate of childbirth. Congress offers a $10,000 bonus for every child born to a married couple. The intention, or manifest function, of the bonus is to increase childbearing. Merton pointed out that people's actions can also have *latent functions—unintended* consequences that help a system adjust. Let's suppose that the bonus works, and the birth rate jumps. As a result, the sales of diapers and baby furniture boom. Because the benefits to these businesses were not the intended consequences, they are *latent* functions of the bonus.

Of course, human actions can also hurt a system. Because such consequences usually are unintended, Merton called them *latent dysfunctions*. Let's suppose that the government has failed to specify a stopping point with regard to its bonus system. To collect the bonus, some people keep on having children. The more children they have, however, the more they need the next bonus to survive. Large families become common, and poverty increases. Welfare is reinstated, taxes jump, and the nation erupts in protest. Because these results were not intended, and because they harmed the social system, they represent latent dysfunctions of the bonus program.

Applying Functional Analysis. Now let's apply functional analysis to the U.S. divorce rate. Functionalists stress that industrialization and urbanization undermined the traditional functions of the family. For example, before industrialization, the family was a sort of economic team. On the farm, where most people lived, each member of the family had jobs or "chores" to do. The wife was in charge not only of household tasks but also of raising small animals, such as chickens. Milking cows, collecting eggs, and churning butter were also her responsibility— as were cooking, baking, canning, sewing, darning, washing, and cleaning. The daughters helped her. The husband was responsible for caring for large animals, such as horses and cattle, for planting and harvesting, and for maintaining buildings and tools. The sons helped him. *Together,* they formed an economic unit in which each depended on the others for survival.

The functions that bonded family members to one another also included educating the children, teaching them religion, providing home-based recreation, and caring for the sick and elderly. To see how sharply family functions have changed, look at this example from the 1800s:

> When Phil became sick, he was nursed by Ann, his wife. She cooked for him, fed him, changed the bed linen, bathed him, read to him from the Bible, and gave him his medicine. (She did this in addition to doing the housework and taking care of their six children.) Phil was also surrounded by the children, who shouldered some of his chores while he was sick.
>
> When Phil died, the male neighbors and relatives made the casket while Ann, her mother, and female friends washed and dressed the body. Phil was then "laid out" in the front parlor (the formal living room), where friends, neighbors, and relatives paid their last respects. From there, friends moved his body to the church for the final message and then to the grave they themselves had dug.

As you can see, the family used to have more functions than it does now. Families handled many aspects of life and

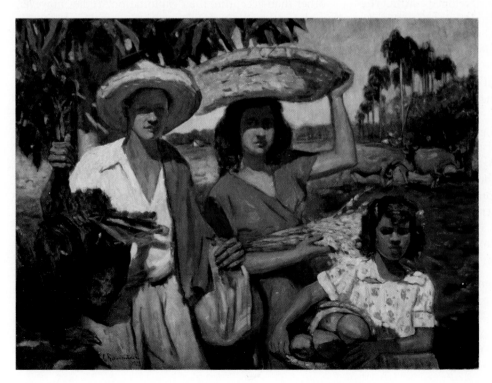

Sociologists who use the *functionalist perspective* stress how industrialization and urbanization undermined the traditional *functions* of the family. Before industrialization, members of the family worked together as an economic unit, as in this painting by Leopoldo Romanach (1958-) of Havana, Cuba. As production moved away from the home, it took with it first the father and, more recently, the mother. One consequence is a major *dysfunction*, the weakening of family ties.

death that we now assign to outside agencies. Similarly, economic production is no longer a cooperative, home-based effort, with husbands and wives depending on one another for their interlocking contributions to a mutual endeavor. In contrast, today's husbands and wives earn individual paychecks and function as separate components in an impersonal, multinational, and even global system. When outside agencies take over family functions, this weakens the "ties that bind." Marriages become more fragile, and divorce increases.

Conflict Theory

Conflict theory provides a third perspective on social life. Unlike the functionalists, who view society as a harmonious whole, with its parts working together, conflict theorists stress that society is composed of groups that are competing with one another for scarce resources. Although on the surface alliances or cooperation may prevail, beneath that surface is a struggle for power.

Karl Marx and Conflict Theory. Karl Marx, the founder of conflict theory, witnessed the Industrial Revolution that transformed Europe. He observed that peasants who had left the land to seek work in cities had to work for wages that provided barely enough to eat. The average worker died at age 30, the average wealthy person at age 50 (Edgerton 1992:87). Shocked by people's deep suffering and their exploitation, Marx began to analyze society and history. As he did so, he developed **conflict theory.** He concluded that the key to human history is *class conflict.* In each society, some small group controls the means of production and exploits those who are not in control. In industrialized societies, the struggle is between the *bourgeoisie,* the small group of capitalists who own the means to produce wealth, and the *proletariat,* the mass of workers who are exploited by the bourgeoisie.

When Marx made his observations, capitalism was in its infancy, and workers were at the mercy of their employers. Workers had none of what we take for granted today: minimum wages, eight-hour days, coffee breaks, five-day work weeks, paid vacations and holidays, medical benefits, sick leave, unemployment compensation, Social Security, and the right to strike. Marx's analysis reminds us that these benefits came not from generous hearts, but from workers forcing concessions from their employers.

Conflict Theory Today. Some sociologists use conflict theory in a much broader sense than Marx did. They examine how conflict permeates every layer of society—whether that be a small group, an organization, a community, or the entire society. When people in a position of authority try to enforce conformity, which their position requires them to do, this creates resentment and resistance. The result is a constant struggle throughout society to determine who has authority over what (Turner 1978; Bartos and Wehr 2002).

Sociologist Lewis Coser (1913–2003) pointed out that conflict is most likely to develop among people who are in close relationships. These people have worked out ways to distribute responsibilities and privileges, power and rewards. Any change in this arrangement can lead to hurt feelings, bitterness, and conflict. Even in intimate relationships, then, people are in a constant balancing act, with conflict lying uneasily just beneath the surface.

Feminists and Conflict Theory. Feminists stress that men and women should have equal rights. As they view relations between men and women, they see a conflict that goes back to the origins of history. Just as Marx stressed conflict between capitalists and workers, so many feminists stress conflict between men and women. Feminists are not united by the conflict perspective, however. Although some focus on the oppression of women and women's struggle against that oppression, feminists tackle a variety of topics and use a variety of theories. (Feminism is discussed in Chapter 10.)

Applying Conflict Theory. To explain why the U.S. divorce rate is high, conflict theorists focus on how men's and women's relationships have changed. For millennia, men dominated women. Women had few alternatives other than accepting their exploitation. Today, however, with industrialization, women can meet their basic survival needs outside of marriage. Industrialization has also fostered a culture in which females participate in social worlds beyond the home. Consequently, today's women, refusing to bear burdens that earlier generations accepted as inevitable, are much more likely to dissolve a marriage that becomes intolerable—or even unsatisfactory.

In sum, the dominance of men over women was once considered natural and right. As women gained education and earnings, their willingness to accept men's domination diminished, and they strived for more power. One consequence has been higher divorce rates as wives grew less inclined to put up with relationships that they defined as unfair. From the conflict perspective, then, our increase in divorce is not a sign that marriage has weakened but, rather, a sign that women are making headway in their historical struggle with men.

Levels of Analysis: Macro and Micro

A major difference among these three theoretical perspectives is their level of analysis. Functionalists and conflict theorists focus on the **macro level;** that is, they examine large-scale patterns of society. In contrast, symbolic interactionists focus on the **micro level,** on **social interaction**—what people do when they are in one another's presence. These levels are summarized in Table 1.1.

To make this distinction between micro and macro levels clearer, let's return to the example of the homeless with which we opened this chapter. To study homeless people, symbolic interactionists would focus on the micro level. They would analyze what homeless people do when they are in shelters and on the streets. They would also analyze their communications, both their talk and their **nonverbal interaction** (gestures, silence, use of space, and so on). The observations I made at the beginning of this chapter about the silence in the homeless shelter, for example, would be of interest to symbolic interactionists.

This micro level, however, would not interest functionalists and conflict theorists. They would focus instead on the macro level. Functionalists would examine how changes in the parts of society have increased homelessness. They might look at how changes in the family (fewer children, more divorce) and economic conditions (inflation, fewer unskilled jobs, loss of jobs overseas) cause homelessness among people who are unable to find jobs and have no family to fall back on. For their part, conflict theorists would stress the struggle between social classes,

especially how the policies of the wealthy force certain groups into unemployment and homelessness. That, they point out, accounts for the disproportionate number of African Americans who are homeless.

Putting the Theoretical Perspectives Together

Which theoretical perspective should we use to study human behavior? Which level of analysis is the correct one? As you have seen, these theoretical perspectives produce contrasting pictures of human life. In the case of divorce, those interpretations are quite different from the commonsense understanding that two people are simply "incompatible." *Because each theory focuses on different features of social life, each provides a distinct interpretation. Consequently, it is necessary to use all three theoretical lenses to analyze human behavior. By combining the contributions of each, we gain a more comprehensive picture of social life.*

How Theory and Research Work Together

Theory cannot stand alone. As sociologist C. Wright Mills (1959) so forcefully argued, if theory isn't connected to research, it will be abstract and empty. It won't represent the

---

Table 1.1   **Major Theoretical Perspectives in Sociology**

Perspective	Usual Level of Analysis	Focus of Analysis	Key Terms	Applying the Perspective to the U.S. Divorce Rate
Symbolic Interactionism	Microsociological—examines small-scale patterns of social interaction	Face-to face interaction; how people use symbols to create social life	Symbols Interaction Meanings Definitions	Industrialization and urbanization changed marital roles and led to a redefinition of love, marriage, children, and divorce.
Functional Analysis (also called functionalism and structural functionalism)	Macrosociological—examines large-scale patterns of society	Relationships among the parts of society; how these parts are functional (have beneficial consequences) or dysfunctional (have negative consequences)	Structure Functions (manifest and latent) Dysfunctions Equilibrium	As social change erodes the traditional functions of the family, family ties weaken, and the divorce rate increases.
Conflict Theory	Macrosociological—examines large-scale patterns of society	The struggle for scarce resources by groups in a society; how the elites use their power to control the weaker groups	Inequality Power Conflict Competition Exploitation	When men control economic life, the divorce rate is low because women find few alternatives to a bad marriage; the high divorce rate reflects a shift in the balance of power between men and women.

way life really is. It is the same for research. Without theory, Mills said, research is also of little value; it is simply a collection of meaningless "facts."

Theory and research, then, go together like a hand and glove. Every theory must be tested, which requires research. And as sociologists do research, they often come up with surprising findings. Those findings must be explained, and for that, we need theory. As sociologists study social life, then, they combine research and theory.

Let's turn now to how sociologists do research.

Doing Sociological Research

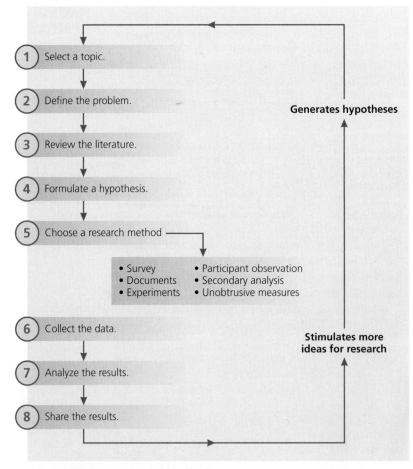 Around the globe, people make assumptions about the way the world "is." Common sense, the things that "everyone knows are true," may or may not be true, however. It takes research to find out. To test your own common sense, read the Down-to-Earth Sociology box on the next page.

Regardless of the topic that we want to investigate, we need to move beyond guesswork and common sense. We want to *know* what is really going on. To find out, sociologists do research on just about every aspect of social life. Let's look at how they do their research.

A Research Model

As shown in Figure 1.3, scientific research follows eight basic steps. This is an ideal model, however, and in the real world of research, some of these steps may run together. Some may even be omitted.

1. *Selecting a topic.* First, what do you want to know more about? Let's choose spouse abuse as our topic.
2. *Defining the problem.* The next step is to narrow the topic. Spouse abuse is too broad; we need to focus on a specific area. For example, you may want to know why men are more likely than women to be the abusers. Or perhaps you want to know what can be done to reduce domestic violence.

3. *Reviewing the literature.* You must review the literature to find out what has been published on the problem. You don't want to waste your time rediscovering what is already known.
4. *Formulating a hypothesis.* The fourth step is to formulate a **hypothesis,** a statement of what you expect to find according to predictions that are based on a theory. A hypothesis predicts a relationship between or among **variables,** factors that vary, or change, from one person or situation to another. For example, the statement "Men who are more socially isolated are more likely to abuse their wives than are men who are more socially integrated" is a hypothesis.

Your hypothesis will need **operational definitions,** that is, precise ways to measure the variables.

Figure 1.3 **The Research Model**

Source: Modification of Figure 2.2 of Schaeffer 1989.

Down-to-Earth Sociology

Enjoying a Sociology Quiz—Sociological Findings Versus Common Sense

SOME FINDINGS OF SOCIOLOGY SUPPORT commonsense understandings of social life, while others contradict them. Can you tell the difference? To enjoy this quiz, complete *all* the questions before turning the page to check your answers.

1. **True/False** More U.S. students are shot to death at school now than ten or fifteen years ago.
2. **True/False** The earnings of U.S. women have just about caught up with those of U.S. men.
3. **True/False** When faced with natural disasters such as floods and earthquakes, people panic, and social organization disintegrates.
4. **True/False** Most rapists are mentally ill.
5. **True/False** Most people on welfare are lazy and looking for a handout. They could work if they wanted to.
6. **True/False** Compared with women, men make more eye contact in face-to-face conversations.
7. **True/False** Couples who live together before marriage are usually more satisfied with their marriages than couples who do not live together before marriage.
8. **True/False** Most husbands of working wives who get laid off from work take up the slack and increase the amount of housework they do.
9. **True/False** Because bicyclists are more likely to wear helmets now than just a few years ago, their rate of head injuries has dropped.
10. **True/False** Students in Japan are under such intense pressure to do well in school that their suicide rate is about double that of U.S. students.

In this example, you would need operational definitions for three variables: social isolation, social integration, and spouse abuse.

5. *Choosing a research method.* The means by which you collect your data is called a **research method** or *research design*). Sociologists use six basic research methods, which are outlined in the next section. You will want to choose the method that will best answer your particular questions.

6. *Collecting the data.* When you gather your data, you have to take care to assure their **validity;** that is, your operational definitions must measure what they are intended to measure. In this case, you must be certain that you really are measuring social isolation, social integration, and spouse abuse—and not something else. Spouse abuse, for example, seems to be obvious. Yet what some people consider to be abuse is not considered abuse by others. Which will you choose? In other words, your operational definitions must be so precise that no one has any question about what you are measuring.

You must also be sure your data are reliable. **Reliability** means that if other researchers use your operational definitions, their findings will be consistent with yours. If your operational definitions are sloppy, husbands who have committed the same act of violence might be included in some research but excluded in other studies. You would end up with erratic results. You might show a 10 percent rate of spouse abuse, but another researcher may conclude that it is 30 percent. This would make your research unreliable.

7. *Analyzing the results.* You can choose from a variety of techniques to analyze the data you gathered. If a hypothesis has been part of your research, it is during this step that you will test it. (Some research, especially that done by participant observation, has no hypothesis. You may know so little about the setting you are going to research that you cannot even specify the variables in advance.)

With today's software, in just seconds you can run tests on your data that used to take days or even

Down-to-Earth Sociology

Sociological Findings Versus Common Sense—Answers to the Sociology Quiz

1. **False** More students were shot to death at U.S. schools in the early 1990s than now (National School Safety Center 2005).

2. **False** Over the years, the wage gap has narrowed, but only slightly. On average, full-time working women earn less than 70 percent of what full-time working men earn. This low figure is actually an improvement over earlier years. See Figures 10.5 and 10.6 on pages 270 and 271.

3. **False** Following disasters, people develop greater co-operation and social organization to deal with the catastrophe. For an example, see the photo essay on pages 108–109.

4. **False** Sociologists compared the psychological profiles of prisoners convicted of rape and prisoners convicted of other crimes. Their profiles were similar. Like robbery, rape is a learned behavior (Scully and Marolla 1984/2005).

5. **False** Most people on welfare are children, the old, the sick, the mentally and physically handicapped or young mothers with few skills. Fewer than 2 percent meet the stereotype of an able-bodied man. See page 213.

6. **False** Women make considerably more eye contact (Henley et al. 1985).

7. **False** The opposite is true. The reason, researchers suggest, is that many couples who cohabit before marriage are less committed to marriage in the first place—and a key to marital success is firm commitment to one another (Larson 1988; Dushl et al. 2003).

8. **False** Most husbands of working wives who get laid off from work *reduce* the amount of housework they do. See page 328 for an explanation.

9. **False** Bicyclists today are more likely to wear helmets, but their rate of head injuries is higher. Apparently, they take more risks because the helmets make them feel safer (Barnes 2001). (Unanticipated consequences of human action are studied by functionalists. See page 16.)

10. **False** The suicide rate of U.S. students is about double that of Japanese students (Haynes and Chalker 1997).

---

weeks. Two basic programs that sociologists and many undergraduates use are Microcase and the Statistical Package for the Social Sciences (SPSS). Some software, such as the Methodologist's Toolchest, provides advice about collecting data and even about ethical issues.

8. *Sharing the results.* To wrap up your research, you will write a report to share your findings with the scientific community. You will review how you did your research, including your operational definitions. You will also show how your findings fit in with the published literature and how they support or refute the theories that apply to your topic. As Table 1.2 on the next page illustrates, sociologists often summarize their findings in tables.

Let's look in greater detail at the fifth step and examine the research methods that sociologists use.

Research Methods

As we review the six research methods (or *research designs*) that sociologists use, we will continue our example of spouse abuse. As you will see, the method you choose will depend on the questions you want to answer. So that you can have a yardstick for comparison, you will want to know what "average" is in your study. The ways to measure average are discussed in Table 1.3 on page 24.

Surveys

Let's suppose you want to know how many wives are abused each year. Some husbands are also abused, but let's assume that you are going to focus on wives. An appropriate method would be the **survey**—asking people a series of questions. Before you begin your research, however, you

Table 1.2 How to Read a Table

Tables summarize information. Because sociological findings are often presented in tables, it is important to understand how to read them. Tables contain six elements: title, headnote, headings, columns, rows, and source. When you understand how these elements fit together, you know how to read a table.

① The **title** states the topic. It is located at the top of the table. What is the title of this table? Please determine your answer before looking at the correct answer at the bottom of the page.

② The **headnote** is not always included in a table. When it is, it is located just below the title. Its purpose is to give more detailed information about how the data were collected or how data are presented in the table. What are the first eight words of the headnote of this table?

③ The **headings** tell what kind of information is contained in the table. There are three headings in this table. What are they? In the second heading, what does *n* = 25 mean?

④ The **columns** present information arranged vertically. What is the fourth number in the second column and the second number in the third column?

⑤ The **rows** present information arranged horizontally. In the fourth row, which husbands are more likely to have less education than their wives?

⑥ The **source** of a table, usually listed at the bottom, provides information on where the data in the table originated. Often, as in this instance, the information is specific enough for you to consult the original source. What is the source for this table?

Comparing Violent and Nonviolent Husbands

Based on interviews with 150 husbands and wives in a Midwestern city who were getting a divorce.

Husband's Achievement and Job Satisfaction	Violent Husbands $n = 25$	Nonviolent Husbands $n = 125$
He started but failed to complete high school or college.	44%	27%
He is very dissatisfied with his job.	44%	18%
His income is a source of constant conflict.	84%	24%
He has less education than his wife.	56%	14%
His job has less prestige than his father-in-law's.	37%	28%

Source: Modification of Table 1 in O'Brien 1975.

Some tables are much more complicated than this one, but all follow the same basic pattern. To apply these concepts to a table with more information, see page 241.

ANSWERS
1. Comparing Violent and Nonviolent Husbands
2. Based on interviews with 150 husbands and wives
3. Husband's Achievement and Job Satisfaction, Violent Husbands, Nonviolent Husbands. The *n* is an abbreviation for number, and *n* = 25 means that 25 violent husbands were in the sample.
4. 56%, 18%
5. Violent Husbands
6. A 1975 article by O'Brien (listed in the References section of this text).

must deal with practical matters that face all researchers. Let's look at these issues.

Selecting a Sample. Ideally, you might want to learn about all wives in the world. Obviously, your resources will not permit such research, and you will have to narrow your **population,** the target group that you are going to study.

Let's assume that your resources allow you to investigate spouse abuse only on your campus. Let's also assume that your college enrollment is large, so you won't be able to survey all the married women who are enrolled. Now you must select a **sample,** individuals from among your target population. How you choose a sample is crucial, for your choice will affect the results of your study. For example, a survey of only women enrolled in introductory sociology courses, or only those in advanced physics classes, would produce skewed results.

Because you want to generalize your findings to your entire campus, you need a sample that is representative of the campus. How do you get a representative sample?

The best way is to obtain a **random sample.** This does not mean that you stand on some campus corner and ask questions of any woman who happens to walk by. *In a random sample, everyone in your population has the same chance of being included in the study.* In this case, because your population is every married woman enrolled in your college, all married women—whether first-year or graduate students, full- or part-time—must have an equal chance of being included in your sample.

How can you get a random sample? First, you need a list of all the married women enrolled in your college. Then you assign a number to each name on the list. Using a table of random numbers, you then determine which of these women become part of your sample. (Tables of random

---

Table 1.3   Three Ways to Measure "Average"

The Mean	The Median	The Mode
The term average seems clear enough. As you learned in grade school, to find the average, you add a group of numbers and then divide the total by the number of cases that were added. For example, assume that the following numbers represent men convicted of battering their wives: 321 229 57 289 136 57 1,795 The total is 2,884. Divided by 7 (the number of cases), the average is 412. Sociologists call this form of average the *mean*. The mean can be deceptive because it is influenced by extreme scores, either low or high. Note that six of the seven cases are less than the mean. Two other ways to compute averages are the median and the mode.	To compute the second average, the *median*, first arrange the cases in order—either from the highest to the lowest or from the lowest to the highest. In this example, that arrangement will produce the following distribution: 57 1,795 57 321 136 289 (229 or 229) 289 136 321 57 1,795 57 Then look for the middle case, the one that falls halfway between the top and the bottom. That number is 229, for three numbers are lower and three numbers are higher. When there is an even number of cases, the median is the halfway mark between the two middle cases.	The third measure of average, the *mode*, is simply the cases that occur the most often. In this instance the mode is 57, which is way off the mark. 57 57 136 229 289 321 1,795 Because the mode is often deceptive and only by chance comes close to either of the other two averages, sociologists seldom use it. In addition, it is obvious that not every distribution of cases has a mode. And if two or more numbers appear with the same frequency, you can have more than one mode.

Doonesbury

Improperly worded questions can steer respondents toward answers that are not their own, thus producing invalid results.

Doonesbury © 1989 G. B. Trudeau. Reprinted with permission of Universal Press Syndicate. All rights reserved.

numbers are available in statistics books, and computer programs also can generate random numbers.)

Because a random sample represents your study's population—in this case, married women enrolled at your college—you can generalize your findings to all the married women students on your campus, even if they were not included in your sample.

What if you want to know only about certain subgroups, such as freshmen and seniors? You could use a stratified random sample. You would need a list of the freshmen and senior married women. Then, using random numbers, you would select a sample from each group. This would allow you to generalize to all the freshmen and senior married women at your college, but you would not be able to draw any conclusions about the sophomores or juniors.

Asking Neutral Questions. After you have decided on your population and sample, your next task is to make certain that your questions are neutral. Your questions must allow **respondents,** the people who respond to a survey, to express their own opinions. Otherwise you will end up with biased answers, which are worthless. For example, if you were to ask, "Don't you think that men who beat their wives should go to prison?" you would be tilting the answers toward agreement with a prison sentence. The Doonesbury cartoon illustrates a more blatant example of biased questions. For examples of flawed research, see the Down-to-Earth Sociology box on the next page.

Types of Questions. You must also decide whether to use closed- or open-ended questions. **Closed-ended questions** are followed by a list of possible answers. This format would work for questions about someone's age (possible ages would be listed), but it wouldn't work for many other items. For example, how could you list all the opinions that people hold about what should be done to spouse abusers? The answers provided for closed-ended questions can miss the respondent's opinions.

As Table 1.4 on the next page illustrates, the alternative is **open-ended questions,** which allow people to answer in their own words. Although open-ended questions allow you to tap the full range of people's opinions, they make it difficult to compare answers. For example, how would you compare these answers to the question "What do you think causes men to abuse their wives?"

"They're sick."

"I think they must have had problems with their mother."

"We ought to string them up!"

Because sociologists find all human behavior to be valid research topics, their research runs from the unusual to the routines of everyday life. Their studies range from broad scale social change, such as the globalization of capitalism, to such events as exhibitions of tattooing, piercing, and body painting. Shown here at the Australian Museum in Sydney is Lucky Rich, displaying his stainless steel teeth.

Down-to-Earth Sociology

Loading the Dice: How *Not* to Do Research

THE METHODS OF SCIENCE LEND themselves to distortion, misrepresentation, and downright fraud. Consider these findings:

Americans overwhelmingly prefer Toyotas to Chryslers.
Americans overwhelmingly prefer Chryslers to Toyotas.

Obviously, these opposite conclusions cannot be true. Yet each comes from so-called scientific surveys. It turns out that *both* findings are misrepresentations. The surveys were conducted by researchers who were biased, not independent and objective.

It turns out that some consumer researchers load the dice. They are hired by firms that have a vested interest in the outcome of the research, and they deliver the results their clients are looking for.

Here are six ways to load the dice.

1. **Choose a biased sample.** If you want to "prove" that Americans prefer Chryslers over Toyotas, interview unem-

ployed union workers who trace their job loss to Japanese imports. The answer is predictable. You'll get what you're looking for.

2. **Ask biased questions.** Even if you choose an unbiased sample, as in the *Doonesbury* cartoon on the preceding page, you can phrase questions in such a way that you direct people to the answer you're looking for. Suppose that you asked the question this way: "We are losing millions of jobs to workers overseas who work for just a few dollars a day. More and more Americans are being fired. Some are even homeless and hungry. Do you prefer a car that gives jobs to Americans, or one that forces our workers to lose their homes?"

Most biases aren't this blatant, of course, but consider this question on a national survey conducted by Republicans:

Is President Bush right in trying to rein in the size and scope of the federal government against the wishes of the big government Democrats?

This question is obviously designed to channel people's thinking toward a predetermined answer—quite contrary

Establishing Rapport. Will victims of abuse really give honest answers to strangers? The answer is yes, but first you must establish rapport ("ruh-POUR"), a feeling of trust, with your respondents. We know from studies of

rape that once rapport is gained (often by first asking non-sensitive questions), victims will talk about personal, sensitive matters.

To go beyond police statistics, each year researchers interview a random sample of 100,000 Americans. They ask them whether they have been victims of burglary, robbery, and so on. After establishing rapport, the researchers ask about rape. They find that rape victims will talk about their experiences. The national crime victimization survey shows that the actual incidence of rape is *three* times higher than the official statistics (*Statistical Abstract* 2005: page 184).

A new technique to gather data on sensitive areas, Computer-Assisted Self-Interviewing, overcomes lingering problems of distrust. In this technique, the interviewer gives a laptop computer to the respondent, then moves aside, while the individual enters his or her own answers into the computer. In some versions of this method, the respondent listens to the questions on a headphone

Table 1.4	Closed- and Open-Ended Questions	
A. Closed-Ended Question	**B. Open-Ended Question**
Which of the following best fits your idea of what should be done to someone who has been convicted of spouse abuse? 1. probation 2. jail time 3. community service 4. counseling 5. divorce 6. nothing—it's a family matter	What do you think should be done to someone who has been convicted of spouse abuse?

to the standards of scientific research. Democrats, by the way, do the same thing.

3. **List biased choices.** Another way to load the dice is to use closed-ended questions that push people into the answers you want. Consider this finding:

> U.S. college students overwhelmingly prefer Levis 501 to the jeans of any competitor.

Sound good? Before you rush out to buy Levis, note what these researchers did: In asking students which jeans would be the most popular in the coming year, their list of choices included no other jeans but Levis 501!

4. **Discard undesirable results.** Researchers can keep silent about results they find embarrassing, or they can continue to survey samples until they find one that matches what they are looking for.

As has been stressed in this chapter, research must be objective if it is to be scientific. Obviously, none of the preceding results qualifies. The underlying problem with the research cited here—and with so many surveys bandied about in the media as fact—is that survey research has become big business. Simply put, the money offered by corporations has corrupted some researchers.

The beginning of the corruption is subtle. Paul Light, dean at the University of Minnesota, put it this way: "A funder will never come to an academic and say, 'I want you to produce finding X, and here's a million dollars to do it.' Rather, the subtext is that if the researchers produce the right finding, more work—and funding—will come their way." He adds, "Once you're on that treadmill, it's hard to get off."

The first four sources of bias are inexcusable, intentional fraud. The next two sources of bias reflect sloppiness, which is also inexcusable in science.

5. **Misunderstand the subjects' world.** This route can lead to errors every bit as great as those just cited. Even researchers who use good samples, word their questions properly, and offer adequate choices can end up with skewed results. They may, for example, fail to anticipate that people may be embarrassed to express an opinion that isn't "politically correct." For example, surveys show that 80 percent of Americans are environmentalists. Most Americans, however, are probably embarrassed to tell a stranger otherwise. Today, that would be like going against the flag, motherhood, and apple pie.

6. **Analyze the data incorrectly.** Even when researchers strive for objectivity, the sample is good, the wording is neutral, and the respondents answer the questions honestly, the results can still be skewed. The researchers may make a mistake in their calculations, such as entering incorrect data into computers. This, too, of course, is inexcusable in science.

Sources: Based on Crossen 1991; Goleman 1993; Barnes 1995; Resnik 2000; "Ask America" 2004.

Sociologists who enter a research setting to discover information are using a research method known as *participant observation*. As discussed in the text, sociologists sometimes conduct research in controversial settings, such as this cockfight in Bangkok.

and answers them on the computer screen. When the respondent clicks the "Submit" button, the interviewer has no idea how the respondent answered any questions (Mosher et al. 2005).

Participant Observation (Fieldwork)

In **participant observation,** or **fieldwork,** the researcher *participates* in a research setting while *observing* what is happening in that setting. Obviously, this method does not mean that you would sit around and watch someone being abused. But if you wanted to learn how abuse has affected the victims' hopes and goals, their dating patterns, or their marriages, you could use participant observation.

For example, if your campus has a crisis intervention center, you may be able to observe victims of spouse abuse from the time they report the attack through their participation in counseling. With good rapport, you may even be able to spend time with them in other settings, observing other aspects of their lives. What they say and how they interact with others may help you understand how the abuse has affected their lives. This, in turn, may give you insight into how to improve college counseling services.

Secondary Analysis

If you were to analyze data that someone else has already collected, you would be doing **secondary analysis.** For example, if you were to examine the original data from a study of women who had been abused by their husbands, you would be doing secondary analysis.

Documents

Documents, or written sources, include books, newspapers, bank records, immigration records, and so on. To study spouse abuse, you might examine police reports to find out how many men in your community have been ar-

rested for abuse. You might also use court records to find out what proportion of those men were charged, convicted, or put on probation. If you wanted to learn about the social and emotional adjustment of the victims, however, these documents would tell you nothing. Other documents, though, might provide answers. For example, a crisis intervention center might have records that contain key information—but gaining access to them is almost impossible. Perhaps an unusually cooperative center might ask victims to keep diaries that you can study later.

Experiments

A lot of people say that abusers need therapy. But no one knows whether therapy really works. Let's suppose that you want to find out. Frankly, no one knows how to change a wife abuser into a loving husband. This may be impossible, but knowing whether therapy works would certainly be a step in the right direction. To find out, you may want to conduct an **experiment,** for experiments are useful for determining cause and effect.

Let's suppose that a judge likes your idea, and she gives you access to men who have been arrested for spouse abuse. You would randomly divide the men into two groups. (See Figure 1.4.) This would help to ensure that their individual characteristics (attitudes, number of arrests, severity of crimes, education, race-ethnicity, age, and so on) are distributed evenly between the groups. You would then arrange for the men in the **experimental group** to receive some sort of therapy. The men in the **control group** would not get therapy.

Your **independent variable,** something that causes a change in another variable, would be therapy. Your **dependent variable,** the variable that might change, would be the men's behavior: whether they abuse women after they get out of jail. To make that determination, you would need to rely on a sloppy operational definition: either reports from the wives or records indicating which men were rearrested

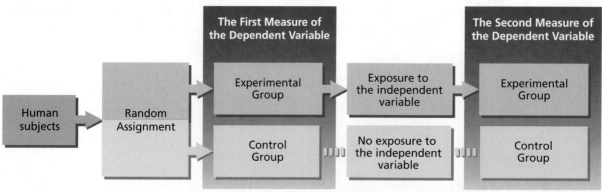

Figure 1.4 **The Experiment**

Source: By the author.

for abuse. This is sloppy because some of the women will not report the abuse, and some of the men who are reported for abuse will not be arrested. Yet it may be the best you can do.

Let's assume that you choose rearrest as your operational definition. If you find that the men who received therapy are *less* likely to be rearrested for abuse, you can attribute the difference to the therapy. If you find *no difference* in rearrest rates, you can conclude that therapy was ineffective. If you find that the men who received the therapy have a *higher* rearrest rate, you can conclude that the therapy backfired.

Unobtrusive Measures

Researchers sometimes use **unobtrusive measures,** observing the behavior of people who do not know they are being studied. For example, researchers have attached infrared devices on shopping carts to track customers' paths through stores. Grocery chains use these findings to place higher-profit items in more strategic locations (McCarthy 1993). Other researchers have studied garbage, measuring whisky consumption in a town that was legally "dry" by counting empty bottles in trashcans (Lee 2000).

It would be considered unethical to use most unobtrusive measures to research spouse abuse. You could, however, analyze 911 calls. Also, if there were a public forum held by abused or abusing spouses on the Internet, you could record and analyze the online conversations. Ethics are still a matter of dispute: To secretly record the behavior of people in public settings, such as a crowd, is generally considered acceptable, but to do so in private settings is not.

Ethics in Sociological Research

In addition to choosing an appropriate research method, then, we must also follow the ethics of sociology, which center on assumptions of science and morality (American Sociological Association 1997). Research ethics require openness (sharing findings with the scientific community), honesty, and truth. Ethics clearly forbid the falsification of results. They also condemn plagiarism, that is, stealing someone else's work. Another ethical guideline is that research subjects should generally be informed that they are being studied and never be harmed by the research. Ethics also require that sociologists protect the anonymity of people who provide private information. Finally, although not all sociologists agree, it generally is considered unethical for researchers to misrepresent themselves.

Sociologists take these ethical standards seriously. To illustrate the extent to which they will go to protect their respondents, consider the research conducted by Mario Brajuha.

Protecting the Subjects: The Brajuha Research

Mario Brajuha, a graduate student at the State University of New York at Stony Brook, was doing participant observation of restaurant workers. He lost his job as a waiter when the restaurant where he was working burned down—a fire of "suspicious origin," as the police said (Brajuha and Hallowell 1986). When detectives learned that Brajuha had taken field notes, they asked to see them. Because he had promised to keep his information confidential, Brajuha refused to hand them over. The district attorney subpoenaed the notes. Brajuha still refused. The district attorney then threatened to put Brajuha in jail. By this time, Brajuha's notes had become rather famous, and unsavory characters—perhaps those who had set the fire—also began to wonder what was in them. They, too, demanded to see them, accompanying their demands with threats of a different nature. Brajuha found himself between a rock and a hard place.

For two years, Brajuha refused to hand over his notes, even though he grew anxious and had to appear at several court hearings. Finally, the district attorney dropped the subpoena. When the two men under investigation for setting the fire died, so did the threats to Brajuha, his wife, and their children.

Misleading the Subjects: The Humphreys Research

Sociologists agree on the necessity to protect respondents, and they applaud the professional manner in which Brajuha handled himself. Although there is less agreement that researchers should not misrepresent themselves, sociologists who violate this norm can become embroiled in ethical controversy. Let's look at the case of Laud Humphreys, whose research forced sociologists to rethink and refine their ethical stance.

Laud Humphreys, a classmate of mine at Washington University in St. Louis, was an Episcopal priest who decided to become a sociologist. For his Ph.D. dissertation, Humphreys (1970, 1971, 1975) studied social interaction in "tearooms," public restrooms where some men go for quick, anonymous sex with other men.

Humphreys found that some restrooms in Forest Park, just across from our campus, were tearooms. He began a participant observation study by hanging around these restrooms. He found that in addition to the two men having sex, a third man—called a "watchqueen"—served as a lookout for police and other unwelcome strangers. Humphreys took on the role of watchqueen, not only watching for strangers but also observing what the men did. He wrote field notes after the encounters.

Humphreys decided that he wanted to know more about the regular lives of these men. For example, what was the significance of the wedding rings that many of the men wore? He came up with an ingenious technique. Many of the men parked their cars near the tearooms, and Humphreys recorded their license plate numbers. A friend in the St. Louis police department gave Humphreys each man's address. About a year later, Humphreys arranged for these men to be included in a medical survey conducted by some of the sociologists on our faculty.

Disguising himself with a different hairstyle and clothing, Humphreys visited the men's homes. He interviewed the men, supposedly for the medical study. He found that they led conventional lives. They voted, mowed their lawns, and took their kids to Little League games. Many reported that their wives were not aroused sexually or were afraid of getting pregnant because their religion did not allow them to use birth control. Humphreys concluded that heterosexual men were also using the tearooms for a form of quick sex.

This study stirred controversy among sociologists and nonsociologists alike. Many sociologists criticized Humphreys, and a national columnist even wrote a scathing denunciation of "sociological snoopers" (Von Hoffman 1970). As the controversy heated up and a court case loomed, Humphreys feared that his list of respondents might be subpoenaed. He gave me the list to take from Missouri to Illinois, where I had begun teaching. When he called and asked me to destroy it, I burned it in my backyard.

Was this research ethical? This question is not decided easily. Although many sociologists sided with Humphreys—and his book reporting the research won a highly acclaimed award—the criticisms mounted. At first, Humphreys vigorously defended his position, but five years later, in a second edition of his book (1975), he stated that he should have identified himself as a researcher.

Values in Sociological Research

Max Weber raised an issue that remains controversial among sociologists. He declared that sociology should be **value free.** By this he meant that a sociologist's **values**—beliefs about what is good or worthwhile in life—should not affect research. Instead, he said, we need objectivity,

© 1984 FarWorks, Inc. All Rights Reserved/Dist. by Creators Syndicate

The Far Side® by Gary Larson © 1984 FarWorks, Inc. All Rights Reserved. The Far Side® and the Larson® signature are registered trademarks of FarWorks, Inc. Used with permission.

"Anthropologists! Anthropologists!"

A major concern of sociologists and other social scientists is that their research methods do not influence their findings. Respondents often change their behavior when they know they are being studied.

total neutrality, for if values influence research, sociological findings will be biased.

Objectivity as an ideal is not a matter of debate in sociology. All sociologists agree that no one should distort data to make them fit preconceived ideas or values. It is equally clear, however, that, like everyone else, sociologists are members of a particular society at a given point in history and are, therefore, infused with values of all sorts. These values inevitably play a role in our research (Duneier 1999:78–79). For example, values are part of the reason that one sociologist chooses to do research on the Mafia while another turns a sociological eye on kindergarten students.

To overcome the distortions that values can cause and that unwittingly can become part of our research, sociologists stress **replication,** the repetition of a study by other researchers to compare results. If values have distorted research findings, replication by other sociologists should uncover the bias and correct it.

Despite this consensus, however, values remain a hotly debated topic in sociology (Buraway 2003; Gans 2003). This debate illustrates again the tension in sociology that we discussed earlier: the goal of analyzing social life versus the goal of social reform. Some sociologists are convinced that research should be directed along paths that will help to reform society, that will alleviate poverty, racism, sexism, and so on. Other sociologists lean strongly toward *basic* or *pure sociology,* research that has no goal beyond understanding social life and testing social theories. They say that nothing but their own interests should direct sociologists to study one topic rather than another. These contrasting views are summarized in Figure 1.5.

In the midst of this controversy, sociologists study the major issues facing our society at this crucial juncture of world history. From racism and sexism to the globalization of capitalism—these are all topics that sociologists study and that we will explore in this book. Sociologists also examine face-to-face interaction—talking, touching, gestures, clothing. These, too, will be the subject of our discussions in the upcoming chapters. This beautiful va-

Figure 1.5 The Debate over Values in Sociological Research

The Purposes of Social Research

To advance understanding of human behavior *versus* To investigate harmful social arrangements

The Uses of Social Research

Can be used by anyone for any purpose *versus* Should be used to reform society

riety in sociology—and the contrast of going from the larger picture to the smaller picture and back again—is part of the reason that sociology holds such fascination for me. I hope that you also find this variety appealing as you read the rest of this book.

Summary *and* Review

The Sociological Perspective

What is the sociological perspective?

The **sociological perspective** stresses that people's social experiences—the groups to which they belong and their experiences within these groups—underlie their behavior. C. Wright Mills referred to this as the intersection of biography (the individual) and history (social factors that influence the individual). P. 4–5.

Origins of Sociology

When did sociology first appear as a separate discipline?

Sociology emerged as a separate discipline in the mid-1800s in western Europe, during the onset of the Industrial Revolution. Industrialization affected all aspects of human existence—where people lived, the nature of their work, how they viewed life, and interpersonal relationships. Early sociologists who focused on these social

changes include Auguste Comte, Herbert Spencer, Karl Marx, Emile Durkheim, Max Weber, Harriet Martineau, and W. E. B. Du Bois. Pp. 5–8.

Sexism in Early Sociology

What was the position of women in early sociology?

Sociology appeared during a historical period of deep sexism. Consequently, the few women who received the education required to become sociologists were ignored. P. 9.

Sociology in North America

When was sociology established in the United States?

The earliest departments of sociology were established in the late 1800s at the universities of Kansas, Chicago, and Atlanta. During the 1940s, the University of Chicago dominated sociology. A tension between social reform and social research and theory ran through sociology, and in its early years, the contributions of women and minorities were largely overlooked. Pp. 9–12.

What is the difference between basic (or pure) and applied sociology?

U.S. sociology has experienced tension between pure or basic sociology, in which the aim is to analyze society, and attempts to use sociology to reform society. Today, these contrasting orientations exist dynamically side by side. **Applied sociology** is the use of sociology to solve problems. Pp. 12–14.

Theoretical Perspectives in Sociology

What is a theory?

A **theory** is a statement about how facts are related to one another. A theory provides a conceptual framework for interpreting facts. P. 14.

What are sociology's major theoretical perspectives?

Sociologists use three primary theoretical frameworks to interpret social life. **Symbolic interactionists** examine how people use symbols to develop and share their views of the world. Symbolic interactionists usually focus on the **micro level**—on small-scale, face-to-face interaction. **Functional analysts,** in contrast, focus on the **macro level**—on large-scale patterns of society. Functional theorists stress that a social system is made up of interrelated parts. When working properly, each part contributes to the stability of the whole, fulfilling a function that contributes to the system's equilibrium. **Conflict theorists** also focus on large-scale patterns of society. They stress that society is composed of competing groups that struggle for scarce resources. Pp. 14–19.

   With each perspective focusing on select features of social life, and each providing a unique interpretation, no single theory is adequate. The combined insights of all three perspectives yield a more comprehensive picture of social life. P. 19.

What is the relationship between theory and research?

Theory and research depend on one another. Sociologists use theory to interpret the data they gather. Theory also generates questions that need to be answered by research, while research, in turn, helps to generate theory. Theory without research is not likely to represent real life, while research without theory is merely a collection of empty facts. P. 19–20.

Doing Sociological Research

Why do we need sociological research when we have common sense?

Common sense is unreliable. Research often shows that commonsense ideas are limited or false. Pp. 20, 21, 22.

What are the eight basic steps in sociological research?

1. Selecting a topic   2. Defining the problem
3. Reviewing the literature   4. Formulating a **hypothesis**   5. Choosing a **research method**
6. Collecting the data   7. Analyzing the results
8. Sharing the results
These steps are explained on pp. 20–22.

Research Methods

How do sociologists gather data?

To gather data, sociologists use six **research methods** (or **research designs**): **surveys, participant observation, secondary analysis, documents, experiments,** and **unobtrusive measures.** Pp. 22–29.

Ethics in Sociological Research

How important are ethics in sociological research?

Ethics are of fundamental concern to sociologists, who are committed to openness, honesty, truth, and protecting their subjects from harm. The Brajuha research on restaurant workers and the Humphreys research on "tearooms" illustrate ethical issues of concern to sociologists. Pp. 29–30.

What value dilemmas do sociologists face?

Max Weber stressed that social research should be **value free:** The researcher's personal beliefs must be set aside to permit objective findings. Like everyone else, however, sociologists are members of a particular society at a given point in history and are infused with **values** of all sorts. To overcome the distortions that values can cause, sociologists stress **replication,** the repetition of a study by other researchers in order to compare results. Values present a second dilemma for researchers: whether to do research solely to analyze human behavior (basic or pure sociology) or to reform harmful social arrangements. P. 30–31.

Thinking Critically

about Chapter 1

1. Do you think that sociologists should try to reform society or study it dispassionately?

2. Of the three theoretical perspectives, which one would you prefer to use if you were a sociologist? Why?

3. Considering the macro- and micro-level approaches in sociology, which one do you think better explains social life? Why?

Additional Resources

Companion Website www.ablongman.com/henslin

- Content Select Research Database for Sociology, with suggested key terms and annotated references
- Link to 2000 Census, with activities
- Flashcards of key terms and concepts

- Flashcards of key terms and concepts
- Practice Tests
- Weblinks
- Interactive Maps

Where Can I Read More on This Topic?

Suggested readings for this chapter are listed at the back of this book.

Culture

OUTLINE

What Is Culture?
Culture and Taken-for-Granted
   Orientations to Life
Practicing Cultural Relativism

**Components of Symbolic
Culture**
Gestures
Language
Language and Perception
Values, Norms, and Sanctions
Folkways and Mores

Many Cultural Worlds
Subcultures
Countercultures

Values in U.S. Society
An Overview of U.S. Values
Value Clusters
Value Contradictions and Social
   Change
Emerging Values
Culture Wars: When Values Clash
Values as Blinders
"Ideal" Versus "Real" Culture

**Technology in the Global
Village**
The New Technology
Cultural Lag and Cultural Change
Technology and Cultural Leveling

Summary and Review

R. C. Gorman, *Night Stories*, 1994

I had never felt heat like this before. This was *northern* Africa, and I wondered what it must be like closer to the equator. Sweat poured off me as the temperature climbed, soaring past 110° Fahrenheit.

As we were herded into the checkpoint—which had no air-conditioning—hundreds of people lunged toward the counter at the rear of the structure. With body crushed against body, we waited as the uniformed officials behind the windows leisurely examined each passport. At times like this, I wondered what I was doing in Africa.

When I first arrived in Morocco, I found the sights that greeted me exotic—not far removed from my memories of *Casablanca, Raiders of the Lost Ark,* and other movies that over the years had become part of my collective memory. The men, the women, and even the children really did wear those white robes that reached down to their feet. What was especially striking was that the women were almost totally covered. Despite the heat, they wore not only full-length gowns, but also head coverings that reached down over their foreheads and veils that covered their faces from the nose down.

All you could see were their eyes—all the same shade of brown. And how short everyone was! The Arab women looked to be, on average, 5 feet, and the men only three or four inches taller. As the only blue-eyed, blond, 6-foot-plus person around, and the only one wearing jeans and a pullover shirt, in a world of white-robed short people I stood out like a creature from another planet. Everyone stared. No matter where I went, they stared. Wherever I looked, I found brown eyes watching me intently. Even staring back at those many dark brown eyes had no effect. It was so different from home, where, if you caught someone staring at you, that person would immediately look embarrassed and glance away.

And lines? The concept apparently didn't even exist. Buying a ticket for a bus or train meant pushing and shoving toward the ticket man (always a man—no women were

I pushed my way forward, forcing my frame into every square inch of vacant space that I could create. At the counter, I shouted in English.

visible in any public position), who took the money from whichever outstretched hand he decided on.

And germs? That notion didn't seem to exist here either. Flies swarmed over the food in the restaurants and over the unwrapped loaves of bread in the stores. Shopkeepers would considerately shoo the flies away before handing me a loaf. They also offered home delivery. I still remember watching a bread vendor deliver a loaf to a woman who stood on a second-floor balcony. She first threw her money to the bread vendor, and he then threw the unwrapped bread up to her. Only, his throw was off. The bread bounced off the wrought-iron balcony railing and landed in the street, which was filled with people, wandering dogs, and the ever-present defecating burros. The vendor simply picked up the unwrapped loaf and threw it again. This certainly wasn't his day, for he missed again. But he made it on his third attempt. The woman smiled as she turned back into her apartment, apparently to prepare the noon meal for her family.

Now, standing in the oppressive heat on the Moroccan-Algerian border, the crowd once again became unruly. Another fight had broken out. And once again, the little man in uniform appeared, shouting and knocking people aside as he forced his way to a little wooden box nailed to the floor. Climbing onto this makeshift platform, he shouted at the crowd, his arms flailing about him. The people fell silent. But just as soon as the man left, the shoving and shouting began again amidst the clamor to get passports stamped.

The situation had become unbearable. His body pressed against mine, the man behind me decided that this was a good time to take a nap. Determining that I made a good support, he placed his arm against my back and leaned his head against his arm. Sweat streamed down my back at the point where his arm and head touched me.

Finally, I realized that I had to abandon U.S. customs. I pushed my way forward, forcing my frame into every square inch of vacant space that I could create. At the counter, I shouted in English. The official looked up at the sound of this strange tongue, and I thrust my long arms over the heads of three people, shoving my passport into his hand.

What Is Culture?

What is culture? The concept is sometimes easier to grasp by description than by definition. For example, suppose you meet a young woman from India who has just arrived in the United States. That her culture is different from yours is immediately evident. You first see it in her clothing, jewelry, makeup, and hairstyle. Next you hear it in her speech. It then becomes apparent by her gestures. Later, you might hear her express unfamiliar beliefs about the world or about what is valuable in life. All of these characteristics are indicative of **culture**—the language, beliefs, values, norms, behaviors, and even material objects that are passed from one generation to the next.

In northern Africa, I was surrounded by a culture quite alien to my own. It was evident in everything I saw and heard. The **material culture**—such things as jewelry, art, buildings, weapons, machines, and even eating utensils, hairstyles, and clothing—provided a sharp contrast to what I was used to seeing. There is nothing inherently "natural" about material culture. That is, it is no more natural (or unnatural) to wear gowns on the street than it is to wear jeans.

I also found myself immersed in a contrasting **nonmaterial culture,** that is, a group's ways of thinking (its beliefs, values, and other assumptions about the world) and doing (its common patterns of behavior, including language, gestures, and other forms of interaction). North African assumptions about pushing others aside to buy a ticket and staring in public are examples of nonmaterial culture. So are U.S. assumptions about not doing either of these things. Like material culture, neither custom is "right." People simply become comfortable with the customs they learn during childhood and—as in the case of my visit to northern Africa—uncomfortable when their basic assumptions about life are challenged.

Culture and Taken-for-Granted Orientations to Life

To develop a sociological perspective, it is essential to understand how culture affects people's lives. If we meet someone from a different culture, the encounter may make us aware of culture's pervasive influence. Attaining the same level of awareness regarding our own culture, however, is quite another matter. *Our* speech, *our* gestures, *our* beliefs, and *our* customs are usually taken for granted. We assume that they are "normal" or "natural," and we almost always accept them without question. As anthropologist Ralph Linton (1936) remarked, "The last thing a fish would ever notice would be water." So also with people: Except in unusual circumstances, the effects of our own culture remain imperceptible to us.

Yet culture's significance is profound; it touches almost every aspect of who and what we are. We came into this life without a language; without values and morality; with no ideas about religion, war, money, love, use of public space, personal boundaries, and so on. We possessed none of these fundamental orientations that we take for granted and that are so essential in determining the type of people we become. Yet by this point in our lives, we all have acquired them. Sociologists call this *culture within us.* These learned and shared ways of believing and of doing (another definition of culture) penetrate our being at an early age and quickly become part of our taken-for-granted assumptions about what normal behavior is. *Culture becomes the lens through which we perceive and evaluate what is going on around us.* Seldom do we question these assumptions, for, like water to a fish, the lens through which we view life remains largely beyond our perception.

The rare instances in which these assumptions are challenged, however, can be upsetting. Although as a sociologist I should be able to look at my own culture from the outside, my trip to Africa quickly revealed how fully I had internalized my culture. My upbringing in Western society had given me strong assumptions about aspects of social life that had become deeply rooted in my being—eye contact with strangers, hygiene, and the use of space. But in this part of Africa these assumptions were useless in helping me navigate everyday life. No longer could I count

on people to stare only surreptitiously, to take precautions against invisible microbes, or to stand in line in an orderly fashion, one behind the other.

As you can tell from the opening vignette, I personally found these different assumptions upsetting, for they violated my basic expectations of "the way people *ought* to be"—although I did not even realize how firmly I held these expectations until they were so abruptly challenged. When my nonmaterial culture failed me—when it no longer enabled me to make sense out of the world—I experienced a disorientation known as **culture shock.** In the case of buying tickets, the fact that I was several inches taller than most Moroccans and thus able to outreach almost everyone helped me adjust partially to their different ways of doing things. But I never did get used to the idea that pushing ahead of others was "right," and I always felt guilty when I used my size to receive preferential treatment.

An important consequence of culture within us is **ethnocentrism,** a tendency to use our own group's ways of doing things as the yardstick for judging others. All of us learn that the ways of our own group are good, right, proper, and even superior to other ways of life. As sociologist William Sumner (1906), who developed this concept, said, "One's own group is the center of everything, and all others are scaled and rated with reference to it."

Ethnocentrism has both positive and negative consequences. On the positive side, it creates in-group loyalties. On the negative side, ethnocentrism can lead to discrimination against people whose ways differ from ours.

The many ways in which culture affects our lives fascinate sociologists. In this chapter, we'll examine how profoundly culture affects everything we are. This will serve as a basis from which you can start to analyze your own assumptions of reality. I should give you a warning at this point: This can result in your gaining a different perspective on social life and your role in it. If so, life will never look the same.

IN SUM To avoid losing track of the ideas under discussion, let's pause for a moment to summarize, and in some instances clarify, the principles we have covered:

1. There is nothing "natural" about material culture. Arabs wear gowns on the street and feel that it is natural to do so; Americans do the same with jeans.
2. There is nothing "natural" about nonmaterial culture; it is just as arbitrary to stand in line as to push and shove.

3. Culture becomes a lens through which we see the world and obtain our perception of reality.

4. Culture provides implicit instructions that tell us what we ought to do and how we ought to think; it provides a fundamental basis for our decision making.

5. Culture also provides a "moral imperative"; that is, the culture that we internalize becomes the "right" way of doing things. (I, for example, believed deeply that it was wrong to push and shove to get ahead of others.)

6. Coming into contact with a radically different culture challenges our basic assumptions about life. (I experienced culture shock when I discovered that my deeply ingrained cultural ideas about hygiene and the use of personal space no longer applied.)

7. Although the particulars of culture differ from one group of people to another, culture itself is universal. That is, all people have culture, for a society cannot exist without developing shared, learned ways of dealing with the challenges of life.

8. All people are ethnocentric, which has both positive and negative consequences.

Practicing Cultural Relativism

To counter our tendency to use our own culture as the standard by which we judge other cultures, we can practice **cultural relativism;** that is, we can try to understand a culture on its own terms. Cultural relativism involves looking at how the elements of a culture fit together without judging those elements as superior or inferior to one's own way of life.

Because we tend to use our own culture as a standard for judging others, cultural relativism presents a challenge to ordinary thinking. For example, most U.S. citizens appear to have strong feelings against raising bulls for the purpose of stabbing them to death in front of crowds that shout "Olé!" According to cultural relativism, however, bullfighting must be viewed from the perspective of the culture in which it takes place—*its* history, *its* folklore, *its* ideas of bravery, and *its* ideas of sex roles.

You still may regard bullfighting as wrong, of course, because U.S. culture, so deeply ingrained in us, has no history of bullfighting. We all possess culturally specific ideas about cruelty to animals, convictions that have evolved slowly and match other elements of our culture. Consequently, practices that once were common—

cock fighting, dog fighting, bear–dog fighting, and so on—have been gradually eliminated.

None of us can be entirely successful at practicing cultural relativism. Look at the Cultural Diversity box on the next page. My best guess is that you will evaluate these "strange" foods through the lens of your own culture. Practicing cultural relativism, however, is an attempt to refocus that lens so we can appreciate other ways of life rather than simply asserting, "Our way is right." As you view the photos on page 40, try to appreciate the cultural differences in standards of beauty.

Although cultural relativism helps us to avoid cultural smugness, this view has come under attack. In a provocative book, *Sick Societies* (1992), anthropologist Robert Edgerton suggests that we develop a scale for evaluating cultures based on their "quality of life," much as we do for U.S. cities. He also asks why we should consider cultures that practice female circumcision, gang rape, or wife beating or cultures that sell little girls into prostitution as morally equivalent to those that do not. Cultural values that result in exploitation, he says, are inferior to those that enhance people's lives.

Edgerton's sharp questions and incisive examples bring us to a topic that comes up repeatedly in this text: the disagreements that arise among scholars as they confront contrasting views of reality. It is such questioning of assumptions that keeps sociology interesting.

Many Americans perceive bullfighting, which is illegal in the United States, as a cruel activity that should be abolished everywhere. To Spaniards and those who have inherited Spanish culture, however, bullfighting is a beautiful, artistic sport in which matador and bull blend into a unifying image of power, courage, and glory. *Cultural relativism* requires that we suspend our own perspectives in order to grasp the perspectives of others, something that is much easier described than attained.

Cultural Diversity *around the* World

You Are What You Eat? An Exploration in Cultural Relativity

HERE IS A CHANCE to test your ethnocentrism and ability to practice cultural relativity. You probably know that the French like to eat snails and that in some Asian cultures, chubby dogs and cats are considered a delicacy ("Ah, lightly browned with a little doggy sauce!"). But did you know about this?

Marston Bates (1967), a zoologist, reports:

I remember once, in the llanos of Colombia, sharing a dish of toasted ants at a remote farmhouse. . . . My host and I fell into conversation about the general question of what people eat or do not eat, and I remarked that in my country people eat the legs of frogs.

The very thought of this filled my ant-eating friends with horror; it was as though I had mentioned some repulsive sex habit.

And then there is the experience of the production coordinator of this text, Dusty Friedman, who told me:

When traveling in Sudan, I ate some interesting things that I wouldn't likely eat now that I'm back in our society. Raw baby camel's liver with chopped herbs was a delicacy. So was camel's milk cheese patties that had been cured in dry camel's dung.

You might be able to see yourself eating frog legs, toasted ants, perhaps raw camel's liver, or even dogs and cats, but this custom may provide a better test of your ethnocentrism and cultural relativity ("Monkey Rescued" 2004).

"Nothing like a little snake blood to get you started in the morning." Food preferences, an essential part of culture, vary around the world, as this photo from Taipei, Taiwan, illustrates.

Maxine Kingston (1975), an English professor whose parents grew up in China, wrote:

"Do you know what people in [the Nantou region of] China eat when they have the money?" my mother began. "They buy into a monkey feast. The eaters sit around a thick wood table with a hole in the middle. Boys bring in the monkey at the end of a pole. Its neck is in a collar at the end of the pole, and it is screaming. Its hands are tied behind it. They clamp the monkey into the table; the whole table fits like another collar around its neck. Using a surgeon's saw, the cooks cut a clean line in a circle at the top of its head. To loosen the bone, they tap with a tiny hammer and wedge here and there with a silver pick. Then an old woman reaches out her hand to the monkey's face and up to its scalp, where she tufts some hairs and lifts off the lid of the skull. The eaters spoon out the brains."

for your Consideration

1. What is your opinion about eating toasted ants? About eating fried frog legs? About eating puppies and kittens? About eating raw monkey brains?

2. If you were reared in U.S. society, more than likely you think that eating frog legs is okay, eating ants is disgusting, and eating dogs, cats, and monkey brains is downright repugnant. How would you apply the concepts of ethnocentrism and cultural relativism to your perception of these customs?

Components of Symbolic Culture

Sociologists sometimes refer to nonmaterial culture as **symbolic culture** because its central component is the symbols that people use. A **symbol** is something to which people attach meaning and that they then use to communicate with one another. Symbols include gestures, language, values, norms, sanctions, folkways, and mores. Let's look at each of these components of symbolic culture.

Standards of Beauty

Standards of beauty vary so greatly from one culture to another that what one group finds attractive, another may not. Yet, in its *ethnocentrism,* each group thinks that its standards are the best—that their appearance reflects what beauty "really" is.

As indicated by these photos, around the world men and women aspire to their group's norms of physical attractiveness. To make themselves appealing to others, they make certain that their appearance reflects those standards.

Tibet

Cameroon

Thailand

New Guinea

Japan

India (Gypsy)

Peru

United States

Gestures

Gestures, using one's body to communicate with others, are shorthand ways to convey messages without using words. Although people in every culture of the world use gestures, a gesture's meaning may change from one culture to another. North Americans, for example, communicate a succinct message by raising the middle finger in a short, upward-stabbing motion. I stress "North Americans," for that gesture does not convey the same message in most parts of the world.

I once was surprised to find that this particular gesture was not universal, having internalized it to such an extent that I thought everyone knew what it meant. When I was comparing gestures with friends in Mexico, however, this gesture drew a blank look from them. After I explained its intended meaning, they laughed and showed me their rudest gesture—placing the hand under the armpit and moving the upper arm up and down. To me, they simply looked as if they were imitating monkeys, but to them the gesture meant "Your mother is a whore," the worst possible insult in that culture.

With the current political, military, and cultural dominance of the United States, "giving the finger" is becoming well known in other cultures. Following 9/11, the United States began to photograph and fingerprint foreign travelers. Feeling insulted, Brazil retaliated by doing the same to U.S. visitors. Angry at this, a U.S. pilot raised his middle finger while being photographed. Having become aware of the meaning of this gesture, Brazilian police arrested him. To gain his release, the pilot had to pay a fine of $13,000 ("Brazil Arrests" . . . 2004).

Gestures not only facilitate communication but also, because their meanings differ around the world, they can lead to misunderstanding, embarrassment, or worse. One time in Mexico, for example, I raised my hand to a certain height to indicate how tall a child was. My hosts began to laugh. It turns out that Mexicans use three hand gestures to indicate height: one for people, a second for animals, and yet another for plants. They were amused because I had ignorantly used the plant gesture to indicate the child's height. (See Figure 2.1.)

To get along in another culture, then, it is important to learn the gestures used by people of that culture. If you don't, not only will you fail to achieve the simplicity of communication that gestures allow but also you may overlook or misunderstand much of what is happening, run the risk of appearing foolish, and possibly offend people. In some cultures, for example, you would provoke deep offense if you were to offer food or a gift with your left hand, because the left hand is reserved for dirty tasks, such as wiping after going to the toilet. Left-handed Americans visiting Arabs, please note!

Suppose for a moment that you are visiting southern Italy. After eating one of the best meals of your life, you are so pleased that when you catch the waiter's eye, you smile broadly and use the standard U.S. "A-OK" gesture of putting your thumb and forefinger together and making a large "**O.**" The waiter looks horrified, and you are struck speechless when the manager asks you to leave. What have you done? Nothing on purpose, of course, but in that culture this gesture refers to a part of the human body that is not mentioned in polite company (Ekman et al. 1984).

Some gestures are so associated with emotional messages that the gesture itself, even when demonstrated out of context, summons up emotions. For example, my introduction to Mexican gestures took place at a dinner table. It was evident that my husband-and-wife hosts were trying to hide their embarrassment at using their culture's obscene gesture at their dinner table. And I felt

Figure 2.1 **Gestures to Indicate Height, Southern Mexico**

Although most gestures are learned, and therefore vary from culture to culture, some gestures that represent fundamental emotions such as sadness, anger, and fear appear to be inborn. This crying child whom I photographed in India differs little from a crying child in China—or the United States or anywhere else on the globe. In a few years, however, this child will demonstrate a variety of gestures highly specific to his Hindu culture.

the same way—not about *their* gesture, of course, which meant nothing to me, but about the one I was teaching them.

Language

Gestures and words go hand in hand, as is evident when you watch people talking. We use gestures to supplement our words, to provide emphasis and a deeper understanding of what we are communicating. Written language lacks the subtle cues that gestures provide, and with online communications so common, we miss these cues. To help supply them, people use "written gestures" that help to convey the feelings that go with their words. These emoticons are the topic of the Down-to-Earth Sociology box on the next page.

The primary way in which people communicate with one another is through **language**—symbols that can be strung together in an infinite number of ways for the purpose of communicating abstract thought. Each word is actually a symbol, a sound to which we have attached a particular meaning. This allows us to use it to communicate with one another. Language itself is universal in the sense that all human groups have language, but there is nothing universal about the meanings given to particular sounds. Thus, like gestures, in different cultures the same

sound may mean something entirely different—or it may have no meaning at all. In German, for example, *gift* means poison, and if you give chocolate to a non-English speaking German and say, "Gift". . .

★ *Because language allows culture to exist,* its significance for human life is difficult to overstate. Consider the following:

Language Allows Human Experience to Be Cumulative   By means of language, we pass on ideas, knowledge, and even attitudes to the next generation. This allows others to build on experiences in which they might never directly participate. Because of this, humans are able to modify their behavior in light of what previous generations have learned. Hence the central sociological significance of language: *Language allows culture to develop by freeing people to move beyond their immediate experiences.*

Without language, human culture would be little more advanced than that of the lower primates. If we communicated by grunts and gestures, we would be limited to a short time span: to events now taking place, those that have just taken place, or those that will take place immediately—a sort of slightly extended present. You can grunt and gesture, for example, that you want a drink of water, but in the absence of language, how could you share ideas concerning past or future events? There would be little or no way to communicate to others what event you had in mind, much less the greater complexities that humans communicate: ideas and feelings about events.

Language Provides a Social or Shared Past Without language, our memories would be extremely limited, for we associate experiences with words and then use words to recall the experience and words to reflect on that experience. Such memories as would exist in the absence of language would be highly individualized, for only rarely and incompletely could we communicate them to others, much less discuss them and agree on something. By attaching words to an event, however, and then using those words to recall it, we are able to discuss the event. As we talk about past events, we develop shared understandings about what those events mean. In short, through talk, people develop a shared past.

Language Provides a Social or Shared Future Language also extends our time horizons forward. Because language enables us to agree on times, dates, and places, it allows us to plan activities with one another. Think about it for a moment. Without language, how could you ever plan future events? How could you possibly communicate goals, times, and plans? Whatever planning could exist would be limited to rudimentary

Down-to-Earth Sociology

Emoticons: "Written Gestures" for Expressing Yourself Online

TALKING ONLINE HAS BECOME A FAVORITE activity of millions of people. Teenagers rehash the day's events with friends; grandparents keep in touch with grandchildren; businesspeople seal their deals with the click of a "send" button. All of them love the speed of online communications. They send an e-mail or an instant message, or post a note in a chat room, and in an instant people across the country or in distant lands can read or respond to it.

There is something nagging about online talk, though. It leaves a dissatisfying taste because it is so one-dimensional. People miss the nuances of emotion and overlays of meaning that we transmit during face-to-face conversations. Lacking are the gestures and tones of voice that give color and life to our communications, the subtleties by which we monitor and communicate submessages.

To help fill this gap, computer users have developed symbols to convey their humor, disappointment, sarcasm, and other moods and attitudes. Although these symbols are not as varied or spontaneous as the nonverbal cues of face-to-face interaction, they are useful. Here are some of them. If you tilt your head to the left as you view them, the symbols will be clearer.

:-)	Smile
:-))	Laugh
:-(	Frowning, or Sad
:-((	Very sad
:,(	Crying
>:-(	Angry, annoyed

:-X	My lips are sealed (or a Kiss)
;-)	Wink, wink—know what I mean?
:-')	Tongue in cheek
:-P	Sticking out your tongue
:-$	Put your money where your mouth is
(:- D	Has a big mouth
:-O	WOW! (Shocked)
#-)	Oh, what a night!

Some correspondents prefer more aesthetically pleasing emoticons. They use the profile version: **:^) :^)) :^(**

Correspondents also use abbreviations to indicate their emotions:

IAB	I Am Bored
ILY	I Love You
JK	Just Kidding
LOL	Laughing Out Loud
OTF	On The Floor (laughing)
ROTF	Rolling On The Floor
ROFLWTIME	Rolling On Floor Laughing With Tears In My Eyes

Another form of emoticons are the many smilies. Each of the symbols below is meant to indicate a particular emotion—from happiness and greed to shock and embarrassment.

With advancing technology, such shorthand might become unnecessary. Now that we can include video in our e-mail, recipients can see our image and hear our voice. Eventually, messages that include verbal and facial cues may replace much written e-mail. As long as written e-mail exists, however, some system of symbols to substitute for gestures will remain.

communications, perhaps to an agreement to meet at a certain place when the sun is in a certain position. But think of the difficulty, perhaps impossibility, of conveying just a slight change in this simple arrangement, such as "I can't make it tomorrow, but my neighbor can take my place, if that's all right with you."

Language Allows Shared Perspectives   Our ability to speak, then, provides a social past and future. These two vital aspects of our humanity represent a watershed that distinguishes us from animals. But speech does much more than this. When humans talk with one another, they are exchanging ideas about events; that is, they are sharing perspectives. Their words are the embodiment of their experiences, distilled into a readily exchangeable form, one that is mutually intelligible for people who have learned that language. Talking about events allows people to arrive at the shared understandings that form the basis of social life. Not sharing a language while residing alongside one another, however, invites miscommunication and suspicion. This risk, which comes with living in a diverse society, is discussed in the Cultural Diversity box below.

Language Allows Complex, Shared, Goal-Directed Behavior Common understandings also enable people to establish a *purpose* for getting together. Let's suppose you want to go on a picnic. You use speech not only to plan the picnic but also to decide on reasons for the picnic—which may be anything from "because it's a nice day and it shouldn't be wasted studying" to "because it's my birthday." Language permits you to blend individual activities into an integrated sequence. In other words, through discussion you decide where you will go; who will drive; who

Cultural Diversity *in the* United States

Miami—Language in a Changing City

Florida

SINCE CASTRO SEIZED POWER IN CUBA in 1959, the city of Miami has been transformed from a quiet southern city to a Latin American mecca. Nothing reflects Miami's essential character today as much as its long-simmering feud over language: English versus Spanish. Half of the city's 360,000 residents have trouble speaking English. Only *one-fourth* of Miami residents speak English at home.

As this chapter stresses, language is a primary means by which people learn—and communicate—their social worlds. Consequently, language differences in Miami reflect not only cultural diversity but also the separate social worlds of the city's inhabitants.

Although its ethnic stew makes Miami culturally one of the richest cities in the United States, the language gap sometimes creates misunderstanding and anger. The aggravation felt by Anglos—which often seems tinged with hostility—is seen in the bumper stickers that used

Mural from Miami.

to read, "Will the Last American Out Please Bring the Flag?"

Latinos, now a majority in Miami, are similarly frustrated. Many think that Anglos should be able to speak at least some Spanish. Nicaraguan immigrant Pedro Falcon, for example, is studying English and wonders why more people don't try to learn his language. "Miami is the capital of Latin America," he says. "The population speaks Spanish."

Language and cultural flare-ups sometimes make headlines in the city. Latinos were outraged when an employee

at the Coral Gables Board of Realtors lost her job for speaking Spanish at the office. And protesters swarmed a Publix supermarket after a cashier was fired for chatting with a friend in Spanish.

What's happening in Miami, says University of Chicago sociologist Douglas Massey, is what happened in cities such as Chicago a hundred years ago. Then, as now, the rate of immigration exceeded the speed with which new residents learned English, creating a pile-up effect in the proportion of non-English speakers. "Becoming comfortable with English is a slow process," he points out, "whereas immigration is fast."

Massey expects Miami's percentage of non-English speakers to grow. But he says that this "doesn't mean that Miami is going to end up being a Spanish-speaking city." Instead, Massey believes that bilingualism will prevail. He says, "The people who get ahead are not monolingual English speakers or monolingual Spanish speakers. They're people who speak both languages."

In the meantime, Miami officials have tried to resolve the controversy over language by declaring English to be the official language of Miami. In at least one small way, they have succeeded. When we tried to get a photograph of "Bienvenidos a Miami" for this box, we discovered that such a sign would be illegal!

Source: Based on Sharp 1992; Usdansky 1992.

will bring the hamburgers, chips, and soda; where you will meet; and so on. Only because of language can you participate in such a picnic—or build bridges and roads, or attend college classes.

IN SUM The sociological significance of language is that it takes us beyond the world of apes and allows culture to develop. Language frees us from the present, actually giving us a social past and a social future. That is, language gives us the capacity to share understandings about the past and to develop shared perceptions about the future. Language also allows us to establish underlying purposes for our activities. In short, *language is the basis of culture.* ✳

Language and Perception: The Sapir-Whorf Hypothesis

In the 1930s, two anthropologists, Edward Sapir and Benjamin Whorf, became intrigued when they noted that the Hopi Indians of the southwestern United States had no words to distinguish among the past, the present, and the future. English, in contrast—as well as French, Spanish, Swahili, and other languages—distinguishes carefully among these three time frames. From this observation, Sapir and Whorf concluded that the commonsense idea that words are merely labels that people attach to things is wrong. *Language, they concluded, has embedded within it ways of looking at the world.* Language, they said, not only expresses our thoughts but also shapes the way we think. Words not only express what we perceive but also help to determine what we perceive. When we learn a language, we learn not only words but also ways of thinking and perceiving (Sapir 1949; Whorf 1956).

The **Sapir-Whorf hypothesis** reverses common sense: It indicates that rather than objects and events forcing themselves onto our consciousness, it is our language that determines our consciousness, and hence our perception of objects and events. The racial-ethnic terms provided by our culture, for example, influence how we see both ourselves and others, a point that is discussed in the Cultural Diversity box below.

Cultural Diversity *in the* United States

Race and Language: Searching for Self-Labels

THE GROUPS THAT DOMINATE SOCIETY often determine the names that are used to refer to racial-ethnic groups. If those names become associated with oppression, they take on negative meanings. For example, the terms *Negro* and *colored people* came to be associated with submissiveness and low status. To overcome these meanings, those referred to by these terms began to identify themselves as *black* or *African American*. They infused these new terms with respect—a basic source of self-esteem that they felt the old terms denied them.

In a twist, African Americans—and to a lesser extent Latinos, Asian Americans, and Native Americans—have changed the rejected term *colored people* to *people of color*. Those who embrace this modified term are imbuing it with meanings that offer an identity of respect. The term also has political meanings. It indicates bonds that cross racial-ethnic lines, a growing sense of mutual ties and identity rooted in historical oppression.

There is *always* disagreement about racial-ethnic terms, and this one is no exception. Although most rejected the term *colored people,* some found in it a sense of respect and claimed it for themselves. The acronym NAACP, for example, stands for the National Association for the Advancement of Colored People. The new term, *people of color,* arouses similar feelings. Some individuals whom this term would include claim that it is inappropriate. They point out that this new label still makes color the primary identifier of people. They stress that humans transcend race-ethnicity, that what we have in common as human beings goes much deeper than what you see on the surface. They stress that we should avoid terms that focus on differences in the pigmentation of our skin.

The language of self-reference in a society that is so conscious of skin color is an ongoing issue. As long as our society continues to emphasize such superficial differences, the search for adequate terms is not likely to ever be "finished." In this quest for terms that strike the right chord, the term *people of color* may become a historical footnote. If it does, it will be replaced by another term that indicates a changing self-identification in a changing historical context.

Sociologist Eviatar Zerubavel (1991) gives a good example: Hebrew, his native language, does not have separate words for jam and jelly. Both go by the same term, and only when Zerubavel learned English could he "see" this difference, which is "obvious" to native English speakers. Similarly, if you learn to classify students as Jocks, Goths, Stoners, Skaters, and Preps, you will perceive students in an entirely different way from someone who does not know these classifications.

Although Sapir and Whorf's observation that the Hopi do not have tenses was wrong (Edgerton 1992:27), they stumbled onto a major truth about social life. Learning a language means not only learning words but also acquiring the perceptions embedded in that language. In other words, language both reflects and shapes cultural experiences.

Values, Norms, and Sanctions

To learn a culture is to learn people's **values,** their ideas of what is desirable in life. When we uncover people's values, we learn a great deal about them, for values are the standards by which people define what is good and bad, beautiful and ugly. Values underlie our preferences, guide our choices, and indicate what we hold worthwhile in life.

Every group develops expectations concerning the right ways to reflect its values. Sociologists use the term **norms** to describe those expectations (or rules of behavior) that develop out of a group's values. They use the term **sanctions** to refer to the reactions people get for following or breaking norms. A **positive sanction** expresses approval for following a norm, while a **negative sanction** reflects disapproval for breaking a norm. Positive sanctions can be material, such as a prize, a trophy, or money, but in everyday life they usually consist of hugs, smiles, a pat on the back, encouraging words, or even handshakes or "high-fives." Negative sanctions can also be material—being given a fine in court is one example—but they, too, are more likely to be symbolic: harsh words or gestures such as frowns, stares, clenched jaws,

or raised fists. Getting a raise at work is a positive sanction, indicating that you have followed the norms clustering around work values. Getting fired, however, is a negative sanction, indicating that you have violated those norms. The North American finger gesture discussed earlier is, of course, a negative sanction.

Because people can find norms stifling, some cultures relieve the pressure through *moral holidays,* specified times when people are allowed to break norms. Moral holidays, such as Mardi Gras, often center on getting drunk and being rowdy. Some activities for which people would otherwise be arrested are permitted—and expected—including public drunkenness and some nudity. The norms are never completely dropped, however, just loosened a bit. Go too far, and the police step in.

Folkways and Mores

Norms that are not strictly enforced are called **folkways.** We expect people to comply with folkways, but we are likely to shrug our shoulders and not make a big deal about it if they don't. If someone insists on passing you on the right side of the sidewalk, for example, you are unlikely to take corrective action—although if the sidewalk is crowded and you must move out of the way, you might give the person a dirty look.

Other norms, however, are taken much more seriously. We think of them as essential to our core values, and we insist on conformity. These are called **mores** ("MORE-rays"). A person who steals, rapes, or kills has violated some of society's most important mores. As sociologist Ian Robertson (1987:62) put it,

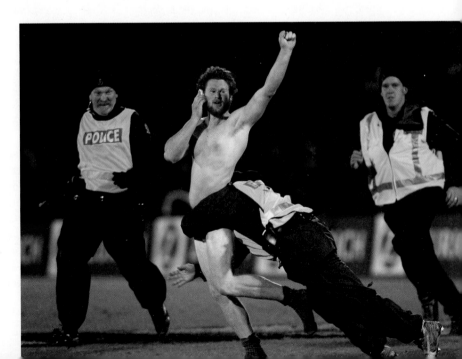

The violation of *mores* is a serious matter. In this case, it is serious enough that the police at this rugby match in Dublin, Ireland, have swung into action to protect the public from seeing a "disgraceful" sight, at least one so designated by this group.

A man who walks down a street wearing nothing on the upper half of his body is violating a folkway; a man who walks down the street wearing nothing on the lower half of his body is violating one of our most important mores, the requirement that people cover their genitals and buttocks in public.

It should also be noted that one group's folkways may be another group's mores. Although a man walking down the street with the upper half of his body uncovered is deviating from a folkway, a woman doing the same thing is violating the culture's mores. In addition, the folkways and mores of a subculture (discussed in the next section) may be the opposite of those of mainstream culture. For example, to walk down the sidewalk in a nudist camp with the entire body uncovered would conform to that subculture's folkways.

A **taboo** refers to a norm so strongly ingrained that even the thought of its violation is greeted with revulsion. Eating human flesh and having sex with one's parents are examples of such behaviors. When someone breaks a taboo, the individual is usually judged unfit to live in the same society as others. The sanctions are severe and may include prison, banishment, or death.

Many Cultural Worlds

Subcultures

What common condition do you think this doctor is describing? Here is what he said:

> [It accompanies] diaphragmatic pleurisy, pneumonia, uremia, or alcoholism . . . Abdominal causes include disorders of the stomach, and esophagus, bowel diseases, pancreatitis, pregnancy, bladder irritation, hepatic metastases, or hepatitis. Thoracic and mediastinal lesions or surgery may be responsible. Posterior fossa tumors or infarcts may stimulate centers in the medulla oblongata. (Chambliss 2003:443)

My best guess is that you don't have the slightest idea what this doctor is talking about. For most of us, he might as well be speaking Greek. Physicians who are lecturing students in medical school, however, talk like this. This doctor is describing hiccups!

Physicians form a **subculture,** *a world within the larger world of the dominant culture.* Subcultures consist of people whose experiences have led them to have distinctive

ways of looking at life or some aspect of it. Even if we cannot understand the preceding quote, it makes us aware that the physician's view of life is not quite the same as ours.

U.S. society contains tens of thousands of subcultures. Some are as broad as the way of life we associate with teenagers, others as narrow as those we associate with body builders—or with physicians. Some U.S. ethnic groups also form subcultures; their values, norms, and foods set them apart. So might their religion, language, and clothing. Occupational groups also form subcultures, as anyone who has hung out with artists (McCall 1980), construction workers (Haas 1972), or undertakers (Thompson 2005) can attest. Even sociologists form a subculture. As you are learning, they use a unique language to make sense of the world.

For a visual depiction of subcultures, see the photo montage on the next two pages.

Countercultures

Consider this quote from another subculture:

> If everyone applying for welfare had to supply a doctor's certificate of sterilization, if everyone who had committed a felony were sterilized, if anyone who had mental illness to any degree were sterilized—then our economy could easily take care of these people for the rest of their lives, giving them a decent living standard—but getting them out of the way. That way there would be no children abused, no surplus population, and, after a while, no pollution. . . .
>
> Now let's talk about stupidity. The level of intellect in this country is going down, generation after generation. The average IQ is always 100 because that is the accepted average. However, the kid with a 100 IQ today would have tested out at 70 when I was a lad. You get the concept . . . marching morons. . . .
>
> When the world system collapses, it'll be good people like you who will be shooting people in the streets to feed their families. (Zellner 1995:58, 65)

Welcome to the world of the survivalists, where the message is much clearer than that of the physicians—and much more disturbing.

The values and norms of most subcultures blend in with mainstream society. In some cases, however, such as these survivalists, some of the group's values and norms place it at odds with the dominant culture. Sociologists use the term **counterculture** to refer to such groups. Another example would be Satanists. To better see this distinction, consider motorcycle enthusiasts and motorcycle gangs.

Looking at Subcultures

ubcultures can form around any interest or activity. Each subculture has its own values and norms that its members share, giving them a common identity. Each also has special terms that pinpoint the group's corner of life and that its members use to communicate with one another. Some of us belong to several subcultures simultaneously.

As you can see from these photos, most subcultures are compatible with the values of the dominant or mainstream culture. They represent specialized interests around which its members have chosen to build tiny worlds. Some subcultures, however, conflict with the mainstream culture. Sociologists give the name counterculture to subcultures whose values (such as those of outlaw motorcyclists) or activities and goals (such as those of terrorists) are opposed to the mainstream culture. Countercultures, however, are exceptional, and few of us belong to them.

Membership in this subculture is not easily awarded. Not only must **high-steel iron-workers** prove that they are able to work at great heights but also that they fit into the group socially. Newcomers are tested by members of the group, and they must demonstrate that they can take joking without offense.

This Native American also represents a subculture within this subculture, for many Mohawk Native Americans specialize in this occupation.

The **cabbies'** subculture, centering on their occupational activities and interest, is also broken into smaller subcultures that reflect their experiences of race-ethnicity.

Participants in the **rodeo** subculture "advertise" their membership by wearing special clothing. The clothing symbolizes a set of values that unites its members. Among those values is the awarding of hyper-masculine status through the conquest of animals—or in this instance, the attempted conquest.

Values and interests are perhaps the two main characteristics of subcultures. What values and interests distinguish the **modeling** subculture?

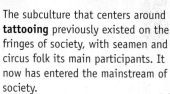

This subculture, with its fierce traditions, used to consist of white men. The subculture's painful adjustment to changed times is evident in its participants, name being changed from firemen to **fire-fighters.**

The subculture that centers around **tattooing** previously existed on the fringes of society, with seamen and circus folk its main participants. It now has entered the mainstream of society.

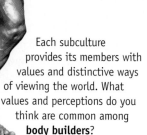

Each subculture provides its members with values and distinctive ways of viewing the world. What values and perceptions do you think are common among **body builders**?

The subculture of **future farmers,** in decline for over 100 years, remains vibrant in some rural areas.

Why would someone decorate themselves like this? Among the many reasons, one is to show their solidarity with the **football subculture.**

Motorcycle enthusiasts—who emphasize personal freedom and speed *and* affirm cultural values of success—are members of a subculture. In contrast, the Hell's Angels not only stress freedom and speed but also value dirtiness and contempt toward women and work. This makes them a counterculture (Watson 1988).

An assault on core values is always met with resistance. To affirm their own values, members of the mainstream culture may ridicule, isolate, or even attack members of the counterculture. The Mormons, for example, were driven out of several states before they finally settled in Utah, which was then a wilderness. Even there, the federal government would not let them practice *polygyny* (one man having more than one wife); Utah's statehood was made conditional on its acceptance of monogamy (Anderson 1942/1966).

Values in U.S. Society

An Overview of U.S. Values

As you know, the United States is a **pluralistic society,** made up of many different groups. The United States has numerous religious and racial-ethnic groups, as well as countless interest groups that focus on such divergent activities as collecting Barbie dolls and hunting deer. This state of affairs makes the job of specifying U.S. values difficult. Nonetheless, sociologists have tried to identify the underlying core values that are shared by the many groups that make up U.S. society. Sociologist Robin Williams (1965) identified the following:

1. *Achievement and success.* Americans place a high value on personal achievement, especially outdoing others. This value includes getting ahead at work and school and attaining wealth, power, and prestige.
2. *Individualism.* Americans prize success that comes from individual efforts and initiative. They cherish the ideal that an individual can rise from the bottom of society to its very top. If someone fails to "get ahead," Americans generally find fault with that individual rather than with the social system for placing roadblocks in his or her path.
3. *Activity and work.* Americans expect people to work hard and to be busy doing some activity even when not at work. This value is becoming less important.
4. *Efficiency and practicality.* Americans award high marks for getting things done efficiently. Even in

everyday life, Americans consider it important to do things fast, and they seek ways to increase efficiency.
5. *Science and technology.* Americans have a passion for applied science, for using science to control nature—to tame rivers and harness winds—and to develop new technology, from video iPods to Segways.
6. *Progress.* Americans expect rapid technological change. They believe that they should constantly build "more and better" gadgets that will help them move toward some vague goal called "progress."
7. *Material comfort.* Americans expect a high level of material comfort. This comfort includes not only good nutrition, medical care, and housing but also late-model cars and recreational playthings—from Land Rovers to X-boxes.
8. *Humanitarianism.* Americans emphasize helpfulness, personal kindness, aid in mass disasters, and organized philanthropy.
9. *Freedom.* This core value pervades U.S. life. It underscored the American Revolution, and Americans pride themselves on their personal freedom. The Mass Media in Social Life box on the next page highlights an interesting study on how this core value applies to Native Americans.
10. *Democracy.* By this term, Americans refer to majority rule, to the right of everyone to express an opinion, and to representative government.
11. *Equality.* It is impossible to understand Americans without being aware of the central role that the value of equality plays in their lives.
12. *Racism and group superiority.* Although it contradicts freedom, democracy, and equality, Americans value some groups more than others and have done so throughout their history. The slaughter of Native Americans and the enslaving of Africans are the most notorious examples.

In an earlier publication, I updated Williams' analysis by adding these three values:

13. *Education.* Americans are expected to go as far in school as their abilities and finances allow. Over the years, the definition of an "adequate" education has changed, and today a college education is considered an appropriate goal for most Americans.
14. *Religiosity.* There is a feeling that every true American ought to be religious. This does not mean that everyone is expected to join a church, synagogue, or mosque, but that everyone ought to acknowledge a

belief in a Supreme Being and follow some set of matching precepts. This value is so pervasive that Americans stamp "In God We Trust" on their money and declare in their national pledge of allegiance that they are "one nation under God."

15. *Romantic love.* Americans feel that the only proper basis for marriage is romantic love. Songs, literature, mass media, and folk beliefs all stress this value. They especially delight in the theme that "love conquers all."

mass Media in social life

Why Do Native Americans Like Westerns?

U.S. audiences (and even German, French, and Japanese ones) devour Western movies. In the United States, it is easy to see why Anglos might like Westerns. It is they who are portrayed as heroes who tame the wilderness and defend themselves from the attacks of cruel, savage Indians who are intent on their destruction. But why would Indians like Westerns?

Sociologist JoEllen Shively, a Chippewa who grew up on Indian reservations in Montana and North Dakota, observed that Westerns are so popular that Native Americans bring bags of paperbacks into taverns to trade with one another. They even call each other "cowboy."

Intrigued, Shively decided to investigate the matter by showing a Western to adult Native Americans and Anglos in a reservation town. She matched the groups in education, age, income, and percentage of unemployment. To select the movie, Shively (1991, 1992) previewed more than seventy Westerns. She chose a John Wayne movie, *The Searchers,* because it not only focuses on conflict between Indians and cowboys but also shows the cowboys defeating the Indians. After the movie the viewers filled out questionnaires, and Shively interviewed them.

She found something surprising: *All* Native Americans and Anglos identified with the cowboys; *none* identified with the Indians. Anglos and Native Americans, however, identified with the cowboys in different ways. Each projected a different fantasy onto the story. While Anglos saw the movie as an accurate portrayal of the Old West and a justification of their own status in society, Native Americans saw it as embodying a free, natural way of life. In fact, Native Americans said that they were the "real cowboys." They said, "Westerns relate to the way I wish I could live"; "He's not tied down to an eight-to-five job, day after day"; "He's his own man."

Shively adds,

What appears to make Westerns meaningful to Indians is the fantasy of being free and independent like the cowboy. . . . Indians . . . find a fantasy in the cowboy story in which the important parts of their ways of life triumph and are morally good, validating their own cultural group in the context of a dramatically satisfying story.

To express their real identity—a combination of marginality on the one hand,

Although he was often portrayed as an Anglo who kills Indians, John Wayne is popular among Indian men. These men tend to identify with the cowboys, who reflect their values of bravery, autonomy, and toughness.

with a set of values which are about the land, autonomy, and being free—they (use) a cultural vehicle written for Anglos about Anglos, but it is one in which Indians invest a distinctive set of meanings that speak to their own experience, which they can read in a manner that affirms a way of life they value, or a fantasy they hold to.

In other words, values, not ethnicity, are the central issue. If a Native American film industry were to portray Native Americans with the same values that the Anglo movie industry projects onto cowboys, then Native Americans would identify with their own group. Thus, says Shively, Native Americans make cowboys "honorary Indians," for the cowboys express their values of bravery, autonomy, and toughness.

Value Clusters

As you can see, values are not independent units; some cluster together to form a larger whole. In the **value cluster** surrounding success, for example, we find hard work, education, efficiency, material comfort, and individualism bound up together. Americans are expected to go far in school, to work hard afterward, to be efficient, and then to attain a high level of material comfort, which, in turn, demonstrates success. Success is attributed to the individual's efforts; lack of success is blamed on his or her faults.

Value Contradictions and Social Change

Not all values fall into neat, integrated packages. Some even contradict one another. The value of group superiority contradicts freedom, democracy, and equality, producing a **value contradiction.** There simply cannot be full expression of freedom, democracy, and equality along with racism and sexism. Something has to give. One way in which Americans sidestepped this contradiction in the past was to say that freedom, democracy, and equality applied only to some groups. The contradiction was bound to surface over time, however, and so it did with the Civil War and the women's liberation movement. *It is precisely at the point of value contradictions, then, that one can see a major force for social change in a society.*

Emerging Values

A value cluster of four interrelated core values—leisure, self-fulfillment, physical fitness, and youthfulness—is emerging in the United States. A fifth core value—concern for the environment—is also emerging.

1. *Leisure.* The emergence of leisure as a value is reflected in a huge recreation industry—from computer games, boats, and spa retreats to sports arenas, home entertainment systems, and luxury cruises.
2. *Self-fulfillment.* This value is reflected in the "human potential" movement, which emphasizes becoming "all one can be," and in books and talk shows that focus on "self-help," "relating," and "personal development."
3. *Physical fitness.* Physical fitness is not a new U.S. value, but its increased emphasis is moving it into this emerging cluster. This trend is evident in the emphasis on organic foods; concerns about weight and diet; the many joggers, cyclists, and backpackers; and countless health clubs and physical fitness centers.
4. *Youthfulness.* While valuing youth and disparaging old age are not new, some note a new sense of urgency. They attribute this to the huge number of aging baby boomers, who, aghast at the physical changes that accompany their advancing years, attempt to deny or at least postpone their biological fate. An extreme view is represented by a physician who claims that

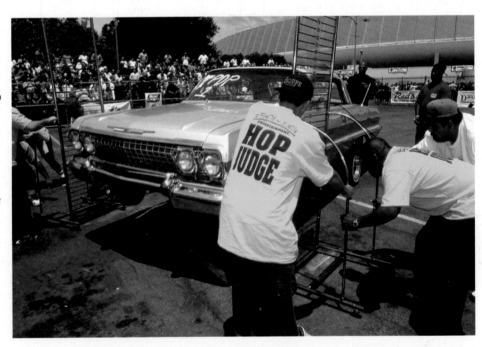

The many groups that comprise the United States contribute to its culture. As the number of Latinos in the United States increases, Latinos are making a greater impact on music, art, and literature. This is also true of other areas of everyday life, such as this car-hopping contest in California. Cars are outfitted with bionic hydraulic systems, and contestants compete to see whose vehicles can hop the highest or shimmy the most erratically from tire to tire.

"aging is not a normal life event, but a disease" (Cowley 1996). It is not surprising, then, that techniques for enhancing and maintaining a youthful appearance—from cosmetic surgery to Botox injections—have become popular.

This emerging value cluster is a response to fundamental changes in U.S. society. Americans used to be preoccupied with forging a nation and fighting for economic survival. They now have come to a point in their economic development at which millions of people are freed from long hours of work and millions more are able to retire from work at an age when they anticipate decades of life ahead of them. This value cluster centers on helping people to maintain their health and vigor during their younger years and enabling them to enjoy their years of retirement.

5. *Concern for the environment.* During most of U.S. history, the environment was viewed as something to be exploited—a wilderness to be settled, forests to be chopped down, rivers and lakes to be fished, and animals to be hunted. One result was the near extinction of the bison and the extinction in 1915 of the passenger pigeon, a bird previously so abundant that its annual migration would darken the skies for days. Today, Americans have developed a genuine and (we can hope) long-term concern for the environment.

This emerging value of environmental concern is related to the current stage of U.S. economic development: People act on environmental concerns only after they meet basic needs. At this point in their development, for example, the world's poor nations have a difficult time "affording" this value.

Culture Wars: When Values Clash

Changes in core values are met with strong resistance by the people who hold them dear. They see the change as a threat to their way of life, an undermining of their present and a hazard to their future. Efforts to change gender roles, for example, arouse intense controversy, as does support for the marriage of homosexuals. Alarmed at such onslaughts to their values, traditionalists fiercely defend historical family relationships and the gender roles they grew up with. Today's clash in values is so severe that the term "culture wars" has been coined to refer to it. Compared with the violence directed against the Mormons, however, today's reactions to such controversies are mild.

Values as Blinders

Just as values and their supporting beliefs paint a unique picture of reality, so they also form a view of what life *ought* to be like. Americans value individualism so highly, for example, that they tend to see everyone as equally free

Values, both those held by individuals and those that represent a nation or people, can undergo deep shifts. It is difficult for many of us to grasp the pride with which earlier Americans destroyed trees that took thousands of years to grow, are located only on one tiny speck of the globe, and that we today consider part of the nation's and world's heritage. But this is a value statement, representing current views. The pride expressed on these woodcutters' faces represents another set of values entirely.

to pursue the goal of success. This value blinds them to the many circumstances that keep people from reaching this goal. The dire consequences of family poverty, parents' low education, and dead-end jobs tend to drop from sight. Instead, Americans cling to the notion that anyone can make it—if they put forth enough effort. And they "know" they are right, for every day, dangling before their eyes are enticing stories of individuals who have succeeded despite huge handicaps.

"Ideal" Versus "Real" Culture

Many of the norms that surround cultural values are followed only partially. Differences always exist between a group's ideals and what its members actually do. Consequently, sociologists use the term **ideal culture** to refer to the values, norms, and goals that a group considers ideal, worth aspiring to. Success, for example, is part of ideal culture. Americans glorify academic progress, hard work, and the display of material goods as signs of individual achievement. What people actually do, however, usually falls short of the cultural ideal. Compared with their abilities, for example, most people don't work as hard as they could or go as far as they could in school. To refer to the norms and values that people actually follow, sociologists use the term **real culture.**

Technology in the Global Village

The New Technology

The gestures, language, values, folkways, and mores that we have discussed—all are part of symbolic or nonmaterial culture. Culture, as you recall, also has a material aspect—a group's *things,* from its houses to its toys. Central to a group's material culture is its technology. In its simplest sense, **technology** can be equated with tools. In a broader sense, technology also includes the skills or procedures necessary to make and use those tools.

We can use the term **new technology** to refer to an emerging technology that has a significant impact on social life. People develop minor technologies all the time. Most are slight modifications of existing technologies. Occasionally, however, they develop a technology that makes a major impact on human life. It is primarily to these that the term *new technology* refers. For people 500 years ago, the new technology was the printing press. For

us, the new technology consists of computers, satellites, and the electronic media.

The sociological significance of technology goes far beyond the tool itself. *Technology sets a framework for a group's nonmaterial culture.* If a group's technology changes, so do the ways people think and how they relate to one another. An example is gender relations. Through the centuries and throughout the world, it has been the custom (the nonmaterial culture of a group) for men to dominate women. Today, with instantaneous communications (the material culture), this custom has become much more difficult to maintain. For example, when women from many nations gathered in Beijing for a U.N. conference in 1995, satellites instantly transmitted their grievances around the globe. Such communications both convey and create discontent, as well as a feeling of sisterhood, motivating women to agitate for social change.

In today's world, the long-accepted idea that it is proper to withhold rights on the basis of someone's sex can no longer hold. What is usually invisible in this revolutionary change is the role of the new technology, which joins the world's nations into a global communications network.

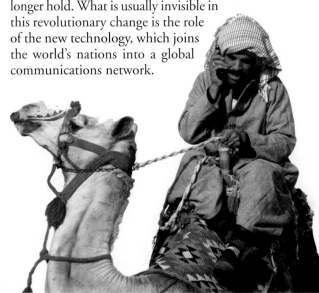

The adoption of new forms of communication by people who not long ago were cut off from events in the rest of the world is bound to change their *nonmaterial culture.* How do you think that this man's thinking and views of the world are changing?

Cultural Lag and Cultural Change

About three generations ago, sociologist William Ogburn (1922/1938), a functional analyst, coined the term **cultural lag.** By this Ogburn meant that not all parts of a culture change at the same pace. When some part of a culture changes, other parts lag behind.

Ogburn pointed out that *a group's material culture usually changes first, with the nonmaterial culture lagging behind,* playing a game of catch-up. For example, when we get sick, we could type our symptoms into a computer and get a printout of our diagnosis and a recommended course of treatment. In fact, in some tests, computers outperform physicians. Yet our customs have not caught up with our technology, and we continue to visit the doctor's office.

Sometimes nonmaterial culture never catches up. Instead, we rigorously hold on to some outmoded form, one that once was needed but long ago was bypassed by new technology. A striking example is our nine-month school year. Have you ever wondered why it is nine months long and why we take summers off? For most of us this is "just the way it's always been," and we have never questioned it. But there is more to this custom than meets the eye, for it is an example of cultural lag.

In the late 1800s, when universal schooling came about, the school year matched the technology of the time, which was labor-intensive. Most parents were farmers, and for survival they needed their children's help at the crucial times of planting and harvesting. Today, generations later, when few people farm and there is no need for the school year to be so short, we still live with this cultural lag.

Technology and Cultural Leveling

For most of human history, communication was limited and travel slow. Consequently, in their relative isolation, human groups developed highly distinctive ways of life as they responded to the particular situations they faced. The unique characteristics they developed that distinguished one culture from another tended to change little over time. The Tasmanians, who lived on a remote island off the coast of Australia, provide an extreme example. For thousands of years they had no contact with other people. They were so isolated that they did not even know how to make clothing or fire (Edgerton 1992).

Except in such rare instances humans have always had *some* contact with other groups. During these contacts, people learn from one another, adapting some part of the other's way of life. In this process, called **cultural diffusion,** groups are most open to a change in their technology or material culture. They usually are eager, for example, to adopt superior weapons and tools. In remote jungles in South America one can find metal cooking pots, steel axes, and even bits of clothing spun in mills in South Carolina. Although the direction of cultural diffusion today is primarily from the West to other parts of the world,

cultural diffusion is not a one-way street—as bagels, woks, hammocks, and sushi bars in the United States attest.

With today's travel and communications, cultural diffusion is occurring rapidly. Air travel has made it possible to journey around the globe in a matter of hours. In the not-so-distant past, a trip from the United States to Africa was so unusual that only a few adventurous people made it, and newspapers would herald their feat. Today, hundreds of thousands make the trip each year.

The changes in communication are no less vast. Communication used to be limited to face-to-face speech, written messages that were passed from hand to hand, and visual signals, such as smoke, or light that was reflected from mirrors. Despite newspapers, people in some parts of the United States did not hear that the Civil War had ended until weeks and even months after it was over. Today's electronic communications transmit messages across the globe in a matter of seconds, and we learn almost instantaneously what is happening on the other side of the world. During Gulf War II, reporters traveled with U.S. soldiers, and for the first time in history the public was able to view live video reports of battles and deaths as they occurred.

Travel and communication now unite us to such an extent that there is almost no "other side of the world" anymore. One result is **cultural leveling,** a process in which cultures become similar to one another. The globalization of capitalism is bringing both technology and Western culture to the rest of the world. Japan, for example, has adopted not only capitalism but also Western forms of dress and music. These changes, which have been "superimposed" on traditional Japanese culture, have transformed Japan into a blend of Western and Eastern cultures.

Cultural leveling is occurring rapidly around the world, as is apparent to any traveler. The Golden Arches of McDonald's welcome today's visitors to Tokyo, Paris, London, Madrid, Moscow, Hong Kong, and Beijing. In Mexico, the most popular piñatas are no longer donkeys but, instead, Mickey Mouse and Fred Flintstone (Beckett 1996). When I visited a jungle village in India—no electricity, no running water, and so remote that the only entrance was by a footpath—I saw a young man sporting a cap with the Nike emblem.

Although the bridging of geography and culture by electronic signals and the exportation of Western icons do not in and of themselves mark the end of traditional cultures, the inevitable result is some degree of *cultural leveling,* some blander, less distinctive way of life—U.S. culture with French, Japanese, and Brazilian accents, so to speak. Although the "cultural accent" remains, something vital is lost forever.

Summary *and* Review

What Is Culture?

All human groups possess **culture**—language, beliefs, values, norms, and material objects that are passed from one generation to the next. **Material culture** consists of objects (art, buildings, clothing, tools). **Nonmaterial** (or **symbolic**) **culture** is a group's ways of thinking and their patterns of behavior. **Ideal culture** is a group's ideal values, norms, and goals. **Real culture** is their actual behavior, which often falls short of their cultural ideals. Pp. 36–38.

What are cultural relativism and ethnocentrism?

People are naturally **ethnocentric;** that is, they use their own culture as a yardstick for judging the ways of others. In contrast, those who embrace **cultural relativism** try to understand other cultures on those cultures' own terms. Pp. 38–39.

Components of Symbolic Culture

What are the components of nonmaterial culture?

The central component is **symbols,** anything to which people attach meaning and use to communicate with others. Universally, the symbols of nonmaterial culture are **gestures, language, values, norms, sanctions, folkways,** and **mores.** Pp. 39–42.

Why is language so significant to culture?

Language allows human experience to be goal-directed, cooperative, and cumulative. It also lets humans move beyond the present and share past, future, and other common perspectives. According to the **Sapir-Whorf hypothesis,** language even shapes our thoughts and perceptions. Pp. 42–46.

How do values, norms, sanctions, folkways, and mores reflect culture?

All groups have **values,** standards by which they define what is desirable or undesirable, and **norms,** rules or expectations about behavior. Groups use **positive sanctions** to show approval of those who follow their norms, and **negative sanctions** to show disapproval of those who do not. Norms that are not strictly enforced are called **folkways,** while **mores** are norms to which groups demand conformity because they reflect core values. Pp. 46–47.

Many Cultural Worlds

How do subcultures and countercultures differ?

A **subculture** is a group whose values and related behaviors distinguish its members from the general culture. A **counterculture** holds values that stand in opposition to those of the dominant culture. Pp. 47–50.

Values in U.S. Society

What are the core U.S. values?

Although the United States is a **pluralistic society,** made up of many groups, each with its own set of values, certain values dominate: achievement and success, individualism, activity and work, efficiency and practicality, science and technology, progress, material comfort, equality, freedom, democracy, humanitarianism, racism and group superiority, education, religiosity, and romantic love. Some values cluster together (**value clusters**) to form a larger whole. **Value contradictions** (such as equality and racism) indicate areas of tension, which are likely points of social change. Leisure, self-fulfillment, physical fitness, youthfulness, and concern for the environment are emerging core values. Changes in a society's values do not come without opposition. Pp. 50–54.

Technology in the Global Village

How is technology changing culture?

William Ogburn coined the term **cultural lag** to refer to how a group's nonmaterial culture lags behind its changing technology. With today's technological advances in travel and communication, **cultural diffusion** is occurring rapidly. This leads to **cultural leveling,** whereby many groups are adopting Western culture in place of their own customs. Much of the richness of the world's diverse cultures is being lost in the process. Pp. 54–55.

Thinking Critically
about Chapter 2

1. Do you favor ethnocentrism or cultural relativism? Explain your position.
2. Do you think that the language change in Miami, Florida (discussed on page 44), is an indicator of the future of the United States? Why or why not?
3. Are you a member of any subcultures? Which one(s)? Why do you think that your group is a subculture? What is your group's relationship to the mainstream culture?

Additional Resources

Companion Website www.ablongman.com/henslin

- Content Select Research Database for Sociology, with suggested key terms and annotated references
- Link to 2000 Census, with activities
- Flashcards of key terms and concepts

- Practice Tests
- Weblinks
- Interactive Maps

Where Can I Read More on This Topic?

Suggested readings for this chapter are listed at the back of this book.

Socialization

Simon Silva, *Orgullo de Familia*, 1997

What is Human Nature?
Feral Children
Isolated Children
Institutionalized Children
Deprived Animals

Socialization into the Self and Mind
Cooley and the Looking-Glass Self
Mead and Role-Taking
Piaget and the Development of Reasoning
Global Aspects of the Self and Reasoning

Learning Personality and Emotions
Freud and the Development of Personality
Socialization and Emotions
Society Within Us: The Self and Emotions as Social Control

Socialization into Gender
Gender Messages in the Family
Gender Messages from Peers
Gender Messages in the Mass Media

Agents of Socialization
The Family
The Neighborhood
Religion
Day Care
The School and Peer Groups
The Workplace

Resocialization
Total Institutions

Socialization Through the Life Course
Childhood
Adolescence
Transitional Adulthood
The Middle Years
The Older Years

Are We Prisoners of Socialization?

Summary and Review

The old man was horrified when he found out. Life had never been good since his daughter lost her hearing when she was just two years old. She couldn't even talk—just fluttered her hands around trying to tell him things. Over the years, he had gotten used to that. But now . . . he shuddered at the thought of her being pregnant. No one would be willing to marry her; he knew that. And the neighbors, their tongues would never stop wagging. Everywhere he went, he could hear people talking behind his back.

If only his wife were still alive, maybe she could come up with something. What should he do? He couldn't just kick his daughter out into the street.

After the baby was born, the old man tried to shake his feelings, but they wouldn't let loose. Isabelle was a pretty name, but every time he looked at the baby, he felt sick to his stomach.

He hated doing it, but there was no way out. His daughter and her baby would have to live in the attic.

Unfortunately, this is a true story. Isabelle was discovered in Ohio in 1938 when she was about 6-years old, living in a dark room with her deaf-mute mother. Isabelle couldn't talk, but she did use gestures to communicate with her mother. An inadequate diet

Her behavior toward strangers, especially men, was almost that of a wild animal, manifesting much fear and hostility.

and lack of sunshine had given Isabelle a disease called rickets. Her legs

were so bowed that as she stood erect the soles of her shoes came nearly flat together, and she got about with a skittering gait. Her behavior toward strangers, especially men, was almost that of a wild animal, manifesting much fear and hostility. In lieu of speech she made only a strange croaking sound. (Davis 1940/2005:138–139)

When the newspapers reported this case, sociologist Kingsley Davis decided to find out what had happened to Isabelle. We'll come back to that later, but first let's use the case of Isabelle to gain insight into what human nature is.

What Is Human Nature?

For centuries, people have been intrigued by the question of what is human about human nature. How much of people's characteristics comes from "nature" (heredity) and how much from "nurture" (the **social environment,** contact with others)? One way to answer this question is to study identical twins who have been reared apart. See the Down-to-Earth Sociology box on the next page for a fascinating account of identical twins who were separated at birth. Another way is to study children who have had little human contact. Let's consider such children.

Feral Children

Over the centuries, people have occasionally found children living in the woods. Supposedly, these children could not speak; they bit, scratched, growled, and walked on all fours. They drank by lapping water, ate grass, tore ravenously at raw meat, and showed an insensitivity to pain and cold. These stories of what are called *feral children* sound like pure fiction, and it is easy to dismiss them as a type of folk myth.

Because of what happened in 1798, however, we can't be so sure. In that year, a child who walked on all fours and could not speak was found in the forests of Aveyron, France. "The wild boy of Aveyron," as this child became known, would have been simply another of those legends, except that French scientists took the child to a laboratory and studied him. Like the earlier informal reports, this child, too, gave no indication of feeling the cold. Most startling, though, the boy would growl when he saw a small animal, pounce on it, and devour it uncooked. Even today, the scientists' detailed reports make fascinating reading (Itard 1962).

Ever since I read Itard's account of this boy, I've been fascinated by feral children, especially the seemingly fantastic possibility that animals could rear human children. In 2002, I received a private report that a feral child had been found in the jungles of Cambodia. When I had the opportunity the following year to visit the child and interview his caregivers, I grabbed it. The boy's photo is on this page.

If animals really have raised children, the sociological question is: If we were untouched by society, would we be like feral children? By nature, would our behavior be like that of wild animals? Unable to study feral children, sociologists have studied children like Isabelle who were reared in isolation.

Isolated Children

Reports of isolated children have been well documented. What can they tell us about human nature? We can first conclude that humans have no natural language, for Isabelle and others like her are unable to speak.

But maybe Isabelle was mentally impaired. This is what people first thought, for she scored close to zero on her first intelligence test. But after a few months of intensive language training, Isabelle was able to speak in short sentences. In about a year, she could write a few words, do simple addition, and retell stories after hearing them. Seven months later, she had a vocabulary of almost 2,000 words. It took only two years for Isabelle to reach the intellectual level normal for her age. She then went on to school, where she was "bright, cheerful, energetic . . . and participated in all school activities as normally as other children" (Davis 1940/2005:139).

Institutionalized Children

Other than language, what else is required for a child to develop into what we consider a healthy, balanced, intelligent human being? We find part of the answer in an intriguing experiment from the 1930s. Back then, parents died a lot younger, and orphanages were sprinkled throughout the United States. Children reared in orphanages often had difficulty establishing close bonds with others—and they tended to have low IQs. "Common

One of the reasons I went to Cambodia was to interview a feral child—the boy shown here—who supposedly had been raised by monkeys. When I arrived at the remote location where the boy was living, I was disappointed to find that the story was only partially true. During its reign of terror, the Khmer Rouge had shot and killed the boy's parents, leaving him, at about the age of two, abandoned on an island. Some months later, villagers found him in the care of monkeys. They shot the female monkey who was carrying the boy. Not quite a feral child—but the closest I'll ever come to one.

Down-to-Earth Sociology

Heredity or Environment? The Case of Oskar and Jack, Identical Twins

IDENTICAL TWINS SHARE EXACTLY THE SAME GENETIC heredity. One fertilized egg divides to produce two embryos. If heredity determines personality—or attitudes, temperament, skills, and intelligence—then identical twins should be identical not only in their looks but also in these characteristics.

The fascinating case of Oskar and Jack helps us unravel this mystery. From their experience, we can see the far-reaching effects of the environment—how social experiences take precedence over biology.

Oskar Stohr and Jack Yufe are identical twins born in 1932 to a Jewish father and a Catholic mother. They were separated as babies after their parents divorced. Oskar was reared in Czechoslovakia by his mother's mother, who was a strict Catholic. When Oskar was a toddler, Hitler annexed this area of Czechoslovakia, and Oskar learned to love Hitler and to hate Jews. He joined the Hitler Youth (a sort of Boy Scout organization, except that this one was designed to instill the "virtues" of patriotism, loyalty, obedience—and hatred).

Jack's upbringing was a mirror image of Oskar's. Reared in Trinidad by his father, he learned loyalty to Jews and hatred of Hitler and the Nazis. After the war, Jack and his father moved to Israel. When he was 17, Jack joined a kibbutz, and later, served in the Israeli army.

In 1954, the two brothers met. It was a short meeting, and Jack had been warned not to tell Oskar that they were Jews. Twenty-five years later, in 1979, when they were 47 years old, social scientists at the University of Minnesota brought them together again. These researchers figured that because Oskar and Jack had the same genes, any differences they showed would have to be the result of their environment—their different social experiences.

The question of the relative influence of heredity and the environment in human behavior has fascinated and plagued researchers. To try to answer this question, researchers have studied identical twins. Some human behaviors, such as beliefs, political and otherwise, are clearly due to the environment, but uncertainty remains about the origin of other behaviors.

Not only did Oskar and Jack hold different attitudes toward the war, Hitler, and Jews, but also their basic orientations to life were different. In their politics, Oskar was conservative, while Jack was more liberal. Oskar enjoyed leisure, while Jack was a workaholic. And, as you can predict, Jack was very proud of being a Jew. Oskar, who by this time knew that he was a Jew, wouldn't even mention it.

That would seem to settle the matter. But there was another side. The researchers also found that Oskar and Jack had both excelled at sports as children, but had difficulty with math. They also had the same rate of speech, and both liked sweet liqueur and spicy foods. Strangely, both flushed the toilet both before and after using it and enjoyed startling people by sneezing in crowded elevators.

Sources: Based on Begley 1979; Chen 1979; Wright 1995; Segal 2000.

for your Consideration

Heredity or environment? How much influence does each one have? The question is not yet settled, but at this point it seems fair to conclude that the *limits* of certain physical and mental abilities are established by heredity (such as ability at sports and aptitude for mathematics), while such basic orientations to life as attitudes are the result of the environment. We can put it this way: For some parts of life, the blueprint is drawn by heredity; but even here the environment can redraw those lines. For other parts, the individual is a blank slate, and it is up to the environment to determine what is written on that slate.

sense" (which we noted in Chapter 1 is unreliable) told everyone that the cause of mental retardation is biological ("They're just born that way"). Two psychologists, H. M. Skeels and H. B. Dye (1939), however, began to suspect a social cause.

For background on their experiment, Skeels (1966) provides this account of a "good" orphanage in Iowa during the 1930s, where he and Dye were consultants:

> **Until about six months, they were cared for in the infant nursery. The babies were kept in standard hospital cribs that often had protective sheeting on the sides, thus effectively limiting visual stimulation; no toys or other objects were hung in the infants' line of vision. Human interactions were limited to busy nurses who, with the speed born of practice and necessity, changed diapers or bedding, bathed and medicated the infants, and fed them efficiently with propped bottles.**

Perhaps, thought Skeels and Dye, the absence of stimulating social interaction was the problem, not some biological incapacity on the part of the children. To test their controversial idea, they selected thirteen infants whose mental retardation was so obvious that no one wanted to adopt them. They placed them in an institution for the mentally retarded. Each infant, then about 19 months old, was assigned to a separate ward of women ranging in mental age from 5 to 12 and in chronological age from 18 to 50. The women were pleased with this arrangement. Not only did they take care of the infants' physical needs—diapering, feeding, and so on—but also they loved to play with the children. They cuddled them and showered them with attention. They even competed to see which ward would have "its baby" walking or talking first. Each child had one woman who became

> particularly attached to him [or her] and figuratively "adopted" him [or her]. As a consequence, an intense one-to-one adult-child relationship developed, which was supplemented by the less intense but frequent interactions with the other adults in the environment. Each child had some one person with whom he [or she] was identified and who was particularly interested in him [or her] and his [or her] achievements. (Skeels 1966)

The researchers left a control group of twelve infants at the orphanage. These infants were also retarded, but they were higher in intelligence than the other thirteen. They received the usual care. Two and a half years later, Skeels and Dye tested all the children's intelligence. Their findings were

startling: Those assigned to the retarded women had gained an average of 28 IQ points, while those who remained in the orphanage had lost 30 points.

What happened after these children were grown? Did these initial differences matter? Twenty-one years later, Skeels and Dye did a follow-up study. Those in the control group who had remained in the orphanage had, on average, less than a third-grade education. Four still lived in state institutions, while the others held low-level jobs. Only two had married. In contrast, the average level of education for the thirteen individuals in the experimental group was twelve grades (about normal for that period). Five had completed one or more years of college. One had even gone to graduate school. Eleven had married. All thirteen were self-supporting or were homemakers (Skeels 1966). Apparently, then, one characteristic that we take for granted as being a basic "human" trait—high intelligence—depends on early close relations with other humans.

A recent experiment in India confirms the Skeels and Dye research. Many of India's orphanages are similar to the ones that Skeels and Dye studied—-dismal places where unattended children lie in bed all day. When experimenters added stimulating play and interaction to the children's activities, the children's motor skills improved and their IQs increased (Taneja et al. 2002).

Let's consider one other case, the story of Genie:

> **In 1970, California authorities found Genie, a 13-year-old girl who had been kept locked in a small room and tied to a chair since she was 20 months old. Apparently her 70-year-old father hated children, and had probably caused the death of two of Genie's siblings. Her 50-year-old mother was partially blind and was frightened of her husband. Genie could not speak, did not know how to chew, and was unable to stand upright. On intelligence tests, she scored at the level of a 1-year-old. After intensive training, Genie learned to walk and use simple sentences (although they were garbled). As she grew up, her language remained primitive, she took anyone's property if it appealed to her, and she went to the bathroom wherever she wanted. At the age of 21, Genie went to live in a home for adults who cannot live alone. (Pines 1981)**

From Genie's pathetic story, we can conclude that early interaction with other humans is necessary to establish intelligence and the ability to experience close bonds with others. In addition, to develop high intelligence and the ability to be sociable and follow social norms, there is apparently a period prior to age 13 in which children must develop language and human bonding.

Deprived Animals

Finally, let's consider animals that have been deprived of normal interaction. In a series of experiments with rhesus monkeys, psychologists Harry and Margaret Harlow demonstrated the importance of early learning. The Harlows (1962) raised baby monkeys in isolation. They gave each monkey two artificial mothers, shown in the photograph below. One "mother" was only a wire frame with a wooden head, but it did have a nipple from which the baby could nurse. The frame of the other "mother," which had no bottle, was covered with soft terrycloth. To obtain food, the baby monkeys nursed at the wire frame.

When the Harlows (1965) frightened the babies with a mechanical bear or dog, the monkeys did not run to the wire frame "mother." Instead, they would cling pathetically to their terrycloth "mother." The Harlows concluded that infant–mother bonding is not the result of feeding but, rather, what they termed "intimate physical contact." To most of us, this phrase means cuddling.

In one of their many experiments, the Harlows isolated baby monkeys for different lengths of time. They found that when monkeys were isolated for shorter periods (about three months), they were able to overcome the effects of their isolation. Those isolated for six months or more, however, were unable to adjust to normal monkey life. They could not play or engage in pretend fights, and the other monkeys rejected them. In other words, the longer the period of isolation, the more difficult its effects are to overcome. In addition, a critical learning stage may

exist: If that stage is missed, it may be impossible to compensate for what has been lost. This may have been the case with Genie.

Because humans are not monkeys, we must be careful about extrapolating from animal studies to human behavior. The Harlow experiments, however, support what we know about children who are reared in isolation.

IN SUM Society makes us human. Apparently, babies do not develop "naturally" into human adults. Although their bodies grow, if children are reared in isolation, they become little more than big animals. Without the concepts that language provides, they can't experience or even grasp relationships between people (the "connections" we call brother, sister, parent, friend, teacher, and so on). And without warm, friendly interaction, they don't become "friendly" in the accepted sense of the term; nor do they cooperate with others. In short, it is through human contact that people learn to be members of the human community. This process by which we learn the ways of society (or of particular groups), called **socialization,** is what sociologists have in mind when they say "Society makes us human."

Socialization into the Self and Mind

At birth, we have no idea that we are separate beings. We don't even know that we are a he or a she. How do we develop a **self,** our image of who we are? How do we develop our ability to reason? Let's see how this occurs.

Cooley and the Looking-Glass Self

Back in the 1800s, Charles Horton Cooley (1864–1929), a symbolic interactionist who taught at the University of Michigan, concluded that this unique aspect of "humanness" is socially created; that is, *our sense of self develops from interaction with others.* Cooley (1902) coined the term **looking-glass self** to describe the process by which our sense of self develops. He summarized this idea in the following couplet:

> *Each to each a looking-glass*
> *Reflects the other that doth pass.*

The looking-glass self contains three elements:

1. *We imagine how we appear to those around us.* For example, we may think that others see us as witty or dull.

Like humans, monkeys need interaction to thrive. Those raised in isolation are unable to interact satisfactorily with other monkeys. In this photograph, we see one of the monkeys described in the text. Purposefully frightened by the experimenter, the monkey has taken refuge in the soft terrycloth draped over an artificial "mother."

2. *We interpret others' reactions.* We come to conclusions about how others evaluate us. Do they like us for being witty? Do they dislike us for being dull?

3. *We develop a self-concept.* How we interpret others' reactions to us frames our feelings and ideas about ourselves. A favorable reflection in this *social mirror* leads to a positive self-concept; a negative reflection leads to a negative self-concept.

Note that the development of the self does *not* depend on accurate evaluations. Even if we grossly misinterpret how others think about us, those misjudgments become part of our self-concept. Note also that *although the self-concept begins in childhood, its development is an ongoing, lifelong process.* The three steps of the looking-glass self are part of our everyday lives: As we monitor how other people react to us, we continually modify the self. The self, then, is never a finished product but is always in process, even into old age.

Mead and Role-Taking

Another symbolic interactionist, George Herbert Mead (1863–1931), who taught at the University of Chicago, added that play is crucial to the development of the self. In play, children learn to **take the role of the other,** that is, to put themselves in someone else's shoes—to understand how someone else feels and thinks and to anticipate how that person will act. Only gradually do children attain this ability (Mead 1934). Psychologist John

Mead analyzed *taking the role of the other* as an essential part of learning to be a full-fledged member of society. At first, we are able to take the role only of *significant others,* as this child is doing. Later we develop the capacity to take the role of *the generalized other,* which is essential not only for extended cooperation but also for the control of antisocial desires.

Flavel (1968) asked 8- and 14-year-olds to explain a board game to some children who were blindfolded and to others who were not. The 8-year-olds gave the same instructions to everyone, but the 14-year-olds gave more detailed instructions to those who were blindfolded. The younger children could not yet take the role of the other, while the older children could.

As they develop this ability, at first children are able to take only the role of **significant others,** individuals who have significant influence on their lives, such as parents or siblings. By assuming their roles during play, such as by dressing up in their parents' clothing, children cultivate the ability to put themselves in the place of significant others.

As the self gradually develops, children internalize the expectations of more and more people. The ability to take roles eventually extends to being able to take the role of "the group as a whole." Mead used the term **generalized other** to refer to this, our perception of how people in general think of us.

To take the role of others is essential if we are to become cooperative members of human groups—whether they be our family, friends, or co-workers. This ability allows us to modify our behavior by anticipating how others will react—something Genie never learned.

Learning to take the role of the other goes through three stages (see Figure 3.1):

1. *Imitation.* Children under age 3 can only mimic others. They do not yet have a sense of self separate from others, and they can only imitate people's gestures and words. (This stage is actually not role taking, but it prepares the child for it.)

2. *Play.* From the age of about 3 to 6, children pretend to take the roles of specific people. They might pretend that they are a firefighter, a nurse, a wrestler, Supergirl, Spiderman, a princess, and so on. They also like costumes at this stage and enjoy dressing up in their parents' clothing or tying a towel around their neck to "become" Spiderman or Wonder Woman.

3. *Games.* This third stage, organized play, or team games, begins roughly with the early school years. The significance for the self is that to play these games, the individual must be able to take multiple roles. One of Mead's favorite examples was that of a baseball game, in which each player must be able to take the role of all the other players. To play baseball, the child must not only know his or her own role but also be able to anticipate who will do what when the ball is hit or thrown.

Figure 3.1 How We Learn to Take the Role of the Other: Mead's Three Stages

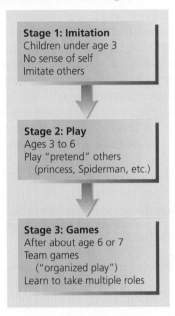

Stage 1: Imitation
Children under age 3
No sense of self
Imitate others

Stage 2: Play
Ages 3 to 6
Play "pretend" others
(princess, Spiderman, etc.)

Stage 3: Games
After about age 6 or 7
Team games
("organized play")
Learn to take multiple roles

Mead also said there were two parts to the self: the "I" and the "me." *The "I" is the self as subject,* the active, spontaneous, creative part of the self. In contrast, *the "me" is the self as object.* It is made up of the attitudes we internalize from our interactions with others. Mead chose these pronouns because in English "I" is the active agent, as in "I shoved him," while "me" is the object of action, as in "He shoved me." Mead stressed that we are not passive in the socialization process. We are not like robots, passively absorbing the responses of others. Rather, our "I" is active. It evaluates the reactions of others and organizes them into a unified whole.

Mead also drew a conclusion that some find startling: *Not only the self but also the human mind is a social product.* Mead stressed that we cannot think without symbols. But where do these symbols come from? Only from society, which gives us our symbols by giving us language. If society did not provide the symbols, we would not be able to think and thus would not possess what we call the mind. Mind, then, like language, is a product of society.

Piaget and the Development of Reasoning

An essential part of being human is our ability to reason. How do we learn this skill?

This question intrigued Jean Piaget (1896–1980), a Swiss psychologist, who noticed that young children give similar wrong answers on intelligence tests. He thought that younger children might be using some sort of consistent but incorrect reasoning to figure out their answers. Perhaps children go through a natural process as they learn how to reason (Piaget 1950, 1954; Flavel et al. 2002).

After years of testing, Piaget concluded that children go through four stages as they develop the ability to reason. (If you mentally substitute "reasoning skills" for the term *operational* in the following explanations, Piaget's findings will be easier to understand.)

1. **The sensorimotor stage** (from birth to about age 2) During this stage, understanding is limited to direct contact with the environment—sucking, touching, listening, looking. Infants do not think, in any sense that we understand. For example, infants cannot recognize cause and effect.

To help his students understand the term *generalized other,* Mead used baseball as an illustration. Why are team sports and organized games such excellent examples to use in explaining this concept?

2. **The preoperational stage** (from about age 2 to age 7) During this stage, children *develop the ability to use symbols.* They do not yet understand common concepts, however, such as size, speed, or causation. Although they can count, they do not really understand what numbers mean. Nor do they yet have the ability to take the role of the other. Piaget asked preoperational children to describe a clay model of a mountain range. They did just fine. But when he asked them to describe how the mountain range looked from where another child was sitting, they couldn't do it. They could only repeat what they saw from their view.

3. **The concrete operational stage** (from the age of about 7 to 12) Although reasoning abilities are more developed, they remain *concrete.* Children can now understand numbers, causation, and speed, and they are able to take the role of the other and to participate in team games. Without concrete examples, however, they are unable to talk about concepts such as truth, honesty, or justice. They can explain why Jane's answer was a lie, but they cannot describe what truth itself is.

4. **The formal operational stage** (after the age of about 12) Children are now capable of abstract thinking. They can talk about concepts, come to conclusions based on general principles, and use rules to solve abstract problems. During this stage, children are likely to become young philosophers (Kagan 1984). If shown a photo of a slave, for example, a child at the concrete operational stage might have said, "That's wrong!" However, a child at the formal operational stage is likely to add, "If our country was founded on equality, how could people have owned slaves?"

Global Aspects of the Self and Reasoning

Cooley's conclusions about the looking-glass self appear to be universal. So do Mead's conclusions about role taking and the mind as a social product, although researchers are finding that the self may develop earlier than Mead indicated. The stages of reasoning that Piaget identified are also probably universal, but researchers have found that the ages at which individuals enter the stages differ from one person to another and that the stages are not as distinct as Piaget concluded (Flavel et al. 2002). Even during the sensorimotor stage, for example, children show early signs of reasoning, which may indicate an innate ability that is wired into the brain. Although Piaget's theory is being refined, his contribution remains: *A basic structure underlies the way we develop reasoning, and children all over the world begin with the concrete and move to the abstract.*

Interestingly, some people seem to get stuck in the concreteness of the third stage and never reach the fourth stage of abstract thinking (Kohlberg and Gilligan 1971; Suizzo 2000). College, for example, nurtures the fourth stage, and most people without this experience apparently have less ability for abstract thought. Social experiences, then, can modify these stages. Also, there is much that we don't yet know about how culture influences the way we think, a topic explored in the Cultural Diversity box on page 68.

Learning Personality and Emotions

Our personality and emotions are vital aspects of who we are. Let's look at how we learn these essential aspects of our being.

Freud and the Development of Personality

Along with the development of our mind and the self comes the development of our personality. Sigmund Freud (1856–1939) developed a theory of the origin of personality that has had a major impact on Western thought. Freud was a physician in Vienna in the early 1900s who founded *psychoanalysis,* a technique for treating emotional problems through long-term, intensive exploration of the subconscious mind. Let's look at his theory.

Freud believed that personality consists of three elements. Each child is born with the first element, an **id,** Freud's term for inborn drives that cause us to seek self-gratification. The id of the newborn is evident in its cries of hunger or pain. The pleasure-seeking id operates throughout life. It demands the immediate fulfillment of basic needs: attention, food, safety, sex, and so on.

The id's drive for immediate gratification, however, runs into a roadblock: primarily the needs of other people, especially those of the parents. To adapt to these constraints, a second component of the personality emerges, which Freud called the ego. The **ego** is the balancing force between the id and the demands of society that suppress it. The ego also serves to balance the id and the **superego,** the third component of the personality, more commonly called the *conscience.*

The superego represents *culture within us,* the norms and values we have internalized from our social groups. As the *moral* component of the personality, the superego provokes feelings of guilt or shame when we break social rules or pride and self-satisfaction when we follow them.

According to Freud, when the id gets out of hand, we follow our desires for pleasure and break society's norms. When the superego gets out of hand, we become overly rigid in following those norms, finding ourselves bound in a straitjacket of rules that inhibit our lives. The ego, the balancing force, tries to prevent either the superego or the id from dominating. In the emotionally healthy individual, the ego succeeds in balancing these conflicting demands of the id and the superego. In the maladjusted individual, however, the ego fails to control the conflict between the id and the superego. Either the id or the superego dominates this person, leading to internal confusion and problem behaviors.

Sociological Evaluation Sociologists appreciate Freud's emphasis on socialization—that the social group into which we are born transmits norms and values that restrain our biological drives. Sociologists, however, object to the view that inborn and subconscious motivations are the primary reasons for human behavior. *This denies the central principle of sociology:* that factors such as social class (income, education, and occupation) and people's roles in groups underlie their behavior (Epstein 1988; Bush and Simmons 1990).

Feminist sociologists have been especially critical of Freud. Although what we just summarized applies to both females and males, Freud assumed that what is "male" is "normal." He even said that females are inferior, castrated males (Chodorow 1990; Gerhard 2000). It is obvious that sociologists need to continue to research how we develop personality.

Socialization and Emotions

Emotions, too, are an essential aspect of who we become. Sociologists who research this area of our "humanness" find that emotions are also not simply the results of biology. Like the development of the mind, emotions also depend on socialization (Hochschild 1975, 1983; Reiser 1999; Barbalet 2002). This may sound strange. Don't all people get angry? Doesn't everyone cry? Don't we all feel guilt, shame, sadness, happiness, fear? What has socialization to do with emotions?

Global Emotions At first, it may look as though socialization is not relevant. Paul Ekman (1980), an anthropologist, studied emotions in several countries. He concluded that everyone experiences six basic emotions:

Sports are a powerful agent of socialization. That sumo wrestling teaches a form of masculinity should be apparent from this photo. What else do you think these boys are learning?

anger, disgust, fear, happiness, sadness, and surprise—and we all show the same facial expressions when we feel these emotions. A person from Zimbabwe, for example, could tell from just the look on an American's face that she is angry, disgusted, or fearful, and we could tell from the Zimbabwean's face that he is happy, sad, or surprised. Because we all show the same facial expressions when we experience these six emotions, Ekman concluded that they are built into our biology, "a product of our genes."

Expressing Emotions The existence of universal facial expressions for these basic emotions does *not* mean that socialization has no effect on how we express them. Facial expressions are only one way in which we show emotions. Other ways vary with gender. For example, U.S. women are allowed to express their emotions more freely, while U.S. men are expected to be more reserved. To express sudden happiness or delighted surprise, for example, women are allowed to make "squeals of glee" in public places. Men are not. Such an expression would be a fundamental violation of their gender role.

Then there are culture, social class, and relationships. Consider culture. Two close Japanese friends who meet after a long separation don't shake hands or hug—they

Cultural Diversity *around the* World

Do You See What I See? Eastern and Western Ways of Perceiving and Thinking

WHICH TWO OF THESE ITEMS go together: a panda, a monkey, and a banana? Please answer before you read further.

You probably said the panda and the monkey. Both are animals, while the banana is a fruit. This is logical.

At least this is the logic of Westerners, and it is difficult for us to see how the answer could be anything else. Someone from Japan, however, is likely to reply that the monkey and the banana go together.

Why? Whereas Westerners typically see categories (animals and fruit), Asians typically see relationships (monkeys eat bananas).

In one study, Japanese and U.S. students were shown a picture of an aquarium that contained one big, fast-moving fish and several smaller fish, along with plants, a rock, and bubbles. Later, when the students were asked what they had seen, the Japanese students were 60 percent more likely to remember background elements. They also referred more to relationships, such as "the little pink fish was in front of the blue rock."

The students were also shown 96 objects and asked which of them had been in the picture. The Japanese students did much better at remembering when the object was shown in its original surroundings. The U.S. students, in

The World

What do you see when you look at this aquarium? Perception depends not only on biology but also on culture.

contrast, had not noticed the background.

Westerners pay more attention to the focal object, in this case the fish, while Asians are more attuned to the overall surroundings. The implications of this difference run deep: Easterners attribute less causation to actors and more to context, while Westerners minimize the context and place greater emphasis on individual actors.

Differences in how Westerners and Easterners perceive the world and think about it are just being uncovered. We know practically nothing about how these differences originate. Because these initial findings indicate deep, culturally based, fundamental differences in perception and thinking, this should prove to be a fascinating area of research.

Source: Based on Nisbett 2003.

for your Consideration

In our global village, differences in perception and thinking can have potentially devastating effects. Consider a crisis between the United States and North Korea. How might Easterners and Westerners see the matter differently? How might they attribute cause differently and, without knowing it, "talk past one another"?

---

bow. Two Arab men will kiss. Social class is also significant, for it cuts across many other lines, even gender. Upon seeing a friend after a long absence, upper-class women and men are likely to be more reserved in expressing their delight than are lower-class women and men. Relationships also make a big difference. We express our emotions more openly if we are with close friends, more guardedly if we are at a staff meeting with the corporate CEO. A good part of childhood socialization centers on learning these "norms of emotion," how to express our emotions in a variety of settings.

What We Feel The matter goes deeper than this. Socialization not only leads to different ways of expressing emotions but even affects *what* we feel (Clark 1997; Shields 2002). People in one culture may even learn to experience feelings that are unknown in another culture. For example, the Ifaluk, who live on the Western Caroline Islands of Micronesia, use the word *fago* to refer to the feelings they have when they see someone suffer. This comes close to what we call *sympathy* or *compassion*. But the Ifaluk also use this term to refer to what they feel when they are with someone who has high status, someone they highly respect or admire (Kagan 1984). To us, these are two distinct emotions, and they require separate terms.

Research Needed   Although Ekman identified only six emotions that are universal in feeling and facial expression, I suspect that other emotions are common to people around the world—and that everyone shows similar facial expressions when they experience them. I suggest that feelings of helplessness, despair, confusion, and shock are among these universal emotions. We need cross-cultural research to find out whether this is so. We also need research into how children learn to feel and express emotions.

Society Within Us: The Self and Emotions as Social Control

Much of our socialization is intended to turn us into conforming members of society. Socialization into the self and emotions is an essential part of this process, for both the self and our emotions mold our behavior. Although we like to think that we are "free," consider for a moment just some of the factors that influence how we act: the expectations of our friends and parents, or neighbors and teachers; classroom norms and college rules; city, federal, and state laws. For example, if in a moment of intense frustration or out of a devilish desire to shock people, you wanted to tear off your clothes and run naked down the street, what would stop you?

The answer is your socialization—*society within you.* Your experiences in society have resulted in a self that thinks along certain lines and feels particular emotions. This helps to keep you in line. Thoughts such as "Would I get kicked out of school?" and "What would my friends (parents) think if they found out?" represent an awareness of the self in relationship to others. So does the desire to avoid feelings of shame and embarrassment. Our *social mirror,* then—the result of being socialized into a self and emotions—sets up effective controls over our behavior. In fact, socialization into self and emotions is so effective that some people feel embarrassed just thinking about running nude in public!

IN SUM | Socialization is essential for our development as human beings. From interaction with others, we learn how to think, reason, and feel. The net result is the shaping of our behavior—including our thinking and emotions—according to cultural standards. This is what sociologists mean when they refer to *society within us.*

Socialization into Gender

To channel our behavior, society also uses **gender socialization.** By expecting different attitudes and behaviors from us *because* we are male or female, the human group nudges boys and girls in separate directions in life. This foundation of contrasting attitudes and behaviors is so well established that as adults, most of us act, think, and even feel according to our culture's guidelines of what is appropriate for our sex.

The significance of gender in social life is emphasized throughout this book, and we focus specifically on gender in Chapter 10. For now, though, let's consider some of the "gender messages" that we get from our family and the mass media.

Gender Messages in the Family

Our parents are the first significant others who teach us our role in this symbolic division of the world. Their own gender orientations have become embedded so firmly that they do most of this teaching without even being aware of what they are doing. This is illustrated by a classic study by psychologists Susan Goldberg and Michael Lewis (1969), whose results have been confirmed by other researchers (Fagot et al. 1985; Connors 1996).

Goldberg and Lewis asked mothers to bring their 6-month-old infants into their laboratory, supposedly to observe the infants' development. Covertly, however, these researchers also observed the mothers. They found that the mothers kept their daughters closer to them. They also touched their daughters more and spoke to them more frequently than they did to their sons.

By the time the children were 13 months old, the girls stayed closer to their mothers during play, and they returned to their mothers sooner and more often than the boys did. When Goldberg and Lewis set up a barrier to separate the children from their mothers, who were holding toys, the girls were more likely to cry and motion for help; the boys were more likely to try to climb over the barrier. Goldberg and Lewis concluded that in our society mothers subconsciously reward their daughters for being passive and dependent, their sons for being active and independent.

These lessons continue throughout childhood. On the basis of their sex, children are given different kinds of toys. Parents let their preschool sons roam farther from home than their preschool daughters, and they subtly encourage the boys to participate in more rough-and-tumble play—

even to get dirtier and to be more defiant (Gilman 1911/1971; Henslin 2005).

We should note, however, that some sociologists would consider biology to be the cause of these behaviors, proposing that Goldberg and Lewis were simply observing innate differences in the children. In short, were the mothers creating those behaviors (the boys wanting to get down and play more, and the girls wanting to be hugged more), or were they responding to natural differences in their children? It is similarly the case with toys. In an intriguing experiment with monkeys, researchers discovered that male monkeys prefer cars and balls more than do female monkeys, who are more likely to prefer dolls and pots (Alexander and Hines 2002). We shall return to this controversial issue in Chapter 10.

Gender Messages from Peers

Sociologists stress how this sorting process that begins in the family is reinforced as the child is exposed to other aspects of society. Of those other influences, one of the most powerful is the **peer group,** individuals of roughly the same age who are linked by common interests. Examples of peer groups are friends, classmates, and "the kids in the neighborhood." Consider how girls and boys teach one another what it means to be a female or a male in U.S. society.

Let's eavesdrop on a conversation between two eighth-grade girls studied by sociologist Donna Eder (2005). You can see how these girls are reinforcing gender images of appearance and behavior:

CINDY: The only thing that makes her look anything is all the makeup . . .

PENNY: She had a picture, and she's standing like this. (Poses with one hand on her hip and one by her head)

CINDY: Her face is probably this skinny, but it looks that big 'cause of all the makeup she has on it.

PENNY: She's ugly, ugly, ugly.

Boys, of course, also reinforce cultural expectations of gender (Pascoe 2003). When sociologist Melissa Milkie (1994) studied junior high school boys, she found that much of their talk centered on movies and TV programs. Of the many images they saw, the boys would single out those involving sex and violence. They would amuse one another by repeating lines, acting out parts, and joking and laughing about what they had seen.

If you know boys in their early teens, you've probably seen behavior like this. You may have been amused or even have shaken your head in disapproval. As a sociologist, however, Milkie peered beneath the surface. She concluded that the boys were using media images to develop their identity as males. They had gotten the message: To be a "real" male is to be obsessed with sex and violence. Not to joke and laugh about murder and promiscuous sex would have marked a boy as a "weenie," a label to be avoided at all costs.

Gender Messages in the Mass Media

Sociologists stress how this sorting process that begins in the family is reinforced as the child is exposed to other aspects of society. Especially important are the **mass media,** forms of communication that are directed to large audiences. Let's look at how images on television and in video games reinforce society's expectations of gender.

Television Television reinforces stereotypes of the sexes. On prime-time television, male characters outnumber female characters. Male characters are also more likely to be portrayed in higher-status positions (Glascock

The *gender roles* that we learn during childhood become part of our basic orientations to life. Although we refine these roles as we grow older, they remain built around the framework established during childhood.

Frank and Ernest

SOON WE'LL GIVE UP DOLLS AND HOPSCOTCH---BUT THEY'LL BE INTO FOOTBALL FOREVER.

www.cartoonistgroup.com

2001). Sports news also maintains traditional stereotypes. Sociologists who studied the content of televised sports news in Los Angeles found that women athletes receive little coverage (Messner et al. 2003). When they do, they are sometimes trivialized by male newscasters, who focus on humorous events in women's sports or turn the woman athlete into a sexual object. Newscasters even manage to emphasize breasts and bras and to engage in locker-room humor.

Stereotype-breaking characters, in contrast, are a sign of changing times. In comedies, women are more verbally aggressive than men (Glascock 2001). The powers of the teenager *Buffy, The Vampire Slayer,* were also remarkable. On *Alias,* Sydney Bristow exhibits extraordinary strength. In cartoons, Kim Possible divides her time between cheerleading practice and saving the world from evil, while, also with tongue in cheek, the Powerpuff Girls are touted as "the most elite kindergarten crime-fighting force ever assembled." This new gender portrayal continues in a variety of programs, such as *Totally Spies.*

The gender messages on these programs are mixed. Girls are powerful, but they have to be skinny and gorgeous and wear the latest fashions, too. This is almost impossible to replicate in real life.

Video Games   The popularity of video games has surged. Even one-fourth of 4- to 6-year-olds play them for an average of an hour a day (Rideout and Vandewater 2003). College students, especially men, relieve stress by escaping into video games (Jones 2003).

Although sociologists have begun to study how the sexes are portrayed in these games, their influence on the players' ideas of gender is still unknown (Dietz 2000; Berger 2002). Because these games are on the cutting edge of society, they sometimes also reflect cutting-edge changes in sex roles, the topic of the Mass Media in Social Life box on the next page.

IN SUM All of us are born into a society in which "male" and "female" are significant symbols. Sorted into separate groups from early childhood, girls and boys learn different ideas of what to expect of themselves and of one another. These gender messages, first transmitted by the family, are reinforced by other social institutions. Each of us learns the meaning that our society associates with the sexes. These images become integrated into our views of the world, forming a picture of "how" males and females "are," and forcing an interpretation of the world in terms

of gender. Because gender serves as a primary basis for **social inequality**—giving privileges and obligations to one group of people while denying them to another—gender images are especially important to understand.

Agents of Socialization

People and groups that influence our orientations to life—our self-concept, emotions, attitudes, and behavior—are called **agents of socialization.** We have already considered how three of these agents–the family, our peers, and the mass media–influence our ideas of gender. Now we'll look more closely at how agents of socialization prepare us to take our place in society. We shall first consider the family, and then the neighborhood, religion, day care, school and peers, and the workplace.

The Family

One of the main findings of sociologists concerns the way socialization depends on a family's social class. In a study of how working-class and middle-class parents rear their children, sociologist Melvin Kohn (1959, 1963, 1976, 1977; Kohn et al. 1986) found that working-class parents are mainly concerned that their children stay out of trouble. They also tend to use physical punishment. Middle-class parents, in contrast, focus more on developing their children's curiosity, self-expression, and self-control. They are more likely to reason with their children than to use physical punishment.

These findings presented a sociological puzzle. Just why would working-class and middle-class parents rear their children so differently? Kohn knew that life experiences of some sort held the key to solving the puzzle, and he found that key in the world of work. Bosses usually tell blue-collar workers exactly what to do. Since blue-collar parents expect their children's lives to be like theirs, they stress obedience. At their work, in contrast, middle-class parents take more initiative. Expecting their children to work at similar jobs, middle-class parents socialize them into the qualities they have found valuable.

Kohn was still puzzled, however, for some working-class parents act more like middle-class parents, and vice versa. As Kohn probed this puzzle, the pieces fell into place. The explanation was the parents' type of job. Middle-class office workers, for example, have little freedom and are closely supervised. Kohn found that they follow the working-class pattern of child rearing, putting stress on outward conformity. And some blue-collar workers, such as those

mass Media in social life

Lara Croft, Tomb Raider: Changing Images of Women in the Mass Media

The mass media reflect women's changing role in society. Portrayals of women as passive, as subordinate, or as mere background objects remain, but a new image has broken through. Although this new image exaggerates changes, it also illustrates a fundamental change in gender relations. Lara Croft is an outstanding example of this change.

Like books and magazines, video games are made available to a mass audience. And with digital advances, they have crossed the line from what is traditionally thought of as games to something that more closely resembles interactive movies. Costing an average of $10 million to produce and another $10 million to market, video games now have intricate subplots and use celebrity voices for the characters (Nussenbaum 2004).

Sociologically, what is significant is that the *content* of video games socializes their users. As they play, gamers are exposed not only to action but also to ideas and images. The gender images of video games communicate powerful messages, just as they do in other forms of the mass media.

Lara Croft, an adventure-seeking archeologist and star of *Tomb Raider* and its many sequels, is the essence of the new gender image. Lara is smart, strong, and able to utterly vanquish foes. With both guns blazing, she is the cowboy of the twenty-first century, the term *cowboy* being purposefully chosen, as Lara breaks stereotypical gender roles and dominates what previously was the domain of men.

The mass media not only reflect gender stereotypes but also they play a role in changing them. Sometimes they do both simultaneously. The images of Lara Croft not only reflect women's changing role in society, but also, by exaggerating the change, they mold new stereotypes.

She was the first female protagonist in a field of muscle-rippling, gun-toting macho caricatures (Taylor 1999).

Yet the old remains powerfully encapsulated in the new. As the photos on this page make evident, Lara is a fantasy girl for young men of the digital generation. No matter her foe, no matter her predicament, Lara oozes sex. Her form-fitting outfits, which flatter her voluptuous physique, reflect the mental images of the men who fashioned this digital character.

Lara has caught young men's fancy to such an extent that they have bombarded corporate headquarters with questions about her personal life. Lara is the star of two movies and a comic book. There is even a Lara Croft candy bar.

for your Consideration

A sociologist who reviewed this text said, "It seems that for women to be defined as equal, we have to become symbolic males—warriors with breasts." Why is gender change mostly one-way—females adopting traditional male characteristics? To see why men get to keep their gender roles, these two questions should help: Who is moving into the traditional territory of the other? Do people prefer to imitate power or powerlessness?

Finally, consider just how far stereotypes have actually been left behind. The ultimate goal of the video game, after foes are vanquished, is to see Lara in a nightie.

who do home repairs, have a good deal of freedom. These workers follow the middle-class model in rearing their children (Pearlin and Kohn 1966; Kohn and Schooler 1969).

The Neighborhood

As all parents know, some neighborhoods are better for their children than others. Parents try to move to those neighborhoods—if they can afford them. Their commonsense evaluations are borne out by sociological research. Children from poor neighborhoods are more likely to get in trouble with the law, to become pregnant, to drop out of school, and even to have worse mental health in later life (Wilson 1987; Brooks-Gunn et al. 1997; Sampson et al. 2001; Wheaton and Clarke 2003).

Sociologists have also documented that the residents of more affluent neighborhoods watch out for the children more than do the residents of poor neighborhoods (Sampson et al. 1999). This isn't because the adults in poor neighborhoods care less about children. Rather, the more affluent neighborhoods have less transition, so the adults are more likely to know the local children and their parents. This better equips them to help keep the children safe and out of trouble.

Religion

By influencing values, religion becomes a key component in people's ideas of right and wrong. Religion is so important to Americans that 65 percent belong to a local congregation, and during a typical week, two of every five Americans attend a religious service (*Statistical Abstract* 2003:Table 80). Religion is significant even for people who are reared in nonreligious homes; religious ideas pervade U.S. society, providing basic ideas of morality for us all.

The influence of religion extends to many areas of our lives. For example, participation in religious services teaches us not only beliefs about the hereafter but also ideas about what kinds of dress, speech, and manners are appropriate for formal occasions. Religion is so significant that we shall examine its influence in a separate chapter (Chapter 13).

Day Care

It is rare for social science research to make national news, but occasionally it does. This is what happened when researchers reported findings from their study of 1,300 children in ten cities. They had observed the children from infancy into kindergarten both at home and at day care. (*Day care* was defined as any care other than by the mother, including care by other relatives and the father.) The researchers had also videotaped and made detailed notes on the children's interaction with their mothers (National

Institute of Child Health and Human Development 1999; Guensburg 2001). What caught the media's attention? Children who spend more hours in day care have weaker bonds with their mothers. In addition, they are more likely to fight, to be cruel, and to be "mean." In contrast, children who spend less time in day care are more cooperative and more affectionate to their mothers. This holds true regardless of the quality of the day care, the family's social class, or whether the child is a girl or a boy.

This study was designed well, and its findings are without dispute. But how do we explain them? The cause could be time spent in day care. The researchers suggest that mothers who spend less time with their children are less responsive to their children's emotional needs because they are less familiar with their children's "signaling systems." But maybe the cause isn't day care. Perhaps mothers who put their children in day care for more hours are less sensitive to their children in the first place. Or perhaps employed mothers are less likely to meet their children's emotional needs because they are more tired and stressed than mothers who stay at home. From this study, we can't determine the cause of the weaker bonding and the behavioral problems.

These researchers also uncovered a positive side to day care. They found that children who spend more hours in day care score higher on language tests (Guensburg 2001). Other researchers have found similar improvement in language skills, especially for children from low-income homes, as well as those from dysfunctional families—those with alcoholic, inept, or abusive parents (Scarr and Eisenberg 1993).

As is obvious, we need more studies to be able to pinpoint the influences of day care. Although this longitudinal study is far from encouraging, it gives us no reason to conclude that day care is producing a generation of "smart but mean" children.

The School and Peer Groups

As a child's experiences with agents of socialization broaden, the influence of the family lessens. Entry into school is one of those significant steps in this transfer of allegiance and learning of new values. The new ways of looking at the world can even replace those the child learns at home, the topic of the Cultural Diversity box on the next page.

When sociologists Patricia and Peter Adler (1998) observed children at two elementary schools in Colorado, they saw how children separate themselves by sex and develop their own worlds with unique norms. The norms that made boys popular were athletic ability, coolness, and toughness. For girls, popularity was based on family background,

Cultural Diversity *in the* United States

Caught Between Two Worlds

IT IS A STRUGGLE TO LEARN a new culture, for its behaviors and ways of thinking contrast with the ones already learned. This can lead to inner turmoil. One way to handle the conflict is to cut ties with your first culture. This, however, can create a sense of loss, perhaps one that is recognized only later in life.

Richard Rodriguez, a literature professor and essayist, was born to working-class Mexican immigrants. Wanting their son to be successful in their adopted land, his parents named him Richard instead of Ricardo. While his English-Spanish hybrid name indicates the parents' aspirations for their son, it was also an omen of the conflict that Richard would experience.

Like other children of Mexican immigrants, Richard's first language was Spanish—a rich mother tongue that introduced him to the world. Until the age of 5, when he began school, Richard knew only fifty words in English. He describes what happened when he began school:

> The change came gradually but early. When I was beginning grade school, I noted to myself the fact that the classroom environment was so different in its styles and assumptions from my own family environment that survival would essentially entail a choice between both worlds. When I became a student, I was literally "remade"; neither I nor my teachers considered anything I had known before as relevant. I had to forget most of what my culture had provided, because to remember it was a disadvantage. The past and its cultural values became detachable, like a piece of clothing grown heavy on a warm day and finally put away.

As happened to millions of immigrants before him, whose parents spoke German, Polish, Italian, and so on, learning English eroded family and class ties and ate away at his ethnic roots. For him, language and education were not simply devices that eased the transition to the dominant culture. Instead, they slashed at the roots that had given him life.

To face conflicting cultures is to confront a fork in the road. Some turn one way and withdraw from the new culture—a clue that helps to explain why so many Latinos drop

out of U.S. schools. Others go in the opposite direction. Cutting ties with their family and cultural roots, they wholeheartedly adopt the new culture. Rodriguez took the second road. He excelled in his new language—so well, in fact, that he graduated from Stanford University and then became a graduate student in English at the University of California at Berkeley. He was even awarded a prestigious Fulbright fellowship to study English Renaissance literature at the British Museum.

But the past wouldn't let Rodriguez alone. Prospective employers were impressed with his knowledge of Renaissance literature. At job interviews, however, they would skip over the Renaissance training and ask him if he would teach the Mexican novel and be an adviser to Latino students. Rodriguez was also haunted by the image of his grandmother, the warmth of the culture he had left behind, and the language and thought to which he had become a stranger.

Richard Rodriguez represents millions of immigrants—not just those of Latino origin but those from other cultures, too—who want to be a part of life in the United States without betraying their past. They fear that to integrate into U.S. culture is to lose their roots. They are caught between two cultures, each beckoning, each offering rich rewards.

Sources: Based on Rodriguez 1975, 1982, 1990, 1991, 1995.

for your Consideration

I saw this conflict firsthand with my father, who did not learn English until after the seventh grade (his last in school): German was left behind, but broken English and awkward expressions remained for a lifetime. Then there were the lingering emotional connections to old ways, as well as the suspicions, haughtiness, and slights of more assimilated Americans. His longing for security by grasping the past was combined with his wanting to succeed in the everyday reality of the new culture. Have you seen anything similar?

physical appearance (clothing and use of makeup), and the ability to attract popular boys. In this children's subculture, academic achievement pulled in opposite directions: For boys, high grades lowered their popularity, but for girls, good grades increased their standing among peers.

You know from your own experience how compelling peer groups are. It is almost impossible to go against a peer group, whose cardinal rule seems to be "conformity or rejection." Anyone who doesn't do what the others want becomes an "outsider," a "nonmember," an "outcast." For preteens and teens just learning their way around in the world, it is not surprising that the peer group dominates.

As a result, the standards of our peer groups tend to dominate our lives. If your peers, for example, listen to rap, heavy metal, rock and roll, country, or gospel, it is almost inevitable that you also prefer that kind of music. It is the same for other kinds of music, clothing styles, and dating standards. Peer influences also extend to behaviors that violate social norms. If your peers are college-bound and upwardly striving, that is most likely what you will be; but if they use drugs, cheat, and steal, you are likely to do so, too.

The Workplace

Another agent of socialization that comes into play somewhat later in life is the workplace. Those initial part-time jobs that we get in high school and college are much more than just a way to earn a few dollars. From the people we rub shoulders with at work, we learn not only a set of skills but also perspectives on the world.

Most of us eventually become committed to some particular line of work, often after trying out various jobs. This may involve **anticipatory socialization,** learning to play a role before entering it. Anticipatory socialization is a sort of rehearsal for some future activity. We may talk to people who work in a career, read novels about them, or take a summer internship. This allows us to identify gradually with the role, to become aware of what would be expected of us. Sometimes this helps people avoid committing themselves to an unrewarding career, as with some of my students who tried student teaching, found that they couldn't stand it, and then moved on to other fields that were more to their liking.

An intriguing aspect of work as a socializing agent is that the more you participate in a line of work, the more the work becomes a part of your self-concept. Eventually, you come to think of yourself so much in terms of the job that if someone asks you to describe yourself, you are likely to include the job in your self-description. You might say, "I'm a teacher," "I'm a nurse," or "I'm a sociologist."

Resocialization

What does a woman who has just become a nun have in common with a man who has just divorced? The answer is that they both are undergoing **resocialization;** that is, they are learning new norms, values, attitudes, and behaviors to match their new situation in life. In its most common form, resocialization occurs each time we learn something contrary to our previous experiences. A new boss who insists on a different way of doing things is resocializing you. Most resocialization is mild, involving only a slight modification of things we have already learned.

Resocialization can also be intense. People who join Alcoholics Anonymous (AA), for example, are surrounded by reformed drinkers who affirm the destructive effects of excessive drinking. Some students experience an intense period of resocialization when they leave high school and start college—especially during those initially scary days before they find companions, start to fit in, and feel comfortable. To join a cult or to begin psychotherapy is even more profound, for these events expose people to ideas that conflict with their previous ways of looking at the world. If these ideas "take," not only does the individual's behavior change but also he or she learns a fundamentally different way of looking at life.

Total Institutions

Relatively few of us experience the powerful agent of socialization that sociologist Erving Goffman (1961) called the **total institution.** He coined this term to refer to a place in which people are cut off from the rest of society and where they come under almost total control of the officials who are in charge. Boot camps, prisons, concentration camps, convents, some religious cults, and some boarding schools, such as West Point, are total institutions.

A person entering a total institution is greeted with a **degradation ceremony** (Garfinkel 1956), an attempt to remake the self by stripping away the individual's current identity and stamping a new one in its place. This unwelcome greeting may involve fingerprinting, photographing, shaving the head, and banning the individual's *personal identity kit* (items such as jewelry, hairstyles, clothing, and other body decorations used to express individuality). Newcomers may be ordered to strip, undergo an examination (often in a humiliating, semipublic setting), and then to put on a uniform that designates their new status.

Total institutions are isolated from the public. The walls, bars, gates, and guards not only keep the inmates in but also keep outsiders out. Staff members closely supervise every aspect of the residents' lives. Eating, sleeping, showering, and recreation—all are standardized. Preexisting statuses are suppressed, and inmates learn that their previous roles such as spouse, parent, worker, or student mean nothing. The only thing that counts is their current role.

No one leaves a total institution unscathed, for the experience brands an indelible mark on the individual's self and colors the way he or she sees the world. Boot camp, as described in the Down-to-Earth Sociology box below, is brutal but swift. Prison, in contrast, is brutal

Down-to-Earth Sociology

Boot Camp as a Total Institution

THE BUS ARRIVES AT PARRIS ISLAND, South Carolina, at 3 A.M. The early hour is no accident. The recruits are groggy, confused. Up to a few hours ago, the boys were ordinary civilians. Now, a sergeant sneeringly calls them "maggots," their heads are buzzed (25 seconds per recruit), and they are thrust quickly into the harsh world of Marine boot camp.

Buzzing the boys' hair is just the first step in stripping away their identity so that the Marines can stamp a new one in its place. The uniform serves the same purpose. So does the ban on using the first person "I." Even a simple request must be made in precise Marine protocol or it will not be acknowledged. ("Sir, Recruit Jones requests permission to make a head call, Sir.")

Every intense moment of the next eleven weeks reminds the recruits that they are joining a subculture of self-discipline. Here pleasure is suspect, and sacrifice is good. As they learn the Marine way of talking, walking, and thinking, they are denied the diversions they once took for granted: television, cigarettes, cars, candy, soft drinks, video games, music, alcohol, drugs, and sex.

Lessons are bestowed with fierce intensity. When Sgt. Carey checks brass belt buckles, Recruit Robert Shelton nervously blurts, "I don't have one." Sgt. Carey's face grows red as the veins in his neck bulge. "I?" he says, his face just inches from the recruit. With spittle flying from his mouth, he screams, "'I' is gone!"

"Nobody's an individual" is the lesson that is driven home again and again. "You are a team, a Marine. Not a civilian. Not black or white, not Hispanic or Indian or some hyphenated American—but a Marine. You will live like a Marine, fight like a Marine, and, if necessary, die like a Marine."

Each day begins before dawn with close-order formations. The rest of the day is filled with training in hand-to-hand

Resocialization *is often a gentle process. Usually we are gradually exposed to different ways of thinking and doing. Sometimes, however,* resocialization *can be swift and brutal, as it is during boot camp in the Marines. This private at Parris Island is learning a world vastly unlike the civilian world he left behind.*

combat, marching, running, calisthenics, Marine history, and—always—following orders.

"An M-16 can blow someone's head off at 500 meters," Sgt. Norman says. "That's beautiful, isn't it?"

"Yes, sir!" shout the platoon's fifty-nine voices.

"Pick your nose!" Simultaneously, fifty-nine index fingers shoot into nostrils.

The pressure to conform is intense. Those who are sent packing for insubordination or suicidal tendencies are mocked in cadence during drills. ("Hope you like the sights you see / Parris Island casualty.") As lights go out at 9 P.M., the exhausted recruits perform the day's last task: The entire platoon, in unison, chants the virtues of the Marines.

Recruits are constantly scrutinized. Subperformance is not accepted, whether it be a dirty rifle or a loose thread on a uniform. The subperformer is shouted at, derided, humiliated. The group suffers for the individual. If a recruit is slow, the entire platoon is punished.

One of the new Marines (until graduation, they are recruits, not Marines) says, "I feel like I've joined a new society or religion."

He has.

Source: Based on Garfinkel 1956; Goffman 1961; Ricks 1995; Dyer 2005.

for your Consideration

Of what significance is the recruits' degradation ceremony? Why are recruits not allowed video games, cigarettes, or calls home? Why are the Marines so unfair as to punish an entire platoon for the failure of an individual? Use concepts in this chapter to explain why the system works.

and prolonged. Neither recruit nor prisoner, however, has difficulty in recognizing how the institution has affected the self.

Socialization Through the Life Course

You are at a particular stage in your life now, and college is a good part of it. You know that you have more stages ahead of you as you go through life. These stages, from birth to death, are called the **life course** (Elder 1975, 1999). The sociological significance of the life course is twofold. First, as you pass through a stage, it affects your behavior and orientations. You simply don't think about life in the same way when you are 30, are married, and have children and a mortgage as you do when you are 18 or 20, single, and in college. (Actually, you don't even see life the same as a freshman and as a senior.) Second, your life course differs by social location. Your social class, race-ethnicity, and gender, for example, map out distinctive worlds of experience. Consequently, the typical life course differs for males and females, the rich and the poor, and so on. To emphasize this major sociological point, in the sketch that follows, I will stress the *historical* setting of people's lives. Because of your particular social location, your own life course may differ from this sketch, which is a composite of stages that others have suggested (Levinson 1978; Carr et al. 1995; Lee 2001).

Childhood (From Birth to About Age 12)

Consider how different your childhood would have been if you had grown up in another historical time. Historian Philippe Ariès (1965) noticed that in European paintings from about 1000 to 1800 A.D., children were always dressed in adult clothing. If they were not depicted stiffly posed, as in a family portrait, they were shown doing adult activities.

From this, Ariès drew a conclusion that sparked a debate among historians: that during this time in Europe childhood was not regarded as a special time of life. He said that adults viewed children as miniature adults and put them to work at very early ages. At the age of 7, for example, a boy might leave home for good to learn to be a jeweler or a stonecutter. A girl, in contrast, stayed home, but by the age of 7 she was expected to assume her share of the household tasks. She might marry in her early teens, or even earlier. Historians do not deny that these were the customs of that time, but some say that Ariès' conclusion is ridiculous. They say that other evidence of that period indicates that childhood was viewed as a special time of life (Orme 2002).

In contemporary Western societies such as the United States, children are viewed as innocent and in need of protection from adult responsibilities. Ideas of childhood vary historically and cross–culturally. From paintings, such as this 1605 portrait of Lady Tasburgh and her children, some historians conclude that Europeans once viewed children as miniature adults who assumed adult roles at the earliest opportunity.

Having children work like adults did not disappear with the Middle Ages. It is still common in the Least Industrialized Nations. The photo essay on pages 184–185 provides a startling example of this practice, reflecting not just different activities but also a view of children worlds apart from the one common in the Most Industrialized Nations.

In earlier centuries, parents and teachers also considered it their moral duty to terrorize children to keep them in line. They would lock children in dark closets, frighten them with bedtime stories of death and hellfire, and force them to witness gruesome events. Consider this:

> A common moral lesson involved taking children to visit the gibbet [an upraised post on which executed bodies were left hanging from chains], where they were forced to inspect rotting corpses hanging there as an example of what happens to bad children when they grow up. Whole classes were taken out of school to witness hangings, and parents would often whip their children afterwards to make them remember what they had seen. (DeMause 1975)

Industrialization transformed the way we see children. When children have the leisure to go to school, they come to be thought of as tender and innocent, as needing more adult care, comfort, and protection. Over time, such attitudes of dependency grow, and today we view children as needing gentle guidance if they are to develop emotionally, intellectually, morally, even physically. We take our view for granted—after all it is only "common sense." Yet, as you can see, our view is not "natural"; it is, instead, rooted in our geography and history.

IN SUM Childhood is more than biology. Everyone's childhood occurs at some point in history and is embedded in particular social locations, especially social class and gender. *These social factors are as vital as our biology, for they determine what childhood will be like for us.* Although a child's *biological* characteristics (such as being small and dependent) are universal, the child's *social* experiences (the kind of life the child lives) are not. Thus, sociologists say that childhood varies from culture to culture.

Adolescence (Ages 13–17)

In earlier centuries, societies did not mark out adolescence as a distinct time of life. People simply moved from childhood into young adulthood, with no stopover in between. The Industrial Revolution brought such an abundance of material surpluses, however, that for the first time in history, millions of people in their teens

were able to remain outside the labor force. At the same time, education became a more important factor in achieving success. The convergence of these two forces in industrialized societies created a gap between childhood and adulthood. In the early 1900s, the term *adolescence* was coined to indicate this new stage in life (Hall 1904).

To ground the self-identity and mark the passage of children into adulthood, tribal societies hold *initiation rites.* In the industrialized world, however, adolescents must "find" themselves on their own. As they attempt to carve out an identity that is distinct from both the "younger" world being left behind and the "older" world that is still out of range, adolescents develop their own subcultures, with distinctive clothing, hairstyles, language, gestures, and music. We usually fail to realize that contemporary society, not biology, created the period of inner turmoil that we call *adolescence.*

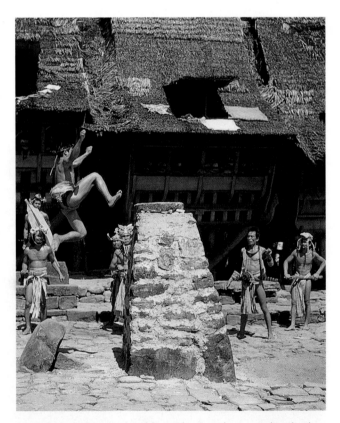

In many societies, manhood is not bestowed upon males simply because they reach a certain age. Manhood, rather, signifies a standing in the community that must be achieved. Shown here is an initiation ceremony in Indonesia, where boys must jump over this barrier to lay claim to the status of manhood.

Transitional Adulthood (Ages 18–29)

If society invented adolescence, can it also invent other periods of life? As Figure 3.2 illustrates, this is actually happening now. Postindustrial societies are adding a period of extended youth to the life course, which sociologists call **transitional adulthood** (also known as *adultolescence*). After high school, millions of young adults go to college, where they postpone adult responsibilities. They are mostly freed from the control of their parents, yet they don't have to support themselves. Even after college, many return home, so they can live cheaply while they establish themselves in a career—and, of course, continue to "find themselves." During this time, people are "neither psychological adolescents nor sociological adults" (Keniston 1971). At some point during this period of extended youth, young adults gradually ease into adult responsibilities. They take a full-time job, become serious about a career, engage in courtship rituals, get married—and go into debt.

The Middle Years (Ages 30–65)

The Early Middle Years (Ages 30–49)   During the early middle years, most people are more sure of both themselves and their goals in life. As with any point in the life

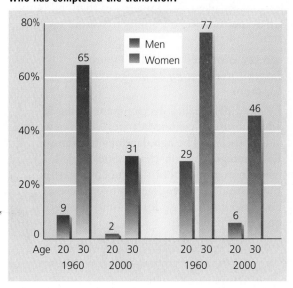

Figure 3.2   Transitional Adulthood: A New Stage in the Life Course

Who has completed the transition?

The percent who have completed the transition to adulthood, as measured by leaving home, finishing school, getting married, having a child, and being financially independent.

Source: Furstenburg et al. 2004.

course, however, the self can receive severe jolts. Common in this period are divorce and losing jobs. It may take years for the self to stabilize after such ruptures.

The early middle years pose a special challenge for many U.S. women, who have been given the message, especially by the media, that they can "have it all." They can be superworkers, superwives, and supermoms all rolled into one. The reality, however, usually consists of conflicting pressures—too little time and too many demands. Something has to give. Attempts to resolve this dilemma are often compounded by another hard reality: that during gender socialization, their husbands learned that child care and housework are not "masculine." In short, adjustments continue in this and all phases of life.

The Later Middle Years (Ages 50–65)   During the later middle years, health problems and mortality begin to loom large as people feel their bodies change, especially if they watch their parents become frail, fall ill, and die. The consequence is a fundamental reorientation in thinking—*from time since birth to time left to live* (Neugarten 1976). With this changed orientation, people attempt to evaluate the past and come to terms with what lies ahead. They compare what they have accomplished with how far they had hoped to go. Many people also find themselves caring not only for their own children but also for their aging parents. Because of this set of burdens, which is often crushing, people in the later middle years sometimes are called the "sandwich generation."

Life during this stage isn't stressful for everyone. Many find late middle age to be the most comfortable period of their lives. They enjoy job security and a standard of living that is higher than ever before; they have a bigger house (one that may even be paid for), newer cars, longer and more exotic vacations. The children are grown, the self is firmly planted, and fewer upheavals are likely to occur.

As they anticipate the next stage of life, however, most people do not like what they see.

The Older Years (About 65 On)

In industrialized societies, the older years begin around the mid-60s. This, too, is recent, for in agricultural societies, when most people died early, old age was thought to begin at around age 40. Industrialization brought improved nutrition and public health, which prolonged life. Today, people in good health who are over the age of 65 often experience this period not as old age, but as an extension of the middle years. People who continue to work or to do things they enjoy are less likely to perceive themselves as old (Neugarten 1977). Although frequency of sex declines, most men and women in their 60s and 70s are sexually active (Denney and Quadagno 1992).

Because we have a self and can reason abstractly, we can contemplate death. Initially, we regard death as a vague notion, a remote possibility. But as people see their friends die and find their own bodies no longer function as before, the thought of death becomes less abstract. Increasingly during this stage in the life course, people feel that "time is closing in" on them.

Are We Prisoners of Socialization?

From our discussion of socialization, you might conclude that sociologists think of people as robots: The socialization goes in, and the behavior comes out. People cannot help what they do, think, or feel, for everything is a result of their exposure to socializing agents.

Sociologists do *not* think of people in this way. Although socialization is powerful and profoundly affects us all, we have a self. Established in childhood and continually modified by later experience, the self is dynamic.

It is not a sponge that passively absorbs influences from the environment but, rather, a vigorous, essential part of our being that allows us to act upon our environment.

Indeed, it is precisely because individuals are not robots that their behavior is so hard to predict. The countless reactions of other people merge in each of us. As the self develops, each person internalizes or "puts together" these innumerable reactions, producing a unique whole called the *individual.* Each unique individual uses his or her own mind to reason and to make choices in life.

In this way, *each of us is actively involved in the construction of the self.* For example, although our experiences in the family lay down the basic elements of our personality, including fundamental orientations to life, we are not doomed to keep those orientations if we do not like them. We can purposely expose ourselves to groups and ideas that we prefer. Those experiences, in turn, will have their own effects on our self. In short, although socialization is powerful, we can change even the self within the limitations of the framework laid down by our social location. And that self—along with the options available within society—is the key to our behavior.

Summary *and* Review

What Is Human Nature?

How much of our human characteristics comes from "nature" (heredity) and how much from "nurture" (the social environment)?

Observations of isolated and institutionalized children help to answer this question, as do experiments with monkeys that were raised in isolation. Language and intimate social interaction—aspects of "nurture"—are essential to the development of what we consider to be human characteristics. Pp. 60–63.

Socialization into the Self, Mind, and Emotions

How do we acquire a self and reasoning skills?

Humans are born with the *capacity* to develop a **self,** but the self must be socially constructed; that is, its contents depend on social interaction. According to Charles Horton Cooley's concept of the **looking-glass self,** our self develops as we internalize others' reactions to us. George Herbert Mead identified the ability to **take the role of the other** as essential to the development of the self. Mead concluded that even the mind is a social product. Jean Piaget identified four stages that children go through as they develop the ability to reason. Pp. 63–66

How do sociologists evaluate Freud's psychoanalytic theory of personality development?

Freud viewed personality development as the result of one's **id** (inborn, self-centered desires) clashing with the demands of society. The **ego** develops to balance the id and the **superego,** the conscience. Sociologists, in contrast, do not examine inborn or subconscious motivations but, instead, how *social* factors—social class, gender, religion, education, and so forth—underlie personality development. Pp. 66–67.

How does socialization influence emotions?

Socialization influences *not only how we express our emotions but also what emotions we feel.* Socialization into emotions is one of the means by which society produces conformity. Pp. 67–69.

Socialization into Gender

How does gender socialization affect our sense of self?

Gender socialization—sorting males and females into different roles—is a primary means of controlling human behavior. Children receive messages about gender even in infancy. A society's ideals of sex-linked behaviors are reinforced by its social institutions. Pp. 69–71.

Agents of Socialization

What are the main agents of socialization?

Agents of socialization include the **mass media,** family, the neighborhood, religion, day care, school, **peer groups,** and the workplace. Each has its particular influences in socializing us into becoming full-fledged members of society. Pp. 71–75.

Resocialization

What is resocialization?

Resocialization is the process of learning new norms, values, attitudes, and behavior. Most resocialization is voluntary, but some, as with residents of **total institutions,** is involuntary. Pp. 75–77.

Socialization Through the Life Course

Does socialization end when we enter adulthood?

Socialization occurs throughout the life course. In industrialized societies, the **life course** can be divided into childhood, adolescence, young adulthood, the middle years, and the older years. The West is adding a new stage, **transitional adulthood.** Life course patterns vary by social location such as history, gender, race-ethnicity, and social class. Pp. 77–80.

Are We Prisoners of Socialization?

Although socialization is powerful, we are not merely the sum of our socialization experiences. Just as socialization influences human behavior, so humans act on their environment and influence even their self-concept. P. 80.

Thinking Critically
about Chapter 3

1. What three agents of socialization have influenced you the most? Can you pinpoint their influence on your attitudes, beliefs, values, or other orientations to life?
2. Summarize your views of gender. What in your socialization has led you to have these views?
3. What is your location in the life course? How does the text's summary of that location match your experiences? Explain the similarities and differences.

Additional Resources

Companion Website www.ablongman.com/henslin

- Content Select Research Database for Sociology, with suggested key terms and annotated references
- Link to 2000 Census, with activities
- Flashcards of key terms and concepts
- Practice Tests
- Weblinks
- Interactive Maps

Where Can I Read More on This Topic?

Suggested readings for this chapter are listed at the back of this book.

Social Structure and Social Interaction

CHAPTER

4

OUTLINE

Levels of Sociological Analysis
Macrosociology and Microsociology

**The Macrosociological
Perspective: Social Structure**
Culture
Social Class
Social Status
Roles
Groups
Social Institutions
Societies—and Their
  Transformations
Biotech Society: Is a New Type of
  Society Emerging?
What Holds Society Together?

**The Microsociological
Perspective: Social Interaction
in Everyday Life**
Stereotypes
Personal Space
Dramaturgy: The Presentation of
  Self in Everyday Life
Ethnomethodology: Uncovering
  Background Assumptions
The Social Construction of Reality
Social Interaction on the Internet

**The Need for Both
Macrosociology and
Microsociology**

Summary and Review

Jacob Lawrence, *Street Scene (Boy with Kite)*, 1962

My curiosity had gotten the better of me. When the sociology convention finished, I climbed aboard the first city bus that came along. I didn't know where the bus was going, and I didn't know where I was going to spend the night.

"Maybe I overdid it this time," I thought as the bus began winding down streets I had never seen before. Actually, this was my first visit to Washington, D.C., so everything was unfamiliar to me. I had no destination, no plans, not even a map. I carried no billfold, just a driver's license shoved into my jeans for emergency identification, some pocket change, and a $10 bill tucked into my sock. My goal was simple: If I saw something interesting, I would get off and check it out.

"Nothing but the usual things," I mused, as we passed row after row of apartment buildings and stores. I could see myself riding buses the entire night. Then something caught my eye. Nothing spectacular—just groups of people clustered around a large circular area where several streets intersected.

I climbed off the bus and made my way to what turned out to be Dupont Circle. I took a seat on a sidewalk bench and began to observe what was going on around me. As the scene came into focus, I noticed several streetcorner men drinking and joking with one another. One of the men broke from his companions and sat down next to me. As we talked, I mostly listened.

Suddenly one of the men jumped up, smashed the empty bottle against the sidewalk, and . . .

As night fell, the men said that they wanted to get another bottle of wine. I contributed. They counted their money and asked if I wanted to go with them.

Although I felt my stomach churning—a combination of hesitation and fear—I heard a confident "Sure!" come out of my mouth. As we left the circle, the three men began to cut through an alley. "Oh, no," I thought. "This isn't what I had in mind."

I had but a split second to make a decision. I found myself continuing to walk with the men but holding back half a step so that none of the three was behind me. As we walked, they passed around the remnants of their bottle. When my turn came, I didn't know what to do. I shuddered to think about the diseases lurking within that bottle. I made another quick decision. In the

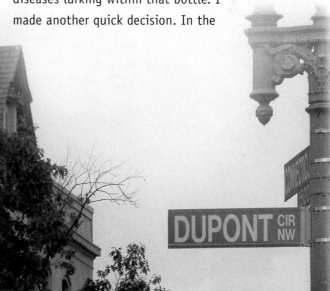

semidarkness, I faked it, letting only my thumb and forefinger touch my lips and nothing enter my mouth.

When we returned to Dupont Circle, we sat on the benches, and the men passed around their new bottle of Thunderbird. I couldn't fake it in the light, so I passed, pointing at my stomach to indicate that I was having digestive problems.

Suddenly, one of the men jumped up, smashed the emptied bottle against the sidewalk, and thrust the jagged neck outward in a menacing gesture. He glared straight ahead at another bench, where he had spotted someone with whom he had some sort of unfinished business. As the other men told him to cool it, I moved slightly to one side of the group—ready to flee, just in case.

Levels of Sociological Analysis

In this sociological adventure, I almost got myself in over my head. Fortunately, it turned out all right. The man's "enemy" didn't look our way, he sat the broken bottle down next to the bench "just in case he needed it," and my introduction to a life that up to then I had only read about continued until dawn.

Sociologists Elliot Liebow (1967/1999), Mitchell Duneier (1999), and Elijah Anderson (1978, 1990, 2006) have written fascinating accounts about men like my companions from that evening. Although streetcorner men may appear to be disorganized—simply coming and going as they please and doing whatever feels good at the moment—sociologists have analyzed how, like us, these men are influenced by the norms and beliefs of our society. This will become more apparent as we examine the two levels of analysis that sociologists use.

Macrosociology and Microsociology

The first level, **macrosociology**, focuses on broad features of society. Sociologists who use this approach analyze such things as social class and how groups are related to one another. If macrosociologists were to analyze streetcorner men, for example, they would stress

Sociologists use both macro and micro levels of analysis to study social life. Those who use *macrosociology* to analyze the homeless—or any human behavior—focus on broad aspects of society, such as the economy and social classes. Sociologists who use the *microsociological approach,* analyze how people interact with one another. This photo illustrates social structure—the disparities between power and powerlessness are amply evident. It also illustrates the micro level—the isolation of these homeless men.

that these men are located at the bottom of the U.S. social class system. Their low status means that many opportunities are closed to them: The men have few job skills, little education, hardly anything to offer an employer. As "able-bodied" men, however, they are not eligible for welfare—even for a two-year limit—so they hustle to survive. As a consequence, they spend their lives on the streets.

Conflict theory and functionalism, both of which focus on the broader picture, are examples of this macrosociological approach. The goal of these theories is to examine the large-scale social forces that influence people.

The second approach **microsociology,** examines **social interaction,** what people do when they come together. Sociologists who use this approach are likely to focus on the men's rules or "codes" for getting along; their survival strategies ("hustles"); how they divide up money, wine, or whatever other resources they have; their relationships with girlfriends, family, and friends; where they spend their time and what they do there; their language; their pecking order; and so on. With its focus on face-to-face interaction, symbolic interactionism is an example of microsociology.

Because each approach has a different focus, macrosociology and microsociology yield distinctive perspectives, and both are needed to gain a fuller understanding of social life. We cannot adequately understand streetcorner men, for example, without using *macrosociology.* It is essential that we place the men within the broad context of how groups in U.S. society are related to one another, for, as is true for ourselves, the social class of these men helps to shape their attitudes and behavior. Nor can we adequately understand these men without *microsociology,* for their everyday situations also form a significant part of their lives—as they do for all of us.

Let's look in more detail at how these two approaches in sociology work together to help us understand social life.

The Macrosociological Perspective: Social Structure

To better understand human behavior, we need to understand *social structure,* the framework of society that was already laid out before you were born.

Social structure refers to the typical patterns of a group, such as its usual relationships between men and women or students and teachers. *The sociological significance of social structure is that it guides our behavior.*

Because this term may seem vague, let's consider how you experience social structure in your own life. As I write this, I do not know your race-ethnicity. I do not know your religion. I do not know whether you are young or old, tall or short, male or female. I do not know whether you were reared on a farm, in the suburbs, or in the inner city. I do not know whether you went to a public high school or to an exclusive prep school. But I do know that you are in college. And this, alone, tells me a great deal about you.

From this one piece of information, I can assume that the social structure of your college is now shaping what you do. For example, let's suppose that today you felt euphoric over some great news. I can be fairly certain (not absolutely, mind you, but relatively certain) that when you entered the classroom, social structure overrode your mood. That is, instead of shouting at the top of your lungs and joyously throwing this book into the air, you entered the classroom in a fairly subdued manner and took your seat.

The same social structure influences your instructor, even if he or she, on the one hand, is facing a divorce or has a child dying of cancer or, on the other hand, has just been awarded a promotion or a million-dollar grant. The instructor may feel like either retreating into seclusion or celebrating wildly, but most likely, he or she will conduct class in the usual manner. In short, social structure tends to override personal feelings and desires.

Just as social structure influences you and your instructor, so it establishes limits for street people. They, too, find themselves in a specific location in the U.S. social structure—although their location is quite different from yours or your instructor's. Consequently, they are affected in different ways. Nothing about their social location leads them to take notes or to lecture. Their behaviors, however, are as logical an outcome of where they find themselves in the social structure as are your own. In their position in the social structure, it is just as "natural" to drink wine all night as it is for you to stay up studying all night for a crucial examination. It is just as "natural" for you to nod and say "Excuse me" when you enter a crowded classroom late and have to claim a desk on which someone has already placed books as it is for them to break off the neck of a wine bottle and glare at an enemy.

In short, people learn certain behaviors and attitudes because of their location in the social structure (whether they be privileged, deprived, or in between), and they act accordingly. This is equally true of street people and ourselves. *The differences in behavior and attitudes are due not to biology (race, sex, or any other supposed genetic factors) but to people's location in the social structure.* Switch places with street people, and watch your behaviors and attitudes change!

To better understand social structure, read the Down-to-Earth Sociology box on football below.

Because social structure so crucially affects who we are and what we are like, let's look more closely at its major components: culture, social class, social status, roles, groups, social institutions, and societies.

Down-to-Earth Sociology

College Football as Social Structure

TO GAIN A BETTER IDEA OF WHAT *SOCIAL STRUCTURE* IS, think of college football (see Dobriner 1969a). You probably know the various positions on the team: center, guards, tackles, ends, quarterback, running backs, and the like. Each is a *status;* that is, each is a social position. For each of these statuses, there is a *role;* that is, each of these positions has certain expectations and responsibilities attached to it. The center is expected to snap the ball, the quarterback to pass it, the guards to block, the tackles to tackle or block, the ends to receive passes, and so on. Those role expectations guide each player's actions; that is, the players try to do what their particular role requires.

Let's suppose that football is your favorite sport and you never miss a home game at your college. Let's also suppose that you graduate, get a great job, and move across the country. Five years later, you return to your campus for a nostalgic visit. The climax of your visit is the biggest football game of the season. When you get to the game, you might be surprised to see a different coach, but you are not surprised that each playing position is occupied by people you don't know, for all the players you knew have graduated, and their places have been filled by others.

This scenario mirrors *social structure,* the framework around which a group exists. In football, that framework consists of the coaching staff and the eleven playing positions. The game does not depend on any particular individual, but, rather, on *social statuses,* the positions that the individuals occupy. When someone leaves a position, the game can go on because someone else takes over that

position or status and plays the role. The game will continue even though not a single individual remains from one period of time to the next. Notre Dame's football team endures today even though Knute Rockne, the Gipper, and his teammates are long dead.

Even though you may not play football, you nevertheless live your life within a clearly established social structure. The statuses that you occupy and the roles you play were already in place before you were born. You take your particular positions in life, others do the same, and society goes about its business. Although the specifics change with time, the game—whether that of football or of life—goes on.

▮ Figure 4.1 **Team Positions (Statuses) in Football**

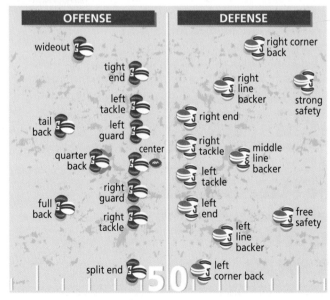

OFFENSE

wideout
tight end
left tackle
tail back
left guard
quarter back
center
right guard
full back
right tackle
split end

DEFENSE

right corner back
right line backer
strong safety
right end
right tackle
middle line backer
left tackle
left end
left line backer
free safety
left corner back

Culture

In Chapter 2, we considered culture's far-reaching effects on our lives. At this point, let's simply summarize its main impact. Sociologists use the term *culture* to refer to a group's language, beliefs, values, behaviors, and even gestures. Culture also includes the material objects that a group uses. Culture is the broadest framework that determines what kind of people we become. If we are reared in Chinese, Arab, or U.S. culture, we will grow up to be like most Chinese, Arabs, or Americans. On the outside, we will look and act like them; and on the inside, we will think and feel like them.

Social Class

To understand people, we must examine the social locations that they hold in life. Especially significant is *social class*, which is based on income, education, and occupational prestige. Large numbers of people who have similar amounts of income and education and who work at jobs that are roughly equivalent in prestige make up a **social class.** It is hard to overemphasize this aspect of social structure, for our social class influences not only our behaviors but even our ideas and attitudes. We have this in common, then, with the street people described in the opening vignette: We both are influenced by our location in the social class structure. Theirs may be a considerably less privileged position, but it has no less influence on their lives. Social class is so significant that we will spend an entire chapter (Chapter 8) on this topic.

Social Status

When you hear the word *status,* you are likely to think of prestige. These two words are welded together in common thinking. As you saw in the box on football, however, sociologists use **status** in a different way–to refer to the *position* that someone occupies. That position may carry a great deal of prestige, as in the case of a judge or an astronaut, or it may bring very little prestige, as in the case of a convenience store clerk or a waitress. The status may also be looked down on, as in the case of a streetcorner man, an ex-convict, or a thief.

All of us occupy several positions at the same time. You may simultaneously be a son or daughter, a worker, a date, and a student. Sociologists use the term **status set** to refer to all the statuses or positions that you occupy. Obviously, your status set changes as your particular statuses change: For example, if you graduate from college and take a full-time job, get married, buy a home, have children, and so on, your status set changes to include the positions of worker, spouse, homeowner, and parent.

Like other aspects of social structure, statuses are part of our basic framework of living in society. The example I gave of students and teachers who come to class and do what others expect of them despite their particular circumstances and moods illustrates how statuses affect our actions—and those of the people around us. Our statuses—whether daughter or son, worker or date—serve as guides for our behavior.

Ascribed and Achieved Statuses An **ascribed status** is involuntary. You do not ask for it, nor can you choose it. You inherit some ascribed statuses at birth, such as your race-ethnicity, sex, and the social class of your parents, as well as your statuses as female or male, daughter or son, and niece or nephew. Others, such as teenager and senior citizen, are related to the life course and are given to you later in life.

Achieved statuses, in contrast, are voluntary. These you earn or accomplish. As a result of your efforts, you become a student, a friend, a spouse, a rabbi, minister, priest, or nun. Or, for lack of effort (or for efforts that others fail to appreciate), you become a school dropout, a former friend, an ex-spouse, or a defrocked rabbi, priest, or nun. In other words, achieved statuses can be either positive or negative; both college president and bank robber are achieved statuses.

Each status provides guidelines for how we are to act and feel. Like other aspects of social structure, statuses set limits on what we can and cannot do. Because social statuses are an essential part of social structure, they are found in all human groups.

Status Symbols People who are pleased with their social status often want others to recognize their particular position. To elicit this recognition, they use **status symbols,** signs that identify a status. For example, people wear wedding rings to announce their marital status; uniforms, guns, and badges to proclaim that they are police officers (and not so subtly to let you know that their status gives them authority over you); and "backward" collars to declare that they are Lutheran ministers or Roman Catholic or Episcopal priests.

Some social statuses are negative, and so, therefore, are their status symbols. The scarlet letter in Nathaniel Hawthorne's book by the same title is one example. Another is the CONVICTED DUI (Driving Under the

Influence) bumper sticker that some U.S. courts require convicted drunk drivers to display if they wish to avoid a jail sentence.

All of us use status symbols to announce our statuses to others and to help smooth our interactions in everyday life. You might consider what your own status symbols communicate. For example, how does your clothing announce your statuses of sex, age, and college student?

Master Statuses　A **master status** is one that cuts across the other statuses you hold. Some master statuses are ascribed. An example is your sex. Whatever you do, people perceive you as a male or as a female. If you are working your way through college by flipping burgers,

people see you not only as a burger flipper and a student but also as a *male* or *female* burger flipper and a *male* or *female* college student. Other master statuses are race and age.

Some master statuses are achieved. If you become very, very wealthy (and it doesn't matter whether your wealth comes from a successful invention or from winning the lottery—it is still *achieved* as far as sociologists are concerned), your wealth is likely to become a master status. For example, people might say, "She is a very rich burger flipper"—or, more likely, "She's very rich, and she used to flip burgers!"

Similarly, people who become disfigured find, to their dismay, that their condition becomes a master status. For example, a person whose face is scarred from severe burns will be viewed through this unwelcome master status regardless of his or her occupation or accomplishments. Similarly, people who are confined to wheelchairs can attest to how this handicap overrides all their other statuses and influences others' perceptions of everything they do.

Although our statuses usually fit together fairly well, some people have a contradiction or mismatch between their statuses. This is known as **status inconsistency** (or discrepancy). A 14-year-old college student is an example. So is a 40-year-old married woman who is dating a 19-year-old college sophomore.

These examples reveal an essential aspect of social statuses: Like other components of social structure, they come with built-in *norms* (that is, expectations) that guide our behavior. When statuses mesh well, as they usually do, we know what to expect of people. Status inconsistency, however, upsets our expectations. In the preceding examples, how are you supposed to act? Are you supposed to treat the 14-year-old as you would a young teenager or as you would your college classmate? Do you react to the married woman as you would to the mother of your friend or as you would to a classmate's date?

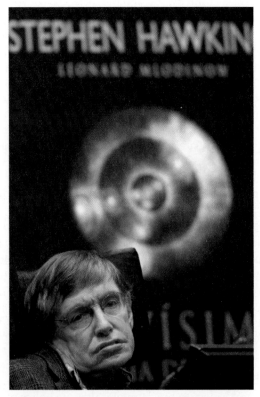

Master statuses are those that overshadow our other statuses. Shown here is Stephen Hawking, who is severely disabled by Lou Gehrig's disease. For many, his *master status* is that of a person with disabilities. Because Hawking is one of the greatest physicists who has ever lived, however, his outstanding achievements have given him another *master status*, that of world-class physicist in the ranking of Einstein.

Roles

All the world's a stage
And all the men and women merely players.
They have their exits and their entrances;
And one man in his time plays many parts . . .
—*(William Shakespeare,* As You Like It, *Act II, Scene 7)*

Like Shakespeare, sociologists see roles as essential to social life. When you were born, **roles**—the behaviors, obligations, and privileges attached to a status—were already set up for you. Society was waiting with outstretched arms to teach you how it expected you to act as a boy or a girl. And whether you were born poor, rich, or somewhere in between, that, too, attached certain behaviors, obligations, and privileges to your statuses.

The difference between role and status is that you *occupy* a status, but you *play* a role (Linton 1936). For example, being a son or daughter is your status, but your expectations of receiving food and shelter from your parents—as well as their expectations that you show respect to them—are part of your role.

Roles are like a fence. They allow us a certain amount of freedom, but for most of us, that freedom doesn't go very far. Suppose that a woman decides that she is not going to wear dresses or a man that he will not wear suits and ties—regardless of what anyone says. In most situations, they'll stick to their decision. When a formal occasion comes along, however, such as a family wedding or a funeral, they likely will cave in to norms that they find overwhelming. Almost all of us follow the guidelines for what is "appropriate" for our roles. Few of us are bothered by such constraints, for our socialization is so thorough that we usually *want* to do what our roles indicate is appropriate.

The sociological significance of roles is that they lay out what is expected of people. As individuals throughout society perform their roles, those roles mesh together to form this thing called *society*. As Shakespeare put it, people's roles provide "their exits and their entrances" on the stage of life. In short, roles are remarkably effective at keeping people in line—telling them when they should "enter" and when they should "exit," as well as what to do in between.

Groups

A **group** consists of people who regularly interact with one another. Ordinarily, the members of a group share similar values, norms, and expectations. Just as our social class, statuses, and roles influence our actions, so, too, the groups to which we belong are powerful forces in our lives. In fact, *to belong to a group is to yield to others the right to make certain decisions about our behavior.* If we belong to a group, we assume an obligation to act according to the expectations of other members of that group.

Let's look in greater detail at the next component of social structure, social institutions.

Social Institutions

At first glance, the term *social institution* may seem to have little relevance for your life. The term appears so cold and abstract. In fact, however, **social institutions**—the ways that each society develops to meet its basic needs—vitally affect our life. By weaving the fabric of society, social institutions shape our behavior. They even influence our thoughts. How can this be? Consider what social institutions are: the family, religion, education, economics, medicine, politics, law, science, the military, and the mass media.

In industrialized societies, social institutions tend to be more formal; in tribal societies, they are more informal. Education in industrialized societies, for example, is highly structured, while in tribal societies it usually consists of informally learning what adults do. Figure 4.2 on the next page summarizes the basic social institutions. Note that each institution has its own groups, statuses, values, and norms. Social institutions are so significant that Part IV of this book focuses on them.

Societies—and Their Transformations

How did our society develop? You know that it didn't spring full-blown on the human scene. To better understand this framework that surrounds us, that sets the stage for our experiences in life, let's trace the evolution of societies. Figure 4.3 on page 91 illustrates how changes in technology brought extensive changes to **society**—people who share a culture and a territory. As we review these sweeping changes, picture yourself as a member of each society. Consider how different your life would be—how your thinking, values, and view of the world would be transformed.

Hunting and Gathering Societies Societies with the fewest social divisions are called **hunting and gathering societies.** As the name implies, these groups depend on hunting and gathering for their survival. (The "gatherers" do not plant but only gather what food is already there.) Because an area cannot support a large number of people who hunt animals and gather plants, hunting and gathering societies are small. They usually consist of twenty-five to forty people. They are also nomadic, for as their food

Figure 4.2 Social Institutions in Industrial and Postindustrial Societies

Social Institution	Basic Needs	Some Groups or Organizations	Some Statuses	Some Values	Some Norms
Family	Regulate reproduction, socialize and protect children	Relatives, kinship groups	Daughter, son, father, mother, brother, sister, aunt, uncle, grandparent	Sexual fidelity, providing for your family, keeping a clean house, respect for parents	Have only as many children as you can afford, be faithful to your spouse
Religion	Concerns about life after death, the meaning of suffering and loss; desire to connect with the Creator	Congregation, synagogue, mosque, denomination, charity	Priest, minister, rabbi, imam, worshipper, teacher, disciple, missionary, prophet, convert	Reading and adhering to holy texts such as the Bible, the Koran, and the Torah; honoring God	Attend worship services, contribute money, follow the teachings
Education	Transmit knowledge and skills across generations	School, college, student senate, sports team, PTA, teachers' union	Teacher, student, dean, principal, football player, cheerleader	Academic honesty, good grades, being "cool"	Do homework, prepare lectures, don't snitch on classmates
Economy	Produce and distribute goods and services	Credit unions, banks, credit card companies, buying clubs	Worker, boss, buyer, seller, creditor, debtor, advertiser	Making money, paying bills on time, producing efficiently	Maximize profits, "the customer is always right," work hard
Medicine	Heal the sick and injured, care for the dying	AMA, hospitals, pharmacies, insurance companies, HMOs	Doctor, nurse, patient, pharmacist, medical insurer	Hippocratic oath, staying in good health, following doctor's orders	Don't exploit patients, give best medical care available
Politics	Allocate power, determine authority, prevent chaos	Political party, congress, parliament, monarchy	President, senator, lobbyist, voter, candidate, spin doctor	Majority rule, the right to vote as a sacred trust	One vote per person, voting as a privilege and a right
Law	Maintain social order	Police, courts, prisons	Judge, police officer, lawyer, defendant, prison guard	Trial by one's peers, innocence until proven guilty	Give true testimony, follow the rules of evidence
Science	Master the environment	Local, state, regional, national, and international associations	Scientist, researcher, technician, administrator, journal editor	Unbiased research, open dissemination of research findings, originality	Follow scientific method, be objective, disclose findings, don't plagiarize
Military	Protection from enemies, support of national interests	Army, navy, air force, marines, coast guard, national guard	Soldier, recruit, enlisted person, officer, prisoner, spy	To die for one's country is an honor, obedience unto death	Be ready to go to war, obey superiors, don't question orders
Mass Media (an emerging institution)	Disseminate information, mold public opinion, report events	TV networks, radio stations, publishers, association of bloggers	Journalist, newscaster, author, editor, publisher, blogger	Timeliness, accuracy, large audiences, freedom of the press	Be accurate, fair, timely, and profitable

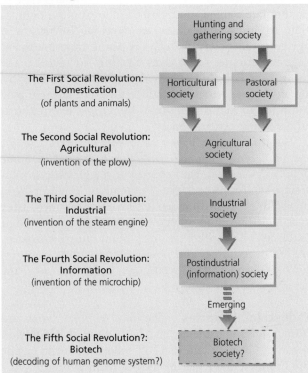

Figure 4.3 **The Social Transformations of Society**

Hunting and gathering society

The First Social Revolution: Domestication (of plants and animals)
→ Horticultural society
→ Pastoral society

The Second Social Revolution: Agricultural (invention of the plow)
→ Agricultural society

The Third Social Revolution: Industrial (invention of the steam engine)
→ Industrial society

The Fourth Social Revolution: Information (invention of the microchip)
→ Postindustrial (information) society

Emerging

The Fifth Social Revolution?: Biotech (decoding of human genome system?)
→ Biotech society?

Source: By the author.

ing the second branching is *horticulture,* or plant cultivation. **Horticultural societies** (also called gardening societies) are based on the *cultivation of plants by the use of hand tools.* Because they no longer had to abandon an area as the food supply gave out, these groups developed permanent settlements.

We can call the domestication of animals and plants the *first social revolution,* for, as shown in Figure 4.4 on the next page, it transformed human society. With dependable sources of food, human groups became larger. Because not everyone had to produce food, a specialized *division of labor* evolved: Some people made jewelry, others tools, others weapons, and so on. This production of objects, in turn, stimulated trade, and people began to accumulate gold, jewelry, and utensils as well as herds of animals.

The primary significance of these changes is that they set the stage for social inequality. Feuds and wars erupted, for groups now had material goods to fight about. War, in turn, opened the door to slavery, for people found it convenient to let captives from their battles do their drudge work. As individuals passed their possessions on to their descendants, wealth grew more concentrated. So did power, and for the first time, some people became chiefs.

supply dwindles, they move to another location (Lenski and Lenski 1987).

Of all societies, hunters and gatherers are the most egalitarian. Because what they hunt and gather is perishable, they can't accumulate possessions. Consequently, no one becomes wealthier than anyone else. There are no rulers, and most decisions are arrived at through discussion.

Pastoral and Horticultural Societies About ten thousand years ago, some groups found that they could tame and breed some of the animals they hunted, others that they could cultivate plants. As a result, hunting and gathering societies branched in two directions.

The key to understanding the first branching is the word *pasture;* **pastoral societies** (also called herding societies) are based on the *pasturing of animals.* Groups that took this turn remained nomadic, for they followed their animals to fresh pasture. The key to understand-

The simplest forms of societies are called *hunting and gathering societies.* Members of these societies have adapted well to their environments, and they have more leisure than the members of other societies. Shown here is a member of the Kayapó tribe in the rainforest of Brazil.

Figure 4.4 Consequences of Animal Domestication and Plant Cultivation

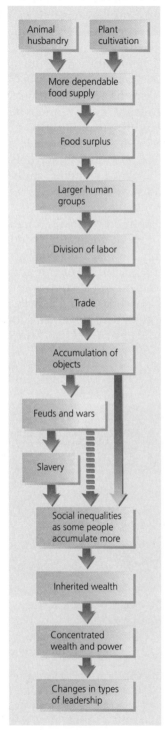

Source: By the author.

Agricultural Societies When the plow was invented about five or six thousand years ago, it ushered in a *second social revolution.* The plow enabled people to accumulate a huge food surplus, allowing the population to grow and cities to develop. In this new **agricultural society,** many more people were able to engage in activities other than farming—to develop the things popularly known as "culture," such as philosophy, art, music, literature, and architecture. The changes were so profound that this period is sometimes referred to as "the dawn of civilization."

Social inequality, which up to now had been sporadic and mild, became a fundamental feature of social life. Some people managed to gain control of the growing surplus resources. To protect their expanding privileges and power, this elite surrounded itself with armed men. They even levied taxes on others, who now had become their "subjects." As conflict theorists point out, this concentration of resources and power, along with the oppression of people who were not in power, was the forerunner of the state.

Industrial Societies The *third social revolution* also turned society upside down. The **Industrial Revolution** began in Great Britain in 1765, where the steam engine was first used to run machinery. Before this time, a few machines had been used to harness nature (such as wind and water mills), but most had depended on power from humans and animals. This new form of production in the **industrial society** was far more efficient than anything the world had ever seen. It brought even greater surplus and, with it, even greater social inequality. The individuals who first used the new technology accumulated immense wealth. The masses, in contrast, were thrown off the land as feudal society broke up. They moved to the cities, where they faced the choice of stealing, starving, or working for wages barely adequate to sustain life (the equivalent of a loaf of bread for a day's work).

Through a bitter struggle, one that went on too long for us to review it here, workers gradually attained their demands for better working conditions, reversing the earlier pattern of growing inequality. The indicators of greater equality in later industrial societies are extensive: widespread ownership of homes and automobiles, access to libraries and education, better housing, greater variety of food, and a much longer life for the average person. On an even broader level, indicators include the abolition of slavery, the shift from monarchies and dictatorships to more representative political systems, the right to vote, the right

The sociological significance of the social revolutions discussed in the text is that the type of society in which we live determines the kind of people we become. It is obvious, for example, that the orientations to life of this worker would differ markedly from those of the man shown on page 91. This classic scene is from Charlie Chaplin's *Modern Times*.

to be tried by a jury of one's peers and to cross-examine witnesses, and greater rights for women and minorities.

Postindustrial (Information) Societies   Today, a new type of society has emerged. The basic trend in advanced industrial societies is away from production and manufacturing and toward service industries. The United States was the first country to have more than half its work force employed in service industries—health, education, research, the government, counseling, banking and investments, sales, law, and the mass media. Australia, New Zealand, western Europe, and Japan soon followed. The term **postindustrial** (or **information**) **society** refers to this new type of society—one based on information, services, and the latest technology rather than on raw materials and manufacturing (Bell 1973; Lipset 1979; Toffler 1980).

The basic component of the postindustrial society is information. People who offer services either provide or apply information. Teachers pass on knowledge to students, while lawyers, physicians, bankers, and interior decorators sell their specialized knowledge of law, medicine, money, and color schemes. Unlike factory workers in an industrial society, workers in service industries don't *produce* anything. Rather, they transmit or apply knowledge to provide services that others are willing to pay for.

Perhaps in years to come, social analysts will refer to these changes as the *fourth social revolution*. Based on the computer chip, the information revolution is transforming society—and, with it, our social relationships. Because of this tiny device, we can talk to people in other countries while we ride in cars, trucks, and airplanes; we can peer farther into space than ever before; and millions of children can spend countless hours battling virtual video villains. Our shopping patterns are also changing, and we now spend several billion dollars a year on Internet purchases. (For a review of other changes, see the section on the computer in Chapter 15, pages 434–436.) Although the full implications of the information explosion are still unknown, with history as our guide, we can predict that the changes will be so extensive that even our attitudes about the self and life will be transformed.

Biotech Society: Is a New Type of Society Emerging?

Can you believe these new products?

> Tobacco that fights cancer. ("Yes, smoke your way to health!")
>
> Corn that fights herpes and is a contraceptive. ("Corn flakes in the morning—and safe sex all day!")
>
> Goats whose milk contains spider silk (to make fishing lines and body armor). ("Got milk? The best bulletproofing.")
>
> Animals that are part human: Human genes have been inserted into animal genes, so they produce medicines for humans—and creamier mozzarella cheese (Elias 2001). (You can write your own jingle for this one.)

I know that this sounds like science fiction, but we *already* have the goats that make spider silk and the part-human animals that produce medicine (Kristoff 2002; Osborne 2002). The others are being developed. Some suggest that the changes in which we are immersed are revolutionary, that we are entering another new type of society (Holloway 2002; Oliver 2003). In this new **biotech society,** the economy will center on applying and altering genetic structures—both plant and animal—to produce food, medicine, and materials.

If there is a new society, then when did it begin? There are no firm edges to new societies, for each new one overlaps the one it is replacing. The biotech society could have begun in 1953, when Francis Crick and James Watson identified the double-helix structure of DNA. Or perhaps historians will trace the date to the decoding of the human genome in 2001.

Whether the changes that are swirling around us are part of a new type of society is not the main point. *The sociological significance of these changes is that just as the larger group called society always profoundly affects people's thinking and behavior, so, too, these recent developments will do the same for us.* As society is transformed, we will be swept along with it. The changes will be so extensive that they will transform even the ways we think about the self and life.

Projecting a new type of society so soon after the arrival of the information society is risky. The wedding of genetics and economics could turn out to be simply another aspect of our information society—or we may have just stepped into a new type of society. In either case, we can anticipate revolutionary changes in health care (prevention, instead of treating disease) and, with cloning and bioengineering, perhaps even changes in the human species. The Sociology and the New Technology box on the next page examines implications of cloning.

IN SUM | Our society sets boundaries around our lives. By laying out a framework of social statuses, roles, groups, and social institutions, society establishes the values and beliefs that prevail. It also determines the type and extent of social inequality. These factors, in turn, set the stage for relationships between men and women, the young and the elderly, racial and ethnic groups, the rich and the poor, and so on.

It is difficult to overstate the sociological principle that the type of society in which we live is the fundamental reason why we become who we are—why we feel about things the way we do, and even why we think our particular thoughts. On the obvious level, if you lived in an agrarian society, you would not be taking this course. On a deeper level, you would not feel the same about life or hold your particular aspirations for the future.

What Holds Society Together?

With its many, often conflicting, groups and its extensive social change, how can a society manage to hold together? Let's examine two answers that sociologists have proposed.

Mechanical and Organic Solidarity Sociologist Emile Durkheim (1893/1933) found the key to **social integration**—the degree to which members of a society are united by shared values and other social bonds—in what he called **mechanical solidarity.** By this term, Durkheim meant that people who perform similar tasks develop a shared consciousness. Think of a farming community in which everyone is involved in planting, cultivating, and harvesting. Members of this group have so much in common that they know how almost everyone in the community feels about life.

As societies get larger, their **division of labor** (how they divide up work) becomes more specialized. Some people mine gold, others turn it into jewelry, while still others sell it. This division of labor makes people depend on one another, for the work of each person contributes to the whole.

Durkheim called this new form of solidarity based on interdependence **organic solidarity.** To see why he used this term, think about how you depend on your teacher to guide you through this introductory course in sociology. At the same time, your teacher needs you and other students in order to have a job. You and your teacher are *like organs* in the same body. Although each of you performs different tasks, you depend on one another. This creates a form of unity.

Gemeinschaft and Gesellschaft Ferdinand Tönnies (1887/1988) also analyzed this fundamental change. He used the term **Gemeinschaft** (Guh-MINE-shoft), or "intimate community," to describe village life, the type of society in which everyone knows everyone else. He noted that in the society that was emerging, the personal ties, kinship connections, and lifelong friendships that marked village life were being crowded out by short-term relationships, individual accomplishments, and self-interest. Tönnies called this new type of society **Gesellschaft** (Guh-ZELL-shoft), or "impersonal association." He did not mean that we no longer have intimate ties to family and friends but, rather, that these ties have shrunk in importance. Contracts, for example, replace handshakes, and work doesn't center on friends and family but on strangers and short-term acquaintances.

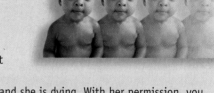

> SOCIOLOGY *and the* NEW TECHNOLOGY

"So, You Want to Be Yourself?" Cloning in the Coming Biotech Society

No type of society ends abruptly. The edges are fuzzy, and one overlaps the other. As the information society matures, it looks as though it is being overtaken by a biotech society. Let's try to peer over the edge of our current society to catch a glimpse of the one that may be coming. What will life be like? We could examine many issues, but since space is limited, let's consider just one: cloning.

Consider this scenario:

Your four-year-old daughter has drowned, and you can't get over your sorrow. You go to the regional cloning clinic, where you have stored DNA from all members of your family. You pay the standard fee, and the director hires a surrogate mother to bring your daughter back as a newborn.

Will cloning humans become a reality? Since human embryos have already been cloned, it seems inevitable that some group somewhere will complete the process. If cloning humans becomes routine—well, consider these scenarios:

- Suppose that a couple can't have children. Testing shows that the husband is sterile. The couple talk about their dilemma, and the wife agrees to have her husband's genetic material implanted into one of her eggs. Would this woman, in effect, be rearing her husband as a little boy?

- Or suppose that you love your mother dearly, and she is dying. With her permission, you decide to clone her. Who is the clone? Would you be rearing your own mother?
- What if a woman gave birth to her own clone? Would the clone be her daughter or her sister?

When genetic duplicates appear, the questions of what humans are, what their relationship is to their "parents," and indeed what "parents" and "children" are, will be brought up at every kitchen table.

Source: Based on Kaebnick 2000; McGee 2000; Bjerklie et al. 2001; Davis 2001; Weiss 2004; Regalado 2005.

for your Consideration

As these scenarios show, the issue of cloning brings up profound questions. Perhaps the most weighty concerns the future of society. Let's suppose that mass cloning becomes possible.

Many people object that cloning is immoral, but some will argue the opposite. They will ask why we should leave human reproduction to people who have inferior traits—genetic diseases, low IQs, perhaps even the propensity for crime and violence. They will suggest that we select people with the finer characteristics—high creative ability, high intelligence, compassion, and a propensity for peace.

Let's assume that scientists have traced these characteristics—as well as the ability and appreciation for poetry, music, mathematics, architecture, and love—to genetics. Do you think that it should be our moral obligation to populate society with people like this? To try to build a society that is better for all—one without terrorism, war, violence, and greed? Could this perhaps even be our evolutionary destiny?

IN SUM Whether the terms are *Gemeinschaft* and *Gesellschaft* or *mechanical solidarity* and *organic solidarity,* they indicate that as societies change, so do people's orientations to life. *The sociological point is that social structure sets the context for what we do, feel, and think and ultimately,* *then, for the kind of people we become.* As you read the Cultural Diversity box on the next page, which describes one of the few remaining *Gemeinschaft* societies in the United States, think about how fundamentally different you would be had you been reared in an Amish family.

Cultural Diversity *in the* United States

The Amish: *Gemeinschaft* Community in a *Gesellschaft* Society

IN FERDINAND TÖNNIES' TERM, the United States is a *Gesellschaft* society. Impersonal associations pervade our everyday life. Local, state, and federal governments regulate many activities. Corporations hire and fire people not on the basis of personal relationships, but on the basis of the bottom line. And, perhaps even more significantly, millions of Americans do not even know their neighbors.

Within the United States, a handful of small communities exhibits characteristics that are quite distinct from those of the mainstream society. One such community is the Old Order Amish, followers of a sect that broke away from the Swiss-German Mennonite church in the 1600s, and settled in Pennsylvania around 1727. Today, about 150,000 Old Order Amish live in the United States. About 75 percent live in just three states: Pennsylvania, Ohio, and Indiana. The largest concentration, about 22,000, reside in Lancaster County, Pennsylvania. The Amish, who believe that birth control is wrong, have doubled in population in just the past two decades.

Because Amish farmers use horses instead of tractors, most of their farms are one hundred acres or less. To the five million tourists who pass through Lancaster County each year, the rolling green pastures, white farmhouses, simple barns, horse-drawn buggies, and clotheslines hung with somber-colored garments convey a sense of peace and innocence reminiscent of another era. Although just sixty-five miles from Philadelphia, "Amish country" is a world away.

Amish life is based on separation from the world—an idea taken from Christ's Sermon on the Mount—and obedience to the church's teachings and leaders. This rejection of worldly concerns, writes sociologist Donald Kraybill in *The Riddle of Amish Culture* (2002), "provides the foundation of such Amish values as humility, faithfulness, thrift, tradition, communal goals, joy of work, a slow-paced life, and trust in divine providence."

The *Gemeinschaft* of village life that has been largely lost to industrialization remains a vibrant part of Amish life. The Amish make their decisions during weekly meetings, where, by consensus, they follow a set of rules, or *Ordnung,* to guide their behavior. Religion and discipline are the glue that holds the Amish together. Brotherly love and the welfare of the community are paramount values. In times of birth, sickness, and death, neighbors pitch in with the chores. In these ways, they maintain the bonds of intimate community.

The Amish are bound by other ties, including language (a dialect of German known as Pennsylvania Dutch), plain clothing—often black, whose style has remained unchanged for almost 300 years—and church-sponsored schools. Nearly all Amish marry, and divorce is forbidden. The family is a vital ingredient in Amish life; all major events take place in the home, including weddings, births, funerals, and church services. Amish children attend church schools, but only until the age of 13. (In 1972, the Supreme Court ruled that Amish parents had the right to take their children out of school after the eighth grade.) To go to school beyond the eighth grade would expose them to values and "worldly concerns" that would drive a wedge between the children and their community. The Amish believe that violence is bad, even personal self-defense, and they register as conscientious objectors during times of war. They pay no social security, and they receive no government benefits.

The Amish cannot resist all change, of course. Instead, they try to adapt to change in ways that will least disrupt their core values. Because urban sprawl has driven up the price of farmland, about half of Amish men work at jobs other than farming, most in farm-related businesses or in woodcrafts. They go to great lengths to avoid leaving the home. The Amish believe that when a husband works away from home, all aspects of life change—from the marital relationship to the care of the children—certainly an astute sociological insight. They also believe that if a man receives a paycheck, he will think that his work is of more value than his wife's. For the Amish, intimate, or *Gemeinschaft,* society is essential for maintaining their way of life.

Sources: Hostetler 1980; Aeppel 1996; Kephart and Zellner 2001; Kraybill 1989, 2002; Dawley 2003; Savells 2005.

The warm, more intimate relationships of *Gemeinschaft* society are apparent in this restaurant in Salzburg, Austria. The more impersonal relationships of *Gesellschaft* society are evident in this café in Bangkok, Thailand, where, ignoring one another, the customers engage in electronic interactions.

The Microsociological Perspective: Social Interaction in Everyday Life

Whereas the macrosociological approach stresses the broad features of society, the microsociological approach has a narrower focus.

Microsociologists examine *face-to-face interaction*—what people do when they are in one another's presence. Let's examine some of the areas of social life that microsociologists study.

Stereotypes

You are familiar with how strong first impressions are and the way they set the tone for interaction. When you first meet someone, you cannot help but notice certain features, especially the person's sex, race, age, and clothing. Despite your best intentions, your assumptions about these characteristics shape your first impressions. They also affect how you act toward that person—and, in turn, how that person acts toward you. These fascinating aspects of our social interaction are discussed in the Down-to-Earth Sociology box on the next page.

Personal Space

We all surround ourselves with a "personal bubble" that we go to great lengths to protect. We open the bubble to intimates—to our friends, children, parents, and so on—but we are careful to keep most people out of this space. When we stand in lines, for example, we make certain there is enough space so that we don't touch the person in front of us and aren't touched by the person behind us.

The amount of space that people prefer varies from one culture to another. Anthropologist Edward Hall (1959; Hall and Hall 2005) recounts a conversation with a man from South America who had attended one of his lectures:

> He came to the front of the class at the end of the lecture. . . . We started out facing each other, and as he talked I became dimly aware that he was standing a little too close and that I was beginning to back up. . . . By experimenting I was able to observe that as I moved away slightly, there was an associated shift in the pattern of interaction. He had more trouble expressing himself. If I shifted to where I felt comfortable (about twenty-one inches), he looked somewhat puzzled and hurt.

Down-to-Earth Sociology

Beauty May Be Only Skin Deep, But Its Effects Go On Forever: Stereotypes in Everyday Life

MARK SNYDER, A PSYCHOLOGIST, wondered whether **stereotypes**—our assumptions of what people are like—might be self-fulfilling. He came up with an ingenious way to test this idea. He (1993) gave college men a Polaroid snapshot of a woman (supposedly taken just moments before) and told them that he would introduce them to her after they talked with her on the telephone. Actually, the photographs—showing either a pretty or a homely woman—had been prepared before the experiment began. The photo was not of the woman the men would talk to.

Stereotypes came into play immediately. As Snyder gave each man the photograph, he asked him what he

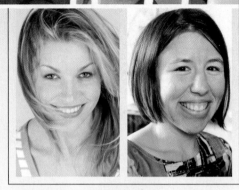

Physical attractiveness underlies much of our social interaction in everyday life. The experiment reviewed in this box illustrates how college men modified their interactions on the basis of attractiveness. How do you think men would modify their interactions if they were to meet the two women in these photographs? How about women? Would they change their interactions in the same way?

thought the woman would be like. The men who saw the photograph of the attractive woman said that they expected to meet a poised, humorous, outgoing woman. The men who had been given a photo of the unattractive woman described her as awkward, serious, and unsociable.

The men's stereotypes influenced the way they spoke on the telephone to the women, who did not know about the photographs. The men who had seen the photograph of a pretty woman were warm, friendly, and humorous. This, in turn, affected the women they spoke to, for they responded in a warm, friendly, outgoing manner. And the men who had seen the photograph of a homely woman? On the phone, they

---

After Hall (1969; Hall and Hall 2005) analyzed situations like this, he observed that North Americans use four different "distance zones":

1. *Intimate distance.* This is the zone that the South American unwittingly invaded. It extends to about 18 inches from our bodies. We reserve this space for comforting, protecting, hugging, intimate touching, and lovemaking.
2. *Personal distance.* This zone extends from 18 inches to 4 feet. We reserve it for friends and acquaintances and ordinary conversations. This is the zone in which Hall would have preferred speaking with the South American.
3. *Social distance.* This zone, extending out from us about 4 to 12 feet, marks impersonal or formal relationships. We use this zone for such things as job interviews.

4. *Public distance.* This zone, extending beyond 12 feet, marks even more formal relationships. It is used to separate dignitaries and public speakers from the general public.

Let's now turn to dramaturgy, a special focus of microsociology.

Dramaturgy: The Presentation of Self in Everyday Life

It was their big day, two years in the making. Jennifer Mackey wore a white wedding gown adorned with an 11-foot train and 24,000 seed pearls that she and her mother had sewn onto the dress. Next to her at the altar in Lexington, Kentucky, stood her intended, Jeffrey Degler, in black tie. They said their vows, and then turned to gaze for a moment at the four hundred guests.

were cold, reserved, and humorless, and the women they spoke to became cool, reserved, and humorless. Keep in mind that the women did not know that their looks had been evaluated—and that the photographs were not even of them. In short, stereotypes tend to produce behaviors that match the stereotype. This principle is illustrated in Figure 4.5.

Although beauty might be only skin deep, its consequences permeate our lives (Katz 2005). Beauty bestows an advantage in everyday interaction, but it also has other effects. For one, if you are physically attractive, you are likely to make more money. Researchers in both Holland and the United States found that advertising firms with better-looking executives have higher revenues (Bosman et al. 1997; Pfann et al. 2000). The reason? The researchers suggest that people are more willing to associate with individuals whom they perceive as good-looking.

for your Consideration

Stereotypes have no single, inevitable effect. They are not magical. People can resist stereotypes and change outcomes. However, these studies do illustrate that stereotypes deeply influence how we react to one another.

Instead of beauty, consider gender and race-ethnicity. How do they affect those who do the stereotyping and those who are stereotyped?

Figure 4.5 **How Self-Fulfilling Stereotypes Work**

We see features of the person, or hear things about the person.

⬇

We fit what we see or hear into stereotypes, and then expect the person to act in certain ways.

⬇

How we expect the person to act shapes our attitudes and actions.

⬇

From how we act, the person gets ideas of how we perceive him or her.

⬇

The behaviors of the person change to match our expectations, thus confirming the stereotype.

Social space is one of the many aspects of social life studied by sociologists who have a microsociological focus. What do you see in common in these two photos?

That's when groomsman Daniel Mackey collapsed. As the shocked organist struggled to play Mendelssohn's "Wedding March," Mr. Mackey's unconscious body was dragged away, his feet striking—loudly—every step of the altar stairs.

"I couldn't believe he would die at my wedding," the bride said. (Hughes 1990)

Sociologist Erving Goffman (1922–1982) added a new twist to microsociology when he developed **dramaturgy** (or dramaturgical analysis). By this term, he meant that social life is like a drama or a stage play: Birth ushers us onto the stage of everyday life, and our socialization consists of learning to perform on that stage. The self that we studied in the previous chapter lies at the center of our performances. We have ideas of how we want others to think of us, and we use our roles in everyday life to communicate those ideas. Goffman called these efforts to manage the impressions that others receive of us **impression management.**

Everyday life, said Goffman, involves playing our assigned roles. We have *front stages* on which to perform them, as did Jennifer and Jeffrey. (By the way, Daniel Mackey didn't die—he had just fainted.) But we don't have to look at weddings to find front stages. Everyday life is filled with them. Where your teacher lectures is a front stage. And if you make an announcement at the dinner table, you are using a front stage. In fact, you spend most of your time on front stages, for a front stage is wherever you deliver your lines. We also have *back stages,* places where we can retreat and let our hair down. When you close the bathroom or bedroom door for privacy, for example, you are entering a back stage.

Everyday life brings with it many roles. The same person may be a student, a teenager, a shopper, a worker, and a date, as well as a daughter or a son. Although a role lays down the basic outline for a performance, it also allows a great deal of flexibility. The particular emphasis or interpretation that we give a role, our "style," is known as **role performance.** Consider your role as son or daughter. You may play the role of ideal daughter or son–being very respectful, coming home at the hours your parents set, and so forth. Or this description may not even come close to your particular role performance.

Ordinarily, our statuses are sufficiently separated that we find minimal conflict between them. Occasionally, however, what is expected of us in one status (our role) is incompatible with what is expected of us in another status. This problem, known as **role conflict,** is illus-

In *dramaturgy,* a specialty within sociology, social life is viewed as similar to the theater. In our everyday lives, we all are actors like those in this cast of *The George Lopez Show.* We, too, perform roles, use props, and deliver lines to fellow actors—who, in turn, do the same.

trated in Figure 4.6, in which family, friendship, student, and work roles come crashing together. Usually, however, we manage to avoid role conflict by segregating our statuses, which in some instances requires an intense juggling act.

Sometimes the *same* status contains incompatible roles, a conflict known as **role strain.** Suppose that you are exceptionally well prepared for a particular class assignment. Although the instructor asks an unusually difficult question, you find yourself knowing the answer when no one else does. If you want to raise your hand, yet don't want to make your fellow students look bad, you will experience role strain. As illustrated in Figure 4.6, the difference between role conflict and role strain is that role conflict is conflict *between roles,* while role strain is conflict *within* a role.

Being an adept role player brings positive recognition from others, something we all covet. To accomplish this, we often use **teamwork**—two or more people working together to make certain a performance goes off as planned. When a performance doesn't come off quite right, how-ever, it may require **face-saving behavior.** We may, for example, ignore flaws in someone's performance, which Goffman defines as *tact.*

Suppose your teacher is about to make an important point. Suppose also that her lecturing has been outstanding and the class is hanging on every word. Just as she pauses for emphasis, her stomach lets out a loud growl. She might then use a *face-saving technique* by remarking, "I was so busy preparing for class that I didn't get breakfast this morning." It is more likely, however, that both class and teacher will simply ignore the sound, both giving the impression that no one heard a thing—a face-saving technique called *studied nonobservance.* This allows the teacher to make the point, or, as Goffman would say, it allows the performance to go on.

Because our own body is so strongly identified with the self, a good part of impression management centers on "body messages." The messages that are attached to various body shapes change over time, but, as explored in the Mass Media in Social Life box on the next two pages, thinness currently screams "desirability."

Figure 4.6   Role Strain and Role Conflict

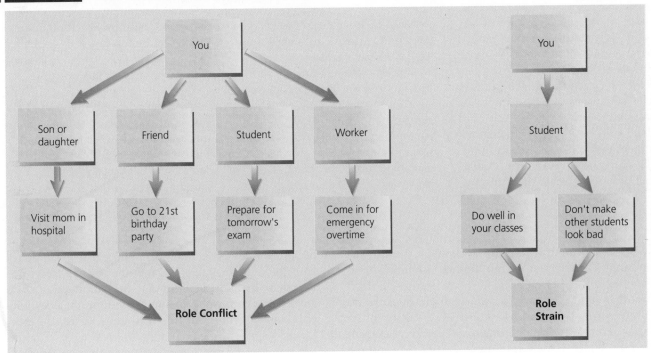

Source: By the author.

mass Media in social life

You Can't Be Thin Enough: Body Images and the Mass Media

An ad for Kellogg's Special K cereal shows an 18-month-old girl wearing nothing but a diaper. She has a worried look on her face. A bubble caption over her head has her asking, "Do I look fat?" (Krane et al. 2001)

When you stand before a mirror, do you like what you see? To make your body more attractive, do you watch your weight or work out? You have ideas about what you should look like. Where did you get them?

TV and magazine ads keep pounding home the message that our bodies aren't good enough, that we've got to improve them. The way to improve them, of course, is to buy the advertised products: wigs, hairpieces, hair transplants, padded brassieres, diet pills, and exercise equipment. Muscular hulks show off machines that magically produce "six-pack abs" and incredible biceps—in just a few minutes a day. Female movie stars effortlessly go through their own tough workouts without even breaking into a sweat. Women and men get the feeling that attractive

All of us contrast the reality we see when we look in the mirror with our culture's ideal body types. Lara Flynn Boyle, a top U.S. actress, represents an ideal body type that has developed in some parts of Western culture. These cultural images often make it difficult for larger people to maintain positive images of their bodies. These twins in Los Angeles, California, have struggled against dominant cultural images.

members of the opposite sex will flock to them if they purchase that wonder-working workout machine.

Although we try to shrug off such messages, knowing that they are designed to sell products, the messages still get our attention. They penetrate our thinking and feelings, helping to shape ideal images of how we "ought" to look. Those models so attractively clothed and coiffed as they walk down

the runway, could they be any thinner? For women, the message is clear: You can't be thin enough. The men's message is also clear: You can't be muscular enough.

Woman or man, your body isn't good enough. It sags where it should be firm. It bulges where it should be smooth. It sticks out where it shouldn't, and it doesn't stick out enough where it should.

Before closing this section, we should note that impression management is not limited to individuals. Families, businesses, colleges, sports teams—in fact, probably all groups—try to manage impressions. So do governments. When on September 11, 2001, terrorists hijacked four commercial airliners and flew three of them into the World Trade Center in New York City and the Pentagon in Washington, D.C., the president was in Florida, speaking at a grade school. For his safety, the

Secret Service rushed him into hiding, first to a military base in Louisiana, then to another base in Nebraska. President Bush first addressed the nation from these secluded locations. To assure the people that the government was still in control, it wouldn't do for the president to speak while in hiding. He had to get back to Washington. The perceived danger to the president was ruled less important than his presence in the White House, and Bush was flown to Washington, escorted by

And—no matter what your weight—it's too much. You've got to be thinner.

Exercise takes time, and getting in shape is painful. Once you do get in shape, if you slack off it seems to take only a few days for your body to sag into its previous slothful, drab appearance. You can't let up, you can't exercise enough, and you can't diet enough.

But who can continue at such a torrid pace, striving for what are unrealistic cultural ideals? A few people, of course, but not many. So liposuction is appealing. Just lie there, put up with a little discomfort, and the doctor will vacuum the fat right out of you. Surgeons can transform flat breasts into super breasts overnight. They can lower receding hairlines and smooth furrowed brows. They remove lumps with their magical tummy tucks, and can take off a decade with their rejuvenating skin peels, face lifts, and Botox injections.

With the impossibly shaped models at *Victoria's Secret* as the standard to which they hold themselves, even teens call the plastic surgeon. Anxious lest their child violate peer ideals and trail behind in her race for popularity, parents foot the bill. Some parents pay $25,000 just to give their daughters a flatter tummy (Gross 1998).

With peer pressure to alter the body already intense, surgeons keep stoking the fire. A sample ad: "No Ifs, Ands or Butts. You Can Change Your Bottom Line in Hours!" Some surgeons even offer gift certificates—so you can give your loved ones liposuction or botox injections along with their greeting card (Dowd 2002).

The thinness craze has moved to the East. Glossy magazines in Japan and China are filled with skinny models and crammed with ads touting diet pills and diet teas. In China, where famine used to abound, a little extra padding was valued as a sign of good health. Today, the obsession is thinness (Rosenthal 1999; Prystay and Fowler 2003). Not-so-subtle ads scream that fat is bad. Some teas come with a package of diet pills. Weight-loss machines, with electrodes attached to acupuncture pressure points, not only reduce fat but also build breasts—or so the advertisers claim.

Not limited by our rules, advertisers in Japan and China push a soap that supposedly "sucks up fat through the skin's pores" (Marshall 1995). What a dream product! After all, even though our TV models smile as they go through their paces, those exercise machines do look like a lot of hard work.

Then there is the other bottom line: Attractiveness does pay off. Economists studied physical attractiveness and earnings. The result? "Good-looking" men and women earn the most, "average-looking" men and women earn more than "plain" people, and the "ugly" are paid a "pittance" (Hamermesh and Biddle 1994). Consider obese women: Their net worth is less than half that of their slimmer sisters ("Fat is a Financial Issue" 2000). "Attractive" women have another cash advantage: They attract and marry higher-earning men.

More popularity *and* more money? Maybe you can't be thin enough after all. Maybe those exercise machines are a good investment. If only we could catch up with the Japanese and develop a soap that would suck the fat right out of our pores. You can practically hear the jingle now.

for your Consideration

What image do you have of your body? How do cultural expectations of "ideal" bodies underlie your image? Can you recall any advertisement or television program that has affected your body image?

What is considered ideal body size differs with historical periods and from one ethnic group to another. The women who posed for 16th century European painters, for example, appear to be "thicker" than the so-called "ideal" young women of today. Why do you think that this difference exists?

Most advertising and television programs that focus on weight are directed at women. Women are more concerned than men about weight, more likely to have eating disorders, and more likely to be dissatisfied with their bodies (Honeycutt 1995; Stinson 2001). Do you think that the targeting of women in advertising creates these attitudes and behaviors? Or do you think that these attitudes and behaviors would exist even if there were no such ads? Why?

U.S. Air Force F-16 fighter jets. That same evening, he addressed the American people from within the symbol of power: the Oval Office.

Ethnomethodology: Uncovering Background Assumptions

Certainly one of the strangest words in sociology is *ethnomethodology*. To understand this term, consider its three basic components. *Ethno* means "folk" or "people"; *method* means how people do something; *ology* means "the study of." Putting them together, then, *ethno/method/ology* means "the study of how people do things." Specifically, **ethnomethodology** is the study of how people use commonsense understandings to make sense of life.

Let's suppose that during a routine office visit, your doctor remarks that your hair is rather long, then takes out a pair of scissors and starts to give you a haircut. You would feel strange about this, for your doctor would be violating **background assumptions**—your ideas about the way life is and the way things ought to work. These assumptions, which lie at the root of everyday life, are so deeply embedded in our consciousness that we are seldom aware of them, and most of us fulfill them unquestioningly. Thus, your doctor does not offer you a haircut, even if he or she is good at cutting hair and you need one!

The founder of ethnomethodology, sociologist Harold Garfinkel, conducted some interesting exercises designed to reveal our background assumptions. Garfinkel (1967) asked his students to act as though they did not understand the basic rules of social life. Some tried to bargain with supermarket clerks; others would inch close to people and stare directly at them. They were met with surprise, bewilderment, even anger. In one exercise, Garfinkel asked students to take words and phrases literally. One conversation went like this:

ACQUAINTANCE: How are you?

STUDENT: How am I in regard to what? My health, my finances, my schoolwork, my peace of mind, my . . .

ACQUAINTANCE: (RED IN THE FACE): Look! I was just trying to be polite. Frankly, I don't give a damn how you are.

Students who are asked to break background assumptions can be highly creative. The young children of one of my students were surprised one morning when they came down for breakfast to find a sheet spread across the living room floor. On it were dishes, silverware, lit candles—and bowls of ice cream. They, too, wondered what was going on, but they dug eagerly into the ice cream before their mother could change her mind.

This is a risky assignment to give students, however, for breaking background assumptions can make people suspicious. When a colleague of mine gave this assignment, a couple of his students began to wash dollar bills in a laundromat. By the time they put the bills in the dryer, the police had arrived.

IN SUM Ethnomethodologists explore background assumptions, the taken-for-granted ideas about the world that underlie our behavior. Most of these assumptions are unstated. We learn these basic rules of social life as we learn our culture, and we violate them only with risk. Deeply

All of us have *background assumptions,* deeply ingrained expectations of how the world operates. They lay the groundwork for what we expect will happen in our interactions. How do you think the background assumptions of these people differ?

embedded in our minds, they give us basic directions for living everyday life.

The Social Construction of Reality

Symbolic interactionists stress how our ideas help determine our reality. In what has become known as *the definition of the situation,* or the **Thomas theorem,** sociologists W. I. and Dorothy S. Thomas (1928) said, "If people define situations as real, they are real in their consequences." Consider the following incident:

> On a visit to Morocco, in northern Africa, I decided to buy a watermelon. When I indicated to the street vendor that the knife he was going to use to cut the watermelon was dirty (encrusted with filth would be more apt), he was very obliging. He immediately bent down and began to swish the knife in a puddle on the street. I shuddered as I looked at the passing burros that were freely urinating and defecating as they went by. Quickly, I indicated by gesture that I preferred my melon uncut after all.

For that vendor, germs did not exist. For me, they did. And each of us acted according to our definition of the situation. My perception and behavior did not come from the fact that germs are real but *because I grew up in a society that teaches they are real.* Microbes, of course, *objectively* exist, and whether or not germs are part of our thought world has no bearing on whether we are infected by them. Our behavior, however, does not depend on the *objective* existence of something but, rather, on our *subjective interpretation,* on our *definition of reality.* In other words, it is not the reality of microbes that impresses itself on us, but society that impresses the reality of microbes on us.

This is what the **social construction of reality** is. Our society, or the social groups to which we belong, holds particular views of life. From our groups (the *social* part of this process), we learn specific ways of looking at life—whether that be our view of Hitler or Osama bin Laden (they're good, they're evil), germs (they exist, they don't exist), or *anything else in life.* In short, through our interactions with others, we *construct reality;* that is, we learn ways of interpreting our experiences in life.

Gynecological Examinations To better understand the social construction of reality, let's consider an extended example.

To do research on vaginal examinations, I interviewed a gynecological nurse who had been present at about 14,000 examinations. I focused on how doctors construct social reality in order to define this examination as nonsexual (Henslin and Biggs 1971/2005). It became apparent that the pelvic examination unfolds much as a stage play does. I will use "he" to refer to the physician because only male physicians participated in this study. Perhaps the results would be different with women gynecologists.

Scene 1 (the patient as person) In this scene, the doctor maintains eye contact with his patient, calls her by name, and discusses her problems in a professional manner. If he decides that a vaginal examination is necessary, he tells a nurse, "Pelvic in room 1." By this statement, he is announcing that a major change will occur in the next scene.

Scene 2 (from person to pelvic) This scene is the depersonalizing stage. In line with the doctor's announcement, the patient begins the transition from a "person" to a "pelvic." The doctor leaves the room, and a female nurse enters to help the patient make the transition. The nurse prepares the "props" for the coming examination and answers any questions the woman might have.

What occurs at this point is essential for the social construction of reality, for *the doctor's absence removes even the suggestion of sexuality.* To undress in front of him could suggest either a striptease or intimacy, thus undermining the reality being so carefully defined: that of nonsexuality.

The patient also wants to remove any hint of sexuality, and during this scene, she may express concern about what to do with her panties. Some mutter to the nurse, "I don't want him to see these." Most women solve the problem by either slipping their panties under their other clothes or placing them in their purse.

Scene 3 (the person as pelvic) This scene opens when the doctor enters the room. Before him is a woman lying on a table, her feet in stirrups, her knees tightly together, and her body covered by a drape sheet. The doctor seats himself on a low stool before the woman and says, "Let your knees fall apart" (rather than the sexually loaded "Spread your legs"), and begins the examination.

The drape sheet is crucial in this process of desexualization, for *it dissociates the pelvic area from the person:* Leaning forward and with the drape sheet above his head, the physician can see only the vagina, not the patient's face. Thus dissociated from the individual, the vagina is dramaturgically transformed into an object of analysis. If the doctor examines the patient's breasts, he also dissociates them from her person by examining them one at a time, with a towel covering the unexamined breast. Like the vagina, each breast becomes an isolated item dissociated from the person.

In this third scene, the patient cooperates in being an object, becoming, for all practical purposes, a pelvis to be examined. She withdraws eye contact from the doctor and usually from the nurse, is likely to stare at the wall or at the ceiling, and avoids initiating conversation.

Scene 4 (from pelvic to person) In this scene, the patient is "repersonalized." The doctor has left the examining room; the patient dresses and fixes her hair and makeup. Her reemergence as a person is indicated by such statements to the nurse as "My dress isn't too wrinkled, is it?" indicating a need for reassurance that the metamorphosis from "pelvic" back to "person" has been completed satisfactorily.

Scene 5 (the patient as person) In this final scene, the patient is once again treated as a person rather than an object. The doctor makes eye contact with her and addresses her by name. She, too, makes eye contact with the doctor, and the usual middle-class interaction patterns are followed. She has been fully restored.

IN SUM To an outsider to our culture, the custom of women going to a male stranger for a vaginal examination might seem bizarre. But not to us. We learn that pelvic examinations are nonsexual. To sustain this definition requires teamwork—patients, doctors, and nurses working together to socially construct reality.

It is not just pelvic examinations or our views of microbes that make up our definitions of reality. Rather, *our behavior depends on how we define reality.* Our definitions (or constructions) provide the basis for what we do and how we feel about life. To understand human behavior, then, we must know how people define reality.

Social Interaction on the Internet

Microsociologists do not limit themselves to studying face-to-face interaction. They are interested in any small-scale interaction, even a child's talk as he or she plays with toys alone. Communications on the Internet, too, aren't exactly face-to-face. One could say that they are face-to-computer, but they can also be viewed as face-to-face with computers in between. (More technically phrased, this would be called computer-mediated face-to-face interaction.)

At this point, there has been little research about interaction on the Net, but what we do know is intriguing. As we saw in the box on "written gestures" in Chapter 2 (page 43), people use emoticons to help communicate the feelings that underlie their online communications. The Sociology and the New Technology box on the next page explores another aspect of Net communications.

The Need for Both Macrosociology and Microsociology

As was noted earlier, both microsociology and macrosociology make vital contributions to our understanding of human behavior. Our understanding of social life would be vastly incomplete without one or the other. The photo essay on pages 108–109 should help to make clear why we need *both* perspectives.

To illustrate this point, let's consider two groups of high school boys studied by sociologist William Chambliss (1973/2005). Both groups attended Hanibal High School. In one group were eight middle-class boys who came from "good" families and were perceived by the community as "going somewhere." Chambliss calls this group the "Saints." The other group consisted of six lower-class boys who were seen as headed down a dead-end road. Chambliss calls this group the "Roughnecks."

Boys in both groups skipped school, got drunk, and did a lot of fighting and vandalism. The Saints were actually somewhat more delinquent, for they were truant more often and engaged in more vandalism. Yet the Saints had a good reputation, while the Roughnecks were perceived by teachers, the police, and the general community as no good and headed for trouble.

The boys' reputations set them on distinct paths. Seven of the eight Saints went on to graduate from college. Three studied for advanced degrees: One finished law school and became active in state politics, one finished medical school, and one went on to earn a Ph.D. The four other college graduates entered managerial or executive training programs with large firms. After his parents divorced, one Saint failed to graduate from high school on time and had to repeat his senior year. Although this boy tried to go to college by attending night school, he never finished. He was unemployed the last time Chambliss saw him.

In contrast, only four of the Roughnecks finished high school. Two of these boys did exceptionally well in sports and were awarded athletic scholarships to college. They both

> ## SOCIOLOGY
> *and the* NEW TECHNOLOGY

When Worlds Collide: Virtual Reality and the Real World

Although the Internet can unite us with strangers, it can divide us from friends and family. As we develop online relationships with people we don't know, we can neglect relationships with people we do know.

Virtual reality is seductive. It can be more appealing to log onto the Net and talk to strangers than to deal with the rigors of interacting with friends and family. The Net allows us to communicate selectively—to say what we want when we want to. We don't have to put up with people's moods and personalities. If we don't like what a "Net friend" says, we can just log off—or strike up a "conversation" with someone more to our liking at the moment. In contrast, with friends, family, and even some acquaintances, we have to put up with many dimensions of their personalities, not all of them pleasant.

Some find the Net-world so alluring that real-world reality pales by comparison. One man became "addicted" to pornography on the Net. Each evening after work, he would ignore his wife and children and seclude himself in his home office. There he would view pornography until it was time to go to bed. Night after night, it was the same. His wife finally gave him an ultimatum: Either he stop viewing his cyber babes, or she would leave. He said that he loved her but couldn't give this up. She left. He turned on his virtual lovers.

The Internet has become a marvelous tool, but some people find it so seductive that they neglect their offline social relationships.

for your Consideration

To what degree has virtual reality replaced your family, friends, networks, and neighborhood? Do you think that our future will see us plugging into the Net and unplugging from family and friends?

---

graduated from college and became high school coaches. Of the two others who graduated from high school, one became a small-time gambler, and the other disappeared "up north," where he was last reported to be driving a truck. The two boys who did not complete high school were convicted of separate murders and sent to prison.

To understand what happened to the Saints and the Roughnecks, we need to grasp *both* social structure and social interaction. Using *macrosociology,* we can place these boys within the larger framework of the U.S. social class system. This reveals how opportunities open or close to people depending on their social class and how people learn different goals as they grow up in different groups.

We can then use *microsociology* to follow their everyday lives. We can see how the Saints manipulated their "good" reputations to skip classes and how their access to automobiles allowed them to protect those reputations by transferring their troublemaking to different communities. In contrast, the Roughnecks, who did not have cars, were highly visible. Their lawbreaking, which was limited to a small area, readily came to the attention of the community. Microsociology also reveals how their respective reputations opened doors of opportunity to the first group of boys while closing them to the other.

It is clear that we need both kinds of sociology, and both are stressed in the following chapters.

When a **Tornado Strikes:**
Social Organization Following a Natural Disaster

a s I was watching television on March 20, 2003, I heard a report that a tornado had hit Camilla, Georgia. "Like a big lawn mower," the report said, it had cut a path of destruction through this little town. In its fury, the tornado had left behind six dead and about 200 injured.

From sociological studies of natural disasters, I knew that immediately after the initial shock the survivors of natural disasters work together to try to restore order to their disrupted lives. I wanted to see this restructuring process first hand. The next morning, I took off for Georgia.

These photos, taken the day after the tornado struck, tell the story of people in the midst of trying to put their lives back together. I was impressed at how little time people spent commiserating about their misfortune and how quickly they took practical steps to restore their lives.

As you look at these photos, try to determine why you need both microsociology and macrosociology to understand what occurs after a natural disaster.

After making sure that their loved ones are safe, one of the next steps people take is to recover their possessions. The cooperation that emerges among people, as documented in the sociological literature on natural disasters, is illustrated here.

© James M. Henslin, all photos

The owners of this house invited me inside to see what the tornado had done to their home. In what had been her dining room, this woman is trying to salvage whatever she can from the rubble. She and her family survived by taking refuge in the bathroom. They had been there only five seconds, she said, when the tornado struck.

In addition to the inquiring sociologist, television teams also were interviewing survivors and photographing the damage. This was the second time in just three years that a tornado had hit this neighborhood.

No building or social institution escapes a tornado as it follows its path of destruction. Just the night before, members of this church had held evening worship service. After the tornado someone mounted a U.S. flag on top of the cross, symbolic of the church members' patriotism and religiosity—and of their enduring hope.

Personsal relationships are essential in putting lives together. Consequently, reminders of these relationships are one of the main possessions that people attempt to salvage. This young man, having just recovered the family photo album, is eagerly reviewing the photos.

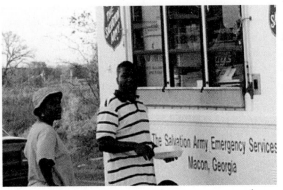

For children, family photos are not as important as toys. This girl has managed to salvage a favorite toy, which will help anchor her to her previous life.

Formal organizations also help the survivors of natural disasters recover. In this neighborhood, I saw representatives of insurance companies, the police, the fire department, and an electrical co-op. The Salvation Army brought meals to the neighborhood.

A sign of the times. Like electricty and gas, cable television also has to be restored as soon as possible.

Summary *and* Review

Levels of Sociological Analysis

What two levels of analysis do sociologists use?

Sociologists use macrosociological and microsociological levels of analysis. In **macrosociology,** the focus is placed on large-scale features of social life, while in **microsociology,** the focus is on **social interaction.** Functionalists and conflict theorists tend to use a macrosociological approach, while symbolic interactionists are more likely to use a microsociological approach. Pp. 84–85.

The Macrosociological Perspective: Social Structure

How does social structure influence behavior?

The term social structure refers to the social envelope that surrounds us and establishes limits on our behavior. Social structure consists of culture, social class, social statuses, roles, groups, social institutions, and societies. Together, these serve as foundations for how we view the world. Pp. 85–86.

Our location in the social structure underlies our perceptions, attitudes, and behaviors. Culture lays the broadest framework, while social class divides people according to income, education, and occupational prestige. Our behaviors and orientations are further influenced by the statuses we occupy, the roles we play, the groups to which we belong, and our experiences with the institutions of our society. These components of society work together to help maintain social order. Pp. 87–89.

What are social institutions?

Social institutions are the standard ways that a society develops to meet its basic needs. As summarized in Figure 4.2 (p. 90), industrial and postindustrial societies have ten social institutions: the family, religion, education, economics, medicine, politics, law, science, the military, and the mass media. Pp. 89, 90.

What social revolutions have transformed society?

The discovery that animals and plants could be domesticated marked the *first* social revolution. This transformed

hunting and gathering societies into **pastoral** and **horticultural societies.** The invention of the plow brought about the *second* social revolution, as societies became **agricultural.** The invention of the steam engine allowed **industrial societies** to develop—the *third* social revolution. The *fourth* social revolution was ushered in by the invention of the microchip. Another new type of society, the **biotech society,** may be emerging. As in the previous social revolutions, little will remain the same. Our attitudes, ideas, expectations, behaviors, relationships—all will be transformed. Pp. 89–95, 96.

What holds society together?

According to Emile Durkheim, people in agricultural societies are united by **mechanical solidarity** (having similar views and feelings). With industrialization comes **organic solidarity** (people depend on one another to do their more specialized jobs). Ferdinand Tönnies pointed out that the informal means of control of *Gemeinschaft* (small, intimate) societies are replaced by formal mechanisms in *Gesellschaft* (larger, more impersonal) societies. P. 95.

The Microsociological Perspective: Social Interaction in Everyday Life

How do stereotypes affect social interaction?

Stereotypes are assumptions of what people are like. When we first meet people, we classify them according to our perceptions of their visible characteristics. Our ideas about those characteristics guide our behavior toward them. Our behavior, in turn, may influence them to behave in ways that reinforce our stereotypes. P. 97.

Do all human groups share a similar sense of personal space?

In examining how people use physical space, symbolic interactionists stress that we surround ourselves with a "personal bubble" that we carefully protect. People from different cultures have "personal bubbles" of varying sizes, so the answer to the question is no. Americans typically use four different "distance zones": intimate, personal, social, and public. Pp. 97–98.

What is dramaturgy?

Erving Goffman developed the term **dramaturgy** (or dramaturgical analysis), in which everyday life is analyzed in terms of the stage. At the core of this analysis is **impression management,** our attempts to control the impressions we make on others. Our performances often call for **teamwork** and **face-saving behavior.** Pp. 98–103.

What is the social construction of reality?

The phrase **the social construction of reality** refers to how we construct our views of the world, which, in turn, underlie our actions. **Ethnomethodology** is the study of how people make sense of everyday life. Ethnomethodologists try to uncover **background assumptions,** our basic ideas about the way life is. Pp. 103–106.

How is the Internet changing social interaction?

The Internet is too new for us to know its full effects on human interaction. There are concerns at this point that virtual relationships may drive a wedge between some Internet users and their real-life relationships. We'll have to wait and see what develops. Pp. 106–107.

The Need for Both Macrosociology and Microsociology

Why are both levels of analysis necessary?

Because each focuses on different aspects of the human experience, both macrosociology and microsociology are necessary for us to understand social life. Pp. 106–109.

Thinking Critically

about Chapter 4

1. The major components of social structure are culture, social class, social status, roles, groups, and social institutions. Use social structure to explain why Native Americans have such a low rate of college graduation. (See Table 9.3 on page 241.)

2. Dramaturgy is a form of microsociology. Use dramaturgy to analyze a situation with which you are intimately familiar (such as interaction with your family or friends, or in one of your college classes).

3. To illustrate why we need both macrosociology and microsociology to understand social life, consider a student getting kicked out of college as an example.

Additional Resources

Companion Website www.ablongman.com/henslin

- Content Select Research Database for Sociology, with suggested key terms and annotated references
- Link to 2000 Census, with activities
- Flashcards of key terms and concepts

- Practice Tests
- Weblinks
- Interactive Maps

Where Can I Read More on This Topic?

Suggested readings for this chapter are listed at the back of this book.

Social Groups and Formal Organizations

OUTLINE

Social Groups
Primary Groups
Secondary Groups
In-Groups and Out-Groups
Reference Groups
Social Networks
A New Group: Electronic
   Communities

Bureaucracies
The Characteristics of
   Bureaucracies
The Perpetuation of Bureaucracies
The Rationalization of Society
Coping with Bureaucracies

Working for the Corporation
Stereotypes and the "Hidden"
   Corporate Culture
U.S. and Japanese Corporations

Group Dynamics
Effects of Group Size on Stability
   and Intimacy
Effects of Group Size on Attitudes
   and Behavior
Leadership
The Power of Peer Pressure: The
   Asch Experiment
The Power of Authority: The
   Milgram Experiment
Global Consequences of Group
   Dynamics: Groupthink

Summary and Review

David Tillinghast, *Human Pyramid of Businesspeople*, 1998

When Kody Scott joined the L.A. Crips, his initiation had two parts. Here's the first:

"How old is you now anyway?"

"Eleven, but I'll be twelve in November."

I never saw the blow to my head come from Huck. Bam! And I was on all fours. . . . Kicked in the stomach, I was on my back counting stars in the blackness. Grabbed by the collar, I was made to stand again. A solid blow to my chest exploded pain on the blank screen that had now become my mind. Bam! Another, then another. Blows rained on me from every direction. . . .

Up until this point not a word had been spoken. . . . Then I just started swinging, with no style or finesse, just anger and the instinct to survive. . . . (This) reflected my ability to represent the set [gang] in hand-to-hand combat. The blows stopped abruptly. . . . My ear was bleeding, and my neck and face were deep red. . . .

Scott's beating was followed immediately by the second part of his initiation. For this, he received the name "Monster," which he carried proudly.

Back in the shack we smoked more pot and drank more beer. I was the center of attention for my acts of aggression.

"Give Kody the pump" [12-gauge pump action shotgun]. . . . Tray Ball spoke with the calm of a football coach. "Tonight we gonna rock they world." Hand slaps were passed around the room. . . . "Kody, you got eight shots, you don't come back to the car unless they all are gone."

"Righteous," I said, eager to show my worth. . . .

Hanging close to buildings, houses, and bushes, we made our way, one after the other, to within spitting distance of the Bloods. . . . Huck and Fly stepped from the shadows simultaneously and were never noticed until it was too late. Boom! Boom! Heavy bodies hitting the ground, confusion, yells of dismay, running, ... By my sixth shot I had advanced past the first fallen bodies and into the

street in pursuit of those who had sought refuge behind cars and trees. . . .

Back in the shack we smoked more pot and drank more beer. I was the center of attention for my acts of aggression. . . .

Tray Ball said. "You got potential, 'cause you eager to learn. Bangin' [being a gang member] ain't no part-time thang, it's full-time, it's a career. It's bein' down when ain't nobody else down with you. It's gettin' caught and not tellin'. Killin' and not caring, and dyin' without fear. It's love for your set and hate for the enemy. You hear what I'm sayin'?"

Scott adds this insightful remark:

Though never verbally stated, death was looked upon as a sort of reward, a badge of honor, especially if one died in some heroic capacity for the hood. . . . The supreme sacrifice was to "take a bullet for a homie" [fellow gang member]. The set functioned as a religion. Nothing held a light to the power of the set. If you died on the trigger you surely were smiled upon by the Crip God.

Source: Excerpts from Scott 1994:8–13, 103.

Social Groups

Groups are the essence of life in society. We become who we are because of our membership in human groups. As we saw in Chapter 3, even our minds are a product of society or, more specifically phrased, of the groups to which we belong.

In this chapter, we'll consider how groups influence our lives and examine the power that groups can wield over us. Although none of us wants to think that we could participate in killings such as those recounted in our opening vignette, don't bet on it. You are going to read some surprising things about groups in this chapter.

First, we need to clarify the concept *group.* Two terms that are sometimes confused with "group" are *aggregate* and *category.* An **aggregate** consists of individuals who temporarily share the same physical space but who do not see themselves as belonging together. People waiting in a checkout line or drivers stopped at a red light are an aggregate. A **category** consists of people who share similar characteristics, such as all college women who wear glasses or all men over 6 feet tall. Unlike groups, the individuals who make up a category neither interact with one another nor take one another into account. The members of a **group,** in contrast, think of themselves as belonging together, and they interact with one another.

Groups affect your life so extensively that they even determine who you are. If you think that this is an exaggeration, read on. Let's begin by looking at the types of groups that make up our society.

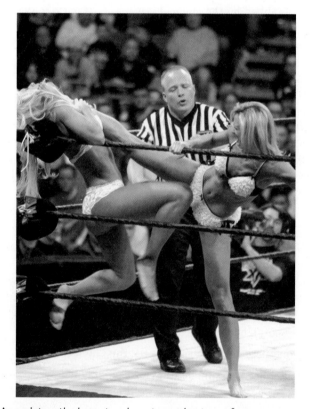

As society—the largest and most complex type of group—changes, so, too, do the groups, activities, and, ultimately, the type of people who form that society. This photo of Stacy Keibler and Torrie Wilson in Madison Square Garden captures some of the changes that U.S. society has been undergoing in recent years. What social changes can you identify from this photo?

Primary Groups

Our first group, the family, gives us our basic orientations to life. Later, among friends, we find more intimacy and an additional sense of belonging. These groups are what sociologist Charles Cooley called **primary groups.** By providing intimate, face-to-face interaction, they give us an identity, a feeling of who we are. As Cooley (1909) put it,

> By primary groups I mean those characterized by intimate face-to-face association and cooperation. They are primary in several senses, but chiefly in that they are fundamental in forming the social nature and ideals of the individual.

Cooley calls primary groups the "springs of life." By this, he means that primary groups, such as the family, friendship groups, and even gangs, are essential to our emotional well-being. As humans, we have an intense need for face-to-face interaction that generates feelings of self-esteem. By offering a sense of belonging and a feeling of being appreciated—and sometimes even loved—primary groups are uniquely equipped to meet this basic need.

Primary groups are also significant because their values and attitudes become fused into our identity. We internalize their views, which then become the lens through which we view life. Even as adults—no matter how far we move away from our childhood roots—early primary groups remain "inside" us. There, they continue to form part of the perspective through which we look out onto the world. Ultimately, then, it is difficult, if not impossible, for us to separate the self from our primary groups, for the self and our groups merge into a "we."

Secondary Groups

Compared with primary groups, **secondary groups** are larger, more anonymous, more formal, and more impersonal. Secondary groups are based on some common interest or activity, and their members are likely to interact on the basis of specific statuses, such as president, manager, worker, or student. Examples are a college class, the American Sociological Association, a factory, and the Democratic Party. Contemporary society could not function without secondary groups. They are part of the way we get our education, make our living, spend our money, and use our leisure time.

As necessary as secondary groups are for contemporary life, they often fail to satisfy our deep needs for intimate association. Consequently, *secondary groups tend to break down into smaller primary groups.* At school and work, we form friendships. Our interaction with our friends is so important that we sometimes feel that if it weren't for them, school or work "would drive us crazy." The primary groups that we form within secondary groups, then, serve as a buffer between us and the demands that secondary groups place on us.

Voluntary Associations   A special type of secondary group is a **voluntary association,** a group made up of volunteers who organize on the basis of some mutual interest. Some are local, consisting of only a few volunteers; some are national, with a paid professional staff; and others are in between.

Americans love voluntary associations and use them to pursue a wide variety of interests. A visitor entering one of the thousands of small towns that dot the U.S. landscape is often greeted by a highway sign proclaiming some of the town's voluntary associations: Girl Scouts, Boy Scouts, Lions, Elks, Knights of Columbus, Chamber of Commerce, American Legion, Veterans of Foreign Wars, and perhaps a host of others. One type of voluntary association is so prevalent that a separate sign sometimes announces which varieties are in the town: Roman Catholic, Baptist, Lutheran, Methodist, Episcopalian, and so on. Not listed on these signs are many other voluntary associations, such as political parties, unions, health clubs, the National Organization for Women, Alcoholics Anonymous, Gamblers Anonymous, Association of Pinto Racers, and Citizens United For or Against This and That.

The Inner Circle and the Iron Law of Oligarchy
An interesting, and disturbing, aspect of voluntary associations is that the leaders often grow distant from their members and become convinced that only the inner circle can be trusted to make the group's important decisions. To see this principle at work, let's look at the Veterans of Foreign Wars (VFW).

Sociologists Elaine Fox and George Arquitt (1985) studied three local posts of the VFW, a national organization of former U.S. soldiers who have served in foreign wars. They found that although the leaders conceal their attitudes from the other members, the inner circle views the rank and file as a bunch of ignorant boozers. Because the leaders can't stand the thought that such people might represent them in the community and at national meetings, a curious situation arises. Although the VFW constitution makes rank-and-file members eligible for top leadership positions, they never become leaders. In fact, the leaders are so effective at controlling who holds these top positions that even before an election, they can tell you who is going to win. "You need to meet Jim," the sociologists were told. "He's the next post commander after Sam does his time."

Categories, Aggregates, Primary and Secondary Groups

Groups have a deep impact on our views, orientations, even what we feel and think about life. Yet, as illustrated by these photos, not everything that appears to be a group is actually a group in the sociological sense.

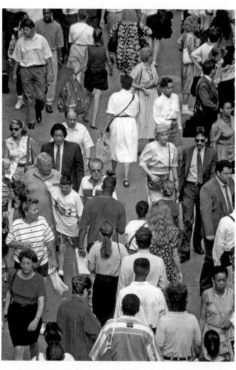

Secondary groups are larger and more anonymous, formal, and impersonal than primary groups. Why is this photo of a political convention an example of a secondary group?

Primary groups such as the family play a key role in the development of the self. As a small group, the family also serves as a buffer from the often-threatening larger group known as society. The family has been of primary significance in forming the basic orientations of this Latino couple, as it will be for their daughter.

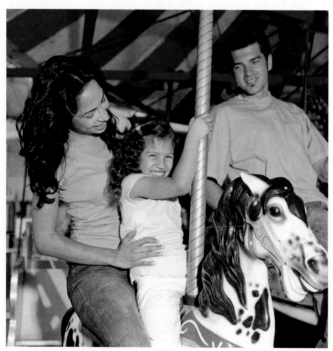

Aggregates are simply people who happen to be in the same place at the same time.

The outstanding trait that these three people have in common does not make them a group, but a **category**.

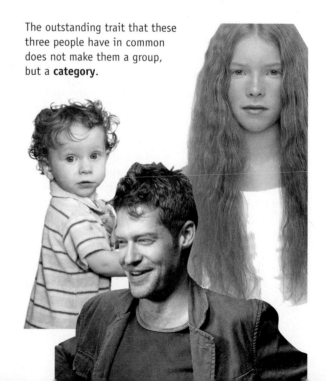

At first, the researchers found this puzzling. The election hadn't been held yet. As they investigated further, they found that leadership is actually determined behind the scenes. The elected leaders appoint their favored people to chair the key committees. This makes the members aware of their accomplishments, and they elect the favored ones as leaders. The inner circle, then, maintains control over the entire organization simply by appointing its own members to highly visible positions.

Like the VFW, most organizations are run by only a few of their members (Cnaan 1991). Building on the term *oligarchy,* a system in which many are ruled by a few, sociologist Robert Michels (1876–1936) coined the term **the iron law of oligarchy** to refer to how organizations come to be dominated by a self-perpetuating elite (Michels 1911/1949). Most members of an organization are passive, and the members of the inner circle keep themselves in power by passing the leadership positions around to one another.

What many find disturbing about the iron law of oligarchy is that people are excluded from leadership because they don't represent the inner circle's values—or, in some instances, their background. This is true even of organizations that are committed to democratic principles. For example, U.S. political parties—supposedly the backbone of the nation's representative government—are run by an inner circle that passes leadership positions from one elite member to another. This principle is also demonstrated by the U.S. Senate. With their control of statewide political machinery and access to free mailing, about 90 percent of U.S. senators who choose to run are reelected (*Statistical Abstract* 2005:Table 395).

In-Groups and Out-Groups

Groups toward which we feel loyalty are called **in-groups;** those toward which we feel antagonism are called **out-groups.** For Monster Kody in our opening vignette, the Crips were an in-group, while the Bloods were an out-group. That the Crips—and we—make such a fundamental division of the world has far-reaching consequences for our lives.

Producing Loyalty, a Sense of Superiority, and Rivalries Identification with a group can generate not only a sense of belonging, but also loyalty and feelings of superiority. These, in turn, often produce rivalries. Usually, the rivalries are mild, such as sports rivalries among nearby towns, in which the most extreme act is likely to be the furtive invasion of the out-group's territory to steal a mascot, paint a rock, or uproot a goal post. The consequences

"So long, Bill. This is my club. You can't come in."

How our participation in social groups shapes our self-concept is a focus of symbolic interactionists. In this process, knowing who we are *not* is as significant as knowing who we are.

of in-group membership also can be discrimination, hatred, and, as we saw in our opening vignette, even participation in murder.

Implications for a Socially Diverse Society The strong identifications with members of our in-groups are the basis of many gender and racial-ethnic divisions. As sociologist Robert Merton (1968) observed, our favoritism leads to biased perception. Following a fascinating double standard, we tend to view the traits of our in-group as virtues while we see those *same* traits in out-groups as vices. Men may perceive an aggressive man as assertive but an aggressive woman as pushy. They may think that a male employee who doesn't speak up "knows when to keep his mouth shut," while they consider a quiet woman as too timid to make it in the business world.

To divide the world into "we" and "they" poses a danger for a pluralistic society. For the Nazis, the Jews were an out-group that came to symbolize evil. One consequence of biased perception is that harming others can come to be seen as justified. The Nazis weren't alone in their views; many ordinary, "good" Germans defended the

Holocaust as "dirty work" that someone had to do (Hughes 1962/2005). This principle might seem to pertain only to the past, but it continues today–and likely always will. Consider what happened following the terrorist attacks of 9/11. Top U.S. politicians (and other Americans) began to view Arabs as sinister, bloodthirsty villains. U.S. officials approved torture "for the sake of good" as an option for U.S. interrogators. In the face of potential attacks, torture, for the sake of the lives it would save, became "dirty work" that someone had to do.

Periods of economic downturn provide fertile ground for promoting divisions among groups. The Nazis took power during a depression so severe that it was wiping out the middle class. If such a depression were to occur in the United States, immigrants would be transformed from "nice people who do jobs that Americans think are beneath them" to "sneaky people who steal jobs from friends and family." A national anti-immigration policy would follow, probably accompanied by a resurgence of hate groups such as the neo-Nazis, skinheads, and the Ku Klux Klan.

In short, to divide the world into in-groups and out-groups is a natural part of social life. But in addition to bringing functional consequences, it can bring dysfunctional ones.

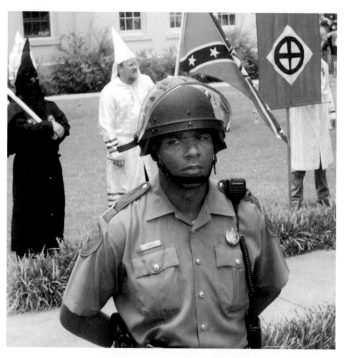

All of us have *reference groups*—the groups we use as standards to evaluate ourselves. How do you think the reference groups of these members of the KKK who are demonstrating in Jaspar, Texas, differ from those of the police officer who is protecting their right of free speech? Although the KKK and this police officer use different groups to evaluate their attitudes and behaviors, the process is the same.

Reference Groups

Suppose you have just been offered a great job. It pays double what you hope to make even after you graduate from college. You have only three days to make up your mind. If you accept it, you will have to drop out of college. As you consider the matter, thoughts like this may go through your mind: "My friends will say I'm a fool if I don't take the job . . . but Dad and Mom will practically go crazy. They've made sacrifices for me, and they'll be crushed if I don't finish college. They've always said I've got to get my education first, that good jobs will always be there. But, then, I'd like to see the look on the faces of those neighbors who said I'd never amount to much!"

This is an example of how people use **reference groups,** the groups we use as standards to evaluate ourselves. Your reference groups may include your family, neighbors, teachers, classmates, co-workers, and the Scouts or the members of a church, mosque, or synagogue. If you are like Monster Kody in our opening vignette, the "set" would be your main reference group. Even a group you don't belong to can be a reference group. For example, if you are thinking about going to graduate school, graduate students or members of the profession you want to join may form a reference group. You would consider their standards as you evaluate your grades or writing skills.

Providing a Yardstick Reference groups exert tremendous influence over our lives. For example, if you want to become a corporate executive, you might start to dress more formally, try to improve your vocabulary, read the *Wall Street Journal,* and change your major to business or law. In contrast, if you want to become a rock musician, you might wear jewelry in several places where you have pierced your body, get elaborate tattoos, dress in ways your parents and many of your peers consider extreme, read *Rolling Stone,* drop out of college, and hang around clubs and rock groups.

Exposure to Contradictory Standards in a Socially Diverse Society From these examples, you can see how we use reference groups to evaluate our behavior. When we see ourselves as measuring up to a reference group's standards, we feel no conflict. If our behavior, or even aspirations, do not match the group's standards, however, the mismatch can lead to inner turmoil. For example, to want

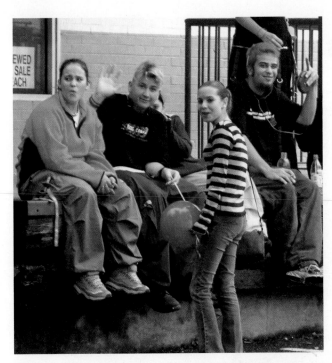

We all use *reference groups* to evaluate our accomplishments, failures, values, and attitudes. We compare what we do and think with what we perceive as normative in our reference groups. What reference groups do you think these teenagers are using?

to become a corporate executive would create no inner conflict for most of us. It would, however, if you had grown up in an Amish home, for the Amish strongly disapprove of such aspirations for their children. They ban high school and college education, three-piece suits, and corporate employment. Similarly, if you wanted to become a soldier and your parents were dedicated pacifists, you likely would feel deep conflict, as your parents would hold quite different aspirations for you.

Given the social diversity of our society and our social mobility, as we grow up many of us are exposed to contradictory ideas and standards from the groups that become significant to us. The "internal recordings" that play contradictory messages from these reference groups, then, are one price we pay for our social mobility.

Social Networks

Although we live in a huge and diverse society, we don't experience social life as a sea of nameless, strange faces. Instead, we interact within social networks. The term **social network** refers to people who are linked to one another. Your social network includes your family, friends, acquaintances, people at work and school, and even your "friends of friends." Think of your social network as lines that extend outward from yourself, gradually ecompassing more and more people.

If you are a member of a large group, you probably associate regularly with a few people within that group. In a sociology class I was teaching at a commuter campus, six women who didn't know one another ended up working together on a project. They got along well, and they began to sit together. Eventually they planned a Christmas party at one of their homes. This type of social network, the clusters within a group, or its internal factions, is called a **clique** (cleek).

The analysis of social networks has moved from theory and laboratory study to the practical world. As you may recall from Chapter 1 (page 14), analyzing social networks was the way that U. S. forces located Saddam Hussein. On a more personal level, a fascinating development in social networks is *facebooking,* the topic of the Down-to-Earth Sociology box on the next page.

Although we live in a huge society, we don't experience social life as a sea of nameless, strange faces. Instead, we interact within social networks. One of the more interesting ways that people are expanding their social networks is *facebooking,* the topic of the Down-to-Earth Sociology box on the next page.

The Small World Phenomenon Social scientists have wondered just how extensive the connections are between social networks. If you list everyone you know, each of those individuals lists everyone he or she knows, and you keep doing this, would almost everyone in the United States eventually be included on those lists?

It would be too cumbersome to test this hypothesis by drawing up such lists, but psychologist Stanley Milgram (1933–1984) came up with an interesting idea. In a classic study known as "the small world phenomenon," Milgram (1967) addressed a letter to "targets:" the wife of a divinity student in Cambridge and a stockbroker in Boston. He sent the letter to "starters," who did not know these people. He asked them to send the letter to someone they knew on a first-name basis, someone they thought might know the "target." The recipients, in turn, were asked to mail the letter to someone they knew who might know the "target," and so on. The question was: Would the letters ever reach the "target"? If so, how long would the chain be?

Think of yourself as part of this study. What would you do if you were a "starter" but the "target" lived in a state in which you know no one? You would send the letter to someone you knew who might know someone in

Down-to-Earth Sociology

Facebooking: The Lazy (But Efficient) Way to Meet Friends

MAKING NEW FRIENDS AND MAINTAINING FRIENDSHIPS can take effort. You have to clean up, put on clothes, leave your room, and engage in conversations. The topic of conversation can move in directions that don't interest you, and people can drop into your group that you don't particularly care for. Situations can arise that make you feel awkward or embarrassed. Maybe you would like to disengage for a few minutes—to take a little power nap or to read a book. You can't do this without offending someone.

Not so with facebooking. You are in charge. Talk with people when you want. Stop when you want.

This is part of the allure of facebooking. The facebook is like an ever-changing, online yearbook. To find people with similar interests, just type in that interest. Your favorite book is Kerouac's *On The Road*? *The DaVinci Code*? Your favorite movie is *Fight Club*? *Barbarella*? You enjoy *J. Crew* or *Wheezer*? Your favorite activity is making out? Fiddling with guns? Looking at pink shoes? And you want to find people who share your interest? Just a mouse-click away.

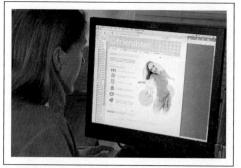

You can even form your own group—and invite others to join it. The group can be as esoteric as you prefer. Some actual groups: "Ann Coulter Fan Club." "Republican Princesses." "Preppy Since Conception." "Cancer Corner" (for students who love to smoke). "I Want to Be a Trophy Wife and You Can't Stop Me." There is even an "anti-group" group.

You see a cute guy or girl, and you want to get to know them. Back in your room, with one click you learn not only their e-mail address, but also the classes they are taking and their interests. This will give you good pick-up info. That person won't even know you're stalking them.

One woman who contacted a man after reading his profile, said "We had all the same interests. Books. Movies. Everything. It was a little weird, though—like dating a website."

Facebooking is free. If you have a school e-mail address, just answer a few questions, post your picture—and start making friends. You can do a search of your own campus or even locate old friends who might be attending college somewhere else.

A photo blinks onto your computer screen, and someone asks to be listed as part of your social network. You consider it for a couple of seconds, faintly recalling the individual from high school, and you click yes. You have just "friended" him.

You have control. You can set the privacy settings to determine who can view which parts of your profile: the contact information, personal information, courses you are taking, and a list of your friends.

Many students find the allure of facebooking irresistible, a new form of creative procrastination. And in college, there is so much to procrastinate from.

Facebooking has a touch of whimsy. The poke option lets you "poke" anyone you want to. No one knows what the "poke" message really means, but it seems to be, "Hey. How ya doin'?" The poke can be a conversation starter, like "zup" (what's up?), a tap on the shoulder as it were.

Then there's The Wall, a virtual "wall" on which friends can scrawl messages. ("MEATHEAD WAS HERE.")

Change your mind about someone? It's so simple to drop them. Just click the "defriend" button. But risky. That's a slap in the face.

Not only do you see a list of your friends but also you can track your social network—the friends of friends, the people you can reach in three or fewer steps. In just three steps, your network could balloon to several thousand.

The usual popularity contest has reared its head, of course. Who has the most friends listed? Some students even contact members they've never met just to ask to be "friended." Larger numbers give them bragging rights. Pathetic, but true. There is something strange about groups that exist only in cyberspace, profiles that might be faked, and friends you may not even know. But life itself is strange.

On the serious side: Facebooking provides a sense of belonging on what can be large, impersonal campuses. It is reassuring to see that you are connected to others—even if most of the connections are in cyberspace.

Based on Copeland 2004; Sales 2004; Schackner 2004; Sege 2005.

that state. This, Milgram reported, is just what happened. Although none of the senders knew the targets, the letters reached the designated individual in an average of just six jumps.

Milgram's study caught the public's fancy, leading to the phrase "six degrees of separation." This expression means that, on average, everyone in the United States is separated by just six individuals. Milgram's conclusions have become so popular that a game, "Six Degrees of Kevin Bacon," was built around it, and the game has spawned countless variants.

Is the Small World Phenomenon an Academic Myth?
But things are not this simple. There is a problem with Milgram's research, as psychologist Judith Kleinfeld (2002a, 2002b) discovered when she decided to replicate Milgram's study. When she went to the archives at Yale University Library to get more details, she found that Milgram had stacked the deck in favor of finding a small world. The "starters" came from mailing lists of people who were likely to have higher incomes and therefore were not representative of average people. In addition, one of the "targets" was a stockbroker, and that person's "starters" were investors in blue-chip stocks. Kleinfeld also found another discrepancy: On average, only 30 percent of the letters reached their "target." In one of Milgram's studies, the success rate was just 5 percent.

Since most letters did *not* reach their targets, even with the deck stacked in favor of success, we can draw the *opposite* conclusion from the one that Milgram reported: People who don't know one another are dramatically separated by social barriers. How great the barriers are is illustrated by another attempt to replicate Milgram's study, this one using e-mail. Only 384 of 24,000 chains reached their targets (Dodds et al. 2003).

As Kleinfeld says, "Rather than living in a small world, we may live in a world that looks a lot like a bowl of lumpy oatmeal, with many small worlds loosely connected and perhaps some small worlds not connected at all." Somehow, I don't think that the phrase, "lumpy oatmeal phenomenon," will become standard, but the criticism of Milgram's research is valid.

Implications for a Socially Diverse Society
Besides geography, the barriers that separate us into many small worlds are primarily those of social class, gender, and race-ethnicity. Overcoming these social barriers is difficult because even our own social networks contribute to social inequality, a topic that we explore in the Cultural Diversity box on the next page.

Implications for Science
Kleinfeld's revelations of Milgram's research reinforce the need of replication, a topic discussed in Chapter 1. For our knowledge of social life, we cannot depend on single studies, for there may be problems of generalizability on the one hand or those of negligence or even fraud on the other. Replication by objective researchers is essential to build and advance solid social knowledge.

A New Group: Electronic Communities

In the 1990s, a new type of human group, the **electronic community,** made its appearance. People "meet" online in chat rooms to communicate on almost any conceivable topic, from donkey racing and bird watching to sociology and quantum physics. Although sociologists have begun to study these groups, at this point we know little about them.

Bureaucracies

About 100 years ago, sociologist Max Weber also noticed that a new type of group was emerging: the *bureaucracy.* To achieve more efficient results, this new form of social organization was shifting the emphasis from personal loyalties to the "bottom line." Bureaucracies have become so common that we now take them for granted, unaware that they are fairly new on the human scene. As we look at the characteristics of bureaucracies, we will also consider their implications for our lives.

The Characteristics of Bureaucracies

What do the Russian army and the U.S. Postal Service have in common? Or the government of Mexico and your college? The sociological answer is that they all are *bureaucracies.* As Weber (1913/1947) pointed out, **bureaucracies** have:

1. *Clear levels, with assignments flowing downward and accountability flowing upward.* Figure 5.1 on page 123 shows the bureaucratic structure of a typical university. Each level assigns responsibilities to the level beneath it, while each lower level is accountable to the level above for fulfilling those assignments.
2. *A division of labor.* Each worker has a specific task to fulfill, and all the tasks are coordinated to accomplish the purpose of the organization. In a college, for example, a teacher does not fix the heating system, the

Cultural Diversity *in the* United States

How Our Own Social Networks Perpetuate Social Inequality

CONSIDER SOME OF THE PRINCIPLES we have reviewed. People tend to form in-groups with which they identify; they use reference groups to evaluate their attitudes and behavior; and they interact in social networks. Our in-groups, reference groups, and social networks are likely to consist of people whose backgrounds are similar to our own. This means that, for most of us, just as social inequality is built into society, so it is built into our own relationships. One consequence is that we tend to perpetuate social inequality.

To see why, suppose that an outstanding job—great pay, interesting work, opportunity for advancement—has just opened up where you work. Who are you going to tell? Most likely it will be someone you know, a friend or at least someone to whom you owe a favor. And most likely your social network is made up of people who look much like yourself—especially their race-ethnicity, age, social class, and probably also, gender. This tends to keep good jobs moving in the direction of people whose characteristics are similar to those of the people already in an organization. You can see how our social networks both reflect the inequality that characterizes our society and help to perpetuate it.

Consider a network of white men who are established in an organization. As they learn of opportunities (jobs, investments, real estate, and so on), they share this information with their networks. Opportunities and good jobs flow to people who have characteristics similar to their own. Those who benefit from this information, in turn, reciprocate with similar information when they learn of it. This bypasses people who have different characteristics, in this example women and minorities, while it perpetuates

Social networks, *which open and close doors of opportunity, are important for careers. Despite the official program of sociology conventions, much of the "real" business centers around renewing and extending social networks.*

the "good old boy'" network. No intentional discrimination need be involved.

To overcome this barrier, women and minorities do *networking*. They try to meet people who can help advance their careers. Like the "good old boys," they go to parties and join clubs, churches, synagogues, mosques, and political parties. African American leaders, for example, cultivate a network of African American leaders. As a result, the network of African American leaders is so tight that one-fifth of the entire national African American leadership are personal acquaintances. Add some "friends of a friend," and *three-fourths* of the entire leadership belong to the same network (Taylor 1992).

Women cultivate a network of women. As a result, some women who reach top positions end up in a circle so tight that the term "new girl" network is being used, especially in the field of law. Remembering those who helped them and sympathetic to those who are trying to get ahead, these women tend to steer business to other women. Like the "good old boys" who preceded them, the new insiders have a ready set of reasons to justify their exclusionary practice (Jacobs 1997).

for your Consideration

The perpetuation of social inequality does not require intentional discrimination. Just as social inequality is built into society, so is it built into our personal relationships. How do you think your own social network helps to perpetuate social inequality? How do you think we can break this cycle? (The key must center on creating diversity in social networks.)

Figure 5.1 | The Typical Bureaucratic Structure of a Medium-Sized University

This is a scaled-down version of a university's bureaucratic structure. The actual lines of a university are likely to be much more complicated than those depicted here. A large university may have a chancellor and several presidents under the chancellor, each president being responsible for a particular campus. Although in this figure extensions of authority are shown only for the Vice President for Administration and the College of Social Sciences, each of the other vice presidents and colleges has similar positions. If the figure were to be extended, departmental secretaries would be shown, and eventually, somewhere, even students.

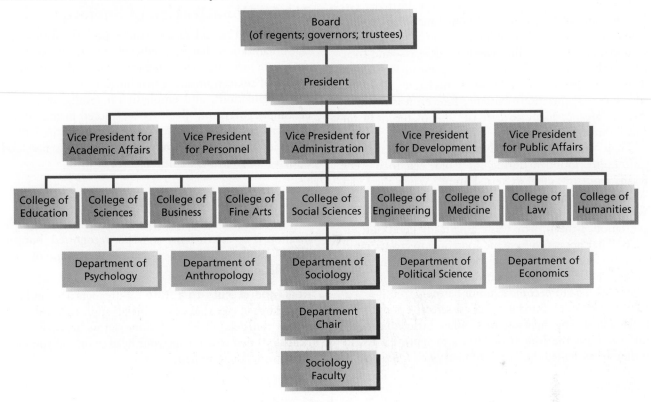

president does not teach, and a secretary does not evaluate textbooks. These tasks are distributed among people who have been trained to do them.

3. *Written rules.* In their attempt to become efficient, bureaucracies stress written procedures. In general, the longer a bureaucracy exists and the larger it grows, the more written rules it has.

4. *Written communications and records.* Records are kept of much of what occurs in a bureaucracy. ("Make sure you send a copy to your supervisor.") Workers also spend a good deal of time sending memos and e-mail back and forth.

5. *Impersonality and replaceability.* It is the position that is important, not the individual who holds the position. You work for the organization, not for the replaceable person who heads some post in the organization.

The Perpetuation of Bureaucracies

Bureaucracies have become a standard feature of our lives because they are a powerful form of social organization. They harness people's energies to reach specific goals. Once in existence, however, bureaucracies tend to take on a life of their own. In a process called **goal displacement,** even after the organization achieves its goal and no longer has a reason to continue, continue it does.

A classic example is the National Foundation for the March of Dimes, organized in the 1930s to fight polio (Sills 1957). At that time, the origin of polio was a mystery. The public was alarmed and fearful, for overnight a healthy child could be stricken with this crippling disease. To raise money to find a cure, the March of Dimes placed posters of children on crutches near cash registers in almost every store in the United States. (See the photo on the next page.)

They raised money beyond the organization's wildest dreams. When Dr. Jonas Salk developed a vaccine for polio in the 1950s, the threat was wiped out almost overnight.

The staff that ran the March of Dimes did not quietly fold up their tents and slip away. Instead, they found a way to keep their jobs by targeting a new enemy: birth defects. But then in 2001, researchers finished mapping the human genome system. Perceiving that some day this information could help to eliminate birth defects—and their jobs—officials of the March of Dimes came up with a new slogan: "Breakthroughs for Babies." This latest goal should ensure the organization's existence forever; it is so vague that we are not likely to ever run out of the need for "breakthroughs."

Then there is NATO (North Atlantic Treaty Organization), founded during the Cold War to prevent Russia from invading western Europe. When the Cold War ended, removing the organization's purpose, the Western powers tried to find a reason to continue their organization. I mean, why waste a perfectly good bureaucracy? They appear to have hit upon one: to create "rapid response forces" to combat terrorism and "rogue nations" (Tyler 2002). To keep this bureaucracy going, they even allowed Russia to become a junior partner.

On a side note: Bureaucracies are sensitive about sociologists analyzing their activities. When I tried to get permission from the March of Dimes to reprint a recent poster, I was denied that permission—*unless I changed my analysis to make it more favorable to the organization.* I kept my analysis, and, finally, several years later, the organization relented and granted permission to reprint the poster below. Sociologists regularly confront such obstacles in their work.

The Rationalization of Society

Weber viewed bureaucracies as such a powerful form of social organization that he predicted they would come to dominate social life. He called this process **the rationalization of society,** meaning that bureaucracies, with their rules, regulations, and emphasis on results, would increasingly govern our lives. As is explored in the Down-to-Earth Sociology box on the next page, in the United States, even cooking is becoming rationalized, as fast-food outlets take over this traditional area of work.

Coping with Bureaucracies

Although in the long run, no other form of social organization is more efficient, as Weber recognized, bureaucracies also have a dark side. Let's look at some of their dysfunctions.

Red Tape: A Rule Is a Rule   Bureaucracies can be so bound by red tape that when officials apply their rules, the results can defy all logic. I came across an example so ridiculous that it can make your head swim—if you don't burst from laughing first.

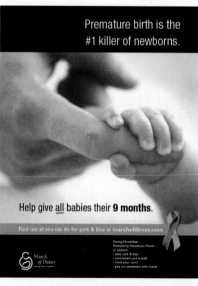

The March of Dimes was founded by President Franklin Roosevelt in the 1930s to fight polio. When a vaccine for polio was discovered in the 1950s, the organization did not declare victory and disband. Instead, its leaders kept the organization intact by creating new goals—fighting birth defects. Sociologists use the term *goal displacement* to refer to this process of adopting new goals.

Down-to-Earth Sociology

The McDonaldization of Society

THE MCDONALD'S restaurants that seem to be all over the United States—and, increasingly, the world—have a significance that goes far beyond the convenience of ready-made hamburgers and milk shakes. As sociologist George Ritzer (1993, 1998, 2001) says, our everyday lives are being "McDonaldized." Let's see what he means by this.

McDonald's in Tokyo, Japan

The McDonaldization of society—the standardization of everyday life—does not refer just to the robotlike assembly of food. As Ritzer points out, this process is occurring throughout society—and it is transforming our lives. Want to do some shopping? Shopping malls offer one-stop shopping in controlled environments. Planning a trip? Travel agencies offer "package" tours. They will transport middle-class Americans to ten European capitals in fourteen days. All visitors experience the same hotels, restaurants, and other scheduled sites—and no one need fear meeting a "real" native. Want to keep up with events? *USA Today* spews out McNews—short, bland, unanalytical pieces that can be digested between gulps of the McShake or the McBurger.

Efficiency brings dependability. You can expect your burger and fries to taste the same whether you buy them in Los Angeles or Beijing. Efficiency also lowers prices. But efficiency does come at a cost. Predictability washes away spontaneity, changing the quality of our lives. It produces a sameness, a bland version of what used to be unique experiences. In my own travels, for example, had I taken packaged tours I never would have had the enjoyable, eye-opening experiences that have added so much to my appreciation of human diversity.

For good or bad, our lives are being McDonaldized, and the predictability of packaged settings seems to be our social destiny. When education is rationalized, no longer will our children have to put up with real professors, who insist on discussing ideas endlessly, who never provide decisive answers, and who come saddled with idiosyncrasies. At some point, such an approach to education is going to be a quaint bit of history. Our programmed education will eliminate the need for discussion of social issues—we will have packaged solutions to social problems, definitive answers that satisfy our need for closure. Computerized courses will teach the same answers to everyone—the approved, "politically correct" ways to think about social issues. Mass testing will ensure that students regurgitate the programmed responses.

Our coming prepackaged society will be efficient, of course. But it also means that we will be trapped in the "iron cage" of bureaucracy—just as Weber warned would happen.

In Spain, the Civil Registry of Barcelona recorded the death of a woman named Maria Antonieta Calvo in 1992. Apparently, Maria's evil brother had reported her dead so he could collect the family inheritance.

When Maria learned that she was supposedly dead, she told the Registry that she was very much alive. The bureaucrats at this agency looked at their records, shook their heads, and insisted that she was dead. Maria then asked lawyers to represent her in court. They all refused—because no dead person can bring a case before a judge.

When Maria's boyfriend asked her to marry him, the couple ran into a serious obstacle: No man in Spain (or elsewhere, I presume) can marry a dead woman—so these bureaucrats said, "So sorry, but no license."

After years of continuing to insist that she was alive, Maria finally got a hearing in court. When the judges looked at Maria, they believed that she really was a living person, and they ordered the Civil Registry to declare her alive.

The ending of this story gets even happier, for now that Maria was alive, she was able to marry her boyfriend. I don't know if the two lived happily ever after, but, after overcoming the bureaucrats, they at least had that chance (BBC Mundo, February 18, 2006).

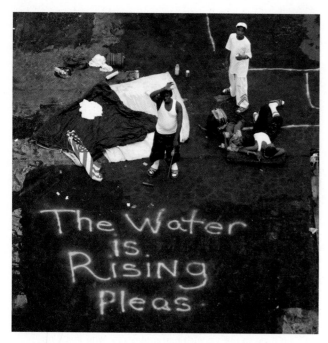

When dealing with the routine, bureaucracies usually function quite efficiently. In emergencies, however, they sometimes fail miserably. This dysfunction was evident during Hurricane Katrina, which hit the U.S. Gulf Coast in 2005. Due to bureaucratic bungling, the pathetic pleas of thousands of people in flooded New Orleans went unanswered.

Bureaucratic Alienation Perceived in terms of roles, rules, and functions rather than as individuals, many workers begin to feel more like objects than people. Marx termed these reactions **alienation,** a result, he said, of workers being cut off from the finished product of their labor. He pointed out that before industrialization, workers used their own tools to produce an entire product, such as a chair or table. Now the capitalists own the tools (machinery, desks, computers) and assign each worker only a single step or two in the entire production process. Relegated to doing repetitive tasks that seem so remote from the final product, workers no longer relate or identify with what they produce. They come to feel estranged not only from their results of their labor but also from their work environment.

Resisting Alienation Because workers would like to feel valued and want to have a sense of control over their work, they resist alienation. Forming primary groups at work is a major form of that resistance. Workers band together in informal settings—at lunch, around desks, or for a drink after work. During those times, they give one another approval for jobs well done and express sympathy for the shared need to put up with cantankerous bosses, meaningless routines, and endless rules. They relate to one another not just as workers but as people who value one another. They flirt, laugh, and tell jokes, and talk about their families and goals. Adding this personal part to their work relationships maintains their sense of being individuals rather than merely cogs in a machine.

Consider a common sight. While visiting an office, you see work areas decorated with family and vacation photos. The sociological implication is that of workers who are striving to resist alienation. By staking a claim to individuality, the workers are rejecting an identity as machines that exist simply to perform functions.

Working for the Corporation

Since you are likely to end up working in a bureaucracy, let's look at how its characteristics may affect your career.

Stereotypes and the "Hidden" Corporate Culture

Who gets ahead in large corporations? Although we might like to think that success comes from intelligence and hard work, many factors other than merit underlie salary increases and promotions. As sociologist Rosabeth Moss Kanter (1977, 1983) stresses, the **corporate culture** contains "hidden values." These values create a self-fulfilling prophecy that affects people's corporate careers.

It works like this: Corporate and department heads have stereotypes about what good workers are like and who will make good colleagues. Not surprisingly, these stereotypes reflect the bosses' own backgrounds; they consist of people who look like them. They give these workers better access to information, networking, and "fast track" positions. These people then perform better and become more committed to the organization—thus confirming the initial expectation or stereotype. In contrast, those who are judged to be outsiders are thought to have lesser abilities. Because of this, they are given fewer opportunities and challenges, as well as less access to information that might help them get ahead. Working at a level beneath their capacity, they come to think poorly of themselves, become less committed to the organization, and don't perform as well—thus confirming the stereotypes the bosses had of them. (You may want to review the discussion of stereotypes on pages 97, 98–99.)

The hidden values and stereotypes that created this self-fulfilling prophecy remain invisible. What people see are the promotions of those with superior performances and greater commitment to the company; they are not aware of the higher and lower expectations that opened and closed opportunities, resulting in these attitudes and accomplishments.

You can see how these hidden values contribute to the *iron law of oligarchy* we just reviewed: Because of this self-fulfilling prophecy, the inner circle reproduces itself by favoring people who "look" like its own members—generally white and male. Women and minorities, who don't match this stereotype, often are "showcased"—placed in highly visible but powerless positions to demonstrate how progressive the company is. These are "slow-track" positions, in which accomplishments seldom come to the attention of top management.

As corporations grapple with their growing diversity, the hidden corporate culture and its stereotypes are likely to give way, but only slowly and grudgingly. In the following Thinking Critically section, we'll consider other aspects of diversity in the workplace.

Thinking Critically

Managing Diversity in the Workplace

Times have changed. The San Jose, California, electronic phone book lists *eight* times more *Nguyens* than *Joneses* (Pauken 2003). More than half of U.S. workers are minorities, immigrants, and women. Diversity in the workplace is much more than skin color. Diversity includes ethnicity, gender, age, religion, social class, and sexual orientation.

In the past, the idea was for people to join the "melting pot," to give up their distinctive traits and become like the dominant group. Today, with the successes of the civil rights and women's movements, people are more likely to prize their distinctive traits. Realizing that assimilation (being absorbed into the dominant culture) is probably not the wave of the future, three out of four Fortune 500 companies have "diversity training." They hold lectures and workshops so that employees can learn to work with colleagues of diverse cultures and racial-ethnic backgrounds.

Coors Brewery is a prime example of this change. Coors went into a financial tailspin after one of the Coors brothers gave a racially charged speech in the 1980s. Today, Coors offers diversity workshops, has sponsored a gay dance, and has paid for a corporate-wide mammography program. In 2004, Coors opposed an amendment to the Colorado constitution to ban same-sex marriages. The company has even had rabbis certify its suds as kosher. Its proud new slogan: "Coors cares" (Cloud 1998). Now, that's quite a change.

What Coors cares about, of course, is the bottom line. It's the same with other corporations. Blatant racism and sexism once made no difference to profitability. Today, they do. To promote profitability, companies must promote diversity—or at least pretend to. The sincerity of corporate leaders is not what's important; diversity in the workplace is.

Diversity training has the potential to build bridges, but it can backfire. Directors of these programs can be so incompetent that they create antagonisms and reinforce stereotypes. The leaders of a diversity training session at the U.S. Department of Transportation, for example, had women grope men as the men ran by. They encouraged blacks and whites to insult one another and to call each other names (Reibstein 1996). The intention may have been good (understanding the other through role reversal and getting hostilities "out in the open"), but the approach was moronic. Instead of healing, such behaviors wound and leave scars.

Pepsi provides a positive example of diversity training. Managers at Pepsi are given the assignment of sponsoring a group of employees who are unlike themselves. Men sponsor women, African Americans sponsor whites, and so on. The executives are expected to try to understand work from the perspective of the people they sponsor, to identify key talent, and to personally mentor at least three people in their group. Accountability is built in—the sponsors have to give updates to executives even higher up (Terhune 2005).

for your Consideration

Do you think that corporations and government agencies should offer diversity training? If so, how can we develop diversity training that fosters mutual respect? Can you suggest practical ways to develop workplaces that are not divided by gender and race-ethnicity?

The growing diversity of the U.S. workforce has created a need for diversity training.

U.S. and Japanese Corporations

How were the Japanese able to recover from the defeat of World War II—including the nuclear destruction of two of their major cities—to become a giant in today's global economy? Some analysts trace part of the answer to the way their corporations are organized. One of these analysts, William Ouchi (1981), pinpointed five ways in which Japanese corporations differ from those of the United States. You will be surprised at how different they are. But are these differences myth or reality?

Hiring and Promoting Teams   In *Japan,* teamwork is central. College graduates who join a corporation are all paid about the same starting salary. They also get raises as a team. To learn about the company, they are rotated as a team through the various levels of the organization. They develop intense loyalty to one another and to their company, for the welfare of one represents the welfare of all. Only in later years are individuals singled out for recognition. When there is an opening in the firm, outsiders are not even considered.

In the *United States,* a worker is hired on the basis of what the firm thinks that individual can contribute. Employees try to outperform each other, and they strive for raises and promotions as signs of personal success. The individual's loyalty is to himself or herself, not to the company. Outsiders are considered for openings in the firm.

Lifetime Security   In *Japan,* lifetime security is taken for granted. Employees can expect to work for the same firm for the rest of their lives. In return for not being laid off or fired, the firm expects employees to be loyal to the company, to stick with it through good and bad times. Workers do not go job shopping, for their careers—and many aspects of their lives—are wrapped up in this one firm.

In the *United States,* lifetime security is unusual. It is limited primarily to teachers and some judges, who receive what is called *tenure.* Companies lay off workers in slow times. To remain competitive, they even reorganize and fire entire divisions. Workers, too, "look out for number one." Job shopping and job hopping are common.

Almost Total Involvement   In *Japan,* work is like a marriage: The worker and the company are committed to each other. The employee supports the company with loyalty and long hours at work, while the company supports its workers with lifetime security, health services, recreation, sports and social events, even a home mortgage. Involvement with the company does not stop when the workers leave the building. They join company study and

exercise groups and are likely to spend evenings socializing with co-workers in bars and restaurants.

In the *United States,* work is a specific, often temporary contract. Workers are hired to do a certain job. When they have done that job, they have fulfilled their obligation to the company. Their after-work hours are their own. They go home to their private lives, which are separate from the firm.

Broad Training   In *Japan,* employees move from one job to another within the company. Not only are they not stuck doing the same thing for years on end but also they gain a larger perspective of the corporation and how the specific jobs they are assigned fit into that bigger picture.

In the *United States,* workers are expected to perform one job, to do it well, and then to be promoted upward to a job with more responsibility. Their understanding of the company is largely tied to the particular corner they occupy, often making it difficult for them to see how their job fits into the overall picture.

Decision Making by Consensus   In *Japan,* decision making is a lengthy process. Each person who will be affected by a decision is consulted. After lengthy deliberations, a consensus emerges, and everyone agrees on which suggestion is superior. This makes workers feel that they are an essential part of the organization, not simply cogs in a giant wheel.

In the *United States,* the person in charge of the unit to be affected does as much consulting with others as he or she thinks necessary and then makes the decision.

The Myth Versus Reality   Peering beneath the surface reveals a reality that is different from the myth that has grown up around the Japanese corporation. Lifetime job security, for example, is elusive, and only about a third of Japanese workers find it. Management by consensus is also a myth. This was not how decisions were made at Sony, one of Japan's most successful companies (Nathan 1999). Akio Morita, Sony's founder, was an entrepreneur from the same mold as Bill Gates. Morita didn't send memos up and down the line, as the myth would have us believe. Instead, he relied on his gut feeling about products. When he thought up the idea of the Walkman, Morita didn't discuss it until consensus emerged—he simply ordered it to be manufactured. And Morita made quick decisions. Over lunch, he decided to buy CBS Records. The cost was $2 billion.

In a surprising move, Japan has turned to U.S. corporations to see why they are more efficient. Flying in the face of their traditions, Japanese corporations have begun to lay off workers and to use merit pay. Although this is

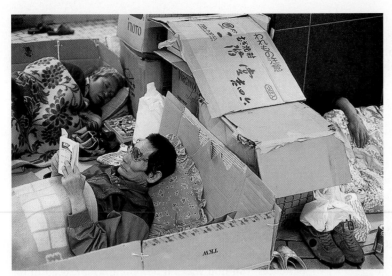

For a time, Americans stood in awe of the Japanese corporate model. The passage of time, however, has revealed serious flaws. Lifetime job security, for example, is a myth. These homeless men are living in the Shinjuko train station in Tokyo. Note how they have followed the Japanese custom of placing their shoes outside before entering their "home."

standard U.S. practice, it had been unthinkable in Japan. Some firms have even cut salaries and demoted managers who didn't meet goals. Perhaps the biggest surprise was Ford's takeover of Mazda. After huge losses, Mazda's creditors decided that Ford knew more about building and marketing cars than Mazda and invited Ford to manage the company (Reitman and Suris 1994).

The real bottom line is that we live in a global marketplace—of ideas as well as products. The likely result of global competition is that both the West and Japan will feed off each other—the one learning greater cooperation in the production process, the other greater internal competition.

Group Dynamics

As you know from personal experience, the lively interaction *within* groups—who does what with whom—has profound consequences for how you adjust to life. Sociologists use the term **group dynamics** to refer to how groups influence us and how we affect groups. Let's consider how the size of a group makes a difference and then examine leadership, conformity, and decision making.

Before doing this, we should see how sociologists define the term *small group*. In a **small group,** there are few enough members that each one can interact directly with all the other members. Small groups can be either primary or secondary. A wife, husband, and children make up a primary small group, as do workers who take their breaks together, while bidders at an auction and the students in an introductory sociology class are secondary small groups.

Effects of Group Size on Stability and Intimacy

Writing in the early 1900s, sociologist Georg Simmel (1858–1918) noted the significance of group size. He used the term **dyad** for the smallest possible group, which consists of two people. Dyads, which include marriages, love affairs, and close friendships, show two distinct qualities. First, they are the most intense or intimate of human groups. Because only two people are involved, the interaction is focused on them. Second, because dyads require that both members participate and be committed, it takes just one member to lose interest for the dyad to collapse. In larger groups, by contrast, even if one member withdraws, the group can continue, for its existence does not depend on any single member (Simmel 1950).

A **triad** is a group of three people. As Simmel noted, the addition of a third person fundamentally changes the group. With three people, interaction between the first two decreases. This can create strain. For example, with the birth of a child, hardly any aspect of a couple's relationship goes untouched. Attention focuses on the baby, and interaction between the husband and wife diminishes. Despite the difficulty that this presents—including in many instances the husband's jealousy that he is getting less attention from his wife—the marriage usually becomes stronger. Although the intensity of interaction is less in triads, they are inherently stronger and give greater stability to a relationship.

Yet, as Simmel noted, triads, too, are inherently unstable. They tend to form **coalitions**—some group members aligning themselves against others. In a triad, it is not uncommon for two members to feel strong bonds and prefer one another. This leaves the third person feeling hurt and excluded. Another characteristic of triads is that they often produce an arbitrator or mediator, someone who tries to settle disagreements between the other two. In one-child families, you can often observe both of these characteristics of triads—coalitions and arbitration.

The general principle is this: *As a small group grows larger, it becomes more stable, but its intensity, or intimacy, decreases.* To see why, look at Figure 5.2. As each new person comes into a group, the connections among people multiply. In a dyad, there is only 1 relationship; in a triad, there are 3; in a group of four, 6; in a group of five, 10. If we expand the group to six, we have 15 relationships, while a group of seven yields 21 relationships. If we continue adding members, we soon are unable to follow the connections: A group of eight has 28 possible relationships; a group of nine, 36 relationships; a group of ten, 45; and so on.

It is not only the number of relationships that makes larger groups more stable. As groups grow, they also tend to develop a more formal structure to accomplish their goals. For example, leaders emerge, and more specialized roles come into play. This often results in such familiar offices as president, secretary, and treasurer. This structure provides a framework that helps the group survive over time.

Effects of Group Size on Attitudes and Behavior

Imagine that your social psychology professors have asked you to join a few students to discuss your adjustment to college life. When you arrive, they tell you that to make the discussion anonymous, they want you to sit unseen in a booth. You will participate in the discussion over an intercom, talking when your microphone comes on. The professors say that they will not listen to the conversation, and they leave.

You find the format somewhat strange, to say the least, but you go along with it. You have not seen the other students in their booths, but when they talk about their experiences, you find yourself becoming wrapped up in the problems they begin to share. One student even mentions how frightening he has found college because of his history of epileptic seizures. Later, you hear this individual breathe heavily into the microphone. Then he stammers and cries for help. A crashing noise follows, and you imagine him lying helpless on the floor.

Nothing but an eerie silence follows. What do you do?

Your professors, John Darley and Bibb Latané (1968), staged the whole thing, but you don't know this. No one had a seizure. In fact, no one was even in the other booths. Everything, except your comments, was on tape.

Some participants were told that they would be discussing the topic with just one other student, others with two, others with three, and so on. Darley and Latané found that all students who thought they were part of a dyad rushed out to help. If they thought they were part of a triad, only 80 percent went to help—and they were slower in leaving the booth. In six-person groups, only 60 percent went to see what was wrong—and they were even slower.

This experiment demonstrates how deeply group size influences our attitudes and behavior: It even affects our willingness to help one another. Students in the dyad knew that it was up to them to help the other student. The professor was gone, and if they didn't help, there was no one else. In the larger groups, including the triad, students felt *a diffusion of responsibility:* Giving help was no more their responsibility than anyone else's.

Figure 5.2 **The Effects of Group Size on Relationships**

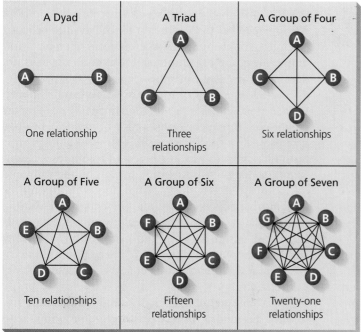

A Dyad — One relationship

A Triad — Three relationships

A Group of Four — Six relationships

A Group of Five — Ten relationships

A Group of Six — Fifteen relationships

A Group of Seven — Twenty-one relationships

You probably have observed the second consequence of group size firsthand. When a group is small, its members act informally, but as the group grows, the members lose their sense of intimacy and become more formal. No longer can the members assume that the others are "insiders" in sympathy with what they say. Now they must take a larger audience into consideration, and instead of merely "talking," they begin to "address" the group. As their speech becomes more formal, their body language stiffens.

You probably have observed a third aspect of group dynamics, too. In the early stages of a party, when only a few people are present, almost everyone talks with everyone else. But as others arrive, the guests break into smaller groups. Some hosts, who want their guests to mix together, make a nuisance of themselves trying to achieve *their* idea of what a group should be like. The division into small groups is inevitable, however, for it follows the basic sociological principles that we have just reviewed. Because the addition of each person rapidly increases connections (in this case, "talk lines"), conversation becomes more difficult. The guests break into smaller groups in which they can see each other and are able to interact comfortably and directly with one another.

Leadership

All of us are influenced by leaders, so it is important to understand leadership. Let's look at how people become leaders, the types of leaders there are, and their different styles of leadership. Before we do this, though, it is important to know that leaders don't necessarily hold formal positions in a group. **Leaders** are simply people who influence the behaviors, opinions, or attitudes of others. Even a group of friends has leaders.

Who Becomes a Leader?   Are leaders born with characteristics that propel them to the forefront of a group? No sociologist would agree with such a premise. In general, people who become leaders are perceived by group members as strongly representing their values or as able to lead a group out of a crisis (Trice and Beyer 1991). Leaders also tend to be more talkative and to express determination and self-confidence.

These findings may not be surprising, as such traits appear to be related to leadership. Researchers, however, have also discovered traits that seem to have no bearing on the ability to lead. For example, taller people and those who are judged better looking are more likely to become leaders (Stodgill 1974; Judge and Cable 2004). The taller and more attractive are also likely to earn more, but that is another story (Deck 1968; Feldman 1972; Katz 2005).

Many other factors underlie people's choice of leaders, most of which are quite subtle. A simple experiment performed by social psychologists Lloyd Howells and Selwyn Becker (1962) uncovered one of these factors. Forming groups of five people who did not know one another, they seated them at a rectangular table, three on one side and two on the other. After discussing a topic for a set period of time, each group chose a leader. The findings are startling: Although only 40 percent of the people sat on the two-person side, 70 percent of the leaders emerged from that side. The simple explanation is that we tend to direct more interactions to people facing us than to people to the side of us.

Types of Leaders   Groups have two types of leaders (Bales 1950, 1953; Cartwright and Zander 1968). The first is easy to recognize. This person, called an **instrumental leader** (or *task-oriented leader*), tries to keep the group moving toward its goals. These leaders try to keep group members from getting sidetracked, reminding them of what they are trying to accomplish. The **expressive leader** (or *socioemotional leader*), in contrast, usually is not recognized as a leader, but he or she certainly is one. This person is likely to crack jokes, to offer sympathy, or to do other things that help to lift the group's morale. Both types of leadership are essential: the one to keep the group on track, the other to increase harmony and minimize conflicts.

It is difficult for the same person to be both an instrumental and an expressive leader, for these roles contradict one another. Because instrumental leaders are task oriented, they sometimes create friction as they prod the group to get on with the job. Their actions often cost them popularity. Expressive leaders, in contrast, who stimulate personal bonds and reduce friction, are usually more popular (Olmsted and Hare 1978).

Leadership Styles   Let's suppose that the president of your college has asked you to head a task force to determine how the college can improve race relations on campus. Although this position requires you to be an instrumental leader, you can adopt a number of **leadership styles,** or ways of expressing yourself as a leader. The three basic styles are those of **authoritarian leader,** one who gives orders; **democratic leader,** one who tries to gain a consensus; and **laissez-faire leader,** one who is highly permissive. Which style should you choose?

Social psychologists Ronald Lippitt and Ralph White (1958) carried out a classic study of these leadership styles. Boys who were matched for IQ, popularity, physical energy, and leadership were assigned to "craft clubs" made up of five boys each. The experimenters trained adult men in the three leadership styles. As the researchers peered through peepholes, taking notes and making movies, each adult rotated among the clubs, playing all three styles to control possible influences of their individual personalities.

The *authoritarian* leaders assigned tasks to the boys and told them exactly what to do. They also praised or condemned the boys' work arbitrarily, giving no explanation for why they judged it good or bad. The *democratic* leaders held discussions with the boys, outlining the steps that would help them reach their goals. They also suggested alternative approaches and let the boys work at their own pace. When they evaluated the projects, they gave "facts" as the bases for their decisions. The *laissez-faire* leaders were passive. They gave the boys almost total freedom to do as they wished. They offered help when asked but made few suggestions. They did not evaluate the boys' projects, either positively or negatively.

The results? The boys who had authoritarian leaders grew dependent on their leader and showed a high degree of internal solidarity. They also became either aggressive or apathetic, with the aggressive boys growing hostile toward their leader. In contrast, the boys who had democratic leaders were friendlier and looked to one another for mutual approval. They did less scapegoating, and when the leader left the room, they continued to work at a steadier pace. The boys with laissez-faire leaders asked more questions, but they made fewer decisions. They were notable for their lack of achievement. The researchers concluded that the democratic style of leadership works best. Their conclusion, however, may have been biased, as the researchers favored a democratic style of leadership in the first place, and they did the research during a highly charged political period called the Cold War (Olmsted and Hare 1978). Apparently, this same bias in studies of leadership continues (Cassel 1999).

You may have noted that only boys and men were involved in this experiment. It is interesting to speculate how the results might differ if we were to repeat the experiment with all-girl groups and with mixed groups of girls and boys—and if we used both men and women as leaders. Maybe you will become the sociologist to study such variations of this classic experiment.

Leadership Styles in Changing Situations Different situations require different styles of leadership. Suppose, for example, that you are leading a dozen backpackers in the Sierra Madre Mountains north of Los Angeles, and it is time to make dinner. A laissez-faire style would be appropriate if the backpackers had brought their own food, or perhaps a democratic style if the meal were to be communally

prepared. Authoritarian leadership—with you telling all the hikers how to prepare their meals—would create resentment. This, in turn, would likely interfere with meeting the primary goal of the group, which in this case is to have a good time while enjoying nature.

Now assume the same group but a different situation: One of your party is lost, and a blizzard is on its way. This situation calls for you to take charge and be authoritarian. To simply shrug your shoulders and say, "You figure it out," would invite disaster—and probably a lawsuit.

The Power of Peer Pressure: The Asch Experiment

How influential are groups in our lives? To answer this, let's look first at *conformity* in the sense of going along with our peers. Our peers have no authority over us, only the influence that we allow.

Imagine that you are taking a course in social psychology with Dr. Solomon Asch and you have agreed to participate in an experiment. As you enter his laboratory, you see seven chairs, five of them already filled by other students. You are given the sixth. Soon the seventh person arrives. Dr. Asch stands at the front of the room next to a covered easel. He explains that he will first show a large card with a vertical line on it, then another card with three vertical lines. Each of you is to tell him which of the three lines matches the line on the first card (see Figure 5.3).

Dr. Asch then uncovers the first card with the single line and the comparison card with the three lines. The correct answer is easy, for two of the lines are obviously wrong, and one is exactly right. Each person, in order, states his or her answer aloud. You all answer correctly. The second trial is just as easy, and you begin to wonder why you are there.

Then on the third trial, something unexpected happens. Just as before, it is easy to tell which lines match. The first student, however, gives a wrong answer. The second gives the same incorrect answer. So do the third and the fourth. By now, you are wondering what is wrong. How will the person next to you answer? You can hardly believe it when he, too, gives the same wrong answer. Then it is your turn, and you give what you know is the right answer. The seventh person also gives the same wrong answer.

On the next trial, the same thing happens. You know that the choice of the other six is wrong. They are giving what to you are obviously wrong answers. You don't know what to think. Why aren't they seeing things the same way you are? Sometimes they do, but in twelve trials they don't. Something is wrong, and you are no longer sure what to do.

Figure 5.3   Asch's Cards

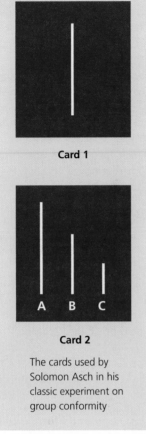

Card 1

Card 2

The cards used by
Solomon Asch in his
classic experiment on
group conformity

Source: Asch 1952: 452–453.

When the eighteenth trial is finished, you heave a sigh of relief. The experiment is finally over, and you are ready to bolt for the door. Dr. Asch walks over to you with a big smile on his face and thanks you for participating in the experiment. He explains that you were the only real subject in the experiment! "The other six were stooges. I paid them to give those answers," he says. Now you feel real relief. Your eyes weren't playing tricks on you after all.

What were the results? Asch (1952) tested fifty people. One third (33 percent) gave in to the group half the time, giving what they knew to be wrong answers. Another two out of five (40 percent) gave wrong answers but not as often. One out of four (25 percent) stuck to their guns and always gave the right answer. I don't know how I would do on this test (if I knew nothing about it in advance), but I like to think that I would be part of

the 25 percent. You probably feel the same way about yourself. But why should we feel that we wouldn't be like *most* people?

The results are disturbing, and more researchers have replicated Asch's experiment than any other study (Levine 1999). In our land of individualism, the group is so powerful that most people are willing to say things that they know are not true. And this was a group of strangers! How much more conformity can we expect when our group consists of friends, people we value highly and depend on for getting along in life? Again, perhaps you will become the sociologist to run that variation of Asch's experiment, perhaps using female subjects.

The Power of Authority: The Milgram Experiment

Even more disturbing are the results of the experiment described in the following Thinking Critically section.

Thinking Critically

If Hitler Asked You to Execute a Stranger, Would You? The Milgram Experiment

Imagine that you are taking a course with Dr. Stanley Milgram (1963, 1965), a former student of Dr. Asch. Assume that you do not know about the Asch experiment and have no reason to be wary. You arrive at the laboratory to participate in a study on punishment and learning. You and a second student draw lots for the roles of "teacher" and "learner." You are to be teacher. When you see that the learner's chair has protruding electrodes, you are glad that you are the teacher. Dr. Milgram shows you the machine you will run. You see that one side of the control panel is marked "Mild Shock, 15 volts," while the center says "Intense Shock, 350 Volts," and the far right side reads "DANGER: SEVERE SHOCK."

"As the teacher, you will read aloud a pair of words," explains Dr. Milgram. "Then you will repeat the first word, and the learner will reply with the second word. If the learner can't remember the word, you press this lever on the shock generator. The shock will serve as punishment, and we can then determine if punishment improves memory." You nod, now very relieved that you haven't been designated the learner.

"Every time the learner makes an error, increase the punishment by 15 volts," instructs Dr. Milgram. Then, seeing the look on your face, he adds, "The shocks can be extremely painful, but they won't cause any permanent tissue damage." He pauses and then says, "I want you to see." You then follow him to the "electric chair," and Dr. Milgram gives you a shock of 45 volts. "There. That wasn't too bad, was it?" "No," you mumble.

The experiment begins. You hope for the learner's sake that he is bright, but unfortunately, he turns out to be rather dull. He gets some answers right, but you have to keep turning up the dial. Each turn makes you more and more uncomfortable. You find yourself hoping that the learner won't miss another answer. But he does. When he received the first shocks, he let out some moans and groans, but now he is screaming in agony. He even protests that he suffers from a heart condition.

How far do you turn that dial?

By now, you probably have guessed that there was no electricity attached to the electrodes and that the "learner" was a stooge who only pretended to feel pain. The purpose of the experiment was to find out at what point people refuse to participate. Does anyone actually turn the lever all the way to "DANGER: SEVERE SHOCK"?

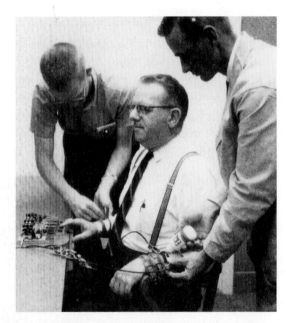

In the 1960s, U.S. social psychologists ran a series of creative but controversial experiments. From this photo of the "learner" being prepared for one of Stanley Milgram's experiments, you can get an idea of how convincing the situation would be for the "teacher."

Milgram wanted the answer because millions of ordinary people did nothing to stop the Nazi slaughter of Jews, gypsies, Slavs, homosexuals, people with disabilities, and others whom the Nazis designated as "inferior." That seeming compliance in the face of all of these deaths seemed bizarre, and Milgram wanted to see how ordinary, intelligent Americans might react in an analogous situation.

Milgram was upset by what he found. Many "teachers" broke into a sweat and protested to the experimenter that this was inhuman and should be stopped. But when the experimenter calmly replied that the experiment must go on, this assurance from an "authority" ("scientist, white coat, university laboratory") was enough for most "teachers" to continue, even though the "learner" screamed in agony. Even "teachers" who were "reduced to twitching, stuttering wrecks" continued to follow orders.

Milgram varied the experiments (Brannigan 2004). He used both men and women. In some experiments, he put the "teachers" and "learners" in the same room, so the "teacher" could clearly see the suffering. In others, he put the "learners" in a separate room, and had them pound and kick the wall during the first shocks and then go silent. The results varied. When there was no verbal feedback from the "learner," 65 percent of the "teachers" pushed the lever all the way to 450 volts. Of those who could see the "learner," 40 percent turned the lever all the way. When Milgram added a second "teacher," a stooge who refused to go along with the experiment, only 5 percent of the "teachers" turned the lever all the way, a result that bears out some of Asch's findings.

A stormy discussion about research ethics erupted. Not only were researchers surprised—and disturbed—by what Milgram found, but also they were alarmed at his methods. Universities began to require that subjects be informed of the nature and purpose of social research. Researchers agreed that to reduce subjects to "twitching, stuttering wrecks" was unethical, and almost all deception was banned.

for your Consideration

What is the connection between Milgram's experiment and the actions of Monster Kody in our opening vignette? Taking into account how significant these findings are, do you think that the scientific community overreacted to Milgram's experiments? Should we allow such research? Consider both the Asch and Milgram experiments, and use symbolic interactionism, functionalism, and conflict theory to explain why groups have such influence over us.

Global Consequences of Group Dynamics: Groupthink

Suppose you are a member of the President's inner circle. It is midnight, and the President has just called an emergency meeting to deal with a terrorist attack. At first, several options are presented. Eventually, these are narrowed to only a couple of choices, and at some point, everyone seems to agree on what now appears to be "the only possible course of action." To express doubts at that juncture will bring you into conflict with all the other important people in the room. To criticize will mark you as not being a "team player." So you keep your mouth shut, with the result that each step commits you—and them—more and more to the "only" course of action.

From the Milgram and Asch experiments, we can see the power of authority and the influence of peers. Under some circumstances, as in this example, this can lead to **groupthink.** Sociologist Irving Janis (1972, 1982) coined this term to refer to the collective tunnel vision that group members sometimes develop. As they begin to think alike, they become convinced that there is only one "right" viewpoint and a single course of action to follow. They take any suggestion of alternatives as a sign of disloyalty. With their perspective narrowed and fully convinced that they are right, they may even put aside moral judgments and disregard risk (Hart 1991; Flippen 1999).

Groupthink can bring serious consequences. Consider the *Columbia* space shuttle disaster of 2003.

Foam broke loose during launch, and engineers were concerned that it might have damaged tiles on the nose cone. Because this would make reentry dangerous, they sent e-mails to NASA officials, warning them about the risk. One engineer even suggested that the crew do a "space walk" to examine the tiles (Vartabedian and Gold 2003). The team in charge of the shuttle, however, disregarded the warnings. Convinced that a piece of foam weighing less than two pounds could not seriously harm the shuttle, they refused to even consider the possibility (Wald and Schwartz 2003). The fiery results of their mental closure were transmitted around the globe.

The consequences of groupthink can be even greater than this. In 1941, President Franklin D. Roosevelt and his chiefs of staff had evidence that the Japanese were preparing to attack Pearl Harbor. They simply refused to believe it and decided to continue naval operations as usual. The destruction of the U.S. naval fleet ushered the United States into World War II. In the war with Vietnam, U.S. officials had evidence of the strength and determination of the North Vietnamese military. They arrogantly threw such evidence aside, refusing to believe that "little, uneducated, barefoot people in pajamas" could defeat the U.S military. In each of these cases, options closed as officials committed themselves to a single course of action. Questioning the decisions would have indicated disloyalty and disregard for "team playing." Those in power plunged ahead, unable to see alternative perspectives. No longer did they try to objectively weigh evidence as it came in; instead, they interpreted everything as supporting their one "correct" decision.

Groupthink knows few bounds. Consider the aftermath of 9/11, when government officials defended torture as moral, "the lesser of two evils." Groupthink narrowed thought to the point that the U.S. Justice Department ruled that the United States was not bound by the Geneva Convention that prohibits torture. Facing protests, the Justice Department backed down (Lewis 2005).

Preventing Groupthink Groupthink is a danger that faces government leaders, who tend to surround themselves with an inner circle that closely reflects their own views. In briefings, written summaries, and "talking points," this inner circle spoon-feeds the leaders carefully selected information. The result is that top leaders, such as the president, become cut off from information that does not support their own opinions.

Perhaps the key to preventing the mental captivity and intellectual paralysis known as groupthink is the widest possible circulation—especially among a nation's top government officials—of research that has been conducted by social scientists who are independent of the government and information that has been gathered freely by media reporters. If this conclusion comes across as an unabashed plug for sociological research and the free exchange of ideas, it is. Giving free rein to diverse opinions can curb groupthink, which—if not prevented—can lead to the destruction of a society and, in today's world of nuclear, chemical, and biological weapons, the obliteration of Earth's inhabitants.

Summary *and* Review

Social Groups

What is a group?

Sociologists use many definitions of groups, but, in general, **groups** are people who think of themselves as belonging together and who interact with one another. P. 114.

How do sociologists classify groups?

Sociologists divide groups into primary groups, secondary groups, in-groups, out-groups, reference groups, and networks. The cooperative, intimate, long-term, face-to-face relationships provided by **primary groups** are fundamental to our sense of self. **Secondary groups** are larger and are more anonymous, formal, and impersonal than primary groups. **In-groups** provide members with a strong sense of identity and belonging. **Out-groups** also foster this identity by showing in-group members what they are *not*. **Reference groups** are groups whose standards we refer to as we evaluate ourselves. **Social networks** consist of social ties that link people together. The new technology has given birth to a new type of group, the **electronic community**. Pp. 115–121.

What is the "iron law of oligarchy"?

Sociologist Robert Michels noted that formal organizations have a tendency to become controlled by an inner circle that limits leadership to its own members. The dominance of a formal organization by an elite inner circle that keeps itself in power is called **the iron law of oligarchy**. P. 115.

Bureaucracies

What are the characteristics of bureaucracies?

A **bureaucracy** consists of an organization arranged in a hierarchy, with a division of labor, written rules, written communications, and impersonality and replaceability of positions. Bureaucracies tend to endure because they are efficient and because of **goal displacement** (when original goals are met, they are replaced with other goals). In a process called **the rationalization of society,** everyday tasks are taken over by bureaucracies. This is happening today with food preparation. Red tape, or obsessive following of rules, is a dysfunction of bureaucracies. Pp. 121–126.

Working for the Corporation

How does the corporate culture affect workers?

The term **corporate culture** refers to an organization's traditions, values, and unwritten norms. Much of corporate culture, such as its hidden values and stereotypes, is not readily visible. People who match a corporation's hidden values tend to be put on tracks that enhance their chances of success, while those who do not match these values tend to be set on a course that minimizes their performance. Pp. 126–127.

How do Japanese and U.S. corporations differ?

The Japanese corporate model contrasts sharply with the U.S. model in hiring and promotion, lifetime security, interaction of workers after work, broad training of workers, and collective decision making. Much of this model is a myth, an idealization of reality, and does not reflect the reality of Japanese corporate life today. Pp. 127–128.

Group Dynamics

How does a group's size affect its dynamics?

The term **group dynamics** refers to how individuals affect groups and how groups influence individuals. In a **small group,** everyone can interact directly with everyone else. As a group grows larger, its intensity decreases, and its stability increases. A **dyad,** which consists of two people, is the most unstable of human groups, but it provides the most intense or intimate relationships. The addition of a third person, forming a **triad,** fundamentally alters relationships. Triads are unstable, as **coalitions** tend to form. Pp. 129–131.

What characterizes a leader?

A **leader** is someone who influences others. **Instrumental leaders** try to keep a group moving toward its goals, even though this causes friction and they lose popularity. **Expressive leaders** focus on creating harmony and raising group morale. Both types are essential to the functioning of groups. P. 131.

What are the three main leadership styles?

Authoritarian leaders give orders, **democratic leaders** try to lead by consensus, and **laissez-faire leaders** are highly permissive. An authoritarian style appears to be more effective in emergency situations, a democratic style works best for most situations, and a laissez-faire style is usually ineffective. Pp. 131–132.

How do groups encourage conformity?

The Asch experiment was cited to illustrate the power of peer pressure, the Milgram experiment to illustrate the influence of authority. Both experiments demonstrate how easily we can succumb to **groupthink,** a kind of collective tunnel vision. Preventing groupthink requires the free circulation of contrasting ideas. Pp. 132–135.

Thinking Critically
about Chapter 5

1. Identify your in-groups and your out-groups. How have your in-groups influenced the way you see the world?

2. You are likely to work for a bureaucracy. How do you think that this will affect your orientations to life? How can you make the "hidden culture" work to your advantage?

3. Milgram's and Asch's experiments illustrate the power of peer pressure. How has peer pressure operated in your life? Think about something that you did not want to do but did anyway because of peer pressure.

Additional Resources

Companion Website www.ablongman.com/henslin

- Content Select Research Database for Sociology, with suggested key terms and annotated references
- Link to 2000 Census, with activities
- Flashcards of key terms and concepts
- Practice Tests
- Weblinks
- Interactive Maps

Where Can I Read More on This Topic?

Suggested readings for this chapter are listed at the back of this book.

Deviance and Social Control

Vincent van Gogh, *Prisoners Exercising*, 1890

What Is Deviance?
How Norms Make Social Life
  Possible
Sanctions
Competing Explanations of
  Deviance: Sociobiology,
  Psychology, and Sociology

**The Symbolic Interactionist
Perspective**
Differential Association Theory
Control Theory
Labeling Theory

The Functionalist Perspective
Can Deviance Really Be Functional
  for Society?
Strain Theory: How Social Values
  Produce Deviance
Illegitimate Opportunity
  Structures: Social Class and
  Crime

The Conflict Perspective
Class, Crime, and the Criminal
  Justice System
Power and Inequality
The Law as an Instrument of
  Oppression

Reactions to Deviance
Street Crime and Prisons
The Decline in Crime
Recidivism
The Death Penalty and Bias
Legal Change
The Medicalization of Deviance:
  Mental Illness
The Homeless Mentally Ill
The Need for a More Humane
  Approach

Summary and Review

In just a few moments I was to meet my first Yanomamö, my first primitive man. What would it be like? . . . I looked up [from my canoe] and gasped when I saw a dozen burly, naked, filthy, hideous men staring at us down the shafts of their drawn arrows. Immense wads of green tobacco were stuck between their lower teeth and lips, making them look even more hideous, and strands of dark-green slime dripped or hung from their noses. We arrived at the village while the men were blowing a hallucinogenic drug up their noses. One of the side effects of the drug is a runny nose. The mucus is always saturated with the green powder, and the Indians usually let it run freely from their nostrils. . . . I just sat there holding my notebook, helpless and pathetic. . . .

The whole situation was depressing, and I wondered why I ever decided to switch from civil engineering to anthropology in the first place. . . . [Soon] I was covered with red pigment, the result of a dozen or so complete examinations. . . . These examinations capped an otherwise grim day. The Indians would blow their noses into their hands, flick as much of the mucus off that would separate in a snap of the wrist, wipe the residue into their hair, and then carefully examine my face, arms, legs, hair, and the contents of my pockets. I said (in their language), "Your hands are dirty"; my comments were met by the Indians in the following way: they would "clean" their hands by spitting a quantity of slimy tobacco juice into them, rub them together, and then proceed with the examination.

They would "clean" their hands by spitting . . . slimy tobacco juice into them.

So went Napoleon Chagnon's eye-opening introduction to the Yanomamö tribe of the rain forests of Brazil. His ensuing months of fieldwork continued to bring surprise after surprise, and often Chagnon (1977) could hardly believe his eyes—or his nose.

If you were to start to list the deviant behaviors of the Yanomamö, what would you include? The way they appear naked in public? Use hallucinogenic drugs? Let mucus hang from their noses? Or the way they rub their hands filled with mucus, spittle, and tobacco juice over a frightened stranger who doesn't dare to protest? Per-haps. But it isn't this simple, for, as we shall see, deviance is relative.

What Is Deviance?

Sociologists use the term **deviance** to refer to any violation of norms, whether the infraction is as minor as exceeding the speed limit, as serious as murder, or as humorous as Chagnon's encounter with the Yanomamö. This deceptively simple definition takes us to the heart of the sociological perspective on deviance, which sociologist Howard S. Becker (1966) described this way: *It is not the act itself, but the reactions to the act, that make something deviant.* Chagnon was frightened by what he saw, but to the Yanomamö, those same behaviors represented normal, everyday life. What was deviant to Chagnon was *conformist* to the Yanomamö. From their viewpoint, you *should* check out strangers as they did, and nakedness is good, as are hallucinogenic drugs and letting mucus be "natural."

Chagnon's abrupt introduction to the Yanomamö allows us to see the *relativity of deviance,* a major point made by symbolic interactionists. Because different groups have different norms, *what is deviant to some is not deviant to others.* (See the photo on this page.) This principle holds both *within* a society as well as across cultures. Thus, acts that are acceptable in one culture—or in one group within a society—may be considered deviant in another culture or by another group within the same society. This idea is explored in the Cultural Diversity box on the next page.

This principle also applies to a specific form of deviance known as **crime,** the violation of rules that have been written into law. In the extreme, an act that is applauded by one group may be so despised by another group that it is punishable by death. Making a huge profit on a business deal is one example. Americans who do this are admired. Like Donald Trump, Jack Welch, and Warren Buffet, they may even write books about their exploits. However, in China, until recently, this same act was a crime called profiteering. Anyone who was found guilty was hung in a public square as a lesson to all.

Unlike the general public, sociologists use the term *deviance* nonjudgmentally, to refer to any act to which people respond negatively. When sociologists use this term, it

I took this photo on the outskirts of Hyderabad, India. Is this man deviant? If this were a U.S. street, he would be. But here? No houses have running water in his neighborhood, and the men, women, and children bathe at the neighborhood water pump. This man, then, would not be deviant in this culture. And yet he is actually mugging for my camera, making the three bystanders laugh. Does this additional factor make this a scene of deviance?

does not mean that they agree that an act is bad, just that people judge the act negatively. To sociologists, then, *all* of us are deviants of one sort or another, for we all violate norms from time to time.

To be considered deviant, a person does not even have to *do* anything. Sociologist Erving Goffman (1963) used the term **stigma** to refer to characteristics that discredit

Cultural Diversity *around the* World

Human Sexuality in Cross-Cultural Perspective

Human sexuality illustrates how a group's *definition* of an act, not the act itself, determines whether it will be considered deviant. Let's look at some examples reported by anthropologist Robert Edgerton (1976).

Norms of sexual behavior vary so widely around the world that what is considered normal in one society may be considered deviant in another. In Kenya, a group called the Pokot place high emphasis on sexual pleasure, and they expect that both a husband and wife will reach orgasm. If a husband does not satisfy his wife, he is in trouble—especially if she thinks that his failure is because of adultery. If she has such suspicions, she and her female friends will sneak up on her husband when he is asleep. The women will tie him up, shout obscenities at him, beat him, and then urinate on him. As a final gesture of their contempt, before releasing him, they will slaughter and eat his favorite ox. The husband's hours of painful humiliation are intended to make him more dutiful concerning his wife's conjugal rights.

People can also become deviants for failing to understand that the group's ideal norms may not be its real norms. As with many groups, the Zapotec Indians of Mexico

profess that sexual relations should take place exclusively between husband and wife. Yet the *only* person in one Zapotec community who had not had any extramarital affairs was considered deviant. Evidently, these people have an unspoken understanding that married couples will engage in affairs, but be discreet about them. When a wife learns that her husband is having an affair, she usually has one, too.

One Zapotec wife did not follow this covert norm. Instead, she would praise her own virtue to her husband—and then voice the familiar "headache" excuse. She also told other wives the names of the women their husbands were sleeping with. As a result, this virtuous woman was condemned by everyone in the village. Clearly, real norms can conflict with ideal norms—another illustration of the gap between ideal and real culture.

for your Consideration

How do the behaviors of the Pokot wife and husband look from the perspective of U.S. norms? Are there U.S. norms in the first place? How about the Zapotec woman? The rest of the Zapotec community? How does cultural relativity (discussed in Chapter 2, pages 38–39) apply?

people. These include violations of norms of ability (blindness, deafness, mental handicaps) and norms of appearance (a facial birthmark, obesity). They also include involuntary memberships, such as being a victim of AIDS or the brother of a rapist. The stigma can become a master status, a sort of screen through which all aspects of the person are viewed. Recall from Chapter 4 that a master status cuts across all other statuses that a person occupies.

How Norms Make Social Life Possible

No human group can exist without norms, for *norms make social life possible by making behavior predictable.* What would life be like if you could not predict what others

would do? Imagine for a moment that you have gone to a store to purchase milk:

> Suppose the clerk says, "I won't sell you any milk. We're overstocked with soda, and I'm not going to sell anyone milk until our soda inventory is reduced."
>
> You don't like it, but you decide to buy a case of soda. At the checkout, the clerk says, "I hope you don't mind, but there's a $5 service charge on every fifteenth customer." You, of course, are the fifteenth.
>
> Just as you start to leave, another clerk stops you and says, "We're not working any more. We decided to have a party." Suddenly a CD player begins to blast, and everyone in the store begins to dance. "Oh, good, you've brought the

soda," says one clerk, who takes your package and passes sodas all around.

Life is not like this, of course. You can depend on grocery clerks to sell you milk. You can also depend on paying the same price as everyone else and not being forced to attend a party in the store. Why can you depend on this? Because we are socialized to follow norms, to play the basic roles that society assigns to us.

Without norms, we would have social chaos. Norms lay out the basic guidelines for how we should play our roles and interact with others. In short, norms bring about **social order,** a group's customary social arrangements. Our lives are based on these arrangements, which is why deviance often is perceived as so threatening: Deviance undermines predictability, the foundation of social life. Consequently, human groups develop a system of **social control**—formal and informal means of enforcing norms.

Sanctions

As we discussed in Chapter 2, people do not enforce folkways strictly, but they become very upset when people break mores (MORE-ays). Actions showing disapproval of deviance, called **negative sanctions,** range from frowns and gossip for breaking folkways to imprisonment and capital

punishment for breaking mores. In general, the more seriously a group takes a norm, the harsher the penalty is for violating it. In contrast, **positive sanctions**—from smiles to formal awards—are used to reward people for conforming to norms. Getting a raise is a positive sanction; being fired is a negative sanction. Getting an A in intro to sociology is a positive sanction; getting an F is a negative one.

Most negative sanctions are informal. You probably merely stare when someone dresses in what you consider to be inappropriate clothing or just gossip if a married person you know spends the night with someone other than his or her spouse. Whether you consider the breaking of a norm simply an amusing matter that warrants no severe sanction or a serious infraction that does, however, depends on your perspective. If a woman appears at your college graduation ceremonies in a bikini, you may stare and laugh, but if this is *your* mother, you are likely to feel that different sanctions are appropriate. Similarly, if it is *your* father who spends the night with an 18-year-old college freshman, you are likely to do more than gossip.

IN SUM In sociology, the term deviance refers to all violations of social rules, regardless of their seriousness. The term is neutral, not a judgment about the behavior. Deviance is relative, for what is deviant in one group may be conformist in another. Consequently, we must consider deviance from within a group's own framework, for it is their meanings that underlie their behavior. The following Thinking Critically section focuses on this issue.

Thinking Critically

Is It Rape, or Is It Marriage? A Study in Culture Clash

Surrounded by cornfields, Lincoln, Nebraska, is about as provincial as state capitals get. Most of its residents have little experience with people from different ways of life. Their baptism into cultural diversity came as a shock.

The wedding was traditional and followed millennia-old Islamic practices (Annin and Hamilton 1996). A 39-year-old immigrant from Iraq had arranged for his two eldest daughters, ages 13 and 14, to marry two fellow Iraqi immigrants, ages 28 and 34. A Muslim cleric flew in from Ohio to perform the ceremony.

Nebraska went into shock. So did the immigrants. What is marriage in Iraq is rape in Nebraska. The husbands were charged with rape, the girls' father with child abuse, and their mother with contributing to the delinquency of minors.

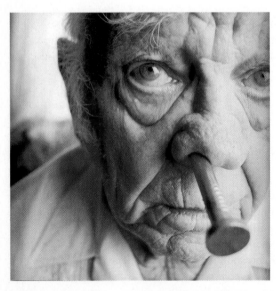

Much of our interaction is based on *background assumptions*, the unwritten, taken-for-granted "rules" that underlie our everyday lives. We don't have a "rule" that specifies "Adults, don't shove a spike up your nose," yet we all know that this rule exists. Shown here is Melvin Burkhart from Gibsonton, Florida, whose claim to fame is breaking this particular unspecified rule.

Culture conflict centered around parents giving girls like this in marriage to men 15 to 20 years older.

The event made front-page news in Saudi Arabia, where people shook their heads in amazement at Americans. Nebraskans shook their heads in amazement, too.

In Fresno, California, a young Hmong immigrant took a group of friends to a local college campus. There, they picked up the Hmong girl whom he had selected to be his wife (Sherman 1988; Lacayo 1993). The young men brought her to his house, where he had sex with her. The young woman, however, was not in agreement with this plan.

The Hmong call this *zij poj niam*, "marriage by capture." For them, this is an acceptable form of mate selection, one that mirrors Hmong courtship ideals of strong men and virtuous, resistant women. The Fresno District Attorney, however, called it kidnapping and rape.

for your Consideration

To apply *symbolic interactionism* to these real-life dramas, ask how the perspectives of the people involved explain why they did what they did. To apply *functionalism*, ask how the U.S. laws that were violated are "functional" (that is, what are their benefits, to whom?). To apply *conflict theory*, ask what groups are in conflict in these examples. (Do not focus on the individuals involved, but on the groups to which they belong.)

Understanding events in terms of different theoretical perspectives does not tell us what reaction is "right" when cultures clash. Science can analyze causes and consequences, but it cannot answer questions of what is "right" or moral. Any "ought" that you feel about these cases comes from your values—which brings us to the initial issue: the relativity of deviance.

Competing Explanations of Deviance: Sociobiology, Psychology, and Sociology

If social life is to exist, norms are essential. So why do people violate them? To better understand the reasons, it is useful to know how sociological explanations differ from biological and psychological ones.

Sociobiologists explain deviance by looking for answers *within* people. They assume that some people have **genetic predispositions** to become deviant, that they are born with characteristics that lead them to become juvenile delinquents and criminals (Lombroso 1911; Wilson and Herrnstein 1985; Lalumiere and Quinsey 2000; Williams and McShane 2004). Among their explanations are the following three theories: (1) intelligence—low intelligence leads to crime; (2) the "XYY" theory—an extra Y chromosome in males leads to crime; and (3) body type—people with "squarish, muscular" bodies are more likely to commit **street crime,** acts such as mugging, rape, and burglary.

How have these theories held up? We should first note that most people who have these supposedly "causal" characteristics do not become criminals. Regarding intelligence, you already know that some criminals are very intelligent, and that most people of low intelligence do not commit crimes. Regarding the extra Y chromosome, most men who commit crimes have the normal XY chromosome combination, and most men with the XYY combination do not become criminals. No women have this combination of genes, so this explanation can't even be applied to female criminals. Regarding body type, criminals exhibit the full range of body types, and most people with "squarish, muscular" bodies do not become street criminals.

Psychologists also focus on conditions *within* the individual. They examine what are called **personality disorders.** Their supposition is that deviating individuals have deviating personalities (Heilbrun 1990; Barnes 2001; Williams and McShane 2004) and that subconscious motives drive people to deviance. No specific childhood experience, however, is invariably linked with deviance. For example, children who had "bad toilet training," "suffocating mothers," or "emotionally aloof fathers" may become embezzling bookkeepers—or good accountants. Just as college students, teachers, and police officers represent a variety of bad—and good—childhood experiences, so do deviants. Similarly, people with "suppressed anger" can become freeway snipers or military heroes—or anything else. In short, there is no inevitable outcome of any childhood experience. Deviance is not associated with any particular personality.

Sociologists, in contrast, search for factors *outside* the individual. They look for *social* influences that "recruit" people to break norms. To account for why people commit crimes, for example, sociologists examine such external influences as socialization, membership in subcultures, and social class. *Social class*, a concept that we will discuss in depth in Chapter 8, refers to people's relative standing in terms of education, occupation, and especially income and wealth.

The point stressed earlier–that deviance is relative–leads sociologists to ask a crucial question: Why should we expect to find something constant within people to account for a behavior that is conforming in one society and deviant in another?

To see how sociologists explain deviance, let's contrast the three sociological perspectives: symbolic interactionism, functionalism, and conflict theory.

The Symbolic Interactionist Perspective

As we examine symbolic interactionism, it will become more evident why sociologists are not satisfied with explanations that are rooted in biology or personality. A basic principle of symbolic interactionism is this: We act according to how we interpret situations, not according to blind dispositions. Let's consider how our membership in groups influences our views of life and, from those, our behavior.

Differential Association Theory

The Theory Contrary to theories built around biology and personality, sociologists stress that people *learn* deviance. Edwin Sutherland coined the term **differential association** to indicate that we learn to deviate from or to conform to society's norms mostly by the *different* groups we *associate* with (Sutherland 1924, 1947; Sutherland et al. 1992). On the most obvious level, some boys and girls join Satan's Servants, while others join the Scouts. As sociologists have repeatedly demonstrated, what we learn influences us toward or away from deviance (Alarid et al. 2000; Laub and Sampson 2004).

Sutherland's theory is actually more complicated than this, but basically he said that deviance is learned. This goes directly against the view that deviance is due to biology or personality. Sutherland stressed that the different groups with which we associate (our "*differenti*al association") give us messages about conformity and deviance. We may receive mixed messages, but we end up with more of one than the other (an "excess of definitions," as Sutherland put it). The end result is an imbalance—attitudes that tilt us more in one direction than the other. Consequently, we conform or deviate.

Families Since our family is so important for teaching us attitudes, it probably is obvious to you that the family makes a big difference in whether we learn deviance or

conformity. Researchers have confirmed this informal observation. They have found that delinquents are more likely to come from families that get in trouble with the law. Of the many statistics that show this, one stands out: Of all jail inmates across the United States, about *half* have a father, mother, brother, or sister who has served time in prison (*Sourcebook of Criminal Justice Statistics* 2003: Table 6.0011). In short, families that are involved in crime tend to set their children on a lawbreaking path.

Friends, Neighborhoods, and Subcultures Most people don't know the term *differential association*, but they do know how it works. Most parents want to move out of "bad" neighborhoods because they know that if their kids have delinquent friends, they are likely to become delinquent, too. Sociological research supports this common observation (Miller 1958; Baskin and Sommers 1998; Sampson et al. 2001). Some neighborhoods even develop a subculture of violence. There, even a teasing remark can mean instant death. If the neighbors feel that a victim deserved to be killed, they refuse to testify because "he got what was coming to him" (Kubrin and Weitzer 2003).

Some neighborhoods even develop subcultures in which killing is considered an honorable act:

> Sociologist Ruth Horowitz (1983, 2005), who did participant observation in a lower-class Chicano neighborhood in Chicago, discovered how associating with people who have a certain concept of "honor" can propel young men to deviance. The formula is simple. "A real man has honor. An insult is a threat to one's honor. Therefore, not to stand up to someone is to be less than a real man."
>
> Now suppose you are a young man growing up in this neighborhood. You likely would do a fair amount of fighting, for you would interpret many things as attacks on your honor. You might even carry a knife or a gun, for words and fists wouldn't always be sufficient. Along with members of your group, you would define fighting, knifing, and shooting quite differently from the way most people do.

Members of the Mafia also intertwine ideas of manliness with violence. For them, *to kill is a measure of their manhood*. Not all killings are accorded the same respect, however, for "the more awesome and potent the victim, the more worthy and meritorious the killer" (Arlacchi 1980). Some killings are done to enforce norms. A member of the Mafia who gives information to the police, for example, has violated *omertá* (the Mafia's vow of secrecy). This offense can never be tolerated, for it threatens the very existence of the group. Mafia killings further illustrate just

To experience a sense of belonging is a basic human need. Membership in groups, especially peer groups, is a primary way that people meet this need. Regardless of the orientation of the group—whether to conformity or to deviance—the process is the same. Shown here are members of the Mara Salvatrucha street gang in San Salvador's Tonatepeque penitentiary for underage prisoners.

how relative deviance is. Although killing is deviant to mainstream society, for members of the Mafia, *not* to kill after certain rules are broken—such as when someone "squeals" to the cops—is the deviant act.

Prison or Freedom? As was mentioned in Chapter 3, an issue that comes up over and over again in sociology is whether we are prisoners of socialization. Symbolic interactionists stress that we are not mere pawns in the hands of others. We are not destined by our group memberships to think and act as our groups dictate. Rather, we *help to produce our own orientations to life.* By joining one group rather than another (differential association), for example, we help to shape the self. For instance, one college student may join a feminist group that is trying to improve the treatment of women on campus; another may associate with a group of women who shoplift on weekends. Their choice of groups points them in different directions. The one who associates with shoplifters may become even more oriented toward criminal activities, while the one who joins the feminist group may develop an even greater interest in bringing about social change.

Control Theory

Inside most of us, it seems, are strong desires to do things that would get us in trouble—inner drives, temptations, urges, hostilities, and so on. Yet most of us stifle these desires most of the time. Why?

The Theory Sociologist Walter Reckless (1973), who developed **control theory,** stresses that two control systems work against our motivations to deviate. Our *inner controls* include our internalized morality—conscience, religious principles, ideas of right and wrong. Inner controls also include fear of punishment, feelings of integrity, and the desire to be a "good" person (Hirschi 1969; Rogers 1977; Williams and McShane 2004). Our *outer controls* consist of people—such as family, friends, and the police—who influence us not to deviate.

The stronger our bonds are with society, the more effective our inner controls are (Hirschi 1969). Bonds are based on *attachments* (feeling affection and respect for people who conform to mainstream norms), *commitments* (having a stake in society that you don't want to risk, such as a respected place in your family, a good standing at college, a good job), *involvements* (putting time and energy into approved activities), and *beliefs* (believing that certain actions are morally wrong).

This theory can be summarized as *self*-control, says sociologist Travis Hirschi. The key to learning high self-control is socialization, especially in childhood. Parents help their children to develop self-control by supervising them and punishing their deviant acts (Gottfredson and Hirschi 1990).

Applying the Theory

Suppose that some friends have invited you to a nightclub. When you get there, you notice that everyone seems unusually happy—giddy would be a better word. They seem to be euphoric in their animated conversations and dancing. Your friends tell you that almost everyone here has taken the drug Ecstasy, and they invite you to take some with them.

What do you do? Let's not explore the question of whether taking Ecstasy in this setting is a deviant or a conforming act. That is a different question. Instead, concentrate on the pushes and pulls you would feel. The pushes toward taking the drug: your friends, the setting, and your curiosity. Then there are the inner controls: the inner voices of your conscience and your parents, perhaps of your teachers, as well as your fears of arrest and of the dangers of illegal drugs. There are also the outer controls—perhaps the uniformed security guard looking in your direction.

So what *did* you do? Which was stronger: your inner and outer controls or the pushes and pulls toward taking the drug? It is you who can best weigh these forces, for they differ with each of us.

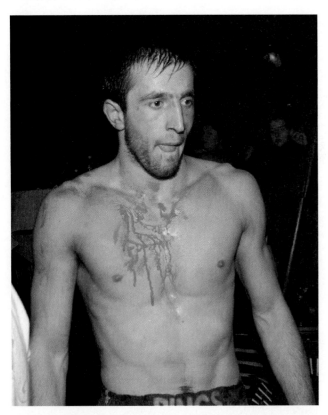

The social control of deviance takes many forms some rather subtle. With its mayhem, "cage fighting" might look like the opposite of social control, but it is a way to channel aggressive impulses in a way that leaves no vendetta, feud, or "score to settle."

Labeling Theory

Symbolic interactionists have developed **labeling theory,** which focuses on the significance of the labels (names, reputations) that we are given. Labels tend to become a part of our self-concept and help to set us on paths that either propel us into or divert us from deviance. Let's look at how people react to society's labels—from "whore" and "pervert" to "cheat" and "slob."

Rejecting Labels: How People Neutralize Deviance

Most people resist the negative labels that others try to pin on them. Some are so successful that even though they persist in deviance, they still consider themselves conformists. For example, even though they beat up people and vandalize property, some delinquents consider themselves to be conforming members of society. How do they do it?

Sociologists Gresham Sykes and David Matza (1957/1988) studied boys like this. They found that they use five **techniques of neutralization** to deflect society's norms:

Denial of Responsibility. Some boys said, "I'm not responsible for what happened because . . ." and then were quite creative about the "becauses." Some said that what happened was an "accident." Other boys saw themselves as "victims" of society. What else could you expect? They were like billiard balls shot around the pool table of life.

Denial of Injury. Another favorite explanation of the boys was "What I did wasn't wrong because no one got hurt." They would define vandalism as "mischief," gang fights as a "private quarrel," and stealing cars as "borrowing." They might acknowledge that what they did was illegal but claim that they were "just having a little fun."

Denial of a Victim. Some boys thought of themselves as avengers. Vandalizing a teacher's car was done to get revenge for an unfair grade, while shoplifting was a way to even the score with "crooked" store owners. In short, even if the boys did accept responsibility and admit that someone did get hurt, they protected their self-concept by claiming that the people "deserved what they got."

Condemnation of the Condemners. Another technique the boys used was to deny that others had the right to judge them. They might accuse people who pointed their fingers at them of being "a bunch of hypocrites": The police were "on the take," teachers had "pets," and parents cheated on their taxes. In short, they said, "Who are they to accuse me of something?"

Appeal to Higher Loyalties. A final technique the boys used to justify antisocial activities was to consider loyalty to the gang more important than following the norms of society. They might say, "I had to help my friends. That's why I got in the fight." Not incidentally, the boy may have shot two members of a rival group as well as a bystander!

■ ◣ ■ **IN SUM** These five techniques of neutralization have implications far beyond these boys, for it is not only delinquents who try to neutralize the norms of mainstream society. Look again at these five techniques—don't they sound familiar? (1) "I couldn't help myself"; (2) "Who really got hurt?"; (3) "Don't you think she deserved that, after what *she* did?"; (4) "Who are *you* to talk?"; and (5) "I had to help my friends—wouldn't you have done the same thing?" All of us attempt to neutralize the moral demands of society, for neutralization helps us to sleep at night.

Embracing Labels: The Example of Outlaw Bikers

Although most of us resist others' attempts to label us as deviant, there are those who revel in a deviant identity. Some teenagers, for example, make certain by their clothing, choice of music, and hairstyles that no one misses their rejection of adult norms. Their status among fellow members of a subculture—within which they are almost obsessive conformists—is vastly more important than any status outside it.

One of the best examples of a group that embraces deviance is motorcycle gangs. Sociologist Mark Watson (1980/2006) did participant observation with outlaw bikers. He rebuilt Harleys with them, hung around their bars and homes, and went on "runs" (trips) with them. He concluded that outlaw bikers see the world as "hostile, weak, and effeminate." They pride themselves on looking "dirty, mean, and generally undesirable" and take pleasure in provoking shocked reactions to their appearance. Holding the conventional world in contempt, they also pride themselves on getting into trouble, laughing at death, and treating women as lesser beings whose primary value is to provide them with services—especially sex. Outlaw bikers also regard themselves as losers, a factor that becomes woven into their unusual embrace of deviance.

The Power of Labels: The Saints and the Roughnecks

We can see how powerful labeling is by referring back to the study of the "Saints" and the "Roughnecks" that was cited in Chapter 4 (pages 106–107). As you recall, both groups of high school boys were "constantly occupied with truancy, drinking, wild parties, petty theft, and vandalism." Yet their teachers looked on the Saints as "headed for success" and the Roughnecks as "headed for trouble." By the time they finished high school, not one Saint had been arrested, while the Roughnecks had been in constant trouble with the police.

Why did the community see these boys so differently? William Chambliss (1973/2005) concluded that this split vision was due to *social class.* As symbolic interactionists emphasize, social class vitally affects our perceptions and behavior. The Saints came from respectable, middle-class families; the Roughnecks from less respectable, working-class families. These backgrounds led teachers and the authorities to expect good behavior from the Saints but trouble from the Roughnecks. And like the rest of us, teachers and police saw what they expected to see.

The boys' social class also affected their visibility. The Saints had automobiles, and they did their drinking and vandalism outside of town. Without cars, the Roughnecks hung around their own street corners, where their boisterous behavior drew the attention of police and confirmed the ideas that community members already had of them.

The boys' social class also equipped them with distinct *styles of interaction.* When police or teachers questioned them, the Saints were apologetic. Their show of respect for authority elicited a positive reaction from teachers and police, allowing the Saints to escape school and legal problems. The Roughnecks, said Chambliss, were "almost the polar opposite." When questioned, they were hostile. Even when they tried to assume a respectful attitude, everyone could see through it. Consequently, while teachers and police let the Saints off with warnings, they came down hard on the Roughnecks.

Although what happens in life is not determined by labels alone, the Saints and the Roughnecks did live up to the labels that the community gave them. As you recall, all but one of the Saints went on to college. One earned a Ph.D., one became a lawyer, one a doctor, and the others business managers. In contrast, only two of the Roughnecks went to college. They earned athletic scholarships and became coaches. The other Roughnecks did not fare so well. Two of them dropped out of high school, later became involved in separate killings, and were sent to prison. One became a local bookie, and no one knows the whereabouts of the other.

How do labels work? Although the matter is complex, because it involves the self-concept and reactions that vary from one individual to another, we can note that labels open and close doors of opportunity. Unlike its use in sociology, the label *deviant* is a judgmental term in everyday usage. This label can lock people out of conforming groups and push them into almost exclusive contact with people who have similar labels.

IN SUM Symbolic interactionists examine how people's definitions of the situation underlie their deviating from or conforming to social norms. They focus on group membership (differential association), how people balance pressures to conform and to deviate (control theory), and the significance of the labels that are given to people (labeling theory).

The Functionalist Perspective

When we think of deviance, its dysfunctions are likely to come to mind. Functionalists, in contrast, are as likely to stress the functions of deviance as they are to emphasize its dysfunctions.

Can Deviance Really Be Functional for Society?

Most of us are upset by deviance, especially crime, and assume that society would be better off without it. The classic functionalist theorist Emile Durkheim (1893/1933, 1895/1964), however, came to a surprising conclusion. Deviance, he said, including crime, is functional for society, for it contributes to the social order. Its three main functions are:

1. *Deviance clarifies moral boundaries and affirms norms.* A group's ideas about how people should act and think mark its *moral boundaries.* Deviant acts challenge those boundaries. To call a member into account is to say, in effect, "You broke an important rule, and we cannot tolerate that." To punish deviants affirms the group's norms and clarifies what it means to be a member of the group.
2. *Deviance promotes social unity.* To affirm the group's moral boundaries by punishing deviants fosters a "we" feeling among the group's members. In saying, "You can't get by with that," the group collectively affirms the rightness of its own ways.
3. *Deviance promotes social change.* Groups do not always agree on what to do with people who push beyond their accepted ways of doing things. Some group members may even approve of the rule-breaking behavior. Boundary violations that gain enough support become new, acceptable behaviors. Thus, deviance may force a group to rethink and redefine its moral boundaries, helping groups—and whole societies—to change their customary ways.

Strain Theory: How Social Values Produce Deviance

Functionalists argue that crime is a *natural* part of society, not an aberration or some alien element in our midst. Indeed, they say, some mainstream values actually generate crime. To understand what they mean, consider what sociologists Richard Cloward and Lloyd Ohlin (1960) identified as the crucial problem of the industrialized world: the need to locate and train the most talented people of every generation—whether they were born into wealth or into poverty—so that they can take over the key technical jobs of modern society. When children are born, no one knows which ones will have the ability to become dentists, nuclear physicists, or engineers. To get the most talented people to compete with one another, society tries to motivate *everyone* to strive for success. It does this by arousing discontent—making people feel dissatisfied with what they have so that they will try to "better" themselves.

Most people, then, end up with strong desires to reach **cultural goals** such as wealth or high status or to achieve whatever other objectives society holds out for them. Not everyone, however, has equal access to society's **institutionalized means,** the legitimate ways of achieving success. Some people, for example, find their path to education and good jobs blocked. These people experience *strain* or frustration, which may motivate them to take a deviant path.

This perspective, known as **strain theory,** was developed by sociologist Robert Merton (1956, 1968). People who experience strain, he said, are likely to feel *anomie,* a sense of normlessness. Because mainstream norms (work, education) don't seem to be getting them anywhere, people who experience strain find it difficult to identify with mainstream norms. They may even feel wronged by the system, and its rules may seem illegitimate (Anderson 1978).

Table 6.1 compares people's reactions to cultural goals and institutionalized means. The first reaction, which Merton said is the most common, is *conformity,* using socially acceptable means to try to reach cultural goals. In industrialized societies, most people try to get good jobs, a good education, and so on. If well-paid jobs are unavailable, they take less desirable jobs. If they are denied

| Table 6.1 | How People Match Their Goals to Their Means | | |

Do They Feel the Strain That Leads to Anomie?	Mode of Adaptation	Cultural Goals	Institutionalized Means
No	Conformity	Accept	Accept
Yes	**Deviant Paths:**		
	1. Innovation	Accept	Reject
	2. Ritualism	Reject	Accept
	3. Retreatism	Reject	Reject
	4. Rebellion	Reject/Replace	Reject/Replace

access to Harvard or Stanford, they go to a state university. Others take night classes and go to vocational schools. In short, most people take the socially acceptable road.

Four Deviant Paths The remaining four responses, which are deviant, represent reactions to strain. Let's look at each. *Innovators* are people who accept the goals of society but use illegitimate means to try to reach them. Crack dealers, for instance, accept the goal of achieving wealth, but they reject the legitimate avenues for doing so. Other examples are embezzlers, robbers, and con artists.

The second deviant path is taken by people who become discouraged and give up on achieving cultural goals. Yet they still cling to conventional rules of conduct. Merton called this response *ritualism*. Although ritualists have given up on getting ahead at work, they survive by following the rules of their job. Teachers whose idealism is shattered (who are said to suffer from "burnout"), for example, remain in the classroom, where they teach without enthusiasm. Their response is considered deviant because they cling to the job although they have abandoned the goal, which may have been to stimulate young minds or to make the world a better place.

People who choose the third deviant path, *retreatism*, reject both the cultural goals and the institutionalized means of achieving them. Those who drop out of the pursuit of success by way of alcohol or drugs are retreatists. Although their withdrawal takes a much different form, women who enter a convent or men a monastery are also retreatists.

The final type of deviant response is *rebellion*. Convinced that their society is corrupt, rebels, like retreatists, reject both society's goals and its institutionalized means. Unlike retreatists, however, they seek to give society new goals. Revolutionaries are the most committed type of rebels.

IN SUM | *Strain theory* underscores the sociological principle that deviants are the product of society. Mainstream social values (cultural goals and institutionalized means to reach those goals) can produce strain (frustration, dissatisfaction). People who feel this strain are more likely than others to take the deviant (nonconforming) paths summarized in Table 6.1.

Illegitimate Opportunity Structures: Social Class and Crime

One of the more interesting sociological discoveries in the study of deviance is the finding that the social classes have distinct styles of crime. Let's see how unequal access to the institutionalized means to success helps to explain this.

Street Crime Functionalists point out that industrialized societies have no trouble socializing the poor into wanting to own things. Like others, the poor are bombarded with messages urging them to buy everything from X Boxes and iPods to designer jeans and new cars. Television and movies show images of middle-class people enjoying luxurious lives. These images reinforce the myth that all full-fledged Americans can afford society's many goods and services.

In contrast, the school system, the most common route to success, often fails the poor. The middle class runs it, and there the children of the poor confront a bewildering world, one that is at odds with their background. Their speech, with its nonstandard grammar, is often sprinkled with what the middle class considers obscenities. Their ideas of punctuality, as well as their poor preparation in paper-and-pencil skills, are also a mismatch with their new environment. Facing such barriers, the poor are more likely than their more privileged counterparts to drop out of school. Educational failure, in turn, closes the door on many legitimate avenues to financial success.

Not infrequently, however, a different door opens to the poor, one that sociologists Richard Cloward and Lloyd Ohlin (1960) called **illegitimate opportunity structures.** Woven into the texture of life in urban slums, for example, are robbery, burglary, drug dealing, prostitution, pimping, gambling, and other remunerative crimes, commonly called "hustles" (Liebow 1967/1999; Anderson 1978, 1990, 2006; Bourgois 1994). For many of the poor, the "hustler" is a role model—glamorous, in control, the image of "easy money," one of the few people in the area who comes close to attaining the cultural goal of success. For such reasons, then, these activities attract disproportionate numbers of the poor. As is discussed in the Down-to-Earth Sociology box below, gangs are one way that the illegitimate opportunity structure beckons disadvantaged youth.

White-Collar Crime The more privileged social classes are not crime-free, of course, but for them, different illegitimate opportunities beckon. They find *other forms* of crime to be functional. Physicians, for example, don't hold up cabbies, but many do cheat Medicare. You've heard about bookkeepers who embezzle from their employers and corporate officers who manipulate stock prices. In other words, rather than mugging, pimping, and burglary, the more privileged encounter "opportunities" for evading income tax, bribing public officials, embezzling, and so on. Sociologist Edwin Sutherland (1949) coined the term **white-collar crime** to refer to crimes that people of respectable and high social status commit in the course of their occupations.

A special form of white-collar crime is **corporate crime,** crimes committed by executives to benefit their corporation. For example, to increase corporate profits, Sears executives

Down-to-Earth Sociology

Islands in the Street: Urban Gangs in the United States

FOR MORE THAN TEN YEARS, SOCIOLOGIST Martín Sánchez Jankowski (1991) did participant observation of thirty-seven African American, Chicano, Dominican, Irish, Jamaican, and Puerto Rican gangs in Boston, Los Angeles, and New York City. The gangs earned money through gambling, arson, mugging, armed robbery, and selling moonshine, drugs, guns, stolen car parts, and protection. Jankowski ate, slept, and sometimes fought with the gangs, but by mutual agreement he did not participate in drug dealing or in other illegal activities. He was seriously injured twice during the study.

Contrary to stereotypes, Jankowski did not find that the motive for joining a gang was to escape a broken home (there were as many members from intact families as from broken homes) or to seek a substitute family (the same number of boys said they were close to their families as those that said they were not). Rather, the boys joined to gain access to money, to have recreation (including girls and drugs), to maintain anonymity in committing crimes, to get protection, and to help the community. This last reason

may seem surprising, but in some neighborhoods, gangs protect residents from outsiders and spearhead political change (Kontos et al. 2003). The boys also saw the gang as an alternative to the dead-end—and deadening—jobs held by their parents.

Neighborhood residents are ambivalent about gangs. On the one hand, they fear the violence. On the other hand, many of the adults once belonged to gangs, the gangs often provide better protection than the police, and gang members are the children of people who live in the neighborhood.

Particular gangs will come and go, but gangs will likely always remain part of the city. As functionalists point out, gangs fulfill needs of poor youth who live on the margins of society.

for your Consideration

What are the functions that gangs fulfill (the needs they meet)? Suppose that you have been hired as an urban planner by the City of Los Angeles. How could you arrange to meet the needs that gangs fulfill in ways that minimize violence and encourage youth to follow mainstream norms?

defrauded the poor of over $100 million. Their victims were so poor that they had filed for bankruptcy. To avoid a criminal trial, Sears pleaded guilty. This frightened the parent companies of Macy's and Bloomingdale's, which had similar deceptive practices, and they settled with their debtors out of court (McCormick 1999a). Similarly, Citigroup had to pay $70 million for preying on the poor (O'Brien 2004).

One of the most notorious corporate crimes was the decision by Firestone executives to let faulty tires remain on U.S. vehicles—even though they were recalling the tires in Saudi Arabia and Venezuela. These tires cost the lives of about 200 Americans (White et al. 2001).

Seldom is corporate crime taken seriously, even when it results in death. No Firestone or Ford executive went to jail. Consider this: Under federal law, causing the death of a worker by willfully violating safety rules is a misdemeanor punishable by up to six months in prison. Yet to harass a wild burro on federal lands is punishable by a year in prison (Barstow and Bergman 2003).

At $400 billion a year (Reiman 2004), "crime in the suites" actually costs more than "crime in the streets." This refers only to dollar costs. No one has yet figured out a way to compare, for example, the suffering experienced by a rape victim with the pain felt by an elderly couple who have lost their life savings to white-collar fraud.

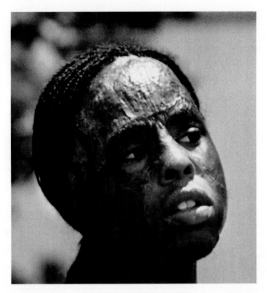

Most white-collar crime is a harmless nuisance, but some brings horrible costs. Shown here is Alisha Parker, who, with three siblings, was burned when the gas tank of her 1979 Chevrolet Malibu exploded after a rear-end collision. Although General Motors executives knew about the problem with the Malibu gas tanks, they had ignored it. Outraged at the callousness of GM's conduct, the jury awarded these victims the staggering sum of $4.9 billion.

Figure 6.1 **Some States Are Safer: Violent Crime in the United States**

Violent crimes are murder, rape, robbery, and aggravated assault. The U.S. average is 495 per 100,000 people, but the rate varies widely among the states. The chances of becoming a victim of these crimes are *ten* times higher in South Carolina, the most dangerous state, than in North Dakota, the safest state. Washington, D.C., not a state, is in a class by itself. Its rate of 1,633 is more than three times the national average and over 20 times North Dakota's rate.

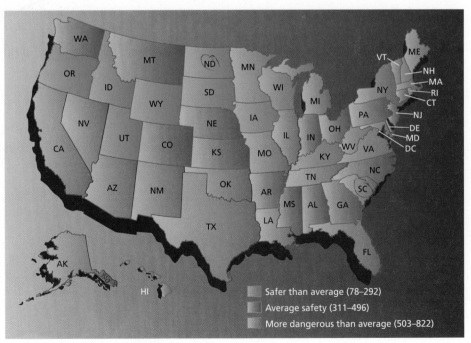

Safer than average (78–292)
Average safety (311–496)
More dangerous than average (503–822)

Source: By the author. Based on *Statistical Abstract* 2005:Table 291.

The greatest concern of Americans, however, is street crime. They fear the violent stranger who will change their life forever. As the Social Map on page 151 shows, the chances of such an encounter depend on where you live. From this map, you can see that entire regions are safer or more dangerous than others. In general, the northern states are the safest and the southern states the most dangerous.

Gender and Crime A major change in the nature of crime is the growing number of female offenders. As Table 6.2 shows, women are committing a larger percentage of criminal acts—from stealing cars to possessing illegal weapons. The basic reason for this increase is women's changed social location. As more women work in factories, corporations, and the professions, their opportunities for crime increase. Like men, women are also enticed by illegitimate opportunities.

IN SUM Functionalists conclude that much street crime is the consequence of socializing everyone into equating success with owning material possessions, while denying many in the lower social classes the legitimate means to attain that success. People from different social classes encounter different opportunities to commit crimes. The growing crime rates of women illustrate how changing gender roles are giving more women access to illegitimate opportunities.

The Conflict Perspective

Class, Crime, and the Criminal Justice System

> Two leading U.S. aerospace companies, Hughes Electronics and Boeing Satellite Systems, were accused of illegally exporting missile technology to China. The technology places the United States at risk, for it allowed China to improve its delivery system for nuclear weapons. The two companies pleaded guilty and paid fines. No executives went to jail. (Gerth 2003)

Social class divides people in such distinct ways of life that even crime and punishment differ by social class. Shown here is Martha Stewart after her release from prison, as she shows off her ankle monitoring device during a news conference. Stewart has good reason to laugh. For her conviction for obstructing justice in the investigation of her illegal stock trading, she served 5 months in a prison consisting of a campuslike collection of cottages in the West Virginia mountains.

Table 6.2 Women and Crime: What a Difference Ten Years Make

Of all those arrested, what percentage are women?

Crime	1992	2002[1]	Change
Car Theft	10.8%	16.4%	+52%
Burglary	9.2%	13.2%	+43%
Stolen Property[2]	12.5%	17.9%	+43%
Aggravated Assault	14.8%	20.3%	+37%
Drunken Driving	13.8%	17.4%	+26%
Robbery	8.5%	10.1%	+19%
Forgery and Counterfeiting	34.7%	39.9%	+15%
Larceny/Theft	32.1%	36.9%	+15%
Arson	13.4%	15.1%	+13%
Illegal Drugs	16.4%	18.0%	+10%
Fraud	42.1%	45.5%	+8%
Illegal Weapons[3]	7.5%	8.1%	+8%

[1] Latest year available; national U.S. arrests.
[2] Buying, receiving, possessing.
[3] Carrying, possessing.
Source: By the author. Based on *Statistical Abstract* 1994:Table 317; 2005:Table 309.

Contrast this corporate crime—which places you in danger—with newspaper reports about young people who are sentenced to several years in prison for stealing cars. How can a legal system that is supposed to provide "justice for all" be so inconsistent? According to conflict theorists, this question is central to the analysis of crime and the **criminal justice system**—the police, courts, and prisons that deal with people who are accused of having committed crimes. Let's see what answer conflict theorists have.

Power and Inequality

Conflict theorists regard power and social inequality as the main characteristics of society. They stress that the power elite that runs society also controls the criminal justice system. This group makes certain that laws are passed that will protect its position in society. Other norms, such as

those that govern informal behavior (chewing with a closed mouth, appearing in public with combed hair, and so on), may come from other sources, but they simply are not as important. Such norms influence our everyday behavior, but they do not determine who has power or who gets sent to prison.

Conflict theorists see the most fundamental division in capitalist society as that between the few who own the means of production and the many who do not, those who sell their labor and the privileged few who buy it. Those who buy labor, and thereby control workers, make up the **capitalist class;** those who sell their labor form the **working class.** Toward the most depressed end of the working class is the **marginal working class**–people who have few skills, who are subject to layoffs, and whose jobs are low paying, part time, or seasonal. This class is marked by unemployment and poverty. From its ranks come most of the prison inmates in the United States. Desperate, these people commit street crimes, and because their crimes threaten the social order that keeps the elite in power, they are punished severely.

The Law as an Instrument of Oppression

According to conflict theorists, the idea that the law operates impartially and administers a code that is shared by all is a cultural myth promoted by the capitalist class. These theorists see the law as an instrument of oppression, a tool designed by the powerful to maintain their privileged position (Spitzer 1975; Reiman 2004; Chambliss 2000, 2006). Because the working class has the potential to rebel and overthrow the current social order, the law comes down hard on members of this class when they get out of line.

For this reason, the criminal justice system does not focus on the owners of corporations and the harm they do through unsafe products, pollution, and price manipulations. Instead, it directs its energies against violations by the working class. The violations of the capitalist class cannot be ignored totally, however, for if they become too outrageous or oppressive, the working class might rise up and revolt. To prevent this, a flagrant violation by a member of the capitalist class is occasionally prosecuted. The publicity given to the case helps to stabilize the social system by providing evidence of the "fairness" of the criminal justice system.

Usually, however, the powerful are able to bypass the courts altogether, appearing instead before an agency that has no power to imprison (such as the Federal Trade Commission). People from wealthy backgrounds who sympathize with the intricacies of the corporate world direct these agencies. It is they who oversee most cases of manipulating the price of stocks, insider trading, violating

By using hyperbole to create humor, the cartoonist comments on the social class disparity of our criminal justice system.

fiduciary duty, and so on. Is it surprising, then, that the typical sanction for corporate crime is a token fine?

When groups that have been denied access to power gain that access, we can expect to see changes in the legal system. This is precisely what is occurring now. Racial-ethnic minorities and homosexuals, for example, have more political power today than ever before. In line with conflict theory, a new category called *hate crime* has been formulated. We analyze this change in a different context on pages 160–161.

IN SUM | From the perspective of conflict theory, the small penalties that are imposed for crimes committed by the powerful are typical of a legal system that has been designed by the elite (capitalists) to keep themselves in power, to control workers, and, ultimately, to stabilize the social order. From this perspective, law enforcement is a cultural device through which the capitalist class carries out self-protective and repressive policies.

Reactions to Deviance

Whether it is cheating on a sociology quiz or holding up a liquor store, any violation of norms invites reaction. Let's look at some of these reactions.

Street Crime and Prisons

Today, we don't make people wear scarlet letters, but we do remove them from society and make them wear prison uniforms. And we still use degradation ceremonies—in this case, a public trial and an announcement (the sentencing) that someone is "unfit" to live among "decent, law-abiding people" for some specified period of time.

Figure 6.2 illustrates the remarkable growth in the U.S. prison population. The number of prisoners is actually higher than the total shown in this figure. If we add jail inmates, the total comes to over two million people—one out of every 143 citizens. Not only does the United States have more prisoners than any other nation, but also it has a larger percentage of its population in prison as well (Pager 2003; Fernandez-Kelly 2004). To keep up with the growth in prisoners, the states have even hired private companies to operate jails for them. About 100,000 prisoners are in these "private" jails (Harrison and Beck 2005:Table 3).

To see how U.S. prisoners compare with the U.S. population, look at Table 6.3. Several things may strike you. Almost all prisoners (87 percent) are ages 18 to 44, and almost all of them are men. Then there is this remarkable statistic: Although African Americans make up just 12.2 percent of the U.S. population, close to half of all prisoners are African Americans. On any given day, about one out of eight African American men ages 20 to 34 is in jail or prison (Butterfield 2003). Finally, you might note how marriage—one of the major techniques society has of "anchoring" us—provides protection from prison.

As I mentioned earlier, social class funnels some people into the criminal justice system and others away from it. Look at the education totals on this table. You can see how the chances of ending up in prison are higher for people who do not complete high school—and how unlikely it is for a college graduate to have this unwelcome destination in life.

Figure 6.2 How Much Is Enough? The Explosion in the Number of U.S. Prisoners

To better understand how remarkable this change is, compare the prison growth with the growth of the U.S. population. Between 1970 and 2000, the U.S. population grew 38 percent, while the U.S. prison population grew *16 times* as fast (605 percent). If the U.S. prison population had grown at the same rate as the U.S. population, there would be about 270,000 prisoners, one fifth of the actual number. (Or if the U.S. population had increased at the same rate as that of U.S. prisoners, the U.S. population would be 1,423,000,000—more than the population of China.)

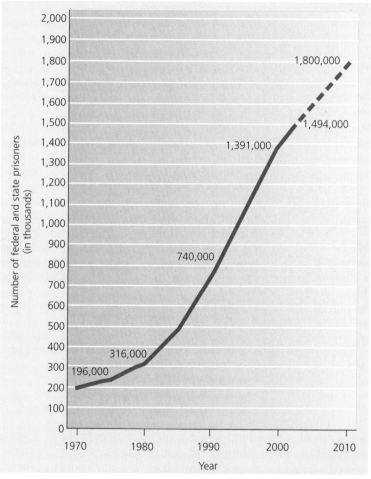

Source: By the author. Based on *Statistical Abstract* 1995:Table 349, 2005:Table 336. Harrison and Beck 2005:Table 2. The broken line is the author's estimate.

For about the past 20 years, the United States has followed a "get tough" policy. "Three strikes and you're out" laws (a mandatory sentence, sometimes life imprisonment, upon conviction for a third felony) have become common. While few of us would feel sympathy if a man convicted of a third brutal rape or a third murder were sent to prison

Table 6.3 Inmates in U.S. State Prisons

Characteristics	Percentage of Prisoners with These Characteristics	Percentage of U.S. Population with These Characteristics
Age		
18–24	26.4%	9.9%
25–34	35.4%	13.9%
35–44	25.2%	15.3%
45–54	10.4%	14.0%
55 and older	1.0%	21.9%
Race-Ethnicity		
African American	46.3%	12.2%
White	35.8%	68.0%
Latino	16.1%	13.7%
Native Americans	0.8%	4.1%
Asian Americans	1.0%	0.8%
Sex		
Male	89.6%	49.1%
Female	10.4%	50.9%
Marital Status		
Never Married	59.8%	24.4%
Divorced	15.5%	10.1%
Married	17.3%	58.8%
Widowed	1.1%	6.6%
Education		
Less than high school	44.0%	15.4%
High school graduate	43.2%	32.0%
Some college	9.6%	25.4%
College graduate (BA or higher)	3.1%	27.2%

Sources: *Sourcebook of Criminal Justice Statistics* 2003:Tables 6.000b, 6.28; *Statistical Abstract* 2005:Tables 11, 51, 53, 214; Figure 12.5 of this text.

for life, as discussed in the following Thinking Critically section, these laws have had unanticipated consequences.

Thinking Critically

"Three Strikes and You're Out!": Unintended Consequences of Well-Intended Laws

In the 1980s, violent crime soared. Americans grew fearful, and they demanded that their lawmakers do something. Politicians heard the message, and they responded by passing the "three strikes" law. Anyone who is convicted of a third felony receives an automatic mandatory sentence. Judges are not allowed to consider the circumstances. Some mandatory sentences carry life imprisonment.

In their haste to appease the public, the politicians did not limit these laws to *violent* crimes. And they did not consider that some minor crimes are considered felonies. As the functionalists would say, this has led to unanticipated consequences.

Here are some actual cases (Cloud 1998).

- In California, a 21-year-old anthropology major was sentenced to 10 years for mailing sheets of LSD to her boyfriend.

- In Los Angeles, a 27-year-old man was sentenced to 25 years for stealing a pizza.
- In New York City, a man who was about to be sentenced for selling crack said to the judge, "I'm only 19. This is terrible." He then hurled himself out of a courtroom window, plunging to his death sixteen stories below.
- In Sacramento, a man who passed himself off as Tiger Woods to go on a $17,000 shopping spree was sentenced to 200 years in prison (Reuters 2001).
- In California, a man who stole nine videotapes from Kmart was sentenced to 50 years in prison without parole. He appealed to the U.S. Supreme Court, which upheld his sentence (Greenhouse 2003).

for your Consideration

Apply the symbolic interactionist, functionalist, and conflict perspectives to mandatory sentencing. For *symbolic interactionism*, what do these laws represent to the public? How does your answer differ depending on what part of "the public" you are referring to? For *functionalism*, who benefits from these laws? What are some of their dysfunctions? For the *conflict perspective*, what groups are in conflict? Who has the power to enforce their will on others?

The Decline in Crime

As you saw in Figure 6.2, judges have put more and more people in prison. In addition, legislators passed the three-strikes laws and reduced early releases of prisoners. As these changes occurred, the crime rate dropped sharply, which has led to a controversy in sociology. Some sociologists conclude that getting tough on criminals was the main reason for the drop in crime (Conklin 2003). Other sociologists place greater emphasis on

higher employment and a drop in drug use (Rosenfeld 2002; Reiman 2004). This matter is not yet settled, but both tough sentencing and the economy seem to be important factors.

Recidivism

A major problem with prisons is that they fail to teach their clients to stay away from crime. Our **recidivism rate**—the percentage of former prisoners who are rearrested—is high. For those who are sentenced to prison for crimes of violence, within just three years of their release, two out of three (62 percent) are rearrested, and half (52 percent) are back in prison. The recidivism rate for people convicted of property offenses is even higher (*Sourcebook of Criminal Justice* Statistics 2002:Table 6.44). Figure 6.3 shows recidivism by type of crime. It is safe to conclude that if—and this is a big if—the purpose of prisons is to teach people that crime doesn't pay, then prisons are colossal failures.

Beneath the humor of this cartoon lies a serious point about the high recidivism of U.S. prisoners.

Figure 6.3   Recidivism of U.S. Prisoners

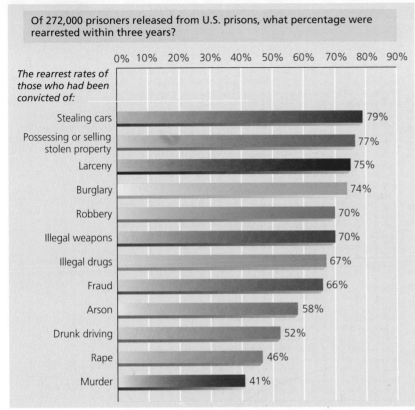

Of 272,000 prisoners released from U.S. prisons, what percentage were rearrested within three years?

The rearrest rates of those who had been convicted of:

Stealing cars	79%
Possessing or selling stolen property	77%
Larceny	75%
Burglary	74%
Robbery	70%
Illegal weapons	70%
Illegal drugs	67%
Fraud	66%
Arson	58%
Drunk driving	52%
Rape	46%
Murder	41%

Note: The individuals were not necessarily rearrested for the same crime for which they had originally been imprisoned.
Source: By the author. Based on *Sourcebook of Criminal Justice Statistics* 2002:Table 6.44.

The Death Penalty and Bias

Capital punishment, the death penalty, is the most extreme measure the state takes. The death penalty is mired in controversy, arousing impassioned opposition and support on both moral and philosophical grounds. Advances in DNA testing have given opponents of the death penalty a strong argument: Innocent people have been executed. Others are passionate about retaining the death penalty, pointing to such crimes as those of the serial killers discussed in the Down-to-Earth Sociology box on the next page.

Apart from anyone's personal position on the death penalty, it certainly is clear that the death penalty is not administered evenly. Consider geography: As the Social Map below shows *where* people commit murder greatly affects their chances of being put to death.

Figure 6.4
Executions in the United States

Executions since 1977, when the death penalty was reinstated.

Source: By the author. Based on *Statistical Abstract* 2005:Table 342.

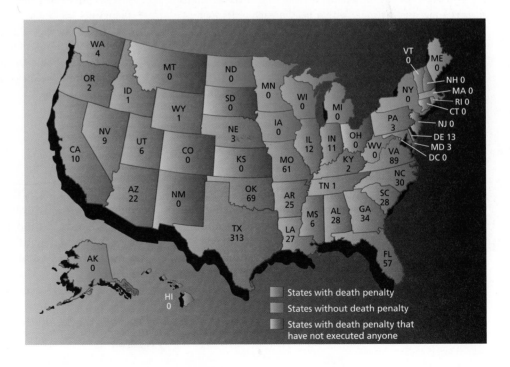

Down-to-Earth Sociology

The Killer Next Door: Serial Murderers in Our Midst

I WAS STUNNED BY THE IMAGES. Television cameras showed the Houston police digging up dozens of bodies in a boat storage shed. Fascinated, I waited impatiently for spring break. A few days later, I drove from Illinois to Houston, where 33-year-old Dean Corll had befriended Elmer Wayne Henley and David Brooks, two teenagers from broken homes. Together, they had killed 27 boys. Elmer and David would pick up young hitchhikers and deliver them to Corll to rape and kill. Sometimes they even brought him their high school classmates.

I talked to one of Elmer's neighbors, as he was painting his front porch. His 15-year-old son had gone to get a haircut one Saturday morning; it was the last time he had seen his son alive. The police insisted that the boy had run away, and they refused to investigate. On a city map, I plotted the locations of the homes of the local murder victims. Many clustered around the homes of the teenage killers.

I was going to spend my coming sabbatical writing a novel on this case, but, to be frank, I became frightened and didn't write the book. I didn't know if I could recover psychologically if I were to immerse myself in grisly details day after day for months on end. One of these details was a piece of plywood, with a hole in each of its four corners. Corll and the boys would spread-eagle their victims handcuffed to the plywood. There, they would torture and rape the boys (no girl victims) for hours. Sometimes, they would even pause to order pizza.

My interviews confirmed what has since become common knowledge about serial killers: They lead double lives so successfully that their friends and family are unaware of their criminal activities. Henley's mother swore to me that her son was a good boy and couldn't possibly be guilty. Some of his high school friends told me the same thing. They stressed that Elmer couldn't be involved in homosexual rape and murder because he was interested only in girls. I conducted my interviews in Henley's bedroom, and for proof of what they told me, his friends pointed to a pair of girls' panties that were draped across a lamp shade.

Serial murder is the killing of several victims in three or more separate events. The murders may occur over several days, weeks, or years. The elapsed time between murders distinguishes serial killers from *mass murderers*, who do their killing all at once. Here are some infamous examples:

- Between 1962 and 1964, Albert De Salvo ("the Boston Strangler") raped and killed 13 women.
- During the 1960s and 1970s, Ted Bundy raped and killed dozens of women in four states.
- In the 1970s, John Wayne Gacy raped and killed 33 young men in Chicago.
- Between 1979 and 1981, Wayne Williams killed 28 boys and young men in Atlanta.
- During the 1980s and 1990s, the "Green River" killer scattered the bodies of prostitutes around the countryside near Seattle, Washington. In 2003, Gary Ridgway was convicted of the crimes and given 48 consecutive life sentences for killing 48 women.

The death penalty also shows social class bias. As you know from news reports on murder and sentencing, it is rare for a rich person to be sentenced to death. Although the government does not collect statistics on social class and the death penalty, this common observation is borne out by the average education of the prisoners on death row. *Most* prisoners on death row (52%) have not finished high school (*Sourcebook of Criminal Justice Statistics* 2003:Table 6.78).

Figure 6.5 on page 160 shows gender bias in the death penalty. It is almost unheard of for a woman to be sentenced to death. Although women commit 11.6 percent of the murders, they make up only 1.6 percent of death row inmates. It is possible that this statistic reflects not only gender bias but also the relative brutality of the women's murders. We need research to determine this.

The bias that once put a stop to the death penalty was flagrant. Seeing this bias in the courtroom, Donald

- In 2005, in Wichita, Kansas, Dennis Rader was charged as the BTK (Bind, Torture, and Kill) strangler, a name he had proudly given himself. His 10 killings spanned 1974 to 1991.
- The serial killer with the most victims appears to be Harold Shipman of Manchester, England. From 1977 to 2000, this quiet, unassuming physician killed 230 to 275 of his elderly women patients. While making house calls, he gave the women lethal injections.
- One of the most bizarre serial killers was Jeffrey Dahmer of Milwaukee. Dahmer fried and ate parts of his victims. So he wouldn't go hungry, he kept body parts in his freezer.

Almost all serial killers are men, but an occasional woman joins this list of infamy:

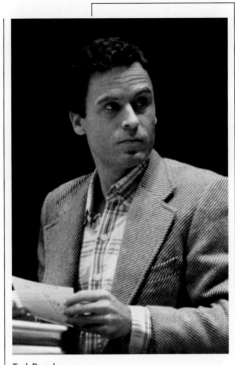

Ted Bundy

- In North Carolina, Blanche Taylor Moore used arsenic to kill her father, her first husband, and a boyfriend. She was tripped up in 1986 when she tried to poison her current husband.
- In 1987 and 1988, Dorothea Montalvo Puente, who operated a boarding house in Sacramento, killed 7 of her boarders. Her motive was to collect their Social Security checks.
- In Missouri, from 1986 to 1989, Faye Copeland and her husband killed 5 transient men.
- In the late 1980s and early 1990s, Aileen Wuornos, hitchhiking along Florida's freeways, killed 7 men after having sex with them.

Many serial killers are motivated by lust and are sexually aroused by killing, so the FBI sometimes uses the term "lust murder." As with Ted Bundy and Jeffrey Dahmer, some have sex with their dead victims. Bundy returned day after day to the countryside to copulate with the corpses of his victims. Other serial killers, however, like Dorothea Puente, are more "garden variety"—motivated by greed and killing for money.

Is serial murder more common now than it used to be? Not likely. In the past, police departments had little communication with one another. When killings occurred in different jurisdictions, seldom did anyone connect them. Today's more efficient communications, investigative techniques, and DNA matching make it easier for the police to conclude that a serial killer is operating in an area. Part of the perception that there are more serial killers today is also due to ignorance of our history: In our frontier past, serial killers went from ranch to ranch (and mass murderers wiped out entire villages of Native Americans).

for your Consideration

Do you think that serial killers should be given the death penalty? Why or why not? How do your social locations influence your opinion?

Partington (1965), a Virginia lawyer, decided to document it. He found that 2,798 men had been convicted for rape and attempted rape in Virginia between 1908 and 1963—56 percent whites and 44 percent blacks. For attempted rape, 13 had been executed. For rape, 41 men had been executed. *All those executed were black.* Not one of the whites was executed.

After listening to evidence like this, in 1972 the Supreme Court ruled in *Furman* v. *Georgia* that the

death penalty was unconstitutionally applied. The execution of prisoners stopped—but not for long. The states wrote new laws, and in 1977 they again began to execute prisoners. Since then, 65 percent of those put to death have been white and 35 percent African American (*Statistical Abstract* 2005:Table 341). (Latinos are evidently counted as whites in this statistic.) Table 6.4 on the next page shows the race-ethnicity of the prisoners who are on death row.

Figure 6.5 Women and Men on Death Row

98.4%

1.6%

Men   Women

Source: By the author. Based on *Sourcebook of Criminal Justice Statistics* 2005: Table 6.81.

Table 6.4 The Racial-Ethnic Makeup of the 3,486 Prisoners on Death Row

	Percentage	
	on Death Row	in U.S. Population
Whites	46%	68%
African Americans	42%	12%
Latinos	10%	14%
Native Americans	1%	1%
Asian Americans	1%	4%

Source: By the author. Based on Sourcebook of *Criminal Justice Statistics* 2005:Table 6.80 and Figure 12.5 of this text.

Legal Change

Did you know that it is a crime in Iran for women to wear makeup? A crime in Florida for merchants to sell alcohol before 1 P.M. on Sundays? Illegal in Wells, Maine, to advertise on tombstones? As has been stressed in this chapter, deviance, including the form called *crime*, is relative. It varies from one society to another, and from group to group within a society. Crime also varies from one time period to another, as opinions change or as different groups gain access to power.

Let's consider legal change.

Thinking Critically

Changing Views: Making Hate a Crime

Because crime is whatever acts authorities choose to pass laws against, new crimes emerge from time to time. A prime example is juvenile delinquency, which Illinois lawmakers designated as a separate type of crime in 1899. Juveniles committed crimes before this time, of course, but youths were not considered to be a separate type of lawbreaker. They were just young people who committed crimes, and they were treated the same as adults who committed the same crime. Sometimes new technology brings new crimes. Motor vehicle theft, a separate crime in the United States, obviously did not exist before the automobile was invented.

In the 1980s, another new crime was born when state governments developed the classification **hate crime.** This is a crime that is motivated by bias (dislike, hatred) against someone's race-ethnicity, religion, sexual orientation, disability, or national origin. Before this, of course, people attacked others or destroyed their property out of these same motivations, but in those cases, the motivation was not the issue. If someone injured or killed another person because of that person's race-ethnicity, religion, sexual orientation, national origin, or disability, he or she was charged with assault or murder. Today, motivation has become a central issue, and hate crimes carry more severe sentences than do the same acts that do not have hatred as their motive. Table 6.5 summarizes the victims of hate crimes.

We can be certain that the "evolution" of crime is not yet complete. As society changes and as different groups gain access to power, we can expect the definitions of crime to change accordingly.

Table 6.5 Hate Crimes

Directed Against	Number of Victims
Race-Ethnicity	
African Americans	3,076
Whites	910
Latinos	639
Asian Americans	280
Native Americans	72
Religion	
Jews	1,084
Muslims	174
Catholics	71
Protestants	58
Sexual Orientation	
Male Homosexual	984
Female Homosexual	221
Homosexuals (general)	267
Heterosexuals	26
Bisexual	15
Disabilities	
Mental	30
Physical	20

The latest year available is 2002.
Source: Statistical Abstract 2005:Table 301.

for your Consideration

Why should we have a separate classification called hate crime? Why aren't the crimes of assault, robbery, and murder adequate? As one analyst (Sullivan 1999) said, "Was the brutal murder of gay college student Matthew Shepard [a hate crime] in Laramie, Wyoming, in 1998 worse than the abduction, rape, and murder of an eight-year-old Laramie girl [not a hate crime] by a pedophile that same year?"

How do you think your social location (race-ethnicity, gender, social class, sexual orientation, or physical ability) affects your opinion?

The Medicalization of Deviance: Mental Illness

Another way in which society deals with deviance is to "medicalize" it. Let's look at what this entails.

Neither Mental Nor Illness? To *medicalize* something is to make it a medical matter, to classify it as a form of illness that properly belongs in the care of physicians. For the past hundred years or so, especially since the time of Sigmund Freud (1856–1939), the Viennese physician who founded psychoanalysis, there has been a growing tendency toward the **medicalization of deviance.** In this view, deviance, including crime, is a sign of mental sickness. Rape, murder, stealing, cheating, and so on are external symptoms of internal disorders, consequences of a confused or tortured mind.

Thomas Szasz (1986, 1996, 1998), a renegade in his profession of psychiatry, argues that *mental illnesses are neither mental nor illnesses. They are simply problem behaviors.* Some forms of so-called mental illnesses have organic causes; that is, they are *physical* illnesses that result in unusual perceptions or behavior. Some depression, for example, is caused by a chemical imbalance in the brain; this can be treated by drugs. The depression, however, may show itself as crying, long-term sadness, and lack of interest in family, work, school, or one's appearance. When someone becomes deviant in ways that disturb others *and* when these others cannot find a satisfying explanation for why the person is "like that," a "sickness in the head" is often taken as the cause of the unacceptable behavior.

All of us have troubles. Some of us face a constant barrage of problems as we go through life. Most of us continue the struggle, encouraged perhaps by relatives and friends and motivated by job, family responsibilities, religious faith, and life goals. Even when the odds seem hopeless, we carry on, not perfectly, but as best we can.

Some people, however, fail to cope well with life's challenges. Overwhelmed, they become depressed, uncooperative, or hostile. Some strike out at others, while some, in Merton's terms, become retreatists and withdraw into their apartments or homes, not wanting to come out. These are *behaviors, not mental illnesses,* stresses Szasz. They may be inappropriate coping devices, but they are coping devices, nevertheless, not mental illnesses. Thus, Szasz concludes that "mental illness" is a myth foisted on a naive public by a medical profession that uses pseudoscientific jargon in order to expand its area of control and force nonconforming people to accept society's definitions of "normal."

Szasz's extreme claim forces us to look anew at the forms of deviance that we usually refer to as mental illness. To explain behavior that people find bizarre, he directs our attention not to causes hidden deep within the "subconscious" but, instead, to how people learn such behaviors. To ask, "What is the origin of inappropriate or bizarre behavior?" then becomes similar to asking, "Why do some women steal?" "Why do some men rape?" "Why do some teenagers cuss their parents and stalk out of the room, slamming the door?" *The answers depend on those people's particular experiences in life, not on an illness in their mind.* In short, some sociologists find Szasz's renegade analysis refreshing because it indicates that *social experiences,* not some illness of the mind, underlie bizarre behaviors—as well as deviance in general.

The Homeless Mentally Ill

Jamie was sitting on a low wall surrounding the landscaped courtyard of an exclusive restaurant. She appeared unaware of the stares that were elicited by her many layers of mismatched clothing, her dirty face, and the shopping cart that overflowed with her meager possessions.

Every once in a while Jamie would pause, concentrate, and point to the street, slowly moving her finger horizontally. I asked her what she was doing.

"I'm directing traffic," she replied. "I control where the cars go. Look, that one turned right there," she said, now withdrawing her finger.

"Really?" I said.

After a while she confided that her cart talked to her.

"Really?" I said again.

"Yes," she replied. "You can hear it, too." At that, she pushed the shopping cart a bit.

"Did you hear that?" she asked.

When I shook my head, she demonstrated again.

Then it hit me. She was referring to the squeaking wheels!

I nodded.

When I left, Jamie was pointing to the sky, for, as she told me, she also controlled the flight of airplanes.

To most of us, Jamie's behavior and thinking are bizarre. They simply do not match any reality we know. Could you or I become like Jamie?

Suppose for a bitter moment that you are homeless and have to live on the streets. You have no money, no place to sleep, no bathroom. You do not know *if* you are going to eat, much less where. You have no friends or anyone you can trust, and you live in constant fear of rape and other violence. Do you think this might be enough to drive you over the edge?

Consider just the problems involved in not having a place to bathe. (Shelters are often so dangerous that many homeless people prefer to sleep in public settings.) At first, you try to wash in the rest rooms of gas stations, bars, the bus station, or a shopping center. But you are dirty, and people stare when you enter and call the management when they see you wash your feet in the sink. You are thrown out and told in no uncertain terms never to come back. So you get dirtier and dirtier. Eventually, you come to think of being dirty as a fact of life. Soon, maybe, you don't even care. The stares no longer bother you—at least not as much.

No one will talk to you, and you withdraw more and more into yourself. You begin to build a fantasy life. You talk openly to yourself. People stare, but so what? They stare anyway. Besides, they are no longer important to you.

Jamie might be mentally ill. Some organic problem, such as a chemical imbalance in her brain, might underlie her behavior. But perhaps not. How long would it take you to exhibit bizarre behaviors if you were homeless—and hopeless? The point is that *just being on the streets can cause mental illness*—or whatever we want to label socially inappropriate behaviors that we find difficult to classify. *Homelessness and mental illness are reciprocal:* Just as "mental illness" can cause homelessness, so the trials of being homeless, of living on cold, hostile streets, can lead to unusual and unacceptable thinking and behaviors.

The Need for a More Humane Approach

As Durkheim (1895/1964:68) pointed out, deviance is inevitable—even in a group of saints:

> Imagine a society of saints, a perfect cloister of exemplary individuals. Crimes, properly so called, will there be unknown; but faults which appear [invisible] to the layman will create there the same scandal that the ordinary offense does in ordinary [society].

With deviance inevitable, one measure of a society is how it treats its deviants. Our prisons certainly don't say much good about U.S. society. Filled with the poor, they are warehouses of the unwanted. They reflect patterns of broad discrimination in our larger society. White-collar criminals continue to get by with a slap on the wrist, while street criminals are punished severely. Some deviants, who fail to meet current standards of admission to either prison or mental hospital, take refuge in shelters, as well as in cardboard boxes tucked away in urban recesses. Although no one has *the* answer, it does not take much reflection to see that there are more humane approaches than these.

Because deviance is inevitable, the larger issues are to find ways to protect people from deviant behaviors that are harmful to themselves or others, to tolerate those behaviors that are not harmful, and to develop systems of fairer treatment for deviants. In the absence of fundamental changes that would bring about a truly equitable social system, most efforts are, unfortunately, like putting a Band Aid on a gunshot wound. What we need is a more humane social system, one that would prevent the social inequalities that are the focus of the next four chapters.

People whose behaviors violate norms often are called mentally ill. "Why else would they do such things?" is a common response to deviant behaviors that we don't understand. Mental illness is a label that contains the assumption that there is something wrong "within" people that "causes" their disapproved behavior. The surprise with this man, who changed his legal name to "Scary Guy," is that he speaks at schools across the country, where he promotes acceptance, awareness, love, and understanding.

Summary *and* Review

What Is Deviance?

From a sociological perspective, **deviance** (the violation of norms) is relative. What people consider deviant varies from one culture to another and from group to group within the same society. As symbolic interactionists stress, it is not the act, but the reactions to the act, that make something deviant. All groups develop systems of **social control** to punish **deviants**—those who violate their norms. Pp. 140–143.

How do sociological and individualistic explanations of deviance differ?

To explain why people deviate, sociobiologists and psychologists look for reasons *within* the individual, such as **genetic predispositions** or **personality disorders.** Sociologists, in contrast, look for explanations *outside* the individual, in social experiences. P. 143.

The Symbolic Interactionist Perspective

How do symbolic interactionists explain deviance?

Symbolic interactionists have developed several theories to explain deviance such as **crime** (the violation of norms that have been written into law). According to **differential association theory,** people learn to deviate by associating with others. According to **control theory,** each of us is propelled toward deviance, but most of us conform because of an effective system of inner and outer controls. People who have less effective controls deviate. Pp. 144–146.

   Labeling theory focuses on how labels (names, reputations) help to funnel people into or away from deviance. People who commit deviant acts often use **techniques of neutralization** to continue to think of themselves as conformists. Pp. 146–148.

The Functionalist Perspective

How do functionalists explain deviance?

Functionalists point out that deviance, including criminal acts, is functional for society. Functions include affirming norms and promoting social unity and social change. According to **strain theory,** societies socialize their members into desiring **cultural goals.** Many people are unable to achieve these goals in socially acceptable ways—that is, by **institutionalized means.** *Deviants,* then, are people who either give up on the goals or use deviant means to attain them. Merton identified five types of responses to cultural goals and institutionalized means: conformity, innovation, ritualism, retreatism, and rebellion. **Illegitimate opportunity theory** stresses that some people have easier access to illegal means of achieving goals. Pp. 148–152.

The Conflict Perspective

How do conflict theorists explain deviance?

Conflict theorists take the position that the group in power (the **capitalist class**) imposes its definitions of deviance on other groups (the **working class** and the **marginal working class**). From the conflict perspective, the law is an instrument of oppression used to maintain the power and privilege of the few over the many. The marginal working class has little income, is desperate, and commits highly visible property crimes. The ruling class directs the **criminal justice system,** using it to punish the crimes of the poor while diverting its own criminal activities away from this punitive system. Pp. 152–153.

Reactions to Deviance

What are common reactions to deviance in the United States?

In following a "get-tough" policy, the United States has imprisoned millions of people. African Americans and Latinos make up a disproportionate percentage of U.S. prisoners. The death penalty shows biases by geography, social class, race-ethnicity, and gender. In line with conflict theory, as groups gain political power, their views are reflected in the criminal code. **Hate crime** legislation was considered in this context. Pp. 154–161.

What is the medicalization of deviance?

The medical profession has attempted to **medicalize** many forms of deviance, asserting that they represent mental illnesses. Thomas Szasz disagrees, claiming that they are problem behaviors, not mental illnesses. Research on homeless people illustrates how problems in living can lead to bizarre behavior and thinking. Pp. 161–163.

Thinking Critically
about Chapter 6

1. Select some form of deviance with which you are personally familiar. (It does not have to be your own—it can be something that someone you know did.) Choose one of the three theoretical perspectives to explain what happened.

2. As is explained in the text, deviance can be mild. Recall some instance in which you broke a social rule in dress, etiquette, or speech. What was the reaction? Why do you think people reacted like that? What was your reaction to their reactions?

3. What do you think should be done about the U.S. crime problem?

Additional Resources

Companion Website www.ablongman.com/henslin

- Content Select Research Database for Sociology, with suggested key terms and annotated references
- Link to 2000 Census, with activities
- Flashcards of key terms and concepts

- Practice Tests
- Weblinks
- Interactive Maps

Where Can I Read More on This Topic?

Suggested readings for this chapter are listed at the back of this book.

Global Stratification

Franklin McMahon, *Farmers Work in Rice Paddies in Taiwan*

OUTLINE

Systems of Social Stratification
Slavery
Caste
Class
Global Stratification and the Status of Females

What Determines Social Class?
Karl Marx: The Means of Production
Max Weber: Property, Prestige, and Power

Why Is Social Stratification Universal?
The Functionalist Perspective: Motivating Qualified People
The Conflict Perspective: Class Conflict and Scarce Resources
Lenski's Synthesis

How Do Elites Maintain Stratification?
Ideology Versus Force

Comparative Social Stratification
Social Stratification in Great Britain
Social Stratification in the Former Soviet Union

Global Stratification: Three Worlds
The Most Industrialized Nations
The Industrializing Nations
The Least Industrialized Nations

How Did the World's Nations Become Stratified?
Colonialism
World System Theory
Culture of Poverty
Evaluating the Theories

Maintaining Global Stratification
Neocolonialism
Multinational Corporations
Technology and Global Domination
A Concluding Note

Summary and Review

For Getu Mulleta, 33, and his wife, Zenebu, 28, of rural Ethiopia, life is a constant struggle to keep themselves and their seven children from starving. They live in a 320-square-foot manure-plastered hut with no electricity, gas, or running water. They have a radio, but the battery is dead. The family farms teff, a grain, and survives on $130 a year.

The Mulletas' poverty is not due to a lack of hard work. Getu works about 80 hours a week, while Zenebu puts in even more hours. "Housework" for Zenebu includes fetching water, making fuel pellets out of cow dung for the open fire over which she cooks the family's food, and cleaning animal stables. Like other Ethiopian women, she eats after the men.

In Ethiopia, the average male can expect to live to age 48, the average female to 50.

The Mulletas' most valuable possession is their oxen. Their wishes for the future: more animals, better seed, and a second set of clothing.

* * * * * *

Springfield, Illinois, is home to the Kellys—Rick, 36, Patti, 34, Julie, 10, and Michael, 7. The Kellys live in a four-bedroom, 2-1/2 bath, 2,330-square-foot, carpeted ranch-style house, with a fireplace, central heating and air conditioning, a basement, and a two-car garage. Their home is equipped with a refrigerator, washing machine, clothes dryer, dishwasher, garbage disposal, vacuum cleaner, food processor, microwave, and toaster. They also own six telephones (three cellular), four color televisions, three radios, two CD players, a digital camera, digital camcorder, DVD player, iPod, X-box, and a computer, printer, scanner, and fax machine, not to mention two blow dryers, an answering machine, a blender, an electric can opener, and four electric toothbrushes. This count doesn't include the stereo-radio-CD players in their pickup truck and SUV.

Rick works 40 hours a week as a cable splicer for a telephone company. Patti teaches school part time. Together they make $51,680, plus benefits. The Kellys can choose from among dozens of super-stocked supermarkets. They spend $4,431 for food they eat at home, and another $3,014 eating out, a total of 14 percent of their annual income.

> **They live in a 320-square-foot manure-plastered hut with no electricity, gas, or running water.**

In the United States, the average life expectancy is 75 for males, 81 for females.

On the Kellys' wish list are a new SUV with satellite radio, a 160-gigabyte laptop with Bluetooth wi-fi, a 50-inch plasma TV with TiVo and surround sound, a DVD camcorder, a boat, a motor home, an ATV, and, oh, yes, farther down the road, an in-ground heated swimming pool. They also have their eye on purchasing a cabin at a nearby lake.

Sources: Menzel 1994; *Population Today* 2004; *Statistical Abstract* 2005:Tables 92, 661, 670, 930.

Systems of Social Stratification

Some of the world's nations are wealthy, others are poor, and some are in between. This division of nations, as well as the layering of groups of people within a nation, is called *social stratification.* Social stratification is one of the most significant topics we discuss in this book, for it affects our life chances—as you saw in the opening vignette—from our access to material possessions to the age at which we die.

Social stratification also affects the way we think about life. If you had been born into the Ethiopian family in our opening vignette, for example, you would be illiterate and would assume that your children would be as well. You also would expect hunger to be a part of life and would not expect all of your children to survive. Contrast this with the expectations of a typical American parent—not only that their children will be well-fed and reach adulthood, but also that they will go to college. You can see how social stratification brings with it ideas of what we can expect out of life.

Social stratification is a system in which groups of people are divided into layers according to their relative property, prestige, and power. It is important to emphasize that social stratification does not refer to individuals. It is a way of ranking large groups of people into a hierarchy according to their relative privileges.

It also is important to note that *every society stratifies its members.* Some societies have greater inequality than others, but social stratification is universal. In addition, in every society of the world, *gender* is a basis for stratifying people. On the basis of their gender, people are either allowed or denied access to the good things offered by their society.

Let's consider three systems of social stratification: slavery, caste, and class.

Slavery

Slavery, whose essential characteristic is that *some individuals own other people,* has been common in world history. The Old Testament even lays out rules for how the Israelites should treat their slaves. The Romans also had slaves, as did the Africans and the Greeks. Slavery was the most common in agricultural societies and the least common among nomads, especially hunters and gatherers (Landtman 1938/1968). As we examine the major causes and conditions of slavery, you will see how remarkably slavery has varied around the world.

Causes of Slavery. Contrary to popular assumption, slavery was usually based not on racism but on one of three other factors. The first was *debt.* In some cultures, creditors would enslave people who could not pay their debts. The second was *crime.* Instead of being killed, a murderer or thief might be enslaved by the victim's family as compensation

Under slavery, humans are sold like a commodity. This 1784 announcement reveals that slaves could be bought for cash or exchanged for produce (crops).

for their loss. The third was *war.* When one group of people conquered another, they often enslaved some of the vanquished (Starna and Watkins 1991). Historian Gerda Lerner (1986) notes that the first people who were enslaved through warfare were women. When tribal men raided a village or camp, they killed the men, raped the women, and then brought the women back as slaves. The women were valued for sexual purposes, for reproduction, and for their labor.

Roughly twenty-five hundred years ago, when Greece was but a collection of city-states, slavery was common. A city that became powerful and conquered another city would enslave some of the vanquished. Both slaves and slaveholders were Greek. Similarly, when Rome became the supreme power of the Mediterranean area about two thousand years ago, following the custom of the time, the Romans enslaved some of the Greeks they had conquered. More educated than their conquerors, some of these slaves served as tutors in Roman homes. Slavery, then, was a sign of debt, of crime, of defeat in battle. It was not a sign that the slave was inherently inferior.

Conditions of Slavery. The conditions of slavery have varied widely around the world. *In some cases, slavery was temporary.* Slaves of the Israelites were set free in the year of jubilee, which occurred every fifty years. Roman slaves ordinarily had the right to buy themselves out of slavery. They knew what their purchase price was, and some were able to meet this price by striking a bargain with their owner and selling their services to others. In most instances, however, slavery was a lifelong condition. Some criminals, for example, became slaves when they were given life sentences as oarsmen on Roman war ships. There they served until death, which often came quickly to those in this exhausting service.

Slavery was not necessarily inheritable. In most places, the children of slaves were automatically slaves themselves. But in some instances, the child of a slave who served a rich family might even be adopted by that family, becoming an heir who bore the family name along with the other sons or daughters of the household. In ancient Mexico, the children of slaves were always free (Landtman 1938/ 1968:271).

Slaves were not necessarily powerless and poor. In almost all instances, slaves owned no property and had no power. Among some groups, however, slaves could accumulate property and even rise to high positions in the community. Occasionally, a slave might even become wealthy, loan money to the master, and, while still a slave, own slaves

himself or herself (Landtman 1938/1968). This situation, however, was rare.

Slavery in the New World. With a growing need for labor, some colonists tried to enslave Indians. This attempt failed miserably. One reason was that when Indians escaped, they knew how to survive in the wilderness and were able to make their way back to their tribe. The colonists then turned to Africans, who were being brought to North and South America by the Dutch, English, Portuguese, and Spanish.

Because slavery has a broad range of causes, some analysts conclude that racism didn't lead to slavery but, rather, slavery led to racism. Finding it profitable to make people slaves for life, U.S. slave owners developed an **ideology,** beliefs that justify social arrangements. Ideology leads to a picture of the world that makes current social arrangements seem inevitable, necessary, and fair. The colonists developed the view that the slaves were inferior. Some even said that they were not fully human. In short, the colonists wove elaborate justifications for slavery, built on the presumed superiority of their own group.

To make slavery even more profitable, slave states passed laws that made slavery *inheritable;* that is, the babies born to slaves became the property of the slave owners (Stampp 1956). These children could be sold, bartered, or traded. To strengthen their control, slave states passed laws making it illegal for slaves to hold meetings or to be away from the master's premises without carrying a pass (Lerner 1972). As sociologist W. E. B. Du Bois (1935/1992:12) noted, "gradually the entire white South became an armed camp to keep Negroes in slavery and to kill the black rebel."

The Civil War did not end legal discrimination. For example, until 1954, the states operated two separate school systems. Even until the 1950s, to keep the races from "mixing," it was illegal in Mississippi for a white and an African American to sit together on the same seat of a car! The reason there was no outright ban on blacks and whites being in the same car was to allow for African American chauffeurs.

Slavery Today. Slavery has again reared its ugly head, this time in the Ivory Coast, Mauritania, Niger, and Sudan. This region has a long history of slavery, and not until the 1980s was slavery made illegal in Mauritania and Sudan (Ayittey 1998). It took until 2004 for slavery to be banned in Niger (Andersson 2005). Although officially abolished, slavery continues, the topic of the Mass Media box on the next page.

mass **Media** **in social life**

What Price Freedom? Slavery Today

Children of the Dinka tribe in rural Sudan don't go to school. They work. Their families depend on them to tend the cattle that are so important to their way of life.

> On the morning of the raid, ten-year-old Adhieu had been watching the cattle. "We were very happy because we would soon leave the cattle camps and return home to our parents. But in the morning, there was shooting. There was yelling and crying everywhere. My uncle grabbed me by the hand, and we ran. We swam across the river. I saw some children drowning. We hid behind a rock."

By morning's end, 500 children were either dead or enslaved. Their attackers were their fellow countrymen—Arabs from northern Sudan. The children who were captured were forced to march hundreds of miles north. Some escaped on the way. Others tried to—and were shot (Akol 1998).

Tens of thousands of Dinkas have been killed or enslaved since civil war broke out in Sudan in the 1980s. Yet the Arab-led government—the National Islamic Front—insists that slavery does not exist. It claims that the alleged slavery is an invention of foreign politicians, Christian humanitarians, and hostile foreign media (Akol 1998). But there are too many witnesses and there is too much documentation by human rights groups. There also are devastating accounts by journalists: In the United States, public television (PBS) has even run film footage of captive children in chains. Then there are the slaves who manage to escape, who recount their ordeal in horrifying detail (Dottridge 2001; Salopek 2003).

The United States bombed Kosovo into submission for its crimes against humanity, yet it has remained largely silent in the face of this outrage. A cynic might say that Kosovo was located at a politically strategic spot in Europe, whereas Sudan occupies an area of Africa in which the U.S. and European powers have little interest. A cynic might add that these powers fear Arab retaliation, which might take the form of oil embargoes and terrorism. A cynic might also suggest that outrages against black Africans are not as significant to these powers as those against white Europeans. Finally, a cynic might add that this will change as the oil below the surface in Sudan becomes more important.

Appalled by the lack of response on the part of the world's most powerful governments, private groups have stepped in. Christian Solidarity International (CSI), based in Zurich, Switzerland, uses a controversial technique. Arab "retrievers" go to northern Sudan, where they either buy or abduct slaves. Walking by night and hiding by day, they elude security forces and bring the slaves south. There, CSI pays the retrievers $50 per slave (Mabry 1999).

> As CBS news cameras rolled, the rescuer paid the slave trader $50,000 in Sudanese pounds. At $50 per person, the bundle of bills was enough to free 1,000 slaves. The liberated slaves, mostly women and children, were then free to return to their villages. (Jacobs 1999)

Critics claim that buying slaves, even to free them, encourages slavery. The money provides motivation to enslave people in order to turn around and sell them. Fifty dollars is a lot of money in Sudan, where the average income for an entire year is $1,740 (Haub 2004). It is also the price of two or three goats (Gaviak 2000).

That is a bogus argument, replies CSI. What is intolerable is to leave women and children in slavery where they are deprived of their freedom and families and are beaten and raped by brutal masters.

for your Consideration

What do you think about buying the freedom of slaves? Can you suggest a workable alternative? Why do you think the U.S. government has remained inactive about this issue for so long when it has invaded other countries for human rights abuses? Do you think that perhaps its excursions into such places as Haiti and Kosovo were politically motivated, that they had little to do with human rights? If not, why the silence in the face of slavery?

The media coverage of this issue has motivated many Americans to become active in freeing slaves. Some high schools—and even grade schools—are raising money to participate in slave buy-back programs. If you were a school principal, would you encourage this practice? Why or why not?

In this photo, a representative of the Liason Agency Network (on the left) is buying the freedom of the Sudanese slaves (in the background).

Caste

The second system of social stratification is caste. In a **caste system,** status is determined by birth and is lifelong. Someone who is born into a low-status group will always have low status, no matter how much that person may accomplish in life. In sociological terms, a caste system is built on ascribed status. Achieved status cannot change an individual's place in this system.

Societies with this form of stratification try to make certain that the boundaries between castes remain firm. They

During my research in India, I interviewed this 8-year-old girl. Mahashury is a *bonded laborer* who was exchanged by her parents for a 2,000 rupee loan (about $14). To repay the loan, Mahashury must do construction work for one year. She will receive one meal a day and one set of clothing for the year. Because this centuries-old practice is now illegal, the master bribes Indian officials, who inform him when they are going to inspect the construction site. He then hides his bonded laborers. I was able to interview and photograph Mahashury because her master was absent the day I visited the construction site.

practice **endogamy,** marriage within their own group, and prohibit intermarriage. To reduce contact between castes, they even develop elaborate rules about *ritual pollution,* teaching that contact with inferior castes contaminates the superior caste.

India's Religious Castes. India provides the best example of a caste system. Based not on race but on religion, India's caste system has existed for almost three thousand years (Chandra 1993; Berger 2005). India's four castes are depicted in Table 7.1. These four main castes are subdivided into thousands of subcastes, or *jati.* Each subcaste specializes in a particular occupation. For example, one *jati* washes clothes, another sharpens knives, and yet another repairs shoes.

The lowest group listed on Table 7.1, the Dalit, make up India's "untouchables." If a Dalit touches someone of a higher caste, that person becomes unclean. Even the shadow of an untouchable can contaminate. Early morning and late afternoons are especially risky, for the long shadows of these periods pose a danger to everyone higher up the caste system. Consequently, Dalits are not allowed in some villages during these times. Anyone who becomes contaminated must follow *ablution,* or washing rituals, to restore purity.

Although the Indian government formally abolished the caste system in 1949, centuries-old practices cannot be eliminated so easily, and the caste system remains part of everyday life in India. The ceremonies people follow at births, marriages, and deaths, for example, are dictated by caste (Chandra 1993). The upper castes oppose the upward mobility of the untouchables, sometimes resisting it even with violence (Crosette 1996; Filkins 1997; Deliege 2001).

A U.S. Racial Caste System. Before leaving the subject of caste, we should note that when slavery ended in

Table 7.1 India's Caste System

Caste	Occupation
Brahman	Priests and teachers
Kshatriya	Rulers and soldiers
Vaishya	Merchants and traders
Shudra	Peasants and laborers
Dalit (untouchables)	The outcastes; degrading or polluting labor

In a *caste system*, status is determined by birth and is lifelong. At birth, these women received not only membership in a lower caste but also, because of their gender, a predetermined position in that caste. When I photographed these women, they were carrying sand to the second floor of a house being constructed in Andhra Pradesh, India.

the United States, it was replaced by a *racial caste system*, in which everyone was marked for life from the moment of birth (Berger 1963/2005). In this system, *all* whites, even if they were poor and uneducated, considered themselves to have a higher status than *all* African Americans. As in India and South Africa, the upper caste, fearing pollution from the lower caste, prohibited intermarriage, and insisted on separate schools, hotels, restaurants, and even toilets and drinking fountains in public facilities. When any white met any African American on a Southern sidewalk, the African American had to move aside—which the untouchables of India still must do when they meet someone of a higher caste (Deliege 2001).

Class

As we have seen, stratification systems based on slavery and caste are rigid. The lines drawn between people are firm, and there is little or no movement from one group to another. A **class system,** in contrast, is much more open, for it is based primarily on money or material possessions, which can be acquired. This system, too, is in place at birth, when children are ascribed the status of their parents, but unlike the other systems, individuals can change their social class by what they achieve (or fail to achieve) in life. In addition, no laws specify people's occupations on the basis of birth or prohibit marriage between the classes.

A major characteristic of the class system, then, is its relatively fluid boundaries. A class system allows **social mobility,** movement up or down the class ladder. The potential for improving one's life—or for falling down the class ladder—is a major force that drives people to go far in school and to work hard. In the extreme, the family background that a child inherits at birth may present such obstacles that he or she has little chance of climbing very far, or it may provide such privileges that it makes it almost impossible to fall down the class ladder.

Global Stratification and the Status of Females

In every society of the world, gender is a basis for social stratification. In no society is gender the sole basis for stratifying people, but gender cuts across *all* systems of social stratification—whether slavery, caste, or class (Huber 1990). In all these systems, on the basis of their gender, people are sorted into categories and given different access to the good things available in their society.

Apparently these distinctions always favor males. It is remarkable, for example, that in *every* society of the world, men's earnings are higher than women's. Men's dominance is even more evident when we consider female circumcision (see the box on page 274). That most of the world's illiterate are females also drives home women's relative position in society. Of the several hundred million adults who cannot read, about 60 percent are women (UNESCO 2005). Because gender is such a significant factor in what happens to us in life, we shall focus on it more closely in Chapter 10.

What Determines Social Class?

In the early days of sociology, a disagreement arose about the meaning of social class. Let's compare how Marx and Weber analyzed the issue.

Karl Marx: The Means of Production

As was discussed in Chapter 1, the breakup of the feudal system displaced masses of peasants from their traditional lands and occupations. Fleeing to cities, they competed for the few available jobs. Offered only a pittance for their labor, they wore rags, went hungry, and slept under bridges and in shacks. In contrast, the factory owners built mansions, hired servants, and lived in the lap of luxury. Seeing this great disparity between owners and workers, Karl Marx (1818–1883) concluded that social class depends on a single factor: people's relationship to the **means of production**—the tools, factories, land, and investment capital used to produce wealth (Marx 1844/1964; Marx and Engels 1848/1967).

Marx argued that the distinctions people often make among themselves—such as clothing, speech, education, income, the neighborhood they live in, even the car they drive—are superficial matters. These things camouflage the only dividing line that counts. There are just two classes of people, said Marx: the **bourgeoisie** (*capitalists*), those who own the means of production, and the **proletariat** (*workers*), those who work for the owners. In short, people's relationship to the means of production determines their social class.

Marx did recognize other groups: farmers and peasants; a *lumpenproletariat* (people living on the margin of society, such as beggars, vagrants, and criminals); and a middle group of self-employed professionals. Marx did not consider these groups social classes, however, for they lack **class consciousness**—a shared identity based on their position in the means of production. In other words, they did not perceive themselves as exploited workers whose plight could be solved by collective action. Consequently, Marx thought of these groups as insignificant in the future he foresaw—a workers' revolution that was destined to overthrow capitalism.

The capitalists will grow even wealthier, Marx said, and the hostilities will increase. When workers come to realize that capitalists are the source of their oppression, they will unite and throw off the chains of their oppressors. In a bloody revolution, they will seize the means of production and usher in a classless society, in which no longer will the few grow rich at the expense of the many. What holds back the workers' unity and their revolution is **false class consciousness,** workers mistakenly thinking of themselves as capitalists. For example, workers with a few dollars in the bank may forget that they are workers and instead see themselves as investors or as capitalists who are about to launch a successful business.

Taken at the end of the 1800s, these photos illustrate the contrasting worlds of *social classes* produced by early capitalism. The sleeping boys shown in this classic 1890 photo by Jacob Riis sold newspapers in London. They did not go to school, and they had no home. The children on the right, Cornelius and Gladys Vanderbilt, are shown in front of their parents' estate. They went to school and did not work. You can see how the social locations illustrated in these photos would have produced different orientations to life and, therefore, politics, ideas about marriage, values, and so on—the stuff of which life is made.

The only distinction worth mentioning, then, is whether a person is an owner or a worker. This decides everything else, Marx stressed, for property determines people's lifestyles, shapes their ideas, and establishes their relationships with one another.

Max Weber: Property, Prestige, and Power

Max Weber (1864–1920) was an outspoken critic of Marx. Weber argued that property is only part of the picture. **Social class,** he said, is made up of three components: property, prestige, and power (Gerth and Mills 1958; Weber 1922/1968). Some call these the three *P*'s of social class. (Although Weber used the terms *class, status,* and *power,* some sociologists find *property, prestige,* and *power* to be clearer terms. To make them even clearer, you may wish to substitute *wealth* for *property*.)

Property (or wealth), said Weber, is certainly significant in determining a person's standing in society. On that point he agreed with Marx. But, added Weber, ownership is not the only significant aspect of property. For example, some powerful people, such as managers of corporations, *control* the means of production although they do not *own* them. If managers can control property for their own benefit—awarding themselves huge bonuses and magnificent perks—it makes no practical difference that they do not own the property they so generously use for their own benefit.

Prestige, the second element in Weber's analysis, is often derived from property, for people tend to admire the wealthy. Prestige, however, can be based on other factors. Olympic gold medalists, for example, might not own property, yet they have high prestige. Some are even able to exchange their prestige for property—such as those who are paid a small fortune for endorsing a certain brand of sportswear or for claiming that they start their day with "the breakfast of champions." In other words, property and prestige are not one-way streets: Although property can bring prestige, prestige can also bring property.

Power, the third element of social class, is the ability to control others, even over their objections. Weber agreed with Marx that property is a major source of power, but he added that it is not the only source. For example, prestige can be turned into power. Two well-known examples are actors Arnold Schwarzeneggar, who became governor of California, and Ronald Reagan, who became president of the United States. Figure 7.1 shows how property, prestige, and power are interrelated.

Sisters Venus and Serena Williams have dominated the women's tennis world for over a decade. To determine the social class of athletes as highly successful as the Williams sisters presents a sociological puzzle. With their fame and growing wealth, what do you think their social class is? Why?

The text describes the many relationships among Weber's three components of *social class:* property, prestige, and power. Colin Powell is an example of power that was converted into prestige— which was then converted back into power. Power of course, can be lost, as it was when Powell resigned after disagreeing with the Bush administration.

Figure 7.1 Weber's Three Components of Social Class

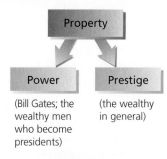

Property

Power | Prestige
(Bill Gates; the wealthy men who become presidents) | (the wealthy in general)

Prestige

Power | Property
(Ronald Reagan) | (Olympic gold medalists who endorse products)

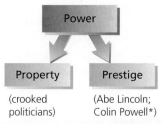

Power

Property | Prestige
(crooked politicians) | (Abe Lincoln; Colin Powell*)

*Colin Powell illustrates the circularity of these components. Powell's power as Chairman of the Joint Chiefs of Staff led to prestige. Powell's prestige, in turn, led to power when he was called from retirement to serve as Secretary of State in George W. Bush's first administration.

IN SUM For Marx, social class was based solely on a person's relationship to the means of production. One is a member of either the bourgeoisie or the proletariat. Weber argued that social class is a combination of property, prestige, and power.

Why Is Social Stratification Universal?

What is it about social life that makes all societies stratified? We shall first look at the explanation proposed by functionalists, which has aroused much controversy in sociology, and then consider explanations proposed by conflict theorists.

The Functionalist Perspective: Motivating Qualified People

Functionalists take the position that the patterns of behavior that characterize a society exist because they are functional for that society. Because social inequality is universal, inequality must help societies survive. But how?

Davis and Moore's Explanation. Two functionalists, Kingsley Davis and Wilbert Moore (1945, 1953), wrestled with this question. They concluded that the stratification of society is inevitable because:

1. Society must make certain that its positions are filled.
2. Some positions are more important than others.
3. The more important positions must be filled by the more qualified people.
4. To motivate the more qualified people to fill these positions, society must offer them greater rewards.

The functionalist argument is straightforward: The position of college president is more important than that of student because the president's decisions affect many more people. Any mistakes that he or she makes carry implications for a large number of people, including many students. College presidents are also accountable for their performance to boards of trustees. It is the same with generals. Their decisions affect many people; sometimes those decisions mean life or death. Generals are accountable to superior generals and to the country's leader.

Why do people accept such high-pressure positions? Why don't they just take less demanding jobs? The answer, said Davis and Moore, is that society offers greater rewards—prestige, salary, and benefits—for its more demanding and accountable positions. To get highly qualified people to compete with one another, some positions offer a salary of $2 million a year, country club membership, a private jet, and a chauffeured limousine. For less demanding positions, a $30,000 salary without fringe benefits is enough to get hundreds of people to compete. If a job requires rigorous training, it, too, must offer more salary and benefits. If you can get the same pay with a high school diploma, why suffer through the many tests and term papers that college requires?

Tumin's Critique of Davis and Moore. Davis and Moore tried to explain *why* social stratification is universal, not justify social inequality. Nevertheless, their view makes many sociologists uncomfortable, for they see it as coming close to justifying the inequalities in society. Its bottom line seems to be: The people who contribute more to society are paid more, while those who contribute less are paid less.

Melvin Tumin (1953) was the first sociologist to point out what he saw as major flaws in the functionalist position. Here are three of his arguments.

First, how do we know that the positions that offer the highest rewards are the most important? Surgeons, for example, earn much more than garbage collectors, but this doesn't mean that garbage collectors are less important to society. Garbage collectors help to prevent contagious diseases, saving thousands of lives. We need independent methods of measuring importance, and we don't have them.

Second, if stratification worked as Davis and Moore described it, society would be a **meritocracy;** that is, positions would be awarded on the basis of merit. But is this what we have? The best predictor of who goes to college, for example, is not ability but income: The more a family earns, the more likely their children are to go to college (Conley 2002). This isn't merit but, rather, inequality built into society. In short, people's positions in society are based on many reasons other than merit.

Third, if social stratification is so functional, it ought to benefit almost everyone. Yet social stratification is *dysfunctional* for many. Think of the people who could have made valuable contributions to society had they not been born in slums and dropped out of school to take menial jobs to help support their families. Then there are the many who, born female, are assigned "women's work," thus ensuring that they do not maximize their mental abilities.

IN SUM Functionalists argue that society works better if its most qualified people hold its most important positions. Therefore, those positions offer higher rewards. For example, to get highly talented people to become surgeons—to undergo years of rigorous training and then cope with life-and-death situations, as well as malpractice suits—society must provide a high payoff.

The Conflict Perspective: Class Conflict and Scarce Resources

Conflict theorists don't just criticize details of the functionalist argument. Rather, they go for the throat and attack its basic premise. Conflict, not function, they stress, is the reason that we have social stratification. Let's look at the major arguments.

Mosca's Argument. Italian sociologist Gaetano Mosca argued that every society will be stratified by power. This is inevitable, he said in an 1896 book titled *The Ruling Class,* because:

1. No society can exist unless it is organized. This requires leadership of some sort to coordinate people's actions and get society's work done.
2. Leadership (or political organization) means inequalities of power. Some people take leadership positions, while others follow.
3. Human nature is self-centered. Therefore, people in power will use their positions to seize greater rewards for themselves.

There is no way around these facts of life, added Mosca. They make social stratification inevitable, and every society will stratify itself along lines of power.

Marx's Argument. If he were alive to hear the functionalist argument, Karl Marx would be enraged. From his point of view, the people in power are not there because of superior traits, as the functionalists would have us believe. This view is simply an ideology that the elite use to justify their being at the top—and to seduce the oppressed into believing that their welfare depends on keeping society stable. Human history is the chronicle of class struggle, of those in power using society's resources to benefit themselves and to oppress those beneath them—and of oppressed groups trying to overcome domination.

Marx predicted that the workers would revolt. The day will come, he said, when class consciousness will overcome the ideology that now blinds workers. When they

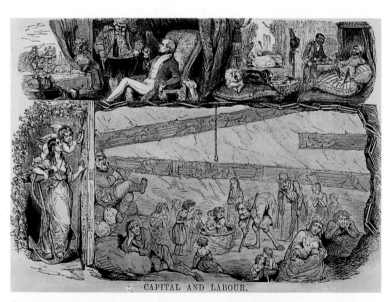

This cartoon of political protest appeared in London newspapers in 1843. It illustrates the severe exploitation of labor that occurred during early capitalism, which stimulated Marx to analyze relations between capitalists and workers.

realize their common oppression, workers will rebel against the capitalists. The struggle to control the means of production may be covert at first, taking the form of work slowdowns or industrial sabotage. Ultimately, however, resistance will break out into the open. The revolution will not be easy, for the bourgeoisie control the police, the military, and even the educational system, where they implant false class consciousness in the minds of the workers' children.

Current Applications of Conflict Theory. Just as Marx focused on overarching historic events—the accumulation of capital and power and the struggle between labor and capitalists—some of today's conflict sociologists are doing the same. Their focus is on the current capitalist triumph on a global level (Sklair 2001). They analyze the use of armed forces to keep capitalist nations dominant and the exploitation of workers as capital is moved from the Most Industrialized Nations to the Least Industrialized Nations.

Some conflict sociologists, in contrast, examine conflict wherever it is found, not just as it relates to capitalists and workers. They examine how groups *within the same class* compete with one another for a larger slice of the pie (Schellenberg 1996; Collins 1988, 1999). Even within the same industry, for example, union will fight against union for higher salaries, shorter hours, and more power. A special focus of research has been conflict between racial-ethnic groups as they compete for education, housing, and even prestige—whatever benefits society has to offer. Another focus has been relations between women and men, which conflict theorists say are best understood as a conflict over power—over who controls society's resources. Unlike functionalists, conflict theorists hold that just beneath the surface of what may appear to be a tranquil society lies conflict that is barely held in check.

Lenski's Synthesis

As you can see, functionalist and conflict theorists disagree sharply. Is it possible to reconcile their views? Sociologist Gerhard Lenski (1966) thought so. He suggested that surplus is the key. He said that the functionalists are right when it comes to groups that don't accumulate a surplus, such as hunting and gathering societies. These societies give a greater share of their resources to those who take on important tasks, such as warriors who risk their lives in battle. It is a different story, said Lenski, with societies that accumulate surpluses. In them, groups fight over the surplus, and the group that

wins becomes an elite. This dominant group rules from the top, controlling the groups below it. In the resulting system of social stratification, where you are born in that society, not personal merit, becomes important.

IN SUM Conflict theorists stress that in every society, groups struggle with one another to gain a larger share of their society's resources. Whenever a group gains power, it uses that power to extract what it can from the groups beneath it. This elite group also uses social institutions to keep itself in power.

How Do Elites Maintain Stratification?

Suppose that you are part of the ruling elite of your society. What can you do to make sure that you don't lose your privileged position? The key lies in controlling ideas and information and, in the least effective means of all, the use of force.

Ideology Versus Force

Medieval Europe provides a good example of the power of ideology. At that time, land was the primary source of wealth—and only the nobility and the church could own it. Almost everyone was a peasant (commoner) who worked for these powerful landowners. The peasants farmed the land, took care of the livestock, and built the roads and bridges. Each year, they had to turn over a designated portion of their crops to their feudal lord. Year after year, for centuries, they did so. Why?

Controlling Ideas. Why didn't the peasants rebel and take over the land themselves? There were many reasons, not the least of which was that the nobility and church controlled the army. Coercion, however, only goes so far, for it breeds hostility and nourishes rebellion. How much more effective it is to get the masses to *want* to do what the ruling elite desires. This is where *ideology* (beliefs that justify the way things are) comes into play, and the nobility and clergy used it to great effect. They developed an ideology known as the **divine right of kings**—the idea that the king's authority comes directly from God. The king delegates authority to nobles, who, as God's representatives, must be obeyed. To disobey is to sin against God; to rebel is to merit both physical punishment on earth and eternal suffering in hell.

The *divine right of kings* was an ideology that made the king God's direct representative on earth—to administer justice and punish evildoers. This theological-political concept was supported by the Roman Catholic Church, whose representatives crowned the king. Depicted here is Charlemagne (742–824), who was crowned by Pope Leo III as king of the Holy Roman Empire.

Controlling people's ideas can be remarkably more effective than using brute force. Although this particular ideology governs few peoples' minds today, the elite in every society develops ideologies to justify its position at the top. For example, around the world schools teach that their country's form of government—*no matter what form of government that is*—is the best. Religious leaders teach that we owe obedience to authority, that laws are to be obeyed. To the degree that their ideologies are accepted by the masses, the elite remain securely in power.

Controlling Information and Using Technology. To maintain their positions of power, elites also try to control information. Fear is a favorite tactic of dictators. To muffle criticism, they imprison, torture, and kill anyone who voices opposition, including reporters who dare to criticize their regime. (Under Saddam Hussein, the penalty for telling a joke about Hussein was having your tongue cut out [Nordland 2003].) Lacking such power, the ruling elites of democracies rely on more covert means. They manipulate the media by selectively releasing information—and by withholding information "in the interest of national security."

The new technology is another tool for the elite. Telephones can be turned into microphones even when they are off the hook. Some spy programs can read the entire contents of a computer in a second, without leaving a trace of evidence that they have done so. Security cameras—"Tiny Brothers"—have sprouted almost everywhere. Face-recognition systems can scan a crowd of thousands, instantly matching the scans with digitized files of individuals. With these devices, the elite can monitor citizens' activities without anyone realizing that they are being observed. Dictatorships have few checks on how they employ such technology, but in democracies, checks and balances, such as requiring court orders for search and seizure, at least partially curb their abuse. The threat of bypassing such restraints on power is always present, as with the Homeland Security laws discussed in Chapter 11 (page 308).

The new technology is a two-edged sword. Just as it gives the elite powerful tools for monitoring citizens, it also makes it more difficult for them to control information. Satellite communications, e-mail, and the Internet pay no respect to international borders, and information flies around the globe in seconds. Internet users have free access to PGP (Pretty Good Privacy), a code that no government has been able to break. Then, too, there is zFone, voice encription for telephone calls, that prevents government agents or others from understanding what people are saying.

IN SUM To maintain stratification within a society, the elite tries to dominate its society's institutions. In a dictatorship, the elite makes the laws. In a democracy, the elite influences the laws. In both, the legal establishment enforces the laws. The elite also controls the police and military and can give orders to crush a rebellion—or even to run the post office or air traffic control if workers strike. Force has its limits, and a nation's elite generally prefers to maintain its stratification system by peaceful means, especially by influencing the thinking of its people.

Comparative Social Stratification

Now that we have examined systems of social stratification, considered why stratification is universal, and looked at how elites keep themselves in power, let's compare social stratification in Great Britain and in the former Soviet Union. In the next chapter, we will look at social stratification in the United States.

Social Stratification in Great Britain

Great Britain is often called England by Americans, but England is only one of the countries that make up the island of Great Britain. The others are Scotland and Wales. In addition, Northern Ireland is part of the United Kingdom of Great Britain and Northern Ireland.

Like other industrialized countries, Great Britain has a class system that can be divided into a lower, a middle, and an upper class. Great Britain's population is about evenly divided between the middle class and the lower (or working) class. A tiny upper class, perhaps 1 percent of the population, is wealthy, powerful, and highly educated.

Compared with Americans, the British are very class conscious. Like Americans, they recognize class distinctions on the basis of the type of car a person drives or the stores someone patronizes. But the most striking characteristics of the British class system are language and education. This often shows up in distinctive speech, which has a powerful impact on British life. Accent almost always betrays class. As soon as someone speaks, the listener is aware of that person's social class—and treats him or her accordingly (Sullivan 1998).

Education is the primary way by which the British perpetuate their class system from one generation to the next. Almost all children go to neighborhood schools. Great Britain's richest 5 percent, however—who own *half* the nation's wealth—send their children to exclusive private boarding schools (which, strangely, they call "public" schools). There the children of the elite are trained in subjects that are considered proper for members of the ruling class. An astounding 50 percent of the students at Oxford and Cambridge, the country's most prestigious universities, come from this 5 percent of the population. To illustrate how powerfully this system of stratified education affects the national life of Great Britain, sociologist Ian Robertson (1987) said,

[E]ighteen former pupils of the most exclusive of them, Eton, have become prime minister. Imagine the chances of a single American high school producing eighteen presidents!

Social Stratification in the Former Soviet Union

Heeding Karl Marx's call for a classless society, Vladimir Ilyich Lenin (1870–1924) and Leon Trotsky (1879–1940) led a revolution in Russia in 1917. They, and the nations that

followed their banner, never claimed to have achieved the ideal of communism, in which all contribute their labor to the common good and receive according to their needs. Instead, they used the term *socialism* to describe the intermediate step between capitalism and communism, in which social classes are abolished but some inequality remains.

To tweak the nose of Uncle Sam, the socialist countries would trumpet their equality and point a finger at glaring inequalities in the United States. These countries, however, also were marked by huge disparities in privilege. Their major basis of stratification was membership in the Communist Party. This often decided who would gain admission to the better schools or obtain the more desirable jobs. The equally qualified son or daughter of a nonmember would be turned down, for such privileges came with demonstrated loyalty to the Party.

The Communist Party, too, was highly stratified. Most members occupied a low level, where they fulfilled such tasks as spying on fellow workers. For this, they might get easier jobs in the factory or occasional access to special stores to purchase hard-to-find goods. The middle level consisted of bureaucrats who were given better than average access to resources and privileges. At the top level was a small elite: Party members who enjoyed not only power but also limousines, imported delicacies, vacation homes, and even servants and hunting lodges. As with other stratification systems around the world, women held lower positions in the Party. This was evident at each year's May Day, when the top members of the Party reviewed the latest weapons paraded in Moscow's Red Square. Photos of these events showed only men.

The leaders of the USSR became frustrated as they saw the West thrive. They struggled with a bloated bureaucracy, the inefficiencies of central planning, workers who did the minimum because they could not be fired, and a military so costly that it spent one of every eight of the nation's rubles (*Statistical Abstract* 1993:1432, table dropped in later editions). Socialist ideology did not call for their citizens to be deprived, and in an attempt to turn things around, the Soviet leadership initiated reforms. They allowed elections to be held in which more than one candidate ran for an office. (Before this, voters had a choice of only one candidate per office.) They also sold huge chunks of state-owned businesses to the public. Overnight, making investments to try to turn a profit changed from being a crime into a respectable goal.

Russia's transition to capitalism took a bizarre twist. As authority broke down, a powerful Mafia emerged. These criminal groups are headed by gangsters, corrupt government officials (including their secret police, the KGB), and crooked businessmen (Tavernise 2002; Varese 2005). In some towns, they buy the entire judicial system—the police force, prosecutors, and judges (Tavernise 2002). They assassinate business leaders, reporters, and politicians who refuse to cooperate (Zarakhovich 2001; Wines 2002). They amass wealth and stash it in offshore retreats, especially in resorts and wintering spots such as Marbella on Spain's Costa del Sol.

Russia's "wild west" days will come to an end as the central government reestablishes its authority. At that time, this group of organized criminals will take its place as part of Russia's new capitalist class.

Global Stratification: Three Worlds

As was noted at the beginning of this chapter, just as the people within a nation are stratified by property, prestige, and power, so are the world's nations. Until recently, a simple model consisting of First, Second, and Third Worlds was used to depict global stratification. *First World* referred to the industrialized capitalist nations, *Second World* to the communist (or socialist) nations, and *Third World* to any nation that did not fit into the first two categories. The breakup of the Soviet Union in 1989 made these terms outdated. In addition, although *first, second,* and *third* did not mean "best," "better," and "worst," they implied it. An alternative classification that some now use—developed, developing, and undeveloped nations—has the same drawback. By calling ourselves "developed," it sounds as though we are mature and the "undeveloped" nations are somehow retarded.

To try to solve this problem, I use more neutral, descriptive terms: *Most Industrialized, Industrializing,* and *Least Industrialized* nations. We can measure industrialization with no judgment implied as to whether a nation's industrialization represents "development," ranks it "first"—or is even desirable at all. The intention is to depict on a global level the three primary dimensions of social stratification: property, prestige, and power. The Most Industrialized Nations have much greater property (wealth), prestige (they are looked up to as world leaders), and power (they usually get their way in international relations). The two families sketched in the opening vignette illustrate the far-reaching effects of global stratification.

The Most Industrialized Nations

The Most Industrialized Nations are the United States and Canada in North America; Great Britain, France, Germany, Switzerland, and the other industrialized nations of western Europe; Japan in Asia; and Australia and New Zealand in the area of the world known as Oceania. Although there are variations in their economic systems, these nations are capitalistic. As Table 7.2 shows, although these nations have only 16 percent of the world's people, they have 31 percent of the earth's land. Their wealth is so enormous that even their poor live better and longer lives than do average citizens of the Least Industrialized Nations. The Social Map on pages 182–183 shows the tremendous disparities in income among the world's nations.

The Industrializing Nations

The Industrializing Nations include most of the nations of the former Soviet Union and its former satellites in eastern Europe. As Table 7.2 shows, these nations account for 20 percent of the earth's land and 16 percent of its people.

The dividing lines between the three "worlds" are soft, making it difficult to know how to classify some nations. This is especially the case with the Industrializing Nations. Exactly how much industrialization must a nation have to be in this category? Although soft, these categories do pinpoint essential differences among nations. Most people who live in the Industrializing Nations have much lower incomes and standards of living than those who live in the Most Industrialized Nations. Most, however, are better off than those who live in the Least Industrialized Nations. For example, on such measures as access to electricity, indoor plumbing, automobiles, telephones, and even food, citizens of the Industrializing Nations rank lower than those in the Most Industrialized Nations, but higher than those in the Least Industrialized

Table 7.2 Distribution of the World's Land and Population

	Land	Population
Most Industrialized Nations	31%	16%
Industralizing Nations	20%	16%
Least Industrialized Nations	49%	68%

Source: Computed from Kurian 1990, 1991, 1992.

Nations. As you saw in the opening vignette, stratification affects even life expectancy.

The benefits of industrialization are uneven. Large numbers of people in the Industrializing Nations remain illiterate and desperately poor. Conditions can be gruesome, as discussed in the following Thinking Critically section.

Thinking Critically

Open Season: Children as Prey

What is childhood like in the Industrializing Nations? The answer depends on who your parents are. If you are the son or daughter of rich parents, childhood can be pleasant—a world filled with luxuries and even servants. If you are born into poverty but live in a rural area where there is plenty to eat, life can still be good—although there may be no books, no television, and little education. If you live in a slum, however, life can be horrible—worse even than in the slums of the Most Industrialized Nations. Let's take a glance at what is happening to children in the slums of Brazil.

Not enough food—this you can take for granted—as well as wife abuse, broken homes, alcoholism, drug abuse, and a lot of crime. From your knowledge of slums in the Most Industrialized Nations, you would expect these things. What you may not expect, however, are the brutal conditions in which Brazilian slum (*favela*) children live.

Sociologist Martha Huggins (Huggins et al. 2002) reports that poverty is so extreme that children and adults swarm over garbage dumps to try to find enough decaying food to keep them alive. You might also be surprised to discover that the owners of some of these dumps hire armed guards to keep the poor out—so that they can sell the garbage for pig food. And you might be shocked to learn that the Brazilian police and death squads murder some of these children. Some shop owners even hire hit men and auction designated victims off to the lowest bidder! The going rate is half a month's salary, figured at the low Brazilian minimum wage.

Life *is* cheap in the poor nations—but death squads for children? To understand this, we must first note that Brazil has a long history of violence. Brazil also has a high rate of poverty, has only a tiny middle class, and is controlled by a small group of families who, under a veneer of democracy, make the country's major decisions. Hordes of homeless children, with no schools or jobs, roam the streets. To survive, they wash windshields, shine shoes, beg, and steal.

The "respectable" classes see these children as nothing but trouble. They hurt business, for customers feel intimidated when they see begging children clustered in front of stores. Some shoplift; others dare to sell items that place them in competition with the stores. With no effective social institutions to care for these children, one solution is to kill them. As Huggins notes, murder sends a clear message—especially if it is accompanied by ritual torture: gouging out the eyes, ripping open the chest, cutting off the genitals, raping the girls, and burning the victim's body.

Not all life is bad in the Industrializing Nations, but this is about as bad as it gets.

for your Consideration

Do you think there is anything the Most Industrialized Nations can do about this situation? Or is it any of their business? Is it, though unfortunate, just an internal affair that is up to the Brazilians to handle as they wish?

The Least Industrialized Nations

In the Least Industrialized Nations, most people are peasant farmers living on farms or in villages. These nations account for 49 percent of the Earth's land and 68 percent of the world's people.

As you can see from the photo on this page, poverty plagues the Least Industrialized Nations. On pages 184–185 are photos I took of people who actually *live* in a city dump. Although wealthy nations have their pockets of poverty, *most*

Homeless people sleeping on the streets is a common sight in India's cities. I took this photo in Chennai (formerly Madras).

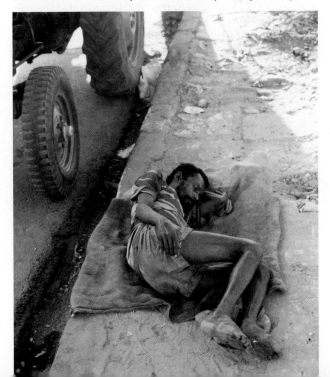

Figure 7.2 **Global Stratification: Income[1] of the World's Nations**

The Most Industrialized Nations

Nation	Income per Person
1 Luxembourg	$53,290
2 Norway	$36,690
3 United States	$36,110
4 Switzerland	$31,840
5 Denmark	$30,600
6 Ireland	$29,570
7 Iceland	$29,240
8 Canada	$28,930
9 Austria	$28,910
10 Netherlands	$28,350
11 Belgium	$28,130
12 Hong Kong (a part of China)	$27,490
13 Australia	$27,440
14 Japan	$27,380
15 France	$27,040
16 Germany	$26,980
17 United Kingdom	$26,580
18 Italy	$26,170
19 Finland	$26,160
20 Sweden	$25,820
21 Singapore	$23,730
22 New Zealand	$20,550
23 Israel	$19,000

The Industrializing Nations

Nation	Income per Person
24 Spain	$21,210
25 Greece	$18,770
26 Slovenia	$18,480
27 Portugal	$17,820
28 Korea, South	$16,960
29 Czech Republic	$14,920
30 Hungary	$13,070
31 Saudi Arabia	$12,660
32 Slovakia	$12,590
33 Estonia	$11,630
34 Mauritius	$10,820
35 Poland	$10,450
36 Argentina	$10,190
37 Lithuania	$10,190
38 Croatia	$10,000
39 South Africa	$9,810
40 Chile	$9,420
41 Latvia	$9,190
42 Equatorial Guinea	$9,110
43 Mexico	$8,800
44 Costa Rica	$8,560
45 Malaysia	$8,500
46 Russia	$8,080
47 Uruguay	$7,710
48 Brazil	$7,450
49 Bulgaria	$7,030
50 Thailand	$6,890
51 Romania	$6,490
52 Colombia	$6,150
53 Venezuela	$5,220

The Least Industrialized Nations

Nation	Income per Person	Nation	Income per Person
54 Botswana[3]	$7,740	69 Ukraine	$4,800
55 Namibia	$6,880	70 El Salvador	$4,790
56 Tunisia	$6,440	71 Turkmenistan	$4,780
57 Macedonia	$6,420	72 Swaziland	$4,730
58 Turkey	$6,300	73 Lebanon	$4,600
59 Dominican Republic	$6,270	74 Paraguay	$4,590
60 Panama	$6,060	75 China	$4,520
61 Kazakstan	$5,630	76 Philippines	$4,450
62 Algeria	$5,530	77 Jordan	$4,180
63 Gabon	$5,530	78 Guatemala	$4,030
64 Belarus	$5,500	79 Guyana	$3,940
65 Belize	$5,490	80 Egypt	$3,810
66 Albania	$4,960	81 Morocco	$3,730
67 Cape Verde	$4,920	82 Jamaica	$3,680
68 Peru	$4,880	83 Sri Lanka	$3,510
		84 Syria	$3,470

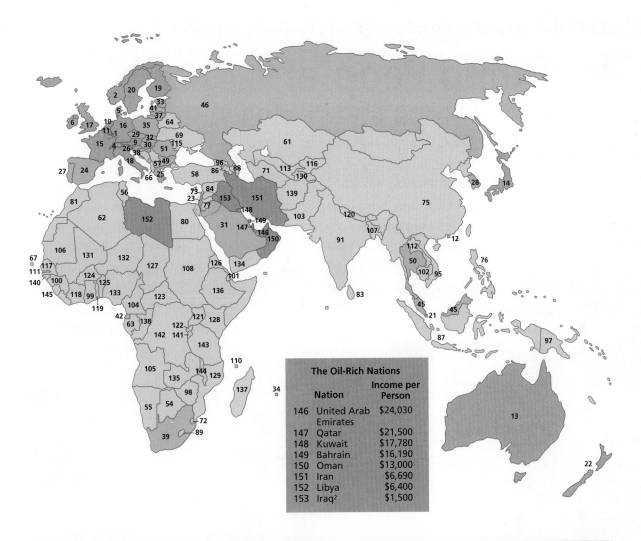

The Oil-Rich Nations

	Nation	Income per Person
146	United Arab Emirates	$24,030
147	Qatar	$21,500
148	Kuwait	$17,780
149	Bahrain	$16,190
150	Oman	$13,000
151	Iran	$6,690
152	Libya	$6,400
153	Iraq[2]	$1,500

The Least Industrialized Nations

	Nation	Income per Person		Nation	Income per Person		Nation	Income per Person		Nation	Income per Person
85	Ecuador	$3,340	101	Djibouti	$2,040	118	Cote d'Ivoire	$1,450	134	Yemen	$800
86	Armenia	$3,230	102	Cambodia	$1,970	119	Togo	$1,450	135	Zambia	$800
87	Indonesia	$3,070	103	Pakistan	$1,960	120	Nepal	$1,370	136	Ethiopia	$780
88	Azerbaijan	$3,010	104	Cameroon	$1,910	121	Uganda	$1,360	137	Madagascar	$730
89	Lesotho	$2,970	105	Angola	$1,840	122	Rwanda	$1,260	138	Congo	$710
90	Cuba	$2,930	106	Mauritania	$1,790	123	Central African Republic	$1,170	139	Afghanistan	$700
91	India	$2,650	107	Bangladesh	$1,770	124	Burkina Faso	$1,090	140	Guinea-Bissau	$680
92	Honduras	$2,540	108	Sudan	$1,740	125	Benin	$1,060	141	Burundi	$630
93	Bolivia	$2,390	109	Mongolia	$1,710	126	Eritrea	$1,040	142	Congo, Democratic Republic	$630
94	Nicaragua	$2,350	110	Comoros	$1,690	127	Chad	$1,010	143	Tanzania	$580
95	Vietnam	$2,300	111	Gambia	$1,660	128	Kenya	$1,010	144	Malawi	$570
96	Georgia	$2,270	112	Laos	$1,660	129	Mozambique	$990	145	Sierra Leone	$500
97	Papua-New Guinea	$2,180	113	Uzbekistan	$1,640	130	Tajikistan	$930			
98	Zimbabwe	$2,180	114	Haiti	$1,610	131	Mali	$860			
99	Ghana	$2,080	115	Moldova	$1,600	132	Niger	$800			
100	Guinea	$2,060	116	Krygyzstan	$1,560	133	Nigeria	$800			
			117	Senegal	$1,540						

[1]Income is the country's per capita gross national product measured in U.S. dollars. Since some totals vary widely from year to year, they must be taken as approximate. [2]Iraq's oil has been disrupted by war. [3]Botswana's relative wealth is based on its diamond mines.

Sources: By the author. Based on *Statistical Abstract* 2005:Table 1336, Haub 2004; data for Afghanistan, Cuba, Iraq, Libya, and Qatar from Central Intelligence Agency 2005.

The Dump People:
Working and Living and Playing in the City Dump of Phnom Penh, Cambodia

went to Phnom Penh, the capital of Cambodia, to inspect orphanages, to see how well the children were being cared for. While there, I was told about people who live in the city dump. *Live* there? I could hardly believe my ears. I knew that people made their living by picking scraps from the city dump, but I didn't know they actually lived among the garbage. This I had to see for myself.

I did. And there I found a highly developed social organization—an intricate support system. Because words are inadequate to depict the abject poverty of the Least Industrialized Nations, these photos can provide more insight into these people's lives than anything I could say.

This is a typical sight—family and friends working together. The trash, which is constantly burning, contains harmful chemicals. Why do people work under such conditions? Because they have few options.
    It is either this or starve.

The people live at the edge of the dump, in homemade huts (visible in the background). This woman, who was on her way home after a day's work, put down her sack of salvaged items to let me take her picture.

After the garbage arrives by truck, people stream around it, struggling to be the first to discover something of value. To sift through the trash the workers use metal picks, like the one the child is holding. Note that children work alongside the adults.

The children who live in the dump also play there. These children are riding bicycles on a "road," a packed, leveled area of garbage that leads to their huts. The huge stacks in the background are piled trash. Note the ubiquitous Nike.

One of my many surprises was to find food stands in the dump. Although this one primarily offers drinks and snacks, others serve more substantial food. One even has chairs for its customers.

I was surprised to learn that ice is delivered to the dump. This woman is using a hand grinder to crush ice for drinks for her customers. The customers, of course, are other people who also live in the dump.

At the day's end, the workers wash at the community pump. This hand pump serves all their water needs—drinking, washing, and cooking. There is no indoor plumbing. The weeds in the background serve that purpose.

Not too many visitors to Phnom Penh tell a cab driver to take them to the **city dump**. The cabbie looked a bit perplexed, but he did as I asked. Two cabs are shown here because my friends insisted on accompanying me.

I know they were curious themselves, but my friends had also discovered that the destinations I want to visit are usually not in the tourist guides, and they wanted to protect me.

people in the Least Industrialized nations live on less than $1,000 a year, in many cases considerably less. *Most* of them have no running water, no indoor plumbing, and no access to trained teachers or physicians. As we will discuss in Chapter 14, the population of most of these nations is mushrooming. This places even greater burdens on their limited resources, causing them to fall farther behind each year.

How Did the World's Nations Become Stratified?

How did the globe become stratified into such distinct worlds? The commonsense answer is that the poorer nations have fewer resources than the richer nations. As with so many commonsense answers, however, this one, too, falls short. Many of the Industrializing and Least Industrialized Nations are rich in natural resources, while one Most Industrialized Nation, Japan, has few. Three theories explain how global stratification came about.

Colonialism

The first theory, **colonialism,** stresses that the countries that industrialized first got the jump on the rest of the world. Beginning in Great Britain about 1750, industrialization spread throughout western Europe. Plowing some of their immense profits into powerful armaments and fast ships, these countries invaded weaker nations, making colonies out of them (Harrison 1993). After subduing these weaker nations, the more powerful countries left behind a controlling force in order to exploit the nations' labor and natural resources. At one point, there was even a free-for-all among the industrialized European countries as they rushed to divide up an entire continent. As they sliced Africa into pieces, even tiny Belgium got into the act and acquired the Congo, which was *seventy-five* times larger than itself.

The purpose of colonialism was to establish *economic colonies*—to exploit the nation's people and resources for the benefit of the "mother" country. The more powerful European countries would plant their national flags in a colony and send their representatives to run the government, but the United States usually chose to plant corporate flags in a colony and let these corporations dominate the territory's government. Central and South America are prime examples. There were exceptions, such as the conquest of the Philippines, which President McKinley said was motivated by the desire "to educate the Filipinos, and uplift and civilize and Christianize them" (Krugman 2002).

Colonialism, then, shaped many of the Least Industrialized Nations. In some instances, the Most Industrialized Nations were so powerful that when dividing their spoils, they drew lines across a map, creating new states without regard for tribal or cultural considerations (Kifner 1999). Britain and France did just this as they divided up North Africa and parts of the Middle East— which is why the national boundaries of Libya, Saudi Arabia, Kuwait, and other countries are so straight. This legacy of European conquests is a background factor in much of today's racial-ethnic and tribal violence: Groups with no history of national identity were incorporated arbitrarily into the same political boundaries.

World System Theory

To explain how global stratification came about, Immanuel Wallerstein (1974, 1979, 1990) proposed a second explanation, called **world system theory.** He analyzed how industrialization led to four groups of nations. The first, the *core nations,* are the countries that industrialized first (Britain, France, Holland, and later Germany). They grew rich and powerful. He calls the second group the *semiperiphery.* The economies of these nations, located around the Mediterranean, stagnated because they grew dependent on trade with the core nations. The economies of the third group, the *periphery,* or fringe nations, developed even less. These are the eastern European countries, which sold cash crops to the core nations. A fourth group of nations was left out of the development of capitalism altogether. This *external area* includes most of Africa and Asia. As capitalism expanded, the relationships among these groups of nations changed. Most notably, Asia is no longer left out of capitalism.

The **globalization of capitalism**—the adoption of capitalism around the world—has created extensive ties among the world's nations. Production and trade are now so interconnected that events around the globe affect us all. Sometimes this is immediate, as happens when a civil war disrupts the flow of oil, or—perish the thought—as would be the case if terrorists managed to get their hands on nuclear weapons. At other times, the effects are like a slow ripple, as when a government adopts new policies that gradually impede its ability to compete in world markets. All of today's societies, then, no matter where they are located, are part of a *world system.*

This interconnection is most evident among nations that do extensive trading with one another. The following Thinking Critically section explores implications of Mexico's *maquiladoras.*

Thinking Critically

When Globalization Comes Home: *Maquiladoras* South of the Border

When Humberto drives his truck among Ciudad Juarez's shanties—patched together from packing crates, discarded tires, and cardboard—women and children flock around him. Humberto is the water man, and his truckload of water means life.

Two hundred thousand Mexicans rush to Juarez each year, fleeing the hopelessness of the rural areas in pursuit of a better life. They didn't have running water or plumbing in the country anyway, and here they have the possibility of a job, a weekly check to buy food for the kids.

The pay is $10 a day.

This may not sound like much, but it is more than twice the minimum daily wage in Mexico.

Assembly-for-export plants, known as *maquiladoras,* dot the Mexican border. The North American Free Trade Agreement (NAFTA) allows U.S. companies to import materials to Mexico without paying tax and to then export the finished products into the United States, again without tax. It's a sweet deal: few taxes and $10 a day for workers starved for jobs. Some get an even sweeter deal. They pay their workers Mexico's minimum wage of $4—for 10-hour days with a 30-minute break (Darweesh 2000).

That these workers live in shacks, with no running water or means of sewage disposal, is not the employers' concern.

Then there is the pollution. Every day, Juarez pumps 75 million gallons of untreated sewage into the Rio Grande. Other *maquiladora* towns along the border do the same.

There is also the loss of jobs for U.S. workers. Six of the fifteen poorest cities in the United States are located on the sewage-infested Rio Grande. NAFTA didn't bring poverty to these cities. They were poor before this treaty, but residents resent the jobs they've seen move across the border (Thompson 2001).

What if the *maquiladora* workers organize and demand better pay? Farther south, even cheaper labor beckons. Guatemala and Honduras will gladly take the *maquiladoras.* So will China, where workers make $1 a day. Mexico has already lost many of its *maquiladora* jobs to places where people even more desperate will work for even less (Luhnow 2004).

Many Mexicans would say that this presentation is one-sided. "Sure there are problems," they say, "but that is always how it is when a country industrializes. Don't you realize that the *maquiladoras* bring jobs to people who have no work? They also bring roads, telephone lines, and electricity to undeveloped areas." "In fact," says Vicente Fox, the president of Mexico, "workers at the *maquiladoras* make more than the average salary in Mexico—and that's what we call fair wages" (Fraser 2001).

for your Consideration

Let's apply our three theoretical perspectives to see where reality lies. Conflict theorists say that capitalists weaken the bargaining power of workers by exploiting divisions among them. In what is known as the *split labor market,* capitalists pit one group of workers against another to lower the cost of labor. How do you think that *maquiladoras* fit this conflict perspective?

A photo taken inside a *maquiladora* in Juarez, Mexico. The workers are assembling electronics parts for automobiles.

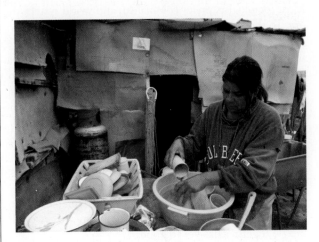

The home of a *maquiladora* worker.

When functionalists analyze a situation, they identify its functions and dysfunctions. What functions and dysfunctions of *maquiladoras* do you see?

Do *maquiladoras* represent exploitation or opportunity? As symbolic interactionists point out, reality is a perspective based on one's experience. What multiple realities do you see here?

Culture of Poverty

A third explanation of global stratification, quite unlike the other two, was proposed by economist John Kenneth Galbraith (1979). Galbraith claimed that the cultures of the Least Industrialized Nations hold them back. Building on the ideas of anthropologist Oscar Lewis (1966a, 1966b), Galbraith argued that some nations are crippled by a **culture of poverty,** a way of life that perpetuates poverty from one generation to the next. He explained it this way: Most of the world's poor people are farmers who live on little plots of land. They barely produce enough food to survive. Living so close to the edge of starvation, they have little room for risk—so they stick closely to tried-and-true, traditional ways. To experiment with new farming techniques could bring disaster, for failure would lead to hunger and death.

Their religion also encourages them to accept their situation, for it teaches fatalism: the belief that an individual's position in life is God's will. In India, the Dalits are taught that they must have done very bad things in a previous life to suffer so. They are supposed to submit to their situation—and perhaps in the next life they'll come back in a more desirable state.

Evaluating the Theories

Most sociologists prefer colonialism and world system theory. To them, an explanation based on a culture of poverty places blame on the victim—the poor nations themselves. It points to characteristics of the poor nations, rather than to international political arrangements that benefit the Most Industrialized Nations at the expense of the poor nations. But even taken together, these theories yield only part of the picture. None of these theories, for example, would have led anyone to expect that after World War II, Japan would become an economic powerhouse: Japan had a religion that stressed fatalism, two of its major cities had been destroyed by atomic bombs, and it been stripped of its colonies.

Each theory, then, yields but a partial explanation, and the grand theorist who will put the many pieces of this puzzle together has yet to appear.

Maintaining Global Stratification

Regardless of how the world's nations became stratified, why do the same countries remain rich year after year while the rest stay poor? Let's look at two explanations of how global stratification is maintained.

Neocolonialism

Sociologist Michael Harrington (1977) argued that colonialism fell out of style and was replaced by **neocolonialism.** When World War II changed public sentiment about sending soldiers and colonists to exploit weaker countries, the Most Industrialized Nations turned to the international markets as a way to control the Least Industrialized Nations.

As many of us learn the hard way, owing a large debt and falling behind on payments puts us at the mercy of our creditors. So it is with neocolonialism. The *policy* of selling weapons and other manufactured goods to the Least Industrialized Nations on credit turns those countries into eternal debtors. The capital they need to develop their own industries goes instead to the debt, which becomes bloated with mounting interest. Keeping these nations in debt forces them to submit to trading terms dictated by the neocolonialists (Carrington 1993; S. Smith 2001).

The oil-rich Middle Eastern nations provide a significant example of neocolonialism. Because of the two Gulf Wars and the terrorism that emanates from this region, it is worth considering Saudi Arabia (*Strategic Energy Policy* 2001; Prashad 2002). Great Britain founded Saudi Arabia, drawing its boundaries and naming the country after the man (Ibn Saud) that it picked to lead it. The Most Industrialized Nations need low-priced oil to control inflation and keep their factories running at a profit—and the Saudis provided it. If other nations pumped less oil—no matter the cause, whether revolution or an attempt to raise prices—the Saudis made up the shortfall.

For decades, this arrangement brought a stable supply of oil at low prices. In return, the United States overlooked human rights violations by the Saudi royal family and propped them in power by selling them high-tech weapons. The appearance of what appear to be real oil shortages accompanied by terrorism and political instability in the Middle East have short-circuited this mutually satisfying arrangement, bringing higher gasoline prices.

Multinational Corporations

Multinational corporations, companies that operate across many national boundaries, also help to maintain the global dominance of the Most Industrialized Nations. In some cases, multinational corporations exploit the Least Industrialized Nations directly. A prime example is the United Fruit Company, which used to control national and local politics in Central America. It ran these nations as fiefdoms for the company's own profit while the U.S. Marines waited in the wings. An occasional invasion to put down dissidents reminded regional politicians of the military power that supported U.S. financial interests.

Most commonly, however, it is simply by doing business that multinational corporations help to maintain international stratification. A single multinational may manage mining operations in several countries, do manufacturing in others, and run marketing networks around the globe. No matter where the profits are made, or where they are reinvested, the primary beneficiaries are the Most Industrialized Nations, especially the one in which the multinational corporation has its world headquarters.

In this game of profits, the elites of the Least Industrialized Nations are essential players (Sklair 2001; Wayne 2003). The multinational corporations funnel money to these elites, who, in return, create what is known as a "favorable business climate"—that is, low taxes and cheap labor. The money paid to the elites is politely called "subsidies" and "offsets"—not bribes. Although most people in the Least Industrialized Nations live in remote villages where they eke out a meager living on small plots of land, the elites of these countries favor urban projects, such as building laboratories and computer centers in the capital city. The elites live a sophisticated upper-class life in the major cities of their home country, with many sending their children to prestigious Western universities, such as Oxford, the Sorbonne, and Harvard.

The money given to the elites (whether by direct payment or by letting the elites share in the investments) helps to maintain stratification. Not only do these payoffs allow the elites to maintain a genteel lifestyle but also they give them the ability to purchase hi-tech weapons. This allows them to continue to oppress their people and to preserve their positions of dominance. The result is a political stability that keeps alive the diabolical partnership between the multinational corporations and the national elites.

This, however, is not the full story. Multinational corporations also play a role in changing international stratification. This is an unintentional byproduct of their worldwide search for cheap resources and labor. When these corporations move manufacturing from the Most Industrialized Nations to the Least Industrialized Nations, not only do they exploit cheap labor but also they bring jobs and money to these nations. Although workers in the Least Industrialized Nations are paid a pittance, it is more than they can earn elsewhere. With new factories come opportunities to develop skills and a capital base.

This does not occur in all nations, but it did in the Pacific Rim nations, nicknamed the "Asian tigers" (Hong Kong, Singapore, South Korea, and Taiwan, with some "emerging tigers" now appearing in this region). In return for providing the "favorable business climate" just mentioned, the multinational corporations invested billions of dollars in this region. These nations now have such a strong capital base that they have begun to rival the older capitalist countries. Subject to capitalism's "boom and bust" cycles, many workers and investors in these nations, including those in the *maquiladoras* that you just read about, will have their dreams smashed as capitalism moves into its next downturn.

Technology and Global Domination

The race between the Most and Least Industrialized Nations to develop and apply the new technologies is like a race between a marathon runner and someone with a broken leg. Can the outcome be in doubt? As the multinational corporations amass profits, they are able to invest huge sums in the latest technology. Gillette, for example, spent $100 million simply so that it could adjust its production "on an hourly basis" (Zachary 1995). These millions came from just one U.S. company. Many Least Industrialized Nations would love to have $100 million to invest in their entire economy, much less to use for finetuning the production of razor blades.

The race is not this simple, however. Although the Most Industrialized Nations have a seemingly insurmountable head start, in a surprise move, some of the Least Industrialized Nations are shortening the distance between themselves and the front runners. India and China are furiously adopting high technology. With cheap telecommunications and the outsourcing of labor by many Western multinational corporations, workers in India and China are able to compete with their Western counterparts (Friedman 2005). Although the maintenance of global domination is not in doubt at this point, it could be on the verge of a major shift from West to East.

Unintended Public Relations If capitalism is too severe in its exploitation, it can trigger counter reactions that can impede its advance toward world domination. Direct defenders of capitalsm are suspect, but sometimes people of good intentions unwttingly serve this purpose. An example is Bono and others who have campaigned for G-8 to forgive the debts owed them by some of the world's poorest nations. The cancelling of debts that results from this publicity is calculated, simply a public announcement of debts that G-8 will never be able to collect anyway. The result, however, is further triumph for capitalism. "How good they are to do this" is a reaction (since, after all, G-8 didn't have to cancel these debts). This act and resulting publicity helps to soften opposition, paving the way for G-8 to replace this debt with new ones, and for this group to continue on the path of world dominaiton.

A Concluding Note

Let's return to the two families in our opening vignette. Remember that these families represent distinct worlds of money and power, that is, global stratification. Their life chances—from access to material possessions to the opportunity for education and even the likely age at which they will die—are affected profoundly by global stratification. This division of the globe into interconnected units of nations with more or less wealth and more or less power and prestige, then, is much more than a matter of theoretical interest. In fact, it is *your* life we are talking about.

Summary and Review

Systems of Social Stratification

What is social stratification?

Social stratification refers to a hierarchy of relative privilege based on property, prestige, and power. Every society stratifies its members, and in every society, men as a group are placed above women as a group. P. 168.

What are the major systems of social stratification?

The major systems of social stratification are slavery, caste, and class. The essential characteristic of **slavery** is that some people own other people. Initially, slavery was based not on race but on debt, punishment, or defeat in battle. Slavery could be temporary or permanent and was not necessarily passed on to one's children. North American slaves had no legal rights, and the system was gradually buttressed by a racist **ideology.** In a **caste system,** status is determined by birth and is lifelong. A **class system** is much more open, for it is based primarily on money or material possessions. Industrialization encourages the formation of class systems. Gender cuts across all forms of social stratification. Pp. 168–173.

What Determines Social Class?

Karl Marx argued that a single factor determines social class: If you own the **means of production,** you belong to the **bourgeoisie** (capitalists); if you do not, you are one of the **proletariat** (workers). Max Weber argued that three elements determine social class: *property, prestige,* and *power.* Pp. 173–175.

Why Is Social Stratification Universal?

To explain why stratification is universal, functionalists Kingsley Davis and Wilbert Moore argued that to attract the most capable people to fill its important positions, society must offer them greater rewards. Melvin Tumin said that if this view were correct, society would be a **meritocracy,** with all positions awarded on the basis of merit. Gaetano Mosca argued that stratification is inevitable because every society must have leadership, which by definition means inequality. Conflict theorists argue that stratification came about because resources are limited and an elite emerges as groups struggle for them. Gerhard Lenski suggested a synthesis between the functionalist and conflict perspectives. Pp. 175–177.

How Do Elites Maintain Stratification?

To maintain social stratification within a nation, the ruling class adopts an ideology that justifies its current arrangements. It also controls information and uses technology. When all else fails, it turns to brute force. Pp. 177–178.

Comparative Social Stratification

What are key characteristics of stratification systems in other nations?

The most striking features of the British class system are speech and education. In Britain, accent reveals social class, and almost all of the elite attend "public" schools (the equivalent of our private schools). In the former Soviet Union, communism was supposed to abolish class distinctions. Instead, it merely ushered in a different set of classes. Pp. 178–180.

Global Stratification: Three Worlds

How are the world's nations stratified?

The model presented here divides the world's nations into three groups: the Most Industrialized, the Industrializing, and the Least Industrialized. This layering represents relative property, prestige, and power. Pp. 180–186.

How the World's Nations Became Stratified

Why are some nations rich and others poor?

The main theories that seek to account for global stratification are **colonialism, world system theory,** and the **culture of poverty.** Pp. 186–188.

Maintaining Global Stratification

How do the elites maintain global stratification?

There are two basic explanations for why the world's countries remain stratified. **Neocolonialism** is the ongoing dominance of the Least Industrialized Nations by the Most Industrialized Nations. The second explanation points to the influence of **multinational corporations.** The new technology gives further advantage to the Most Industrialized Nations. Pp. 188–190.

Thinking Critically
about Chapter 7

1. How do slavery, caste, and class systems of social stratification differ?
2. Why is social stratification universal?
3. Do you think that the low-wage factories of the multinational corporations, located in such countries as Mexico, represent exploitation or opportunity? Why?

Additional Resources

Companion Website   www.ablongman.com/henslin8e

- Content Select Research Database for Sociology, with suggested key terms and annotated references
- Link to 2000 Census, with activities
- Flashcards of key terms and concepts

- Practice Tests
- Weblinks
- Interactive Maps

Where Can I Read More on This Topic?

Suggested readings for this chapter are listed at the back of this book.

Social Class in the United States

Jacob Lawrence, *New Jersey*, 1946

OUTLINE

What Is Social Class?
Property
Power
Prestige
Status Inconsistency

Sociological Models of Social Class
Updating Marx
Updating Weber
Social Class in the Automobile Industry

Consequences of Social Class
Family Life
Education
Religion
Politics
Physical Health
Mental Health

Social Mobility
Three Types of Social Mobility
Women in Studies of Social Mobility
The New Technology and Fears of the Future

Poverty
Drawing the Poverty Line
Who Are the Poor?
Children of Poverty
The Dynamics of Poverty
Welfare Reform
Why Are People Poor?
Where Is Horatio Alger? The Social Functions of a Myth

Summary and Review

Ah, New Orleans, that fabled city on the Mississippi Delta. Images from its rich past floated through my head—pirates, treasure, intrigue. Memories from a pleasant vacation stirred my thoughts—the exotic French Quarter with its enticing aroma of Creole food and sounds of earthy jazz drifting through the air.

The shelter for the homeless, however, forced me back to an un-welcome reality. The shelter was the same as those I had visited in the North, West, and East—only dirtier. The dirt, in fact, was the worst I had encountered during my research, and this shelter was the only one to insist on payment in exchange for sleeping in one of its filthy beds.

The men looked the same—disheveled and hag-gard, wearing that unmistakable expression of de-spair—just like the homeless anywhere in the country. Except for the accent, you wouldn't know what region you were in. Poverty wears the same tired face wher-ever you are, I realized. The accent may differ, but the look remains the same.

I had grown used to the sights and smells of abject poverty. Those no longer surprised me. But after my fit-ful sleep with the homeless, I saw something that did. Just a block or so from the shelter, I was startled by a sight so out of step with the misery and despair I had just experienced that I stopped in midtrack.

Indignation swelled within me. Confronting me were life-size, full-color photos mounted on the transparent

I was startled by a sight so out of step with the misery and despair I had just experienced that I stopped in midtrack.

plexi-glass shelter of a bus stop. Staring back at me were images of finely dressed men and women proudly strutting about as they modeled elegant suits, dresses, diamonds, and furs.

A wave of disgust swept over me. "Something is cockeyed in this society," I thought, my mind refusing to stop juxtaposing these images of extravagance with the desper-ate suffering I had just witnessed. Occasionally the reality of social class hits home with brute force. This was one of those moments.

The disjunction that I felt in New Orleans was triggered by the ads, but it was not the first time that I had experienced this sensation. Whenever my research abruptly transported me from the world of the homeless to one of another social class, I felt a sense of disjointed unreality. Each social class has its own way of being, and because these fundamental orientations to the world contrast so sharply, the classes do not mix well.

What Is Social Class?

If you ask most Americans about their country's social class system, you are likely to get a blank look. If you press the matter, you are likely to get an answer like this: "There are the poor and the rich—and then there are you and I, neither poor nor rich." This is just about as far as most Americans' consciousness of social class goes. Let's try to flesh out this idea.

Our task is made somewhat difficult because sociologists have no clear-cut, agreed-on definition of social class. As was noted in the last chapter, conflict sociologists (of the Marxist orientation) see only two social classes: those who own the means of production and those who do not. The problem with this view, say most sociologists, is that it lumps too many people together. Physicians and corporate executives with incomes of $500,000 a year are lumped together with teenage "order takers" at McDonald's who work for $13,000 a year.

Most sociologists agree with Weber that there is more to social class than just a person's relationship to the means of production. Consequently, most sociologists use the components Weber identified and define **social class** as a large group of people who rank closely to one another in property, prestige, and power. These three elements separate people into different lifestyles, give them different chances in life, and provide them with distinct ways of looking at the self and the world. Let's look at how sociologists measure these three components of social class.

Property (Wealth)

Property comes in many forms, such as buildings, land, animals, machinery, cars, stocks, bonds, businesses, furniture, and bank accounts. When you add up the value of someone's property and subtract that person's debts, you have what sociologists call **wealth.** This term can be misleading, as some of us have little wealth—especially most college students. Nevertheless, if your net total comes to $10, then that is your wealth. (Obviously, wealth as a sociological term does not equal wealthy.)

Distinguishing Between Wealth and Income. Wealth and income are sometimes confused, but they are not the same. Where *wealth* is a person's net worth, **income** is a flow of money. Income can come from a number of sources: usually a business or wages, but also from rent, interest, or royalties, even from alimony, an allowance, or gambling. Some people have much wealth and little income. For example, a farmer may own much land (a form of wealth), but bad weather, combined with the high cost of fertilizers and machinery, can cause the income to dry up. Others have much income and little wealth. An executive with a $250,000 annual income may be debt-ridden. Below the surface prosperity—the exotic vacations, country club membership, private schools for the children, sports cars, and an elegant home—the credit cards may be maxed out, the sports cars in danger of being repossessed, and the mortgage payments "past due." Typically, however, wealth and income go together.

Distribution of Wealth. Who owns the wealth in the United States? One answer, of course, is "everyone." Although this statement has some merit, it overlooks how the nation's wealth is divided among "everyone." Let's look at how property—and also income—are distributed among Americans.

Overall, Americans are worth a hefty sum, about $33 trillion (*Statistical Abstract* 2005:Table 696). This includes all real estate, stocks, bonds, and business assets in the entire country. Figure 8.1 shows how highly concentrated this wealth is. Most wealth, 70 percent, is owned by only *10 percent* of the nation's families. As you can also see from this figure, 1 percent of Americans own one-third of all U.S. assets.

A mere one-half of 1 percent of Americans owns over a quarter of the entire nation's wealth. Very few minorities are numbered among this 0.5 percent. An exception is Oprah Winfrey, who has had an ultra-successful career in entertainment and investing. Worth $1.3 billion, she is the 215th richest person in the United States. Winfrey, who has given millions of dollars to help minority children, is shown here as she is interviewed by David Letterman.

Figure 8.1 Distribution of the Property of Americans

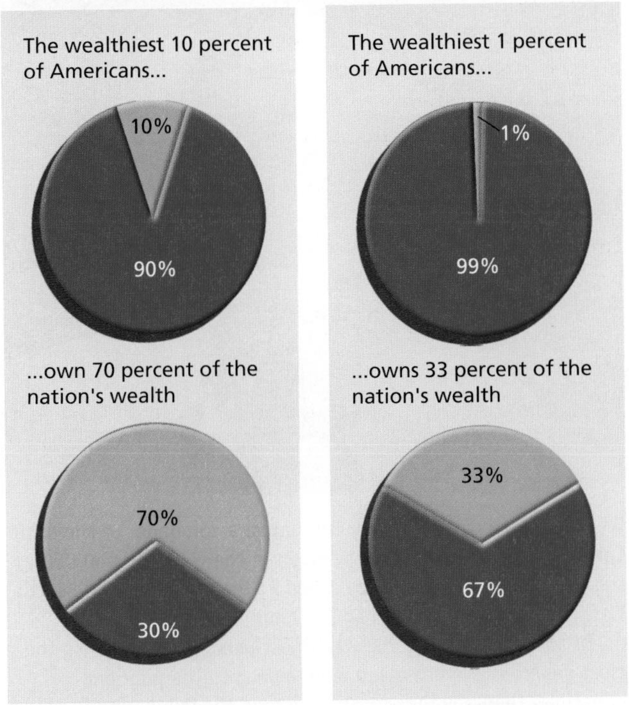

The wealthiest 10 percent of Americans...

10%

90%

...own 70 percent of the nation's wealth

70%

30%

The wealthiest 1 percent of Americans...

1%

99%

...owns 33 percent of the nation's wealth

33%

67%

Source: By the author. Based on Beeghley 2005.

Distribution of Income. How is income distributed in the United States? Economist Paul Samuelson (Samuelson and Nordhaus 2005) put it this way: "If we made an income pyramid out of a child's blocks, with each layer portraying $500 of income, the peak would be far higher than Mount Everest, but most people would be within a few feet of the ground."

Actually, if each block were 1½ inches tall, the typical American would be just 8 *feet off the ground,* for the average per capita income in the United States is about $32,000 per year. (This average income includes every American, even children.) The typical family climbs a little higher, for most families have more than one worker, and together they average about $52,000 a year. Yet compared with the few families who are on the mountain's peak, the average U.S. family would find itself only 13 feet off the ground (*Statistical Abstract* 2005:Tables 653, 670). Figure 8.2 portrays these differences.

The fact that some Americans enjoy the peaks of Mount Everest while most—despite their efforts—make it only 8 to 13 feet up the slope presents a striking image of income inequality in the United States. Another picture emerges

Figure 8.2 Distribution of the Income of Americans

Some U.S. families have incomes that exceed the height of Mt. Everest, 29,028 feet

Average U.S. family income $52,000 or 13 feet

Average U.S. individual income $32,000 or 8 feet

If a 1 1/2 inch child's block equals $500 of income, the average individual's annual income of $32,000 would represent a height of 8 feet. The average family's annual income of $52,000 would represent a height of 13 feet. The income of some families would represent a height greater than that of Mt. Everest.

Source: By the author.

if we divide the U.S. population into five equal groups and rank them from highest to lowest income. As Figure 8.3 shows, the top 20 percent of the population receives *almost half* (47.8 percent) of all income in the United States. In contrast, the bottom 20 percent of Americans receives only 4.2 percent of the nation's income.

Two features of Figure 8.3 are outstanding. First, notice how little change there has been in the distribution of income through the years. Second, look at how income inequality decreased from 1935 to 1970. *Since 1970, the richest 20 percent of U.S. families have grown richer, while the poorest 20 percent have grown poorer.* Despite numerous antipoverty programs, the poorest 20 percent of Americans receive *less* of the nation's income today than they did a generation ago. The richest 20 percent, in contrast, are receiving more, but not as much as they did in 1935.

The most affluent group in the United States is the chief executive officers (CEOs) of the nation's largest corporations. The *Wall Street Journal* surveyed the 350 largest U.S. companies to find out what they paid their CEOs. Their median compensation (including salaries, bonuses, and stock options) came to $5,920,000 a year ("The Boss's Pay" 2005). (Median means that half received more than this amount, and half less.)

The CEOs' income—which does *not* include what they earn from interest, dividends, rents, and capital gains, or the value of their company-paid limousines and

With a fortune of $48 billion, Bill Gates, a cofounder of Microsoft Corporation, is the wealthiest person in the world. His 40,000-square-foot home (sometimes called a "technopalace") in Seattle, Washington, was appraised at $110 million.

In addition to being the wealthiest person, Gates is also the most generous. He has given more money to the poor and minorities than any individual in history. His foundation is now focusing on fighting infectious diseases, developing vaccines, and improving schools.

Figure 8.3 The More Things Change, the More They Stay the Same: The Percentage of the Nation's Income Received by €ach Fifth of U.S. Families

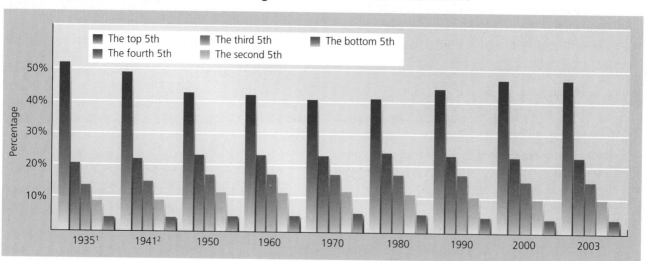

[1] Earliest year available.
[2] No data for 1940.

Source: By the author. Based on *Statistical Abstract* 1960:Table 417; 1970:Table 489; 2006:Table 680.

chauffeurs, airplanes and pilots, and private boxes at the symphony and professional sporting events—is *156 times* higher than the average pay of U.S. workers (*Statistical Abstract* 2005:Table 621). To really see the disparity, consider this: The average U.S. worker would have to work 2,320 *years* to earn the amount paid to the highest-paid executive listed on Table 8.1.

Imagine how you could live with an income like this. And this is precisely the point. Beyond cold numbers lies a dynamic reality that profoundly affects people's lives. The difference in wealth between those at the top and those at the bottom of the U.S. class structure means that these individuals experience vastly different lifestyles. For example, a colleague of mine who was teaching at an exclusive Eastern university piqued his students' curiosity when he lectured on poverty in Latin America. That weekend, one of his students borrowed his parents' corporate jet and pilot, and in class on Monday, he and his friends related their personal observations on poverty in Latin America. Americans who are at the low end of the income ladder, in contrast, lack the funds to travel even to a neighboring town for the weekend: For young parents, choices may revolve around whether to spend the little they have at the laundromat or on milk for the baby. The elderly might have to choose between purchasing the medicines they need or buying food. In short, divisions of wealth represent not "mere" numbers, but choices that make vital differences in people's lives, a topic that is explored in the Down-to-Earth Sociology box on the next page.

Power

Like many people, you may have said to yourself, "Sure, I can vote, but somehow the big decisions are always made despite what I might think. Certainly, *I* don't make the decision to send soldiers to Afghanistan or Iraq. *I* don't launch missiles against Kosovo or Baghdad. *I* don't decide to raise taxes or interest rates. It isn't *I* who decides to change Social Security or Medicare benefits."

And then another part of you may say, "But I do participate in these decisions through my representatives in Congress or by voting for president." True enough—as far as it goes. The trouble is, it just doesn't go far enough. Such views of being a participant in the nation's "big" decisions are a playback of the ideology we learn at an early age—an ideology that Marx said is promoted by the elites to both legitimate and perpetuate their power. Sociologists Daniel Hellinger and Dennis Judd (1991) call this the "democratic façade" that conceals the real source of power in the United States.

Back in the 1950s, sociologist C. Wright Mills (1956) was criticized for insisting that **power**—the ability to carry out your will despite resistance—was concentrated in the hands of a few, for his analysis contradicted the dominant ideology of equality. As was discussed in earlier chapters, Mills coined the term **power elite** to refer to those who make the big decisions in U.S. society.

Mills and others have stressed how wealth and power coalesce in a group of like-minded individuals who share ideologies and values. These individuals belong to the same private clubs, vacation at the same exclusive resorts, and even hire the same bands for their daughters' debutante balls. Their shared backgrounds and vested interests reinforce their view of both the world and their special place in it (Domhoff 1999a, 2002, 2003). This elite wields extraordinary power in U.S. society. Although there are exceptions, *most* U.S. presidents have come from this group—millionaire white men from families with "old money" (Baltzell and Schneiderman 1988).

Continuing in the tradition of Mills, sociologist William Domhoff (1990, 2002) argues that this group is so powerful that no major decision of the U.S. government is made without its approval. He analyzed how this group works behind the scenes with elected officials to determine both the nation's foreign and domestic policy—from setting Social Security taxes to imposing trade tariffs. Although Domhoff's conclusions are controversial—and alarming—they certainly follow logically from the principle that wealth brings power and extreme wealth brings extreme power.

Prestige

Occupations and Prestige. What are you thinking about doing after college? Chances are you don't have the option of lolling under palm trees at the beach. Almost all of us have to choose an occupation and go to work. Look

| Table 8.1 | The Highest-Paid CEOs |
| | |

Compensation	Executive	Company
$88 million	George David	United Technologies
$66 million	Ray Irani	Occidental Petroleum
$51 million	Robert Kovacevich	Wells Fargo
$50 million	Bruce Karatz	KB Home
$47 million	Jeffrey Bleustein	Harley-Davidson
$46 million	Lawrence Ellison	Oracle
$45 million	William Greehey	Valero Energy

Note: Compensation includes salary, bonuses, and stock options.
Source: "The Boss's Pay" 2005.

Down-to-Earth Sociology

How the Super-Rich Live

IT'S GOOD TO SEE HOW OTHER people live. It gives us a different perspective on life. Let's take a glimpse at the life of John Castle (his real name). After earning a degree in physics at MIT and an MBA at Harvard, John went into banking and securities, where he made more than $100 million (Lublin 1999).

Wanting to be connected to someone famous, John bought President John F. Kennedy's "Winter White House," an ocean-front estate in Palm Beach, Florida. John spent $11 million to remodel the 13,000-square-foot house so that it would be more to his liking. Among those changes: adding bathrooms numbers 14 and 15. He likes to show off John F. Kennedy's bed and also the dresser that has the drawer labeled "black underwear," carefully hand-lettered by Rose Kennedy.

At his beachfront estate, John gives what he calls "re-fined feasts" to the glitterati ("On History..." 1999). If he gets tired of such activities—or weary of swimming in the Olympic-size pool where JFK swam the weekend before his assassination—he entertains himself by riding one of his thoroughbred horses at his nearby 10-acre ranch. If this fails to ease his boredom, he can relax aboard his custom-built 42-foot Hinckley yacht.

The yacht is a real source of diversion. John once boarded it for an around-the-world trip. He didn't stay on board, though—just joined the cruise from time to time. A captain

How do the super-rich live? It is difficult to even imagine their lifestyles, but this photo of Jerry Seinfeld's home in East Hampton, New York, helps to give you an idea of how different their lifestyles are from most of us.

and crew kept the vessel on course, and whenever John felt like it he would fly in and stay a few days. Then he would fly back to the States to direct his business. He did this about a dozen times, flying perhaps 150,000 miles. An interesting way to go around the world.

How much does a cus-tom-built Hinckley yacht cost? John can't tell you. As he says, "I don't want to know what anything costs. When you've got enough money, price doesn't make a dif-ference. That's part of the freedom of being rich."

Right. And for John, being rich also means paying $1,000,000 to charter a private jet to fly Spot, his Appaloosa horse, back and forth to the vet. John didn't want Spot to have to endure a long trailer ride. Oh, and of course, there was the cost of Spot's medical treatment, an-other $500,000.

Other wealthy people put John to shame. Wayne Huizenga, the founder of Blockbuster, wanted more elbow room for his estate at Nantucket, so he added the house next door for $2.5 million (Fabrikant 2005). He also bought a 2,000-acre country club, complete with an 18-hole golf course, a 55,000-square-foot clubhouse, and 68 slips for vis-iting vessels. The club is so exclusive that its only members are Wayne and his wife.

---

at Table 8.2 on the next page to see how the career you are considering stacks up in terms of **prestige** (respect or re-gard). Because we are moving toward a global society, this table also shows how the rankings given by Americans com-pare with those of the residents of sixty other countries.

Why do people give more prestige to some jobs than to others? If you look at Table 8.2, you will notice that the jobs at the top share four features:

1. They pay more.
2. They require more education.
3. They entail more abstract thought.

4. They offer greater autonomy (independence, or self-direction).

If you look at the bottom of the list, you can see that people give less prestige to jobs with the opposite char-acteristics—to those that are low-paying, require less preparation or education, involve more physical labor, and are closely supervised. In short, the professions and white-collar jobs are at the top of the list, the blue-collar jobs at the bottom.

One of the more interesting aspects of these rankings is how consistent they are across countries and over time.

Table 8.2 Occupational Prestige: How the United States Compares with 60 Countries

Occupation	United States	Average of 60 Countries	Occupation	United States	Average of 60 Countries
Physician	86	78	Chiropractor	57	62
Supreme court judge	85	82	Athletic coach	53	50
College president	81	86	Social worker	52	56
Astronaut	80	80	Electrician	51	44
Lawyer	75	73	Undertaker	49	34
College professor	74	78	Real estate agent	48	49
Architect	73	72	Mail carrier	47	33
Biologist	73	69	Secretary	46	53
Dentist	72	70	Plumber	45	34
Civil engineer	69	70	Carpenter	43	37
Clergy	69	60	Farmer	40	47
Psychologist	69	66	Barber	36	30
Pharmacist	68	64	Store sales clerk	36	34
High school teacher	66	64	Truck driver	30	33
Registered nurse	66	54	Cab driver	28	28
Professional athlete	65	48	Garbage collector	28	13
Electrical engineer	64	65	Waiter or waitress	28	23
Author	63	62	Bartender	25	23
Veterinarian	62	61	Lives on public aid	25	16
Police officer	61	40	Bill collector	24	27
Sociologist	61	67	Janitor	22	21
Journalist	60	55	Shoe shiner	17	12
Actor or actress	58	52			

Note: For four occupations not located in the 1994 source, the 1991 ratings were used: Supreme court judge, astronaut, athletic coach, and lives on public aid.
Sources: Treiman 1977, Appendices A and D; Nakao and Treas 1991; 1994: Appendix D.

For example, people in every country rank college professors higher than nurses, nurses higher than social workers, and social workers higher than janitors. Similarly, the occupations that were ranked high back in the 1970s still rank high today—and likely will rank high in the years to come.

Displaying Prestige. People want others to acknowledge their prestige. In times past, in some countries, only the emperor and his family could wear purple—for it was the royal color. In France, only the nobility could wear lace. In England, no one could sit while the king was on his throne. Some kings and queens required that subjects walk backward as they left the room—so that no one would "turn their back" on the "royal presence."

Concern with displaying prestige has not let up. For some, it is almost an obsession. Military manuals specify precisely who must salute whom. The U.S. president enters a room only after everyone else attending the function is present (to show that *he* isn't the one waiting for *them*). They must also be standing when he enters. In the courtroom, bailiffs, sometimes armed, make certain that everyone stands when the judge enters.

The display of prestige permeates society. In Los Angeles, some people list their address as Beverly Hills and then add their correct ZIP code. When East Detroit changed its name to East Pointe to play off its proximity to swank Grosse Pointe, property values shot up (Fletcher 1997). Many pay more for clothing that bears a "designer" label. Prestige is often a primary factor in

Acceptable display of prestige and high social position varies over time and from one culture to another. Shown here is Elisabeth d'Autriche, queen of France from 1554 to 1592. It certainly would be difficult to outdress her at a party.

deciding which college to attend. Everyone knows how the prestige of a generic sheepskin from Regional State College compares with a degree from Harvard, Princeton, Yale, or Stanford.

Status symbols vary with social class. Clearly, only the wealthy can afford certain items, such as yachts. But beyond affordability lies a class-based preference in status symbols. For example, people who are striving to be upwardly mobile are quick to flaunt labels, Hummers, Land Rovers, and other material symbols to show that they have "arrived," while the rich, more secure in their status, often downplay such images. The wealthy see designer labels of the "common" classes as cheap and showy. They, of course, flaunt their own status symbols, such as $50,000 Rolex watches. Like the other classes, they, too, try to outdo one another; they boast about who has the longest yacht, how many homes they have, or that they have a helicopter fly them to their meetings or their golf games (Fabrikant 2005).

Status Inconsistency

Ordinarily, a person has a similar rank on all three dimensions of social class: property, prestige, and power. The homeless men in the opening vignette are an example. Such people are **status consistent.** Sometimes the match is not there, however, and someone has a mixture of high and low ranks, a condition called **status inconsistency.** This leads to some interesting situations.

Sociologist Gerhard Lenski (1954, 1966) pointed out that each of us tries to maximize our **status,** our social ranking. Thus, individuals who rank high on one dimension of social class but lower on others want people to judge them on the basis of their highest status. Others, however, who are trying to maximize their own position, may respond to them according to their lowest status.

A classic study of status inconsistency was done by sociologist Ray Gold (1952). He found that after apartment house janitors unionized, they made more money than some of the tenants whose garbage they carried out. Tenants became upset when they saw their janitors driving more expensive cars than they did. Some attempted to "put the janitor in his place" by making "snotty" remarks to him. For their part, the janitors took delight in knowing "dirty" secrets about the tenants, gleaned from their garbage.

Individuals with status inconsistency, then, are likely to confront one frustrating situation after another. They claim the higher status but are handed the lower one. The significance of this condition, said Lenski (1954), is that such people tend to be more politically radical. An example is college professors. Their prestige is very high, as we saw in Table 8.2, but their incomes are relatively low. Hardly anyone in U.S. society is more educated, yet college professors don't even come close to the top of the income pyramid. In line with Lenski's prediction, the politics of most college professors are left of center. This hypothesis may also hold true among academic departments; that is, the higher a department's average pay, the less radical are the members' politics. Teachers in departments of business and medicine, for example, are among the most highly paid in the university—and they also are the most politically conservative.

Instant wealth, the topic of the Down-to Earth Sociology box on the next page, provides an interesting case of status inconsistency.

Sociological Models of Social Class

The question of how many social classes there are is a matter of debate. Sociologists have proposed several models, but no single model has gained

Down-to-Earth Sociology

The Big Win: Life After the Lottery

"IF I JUST WIN THE LOTTERY, LIFE will be good. These problems I've got, they'll be gone. I can just see myself now."

So goes the dream. And many Americans shell out megabucks every week, with the glimmering hope that "Maybe this week, I'll hit it big."

Most are lucky to get $10, or maybe just win another scratch-off ticket.

But there are the big hits. What happens to these winners? Are their lives all wine, roses, and chocolate afterward?

Unfortunately, we don't yet have any systematic studies of the big winners, so I can't tell you what life is like for the average winner. But several themes are apparent from reporters' interviews.

The most common consequence of hitting it big is that life becomes topsy-turvy (Ross 2004). All of us are rooted somewhere. We have connections with others that provide the basis for our orientations to life and how we feel about the world. Sudden wealth can rip these moorings apart, and the resulting *status inconsistency* can lead to a condition sociologists call **anomie.**

First comes the shock. As Mary Sanderson, a telephone operator in Dover, New Hampshire, who won $66 million, said, "I was afraid to believe it was real, and afraid to believe it wasn't." Mary says that she never slept worse than her first night as a multimillionaire. "I spent the whole time crying—and throwing up" (Tresniowski 1999).

Reporters and TV camera operators appear on your doorstep. "What are you going to do with all that money?" they demand. You haven't the slightest idea, but in a daze you mumble something.

Then come the calls. Some are welcome. Your Mom and Dad call to congratulate you. But long-forgotten friends and distant relatives suddenly remember how close they really are to you—and strangely enough, they all have emergencies that your money can solve. You even get calls from strangers who have ailing mothers, terminally ill kids, sick dogs . . .

You have to unplug the phone and get an unlisted number.

Some lottery winners are flooded with marriage proposals. These individuals certainly didn't become more attractive or sexy overnight—or did they? Maybe money makes people sexy.

You can no longer trust people. You don't know what their real motives are. Before, no one could be after your money

Status inconsistency *is common for lottery winners, whose new wealth is vastly greater than the statuses that come with their education and occupation. Shown here are John and Sandy Jarrell of Chicago, after they learned that they were one of 13 families to share a $295 million jackpot. How do you think their $22 million will affect their lives?*

because you didn't have any. You may even fear kidnappers. Before, this wasn't a problem—unless some kidnapper wanted the ransom of a seven-year-old car.

The normal becomes abnormal. Even picking out a wedding gift is a problem. If you give the usual toaster, everyone will think you're stingy. But should you write a check for $25,000? If you do, you'll be invited to every wedding in town—and everyone will expect the same.

Here is what happened to some lottery winners:

As a tip, a customer gave a lottery ticket to Tonda Dickerson, a waitress at the Waffle House in Grand Bay, Alabama. She won $10 million. (Yes, just like the Nicholas Cage movie, *It Could Happen to You.*) Her coworkers sued her, saying that they had always agreed to split such winnings ("House Divided" 1999).

Then there is Michael Klinebiel of Rahway, New Jersey. When he won $2 million, his mother, Phyllis, said that they had pooled $20 a month for years to play the lottery. He said that was true, but his winning ticket wasn't from their pool. He had bought this one on his own. Phyllis sued her son ("Sticky Ticket" 1998).

Frank Capaci, a retired electrician in Streamwood, Illinois, who won $195 million, is no longer welcome at his old neighborhood bar. Two bartenders had collected $5 from customers and driven an hour to Wisconsin to buy tickets. When Frank won, he gave $10,000 to each of them. They said that he promised them more. Also, his former friends say that Capaci started to act "like a big shot," buying rounds of drinks but saying, "Except him," while pointing to someone he didn't like (Annin 1999).

Those who avoid *anomie* seem to be people who don't make sudden changes in their lifestyle or their behavior. They hold onto their old friends, routines, and other anchors in life that give them identity and a sense of belonging. Some even keep their old jobs—not for the money, of course, but because it anchors them to an identity they can count on, one familiar and comfortable.

Sudden wealth, in other words, poses a threat that has to be guarded against.

And I can just hear you say, "I'll take the risk!"

universal support. There are two main models: one that builds on Marx, the other on Weber.

Updating Marx

Marx argued that there are just two classes—capitalists and workers—with membership based solely on a person's relationship to the means of production (see Figure 8.4). As mentioned earlier, sociologists have criticized this view, saying that these categories are too broad. For example, because executives, managers, and supervisors don't own the means of production, they would be classified as workers. But what do these people have in common with assembly-line workers? The category of "capitalist" is also too broad. Some people, for example, employ a thousand workers, and their decisions directly affect a thousand families. Compare these capitalists with a man I know in Godfrey, Illinois, who used to fix cars in his back yard. As Frank gained a following, he quit his regular job, and in a few years, he put up a building with five bays and an office. Frank is now a capitalist, for he employs five or six mechanics and owns the tools and the building (the "means of production"). But what does he have in common with a factory owner who controls the lives of one thousand workers? Not only is Frank's work different but so are his lifestyle and the way he looks at the world.

To resolve this problem, sociologist Erik Wright (1985) suggests that some people are members of more than one class at the same time. They occupy what he calls **contradictory class locations.** By this, Wright means that a person's position in the class structure can generate contradictory interests. For example, the automobile-mechanic-turned-business-owner may want his mechanics

to have higher wages because he, too, has experienced their working conditions. At the same time, his current interests—making profits and remaining competitive with other repair shops—lead him to resist pressures to raise their wages.

Because of such contradictory class locations, Wright modified Marx's model. As summarized in Table 8.3, Wright identifies four classes: (1) *capitalists,* business owners who employ many workers; (2) *petty bourgeoisie,* small business owners; (3) *managers,* who sell their own labor but also exercise authority over other employees; and (4) *workers,* who simply sell their labor to others. As you can see, this model allows finer divisions than the one Marx proposed, yet it maintains the primary distinction between employer and employee.

Updating Weber

Sociologists Joseph Kahl and Dennis Gilbert (Gilbert and Kahl 1998; Gilbert 2003) developed a six-tier model to portray the class structure of the United States and other capitalist countries. Think of this model, illustrated in Figure 8.5 on page 203, as a ladder. Our discussion starts with the highest rung and moves downward. In line with Weber, on each lower rung, you find less property (wealth), less prestige, and less power. Note that in this model, education is also a primary measure of class.

The Capitalist Class. Sitting on the top rung of the class ladder is a powerful elite that consists of just 1 percent of the U.S. population. As you saw in Figure 8.1 on page 195, this capitalist class is so wealthy that it owns one-third of all U.S. assets. *This tiny 1 percent is worth more than the entire bottom 90 percent of the country* (Beeghley 2005).

Power and influence cling to this small elite. They have direct access to top politicians, and their decisions open or close job opportunities for millions of people. They even help to shape the consciousness of the nation: They own our major media and entertainment outlets—newspapers, magazines, radio and television stations, and sports franchises.

Figure 8.4 **Marx's Model of the Social Classes**

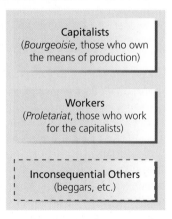

Capitalists
(*Bourgeoisie*, those who own the means of production)

Workers
(*Proletariat*, those who work for the capitalists)

Inconsequential Others
(beggars, etc.)

Table 8.3 **Wright's Modification of Marx's Model of the Social Classes**

1. Capitalists
2. Petty bourgeoisie
3. Managers
4. Workers

Figure 8.5 The U.S. Social Class Ladder

Social Class	Education	Occupation	Income	Percentage of Population
Capitalist	Prestigious university	Investors and heirs, a few top executives	$1,000,000+	1%
Upper Middle	College or university, often with postgraduate study	Professionals and upper managers	$125,000+	15%
Lower Middle	High school or college; often apprenticeship	Semiprofessionals and lower managers, craftspeople, foremen	About $60,000	34%
Working	High school	Factory workers, clerical workers, low-paid retail sales, and craftspeople	About $35,000	30%
Working Poor	Some high school	Laborers, service workers, low-paid salespeople	About $17,000	16%
Underclass	Some high school	Unemployed and part-time, on welfare	Under $10,000	4%

Source: Based on Gilbert and Kahl 1998 and Gilbert 2003; income estimates are modified from Duff 1995.

They also control the boards of directors of our most influential colleges and universities. The super-rich perpetuate themselves in privilege by passing on their assets and social networks to their children.

The capitalist class can be divided into "old" and "new" money. The longer that wealth has been in a family, the more it adds to the family's prestige. The children of "old" money seldom mingle with "common" folk—instead, they attend exclusive private schools, where they learn views of life that support their privileged position. They don't work for wages; instead, many study business or enter the field of law so that they can manage the family fortune. These old-money capitalists (also called "blue bloods") wield vast power as they use their extensive political connections to protect their huge economic empires (Domhoff 1990, 1999a; Sklair 2001).

At the lower end of the capitalist class are the *nouveau riche,* those who have "new money." Although they have made fortunes in business, the stock market, inventions, entertainment, or sports, they are outsiders to the upper class. They have not attended the "right" schools, and they don't share the social networks that come with old money. Not blue bloods, they aren't trusted to have the right orientations to life (Burris 2000). Even their "taste" in clothing and status symbols is suspect (Fabrikant 2005). Donald Trump, whose money is "new," is not listed in the *Social Register,* the "White Pages" of the blue bloods that lists the most prestigious and wealthy one-tenth of 1 percent of the U.S. population. Trump says he "doesn't care," but he reveals his true feelings by adding that his heirs will be in it (Kaufman 1996). He is probably right, for the children of the new-moneyed can ascend into the top part of

Johnny Depp

Jennifer Lopez

Lucy Liu

LeBron James

Sociologists use income, education, and occupational prestige to measure social class. For most people, this classification works well, but not for everyone. Entertainers sometimes are difficult to fit in. To what social class do Depp, Lopez, Liu, and James belong? Johnny Depp makes $10 million a year, Jennifer Lopez $26 million, and Lucy Liu around $5 million. When Lebron James got out of high school, he signed more than $100 million in endorsement contracts, as well as a $4 million contract to play basketball for the Cleveland Cavaliers.

the capitalist class—if they go to the right schools *and* marry old money.

Many in the capitalist class are philanthropic. They establish foundations and give huge sums to "causes." Their motivations vary. Some feel guilty because they have so much while others have so little. Others seek prestige, acclaim, or fame. Still others feel a responsibility—even a sense of fate or purpose—to use their money for doing good. Bill Gates, who has given more money to the poor than any other person, seems to fall into this latter category.

The Upper Middle Class. Of all the classes, the upper middle class is the one most shaped by education. Almost all members of this class have at least a bachelor's degree, and many have postgraduate degrees in business, management, law, or medicine. These people manage the corporations owned by the capitalist class or else operate their own business or profession. As Gilbert and Kahl (1993) say, these positions

may not grant prestige equivalent to a title of nobility in the Germany of Max Weber, but they certainly represent the sign of having "made it" in contemporary America.... Their income is sufficient to purchase houses and cars and travel that become public symbols for all to see and for advertisers to portray with words and pictures that connote success, glamour, and high style.

Consequently, parents and teachers push children to prepare for upper-middle-class jobs. About 15 percent of the population belong to this class.

The Lower Middle Class. About 34 percent of the population belong to the lower middle class. Members of this class have jobs that call for them to follow orders given by those who have upper-middle-class credentials. Their technical and lower-level management positions bring them a good living, although they feel threatened by taxes and inflation. They enjoy a comfortable, mainstream lifestyle, and many anticipate being able to move up the social class ladder.

The distinctions between the lower middle class and the working class on the next rung below are more blurred than those between other classes. In general, however, members of the lower middle class work at jobs that have slightly more prestige, and their incomes are generally higher.

The Working Class.   About 30 percent of the U.S. population belong to this class of relatively unskilled blue-collar and white-collar workers. Compared with the lower middle class, they have less education and lower incomes. Their jobs are less secure, more routine, and more closely supervised. One of their greatest fears is that of being laid off during a recession. With only a high school diploma, the average member of the working class has little hope of climbing up the class ladder. Job changes usually bring "more of the same," so most concentrate on getting ahead by achieving seniority on the job rather than by changing their type of work. They tend to think of themselves as having "real jobs" and regard the "suits" above them as paper pushers who have no practical experience (Morris and Grimes 2005).

The Working Poor.   Members of this class, about 16 percent of the population, work at unskilled, low-paying, temporary and seasonal jobs, such as sharecropping, migrant farm work, housecleaning, and day labor. Most are high school dropouts. Many are functionally illiterate, finding it difficult to read even the want ads. They are not likely to vote (Gilbert and Kahl 1993, 1998; Beeghley 2005), for they believe that no matter what party is elected to office, their situation won't change.

Although they work full time, millions of the working poor depend on help such as food stamps and donations from local food pantries to survive on their meager incomes (O'Hare 1996b). It is easy to see how one can work full time and still be poor. Suppose that you are married and have a baby 3 months old and another child 3 years old. Your spouse stays home to care for them, so earning the income is up to you. But as a high-school dropout, all you can get is a minimum wage job. At $5.15 an hour, you earn $206 for 40 hours. In a year, this comes to $10,712 before deductions. Your nagging fear—and daily nightmare—is of ending up "on the streets."

The Underclass.   On the lowest rung, and with next to no chance of climbing anywhere, is the **underclass.** Concentrated in the inner city, this group has little or no connection with the job market. Those who are employed—and some are—do menial, low-paying, temporary work. Welfare, if it is available, along with food stamps and food pantries, is their main support. Most

members of other classes consider these people the "ne'er-do-wells" of society. About 4 percent of the population fall into this class.

The homeless men described in the opening vignette of this chapter, and the women and children like them, are part of the underclass. These are the people whom most Americans wish would just go away. Their presence on our city streets bothers passersby from the more privileged social classes—which includes just about everyone. "What are those obnoxious, dirty, foul-smelling people doing here, cluttering up my city?" appears to be a common response. Some people react with sympathy and a desire to do something. But what? Almost all of us just shrug our shoulders and look the other way, despairing of a solution and somewhat intimidated by their presence.

The homeless are the "fallout" of our postindustrial economy. In another era, they would have had plenty of work. They would have tended horses, worked on farms, dug ditches, shoveled coal, and run the factory looms. Some would have explored and settled the West. Others would have been lured to California, Alaska, and Australia by the prospect of gold. Today, however, with no frontiers to settle, factory jobs scarce, and farms that are becoming technological marvels, we have little need for unskilled labor.

Social Class in the Automobile Industry

Let's use the automobile industry to illustrate the social class ladder. The Fords, for example, own and control a manufacturing and financial empire whose net worth is truly staggering. Their power matches their wealth, for through their multinational corporation, their decisions affect production and employment in many countries. The family's vast fortune and its accrued power are now several generations old. Consequently, Ford children go to the "right" schools, know how to spend money in the "right" way, and can be trusted to make family and class interests paramount in life. They are without question at the top level of the *capitalist* class.

Next in line come top Ford executives. Although they may have an income of several hundred thousand dollars a year (and some, with stock options and bonuses, earn several million dollars annually), most are new to wealth and power. Consequently, they would be classified at the lower end of the capitalist class.

A husband and wife who own a Ford agency are members of the *upper middle class.* Their income clearly sets them apart from the majority of Americans, and their reputation in the community is enviable. More than likely, they also exert greater-than-average influence in their community, but their capacity to wield power is limited.

A Ford salesperson, as well as the people who work in the dealership office, belongs to the *lower middle class.* Although there are some exceptional salespeople—even a few who make handsome incomes selling prestigious, expensive cars to the capitalist class—those at a run-of-the-mill Ford agency are lower middle class. Compared with the owners of the agency, their income is less, their education is likely to be less, and their work is less prestigious.

Mechanics who repair customers' cars are members of the *working class.* A mechanic who is promoted to supervise the repair shop joins the lower middle class. Those who "detail" used cars (making them appear newer by washing and polishing the car, painting the tires, spraying "new car scent" into the interior, and so on) belong to the *working poor.* Their income and education are low, and the prestige accorded to their work minimal. They are laid off when selling slows down.

Ordinarily, the *underclass* is not represented in the automobile industry. It is conceivable, however, that the agency might hire a member of the underclass to do a specific job such as mowing the grass or cleaning up the used car lot. In general, however, personnel at the agency do not trust members of the underclass and do not want to associate with them—even for a few hours. They prefer to hire someone from the working poor for such jobs.

Consequences of Social Class

Each social class can be thought of as a broad subculture with distinct approaches to life. Social class influences people's family life and their education. It also makes a difference for their religion, politics, and health. Let's look at these consequences of social class.

Family Life

Social class plays a significant role in family life. It even affects our choice of spouse and our chances of getting divorced.

Choice of Husband or Wife. Members of the capitalist class place strong emphasis on family tradition. They stress the family's ancestors, history, and even a sense of purpose or destiny in life (Baltzell 1979; Aldrich 1989). Children of this class learn that their choice of husband or wife affects not just themselves but also the entire family, that their spouse will have an impact on the "family line." Because of these background expectations, the field

of "eligible" marriage partners is much narrower than it is for the children of any other social class. In effect, parents in this class play a strong role in their children's mate selection.

Divorce. The more difficult life of the lower social classes, especially the many tensions that come from insecure jobs and inadequate incomes, leads to higher marital friction and the greater likelihood of divorce. Consequently, children of the poor are more likely to grow up in broken homes.

Education

As we saw in Figure 8.5, education increases as one goes up the social class ladder. It is not just the amount of education that changes with social class but also the type of education. Children of the capitalist class bypass public schools. They attend exclusive private schools, where they are trained to take a commanding role in society. Prep schools such as Phillips Exeter Academy, Groton School, and Woodberry Forest School teach upper-class values and prepare their students for prestigious universities (Higley 2003; Cookson and Persell 2005).

Keenly aware that private schools can be a key to social mobility, some upper-middle-class parents do their best to get their children into the prestigious preschools that feed into these exclusive prep schools. These preschools cost up to $17,000 a year (Gross 2003). The parents even elicit letters of recommendation for their 2- and 3-year-olds. Such parental expectations and resources are major reasons why children from the more privileged classes are more likely to enter and to graduate from college.

Religion

One area of social life that we might think would be unaffected by social class is religion. ("People are just religious, or they are not. What does class have to do with it?") As we shall see in Chapter 13, the classes tend to cluster in different denominations. Episcopalians, for example, are more likely to attract the middle and upper classes, while Baptists draw heavily from the lower classes. Patterns of worship also follow class lines: The lower classes are attracted to more expressive worship services and louder music, while the middle and upper classes prefer more "subdued" worship.

Politics

As has been stressed throughout this text, symbolic interactionists emphasize that people perceive events from their own corner in life. Political views are no exception to this principle, and the rich and the poor walk different political paths. The higher people are on the social class ladder, the more likely they are to vote for Republicans (Burris 2005). In contrast, most members of the working class believe that the government should intervene in the economy to provide jobs and to make citizens financially secure. They are more likely to vote for Democrats. Although the working class is more liberal on *economic* issues (policies that increase government spending), it is more conservative on *social* issues (such as opposing abortion and the Equal Rights Amendment) (Lipset 1959; Houtman 1995). People toward the bottom of the class structure are also less likely to be politically active—to campaign for candidates or even to vote (Soss 1999; Gilbert 2003; Beeghley 2005).

Physical Health

If you want to get a sense of how social class affects health, take a ride on Washington's Metro system. Start in the blighted Southeast section of downtown D.C. For every mile you travel to where the wealthy live in Montgomery County in Maryland, life expectancy rises about a year and a half. By the time you get off, you will find a twenty-year gap between the poor blacks where you started your trip and the rich whites where you ended it (Cohen 2004).

The effects of social class on physical health are startling. The principle is simple: The lower a person's social class, the more likely that individual is to die before the expected age. This principle holds true at all ages. Infants born to the poor are more likely than other infants to die before their first birthday. In old age—whether 75 or 95—a larger proportion of the poor die each year than do the wealthy.

How can social class have such dramatic effects? While there is some controversy over the reasons, there seem to be three basic explanations. First, social class opens and closes doors to medical care. Consider this example:

Terry Takewell (his real name), a 21-year-old diabetic, lived in a trailer park in Somerville, Tennessee. When Zettie Mae Hill, Takewell's neighbor, found the unemployed carpenter drenched with sweat from a fever, she called an ambulance. Takewell was rushed to nearby Methodist Hospital, where, it turned out, he had an outstanding bill of $9,400. A notice posted in the emergency room told staff members to alert supervisors if Takewell ever returned.

When the hospital administrator was informed of the admission, Takewell was already in a hospital bed. The administrator went to Takewell's room, helped him to his feet, and escorted him to the parking lot. There, neighbors found him under a tree and took him home.

Takewell died about twelve hours later.

Zettie Mae Hill is still torn up about it. She wonders whether Takewell would be alive today if she had directed his ambulance to a different hospital. She said, "I didn't think a hospital would just let a person die like that for lack of money." (Based on Ansberry 1988)

Why was Terry Takewell denied medical treatment and his life cut short? The fundamental reason is that health care in the United States is not a citizens' right but a commodity for sale. This gives us a two-tier system of medical care: superior care for those who can afford the cost and inferior care for those who cannot (Budrys 2003). Unlike the middle and upper classes, few poor people have a personal physician, and they often spend hours waiting in crowded public health clinics. After waiting most of a day, some don't even get to see a doctor. Instead, they are told to come back the next day. And when the poor are hospitalized, they are likely to find themselves in understaffed and underfunded public hospitals, treated by rotating interns who do not know them and who cannot follow up on their progress.

A second reason is lifestyles, which are shaped by social class. People in the lower social classes are more likely to smoke, eat food that contains a lot of fat, abuse drugs and alcohol, get little or no exercise, and practice unsafe sex (Chin et al. 2000; Navarro 2002). This, to understate the matter, does not improve their health.

There is a third reason. Life is better for the rich. They have fewer problems and more resources to deal with the ones they have. This gives them a sense of control over their lives, which is a source of both physical and mental health.

Mental Health

From the 1930s until now, sociologists have found that the mental health of the lower classes is worse than that of the higher classes (Faris and Dunham 1939; Srole et al. 1978; Schoenborn 2004). Greater mental problems are part of the higher stress that accompanies poverty. Compared with middle- and upper-class Americans, the poor have less job security and lower wages. They are more likely to divorce, to be the victims of crime, and to have more physical illnesses. Couple these conditions with bill collectors and the threat of eviction, and you can see how they can deal severe blows to people's emotional well-being.

Individuals higher up the social class ladder experience stress in daily life, of course, but their stress is generally less, and their coping resources are greater. Not only can they afford vacations, psychiatrists, and counselors but also *their class position gives them greater control over their lives, a key to good mental health.*

Social class is also significant for mental health care, as you can see from the following Thinking Critically section.

Thinking Critically

Mental Illness and Inequality in Health Care

Standing among the police, I watched as the elderly nude man, looking confused, struggled to put on his clothing. The man had ripped the wires out of the homeless shelter's main electrical box and then led the police on a merry chase as he ran from room to room.

I asked the officers where they were going to take the man, and they replied, "To Malcolm Bliss" (the state hospital). When I commented, "I guess he'll be in there for quite a while," they replied, "Probably just a day or two. We picked him up last week—he was crawling under cars at a traffic light—and they let him out in two days."

The police explained that individuals must be a danger to others or to themselves to be admitted as long-term patients. Visualizing this old man crawling under cars in traffic and thinking about the possibility of electrocution as he ripped out electrical wires with his bare hands, I marveled at the definition of "danger" that the hospital psychiatrists must be using.

Stripped of its veil, the two-tier system of medical care is readily visible. The poor—such as this confused naked man—find it difficult to get into mental hospitals. If they are admitted, they are sent to the dreaded state hospitals. In contrast, private hospitals serve the wealthy and those who have good insurance. The rich are likely to be treated with "talk therapy" (forms of psychotherapy), the poor with "drug therapy" (tranquilizers to make them docile, sometimes known as "medicinal straitjackets").

for your Consideration

How can we improve the treatment of the mentally ill poor? Take into consideration that the public does not want higher taxes. What about the broader, more fundamental issue: that of inequality in health care? Should medical care be a commodity that is sold to those who can afford it? Or do all citizens possess some fundamental right that should guarantee them high-quality health care?

Social Mobility

No aspect of life, then—from marriage to politics—goes untouched by social class. Because life is so much more satisfying in the more privileged classes, people strive to climb the social class ladder. What affects their chances?

Three Types of Social Mobility

There are three basic types of social mobility: intergenerational, structural, and exchange. **Intergenerational mobility** refers to a change that occurs between generations—when grown-up children end up on a different rung of the social class ladder than the one occupied by their parents. If the child of the dealership's owner parties too much, drops out of college, and ends up selling cars, he or she experiences **downward social mobility.** Conversely, if the child of someone who sells used cars graduates from college and buys a Saturn dealership, that person experiences **upward social mobility.** As discussed in the Cultural Diversity box on the next page, social mobility comes at a cost.

We like to think that individual efforts are the reason people move up the social class ladder—and their faults the reason they move down. In these examples, we can identify hard work, sacrifice, and ambition on the one hand versus indolence and drug abuse on the other. Although individual factors such as these do underlie social mobility, sociologists consider **structural mobility** to be the crucial factor. This second basic type of mobility refers to changes in society that cause large numbers of people to move up or down the class ladder.

Cultural Diversity *in the* United States

Social Class and the Upward Social Mobility of African Americans

THE OVERVIEW OF SOCIAL CLASS presented in this chapter doesn't apply equally to all the groups that make up U.S. society. Consider geography: What constitutes the upper class of a town of 5,000 people will be quite different from that of a city of a million. The extremes of wealth and the diversity and prestige of occupations will be less in the small town, where family background is likely to play a more significant role.

So, too, there are differences within racial-ethnic groups. While all racial-ethnic groups are marked by divisions of social class, what constitutes a particular social class will differ from one group to another—as well as from one historical period to another. Consider social class among African Americans (Cole and Omari 2003).

The earliest class divisions can be traced to slavery—to slaves who worked in the fields and those who worked in the "big house." Those

who worked in the plantation home were exposed to more "genteel" manners and forms of speech. Their more privileged position—which brought with it better food, clothing, and lighter work—was often based on skin color. Mulattos, lighter-skinned slaves, were often chosen for this more desirable work. One result was the development of a "mulatto elite," a segment of the slave population that, proud of its distinctiveness, distanced itself from the other slaves. At this time, there also were free blacks. Not only were they able to own property, but some of them even owned black slaves.

After the War Between the States (as the Civil War is known in the South), these two groups, the mulatto elite and the free blacks, became the basis of an upper class. Proud of their earlier status, they distanced themselves from other blacks. From these groups came most of the black professionals.

After World War II, just as with whites, the expansion of the black middle class opened access to a wider range

of occupations and residential neighborhoods. Beginning about 1960, the numbers of African Americans who were middle class surged. Today, more than half of all African American adults work at white-collar jobs. Twenty-two percent of these are at the professional or managerial level (Beeghley 2005). As with members of other racial-ethnic groups, African Americans who move up the social class ladder experience a hidden cost: They feel an uncomfortable distancing from their roots, a separation from significant others—parents, siblings, and childhood friends (hooks 2000). The upwardly mobile individual has entered a world unknown to those left behind.

The cost of upward mobility that comes with trying to straddle two worlds is common to individuals from all groups. What appears to be different for African Americans, however, is a sense of leaving one's racial-ethnic group, and of the necessity—if one is to succeed in the new world—of conforming to a dominant culture. This includes appearance and speech, but also something much deeper—values, aspirations, and ways of evaluating the self. In addition, the increased contact with whites that comes with social mobility often brings a greater sense of deprivation. Whites become a primary reference group, yet racism, mostly subtle and beneath the surface, continues. Awareness that they are not fully accepted in their new world engenders frustration, dissatisfaction, and cynicism among upwardly mobile African Americans.

for your Consideration

If you review the box on upward social mobility on page 74, you will find that Latinos face a similar situation. Why do you think this is? What connection do you see between upward mobility, frustration, and strong racial-ethnic identity? How do you think that the upward mobility of whites is different? Why?

The term *structural mobility* refers to changes in society that push large numbers of people either up or down the social class ladder. A remarkable example was the stock market crash of 1929, when tens of thousands of people suddenly lost immense amounts of wealth. People who once "had it made" found themselves standing on street corners selling apples or, as depicted here, selling their possessions at firesale prices.

To better understand structural mobility, think of how opportunities abounded when computers were invented. New types of jobs appeared overnight. Huge numbers of people attended workshops and took crash courses, switching quickly from blue-collar to white-collar work. Although individual effort certainly was involved—for some seized the opportunity, while others did not—the underlying cause was a change in the *structure* of work. Consider the opposite: how opportunities disappear during a depression, and millions of people are forced downward on the class ladder. In this instance, too, their changed status is due less to individual behavior than to *structural* changes in society.

The third type of social mobility, **exchange mobility,** occurs when large numbers of people move up and down the social class ladder but, on balance, the proportions of the social classes remain about the same. Suppose that a million or so working-class people are trained in some new technology, and they move up the social class ladder. Suppose also that because of a vast surge in imports, about a million skilled workers have to take lower-status jobs. Although millions of people change their social class, there is, in effect, an *exchange* among them. The net result more or less balances out, and the class system remains basically untouched.

Women in Studies of Social Mobility

In classic studies, sociologists concluded that about half of sons passed their fathers; about one-third stayed at the same level, and only about one-sixth moved down the class ladder (Blau and Duncan 1967; Featherman and Hauser 1978; Featherman 1979).

Feminists objected that it wasn't good science to focus on sons and ignore daughters (Davis and Robinson 1988).

They also pointed out that it was wrong to assume women had no class position of their own, that it was not valid to assign wives to the class of their husbands. The defense made by male sociologists of the time was that too few women were in the labor force to make a difference.

With huge numbers of women now working for pay, more recent studies include women (Beeghley 2005). Sociologists Elizabeth Higginbotham and Lynn Weber (1992), for example, studied 200 women from working-class backgrounds who became professionals, managers, and administrators in Memphis. They found that almost without exception, the women's parents had encouraged them while they were still little girls to postpone marriage and get an education. This study confirms how important the family is in the socialization process. It also supports the observation that the primary entry to the upper middle class is a college education. At the same time, if there had not been a *structural* change in society, the millions of new positions that women occupy would not exist.

The New Technology and Fears of the Future

The ladder also leads down, of course, which is precisely what strikes fear in the hearts of many workers. If the United States does not keep pace with global change and remain competitive by producing low-cost, high-quality goods, its economic position will decline. The result will be dwindling opportunities—fewer jobs, shrinking paychecks, and vast downward social mobility.

To compete in this global economic race, the United States is incorporating advanced technology in all spheres of life. While this means good jobs for many, it also implies

The ominous aspect that lurks behind this cute Japanese robot that has learned to ride a bicycle is not immediately visible. As robots become more proficient at performing human tasks, however, they increasingly replace human workers. No one yet knows the end of this process.

that the technologically illiterate are being left behind. This point was driven home to me when I saw the homeless sitting dejected in the shelters. There were our school dropouts, our technological know-nothings. Of what value are they to this new society that is now undergoing its piercing birth pains? They simply have no productive place. Their base of social belonging and self-esteem has been pulled out from under them.

Poverty

Many Americans find the "limitless possibilities" on which the American dream is based to be elusive. As is illustrated in Figure 8.5 on page 203, the working poor and underclass together form about one-fifth of the U.S. population. This percentage translates into a huge number: about 60 million people. Who are these people?

Drawing the Poverty Line

To determine who is poor, the U.S. government draws a **poverty line.** This measure was set in the 1960s, when poor people were thought to spend about one-third of their incomes on food. On the basis of this assumption, each year the government computes a low-cost food budget and multiplies it by 3. Families whose incomes are less than this amount are classified as poor; those whose incomes are higher—even by a dollar—are determined to be "not poor."

This official measure of poverty is grossly inadequate. Poor people actually spend only about 20 percent of their incomes on food, so to determine a poverty line we really ought to multiply their food budget by 5 instead of 3 (Uchitelle 2001). No political party in power wants to do this, as redrawing the line in this way would make it appear that poverty increased under their watch. Another problem with the poverty line is that some mothers work outside the home and have to pay for child care, but they are treated the same as mothers who don't have this expense. The poverty line is also the same for everyone across the nation, even though the cost of living is much higher in New York than in Alabama. In addition, the government does not count food stamps as income.

That a change in the poverty line would instantly make millions of people poor—or take away their poverty—would be laughable if it weren't so serious. (The humor has not been lost on Parker and Hart, as you can see from their sarcastic cartoon.) Although this line is arbitrary, it

WIZARD OF ID

By permission of Johnny Hart and Creators Syndicate.

This cartoon pinpoints the arbitrary nature of the poverty line. This makes me almost think that the creators of the Wizard of Id have been studying sociology.

is the official measure of poverty, and the government uses it to decide who will receive help and who will not. On the basis of this line, let's see who in the United States is poor. Before we do this, though, compare your ideas of the poor with the myths explored in the Down-to-Earth Sociology box on the next page.

Who Are the Poor?

Geography. As you can see from the Social Map below, the poor are not evenly distributed among the states. This map also shows a clustering of poverty in the South, a pattern that has prevailed for more than 100 years.

A second aspect of geography is also significant. About 59 million Americans live in rural areas. Of these, 9 million are poor. At 16 percent, the rate of poverty of rural Americans is higher than the national average of 12 percent. The rural poor are less likely to be single parents and more likely to be married and to have jobs. Compared with urban Americans, the rural poor are less skilled and less educated, and the jobs that are available to them pay less than similar jobs in urban areas (Dudenhefer 1993; Lichter and Crowley 2002).

The greatest predictor of whether Americans are poor is not geography, however; the greatest predictors are

Beyond the awareness of most Americans are the rural poor, such as this family in Kentucky. This family is typical of the rural poor: white and headed by a woman. What do you think the future holds for these children?

race-ethnicity, education, and the sex of the person who heads the family. Let's look at these three factors.

Race-Ethnicity. One of the strongest factors in poverty is race-ethnicity. As Figure 8.7 on the next page

---

Figure 8.6 Patterns of Poverty

Note: Poverty varies tremendously from one state to another. In the extreme, poverty is more than three times more common in Arkansas (18%) than it is in New Hampshire (5.6%).
Source: By the author. Based on *Statistical Abstract* 2005:Table 688.

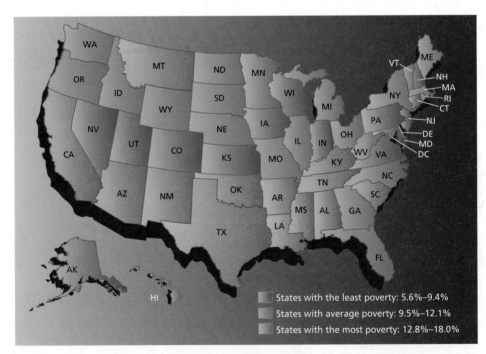

States with the least poverty: 5.6%–9.4%
States with average poverty: 9.5%–12.1%
States with the most poverty: 12.8%–18.0%

Down-to-Earth Sociology

Exploring Myths About the Poor

Myth 1 Most poor people are lazy. They are poor because they do not want to work.
Half of the poor are either too old or too young to work: About 40 percent are under age 18, and another 10 percent are age 65 or older. About 30 percent of the working-age poor work at least half the year.

Myth 2 Poor people are trapped in a cycle of poverty that few escape.
Long-term poverty is rare. Most poverty lasts less than a year (Lichter and Crowley 2002). Only 12 percent remain in poverty for five or more consecutive years (O'Hare 1996a). Most children who are born in poverty are *not* poor as adults (Ruggles 1989; Corcoron 2001).

Myth 3 Most of the poor are African Americans and Latinos.
As shown in Figure 8.7, the poverty rates of African Americans and Latinos are much higher than those of whites. Because there are so many more whites in the U.S. population, however, *most of the poor are white*. Of the 34 million U.S. poor, about 55 percent are white, 20 percent African American, 20 percent Latino, 3 percent Asian American, and 2 percent Native American. (*Statistical Abstract* 2005:Table 682; with adjustments).

Myth 4 Most of the poor are single mothers and their children.
Although about 38 percent of the poor match this stereotype, 34 percent of the poor live in married-couple families, 22 percent live alone or with nonrelatives, and 6 percent live in other settings.

Myth 5 Most of the poor live in the inner city.
This one is close to fact, as about 42 percent do live in the inner city. But 36 percent live in the suburbs, and 22 percent live in small towns and rural areas.

Myth 6 The poor live on welfare.
About half of the income of poor adults comes from wages and pensions, about 25 percent from welfare, and about 22 percent from Social Security.

Sources: Primarily O'Hare 1996a, 1996b, with other sources as indicated.

Figure 8.7 Poverty in the United States, by Age and Race-Ethnicity

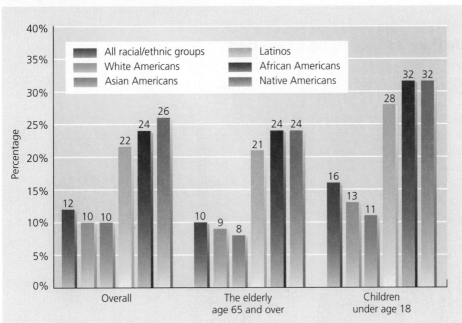

Note: The poverty line on which this figure is based is $18,392 for a family of four.
Source: By the author. Based on Statistical Abstract 2005:Tables 682, 683, 684.

shows, only 10 percent of whites and Asian Americans are poor, but 22 percent of Latinos, 24 percent of African Americans, and 26 percent of Native Americans live in poverty. The stereotype that most poor people are African Americans and Latinos is untrue. Because there are so many more whites in U.S. society, their much lower rate of poverty translates into larger numbers. As a result, most poor people are white.

Education.   You are aware that education is a vital factor in poverty, but you may not have known just how powerful it is. Figure 8.8 shows that only 3 of 100 people who finish college end up in poverty, but one of every five people who drop out of high school is poor. As you can see, the chances that someone will be poor decrease with each higher level of education. This principle applies regardless of race-ethnicity, but this figure also shows that at every level of education, race-ethnicity makes an impact.

The Feminization of Poverty.   One of the best indicators of whether or not a family is poor is family structure. Those least likely to be poor are families that are headed by both the mother and the father. Families headed by only a father or a mother are more likely to

be poor, with poverty the most common among mother-headed families. The reason for this can be summed up in this one statistic: On average, women who head families earn only 70 percent of the income of men who head families (*Statistical Abstract* 2005:Table 674). With our high rate of divorce, combined with more births to single women, the number of mother-headed families has increased over the years. Sociologists call this association of poverty with women *the feminization of poverty*.

Old Age.   As Figure 8.7 on page 213 shows, the elderly are less likely than the general population to be poor. In the past, growing old increased people's chances of being poor, but government policies to redistribute income—Social Security and subsidized housing, food, and medical care—slashed the rate of poverty among the elderly. This figure also shows how the prevailing racial-ethnic patterns carry over into old age. You can see how much more likely an elderly African American or Latino is to be poor than is an elderly white or Asian American.

Children of Poverty

Children are more likely to live in poverty than are adults or the elderly. This holds true regardless of race-ethnicity,

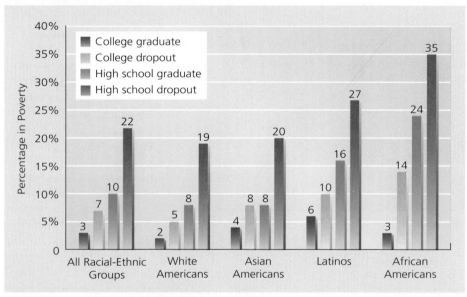

Figure 8.8   Who Ends Up Poor? Poverty by Education and Race-Ethnicity

Source: By the author. Based on *Statistical Abstract* 2005:Table 690.

but from Figure 8.7 on page 213 you can see how much greater poverty is among Latino and African American children. That millions of U.S. children are reared in poverty is shocking when one considers the wealth of this country and the supposed concern for the well-being of children. This tragic aspect of poverty is the topic of the following Thinking Critically section.

Thinking Critically

The Nation's Shame: Children in Poverty

One of the most startling statistics in sociology is shown in Figure 8.7 on page 213. Look at the rate of childhood poverty: For Asian Americans, it is one of nine children; for whites, one of seven or eight; for Latinos, one of five; and for African Americans and Native Americans, an astounding one of three. These percentages translate into incredible numbers—approximately *15 million* children live in poverty: 7 million white children, 3 million Latino children, 3½ million African American children, 300,000 Asian American children, and 250,000 Native American children.

Why do so many U.S. children live in poverty? The main reason, said sociologist and former U.S. Senator Daniel Moynihan (1927–2003), is an increase in births outside marriage. In 1960, one of twenty U.S. children was born to a single woman. Today that total is about *seven times higher*, and single women now account for one of three (34 percent) of all U.S. births. Figure 8.9 shows the striking relationship between births to single women and social class. For women above the poverty line, only 6 percent of births are to single women; for women below the poverty line this rate is *seven* times higher. Sociologists Lee Rainwater and Timothy Smeeding, who note that *the poverty rate of U.S. children is the highest in the industrialized world*, point to another cause: the lack of government support to children.

Regardless of the causes of childhood poverty, what is most significant is that these millions of children face all of the suffering and obstacles to a satisfying life that poverty entails. They are more likely to die in infancy, to be malnourished, to go hungry, to develop more slowly, and to have more health problems. They also are more likely to drop out of school, to become involved in criminal activities, and to have children while still in their teens—thus perpetuating the cycle of poverty.

Sources: Moynihan 1991; *Statistical Abstract* 1997:Table 1338; 2005:Tables 682, 684; Rainwater and Smeeding 2003.

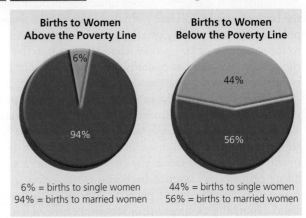

Figure 8.9   Births to Single Mothers

Births to Women Above the Poverty Line

6%

94%

6% = births to single women
94% = births to married women

Births to Women Below the Poverty Line

44%

56%

44% = births to single women
56% = births to married women

Note: Totals were available only for white women.
Source: Murray 1993.

for your Consideration

Many social analysts—liberals and conservatives alike—are alarmed at this high rate of child poverty. They emphasize that it is time to stop blaming the victim, and, instead, to focus on the *structural* factors that underlie this problem. They say that we need three fundamental changes: (1) removing obstacles to employment; (2) improving education; and (3) strengthening the family. Liberals add another factor: more government support for families. What specific programs would *you* recommend?

The Dynamics of Poverty

Some have suggested that the poor tend to get trapped in a **culture of poverty** (Harrington 1962; Lewis 1966a). They assume that the values and behaviors of the poor "make them fundamentally different from other Americans, and that these factors are largely responsible for their continued long-term poverty" (Ruggles 1989:7).

Lurking behind this concept is the idea that the poor are lazy people who bring poverty on themselves. Certainly, some individuals and families match this stereotype—many of us have known them. But is a self-perpetuating culture—one that is transmitted across generations and that locks people in poverty—the basic reason for U.S. poverty?

Researchers who followed 5,000 U.S. families uncovered some surprising findings. Contrary to common stereotypes, most poverty is short-lived, lasting only a year or less. This is because most poverty comes about because of a dramatic life change such as divorce, sudden unemployment, or even the birth of a child (O'Hare 1996a). As Figure 8.10 shows, only 12 percent of poverty lasts five years or longer. Contrary to the stereotype of lazy people who are content to live off the government, the vast majority of poor people don't like poverty, and they do whatever they can to *not* be poor.

Yet from one year to the next, the number of poor people remains about the same. This means that we have *exchange poverty*—the people who move out of poverty are replaced by people who move *into* poverty. Most of these newly poor will also move out of poverty within a year. Some people even bounce back and forth, never quite making it securely out of poverty. Poverty, then, is dynamic, touching a lot more people than the official figures indicate. Although 12 percent of Americans may be poor at any one time, twice that number—about one-fourth of the U.S. population—is or has been poor for at least a year.

Welfare Reform

After decades of criticism, U.S. welfare was restructured in 1996. A federal law—the Personal Responsibility and Work Opportunity Reconciliation Act—requires states to place a lifetime cap on welfare assistance and compels welfare recipients to look for work and to take available jobs. The maximum length of time that someone can collect welfare is five years. In some states, it is less. Unmarried teen parents must attend school and live at home or in some other adult-supervised setting.

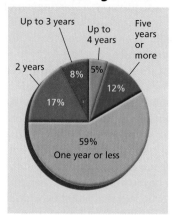

Figure 8.10 How Long Does Poverty Last?

- Up to 3 years — 8%
- Up to 4 years — 5%
- Five years or more — 12%
- 2 years — 17%
- 59% One year or less

Source: Gottschalk et al. 1994:89.

This law set off a storm of criticism. Some called it an attack on the poor. Defenders replied that the new rules would rescue people from poverty. They would transform welfare recipients into self-supporting and hard-working citizens—and reduce welfare costs. National welfare rolls plummeted, dropping by 50 to 60 percent (Cancian et al. 2003; Urban Institute 2005). Two out of five who left welfare also moved out of poverty (Hofferth 2002).

This is only the rosy part of the picture, however. Three of five are still in poverty or are back on welfare. A third of those who were forced off welfare have no jobs (Lichter and Crowley 2002; Hage 2004). Some can't work because they have health problems. Others lack transportation. Some are addicted to drugs and alcohol. Still others are trapped in economically depressed communities where there are no jobs. Then there are those who have jobs but earn so little that they remain in poverty. Consider one of the "success stories":

> JoAnne Sims, 37, lives in Erie, New York, with her 7-year-old daughter Jamine. JoAnne left welfare, and now earns $6.75 an hour as a cook for Head Start. Her 37-hour week brings $239.75 before deductions. With the help of medical benefits and a mother who provides child care, JoAnne "gets by." She says, "From what I hear, a lot of us who went off welfare are still poor . . . let me tell you, it's not easy." (Peterson 2000)

Conflict theorists have an interesting interpretation of welfare. They say that welfare's purpose is not to help people but, rather, to maintain a *reserve labor force*. It is designed to keep the unemployed alive during economic downturns until they are needed during the next economic boom. Reducing the welfare rolls through the 1996 law fits this model, as it occurred during the longest economic boom in U.S. history. Recessions are inevitable, however, and just as inevitable is surging unemployment. In line with conflict theory, we can predict that during the coming recession, welfare rules will be softened—to keep the reserve labor force ready for the next time they are needed.

Why Are People Poor?

Two explanations for poverty compete for our attention. The first, which sociologists prefer, focuses on *social structure*. Sociologists stress that *features of society* deny some people access to education or learning job skills. They emphasize racial-ethnic, age, and gender discrimination, as well as changes in the job market—the closing of plants, the elimination of unskilled jobs, and the increase in marginal jobs that pay poverty wages. In short, some people find their escape routes to a better life blocked.

A competing explanation focuses on the *characteristics of individuals* that are assumed to contribute to poverty. Sociologists reject individualistic explanations such as laziness and lack of intelligence, calling them worthless stereotypes. Individualistic explanations that sociologists reluctantly acknowledge include dropping out of school, bearing children in the teen years, and averaging more children than women in the other social classes. Most sociologists are reluctant to speak of such factors in this context, for they appear to blame the victim, something that sociologists bend over backward not to do.

Where Is Horatio Alger? The Social Functions of a Myth

In the late 1800s, Horatio Alger was one of the country's most talked-about authors. The rags-to-riches exploits of his fictional boy heroes and their amazing successes in overcoming severe odds motivated thousands of boys of that period. Although Alger's characters have disappeared from U.S. literature, they remain alive and well in the psyche of Americans. From abundant real-life examples of people of humble origins who climbed the social class ladder, Americans know that anyone can get ahead by really trying. In fact, they believe that most Americans, including minorities and the working poor, have an average or better-than-average chance of getting ahead—obviously a statistical impossibility (Kluegel and Smith 1986).

The accuracy of the **Horatio Alger myth** is less important than the belief that limitless possibilities exist for everyone. Functionalists would stress that this belief is functional for society. On the one hand, it encourages people to compete for higher positions, or, as the song says, "to reach for the highest star." On the other hand, it places blame for failure squarely on the individual. If you don't make it—in the face of ample opportunities to get ahead—the fault must be your own. The Horatio Alger myth helps to stabilize society: Since the fault is viewed as the individual's, not society's, current social arrangements can be regarded as satisfactory. This reduces pressures to change the system.

As Marx and Weber pointed out, social class penetrates our consciousness, shaping our ideas of life and our "proper" place in society. When the rich look at the world around them, they sense superiority and anticipate control over their own destiny. When the poor look around them, they are more likely to sense defeat and to anticipate that unpredictable forces will batter their lives. Each knows the dominant ideology: that their particular niche in life is due to their own efforts, that the reasons for success—or failure—lie solely with the self. Like fish that don't notice the water, people tend not to perceive the effects of social class on their own lives.

Summary *and* Review

What Is Social Class?
Most sociologists have adopted Weber's definition of **social class:** a large group of people who rank closely to one another in terms of property (wealth), prestige, and power. **Wealth**—consisting of the value of property minus debts—is concentrated in the upper classes. So is *income.* From the 1930s to the 1970s, the trend in the distribution of wealth in the United States was toward greater equality. Since that time, the trend has been toward greater inequality. Pp. 194–197.

Prestige is linked to occupational status. People's rankings of occupational prestige have changed little over the decades and are similar from country to country. Globally, the occupations that bring greater prestige are those that pay more, require more education and abstract thought, and offer greater independence. **Power** is the ability to get your way, even though others resist. C. Wright Mills coined the term **power elite** to refer to the small group that holds the reins of power in business, government, and the military. Pp. 197–200.

What is meant by the term status inconsistency?

Status is social ranking. Most people are **status consistent;** that is, they rank high or low on all three dimensions of social class. People who rank higher on some dimensions than on others are status inconsistent. The frustrations of **status inconsistency** tend to produce political radicalism. P. 200.

Sociological Models of Social Class

What models are used to portray the social classes?

Erik Wright developed a four-class model based on Marx: (1) capitalists (owners of large businesses), (2) petty bourgeoisie (small business owners), (3) managers, and (4) workers. Kahl and Gilbert developed a six-class model based on Weber. At the top is the capitalist class. In descending order are the upper middle class, the lower middle class, the working class, the working poor, and the **underclass.** Pp. 200–206.

Consequences of Social Class

How does social class affect people's lives?

Social class leaves no aspect of life untouched. It affects our chances of living and dying, of getting sick, of receiving good health care, of getting divorced, of getting an education, of participating in politics. Social class even affects our religious affiliation. Pp. 206–208.

Social Mobility

What are the three types of social mobility?

The term **intergenerational mobility** refers to changes in social class from one generation to the next. **Structural mobility** refers to changes in society that lead large numbers of people to change their social class. **Exchange mobility** is the movement of large numbers of people from one class to another with the net result that the relative proportions of the population in the classes remain about the same. Pp. 208–211.

Poverty

Who are the poor?

Poverty is unequally distributed in the United States. Minorities (except Asian Americans), children, woman-headed households, and rural Americans are more likely than others to be poor. The poverty rate of the elderly is less than that of the general population. Pp. 211–216.

Why are people poor?

Some social analysts believe that characteristics of *individuals* cause poverty. Sociologists, in contrast, examine *structural* features of society, such as employment opportunities, to find the causes of poverty. Sociologists generally conclude that life orientations are a consequence, not the cause, of people's position in the social class structure. Pp. 216–217.

How is the Horatio Alger myth functional for society?

The **Horatio Alger myth**—the belief that anyone can get ahead if only he or she tries hard enough—encourages people to strive to get ahead. It also deflects blame for failure from society to the individual. P. 217.

Thinking Critically
about Chapter 8

1. The belief that the United States is the land of opportunity draws millions of legal and illegal immigrants to the United States. How do the materials in this chapter support or undermine this belief?

2. How does social class affect people's lives?

3. What social mobility has your own family experienced? In what ways has this affected your life?

Additional Resources

Companion Website www.ablongman.com/henslin

- Content Select Research Database for Sociology, with suggested key terms and annotated references
- Link to 2000 Census, with activities
- Flashcards of key terms and concepts

- Practice Tests
- Weblinks
- Interactive Maps

Where Can I Read More on This Topic?

Suggested readings for this chapter are listed at the back of this book.

Inequalities of Race and Ethnicity

Laying the Sociological Foundation
Race: Myth and Reality
Ethnic Groups
Minority and Dominant Groups
How People Construct Their Racial-
    Ethnic Identity
Learning Prejudice
Individual and Institutional
    Discrimination

Theories of Prejudice
Psychological Perspectives
Sociological Perspectives

Global Patterns of Intergroup Relations
Genocide
Population Transfer
Internal Colonialism
Segregation
Assimilation
Multiculturalism (Pluralism)

Race and Ethnic Relations in the United States
European Americans
Latinos
African Americans
Asian Americans
Native Americans

Looking Toward The Future
The Immigration Debate
Affirmative Action
Toward a True Multicultural Society

Summary and Review

Pacita Abad, *Filipina: A Racial Identity Crisis*, 1990

Imagine that you are an African American man living in Macon County, Alabama, during the Great Depression of the 1930s. Your home is a little country shack with a dirt floor. You have no electricity or running water. You never finished grade school, and you make a living, such as it is, by doing odd jobs. You haven't been feeling too good lately, but you can't afford a doctor.

Then you hear the fantastic news. You rub your eyes in disbelief. It is just like winning the lottery! If you join Miss Rivers' Lodge (and it is free to join), you will get free physical examinations at Tuskegee University. You will even get free rides to and from the clinic, hot meals on examination days, and free treatment for minor ailments.

You eagerly join Miss Rivers' Lodge.

After your first physical examination, the doctor gives you the bad news. "You've got bad blood," he says. "That's why you've been feeling bad. Miss Rivers will give you some medicine and schedule you for your next exam. I've got to warn you, though. If you go to another doctor, there's no more free exams or medicine."

You can't afford another doctor anyway. You take your medicine and look forward to the next trip to the university.

You have just become part of one of the most callous experiments of all time

What has really happened? You have just become part of what is surely slated to go down in history as one of the most callous medical experiments of all time, outside of the infamous World War II Nazi and Japanese experiments. With heartless disregard for human life, the U.S. Public Health Service told 399 African American men that they had joined a social club and burial society called "Miss Rivers' Lodge." What the men were *not* told was that they had syphilis. For forty years, the "Public Health Service" allowed these men to go without treatment for their syphilis—just "to see what would happen." There was even a control group of 201 men who were free of the disease (Jones 1993).

By the way, you get one more benefit: a free autopsy to determine the ravages of syphilis on your body.

Laying the Sociological Foundation

As unlikely as it seems, this is a true story. It really did happen. Seldom do race and ethnic relations degenerate to this point, but troubled race relations are no stranger to us. Today's newspapers and TV news shows regularly report on racial problems. Sociology can contribute greatly to our understanding of this aspect of social life—and this chapter may be an eye-opener for you. To begin, let's consider to what extent race itself is a myth.

Race: Myth and Reality

With its 6½ billion people, the world offers a fascinating variety of human shapes and colors. People see one another as black, white, red, yellow, and brown. Eyes come in various shades of blue, brown, and green. Lips are thick and thin. Hair is straight, curly, kinky, black, blonde, and red—and, of course, all shades of brown.

As humans spread throughout the world, their adaptations to diverse climates and other living conditions resulted in this profusion of complexions, hair textures and colors, eye hues, and other physical variations. Genetic mutations added distinct characteristics to the peoples of the globe. In this sense, the concept of **race**—a group of people with inherited physical characteristics that distinguish it from another group—is a reality. Humans do, indeed, come in a variety of colors and shapes.

In two senses, however, race is a myth, a fabrication of the human mind. The *first* myth is the idea that any race is superior to others. All races have their geniuses—and their idiots. As with language, no race is superior to another.

Ideas of racial superiority abound, however. They are not only false but also dangerous. Adolf Hitler, for example, believed that the Aryans were a superior race, responsible for the cultural achievements of Europe. The Aryans, he said, were destined to establish a superior culture and usher in a new world order. This destiny required them to avoid the "racial contamination" that would come from breeding with inferior races; therefore, it was necessary to isolate and destroy races that posed a threat to Aryan purity and culture.

Put into practice, Hitler's views left an appalling legacy—the Nazi slaughter of those they deemed inferior: Jews, Slavs, gypsies, homosexuals, and people with mental and physical disabilities. Horrific images of gas ovens and emaciated bodies stacked like cordwood haunted the world's nations. At Nuremberg, the Allies, flush with victory, put the top Nazis on trial, exposing their heinous deeds to a shocked world. Their public executions, everyone assumed, marked the end of such grisly acts.

The reason I selected these photos is to illustrate how seriously we must take all preaching of hatred and of racial supremacy, even though it seems to come from harmless or even humorous sources. The strange-looking person on the left, who is wearing lederhosen, traditional clothing of Bavaria, Germany, is Adolf Hitler. He caused the horrific scene on the right, which greeted the British army when it liberated the concentration camp in Buchenwald, Germany: Thousands of people were dying of starvation and diseases amidst piles of rotting corpses awaiting mass burial.

Obviously, they didn't. In the summer of 1994 in Rwanda, Hutus slaughtered about 800,000 Tutsis—mostly with machetes (Gourevitch 1995). A few years later, the Serbs in Bosnia massacred Muslims, giving us the new term *ethnic cleansing*. As these events sadly attest, **genocide,** the attempt to destroy a group of people because of their presumed race or ethnicity, remains alive and well. Although more recent killings are not accompanied by swastikas and gas ovens, the perpetrators' goal is the same.

The *second* myth is that "pure" races exist. Humans exhibit such a mixture of physical characteristics—in skin color, hair texture, nose shape, head shape, eye color, and so on—that there are no "pure" races. Instead of falling into distinct types that are clearly separate from one another, human characteristics flow endlessly together. The mapping of the human genome system shows that humans are strikingly homogenous, that so-called racial groups differ from one another only once in a thousand subunits of the genome (Angler 2000). As shown in the example of Tiger Woods (discussed in the Cultural Diversity box on the next page), these minute gradations make any attempt to draw lines of race purely arbitrary.

Humans show such remarkable diversity that, as the text explains, there are no pure races. Shown here are Verne Troyer, who weighs about 45 pounds and is 2 feet 8 inches short, and Yao Ming, who weighs 296 pounds and is 7 feet 5 inches tall.

Although large groupings of people can be classified by blood type and gene frequencies, even these classifications do not uncover "race." Rather, "race" is so arbitrary that biologists and anthropologists cannot even agree on how many "races" there are. They have drawn up many lists, each containing a different number. Ashley Montagu (1964, 1999), a physical anthropologist, pointed out that some scientists have classified humans into only two "races," while others have found as many as two thousand. Montagu (1960) himself classified humans into forty "racial" groups. As the Down-to-Earth Sociology box on page 225 illustrates, even a plane ride can change someone's race!

The *idea* of race, of course, is far from a myth. Firmly embedded in our culture, it is a powerful force in our everyday lives. That no race is superior and that even biologists cannot decide how people should be classified into races is not what counts. "I know what I see, and you can't tell me anything different" seems to be the common attitude. As was noted in Chapter 4, sociologists W. I. and D. S. Thomas (1928) observed that "If people define situations as real, they are real in their consequences." In other words, people act on beliefs, not facts. As a result, we will always have people like Hitler and, as illustrated in our opening vignette, officials like those in the U.S. Public Health Service who thought that it was fine to experiment with people whom they deemed inferior. While few people hold such extreme views, most people appear to be ethnocentric enough to believe, at least just a little, that their own race is superior to others.

Ethnic Groups

Whereas people use the term *race* to refer to supposed biological characteristics that distinguish one people from another, **ethnicity** and **ethnic** apply to cultural characteristics. Derived from the word *ethnos* (a Greek word meaning "people" or "nation"), ethnicity and ethnic refer to people who identify with one another on the basis of common ancestry and cultural heritage. Their sense of belonging may center on nation of origin, distinctive foods, clothing, language, music, religion, or family names and relationships.

People often confuse the terms *race* and *ethnic group*. For example, many people, including many Jews, consider Jews a race. Jews, however, are more properly considered an ethnic group, for it is their cultural characteristics, especially their religion, that bind them together. Wherever Jews have lived in the world, they have intermarried.

Cultural Diversity *in the* United States

Tiger Woods and the Emerging Multiracial Identity: Mapping New Ethnic Terrain

TIGER WOODS, PERHAPS THE TOP GOLFER of all time, calls himself Cablinasian. Woods invented this term as a boy to try to explain to himself just who he was—a combination of Caucasian, Black, Indian, and Asian (Leland and Beals 1997; Hall 2001). Woods wants to embrace both sides of his family. To be known by a racial-ethnic identity that applies to just one of his parents is to deny the other parent.

Like many of us, Tiger Woods' heritage is difficult to specify. Analysts who like to quantify ethnic heritage put Woods at one-quarter Thai, one-quarter Chinese, one-quarter white, an eighth Native American, and an eighth African American. From this chapter, you know how ridiculous such computations are, but the sociological question is why many people consider Tiger Woods an African American. The U.S. racial scene is indeed complex, but a good part of the reason is simply that this is the label the media placed on him. "Everyone has to fit somewhere" seems to be our attitude. If they don't, we grow uncomfortable. And for Tiger Woods, the media chose African American.

The United States once had a firm "color line"—barriers between racial-ethnic groups that you didn't dare

Tiger Woods, after making one of his marvelous shots, this one at the Augusta National Golf Club in Augusta, Georgia.

cross, especially in dating or marriage. This invisible barrier has broken down, and today such marriages are common (*Statistical Abstract* 2005:Table 52). Several campuses have interracial student organizations. Harvard has two, one just for students who have one African American parent (Leland and Beals 1997).

As we march into unfamiliar ethnic terrain, our classifications are bursting at the seams. Kwame Anthony Appiah, of Harvard's Philosophy and Afro-American Studies Departments, says, "My mother is English; my father is Ghanaian. My sisters are married to a Nigerian and a Norwegian. I have nephews who range from blond-haired kids to very black kids. They are all first cousins. Now according to the American scheme of things, they're all black—even the guy with blond hair who skis in Oslo" (Wright 1994).

I marvel at what racial experts the U.S. census takers once were. When they took the census, which is done every ten years, they looked at people and assigned them a race. At various points, the census contained these categories: mulatto,

quadroon, octoroon, Negro, black, Mexican, white, Indian, Filipino, Japanese, Chinese, and Hindu. Quadroon (one-fourth black and three-fourths white) and octoroon (one-eighth black and seven-eighths white) proved too difficult to "measure," and these categories were used only in 1890. Mulatto appeared in the 1850 census and lasted until 1930. The Mexican government complained about Mexicans being treated as a race, and this category was used only in 1930. I don't know whose strange idea it was to make Hindu a race, but it lasted for three censuses, from 1920 to 1940 (Bean et al. 2004; Tafoya, Johnson, and Hill 2005).

Today, people are able to choose their own categories—and they have a lot of choices. In the 2000 census, every-one first declared that they were or were not "Spanish/Hispanic/Latino." Then they marked "one or more races" that they "consider themselves to be." They could choose from White; Black, African American, or Negro; American Indian or Alaska Native; Asian Indian, Chinese, Filipino, Japanese, Korean, Vietnamese, Native Hawaiian, Guamanian or Chamorro, Samoan, and other Pacific Islander. If these didn't do it, they could check a box called "Some Other Race" and then write whatever they wanted.

Perhaps the census should list Cablinasian, after all. There should also be ANGEL for African-Norwegian-German-English-Latino Americans, DEVIL for those of Danish-English-Vietnamese-Italian-Lebanese descent, and STUDY for the Swedish-Turkish-Uruguayan-Djibouti-Yugoslavian Americans. As you read farther in this chapter, you will see why these terms make as much sense as the categories we currently use.

for your Consideration

Just why do we count people by "race" anyway? Why not eliminate race from the U.S. census? (Race became a factor in 1790 during the first census when, for purposes of taxation and determining the number of representatives from each state, slaves were counted as three-fifths of whites!) Why is race so important to some people? Perhaps you can use the materials in this chapter to answer these questions.

Down-to-Earth Sociology

Can a Plane Ride Change Your Race?

At the beginning of this text (pages 21–22), I mentioned that common sense and sociology often differ. This is especially so when it comes to race. According to common sense, our racial classifications represent biological differences between people. Sociologists, in contrast, stress that what we call races are *social* classifications, not biological categories.

Sociologists point out that *our "race" depends more on the society in which we live than on our biological characteristics.* For example, the racial categories common in the United States are only one of *numerous* ways by which people around the world classify physical appearances. Although various groups use different categories, each group assumes that its categories are natural, merely a response to visible biology.

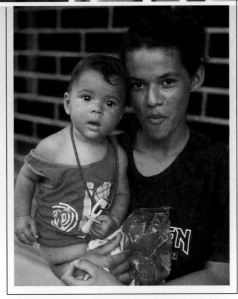

What "race" are these two Brazilians? Is the child of a different "race" than the mother? The text explains why "race" is such an unreliable concept that it changes even with geography.

To better understand this essential sociological point—that race is more social than it is biological—consider this: In the United States, children born to the same parents are all of the same race. "What could be more natural?" Americans assume. But in Brazil, children born to the same parents may be of different races—if their appearances differ. "What could be more natural?" assume Brazilians.

Consider how Americans usually classify a child born to a "black" mother and a "white" father. Why do they usually say that the child is "black"? Wouldn't it be equally as logical to classify the child as "white"? Similarly, if a child has one grandmother who is "black," but all her other ancestors are "white," the child is often considered "black." Yet she has much more "white blood" than "black blood." Why, then, is she considered "black"? Certainly not because of biology. Rather, such thinking is a legacy of slavery. In an attempt to preserve the "purity" of their "race" in the face of numerous children whose fathers were white slave masters and mothers were black slaves, whites classified anyone with even a "drop of black blood" as black. This was actually known as the "one–drop rule."

Even a plane trip can change a person's race. In the city of Salvador in Brazil, people classify one another by color of skin and eyes, breadth of nose and lips, and color and curliness of hair. They use at least seven terms for what we call white and black. Consider again a U.S. child who has "white" and "black" parents. If she flies to Brazil, she is no longer "black"; she now belongs to one of their several "whiter" categories (Fish 1995).

If the girl makes such a flight, would her "race" actually change? Our common sense revolts at this, I know, but it actually would. We want to argue that because her biological characteristics remain unchanged, her race remains unchanged. This is because we think of race as biological, when *race is actually a label we use to describe perceived biological characteristics.* Simply put, the race we "are" depends on our social location—on who is doing the classifying.

"Racial" classifications are also fluid, not fixed. You can see change occurring even now in the classifications that are used in the United States. The category "multiracial," for example, indicates both changing thought and perception.

for your Consideration

How would you explain to "Joe Six-Pack" that race is more a social classification than a biological one? Can you come up with any arguments to refute it? How do you think our racial-ethnic categories will change in the future?

Consequently, Jews in China may have Chinese features, while some Swedish Jews are blue-eyed blonds. This matter is strikingly illustrated in the photo on this page. Ethiopian Jews look so different from European Jews that when they immigrated to Israel many European Jews felt that the Ethiopians could not be *real* Jews.

Minority and Dominant Groups

Sociologist Louis Wirth (1945) defined a **minority group** as people who are singled out for unequal treatment and who regard themselves as objects of collective discrimination. Worldwide, minorities share several conditions: Their physical or cultural traits are held in low esteem by the dominant group, which treats them unfairly, and they tend to marry within their own group (Wagley and Harris 1958). These conditions tend to create a sense of identity among minorities (a feeling of "we-ness"). In many instances, a sense of common destiny emerges (Chandra 1993b).

Surprisingly, a minority group is not necessarily a *numerical* minority. For example, before India's independence in 1947, a handful of British colonial rulers discriminated against tens of millions of Indians. Similarly, when South Africa practiced apartheid, a smaller group of Dutch discriminated against a much larger number of blacks. And all over the world, females are a minority group. Accordingly, sociologists usually refer to those who do the discriminating not as the *majority* but, rather, as the **dominant group,** for they have the greater power, privileges, and social status.

Possessing political power and unified by shared physical and cultural traits, the dominant group uses its position to discriminate against those with different—and supposedly inferior—traits. The dominant group considers its privileged position to be the result of its own innate superiority.

Emergence of Minority Groups. A group becomes a minority in one of two ways. The *first* is through the expansion of political boundaries. With the exception of females, tribal societies contain no minority groups. Everyone shares the same culture, including the same language, and belongs to the same group. When a group expands its political boundaries, however, it produces minority groups if it incorporates people with different customs, languages, values, and physical characteristics into the same political entity and discriminates against them. For example, after defeating Mexico in war in 1848, the United States took over the Southwest. The Mexicans

This photo illustrates the difficulty that assumptions about *race* and *ethnicity* posed for Israel. These Ethiopian Jews, shown here as they arrived in Israel, looked so different from other Jews that it took several years for Israeli authorities to acknowledge this group's "true Jewishness."

living there, who had been the dominant group, were transformed into a minority group, a master status that has influenced their lives ever since. Referring to his ancestors, one Latino said, "We didn't move across the border—the border moved across us."

A *second* way in which a group becomes a minority is by migration. This can be voluntary, as with the millions of people who have chosen to move from Mexico to the United States, or involuntary, as with the millions of Africans who were brought in chains to the United States. (The way females became a minority group represents a third way, but as we will discuss in the next chapter, no one knows just how this occurred.)

How People Construct Their Racial-Ethnic Identity

Some of us have a greater sense of ethnicity than others. Some of us feel firm boundaries between "us" and "them." Others have assimilated so extensively into the mainstream culture that they are only vaguely aware of their ethnic origins. With interethnic marrying common, some do not even know the countries from which their families originated—nor do they care. If asked to identify themselves ethnically, they respond with something like "I'm Heinz 57—German and Irish, with a little Italian and French thrown in—and I think someone said something about being one-sixteenth Indian, too."

Why do some people feel an intense sense of ethnic identity, while others feel hardly any? Figure 9.1 portrays four factors, identified by sociologist Ashley Doane, that heighten or reduce our sense of ethnic identity. From this figure, you can see that the keys are relative size, power,

appearance, and discrimination. If your group is relatively small, has little power, looks different from most people in society, and is an object of discrimination, you will have a heightened sense of ethnic identity. In contrast, if you belong to the dominant group that holds most of the power, look like most people in the society, and feel no discrimination, you are likely to experience a sense of "belonging"—and to wonder why ethnic identity is such a big deal.

We can use the term **ethnic work** to refer to the way people construct their ethnicity. For people who have a strong ethnic identity, this term refers to how they enhance and maintain their group's distinctions—from clothing, food, and language to religious practices and holidays. For people whose ethnic identity is not as firm, it refers to attempts to recover their ethnic heritage, such as trying to trace family lines or visiting the country or region of their family's origin. Millions of Americans are engaged in ethnic work, which has confounded the experts who thought that the United States would be a **melting pot,** with most of its groups quietly blending into a sort of ethnic stew. Because so many Americans have become fascinated with their "roots," in recent years, some analysts have suggested that "tossed salad" is a more appropriate term than "melting pot."

Learning Prejudice

With prejudice and discrimination so significant in social life, let's consider the origin of prejudice and the extent of discrimination.

Distinguishing Between Prejudice and Discrimination. Prejudice and discrimination are common throughout the world. In Mexico, Hispanic Mexicans discriminate against Native American Mexicans; in Israel, Ashkenazi Jews, primarily of European descent, discriminate against Sephardic Jews from the Muslim world. In some places, the elderly discriminate against the young; in others, the young discriminate against the elderly. And all around the world, men discriminate against women.

Discrimination is an *action*—unfair treatment directed against someone. Discrimination can be based on many characteristics: age, sex, height, weight, income, education, marital status, sexual orientation, disease, disability, religion, and politics. When the basis of discrimination is someone's perception of race, it is known as **racism.** Discrimination is often the

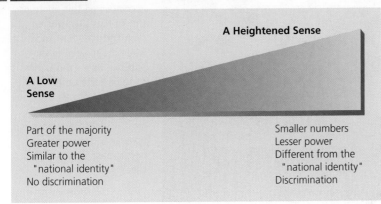

Figure 9.1 **A Sense of Ethnicity**

A Heightened Sense

A Low Sense

Part of the majority	Smaller numbers
Greater power	Lesser power
Similar to the "national identity"	Different from the "national identity"
No discrimination	Discrimination

Source: By the author. Based on Doane 1997.

result of an *attitude* called **prejudice**—a prejudging of some sort, usually in a negative way. There is also *positive prejudice,* which exaggerates the virtues of a group, as when people think that some group (usually their own) is more capable than others. Most prejudice, however, is negative and involves prejudging a group as inferior.

Learning from Association.   As with our other attitudes, we are not born with prejudice. Rather, we learn prejudice from the people around us. In a fascinating study, sociologist Kathleen Blee (2005) interviewed women who were members of the KKK and Aryan Nations. Her first finding is of the "ho hum" variety: Most women were recruited by someone who already belonged to the group. Blee's second finding, however, holds a surprise: Some women learned to be racists *after* they joined the group. They were attracted to the group not because it matched their racist beliefs but because someone they liked belonged to it. Blee found that their racism was not the *cause* of their joining but the *result* of their membership.

The Far-Reaching Nature of Prejudice.   It is amazing how much prejudice people can learn. In a classic article, psychologist Eugene Hartley (1946) asked people how they felt about several racial and ethnic groups. Besides blacks, Jews, and so on, he included the Wallonians, Pireneans, and Danireans—names he had made up. Most people who expressed dislike for Jews and blacks also expressed dislike for these three fictitious groups.

Hartley's study shows that prejudice does not depend on negative experiences with others. It also reveals that people who are prejudiced against one racial or ethnic group also tend to be prejudiced against other groups. People can be, and are, prejudiced against people they have never met—and even against groups that do not exist!

Internalizing Dominant Norms.   People can even learn to be prejudiced against their *own* group. A national survey of black Americans conducted by black interviewers found that African Americans think that lighter-skinned African American women are more attractive than those with darker skin (Hill 2002). Sociologists call this *the internalization of the norms of the dominant group.*

To study the internalization of dominant norms, psychologists Mahzarin Banaji and Anthony Greenwald created the "Implicit Association Test." In one version of this test, good and bad words are flashed on a screen along with photos of African Americans and whites. Most subjects are quicker to associate positive words (such as "love," "peace," and "baby") with whites and negative words (such as "cancer," "bomb," and "devil") with blacks. Here's the clincher: This is true for *both* white and black subjects (Dasgupta et al. 2000; Vedanatam 2005). Apparently, we all learn the *ethnic maps* of our culture, and, along with them, their route to biased perception.

In the 1920s and 1930s, the Ku Klux Klan was a powerful political force in the United States. To get a sense of the prevailing mood at the time, consider the caption that accompanied this photo of the Ku Klux Klan women from Freeport, New York, when it appeared in the papers: "Here's the Ladies in Their Natty Uniforms Marching in the Parade." Which theories would be most useful to explain this upsurge in racism among mainstream whites of the time?

Individual and Institutional Discrimination

Sociologists stress that we need to move beyond thinking in terms of **individual discrimination,** the negative treatment of one person by another. Although such behavior creates problems, it is primarily an issue between individuals. With their focus on the broader picture, sociologists encourage us to examine **institutional discrimination,** that is, to see how discrimination is woven into the fabric of society. Let's look at two examples.

Home Mortgages and Car Loans.   Bank lending provides an excellent illustration of institutional discrimination. As shown in Figure 9.2, race-ethnicity is a significant factor in getting a mortgage. When bankers looked at the statistics shown in this figure, they cried foul. It might *look* like discrimination, they said, but the truth is that whites have better credit histories. To see if this were true, researchers went over the data again, comparing the credit histories of the applicants. The lending gap did narrow a bit, but the bottom line was that even when applicants were identical in all these areas, African Americans and Latinos were *60 percent* more likely than whites to be rejected (Thomas 1992; Passell 1996). African Americans are also likely to be charged more than whites for their mortgages (Avery et al. 2005) and for car loans ("Judge Rules . . ." 2005; Peters and Hakim 2005). In short, it is not a matter of a banker here or there discriminating according to personal prejudices; rather, discrimination is built into the country's financial institutions.

Health Care.   Discrimination does not have to be deliberate. It can occur without the awareness of both those doing the discriminating and those being discriminated against. White patients, for example, are more likely than either Latino or African American patients to receive knee replacements (Skinner et al. 2003) and coronary by-pass surgery (Smedley et al. 2003). Treatment after a heart attack follows a similar pattern. A study of 40,000 patients shows that whites are more likely than blacks to be given cardiac catheterization, a test to detect blockage of blood vessels. This study holds a surprise: both

Figure 9.2   Race-Ethnicity and Mortgages: An Example of Institutional Discrimination

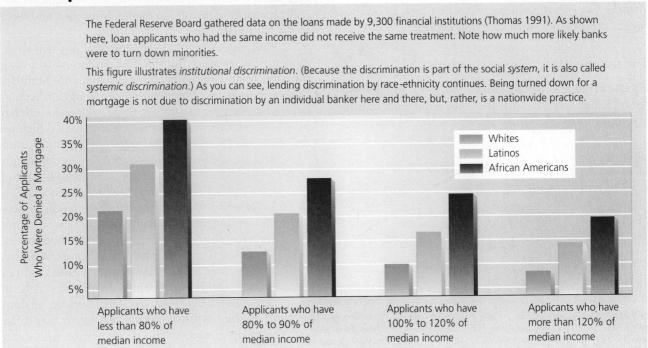

The Federal Reserve Board gathered data on the loans made by 9,300 financial institutions (Thomas 1991). As shown here, loan applicants who had the same income did not receive the same treatment. Note how much more likely banks were to turn down minorities.

This figure illustrates *institutional discrimination*. (Because the discrimination is part of the social *system*, it is also called *systemic discrimination*.) As you can see, lending discrimination by race-ethnicity continues. Being turned down for a mortgage is not due to discrimination by an individual banker here and there, but, rather, is a nationwide practice.

Source: By the author. Based on Thomas 1991.

black *and* white doctors are more likely to give this preventive care to whites (Stolberg 2001).

Researchers do not know why race is a factor in medical decisions. With both white and black doctors involved, we can be certain that physicians *do not intend* to discriminate. In ways we do not yet understand, but which could be related to the implicit bias that apparently comes with the internalization of dominant norms, discrimination is built into the medical delivery system. There, race serves as a subconscious motivation for giving or denying access to advanced medical procedures.

Institutional discrimination, then, is much more than a matter of inconvenience—it even translates into life and death. Table 9.1 also illustrates this point. Here you can see that an African American baby has more than *twice* the chance of dying in infancy as does a white baby, that an African American mother is *four* times as likely to die in childbirth as a white mother, and that African Americans live four to six years less than whites. The reason for these differences is not biology, but *social* factors, in this case largely income—the key factor in determining who has access to better nutrition, housing, and medical care.

Theories of Prejudice

Social scientists have developed several theories to explain prejudice. Let's first look at psychological explanations, then sociological ones.

Psychological Perspectives

Frustration and Scapegoats. In 1939, psychologist John Dollard suggested that prejudice is the result of frustration. People who are unable to strike out at the real source of their frustration (such as unemployment) find someone to blame. This **scapegoat,** often a racial, ethnic, or religious minority that they unfairly blame for their troubles, becomes a target on which they vent their frustrations. Gender and age also provide common bases for scapegoating.

Even mild frustration can increase prejudice. Psychologists Emory Cowen, Judah Landes, and Donald Schaet (1959) measured the prejudice of a sample of students. They then gave the students two puzzles to solve, making sure the students did not have enough time to solve them. After the students had worked furiously on the puzzles, the experimenters shook their heads in disgust and said that they couldn't believe the students hadn't finished such a simple task. They then retested the students and found that their scores on prejudice had increased. The students had directed their frustrations outward, transferring them to people who had nothing to do with the contempt that the experimenters had directed toward them.

The Authoritarian Personality. Have you ever wondered whether personality is a cause of prejudice? Maybe some people are more inclined to be prejudiced, and others more fair-minded. For psychologist Theodor Adorno, who had fled from the Nazis, this was no idle speculation. With the horrors he had observed still fresh in his mind, Adorno wondered whether there might be a certain type of person who is more likely to fall for the racist spewings of people like Hitler, Mussolini, and those in the Ku Klux Klan.

To find out, Adorno (1950) tested about two thousand people, ranging from college professors to prison inmates. To measure their ethnocentrism, anti-Semitism (bias against Jews), and support for strong, authoritarian leaders, he gave them three tests. Adorno found that people who scored high on one test also scored high on the other two. For example, people who agreed with anti-Semitic statements also agreed that governments should be authoritarian and that foreign ways of life posed a threat to the "American" way.

Adorno concluded that highly prejudiced people are insecure conformists. They have deep respect for authority and are submissive to superiors. He termed this the **authoritarian personality.** These people believe that things are either right or wrong. Ambiguity disturbs them, especially in matters of religion or sex. They become anxious when they confront norms and values that differ from their own. Categorizing people who differ from themselves as inferior assures them that their own positions are right.

Table 9.1	**Race and Health**			
	Mother/Child Deaths		**Life Expectancy**	
	Infant Deaths	**Maternal Deaths**	**Males**	**Females**
Whites Americans	5.8	6.0	75.4	80.5
African Americans	14.4	24.9	69.2	76.1

Note: The national database used for this table does not list these totals for other racial-ethnic groups. *White* refers to non-Hispanic whites. *Infant Deaths* refers to the number of deaths per year of infants under 1 year old per 1,000 live births. *Maternal Deaths* refers to the number of deaths per 100,000 women who give birth in a year.
Source: By the author. Based on *Statistical Abstract* 2006:Tables 96,104.

Adorno's research stirred the scientific community, stimulating more than a thousand research studies. In general, the researchers found that people who are older, less educated, less intelligent, and from a lower social class are more likely to be authoritarian. Critics say that this doesn't indicate a particular personality, just that the less educated are more prejudiced—which we already knew (Yinger 1965; Ray 1991). Nevertheless, researchers continue to study this concept (Van Hiel, Pandelaere, and Duriez 2004).

Sociological Perspectives

Sociologists find psychological explanations inadequate. They stress that the key to understanding prejudice cannot be found by looking *inside* people, but rather by examining conditions *outside* them. Therefore, sociologists focus on how social environments influence prejudice. With this background, let's compare functionalist, conflict, and symbolic interactionist perspectives on prejudice.

Functionalism. In a telling scene from a television documentary, journalist Bill Moyers interviewed Fritz Hipler, a Nazi intellectual who at age 29 was put in charge of the entire German film industry. Hipler said that when Hitler came to power, the Germans were no more anti-Semitic than the French, probably less so. He was told to create anti-Semitism. Obediently, Hipler produced movies that contained vivid scenes comparing Jews to rats—their breeding threatening to infest the population.

Why was Hipler told to create hatred? Prejudice and discrimination were functional for the Nazis. Germany was on its knees at this time. It had been defeated in World War I and was being economically devastated by war reparations. The middle class was being destroyed by runaway inflation. The Jews provided a scapegoat, a common enemy against which the Nazis could unite Germany. In addition, the Jews owned businesses, bank accounts, art work, and other property that the Nazis could confiscate. Jews also held key positions (as university professors, reporters, judges, and so on), which the Nazis could replace with their own flunkies. In the end, hatred also showed its dysfunctional side, as the Nazi officials who were hanged at Nuremberg discovered.

Prejudice becomes practically irresistible when state machinery is harnessed to advance the cause of hatred. To produce prejudice, the Nazis exploited government agencies, schools, police, courts, and the mass media. The results were devastating. Recall the identical twins

featured in the Down-to-Earth Sociology box on page 61. Oskar and Jack had been separated as babies. Jack was brought up as a Jew in Trinidad, while Oskar was reared as a Catholic in Czechoslovakia. Under the Nazi regime, Oskar learned to hate Jews, unaware that he himself was a Jew.

That prejudice is functional and is shaped by the social environment was demonstrated by psychologists Muzafer and Carolyn Sherif (1953). In a boys' summer camp, they assigned friends to different cabins and then had the cabins compete in sports. In just a few days, strong in-groups had formed, and even former lifelong friends were calling one another "crybaby" and "sissy" and showing intense dislike for one another.

The Sherif study teaches us several important lessons about social life. Note how it is possible to arrange the social environment to generate negative (or positive) feelings about people, and how prejudice arises if we pit groups against one another in an "I win, you lose" situation. You can also see that prejudice is functional, how it creates in-group solidarity. And, of course, it is obvious how dysfunctional prejudice is, when you observe the way it destroys human relationships.

Conflict Theory. Conflict theorists also analyze how groups are pitted against one another, but they focus on how this arrangement benefits those with power. They begin by noting that workers want better food, health care, housing, and education. To attain these goals, workers need good jobs. If workers are united, they can demand higher wages and better working conditions. If capitalists can keep workers divided, they can hold wages down. To do this, capitalists use two main weapons.

The first weapon is to keep workers insecure. Fear of unemployment works especially well. The unemployed serve as a **reserve labor force** for capitalists. The capitalists draw on the unemployed to expand production during economic booms, and when the economy contracts, they release these workers to rejoin the ranks of the unemployed. The lesson is not lost on workers who have jobs. They fear eviction and having their cars and furniture repossessed. Many know they are just one paycheck away from ending up "on the streets." This helps to keep workers docile.

The second weapon is encouraging and exploiting racial-ethnic divisions. Pitting worker against worker weakens labor's bargaining power. When white workers went on strike in California in the 1800s, owners of factories replaced them with Chinese workers. To break strikes by Japanese workers on plantations in Hawaii, owners used to hire Koreans (Xie and Goyette 2004).

This division of workers along racial-ethnic and gender lines is known as a **split labor market** (Du Bois 1935/1992; Roediger 2002). Although today's exploitation is more subtle, fear and suspicion continue to split workers. Whites are aware that other groups are ready to take their jobs, African Americans often perceive Latinos as competitors, and men know that women are eager to get promoted. All of this helps to make workers more docile.

The consequences are devastating, say conflict theorists. It is just like the boys in the Sherif experiment. African Americans, Latinos, whites, and others see themselves as able to make gains only at the expense of members of the other groups. This rivalry shows up along even finer racial-ethnic lines, such as that in Miami between Haitians and African Americans, who distrust each other as competitors. Divisions among workers deflect anger and hostility away from the power elite and direct these powerful emotions toward other racial and ethnic groups. Instead of recognizing their common class interests and working for their mutual welfare, workers learn to fear and distrust one another.

Symbolic Interactionism. While conflict theorists focus on the role of the capitalist class in exploiting racial and ethnic inequalities, symbolic interactionists examine how labels affect perception and create prejudice.

How Labels Create Prejudice Symbolic interactionists stress that *the labels we learn affect the way we see people.* Labels cause **selective perception;** that is, they lead us to see certain things while they blind us to others. If we apply a label to a group, we tend to perceive its members as all alike. We shake off evidence that doesn't fit (Simpson and Yinger 1972). Racial and ethnic labels are especially powerful. They are shorthand for emotionally charged stereotypes. The term *nigger,* for example, is not neutral. Nor are *cracker, honky, spic, mick, kike, limey, kraut, dago, guinea,* or any of the other scornful words people use to belittle ethnic groups. Such words overpower us with emotions, blocking out rational thought about the people to whom they refer (Allport 1954).

Labels and the Self-Fulfilling Prophecy Some stereotypes not only justify prejudice and discrimination but even produce the behavior depicted in the stereotype. Let's consider Group X. Negative stereotypes characterize the members of Group X as lazy, so they don't deserve good jobs. ("They are lazy and undependable and wouldn't do well.") This attitude creates a *self-fulfilling*

prophecy. Because they are denied jobs that require high dedication and energy, most members of Group X are limited to doing "dirty work," the kind of work thought appropriate for "that kind" of people. Since much dirty work is sporadic, members of Group X are often seen "on the streets." The sight of their idleness reinforces the original stereotype of laziness. The discrimination that created the "laziness" in the first place passes unnoticed.

Global Patterns of Intergroup Relations

Sociologists have studied racial-ethnic relations around the world. They have found six basic patterns that characterize the relationship of dominant groups and minorities. These patterns are shown in Figure 9.3 on the next page. Let's look at each.

Genocide

Last century's two most notorious examples of genocide occurred in Europe and Africa. In Germany during the 1930s and 1940s, Hitler and the Nazis attempted to destroy all Jews. In the 1990s, in Rwanda, the Hutus tried to destroy all Tutsis. One of the horrifying aspects of these slaughters was that those who participated did not crawl out from under a rock someplace. Rather, they were ordinary citizens whose participation was facilitated by labels that singled out the victims as enemies who deserved to die (Huttenbach 1991; Browning 1993; Gross 2001). Here's an example closer to home:

> When gold was discovered in northern California in 1849, the fabled "Forty-Niners" rushed in. With the region already inhabited by 150,000 Native Americans, the white government put a bounty on the heads of "the savages." It even reimbursed the whites for their bullets. The result was the slaughter of 120,000 Native American men, women, and children (Schaefer 2004).

Most Native Americans, however, died not from bullets but from diseases that the whites brought with them. The Native Americans had no immunity against diseases such as measles, smallpox, and the flu (Dobyns 1983; Schaefer 2004). The settlers also ruthlessly destroyed the Native Americans' food supply (buffalos, crops). As a result,

Figure 9.3 Global Patterns of Intergroup Relations: A Continuum

Inhumanity ← → Humanity

Rejection ← → Acceptance

Genocide	Population Transfer	Internal Colonialism	Segregation	Assimilation	Multiculturalism (Pluralism)
The dominant group tries to destroy the minority group (e.g., Germany and Rwanda)	The dominant group expels the minority group (e.g., Native Americans forced to reservations)	The dominant group exploits the minority group (e.g., low-paid, menial work)	The dominant group structures the social institutions to maintain minimal contact with the minority group (e.g., the U.S. South before the 1960s)	The dominant group absorbs the minority group (e.g., American Czechoslovakians)	The dominant group encourages racial and ethnic variation; when successful, there is no longer a dominant group (e.g., Switzerland)

throughout the United States about *95 percent* of Native Americans died (Thornton 1987; Churchill 1997).

Labels are powerful forces in human life. Labels that dehumanize others help people to **compartmentalize**—to separate their acts from their sense of being good and moral people. To regard members of a particular group as less than human means that it is okay to treat them inhumanely. Thus, people can kill—and still retain a good self-concept (Bernard et al. 1971). In short, *labeling the targeted group as inferior or even less than fully human facilitates genocide.*

Population Transfer

There are two types of **population transfer:** indirect and direct. *Indirect transfer* is achieved by making life so unbearable for members of a minority that they leave "voluntarily." Under the bitter conditions of czarist Russia, for example, millions of Jews made this "choice." *Direct transfer* occurs when a dominant group expels a minority. Examples include the U.S. government relocating Native Americans to reservations and transferring Americans of Japanese descent to internment camps during World War II.

In the 1990s, a combination of genocide and population transfer occurred in Bosnia and Kosovo, parts of the former Yugoslavia. A hatred nurtured for centuries had been kept under wraps by Tito's iron-fisted rule from 1944 to 1980. After Tito's death, these suppressed, smoldering hostilities soared to the surface, and Yugoslavia split into warring factions. When the Serbs gained power, Muslims rebelled and began guerilla warfare. The Serbs vented their hatred by what they termed ethnic cleansing: They terrorized villages with killing and rape, forcing survivors to flee in fear.

Internal Colonialism

In Chapter 7, the term *colonialism* was used to refer to one way that the Most Industrialized Nations exploit the Least Industrialized Nations (page 186). Conflict theorists use the term **internal colonialism** to describe the way in

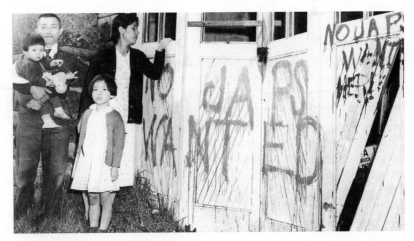

Amid fears that Japanese Americans were "enemies within" who would sabotage industrial and military installations on the West Coast, in the early days of World War II Japanese Americans were transferred to "relocation camps." Many returned home after the war to find that their property had been confiscated or vandalized.

which a country's dominant group exploits minority groups for its economic advantage. The dominant group manipulates the social institutions to suppress minorities and deny them full access to their society's benefits. Slavery, reviewed in Chapter 7, is an extreme example of internal colonialism, as was the South African system of *apartheid*. Although the dominant Afrikaners despised the minority, they found its presence necessary. As Simpson and Yinger (1972) put it, who else would do the hard work?

Segregation

Internal colonialism is often accompanied by **segregation**—the separation of racial or ethnic groups. Segregation allows the dominant group to maintain social distance from the minority and yet to exploit their labor as cooks, cleaners, chauffeurs, housekeepers, nannies, factory workers, and so on. In the U.S. South until the 1960s, by law, African Americans and whites had to use separate public facilities such as hotels, schools, swimming pools, bathrooms, and even drinking fountains. In thirty-eight states, laws prohibited marriage between blacks and whites. Violators could be sent to prison (Mahoney and Kooistra 1995; Crossen 2004b). The last law of this type was repealed in 1967 (Spickard 1989). Yet, in many villages of today's India, an ethnic group, the Dalits (untouchables), is forbidden to use the village pump. Dalit women must walk long distances to streams or pumps outside of the village to fetch their water (author's notes).

Racial-ethnic segregation in housing is still a fact of life for most Americans. In the Cultural Diversity box on the next page, you can see how residential segregation is related to internal colonialism.

Assimilation

Assimilation is the process by which a minority group is absorbed into the mainstream culture. There are two types. In *forced assimilation,* the dominant group refuses to allow the minority to practice its religion, to speak its language, or to follow its customs. Before the fall of the Soviet Union, for example, the dominant group, the Russians, required that Armenian children attend schools where they were taught in Russian. Armenians could celebrate only Russian holidays, not Armenian ones. *Permissible assimilation,* in contrast, allows the minority to adopt the dominant group's patterns in its own way and at its own speed.

Multiculturalism (Pluralism)

A policy of **multiculturalism,** also called **pluralism,** permits or even encourages racial and ethnic variation. The minority groups are able to maintain their separate identities, yet participate freely in the country's social institutions, from education to politics. Switzerland provides an outstanding example of multiculturalism. The Swiss population includes four ethnic groups: French, Italians, Germans, and Romansh. These groups have kept their own languages, and they live peacefully in political and economic unity. Multiculturalism has been so successful that none of these groups can properly be called a minority.

Race and Ethnic Relations in the United States

To write on race-ethnicity is like stepping onto a minefield: One never knows where to expect the next explosion. Even basic terms are controversial. The term African American, for example, is rejected by those who ask why this term doesn't include white immigrants from South Africa. Some people classified as African Americans also reject this term because they identify themselves as blacks. Similarly, some Latinos prefer the term *Hispanic American,* but others reject it, saying that it ignores the Indian side of their heritage. Some would limit the term *Chicanos*—commonly used to refer to Americans from Mexico—to those who have a sense of oppression and ethnic unity; they say that it does not apply to those who have assimilated.

No term that I use here, then, will satisfy everyone. Racial-ethnic identity is fluid, constantly changing, and all terms carry a risk as they take on highly–charged political meanings. Nevertheless, as part of everyday life, we classify ourselves and one another as belonging to distinct racial-ethnic groups. As Figure 9.4 on page 236 shows, on the basis of these self-identifications, whites make up 68 percent of the U.S. population, minorities (African Americans, Asian Americans, Latinos, and Native Americans) 31 percent. The other 1 percent claims membership in two or more racial-ethnic groups.

As you can see from the Social Map on page 237, the distribution of dominant and minority groups among the states seldom comes close to the national average. This is because minority groups tend to be clustered in regions. The extreme distributions are represented by Maine, which has only 4 percent minority, and Hawaii, where minorities outnumber Anglos 77 percent to 23 percent. With this as background, let's review the major groups in the United States, going from the largest to the smallest.

Cultural Diversity *in the* United States *and around the* World

"You Can Work for Us, But You Can't Live Near Us"

NEVER BEFORE HAD SO MANY PEOPLE crowded into the city hall in Glen Cove, Long Island. What drew them was nothing less than the future of their community, which had become an ethnic and social class crucible. At the front sat the well-groomed Long Islanders in their designer clothing. At the back were men in soiled jeans and work boots whose calloused hands bespoke their occupations as landscape laborers and construction workers. Most of them had fled the civil war in El Salvador, seeking safety and jobs in the United States.

The meeting was called to order by the town mayor, the son of Italian immigrants, who had launched a campaign to rid the town of a day labor shape-up area. He had asked the Immigration and Naturalization Service to raid the area where men gathered on the sidewalks in the early mornings to look for day jobs. This evening he proposed an ordinance making it illegal for groups of five or more to assemble on city streets for the purpose of seeking work. City residents testified that the men made cat

Day laborers lined up, soliciting work.

calls at women and urinated in public. They called the shape-up area an eyesore. Representatives of the immigrants countered by affirming the immigrants' constitutional right to freedom of assembly and argued that they were not loitering in the streets but waiting peacefully on the sidewalks.

The larger issue that haunted the Long Islanders, one that they were reluctant to acknowledge publicly but that a few individuals admitted to me privately, was the fear that the immigrants gave the impression that the town was in decline. Such a perception in suburbia jeopardizes real estate values—the bedrock of U.S. middle-class

security. Even the hint of racial or ethnic turnover frightens homeowners and potential buyers. In Glen Cove, this fear led to the campaign to get rid of the shape-up, the single most vivid image of the ethnically distinct people residing in the community.

What was discussed in the town meeting was that the immigrants had been attracted to the area precisely because the suburbanites desired their inexpensive labor. Almost all the landscapers on Long Island are now Salvadoran, and many families depend on immigrant women to clean their houses and take care of their children and elderly. Immigrants, especially from El Salvador and other Latin American countries, toil in the island's restaurants, factories, and laundries, and, at night, cleaning office buildings. They do the jobs that U.S. workers do not want to do or cannot afford to do because the jobs pay too little to support their families.

When the Salvadorans and other immigrants arrived on Long Island, seeking their futures, they first lived in communities with high minority populations. But as the immigrants moved closer to their jobs, their numbers swelled in more traditional bedroom communities like Glen Cove. These other towns also began to adopt "not in my backyard" policies by passing new ordinances or enforcing old ones, even refusing to let undocumented immigrant children attend their public schools. Old-timers felt that such measures could stem the decline in their way of life. What they overlooked was how immigrant labor is preserving their standard of living.

Source: Sarah Maher University of Vermont, *Salvadorans in Suburbia*

European Americans

Perhaps the event that best crystallizes the racial view of the nation's founders occurred at the first Continental Congress of the United States. There, they passed the Naturalization Act of 1790, declaring that only white immigrants could

apply for citizenship. The sense of superiority and privilege of **WASPs** (white Anglo-Saxon Protestants) was not limited to their views of race. They also viewed white Europeans from countries other than England as inferior. They greeted **white ethnics**—immigrants from Europe

Figure 9.4 U.S. Racial-Ethnic Groups

Notes:

[a]The totals in this figure should be taken as broadly accurate only. The totals for groups and even for the U.S. population vary from table to table in the source.

[b]Interestingly, this total is *eight* times higher than all the Irish who live in Ireland.

[c]Includes French Canadian.

[d]Includes "Scottish-Irish."

[e]Most Latinos trace at least part of their ancestry to Europe.

[f]In descending order, the largest groups of Asian Americans are from China, the Philippines, India, Vietnam, Korea, and Japan. See Figure 9.9. Also includes those who identify themselves as Native Hawaiian or Pacific Islander.

[g]Includes Native American, Inuit, and Aleut.

Source: By the author. Based on Statistical Abstract 2005:Tables 13, 47.

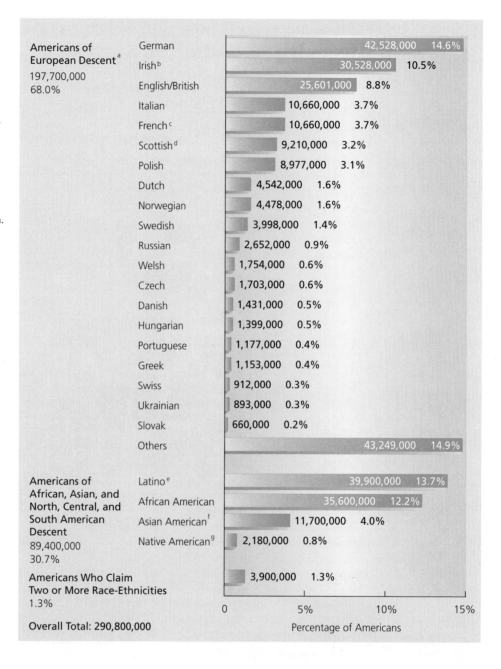

Americans of European Descent[a] 197,700,000 68.0%

Group	Count	Percent
German	42,528,000	14.6%
Irish[b]	30,528,000	10.5%
English/British	25,601,000	8.8%
Italian	10,660,000	3.7%
French[c]	10,660,000	3.7%
Scottish[d]	9,210,000	3.2%
Polish	8,977,000	3.1%
Dutch	4,542,000	1.6%
Norwegian	4,478,000	1.6%
Swedish	3,998,000	1.4%
Russian	2,652,000	0.9%
Welsh	1,754,000	0.6%
Czech	1,703,000	0.6%
Danish	1,431,000	0.5%
Hungarian	1,399,000	0.5%
Portuguese	1,177,000	0.4%
Greek	1,153,000	0.4%
Swiss	912,000	0.3%
Ukrainian	893,000	0.3%
Slovak	660,000	0.2%
Others	43,249,000	14.9%

Americans of African, Asian, and North, Central, and South American Descent 89,400,000 30.7%

Group	Count	Percent
Latino[e]	39,900,000	13.7%
African American	35,600,000	12.2%
Asian American[f]	11,700,000	4.0%
Native American[g]	2,180,000	0.8%

Americans Who Claim Two or More Race-Ethnicities 1.3%

3,900,000 1.3%

Overall Total: 290,800,000

Percentage of Americans

whose language and other customs differed from theirs—with disdain and negative stereotypes. They especially despised the Irish, viewing them as dirty, lazy drunkards, but they also painted Germans, Poles, Jews, Italians, and others with similarly broad disparaging brush strokes.

To get an idea of how intense these feelings were, consider this statement by Benjamin Franklin regarding immigrants from Germany:

Why should the Palatine boors be suffered to swarm into our settlements and by herding together establish their language and manners to the exclusion of ours? Why should Pennsylvania, founded by the English, become a colony of aliens, who will shortly be so numerous as to germanize us instead of our anglifying them? (In Alba and Nee 2003:17)

The cultural and political dominance of the WASPs placed pressure on immigrants to assimilate into the

Figure 9.5 The Distribution of Dominant and Minority Groups

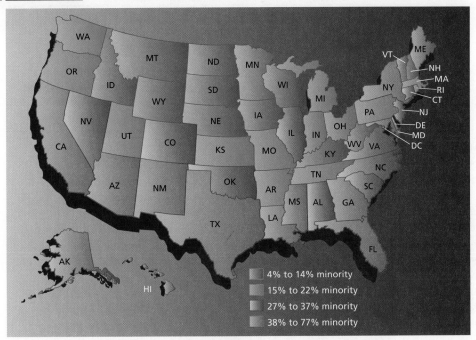

	4% to 14% minority
	15% to 22% minority
	27% to 37% minority
	38% to 77% minority

This social map indicates how unevenly distributed U.S. minority groups are. The extremes are Hawaii with 77 percent minority and Maine with 4 percent minority.

Source: By the author. Based on *Statistical Abstract* 2005:Tables 13, 47.

mainstream culture. The children of most immigrants embraced the new way of life and quickly came to think of themselves as Americans rather than as Germans, French, Hungarians, and so on. They dropped their distinctive customs, especially their language, often viewing them as symbols of shame. This second generation of immigrants was sandwiched between two worlds: that of their parents from "the old country" and their new home. Their children, the third generation, had an easier adjustment, for they had fewer customs to discard. As immigrants from other parts of Europe assimilated into this Anglo culture, the meaning of WASP expanded to include people of this descent.

IN SUM | Because Protestant English immigrants settled the colonies, they established the culture, from the dominant language to the dominant religion. Highly ethnocentric, they regarded as inferior the customs of other groups. Because white Europeans took power, they determined the national agenda to which other ethnic groups had to react and conform. Their institutional and cultural

dominance still sets the stage for current ethnic relations, a topic that is explored in the Down-to-Earth Sociology box on the next page.

Latinos

A Note on Terms. Before reviewing major characteristics of Latinos, it is important to stress that *Latino* and *Hispanic* refer not to a race but to ethnic groups. Latinos may identify themselves racially as black, white, or Native American. With changing self-identifications, some Latinos who have an African heritage even refer to themselves as Afro-Latinos (Navarro 2003).

Numbers, Origins, and Location. When birds still nested in the trees that would be used to build the *Mayflower,* Latinos had already established settlements in Florida and New Mexico (Bretos 1994). Today, Latinos are the largest minority group in the United States. As shown in Figure 9.6 on page 239, about 25 million people trace their origin to Mexico, 3 million to Puerto Rico, over 1 million to Cuba, and over 5 million to Central or South America.

Down-to-Earth Sociology

Unpacking the Invisible Knapsack: Exploring Cultural Privilege

OVERT RACISM IN THE UNITED STATES has dropped sharply, but doors still open and close on the basis of the color of our skin. Whites have a difficult time grasping the idea that good things come their way because they are white. They usually fail to perceive how "whiteness" operates in their own lives.

Peggy McIntosh, of Irish descent, began to wonder why she was so seldom aware of her race-ethnicity, while her African American friends were so conscious of theirs. She realized that people are not highly aware of things that they take for granted—and that "whiteness" is a "taken-for-granted" background assumption of U.S. society. To explore this, she drew up a list of things that she can take for granted because of her "whiteness," what she calls the "invisible knapsack" that she carries with her.

What is in this "knapsack"? What taken-for-granted privileges can most white people in U.S. society assume? Because she is white, McIntosh (1988) says:

1. If I don't do well as a leader, I can be sure people won't say that it is because of my race.
2. When I go shopping, store detectives won't follow me.
3. When I watch television or look at the front page of the paper, I see people of my race positively presented.
4. When I study our national heritage, I see people of my color and am taught that they made our country great.

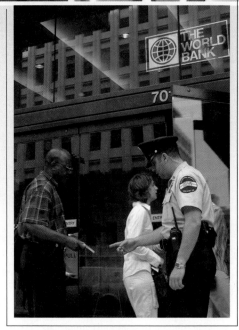

5. When I cash a check or use a credit card, my skin color does not make the clerk think that I may be financially irresponsible.
6. To protect my children, I do not have to teach them to be aware of racism.
7. I can talk with my mouth full and not have people put this down to my color.
8. I can speak at a public meeting without putting my race on trial.
9. I can achieve at something and not be "a credit to my race."
10. I am never asked to speak for all the people of my race.
11. If a traffic cop pulls me over, I can be sure that it isn't because I'm white.
12. I can take a job with an affirmative action employer without people thinking that I got the job because of my race.
13. I can be late to a meeting without people thinking I was late because "That's how *they* are."

for your Consideration

Can you think of other "unearned privileges" of everyday life that come to whites because of their skin color? (McIntosh's list contains 46 items.) Why are whites seldom aware that they carry this invisible knapsack?

Although Latinos are officially tallied at 37 million, another 10 million are living here illegally, about seven million from Mexico and three million from Central and South America (Kronholz 2006). Most Latinos are legal residents, but each year about *1.6 million* Mexicans are apprehended at the border or at points inland and are returned to Mexico (*Statistical Abstract* 2005:Table 313). Several hundred thousand others manage to enter the United States each year. With this vast migration, there are millions more Latinos in the United States than there are Canadians in Canada (33 million). As Figure 9.7 shows, two-thirds live in just four states: California, Texas, Florida, and New York.

The migration of Mexicans across the U.S. border has become a major social issue. As public concern grew, it led to an emotionally-charged debate in the U.S. Congress. One response was to tighten the border, and despite protests from the Mexican government, U.S. officials built a wall at various points on the U.S. side of the border.

Figure 9.6 Geographical Origin of U.S. Latinos

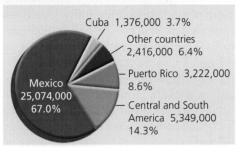

Cuba 1,376,000 3.7%
Other countries 2,416,000 6.4%
Puerto Rico 3,222,000 8.6%
Central and South America 5,349,000 14.3%
Mexico 25,074,000 67.0%

Source: By the author. Based on *Statistical Abstract* 2005:Table 40.

Figure 9.7 Where U.S. Latinos Live

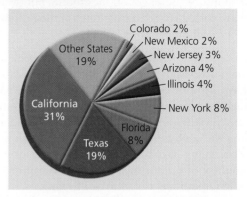

Other States 19%
Colorado 2%
New Mexico 2%
New Jersey 3%
Arizona 4%
Illinois 4%
New York 8%
Florida 8%
Texas 19%
California 31%

Source: By the author. Based on *Statistical Abstract* 2005:Table 21.

Helping to shape the international debate was the arrival of volunteers, calling themselves Minutemen, organized through the Internet to patrol the border. Their arrival in Arizona spread fear among Mexicans and upset U.S. officials, who worried that there would be bloody clashes between the volunteers and the "coyotes" who were smuggling migrants (Peña 2005; Ramos 2005; Rotstein 2005). Despite walls and patrols, as long as there is a need for unskilled labor, this flow of undocumented workers will continue.

Spanish Language. The Spanish language distinguishes most Latinos from other U.S. ethnic groups. With 28 million people speaking Spanish at home, the United States has become one of the largest Spanish-speaking nations in the world (*Statistical Abstract* 2005:Table 48). Because about half of Latinos are unable to speak English or can do so only with difficulty, many millions face a major obstacle to getting good jobs.

The growing use of Spanish has become a matter of controversy. Perceiving the prevalence of Spanish as a threat,

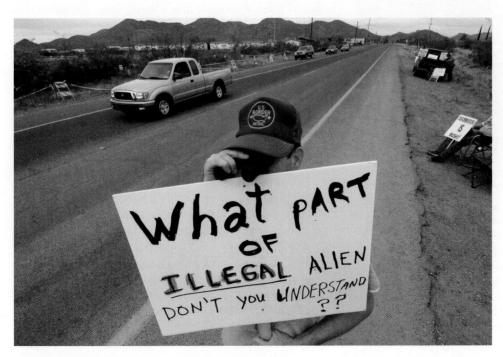

The illegal migration of Mexicans into the United States has become a major social issue. For political reasons, especially that of relations with Mexico, U.S. officials hesitated to close the border. The appearance of citizen patrols proved an embarrassment to politicans and the U.S. Border Patrol.

Senator S. I. Hayakawa of California initiated an English-only movement in 1981. The constitutional amendment that he sponsored never got off the ground, but twenty-six states have passed laws declaring English their official language (Schaefer 2004).

Diversity.   For Latinos, country of origin is highly significant. Those from Puerto Rico, for example, feel that they have little in common with people from Mexico, Venezuela, or El Salvador—just as earlier immigrants from Germany, Sweden, and England felt that they had little in common with one another. A sign of these divisions is the preference many have to refer to themselves in terms of their country of origin, such as Puerto Rican or Cuban American rather than as Latino or Hispanic.

As with other ethnic groups, Latinos are separated by social class. The half-million Cubans who fled Castro's rise to power in 1959, for example, were mostly well-educated, well-to-do professionals or businesspeople. In contrast, the "boat people" who fled later were mostly lower-class refugees, people with whom the earlier arrivals would not have associated in Cuba. The earlier arrivals, who are firmly established in Florida and who control many businesses and financial institutions, distance themselves from the more recent immigrants.

These divisions of national origin and social class present a major obstacle to political unity. One consequence is a severe underrepresentation in politics. Because Latinos make up 13.7 percent of the U.S. population, we might expect 13 or 14 U.S. Senators to be Latino. How many are there? *Two.* In addition, Latinos hold only 6 percent of the seats in the U.S. House of Representatives ("Guide to . . ." 2004; *Statistical Abstract* 2005:Table 396).

The potential political power of Latinos, however, is remarkable, and in coming years we will see more of this potential realized. As Latinos have become more visible in U.S. society and more vocal in their demands for equality, they have come face to face with African Americans, who fear that Latino gains in employment and at the ballot box will come at their expense (Jordan 2006). Together, Latinos and African Americans make up one-fourth of the U.S. population. If these two groups join together, their unity will produce an unstoppable political force.

Comparative Conditions.   Table 9.2 shows how Latinos compare with other groups. You can see that compared with white Americans and Asian Americans, Latinos are worse off on all the indicators of well-being shown in this table. You can also see how similar their rankings on these indicators are to those of African Americans. This table also illustrates the significance of country of origin. You can see that people from Cuba score much higher on these indicators of well-being, while those from Puerto Rico score much lower. Table 9.3 shows that almost half of Latinos do not complete high school, and only 11 percent graduate from college. In a postindustrial society that increasingly requires advanced skills, these totals indicate that a large number of Latinos will be left behind.

When the U.S. government took control of what is now the southwestern United States, Mexicans living there were transformed from the dominant group into a minority group. To try to maintain their culture, *Chicanos,* Americans of Mexican origin, do *ethnic work,* such as this dance by Danza Teocalt at a Cinco de Mayo celebration in Los Angeles. (The Cinco de Mayo— Fifth of May—holiday marks the Mexican army's 1862 defeat of French troops at the city of Puebla.)

African Americans

After slavery was abolished, the Southern states passed legislation (*Jim Crow laws*) to segregate blacks and whites. In 1896, the U.S. Supreme Court ruled in Plessy v. Ferguson that state laws requiring "separate but equal" accommodations for blacks were a reasonable use of state power. Whites used this ruling to strip blacks of the political power they had gained after the Civil War. They prohibited blacks from voting in "white" primaries. It was not until 1944 that the Supreme Court ruled that African Americans could vote in Southern primaries and not until 1954 that they had the legal right to attend the same public schools as whites (Schaefer 2004). Well into the 1960s, the South was still openly—and legally—practicing segregation.

Table 9.2 Race-Ethnicity and Comparative Well-Being[1]

Race-Ethnic Group	Median Family Income	Compared to White Income	Percentage Unemployed	Compared to White Employment	Percentage Below Poverty Line	Compared to White Poverty	Percentage Who Own Their Homes	Compared to White Home Ownership
Whites	$54,633	—	5.2%	—	10.2%	—	72.1%	—
Latinos	$34,185	37% lower	5.2%	The same	21.4%	110% higher	47.5%	34% lower
Country or Area of Origin								
Cuba	NA[2]	NA	3.8%	27% lower	16.5%	62% higher	56.9%	21% lower
Central and South America	NA	NA	5.0%	4% lower	15.2%	49% higher	41.1%	43% lower
Mexico	NA	NA	5.3%	2% higher	22.8%	124% higher	50.0%	31% lower
Puerto Rico	NA	NA	5.8%	12% higher	26.1%	156% higher	35.3%	51% lower
African Americans	$33,525	39% lower	10.8%	108% higher	24.1%	136% higher	47.7%	34% lower
Asian Americans[3]	$60,984	12% higher	4.0%	23% lower	10.1%	1% lower	56.7%	21% lower
Native Americans	$32,866	40% lower	NA	NA	23.9%	134% higher	NA	NA

[1]Data are from 2002 and 2003.
[2]Not Available
[3]Includes Pacific Islanders.
Source: By the author. Based on DeNavas-Walt, Proctor, and Mills 2004; *Statistical Abstract* 2005:Tables 33, 38, 40, 671.

Table 9.3 Race-Ethnicity and Education

Race-Ethnic Group	Less than High School	High School	Some College	College (BA or Higher)	Number Awarded	Percentage of all U.S. Doctorates[1]	Percentage of U.S. Population
Whites	14.6%	30.0%	28.5%	27.0%	26,905	81.0%	68.0%%
Latinos	47.6%	22.1%	19.9%	10.5%	1,432	4.3%	13.7%
Country or Area of Origin							
South America	23.8%	24.0%	27.0%	25.2%	NA	NA	
Cuba	37.0%	20.0%	21.7%	21.2%	NA	NA	
Puerto Rico	36.7%	26.2%	24.6%	12.5%	NA	NA	
Central America	54.0%	19.1%	17.4%	9.5%	NA	NA	
Mexico	54.2%	20.9%	17.5%	7.5%	NA	NA	
African Americans	20.0%	35.2%	27.4%	17.3%	2,397	7.2%	12.2%
Asian Americans	16.8%	18.9%	21.3%	43.1%	2,317	7.0%	4.0%
Native Americans	29.1%	29.2%	30.2%	11.5%	180	0.5%	0.8%

[1]Percentage after the doctorates awarded to nonresidents are deducted from the total.
Source: By the author. Based on *Statistical Abstract* 2005:Tables 34, 37, 38, 41, 283 and Figure 12.5 of this text.

The Struggle for Civil Rights.

It was 1955, in Montgomery, Alabama. As specified by law, whites took the front seats of the bus, and blacks went to the back. As the bus filled up, blacks had to give up their seats to whites.

When Rosa Parks, a 42-year-old African American woman and secretary of the Montgomery NAACP, was told that she would have to stand so that white folks could sit, she refused (Bray 1995). She stubbornly sat there while the bus driver raged and whites felt insulted. Her arrest touched off mass demonstrations, led 50,000 blacks to boycott the city's buses for a year, and thrust an otherwise unknown preacher into a historic role.

Reverend Martin Luther King, Jr., who had majored in sociology at Morehouse College in Atlanta, Georgia, took control. He organized car pools and preached nonviolence. Incensed at this radical organizer and at the stirrings in the normally compliant black community, segregationists also put their beliefs into practice—by bombing the homes of blacks and dynamiting their churches.

Rising Expectations and Civil Strife. The barriers came down, but they came down slowly. Not until 1964 did Congress pass the Civil Rights Act, making it illegal to discriminate in restaurants, hotels, theaters, and other public places. Then in 1965, Congress passed the Voting Rights Act, banning the fraudulent literacy tests that the Southern states had used to keep African Americans from voting.

Encouraged by these gains, African Americans experienced what sociologists call **rising expectations;** that is, they believed that better conditions would soon follow. The lives of the poor among them, however, changed little, if at all. Frustrations built up, finally exploding in Watts in 1965, when people living in that African American ghetto of central Los Angeles took to the streets in the first of what were termed "urban revolts." When King was assassinated by a white supremacist on April 4, 1968, inner cities across the nation erupted in fiery violence. Under threat of the destruction of U.S. cities, Congress passed the sweeping Civil Rights Act of 1968.

Continued Gains. Since then, African Americans have made remarkable gains in politics, education, and jobs. At 9 percent, African Americans have *quadrupled* their membership in the U.S. House of Representatives in the past 30 years (Rich 1986; *Statistical Abstract* 2005:Table 396). As college enrollments increased, the middle class expanded. Today, half of all African American families make more than $35,000 a year. One in three makes more than $50,000 a year, and one in six earns more than $75,000 (*Statistical Abstract* 2005:Table 670). Although their poverty rate is among the highest (see Table 9.2 on page 241), contrary to some stereotypes, the average African American family is *not* poor.

The extent of African American political prominence was highlighted when Jesse Jackson (another sociology

Until the 1960s, the South's public facilities were segregated. Some were reserved for whites only, others for blacks only. This apartheid was broken by blacks and whites who worked together and risked their lives to bring about a fairer society. Shown here is a 1963 sit-in at a Woolworth's lunch counter in Jackson, Mississippi. Sugar, ketchup, and mustard are being poured over the heads of the demonstrators.

major) competed for the Democratic presidential nomination in 1984 and 1988. Political progress was further confirmed in 1989 when L. Douglas Wilder of Virginia became the nation's first elected African American governor. The political prominence of African Americans came to the nation's attention again in 2000 when Alan Keyes competed for the Republican presidential nomination and in 2004 when Barack Obama was elected to the U.S. Senate.

Current Losses. Despite these gains, African Americans continue to lag behind in politics, economics, and education. Only *one* U.S. Senator is African American, but on the basis of the percentage of African Americans in the U.S. population we would expect about 12. As Tables 9.2 and 9.3 on page 241 show, African Americans average only 61 percent of white income, have much more unemployment and poverty, and are less likely to own their home or to have a college educations. That half of African American families have an income over $35,000 is only part of the story. The other part is that about one of every

African Americans are severely underrepresented in Congress. In 2004, Barack Obama became the first African American man to be elected to the U.S. Senate since the period immediately following the Civil War.

⌐ He just became our next PRESIDENT a week ago!! (today is 11/11/08)

five families makes less than $15,000 a year (*Statistical Abstract* 2005:Table 670).

These changes have created two contrasting worlds of African American experience—one educated and affluent, the other uneducated and poor. Concentrated among the poor are those with the least hope, the bleakest future, and the violence that so often dominates the evening news. Homicide rates have dropped to their lowest point in 30 years, but African American males are *five* times as likely to be homicide victims as are white males. Compared with white females, African American females are more than *three* times as likely to be murdered (*Statistical Abstract* 2005:Tables 296, 297). Compared with whites, African Americans are also *eight* times more likely to die from AIDS (*Statistical Abstract* 2005:Table 111).

Race or Social Class? A Sociological Debate. This division of African Americans into "haves" and "have-nots" has fueled a sociological controversy. Sociologist William Julius Wilson (1978, 1987, 2000) argues that social class has become more important than race in determining the life chances of African Americans. Before civil rights legislation, he says, the African American experience was dominated by race. Throughout the United States, African Americans were excluded from avenues of economic advancement: good schools and good jobs. When civil rights legislation opened new opportunities, African Americans seized them. Just as legislation began to open doors to African Americans, however, manufacturing jobs dried up, and many blue-collar jobs were moved to the suburbs. As better-educated African Americans obtained middle-class, white-collar jobs and moved out of the inner city, left behind were the African Americans with poor education and few skills.

Wilson stresses the significance of these two worlds of African American experience. The group that is stuck in the inner city lives in poverty, attends poor schools, and faces dead-end jobs or welfare. This group is filled with hopelessness and despair, combined with apathy or hostility. In contrast, those who have moved up the social class ladder live in comfortable homes in secure neighborhoods. They work at jobs that provide decent incomes, and they send their children to good schools. Their middle-class experiences and lifestyle have changed their views on life, and their aspirations and values have little in common with those of African Americans who remain poor. According to Wilson, then, social class—not race—has become the most significant factor in the lives of African Americans.

Some sociologists reply that this analysis overlooks the discrimination that continues to underlie the African

American experience. They note that even when African Americans do the same work as whites, they average less pay (Willie 1991; Herring 2002). This, they argue, points to racial discrimination, not to social class.

What is the answer to this debate? Wilson would reply that it is not an either-or question. My book is titled *The **Declining** Significance of Race,* he would say, not *The **Absence** of Race.* Certainly, racism is still alive, he would add, but today social class is more central to the African American experience than is racial discrimination. He stresses that for the poor in the inner city we need to provide jobs—for work provides an anchor to a responsible life (Wilson 1996, 2000).

Racism as an Everyday Burden. Today, racism is more subtle than it used to be, but it still walks among us. To study discrimination in the job market, researchers sent out 5,000 resumes in response to help-wanted ads in the Boston and Chicago Sunday papers (Bertrand and Mullainathan 2002). The resumes were identical, except for the names of the job applicants. Some applicants had white-sounding names, such as Emily and Brandon, while others had black-sounding names, such as Lakisha and Jamal. Although the qualifications of the supposed job applicants were identical, the white-sounding names elicited *50 percent* more callbacks than the black-sounding names. The Down-to-Earth Sociology box on the next page presents another study of subtle racism.

African Americans who occupy higher statuses enjoy greater opportunities, and they also face less discrimination. The discrimination that they encounter, however, is no less painful. Unlike whites of the same social class, they feel discrimination constantly hovering over them. Here is how an African American professor puts it:

> [One problem with] being black in America is that you have to spend so much time thinking about stuff that most white people just don't even have to think about. I worry when I get pulled over by a cop. . . . I worry what some white cop is going to think when he walks over to our car, because he's holding on to a gun. And I'm very aware of how many black folks accidentally get shot by cops. I worry when I walk into a store, that someone's going to think I'm in there shoplifting. . . . And I get resentful that I have to think about things that a lot of people, even my very close white friends whose politics are similar to mine, simply don't have to worry about. (Feagin 1999:398)

The following Thinking Critically section highlights a proposal to compensate for injustices to African Americans.

Thinking Critically

Reparations for Slavery: Justice or Foolishness?

The subtitle of this section, "Justice or Foolishness," is intended to frame the stark contrasts that surround the debate about reparations for slavery. The issue itself is simple. The enslavement of millions of Africans was a gross injustice. Because the slaves were never paid for 240 years of work, their descendants should be. This is both a moral and a legal issue.

The argument for reparations, or compensation, contains related matters. The first is that the greater wealth of today's white Americans is built on the centuries of unpaid labor of black slaves (Sidel 2005). The second is that slavery has left a legacy of inequality in education, housing, and income. Proponents of reparations call this the "racial deficit" (Marable 2001; Conley 2002).

Simply put, reparations are a form of back wages. These back wages should be paid either to the descendants of slaves or into a reparations trust fund targeted not to individuals but to black communities with the greatest need.

Opponents of reparations agree that slavery was a horrible crime against humanity. They stress that it occurred a long time ago, however, and that slavery is not simply a black and white issue. It was Africans who sold African prisoners to white slavers in the first place. And consider the problems in figuring out who would get compensation. Would the descendants of free blacks get compensation? How about the descendants of free blacks who owned black slaves? Should reparations be given to the descendants of blacks who immigrated after slavery ended? Or to today's black immigrants?

Then there is the matter of who would pay the reparations. Most U.S. whites are descended from people who moved to the United States after slavery ended. Not only did they have

Down-to-Earth Sociology

Stealth Racism in the Rental Market: What You Reveal by Your Voice

Blatant discrimination has become a thing of the past. There was a time when whites could burn crosses with impunity at the homes of blacks. Some whites even lynched African Americans and Asian Americans without fear of the law. Today, cross burning and lynching will make the national news and the perpetrators will be investigated and prosecuted. If local officials don't make an arrest, the FBI will step in. Similarly, discrimination in public accommodations was once standard. With today's stiff laws and the vigilance of groups such as the NAACP, no hotel, restaurant, or gas station would refuse service on the basis of race-ethnicity.

Racism, however, is not a thing of the past. Although overt racism has been relegated to the back shelves of social life, stealth racism is alive and well, as sociologists have demonstrated (Pager 2003; Ross and Turner 2005). At the University of Pennsylvania, for example, Douglas Massey and the students in his undergraduate course in research methods discussed how Americans often identify one another racially by their speech. In Massey's class were whites who spoke what is called White Middle Class English, African Americans who spoke a dialect known as Black English Vernacular, and other African Americans who spoke middle-class English with a black accent.

The discussion stimulated Massey and his students to investigate how voice is used to discriminate in the housing market. They designed standard identities for the class members who spoke these variants of English, assigning them similar incomes, jobs, and education. They also developed a standard script and translated it into Black English Vernacular. The students called on 79 apartments that were advertised for rent in newspapers. The study was done blindly, with the white and black students not knowing how the others were being treated.

What did they find? Compared with whites, African Americans were less likely to get to talk to rental agents, who often used answering machines to screen calls.

When they did get through, they were less likely to be told that an apartment was available, more likely to have to pay an application fee, and more likely to be asked about their credit history. Students who posed as lower-class blacks (speakers of Black English Vernacular) had the least access to apartments. Figure 9.8 summarizes the percentages of callers who were told an apartment was available.

As you can see from this figure, although both men and women were discriminated against, the discrimination was worse for the women. Sociologists refer to this as the *double bind* that African American women experience: being discriminated against both because they are African American and because they are women.

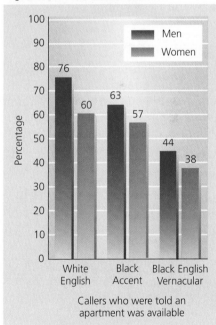

Figure 9.8 **Cloaked Discrimination in Apartment Rentals**

Callers who were told an apartment was available

Source: Massey and Lundy 2001.

nothing to do with slavery—neither did their ancestors. In addition, the money for reparations would come not only from taxes paid by whites but also from taxes paid by Latinos, Asian Americans, and Native Americans. Not incidentally, it would also come from taxes paid by African Americans.

for your Consideration

There are finer points on both sides of the argument, but these are the basic issues. What is your opinion of reparations?

Shelby Steele, a psychologist and an African American, argues that it is time to move beyond "thinking of ourselves as victims." Steele (2001) says that "we need to build a positive black identity, an identity built around ingenuity and personal responsibility. We should busy ourselves with the hard work of development, not try to manipulate white guilt." What do you think of his position?

Our opinions are not located in a social vacuum. They are rooted both in history and in our particular location in society. Can you identify how your social location underlies your opinions about this controversy? To do so, consider your racial-ethnic background, your social class, the ideas of your parents, the opinions of your friends, and when your ancestors arrived in the United States. How do these factors influence your views of what is both moral and logical in this issue?

Asian Americans

I have stressed in this chapter that our racial-ethnic categories are based more on social considerations than on biological ones. This point is again obvious when we examine the category Asian American. As Figure 9.9 shows, those who are called Asian Americans came to the United States from many nations. With no unifying cul-

Figure 9.9 The Country of Origin of Asian Americans

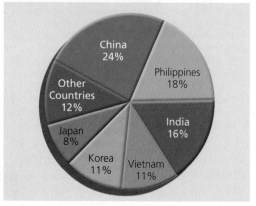

Source: By the author. Based on *Statistical Abstract* 2005:Table 22.

ture or "race," why should these people ever be clustered together in a single category? Think about it. What culture or race-ethnicity do Samoans and Vietnamese have in common? Or Laotians and Pakistanis? Or Native Hawaiians and Chinese? Or people from India and those from Guam? Yet all these groups—and more—are lumped together and called Asian Americans. Apparently, the U.S. government is not satisfied until it is able to pigeonhole everyone into a racial-ethnic category.

Since *Asian American* is a standard term, however, let's look at the characteristics of the 12 million people who are assigned this label.

A Background of Discrimination. From the time they first arrived on these shores, Asian Americans met discrimination. Lured by gold strikes in the West and an urgent need for unskilled workers to build the railroads, 200,000 Chinese immigrated between 1850 and 1880. When the famous golden spike was driven at Promontory, Utah, in 1869 to mark the completion of the railroad to the West Coast, white workers prevented Chinese workers from being in the photo—even though Chinese made up 90 percent of Central Pacific Railroad's labor force (Hsu 1971).

After the railroad was completed, the Chinese took other jobs. Feeling threatened by their cheap labor, Anglos formed vigilante groups to intimidate them. They also used the law. California's 1850 Foreign Miner's Act required Chinese (and Latinos) to pay a fee of $20 a month—when wages were a dollar a day. The California Supreme Court ruled that Chinese could not testify against whites (Carlson and Colburn 1972). In 1882, Congress passed the Chinese Exclusion Act, suspending all Chinese immigration for ten years. Four years later, the Statue of Liberty was dedicated. The tired, the poor, and the huddled masses it was intended to welcome obviously were not Chinese.

When immigrants from Japan arrived, they encountered *spillover bigotry,* a stereotype that lumped Asians together, depicting them as sneaky, lazy, and untrustworthy. After Japan attacked Pearl Harbor in 1941, conditions grew worse for the 110,000 Japanese Americans who called the United States their home. U.S. authorities feared that Japan would invade the United States and that the Japanese Americans would fight on Japan's side. They also feared that Japanese Americans would sabotage military installations on the West Coast. Although no Japanese American had been involved in even a single act of sabotage, on February 19, 1942, President Franklin D. Roosevelt ordered that everyone who was *one-eighth Japanese or more* be confined in special prisons (called "internment camps"). These people were charged with no crime, and they had no trials. Japanese ancestry was sufficient cause for being put in prison.

Diversity. As you can see from Table 9.2 on page 241, the annual income of Asian Americans has outstripped that of whites. This has led to an assumption that all Asian Americans are successful, a stereotype that masks huge ethnic differences. Look at the poverty rate of Asian Americans shown on Table 9.2. Although it is less than that of any other group shown on this table, it means that over a million Asian Americans live in poverty. Like Latinos, country of origin is significant in the distribution of poverty: Poverty is unusual among Chinese and Japanese Americans, but it clusters among Americans from Southeast Asia.

Reasons for Success. The general success of Asian Americans can be traced to three major factors: family life, educational achievement, and assimilation into mainstream culture.

Of all ethnic groups, including whites, Asian American children are the most likely to grow up with two parents and the least likely to be born to a single mother (*Statistical Abstract* 2005:Tables 38, 78). Most grow up in close-knit families that stress self-discipline, thrift, and hard work (Suzuki 1985; Bell 1991). This early socialization provides strong impetus for the other two factors.

The second factor is their high rate of college graduation. As Table 9.3 on page 241 shows, 43 percent of Asian Americans complete college. To realize how stunning this is, compare this with the other groups shown on this table. Their educational achievement, in turn, opens doors to economic success.

Assimilation, the third factor, is indicated by housing and marriage. Asian Americans are more likely than other racial-ethnic groups to live in integrated neighborhoods (Lee 1998). Those who trace their descent from Japan and China—who are the most successful financially—are also the most assimilated. The intermarriage rate of Japanese Americans is so high that two of every three children born to a Japanese American have one parent who is not of Japanese descent (Schaefer 2004). The Chinese are close behind (Alba and Nee 2003).

Asian Americans are becoming more prominent in politics. With more than half of its citizens being Asian American, Hawaii has elected Asian American governors and sent several Asian American senators to Washington, including the two now serving there (Lee 1998, *Statistical Abstract* 2005:Table 296). The first Asian American governor outside of Hawaii is Gary Locke, who in 1996 was elected governor of Washington, a state in which Asian Americans make up less than 6 percent of the population. Locke, who was re-elected in 2000, chose not to run in 2004.

Native Americans

"I don't go so far as to think that the only good Indians are dead Indians, but I believe nine out of ten are—and I shouldn't inquire too closely in the case of the tenth. The most vicious cowboy has more moral principle than the average Indian."
—Teddy Roosevelt, 1886
President of the United States, 1901–1909

Diversity of Groups. This quote from Teddy Roosevelt provides insight into the rampant racism of earlier generations. Yet, even today, thanks to countless grade B Westerns, some Americans view the original inhabitants of what became the United States as wild, uncivilized savages, a single group of people subdivided into separate tribes. The European immigrants to the colonies, however, encountered diverse groups of people with a variety of cultures—from nomadic hunters and gatherers to people who lived in wooden houses in settled agricultural communities. Altogether, they spoke over 700 languages (Schaefer 2004). Each group had its own norms and values—and the usual ethnocentric pride in its own culture. Consider what happened in 1744, when the colonists of Virginia offered college scholarships for "savage" lads. The Iroquois replied:

"Several of our young people were formerly brought up at the colleges of Northern Provinces. They were instructed in all your sciences. But when they came back to us, they were bad runners, ignorant of every means of living in the woods, unable to bear either cold or hunger, knew neither how to build a cabin, take a deer, or kill an enemy. . . . They were totally good for nothing."
They added, "If the English gentlemen would send a dozen or two of their children to Onondaga, the great Council would take care of their education, bring them up in really what was the best manner and make men of them." (Nash 1974; in McLemore 1994)

Native Americans, who numbered about 10 million, had no immunity to the diseases the Europeans brought with them. With deaths due to disease—and warfare, a much lesser cause—their number was reduced to about *one-twentieth* its original size. A hundred years ago, the Native American population reached a low point of a half million. Native Americans, who now number about 2 million (see Figure 9.4 on page 236), speak 150 different languages. Like Latinos and Asian Americans, they do not think of themselves as a single people who fit neatly within a single label (McLemore 1994).

From Treaties to Genocide and Population Transfer. At first, relations between the European settlers and the Native Americans were by and large peaceful. The Native Americans accommodated the strangers, as there was plenty of land for both the newcomers and themselves. As Native Americans were pushed aside and wave after wave of settlers continued to arrive, however, Pontiac, an Ottawa chief, saw the future—and didn't like it. He convinced several tribes to unite in an effort to push the Europeans into the sea. He almost succeeded, but failed when the English were reinforced by fresh troops (McLemore 1994).

A pattern of deception developed. The U.S. government would make treaties to buy some of a tribe's land, with the promise to honor forever the tribe's right to what it had not sold. European immigrants, who continued to pour into the United States, would disregard these boundaries. The tribes would resist, with death tolls on both sides. The U.S. government would then intervene—not to enforce the treaty but to force the tribe off its lands. In its relentless drive westward, the U.S. government embarked on a policy of genocide. It assigned the U.S. cavalry the task of "pacification," which translated into slaughtering Native Americans who "stood in the way" of this territorial expansion.

The acts of cruelty perpetrated by the Europeans against Native Americans appear endless, but two were especially grisly. The first was the distribution of blankets contaminated with smallpox—under the guise of a peace offering. The second was the Trail of Tears, a forced march of a thousand miles from the Carolinas and Georgia to Oklahoma. Fifteen thousand Cherokees were forced to make this midwinter march in light clothing. Conditions were so bad that 4,000 died. The symbolic end to Native American resistance came in 1890 with a massacre at Wounded Knee, South Dakota. Of 350 men, women, and children, the U.S. cavalry gunned down 300, throwing their bodies into a mass grave (Thornton 1987; Lind 1995; Johnson 1998). These acts took place after the U.S. government changed its policy from genocide to population transfer and had begun to confine Native Americans to specified areas called *reservations.*

The Invisible Minority and Self-Determination. Native Americans can truly be called the invisible minority. Because about half live in rural areas and one-third in just three states—Oklahoma, California, and Arizona—most other Americans are hardly conscious of a Native American presence in the United States. The isolation of about half of Native Americans on reservations further reduces their visibility (Schaefer 2004).

The systematic attempts of European Americans to destroy the Native Americans' way of life and their forced resettlement onto reservations continue to have deleterious effects. Table 9.2 on page 241 shows their high rates of both unemployment and poverty. Their rate of suicide is the highest of any racial-ethnic group (Wallace et al. 1996), while their life expectancy is lower than that of the nation as a whole (U.S. Department of Health and Human Services 1990; Lester 1997). Table 9.3 on page 241 shows

The Native Americans stood in the way of the U.S. government's westward expansion. To seize their lands, the government followed a policy of *genocide,* later replaced by *population transfer.* During the massacre of Cheyenne and Arapaho by U.S. Cavalry at Sandy Creek, Colorado, on November 29, 1864, soldiers killed not only warriors but also women and children. They also mutilated the dead, and took scalps. The transcripts of Congress' investigation of this slaughter, available on the Internet, are gripping (Smith 1865). This painting is by Robert Lindneux (1870–1920).

how far their education lags behind that of most groups–only 12 percent graduate from college.

These negative conditions are the consequence of Anglo domination. In the 1800s, U.S. courts ruled that Native Americans did not own the land on which they had been settled and determined that they had no right to develop the land's resources. Native Americans were made wards of the state and treated like children by the Bureau of Indian Affairs (Mohawk 1991; Schaefer 2004). Then, in the 1960s, Native Americans won a series of legal victories that gave them control over reservation lands. As a result, many Native American tribes have opened businesses—ranging from industrial parks serving metropolitan areas to fish canneries.

It is the casinos, though, that have attracted the most attention. In 1988, the federal government passed a law that allowed Native Americans to operate gambling establishments on reservations. Now over 400 tribes operate casinos. They bring in about $18 billion a year, *twice as much as all the casinos in Nevada* (Butterfield 2005). The Oneida tribe of New York, which has only 1,000 members, runs a casino that nets $232,000 a year for each man, woman, and child (Peterson 2003). This huge amount, however, pales in comparison with that of the Pequot of Connecticut. With only 310 members, they bring in more than $2 million a day (Zielbauer 2000). Incredibly, one tribe has only *one* member: She has her own casino (Barlett and Steele 2002).

A highly controversial issue is *separatism.* Because Native Americans were independent peoples when the Europeans arrived and they never willingly joined the United States, many tribes maintain the right to remain separate from the U.S. government and U.S. society. The chief of the Onondaga tribe in New York, a member of the Iroquois Federation, summarizes the issue this way:

> For the whole history of the Iroquois, we have maintained that we are a separate nation. We have never lost a war. Our government still operates. We have refused the U.S. government's reorganization plans for us. We have kept our language and our traditions, and when we fly to Geneva to UN meetings, we carry Hau de no sau nee passports. We made some treaties that lost some land, but that also confirmed our separate-nation status. That the U.S. denies all this doesn't make it any less the case. (Mander 1992)

One of the most significant changes is **pan-Indianism.** This emphasis on common elements that run through Native American cultures is an attempt to develop an identity that goes beyond the tribe. Pan-Indianism ("We are all Indians") is a remarkable example of the plasticity of ethnicity. The label "Indian"—originally imposed by Anglos—is embraced and substituted for individual tribal identities.

Looking Toward the Future

Back in 1903, sociologist W. E. B. Du Bois said, "The problem of the twentieth century is the problem of the color line—the relation of the darker to the lighter races." Incredibly, over a hundred years later, the color line remains one of the most volatile topics facing the nation. From time to time, the color line takes on a different complexion, as with the war on terrorism and the corresponding discrimination directed against people of Middle Eastern descent.

In another hundred years, will yet another sociologist lament that the color of people's skin still affects human relationships? Given our past, it seems that although racial-ethnic walls will diminish, even crumble at some points, the color line is not likely to disappear. Two issues we are currently grappling with are immigration and affirmative action.

The Immigration Debate

Throughout its history, the United States has both welcomed immigration and feared its consequences. The gates opened wide (numerically, if not in attitude) for waves of immigrants in the 1800s and early 1900s. During the past 20 years, a new wave of immigration has brought close to a million new residents to the United States each year. Today, more immigrants (31 million) live in the United States than at any time in the country's history (*Statistical Abstract* 1989:Table 46; 2005:Tables 5, 42).

In contrast to the first wave, which was almost exclusively from western Europe, this second wave is more diverse. In fact, it is changing the U.S. racial-ethnic mix. If current trends in immigration (and birth) persist, in about 50 years the "average" American will trace his or her ancestry to Africa, Asia, South America, the Pacific Islands, the Middle East—almost anywhere but white Europe. This change is discussed in the Cultural Diversity box on the next page.

In some states, the future is arriving much sooner than this. In California, racial-ethnic minorities already constitute the majority. California has 19 million minorities and 16 million whites (*Statistical Abstract* 2005:Table 21). Californians who request new telephone service from Pacific Bell can speak to customer service representatives in Spanish, Korean, Vietnamese, Mandarin, Cantonese—or in English.

As in the past, there is concern that "too many" immigrants will change the character of the United States. "Throughout the history of U.S. immigration," write sociologists Alejandro Portés and Ruben Rumbaut (1990), "a consistent thread has been the fear that the 'alien element' would somehow undermine the institutions of the country and would lead it down the path of disintegration and decay." A hundred years ago, the widespread fear was

Cultural Diversity *in the* United States

Glimpsing the Future: The Shifting U.S. Racial-Ethnic Mix

During the next twenty-five years, the population of the United States is expected to grow by about 22 percent. To see what the U.S. population will look like at the end of that time, can we simply multiply the current racial-ethnic mix by 22 percent? The answer is a resounding no. As you can see from Figure 9.10, some groups will grow much more than others, giving us a different-looking United States. Some of the changes in the U.S. racial-ethnic mix will be dramatic. In twenty-five years, one of every nineteen Americans is expected to have an Asian background, and one of every six a Latino background.

Two basic causes underlie this fundamental shift: immigration and birth rates. Immigration is by far the more important. The racial-ethnic groups have different rates of immigration and birth, and these will change their proportions of the U.S. population. From Figure 9.10, you can see how the proportion of non-Hispanic whites is expected to shrink, that of Native Americans to remain the same, and that of African Americans to increase slightly. With both vast immigration and higher-than-average birth rates, in fifty years almost one of four Americans is expected to be of Latino ancestry.

for your Consideration

This shifting racial-ethnic mix is one of the most significant events occurring in the United States. To better understand its implications, apply the three theoretical perspectives.

Use the *conflict perspective* to identify the groups that are likely to be threatened by this change. Over what resources are struggles likely to develop? What impact do you think this changing mix might have on European Americans? On Latinos? On African Americans? On Asian Americans? On Native Americans? What changes in immigration laws (or their enforcement) can you anticipate?

To apply the *symbolic interactionist perspective*, consider how groups might perceive one another differently as their proportion of the population changes. How do you think that this changed perception will affect people's behavior?

To apply the *functionalist perspective,* try to determine how each racial-ethnic group will benefit from this changing mix. How will other parts of society (such as businesses) benefit? What functions and dysfunctions can you anticipate for politics, economics, education, or religion?

Figure 9.10 Projections of the Racial-Ethnic Makeup of the U.S. Population

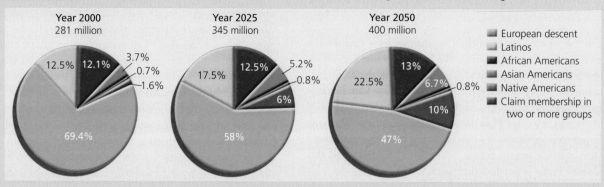

Source: By the author. Based on Bernstein and Bergman 2003; *Statistical Abstract* 2004:Table 16; 2005 Table 16. The projections are modified for 2050 based on the new census category of membership in two or more groups and trends in interethnic marriage.

that the immigrants from southern Europe would bring communism with them. Today, some fear that Spanish-speaking immigrants threaten the primacy of the English language. In addition, the age-old fear that immigrants will take jobs away from native-born Americans remains strong. Finally, minority groups that struggled for political representation fear that newer groups will gain political power at their expense.

Affirmative Action

The role of affirmative action in our multicultural society lies at the center of a national debate about race and ethnic relations. In this policy, initiated by President Kennedy in 1961, goals based on race (and sex) are used in hiring, promotion, and college admission. Sociologist Barbara Reskin (1998) examined the results of affirmative action. She concluded that although it is difficult to separate the results of affirmative action from both economic booms and busts and the greater number of women in the work force, affirmative action has had a modest impact.

The results may have been modest, but the reactions to this program have been anything but modest. Affirmative action has been at the center of controversy for more than a generation. Liberals, both white and minority, say that this program is the most direct way to level the playing field of economic opportunity. If whites are passed over, this is an unfortunate cost that we must pay if we are to make up for past discrimination. In contrast, conservatives, both white and minority, agree that opportunity should be open to all, but claim that putting race (or sex) ahead of an individual's training and ability to perform a job is reverse discrimination. Because of their race (or sex), qualified people who had nothing to do with past inequity are experiencing discrimination. They add that affirmative action stigmatizes the people who benefit from it, because it suggests that they hold their jobs because of race (or sex), rather than personal merit.

This national debate crystallized with a series of controversial rulings. One of the most significant was *Proposition 209,* a 1996 amendment to the California state constitution. This amendment banned preferences to minorities and women in hiring, promotion, and college admissions. Despite appeals by a coalition of civil rights groups, the U.S. Supreme Court upheld this California law.

A second significant ruling was made in 2003, in response to complaints from white applicants who had been denied admission to the University of Michigan. They claimed that they were discriminated against because underrepresented minorities were given extra consideration. The Court's ruling was ambiguous. The goal of racial diversity in a student body is laudable, the Court ruled, and universities can give minorities an edge in admissions. Race, however, can only be a "plus factor." There must be, in the Court's words, "a meaningful individualized review of applicants." Mechanical systems, such as automatically giving extra points because of race, are unconstitutional.

Such a murky message left university officials—and, by extension, those in business and other public and private agencies—scratching their heads. Trying to bring about racial diversity is constitutional, but using quotas and mechanical systems is not. With the Court providing no specific guidelines to bring about affirmative action and its University of Michigan ruling open to different interpretations, we obviously have not yet heard the final word from the U.S. Supreme Court. This issue of the proper role of affirmative action in a multicultural society is likely to remain center stage for quite some time.

Toward a True Multicultural Society

The United States has the potential to become a society in which racial-ethnic groups not only coexist but also respect one another—and thrive—as they work together for mutually beneficial goals. In a true multicultural society, the minority groups that make up the United States will participate fully in the nation's social institutions while maintaining their cultural integrity. Reaching this goal will require that we understand that "the biological differences that divide one race from another add up to a drop in the genetic ocean." For a long time, we have given racial categories an importance they never merited. Now we need to figure out how to reduce them to the irrelevance they deserve. In short, we need to make real the abstraction called equality that we profess to believe (Cose 2000).

The United States is the most racially-ethnically diverse society in the world. This can be our central strength, with our many groups working together to build a harmonious society, a stellar example for the world. Or it can be our Achilles heel, with us breaking into feuding groups, a Balkanized society that marks an ill-fitting end to a grand social experiment. Our reality will probably fall somewhere between these extremes.

Summary and Review

Laying the Sociological Foundation

How is race both a reality and a myth?

In the sense that different groups inherit distinctive physical traits, race is a reality. There is no agreement regarding what constitutes a particular race, however, or even how many races there are. In the sense of one race being superior to another and of there being pure races, race is a myth. The *idea* of race is powerful, shaping basic relationships among people. Pp. 222–226.

How do race and ethnicity differ?

Race refers to inherited biological characteristics, **ethnicity** to cultural ones. Members of ethnic groups identify with one another on the basis of common ancestry and cultural heritage. Pp. 223, 226.

What are minority and dominant groups?

Minority groups are people who are singled out for unequal treatment by members of the **dominant group,** the group with more power, privilege, and social status. Minorities originate with migration, or the expansion of political boundaries. Pp. 226–227.

What heightens racial-ethnic identity, and what is "ethnic work"?

A group's relative size, power, physical characteristics, and amount of discrimination heighten or reduce ethnic identity. **Ethnic work** is the process of constructing an ethnic identity. For people with strong ties to their culture of origin, ethnic work involves enhancing and maintaining group distinctions. For those without a firm ethnic identity, ethnic work is an attempt to recover one's ethnic heritage. P. 227.

Why are people prejudiced?

Prejudice is an attitude, and **discrimination** is an *action.* Like other attitudes, **prejudice** is learned in association with others. Prejudice is so extensive that people can show prejudice against groups that don't even exist. Minorities also internalize the dominant norms, and some show prejudice against their own group. Pp. 227–228.

How do individual and institutional discrimination differ?

Individual discrimination is the negative treatment of one person by another, while **institutional discrimination** is negative treatment that is built into social institutions. Institutional discrimination can occur without the awareness of either the perpetrator or the object of discrimination. Discrimination in health care is one example. Pp. 229–230.

Theories of Prejudice

How do psychologists explain prejudice?

Psychological theories of prejudice stress the **authoritarian personality** and frustration displaced toward **scapegoats.** Pp. 230–231.

How do sociologists explain prejudice?

Sociological theories focus on how different social environments increase or decrease **prejudice.** Functionalists stress the benefits and costs that come from discrimination. Conflict theorists look at how the groups in power exploit racial and ethnic divisions in order to hold down wages and otherwise maintain power. Symbolic interactionists stress how labels create **selective perception** and self-fulfilling prophecies. Pp. 231–232.

Global Patterns of Intergroup Relations

What are the major patterns of minority and dominant group relations?

Beginning with the least humane, they are **genocide, population transfer, internal colonialism, segregation, assimilation,** and **multiculturalism (pluralism).** Pp. 232–234.

Race and Ethnic Relations in the United States

What are the major ethnic groups in the United States?

From largest to smallest, the major ethnic groups are European Americans, Latinos, African Americans, Asian Americans, and Native Americans. Pp. 234, 236.

What are some issues in racial-ethnic relations and characteristics of minority groups?

African Americans are increasingly divided into middle and lower classes, with two sharply contrasting worlds of experience. Latinos are divided by social class and country of origin. On many measures, Asian Americans are better off than white Americans, but their well-being varies with country of origin. For Native Americans, the primary issues are poverty, nationhood, and settling treaty obligations. The overarching issue for minorities is overcoming discrimination. Pp. 235–249.

Looking Toward the Future

What main issues dominate racial-ethnic relations?

The main issues are immigration, affirmative action, and how to develop a true multicultural society. The answers affect our future. Pp. 249–251.

Thinking Critically
about Chapter 9

1. How many races do your friends think there are? Do they think that one race is superior to the others? What do you think their reaction would be to the sociological position that racial categories are primarily social?

2. Over a hundred years ago, sociologist W. E. B. Du Bois said, "The problem of the twentieth century is the problem of the color line—the relation of the darker to the lighter races of men." Why do you think that the color line remains one of the most volatile topics facing the nation?

3. If you were appointed head of the U.S. Civil Service Commission, what policies would you initiate to reduce racial-ethnic strife in the United States? Be ready to explain the sociological principles that might give your proposals a high chance of success.

Additional Resources

Companion Website www.ablongman.com/henslin

- Content Select Research Database for Sociology, with suggested key terms and annotated references
- Link to 2000 Census, with activities
- Flashcards of key terms and concepts
- Practice Tests
- Weblinks
- Interactive Maps

Where Can I Read More on This Topic?

Suggested readings for this chapter are listed at the back of this book.

Inequalities of Gender and Age

Pacita Abad, *Women in Burkah* 1979

INEQUALITIES OF GENDER

Issues of Sex and Gender
Gender Differences in Behavior:
    Biology or Culture?
Opening the Door to Biology

**How Females Became a
Minority Group**
The Origins of Patriarchy

**Gender Inequality in the
United States**
Fighting Back: The Rise of
    Feminism
Gender Inequality in Education
Gender Inequality in Health Care
Gender Inequality in the
    Workplace
Sexual Harassment—and Worse
Gender and Violence

The Changing Face of Politics
Glimpsing the Future—with Hope

INEQUALITIES OF AGING

Aging in Global Perspective
The Social Construction of Aging
Industrialization and the Graying
    of the Globe
The Graying of America

**The Symbolic Interactionist
Perspective**
Ageism: The Concept
Shifting Meanings of Growing Old
Influence of the Mass Media

The Functionalist Perspective
Disengagement Theory
Activity Theory
Continuity Theory

The Conflict Perspective
Social Security Legislation
Intergenerational Conflict

Looking Toward the Future

Summary and Review

In Tunis, the capital of Tunisia, on Africa's northern coast, I met some U.S. college students, with whom I spent a couple of days. They wanted to see the city's red light district, and I wondered whether it would be worth the trip. I already had seen other red light districts, including the unusual one in Amsterdam where the state licenses the women, requires that they have medical checkups (certificates must be posted so that customers can check them), sets their prices, and pays them social security benefits upon retirement. The prostitutes sit behind lighted picture windows while customers stroll along the canal side streets and browse from the outside.

This time the sight turned my stomach.

We ended up on a wharf that extended into the Mediterranean. Each side was lined with a row of one-room wooden shacks, crowded one against the next. In front of each open door stood a young woman. Peering from outside into the dark interiors, I could see that each door led to a tiny room with a well-worn bed.

The wharf was crowded with men who were eyeing the women. Many of them wore sailor uniforms from countries that I couldn't identify.

> **In front of each open door stood a young woman. . . . I could see . . . a well-worn bed.**

As I looked more closely, I could see that some of the women had runny sores on their legs. Incredibly, even with such visible evidence of their disease, customers still sought them out. Evidently, the low price (at that time $2) was too much to resist.

With a sick feeling in my stomach and the desire to vomit, I kept a good distance between myself and the beckoning women. One tour of the two-block area was more than sufficient.

Somewhere nearby, out of sight, I knew that there were men whose wealth derived from exploiting these women who were condemned to short lives punctuated by fear and misery.

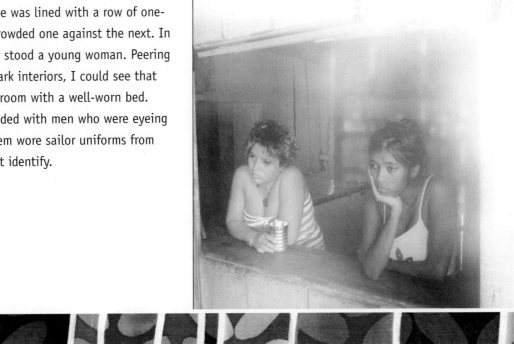

In the previous chapter, we considered how race and ethnicity affect people's well-being and their position in society. In this chapter, we examine how being classified by sex and age makes significant differences in people's lives. Our primary focus is **gender stratification**—males' and females' unequal access to property, prestige, and power—but we also examine the prejudice, discrimination, and hostility that are directed against people because of their age.

Gender and age are especially significant because they are *master statuses,* that is, they cut across all aspects of social life. *We all are labeled male or female and are assigned an age category.* No matter what we attain in life, these labels and categories carry images and expectations about how we should act. They not only guide our behavior but also serve as the basis of power and privilege.

INEQUALITIES OF GENDER

Let's begin by considering the distinction between sex and gender.

Issues of Sex and Gender

When we consider how females and males differ, the first thing that usually comes to mind is **sex,** the *biological characteristics* that distinguish males and females. *Primary sex characteristics* consist of a vagina or a penis and other organs related to reproduction. *Secondary sex characteristics* are the physical distinctions between males and females that are not directly connected with reproduction. Secondary sex characteristics become clearly evident at puberty, when males develop more muscles and a lower voice and gain more body hair and height, while females form more fatty tissue and broader hips and develop larger breasts.

Gender, in contrast, is a *social,* not a biological, characteristic. **Gender** consists of whatever behaviors and attitudes a group considers proper for its males and females. Consequently, gender varies from one society to another. Whereas *sex* refers to male or female, *gender* refers to masculinity or femininity. In short, you inherit your sex, but you learn your gender as you are socialized into the behaviors and attitudes your culture asserts are appropriate for your sex.

As the photo montage on the next page illustrates, these expectations differ around the world. They vary so greatly that some sociologists suggest that we replace the terms *masculinity* and *femininity* with *masculinities* and *femininities.*

The sociological significance of gender is that it is a device by which society controls its members. Gender sorts us, on the basis of sex, into different life experiences. It opens and closes doors to property, power, and even prestige. Like social class, gender is a structural feature of society.

Before examining inequalities of gender, let's consider why the behaviors of men and women differ.

Gender Differences in Behavior: Biology or Culture?

Why are most males more aggressive than most females? Why do women enter "nurturing" occupations such as teaching young children and nursing in far greater numbers than men? To answer such questions, many people respond with some variation of "They're just born that way."

Is this the correct answer? Certainly, biology plays a significant role in our lives. Each of us begins as a fertilized egg. The egg, or ovum, is contributed by our mother, the sperm that fertilizes the egg by our father. At the very moment the egg is fertilized, our sex is determined. Each of us receives twenty-three pairs of chromosomes from the ovum and twenty-three pairs from the sperm. The egg has an X chromosome. If the sperm that fertilizes the egg also has an X chromosome, we become a girl (XX). If the sperm has a Y chromosome, we become a boy (XY).

That's the biology. Now, the sociological question is: Does this biological difference control our behavior? Does it, for example, make females more nurturing and submissive and males more aggressive and domineering? Almost all sociologists take the side of "nurture" in this "nature versus nurture" controversy, but a few do not. The dominant sociological position is that social factors, not biology, are the reasons we do what we do. Our visible differences of sex do not come with meanings built into them. Rather, each human group makes its own interpretation of these physical differences and, on this basis, assigns males and females to separate groups. There, they learn what is expected of them and are given different access to their society's privileges.

Most sociologists find compelling the argument that if biology were the principal factor in human behavior, all around the world we would find women behaving in one way and men in another. In fact, however, ideas of gender

Merida, Mexico

Madaba, Jordan

Standards of Gender

Each human group determines its ideas of "maleness" and "femaleness." As you can see from these photos of four women and four men, standards of gender are arbitrary and vary from one culture to another. Yet, in its ethnocentrism, each group thinks that its preferences reflect what gender "really" is. As indicated here, around the world men and women try to make themselves appealing by aspiring to their group's standards of gender.

Altamira, Brazil

Turmi, Ethiopia

Moran, Kenya

Sichuan Province, Tibet

Chile

India

vary greatly from one culture to another—and, as a result, so do male–female behaviors.

Opening the Door to Biology

The matter of "nature" versus "nurture" is not so easily settled, however, and some sociologists acknowledge that biological factors are involved in some human behavior other than reproduction and childbearing (Udry 2000). Alice Rossi, a feminist sociologist and former president of the American Sociological Association, has suggested that women are better prepared biologically for "mothering" than are men. Rossi (1977, 1984) says that women are more sensitive to the infants' soft skin and to their nonverbal communications. She stresses that the issue is not either biology or society. Instead, nature provides biological predispositions, which are then overlaid with culture.

To see why the door to biology is opening just slightly in sociology, let's consider a medical accident and a study of Vietnam veterans.

A Medical Accident. The drama began in 1963, when 7-month-old identical twin boys were taken to a doctor for a routine circumcision (Money and Ehrhardt 1972). The inept physician, who was using a heated needle, turned the electric current too high and accidentally burned off the penis of one of the boys. You can imagine the parents' disbelief—and then their horror—as the truth sank in.

What can be done in a situation like this? The damage was irreversible. The parents were told that their boy could never have sexual relations. After months of soul-searching and tearful consultations with experts, the parents decided that their son should have a sex-change operation. When he was 22 months old, surgeons castrated the boy, using the skin to construct a vagina. The parents then gave the child a new name, Brenda, dressed him in frilly clothing, let his hair grow long, and began to treat him as a girl. Later, physicians gave Brenda female steroids to promote female pubertal growth (Colapinto 2001).

At first, the results were extremely promising. When the twins were 4 years old, the mother said (remember that the children are biologically identical),

> One thing that really amazes me is that she is so feminine. I've never seen a little girl so neat and tidy. . . . She likes for me to wipe her face. She doesn't like to be dirty, and yet my son is quite different. I can't wash his face for anything . . . She is very proud of herself, when she puts on a new dress,

or I set her hair. . . . She seems to be daintier. (Money and Ehrhardt 1972)

About a year later, the mother described how their daughter imitated her while their son copied his father:

> I found that my son, he chose very masculine things like a fireman or a policeman. . . . He wanted to do what daddy does, work where daddy does, and carry a lunch kit. . . . [My daughter] didn't want any of those things. She wants to be a doctor or a teacher. . . . But none of the things that she ever wanted to be were like policeman or a fireman, and that sort of thing never appealed to her. (Money and Ehrhardt 1972)

If the matter were this clear-cut, we could use this case to conclude that gender is entirely up to nurture. Seldom are things in life so simple, however, and a twist occurs in this story. Despite this promising start and her parents' coaching, Brenda did not adapt well to femininity. She preferred to mimic her father shaving rather than her mother putting on makeup. She rejected dolls and insisted on urinating standing up. Classmates teased her and called her a "cavewoman" because she walked like a boy. At age 14, she was expelled from school for beating up a girl who teased her. Despite estrogen treatment, she was not attracted to boys, and at age 14, in despair over her inner turmoil, she was thinking of suicide. In a tearful confrontation, her father told her about the accident and her sex change.

"All of a sudden, everything clicked. For the first time things made sense, and I understood who and what I was," the twin says of this revelation. David (his new name) then had male hormone shots and later surgery to partially reconstruct a penis. At age 25, he married a woman and adopted her children (Diamond and Sigmundson 1997; Colapinto 2001). There is an unfortunate end to this story, however. In 2004, David committed suicide.

The Vietnam Veterans Study. Time after time, researchers have found that boys and men who have higher levels of testosterone tend to be more aggressive. In one study, researchers compared the testosterone levels of college men in a "rowdy" fraternity with those of men in a fraternity that had a reputation for academic achievement and social responsibility. Men in the "rowdy" fraternity had higher levels of testosterone (Dabbs et al. 1996). The samples that researchers used were small, however, leaving the nagging uncertainty that the findings of a particular study might be due to chance.

Then, in 1985, the U.S. government began a health study of Vietnam veterans. To be certain that the study was representative, the researchers chose a random sample of 4,462 men. Among the data they collected was a measurement of testosterone. This gave sociologists a large random sample to analyze, which is still providing surprising clues about human behavior.

This sample supports earlier studies showing that men who have higher levels of testosterone tend to be more aggressive and to have more problems as a consequence. When the veterans with higher testosterone levels were boys, they were more likely to get in trouble with parents and teachers and to become delinquents. As adults, they are more likely to use hard drugs, to get into fights, to end up in lower-status jobs, and to have more sexual partners. Knowing this, you probably won't be surprised to learn that they are also less likely to marry—certainly, their low-paying jobs and trouble with the police make them less appealing candidates for marriage. Those who do marry are less likely to share problems with their wives. They also are more likely to have affairs, to hit their wives, and to get divorced (Dabbs and Morris 1990; Booth and Dabbs 1993).

Fortunately for us sociologists, the Vietnam veterans study does not leave us with biology as the sole basis for behavior. Not all men with high testosterone get in trouble with the law, do poorly in school, or mistreat their wives. A chief difference, in fact, is social class. High-testosterone men from higher social classes are less likely to be involved in antisocial behaviors than are high-testosterone men from lower social classes (Dabbs and Morris 1990). *Social* factors such as socialization, life goals, and self-definitions play a part. The matter becomes even more complicated, for in some instances men with higher tes-

tosterone have better marriages (Booth, Johnson, and Granger 2004). Discovering how social factors work in combination with testosterone level is of great interest to sociologists.

IN SUM | The findings are preliminary, but significant and provocative. They indicate that human behavior is not a matter of either nature or nurture, but of the two working together. Some behavior that we sociologists usually assume to be due entirely to socialization is apparently influenced by biology. In the years to come, this should prove to be an exciting—and controversial—area of sociological research. One level of research will be to determine if any behaviors are due only to biology. The second level will be to discover the ways that social factors modify biology. The third level will be, in sociologist Janet Chafetz's (1990:30) phrase, to determine how "different" becomes translated into "unequal."

How Females Became a Minority Group

Around the world, gender is *the* primary division between people. To catch a glimpse of how remarkably gender expectations differ with culture, look at the photo essay on pages 260–261.

Every society sets up barriers to provide unequal access to property, power, and prestige on the basis of sex. Consequently, sociologists classify females as a *minority*

Sociologists stress the social factors that underlie human behavior, the experiences that mold us, funneling us into different directions in life. The study of Vietnam veterans discussed in the text is one indication of how the sociological door is opening slowly to also consider biological factors in human behavior. Using a shirt as a stretcher, these soldiers are carrying a wounded buddy from the jungle after heavy fighting near the Cambodian border in Tay Ninh, South Vietnam, on April 6, 1967.

Gender and Work:
Women at Work in India

traveling through India was both a pleasant and an eye-opening experience. The country is incredibly diverse, the people friendly, and the land culturally rich. For this photo essay, wherever I went—whether city, village, or countryside—I took photos of women at work.

From these photos, you can see that Indian women work in a wide variety of occupations. Some of their jobs match traditional Western expectations, and some diverge sharply from our gender stereotypes. Although women in India remain submissive to men—with the women's movement barely able to break the cultural surface—women's occupations are hardly limited to the home. I was surprised at some of the hard, heavy labor that Indian women do.

Indian women are highly visible in public places. A storekeeper is as likely to be a woman as a man. This woman is selling glasses of water at a beach on the Bay of Bengal. The structure on which her glasses rest is built of sand.

The villages of India have no indoor plumbing. Instead, each village has a well with a hand pump, and it is the women's job to fetch the water. This is backbreaking work, for, after pumping the water, the women wrestle the heavy buckets onto their heads and carry them home. This was one of the few occupations I saw that was limited to women.

Women also take care of livestock. It looks as though this woman dressed up and posed for her photo, but this is what she was wearing and doing when I saw her in the field and stopped to talk to her. While the sheep are feeding, her job is primarily to "be" there, to make certain the sheep don't wander off or that no one steals them.

Sweeping the house is traditional work for Western women. So it is in India, but the sweeping has been extended to areas outside the home. These women are sweeping a major intersection in Chennai. When the traffic light changes here, the women will continue sweeping, with the drivers swerving around them. This was one of the few occupations that seems to be limited to women.

As in the West, food preparation in India is traditional women's work. Here, however, food preparation takes an unexpected twist. Having poured rice from the 60-pound sack onto the floor, these women in Chittoor search for pebbles or other foreign objects that might be in the rice.

When I saw this unusual sight, I had to stop and talk to the workers. From historical pictures, I knew that belt-driven machines were common on U.S. farms 100 years ago. This one in Tamil Nadu processes sugar cane. The woman feeds sugar cane into the machine, which disgorges the stalks on one side and sugar cane juice on the other.

I visited quarries in different parts of India, where I found men, women, and children hard at work in the tropical sun. This woman works 8 1/2 hours a day, six days a week. She earns 40 rupees a day (about ninety cents). Men make 60 rupees a day (about $1.35). Like many quarry workers, this woman is a bonded laborer. She must give half of her wages to her master.

This woman belongs to the Dhobi subcaste, whose occupation is washing clothes. She stands waist deep at this same spot doing the same thing day after day. The banks of this canal in Hyderabad are lined with men and women of her caste, who are washing linens for hotels and clothing for more well-to-do families.

A common sight in India is women working on construction crews. As they work on buildings and on highways, they mix cement, unload trucks, carry rubble, and, following Indian culture, carry heavy loads of bricks atop their heads. This photo was taken in Raipur, Chhattisgarh.

group. Because females outnumber males, you may find this strange. The term *minority group* applies, however, because it refers to people who are discriminated against on the basis of physical or cultural characteristics, regardless of their numbers (Hacker 1951). For an overview of gender discrimination in a changing society, see the Cultural Diversity box below.

Have females always been a minority group? Analysts speculate that in some earlier societies women and men may have been social equals. Apparently the horticultural and hunting and gathering societies reviewed in Chapter 4 had less gender discrimination than we have today. In these societies, women may have been equal partners with men, and they may have contributed about 60 percent of the group's total food (Lerner 1986).

How did it happen, then, that around the world, women came to be systematically discriminated against? Let's consider the primary theory that has been proposed.

The Origins of Patriarchy

The major theory of **patriarchy**—men dominating society—points to social consequences of human reproduction (Lerner 1986; Friedl 1990). In early human history, life was short: To balance the high mortality rate and maintain the population required the birth of many children. This brought severe consequences for women. Because only females get pregnant, carry a child for nine months, give birth, and nurse, women were limited in their activities for a considerable part of their lives. To survive, an infant needed a nursing mother. With a child at her breast or in her uterus or one carried on her hip or on her back, women were physically encumbered. Consequently, around the world, women assumed tasks that were associated with the home and child care, while men took over the hunting of large animals and other tasks that required both greater speed and longer absences from the base camp (Huber 1990).

Cultural Diversity *around the* World

"Pssst. You Wanna Buy a Bride?" China in Transition

NGUYEN THI HOAN, AGE 22, thanked her lucky stars. A Vietnamese country girl, she had just arrived in Hanoi to look for work, and while she was still at the bus station a woman offered her a job in a candy factory.

It was a trap. After Nguyen had loaded a few sacks of sugar, the woman took her into the country to "get supplies." There some men took her to China, which was only 100 miles away. Nguyen was put up for auction, along with a 16-year-old Vietnamese girl. Each brought $350. Nguyen was traded from one bride dealer to another until she was taken to a Chinese village. There she was introduced to her new husband, who had paid $700 for her (Marshall 1999).

Why are thousands of women kidnapped and sold as brides in China each year (Rosenthal 2001b)? First, parts of China have a centuries-old tradition of bride selling. Second, China has a shortage of women. The government enforces a "one couple-one child" policy. Since sons are preferred, female infanticide has become common. One result is a shortage of women of marriageable age. In some provinces, for every 100 women there are over 120 men. Yet all the men are expected to marry and produce heirs (Rosenthal 2001b).

Actually, Nguyen was lucky. Some kidnapped women are sold as prostitutes.

Bride selling and forced prostitution are ancient practices. But China is also entering a new era, which is bringing with it new pressures for Chinese women. Ideas of beauty are changing, and blonde, blue-eyed women are becoming a fetish. As a consequence, Chinese women feel a pressure to "Westernize" their bodies. Surgeons promise to give them bigger breasts and Western-looking eyes. A Western style of advertising is gaining ground, too: Ads now show scantily clad women perched on top of sports cars (Chen 1995; Johansson 1999; Yat-ming Sin and Hon-ming Yau 2001).

China in transition . . . It is continuing the old—bride selling—while moving toward the new, Western ideas of beauty and advertising. In both the old and new, women are commodities for the consumption of men.

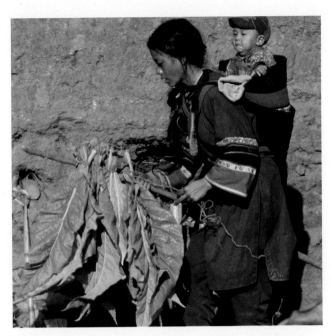

A theory of how patriarchy originated centers on childbirth. Because only women give birth, they assumed tasks associated with home and child care, while men hunted and performed other survival tasks that required greater strength, speed, and absence from home. This woman, who is harvesting tobacco leaves in Shilin, China, also takes care of her child—just as her female ancestors have done for millennia.

As a result, men became dominant. It was the men who left camp to hunt animals, who made contact with other tribes, who traded with these other groups, and who quarreled and waged war with them. It was also the men who made and controlled the instruments of death, the weapons that were used for hunting and warfare. It was the men who accumulated possessions in trade and gained prestige by returning triumphantly with prisoners of war or with large animals to feed the tribe. In contrast, little prestige was given to the routine, taken-for-granted activities of women—who were not perceived as risking their lives for the group. Eventually, men took over society. Their sources of power were their weapons, items of trade, and knowledge gained from contact with other groups. Women became second-class citizens, subject to men's decisions.

Is this theory correct? Remember that the answer lies buried in human history, and there is no way of testing it.

Male dominance may be the result of some entirely different cause. For example, anthropologist Marvin Harris (1977) proposed that because most men are stronger than most women and hand-to-hand combat was necessary in tribal groups, men became the warriors, and women became the reward that enticed men to risk their lives in battle. Frederick Engels proposed that patriarchy came with the development of private property (Lerner 1986; Mezentseva 2001). He could not explain why private property should have produced male dominance, however. Gerda Lerner (1986) suggests that patriarchy may even have had different origins in different places.

Whatever its origins, a circular system of thought evolved. Men came to think of themselves as inherently superior—based on the evidence that they dominated society. They shrouded many of their activities with secrecy and constructed elaborate rules and rituals to avoid "contamination" by females, whom they openly deemed inferior by that time. Even today, patriarchy is always accompanied by cultural supports designed to justify male dominance—such as designating certain activities as "not appropriate" for women.

As tribal societies developed into larger groups, men, who enjoyed their power and privileges, maintained their dominance. Long after hunting and hand-to-hand combat ceased to be routine, and even after large numbers of children were no longer needed to maintain the population, men held on to their power. Male dominance in contemporary societies, then, is a continuation of a millennia-old pattern whose origin is lost in history.

Foot binding, a form of violence against women, was practiced in China. This photo of a woman in Canton, China, is from the early 1900s. The woman's tiny feet, which made it difficult for her to walk, were a status symbol, indicating that her husband was wealthy and did not need her labor. It also made her dependent on him.

Gender Inequality in the United States

Gender inequality is not some accidental, hit-or-miss affair. Rather, the institutions of each society work together to maintain the group's particular forms of inequality. Customs, often venerated throughout history, both justify and maintain these arrangements. Let's take a brief look at how change in this vital area of social life came about.

Fighting Back: The Rise of Feminism

To see how far we have come, it is useful to look back at where we used to be. In early U.S. society, the second-class status of women was taken for granted. A husband and wife were legally one person—him (Chafetz and Dworkin 1986). Women could not vote, buy property in their own name, make legal contracts, or serve on juries. How could times have changed so much that these examples sound like fiction?

A central lesson of conflict theory is that power yields privilege; like a magnet, power draws society's best resources to the elite. Because men tenaciously held onto their privileges and used social institutions to maintain their position, basic rights for women came only through prolonged and bitter struggle.

Feminism, the view that biology is not destiny and that stratification by gender is wrong and should be resisted, met with strong opposition—both by men who had privilege to lose and by women who accepted their current status as morally correct. In 1894, for example, Jeannette Gilder said that women should not have the right to vote because "Politics is too public, too wearing, and too unfitted to the nature of women" (Crossen 2003).

Feminists, then known as suffragists, struggled against such views. In 1916, they founded the National Women's Party, and in 1917 they began to picket the White House. After picketing for six months, the women were arrested. Hundreds were sent to prison, including Lucy Burns, a leader of the National Women's Party. The extent to which these women had threatened male privilege is demonstrated by how she and other protesters were treated in prison.

Two men brought in Dorothy Day [the editor of a periodical that espoused women's rights], twisting her arms above her head. Suddenly they lifted her and brought her body down twice over the back of an iron bench. They had been there a few minutes when Mrs. Lewis, all doubled over like a sack of flour, was thrown in. Her head struck the iron bed

and she fell to the floor senseless. As for Lucy Burns, they handcuffed her wrists and fastened the handcuffs over [her] head to the cell door. (Cowley 1969)

This *first wave* of the women's movement had a radical branch that wanted to reform all the institutions of society and a conservative branch whose concern was to win the vote for women (Freedman 2001). The conservative branch dominated, and after the right to vote was won in 1920, the movement basically dissolved.

The *second wave* began in the 1960s. Sociologist Janet Chafetz (1990) points out that up to this time most women thought of work as a temporary activity intended to fill the time between completing school and getting married. To see how children's books reinforced such thinking, see Figure 10.1. As more women took jobs and began to regard them as careers, however, they began to compare their working conditions with those of men. This shift in their reference group changed the way women viewed their conditions at work. The result was a second wave of protest against gender inequalities. The goals of this second wave (which continues today) are broad, ranging from raising women's pay to changing policies on violence against women.

A *third wave* of feminism is emerging. Three main aspects are apparent. The first is a greater focus on the problems of women in the Least Industrialized Nations (Patel 1997; Spivak 2000). The second is a criticism of the values that dominate work and society. Some feminists argue that competition, calloused emotions, toughness, and independence represent "male" qualities and need to be

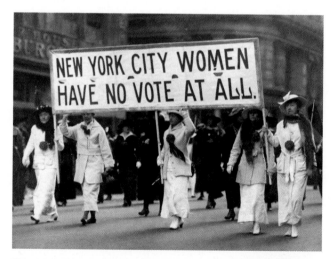

The women's struggle for equal rights has been long and hard. Shown here is a 1919 photo from the first wave of the U.S. women's movement. Only against enormous opposition from men did U.S. women win the right to vote. They first voted in national elections in 1920.

Figure 10.1 **Teaching Gender**

By looking at the past, we get an idea of how far we have come. This illustration from a 1970s children's book shows the mind-set of the day. You can see how children who grew up during this period were taught to view gender and work.

Boys are pilots.

Girls are stewardesses.

Boys are presidents.

Girls are First Ladies.

Boys are doctors.

Girls are nurses.

Boys build houses.

Girls keep houses.

Source: Anthony Cortese, *Provocateur: Images of Women and Minorities in Advertising,* 2nd ed. Boulder, CO: Rowman and Little Publishers, 2003.

replaced with cooperation, openness, connection, and interdependence (England 2000). A third aspect is the removal of impediments to women's experiences of love and sexual pleasure (Gilligan 2002).

Although women enjoy fundamental rights today, gender inequality continues to play a central role in social life. Let's look at gender relations in education, in health care, and at work.

Gender Inequality in Education

Gender inequality in education is not readily apparent. More women than men go to college, and they earn 57 percent of all bachelor's degrees and 59 percent of all master's degrees (*Statistical Abstract* 2005:Table 282). Because men are now lagging behind, some have begun to call for *affirmative action for men*, especially for African American and Native American men (Kleinfeld 2002a).

That men need to catch up with women is certainly a new situation, and in coming years, such programs may

well come into existence. A closer look at the current situation, however, reveals *gender tracking;* that is, degrees tend to follow gender, which reinforces male-female distinctions. Here are two extremes: Men earn 81 percent of bachelor's degrees in the "masculine" field of engineering, while women are awarded 88 percent of bachelor's degrees in the "feminine" field of home economics (*Statistical Abstract* 2005:Table 285). Because gender socialization gives men and women different orientations to life, they enter college with gender-linked aspirations. It is their socialization—not some presumed innate characteristics—that channels men and women into different educational paths. Yet, as discussed in the Down-to-Earth Sociology box on the next page, innate abilities are still a matter of controversy.

If we follow students into graduate school, we see that with each passing year, the proportion of women drops. Table 10.1 on the next page gives us a snapshot of doctoral programs in the sciences. Note how aspirations (enrollment) and accomplishments (doctorates earned) are sex linked. In five of these doctoral programs, men outnumber women,

Down-to-Earth Sociology

The Gender Gap in Math and Science: A National Debate

Overwhelmingly, engineers and scientists are men. Why? A national debate erupted when the president of Harvard University, Larry Summers, suggested that the reason might be innate differences between men and women. In essence, he was suggesting that women's inborn characteristics might make them less qualified to succeed in these endeavors.

Summers' statement landed him squarely on editorial pages throughout the nation. Harvard's Arts and Sciences faculty, which was already upset over what they called his authoritarian manner, took his statement as a "last straw." The faculty met and gave Summers a "no confidence" vote, the equivalent of saying that he should resign. This was the first such repudiation of a president since Harvard was founded in 1636 (Finer 2005).

That Summers had only suggested that biology might be the reason for why men dominate science and engineering indicated that he had touched a sore spot in academia. Among the many who weighed in with replies to Summers was the

Council of the American Sociological Association ("ASA Council . . ." 2005). The council replied that research gives us clear and compelling evidence that social factors, not genetics, are the reason that women have not done as well as men in science and engineering. To support its position, the council made this compelling argument:

Gender differences in test results in math and science abilities have changed over time. There are now hardly any differences in test scores among male and female U.S. students. In Great Britain, girls now outperform boys on these tests. Biology didn't change—but social factors did: more access to courses in school, changed attitudes of school counselors, and more role models for women.

The council added that women's interests change as opportunities open to them. This, too, is social, not biological. As a result, we can expect many more women to enter the fields of science and engineering. These women, unfortunately, will have to struggle against negative stereotypes about their abilities, as their predecessors did.

Table 10.1
Doctorates in Science, By Sex

Field	Students Enrolled		Doctorates Conferred		Completion Ratio* (Higher or Lower Than Expected)	
	Women	Men	Women	Men	Women	Men
Psychology	73%	27%	67%	33%	−8	+22
Biological sciences	54%	46%	45%	55%	−17	+20
Social sciences	52%	48%	45%	55%	−13	+15
Agriculture	44%	56%	31%	69%	−30	+23
Mathematics	36%	64%	29%	71%	−19	+11
Physical sciences	31%	69%	27%	73%	−13	+6
Computer sciences	28%	72%	21%	79%	−25	+10
Engineering	21%	79%	18%	82%	−14	+4

*The formula for the completion ratio is X minus Y divided by Y, where X is the doctorates conferred and Y is the proportion enrolled in a program.

Source: By the author. Based on *Statistical Abstract* 2005:Tables 774, 775.

and in three, women outnumber men. In *all* of them, however, women are less likely to complete the doctorate.

If we follow those who earn doctoral degrees to their teaching careers at colleges and universities, we find gender stratification in rank and pay. Throughout the United States, women are less likely to become full professors, the highest-paying and most prestigious rank. In both private and public colleges, professors average more than twice the salary of instructors (*Statistical Abstract* 2005:Table 278). Even when women do become full professors, on average, their pay is less than that of men who are full professors (Wood 2001).

Figure 10.2 illustrates a remarkable change in education. Note how sharply the proportion of professional degrees earned by women has increased. The greatest change is in dentistry: Across the entire United States, in 1970, only 34 women earned this degree. Today, about 1,700 women become dentists each year.

Gender Inequality in Health Care

Medical researchers were perplexed. Reports were coming in from all over the country: Women were twice as likely as men to die after coronary bypass surgery. Researchers at Cedars-Sinai Medical Center in Los Angeles checked their own records. They found that of 2,300 coronary bypass patients, 4.6 percent of the women died as a result of the surgery, compared with 2.6 percent of the men.

These findings presented a sociological puzzle. To solve it, researchers first turned to biology (Bishop 1990). In coronary bypass surgery, a blood vessel is taken from one part of the body and stitched to an artery on the surface of the heart. Perhaps this operation was more difficult to perform on women because they have smaller arteries. To find out, researchers measured the amount of time that surgeons kept patients on the heart-lung machine while they operated. They were surprised to learn that women spent *less* time on the machine than men. This indicated that the operation was not more difficult to perform on women.

As the researchers probed, a surprising answer emerged: unintended sexual discrimination. Physicians had not taken the chest pains of their women patients as seriously as they took the complaints of their men patients. The physicians were *ten* times more likely to give men exercise stress tests and radioactive heart scans. They also sent men to surgery on the basis of abnormal stress

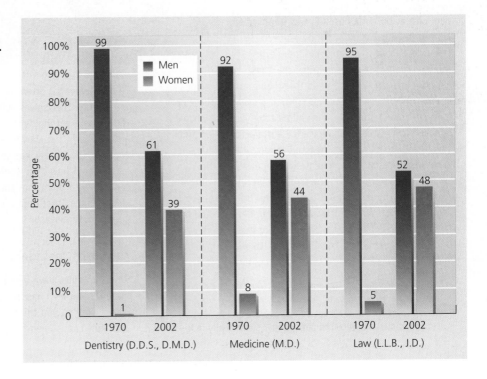

Figure 10.2 **Gender Changes in Professional Degrees**

Source: By the author. Based on *Statistical Abstract* 2006:Table 291.

tests but waited until women showed clear-cut symptoms of heart disease before sending them to surgery. Patients who have surgery after the disease is more advanced are less likely to survive.

As more women become physicians, perhaps this will change. We know that women doctors are more likely to order Pap smears and mammograms (Lurie et al. 1993), so it is likely that they will be more responsive to the health complaints of women.

In the Down-to-Earth Sociology box below, we look at a more blatant form of sexism in medicine.

Gender Inequality in the Workplace

To examine the work setting is to make visible basic relations between men and women. Let's begin with one of the most remarkable areas of gender inequality at work, the pay gap.

The Pay Gap. One of the chief characteristics of the U.S. work force is a steady growth in the numbers of women who work for wages outside the home. Figure 10.3 shows that in 1900, one of five people in the U.S. paid work force was a woman. By 1940, this ratio had grown to one of four; by 1960, to one of three; and today it is almost one of two.

Women who work for wages are not evenly distributed throughout the United States. From the Social Map on the next page, you can see that where a woman lives makes a difference in how likely she is to work outside the home. Why is there such a clustering among the states? The geographical patterns evident in this map

Down-to-Earth Sociology

Cold-Hearted Surgeons and Their Women Victims

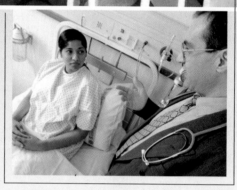

Sociologist Sue Fisher (1986), who did participant observation in a hospital, was surprised to hear surgeons recommend total hysterectomy (removal of both the uterus and the ovaries) *when no cancer was present.* When she asked why, the men doctors explained that the uterus and ovaries are "potentially disease producing." They also said that these organs are unnecessary after the childbearing years, so why not remove them? Doctors who reviewed hysterectomies confirmed this bias: They found that three out of four of these surgeries were, in their term, inappropriate (Broder et al. 2000).

Surgical sexism has a powerful motive: greed. Surgeons make money by performing this surgery. But they have to "sell" the operation, since women, to understate the matter, are reluctant to part with these organs. Here is how one resident explained the "hard sell" to sociologist Diana Scully (1994):

> You have to look for your surgical procedures; you have to go after patients. Because no one is crazy enough to come and say, "Hey, here I am. I want you to operate on me." You have to sometimes convince the patient that she is really sick—if

she is, of course [laughs], and that she is better off with a surgical procedure.

To "convince" a woman to have this surgery, the doctor puts on a serious face and tells her that the examination has turned up fibroids in her uterus—and they might turn into cancer. This statement is often sufficient, for it frightens women, who picture themselves dying from cancer. To clinch the sale, the surgeon withholds the rest of the truth—that fibroids are common, that they most likely will not turn into cancer, and that the patient has several nonsurgical alternatives.

I wonder how men would feel if surgeons systematically suggested to them that they be castrated when they get older—since "that organ is no longer necessary, and it might cause disease."

for your Consideration

Hysterectomies have become so common that one out of three U.S. women has her uterus surgically removed (Elson 2004). Why do you think that surgeons are so quick to operate? How can women find nonsurgical alternatives?

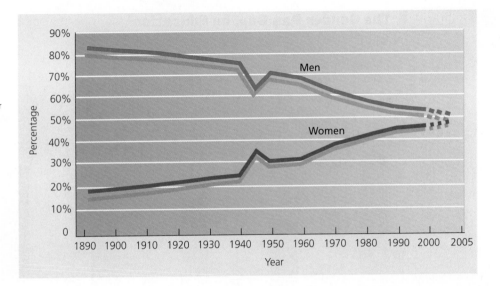

Figure 10.3 **Women's and Men's Proportion of the U.S. Labor Force**

Note: Pre-1940 totals include women 14 and over: totals for 1940 and after are for women 16 and over. Broken lines are the author's projections.
Sources: By the author. Based on 1969 *Handbook on Women Workers,* 1969:10; *Manpower Report to the President,* 1971:203, 205; Mills and Palumbo, 1980:6, 45; *Statistical Abstract* 2005:Table 570.

reflect regional-subcultural differences about which we currently have little understanding.

After college, you might like to take a few years off, travel a bit, and sit under a palm tree and drink piña coladas. But chances are, you are going to go to work instead. Since you have to work, how would you like to earn an extra $635,000 on your job? If this sounds appealing, read

on. I'm going to reveal how you can make an extra $1,300 a month between the ages of 25 and 65.

Is this hard to do? Actually, it is simple for some, but impossible for others. As Figure 10.5 on the next page shows, all you have to do is be born a male and graduate from college. If we compare full-time workers, based on current differences in earnings, this is how much more money the

Figure 10.4 **Women in the Work Force**

Source: By the author. Based on *Statistical Abstract* 2005:Table 574.

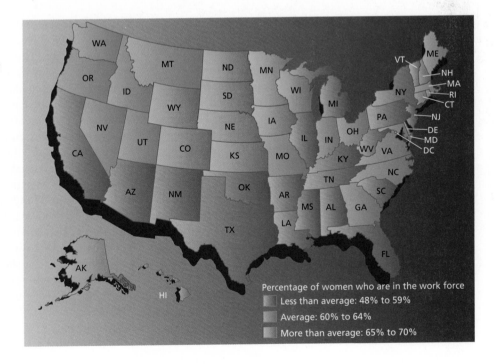

Percentage of women who are in the work force
Less than average: 48% to 59%
Average: 60% to 64%
More than average: 65% to 70%

Figure 10.5 The Gender Pay Gap, by Education[1]

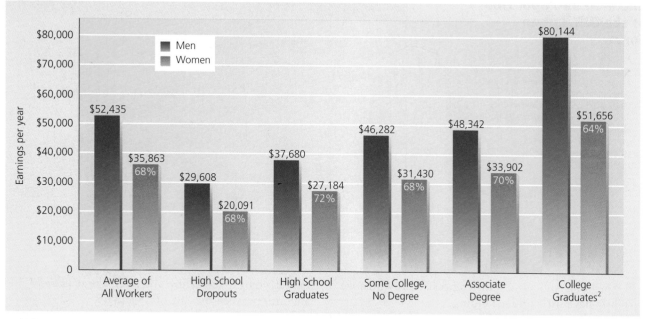

[1]Full-time workers in all fields.
[2]Bachelor's and all higher degrees, including professional degrees.

Source: By the author. Based on *Statistical Abstract* 2005:Table 679.

average male college graduate can expect to earn over the course of his career. Hardly any single factor pinpoints gender discrimination better than this total. You can also see that the pay gap shows up at *all* levels of education.

The pay gap is so great that U.S. women who work full time average *only 70 percent* of what men are paid. As you can see from Figure 10.6, the pay gap used to be even worse. You can also see that the gap closed a bit during the 1980s, but then it grew during the 1990s. Since then, it has held fairly constant, hovering between 65 percent and 70 percent. The gender gap in pay occurs not only in the United States but also in *all* industrialized nations.

If $635,000 additional earnings aren't enough, how would you like to make another $166,000 extra at work? If so, just make sure that you are not only a man but also a *tall* man. Over their lifetimes, men who are over 6 feet tall average $166,000 more than men who are 5 feet 5 inches or less (Judge and Cable 2004). Taller women also make more than shorter women. But even when it comes to height, the gender pay gap persists, and tall men make more than tall women.

What logic can underlie the gender pay gap? Earlier we saw that college degrees are gender linked, so perhaps this gap is due to career choices. Maybe women are more likely to choose lower-paying jobs, such as teaching grade school, while men are more likely to go into better-paying fields, such as business and engineering. Actually, this is true, and researchers have found that about *half* of the gender pay gap is due to such factors. And the balance? It consists of a combination of gender discrimination (Jacobs 2003; Roth 2003) and what is called the "child penalty"—women missing out on work experience and opportunities while they care for children (Hundley 2001; Chaker and Stout 2004).

For college students, the gender gap in pay begins with the first job after graduation. You might know of a particular woman who was offered a higher salary than most men in her class, but she would be an exception. On average, men enjoy a "testosterone bonus," and employers start them out at higher salaries than women (Fuller and Schoenberger 1991; Harris et al. 2005). Depending on your sex, then, you will either benefit from the pay gap or be victimized by it.

Figure 10.6 The Gender Gap Over Time: What Percentage of Men's Income Do Women Earn?

Source: By the author. Based on *Statistical Abstract* 1995:Table 739; 2006:Table 686, and earlier years. The last year for which the source has data is 2003. Broken lines indicate the author's estimates.

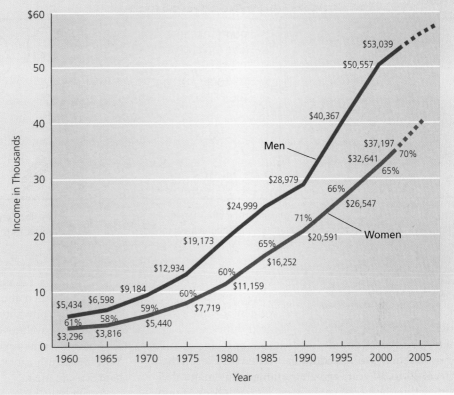

(handwritten note) OR THERE ARE MORE PEOPLE JUST SIMPLY IN THE U.S. w/ THOSE NAMES?

As a final indication of the extent of the U.S. gender pay gap, consider this. Of the nation's top 500 corporations (the so-called "Fortune 500"), only 8 are headed by women (Jones 2005). And 8 is a record-breaking number! I examined the names of the CEOs of the 350 largest U.S. corporations, and I found that your best chance to reach the top is to be named (in this order) John, Robert, James, William, or Charles. Edward, Lawrence, and Richard are also advantageous names. Amber, Katherine, Leticia, and Maria, however, apparently draw a severe penalty. Naming your baby girl John or Robert might seem a little severe, but it could help her reach the top. (I say this only slightly tongue-in-cheek. One of the few women to head a Fortune 500 company—before she was fired and given $21 million severance pay—had a man's first name: Carleton Fiorina of Hewlett-Packard.)

The Cracking Glass Ceiling. What keeps women from breaking through the **glass ceiling,** the mostly invisible barrier that prevents women from reaching the executive suite? Researchers have identified a "pipeline" that leads to the top: the marketing, sales, and production positions that directly affect the corporate bottom line (Hymowitz 2004; DeCrow 2005). Men, who dominate the executive suite, stereotype women as being less capable of leadership than they are (Heilman 2001). Viewing women as good at "support," they steer women into human resources or public relations. There, successful projects are not appreciated in the same way as those that bring corporate profits—and bonuses for their managers.

Another reason the glass ceiling is so powerful is that women lack mentors—successful executives who take an interest in them and teach them the ropes. Lack of a mentor is no trivial matter, for mentors can provide opportunities to develop leadership skills that open the door to the executive suite (Heilman 2001).

The glass ceiling is cracking, however (Solomon 2000; Hymowitz 2004). A look at women who have broken through reveals highly motivated individuals with a fierce competitive spirit who are willing to give up sleep and

Dilbert

One of the frustrations felt by many women in the labor force is that no matter what they do, they hit a glass ceiling. Another is that to succeed they feel forced to abandon characteristics they feel are essential to their self.

recreation for the sake of career advancement. They also learn to play by "men's rules," developing a style that makes men comfortable. Most of these women also have supportive husbands who share household duties and adapt their careers to accommodate the needs of their executive wives (Lublin 1996). In addition, women who began their careers 20 to 30 years ago are running many major divisions within the largest companies. With this background, some of these women will emerge as the new top CEOs (Hymowitz 2004).

Then there is the *glass escalator.* Sociologist Christine Williams (1995) interviewed men and women who worked in traditionally female jobs—as nurses, elementary school teachers, librarians, and social workers. Instead of bumping their heads against a glass ceiling, the men in these occupations found themselves aboard a **glass escalator.** They were given higher-level positions, more desirable work assignments, and higher salaries. The motor that drives the glass escalator is gender: the stereotype that because someone is male he is more capable.

Sexual Harassment—and Worse

Sexual harassment—unwelcome sexual attention at work or at school, which may affect a person's job or school performance or create a hostile environment—was not recognized as a problem until the 1970s. Before this, women considered unwanted sexual comments, touches, looks, and pressure to have sex to be a personal matter.

With the prodding of feminists, women began to perceive unwanted sexual advances at work and school as part of a *structural* problem. That is, they began to realize that the issue was more than a man here or there doing ob-

noxious things because he was attracted to a woman; rather, it was men abusing their positions of authority in order to force unwanted sexual activities on women. Now that women have moved into positions of authority, they, too, have become sexual harassers (Wayne et al. 2001). With most authority vested in men, however, most sexual harassers are men.

As symbolic interactionists stress, labels affect our perception. Because we have the term *sexual harassment,* we perceive actions in a different light than did our predecessors. The meaning of sexual harassment is vague and shifting, however, and court cases constantly change what this term does and does not include. Originally sexual desire was an element of sexual harassment, but it no longer is. This changed when the U.S. Supreme Court considered the lawsuit of a homosexual who had been tormented by his supervisors and fellow workers. The Court ruled that sexual desire is not necessary–that sexual harassment laws also apply to homosexuals who are harassed by heterosexuals while on the job (Felsenthal 1998). By extension, the law applies to heterosexuals who are sexually harassed by homosexuals.

Gender and Violence

The high rate of violence in the United States shocks foreigners and frightens many Americans. Today, fearful of carjackings, many lock their cars even while driving. Fearful of rape and kidnappings, many parents escort their children to school. Lurking behind these fears is the gender inequality of violence—the fact that females are much more likely to be victims of males, not the other way around. Let's briefly review this almost one-way street in gender violence.

Forcible Rape. Being raped is a common fear of U.S. women. This fear is far from groundless. According to FBI statistics, each year 7 of every 10,000 females age 12 and older are raped. From the National Crime Victimization Survey, however, we know that only one-third of rape victims report this crime to the police (*Statistical Abstract* 2005:page 184 and Table 298). A more accurate total, then, is *three* times the official rate, or about 21 victims per 10,000 rather than 7. Despite these high numbers, women are safer now than they were just a few years ago, as rape has been declining for the past decade.

Although the victims of sexual assault include babies and elderly women, the typical victim is 12 to 24 years old. Contrary to stereotypes, most victims know their attacker. Those most likely to be raped are women ages 18 to 19. Only one-third of rapes (32 percent) are committed by strangers (*Statistical Abstract* 2005:Tables 306, 307).

An aspect of rape that is usually overlooked is the rape of men in prison. With prison officials reluctant to let the public know about the horrible conditions behind bars, our studies are far from perfect. Those we have, however, indicate that about 15 to 20 percent of men in prison are raped. From court cases, we know that some guards even punish prisoners by placing them in cells with sexual predators (Donaldson 1993; Lewin 2001b).

Date (Acquaintance) Rape. What has shocked so many about date rape (also known as *acquaintance rape*) is studies showing that it does not consist of a few isolated events (Collymore 2000; Goode 2001). Some researchers even report that most women students experience unwanted, forced, or coerced sex (Kalof 2000). Most samples are inadequate, and the actual numbers are probably much lower. Researchers who did a survey of students in a representative sample of courses at Marietta College, a private school in Ohio, found that 2.5 percent of the women had been physically forced to have sex (Felton et al. 2001). About as many men (23 percent) as women (24 percent) had given in to pressure to have sex when they didn't want to, but—and this is no surprise—none of the men had been physically forced to have sex.

Most date rapes go unreported. A primary reason is that the victim feels partially responsible because she knows the person and was with him voluntarily. However, as a physician who treats victims of date rape said, "Would you feel responsible if someone hit you over the head with a shovel—just because you knew the person?" (Carpenito 1999).

Murder. All over the world, men are more likely than women to be the killers. Figure 10.7 illustrates this gender pattern in U.S. murders. Although females make up

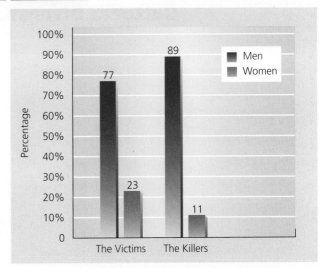

Figure 10.7 **Killers and Their Victims**

Source: By the author. Based on *Statistical Abstract* 2005:Tables 294, 309.

a little over 51 percent of the U.S. population, they don't even come close to making up 51 percent of the nation's killers. Note also that when women are murdered, about nine times out of ten, the killer is a man.

To move beyond the United States for a moment, we can consider "honor killings." In some societies, such as Pakistan, Jordan, and Kurdistan, a woman who is thought to have brought disgrace on her family is killed by a male relative—usually a brother or husband, but often her father or uncles. What threat to the family's honor can be so severe that the men would kill a daughter or wife? The usual reason is sex outside of marriage. In Iraq, even a woman who has been raped is in danger of becoming the victim of an honor killing (Banerjee 2003). Killing the girl or woman removes the "stain" she has brought to the family, and restores the family's honor in the community. Sharing this perspective, the police in these countries generally ignore honor killings, viewing them as family matters.

Violence in the Home. Women are also the typical victims of family violence. Spouse battering, child abuse, and incest are discussed in Chapter 12 (pages 347–349). A particular form of violence against women, genital circumcision, is the focus of the Cultural Diversity box on the next page.

Feminism and Gendered Violence. Feminist sociologists have been especially effective in bringing violence against women to the public's attention. Some use symbolic interactionism, pointing out that to associate

Cultural Diversity *around the* World

Female Circumcision

"Lie down there," the excisor suddenly said to me [when I was 12], pointing to a mat on the ground. No sooner had I laid down than I felt my frail, thin legs grasped by heavy hands and pulled wide apart. . . . Two women on each side of me pinned me to the ground . . . I underwent the ablation of the labia minor and then of the clitoris. The operation seemed to go on forever. I was in the throes of agony, torn apart both physically and psychologically. It was the rule that girls of my age did not weep in this situation. I broke the rule. I cried and screamed with pain. . . !

Afterwards they forced me, not only to walk back to join the other girls who had already been excised, but to dance with them. I was doing my best, but then I fainted. . . . It was a month before I was completely healed. When I was better, everyone mocked me, as I hadn't been brave, they said. (Walker and Parmar 1993:107–108)

Female circumcision is common in parts of Muslim Africa and in some parts of Malaysia and Indonesia. Often called female genital cutting by Westerners, this practice is also known as clitoral excision, clitoridectomy, infibulation, and labia-dectomy, depending on how much of the tissue is removed. Worldwide, between 100 million and 200 million females have been circumcised. In Egypt, 97 percent of the women have been circumcised (Boyle et al. 2001; Douglas 2005).

In some cultures, only the girl's clitoris is cut off; in others, more is removed. In Sudan, the Nubia cut away most of the girl's genitalia, then sew together the remaining outer edges. They bind the girl's legs from her ankles to her waist for several weeks while scar tissue closes up the vagina. They leave a small opening the diameter of a pencil for the passage of urine and menstrual fluids.

Among most groups, the surgery takes place between the ages of 4 and 8. In some cultures, it occurs seven to ten days after birth. In others, it is not performed until girls reach adolescence. Because the surgery is usually done without anesthesia, the pain is so excruciating that adults must hold the girl down. In urban areas, physicians sometimes perform the operation; in rural areas, a neighborhood woman usually does it.

Shock, bleeding, infection, infertility, and death are among the risks. Common side-effects are vaginal spasms, painful intercourse, and lack of orgasms. Urinary tract infections also occur as urine and menstrual flow build up behind the tiny opening.

When a woman marries, the opening is cut wider to permit sexual intercourse. In some groups, this is the husband's

---

strength and virility with violence—as is done in many cultures—is to promote violence. Others use conflict theory. They argue that men are losing power, and that some men turn violently against women as a way to reassert their declining power and status (Reiser 1999; Meltzer 2002).

Solutions. There is no magic bullet for this problem of gendered violence, but to be effective, any solution must break the connection between violence and masculinity. This would require an educational program that encompasses schools, churches, homes, and the media. Given the gun-slinging heroes of the Wild West and other American icons, as well as the violent messages that are so prevalent in the mass media, it is difficult to be optimistic that a change will come any time soon.

Our next topic, women in politics, however, gives us much more reason for optimism.

The Changing Face of Politics

Why don't women, who outnumber men, take political control of the nation? Eight million more women than men are of voting age. As Table 10.2 on page 276 shows, however, men greatly outnumber women in political office. Despite the gains women have made in recent elections, since 1789 over 1,800 men have served in the U.S. Senate but only 33 women, including 14 current senators. Not until 1992 was the first African American woman (Carol Moseley-Braun) elected to the U.S. Senate. No Latina or Asian American woman has yet been elected to the Senate (National Women's Political Caucus 1998; *Statistical Abstract* 2005:Table 396).

Why are women underrepresented in U.S. politics? First, women are still underrepresented in law and business, the careers from which most politicians emerge. Most

responsibility. Before a woman gives birth, the opening is enlarged further. After birth, the vagina is again sutured shut; this cycle of surgically closing and opening begins anew with each birth.

What are the reasons for this custom? Some groups believe that it reduces female sexual desire, making it more likely that a woman will be a virgin at marriage, and, afterward, remain faithful to her husband. Others think that women can't bear children if they aren't circumcised.

Feminists call female circumcision a form of ritual torture to control female sexuality. They point out that men dominate the societies that practice it. Mothers cooperate with the surgery because in these societies an uncircumcised woman is considered impure and is not allowed to marry. Grandmothers insist that the custom continue out of concern that their granddaughters marry well.

The growing opposition to female circumcision has created intense controversy in Africa, perhaps nowhere demonstrated more forcefully than this contrast: On the one hand, fourteen African countries have banned female circumcision

This poster is used in Sudan to try to get parents to stop circumcising their daughters.

(the laws, however, are seldom enforced). On the other hand, to drum up votes for her husband, the wife of the president of Sierra Leone personally sponsored the circumcision of 1,500 girls (Douglas 2005; "Sierra Leone" 2005).

Sources: As cited, and Mahran 1978, 1981; Ebomoyi 1987; Lightfoot-Klein 1989; Merwine 1993; Chalkley 1997; Collymore 2000; "Ethiopia" 2005.

for your Consideration

Do you think that the United States should try to make other nations stop this custom? Or would this be ethnocentric, the imposition of Western values on other cultures? As one Somali woman said, "The Somali woman doesn't need an alien woman telling her how to treat her private parts." Do you think that it is ever legitimate for members of one culture to interfere with another?

How would you respond to those who oppose male circumcision, also a growing movement? How would you respond to those who point out that female circumcision was a custom in Victorian England (Silverman 2004)?

women also find that the irregular hours kept by those who run for office are incompatible with their role as mother. Fathers, in contrast, whose ordinary roles are more likely to take them away from home, are less likely to feel this conflict. Women are also not as likely to have a supportive spouse who is willing to play an unassuming background role while providing solace, encouragement, child care, and voter appeal. Finally, preferring to hold on to their positions of power, men have been reluctant to incorporate women into centers of decision making or to present them as viable candidates.

These conditions are changing. In 2002, a watershed event occurred when Nancy Pelosi was elected by her colleagues as the first woman minority leader—the most powerful woman ever in the House of Representatives. We can also note that more women are becoming corporate executives, and as indicated in Figure 10.2 (on page 267), more

women are also becoming lawyers. In these positions, women are doing more traveling and making statewide and national contacts. Another change is that child care is increasingly seen as a responsibility of both mother and father. This generation, then, is likely to mark a fundamental change in women's political participation, and it appears to be only a matter of time until a woman occupies the Oval Office.

Glimpsing the Future—with Hope

Women's fuller participation in the decision-making processes of our social institutions has shattered stereotypes that tended to limit females to "feminine" activities and push males into "masculine" ones. As structural barriers continue to fall and more activities are degendered, both males and females will be freer to pursue activities that are more compatible with their abilities and desires as individuals.

Table 10.2	**U.S. Women in Political Office**	
	Percentage of Offices Held by Women	Number of Offices Held by Women
National Office		
U.S. Senate	14%	14
U.S. House of Representatives	14%	59
State Office		
Governors	16%	8
Lt. Governors	36%	18
Attorneys general	14%	7
Secretaries of state	20%	10
Treasurers	16%	8
State auditors	14%	7
State legislators	23%	1,654

Sources: National Women's Political Caucus 2005; *Statistical Abstract* 2005:Tables 396, 401, 403.

As females and males develop a new consciousness of both their capacities and their potential, relationships will change. Distinctions between the sexes will not disappear, but there is no legitimate reason for biological differences to be translated into social inequalities. If current trends continue, we

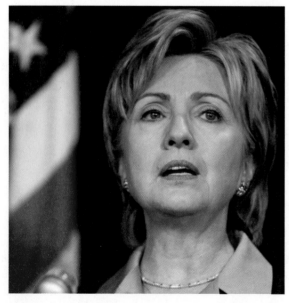

Hillary Clinton broke through the glass ceiling of politics when she was elected Senator from New York. She has her eye on the strongest glass ceiling of all, the presidency of the United States.

may see a growing appreciation of sexual differences coupled with greater equality of opportunity—which has the potential of transforming society (Gilman 1911/1971; Offen 1990). If this happens, as sociologist Alison Jaggar (1990) observed, gender equality will become less a goal than a background condition for living in society.

INEQUALITIES OF AGING

In 1928, Charles Hart, who was working on his Ph.D. in anthropology, did fieldwork with the Tiwi, who lived on an island off the northern coast of Australia. Because every Tiwi belonged to a clan, they assigned Hart to the bird (Jabijabui) clan and told him that a particular woman was his mother. Hart described the woman as "toothless, almost blind, withered." He added that she was "physically quite revolting and mentally rather senile." He then recounted this remarkable event:

[T]oward the end of my time on the islands an incident occurred that surprised me because it suggested that some of them had been taking my presence in the kinship system much more seriously than I had thought. I was approached by a group of about eight or nine senior men. They were the senior members of the Jabijabui clan and they had decided among themselves that the time had come to get rid of the decrepit old woman who had first called me son and whom I now called mother. . . . As I knew, they said, it was Tiwi custom, when an old woman became too feeble to look after herself, to "cover her up." This could only be done by her sons and her brothers and all of them had to agree beforehand, since once it was done they did not want any dissension among the brothers or clansmen, as that might lead to a feud. My "mother" was now completely blind, she was constantly falling over logs or into fires, and they, her senior clansmen, were in agreement that she would be better out of the way. Did I agree?

I already knew about "covering up." The Tiwi, like many other hunting and gathering peoples, sometimes got rid of their ancient and decrepit females. The method was to dig a hole in the ground in some lonely place, put the old woman in the hole and fill it in with earth until only her head was showing. Everybody went away for a day or two and then went back to the hole to discover, to their great surprise, that the old woman was dead, having been too feeble to raise her arms from the earth. Nobody had "killed" her; her death in Tiwi eyes was a natural one. She had been alive when her relatives last saw her. I had never seen it done, though I knew it was the custom, so I asked my brothers if it was necessary for me to attend the "covering up."

They said no and they would do it, but only after they had my agreement. Of course I agreed, and a week or two later we heard in our camp that my "mother" was dead, and we all wailed and put on the trimmings of mourning. (C. W. M. Hart in Hart and Pilling 1979:125–126)

Aging in Global Perspective

We won't deal with the question of whether it was ethical for Hart to agree that the old woman should be "covered up." What is of interest for our purpose is how the Tiwi treated their frail elderly—or, more specifically, their frail *female* elderly. You may have noticed that they "covered up" only their old women. As was noted earlier, throughout the world females are discriminated against. As this case makes evident, in some places, that discrimination extends even to death.

Every society must deal with the problem of people growing old, and of some becoming frail. Although few societies choose to bury old people alive, all societies must decide how to allocate limited resources among their citizens. With the percentage of the population that is old increasing in many nations, these decisions are generating tensions between the generations.

The Social Construction of Aging

The way the Tiwi treated frail elderly women reflects one extreme of how societies cope with aging. Another extreme, one that reflects an entirely different attitude, is illustrated by the Abkhasians, an agricultural people who live in a mountainous region of Georgia, a republic of the former Soviet Union. The Abkhasians pay their elderly high respect and look to them for guidance. They would no more dispense with their elderly by "covering them up" than we would "cover up" a sick child in our culture.

The Abkhasians may be the longest-lived people on earth. Many claim to live past 100—some beyond 120 and even 130 (Benet 1971). Although it is difficult to document the accuracy of these claims (Haslick 1974; Harris 1990), government records indicate that an extraordinary number of Abkhasians do live to a very old age.

Three main factors appear to account for their long lives. The first is their diet, which consists of little meat, much fresh fruit, vegetables, garlic, goat cheese, cornmeal, buttermilk, and wine. The second is their lifelong physical activity. They do slow down after age 80, but even after the age of 100, they still work about four hours a day. The third

factor—a highly developed sense of community—lies at the very heart of Abkhasian culture. From childhood, each individual is integrated into a primary group, and remains so throughout life. There is no such thing as a nursing home, nor do the elderly live alone. Because they continue to work and contribute to the group's welfare, the elderly aren't a burden to anyone. They don't vegetate, nor do they feel the need to "fill time" with bingo and shuffleboard. In short, the elderly feel no sudden rupture between what they "were" and what they "are."

The examples of the Tiwi and the Abkhasians reveal an important sociological principle—that, like gender, aging is *socially constructed*. That is, nothing in the nature of aging summons forth any particular viewpoint. Rather, attitudes toward the aged are rooted in society and therefore differ from one social group to another.

Central to a group's culture are ways of viewing reality. Living for centuries in isolation on Bathurst and Melville Islands off the northern coast of Australia, the Tiwi, featured in the vignette on "covering up," developed a unique culture. Shown here is Wurabuti, who has prepared himself to lead his uncle's funeral dance. To be certain that his uncle's ghost will not recognize him, Wurabuti is wearing a "shirt" painted with ocher and clay, a topknot of cockatoo feathers, and a beard of goose feathers.

When does old age begin? And what activities are appropriate for the elderly? From this photo that I took of Munimah, a 65-year-old bonded laborer in Chennai, India, you can see how culturally relative these questions are. No one in Chennai thinks it is extraordinary that this woman makes her living by carrying heavy rocks all day in the burning, tropical sun. Working next to her in the quarry is her 18-year-old son, who breaks the rocks into the size that his mother carries.

Industrialization and the Graying of the Globe

As was noted in previous chapters, industrialization is a worldwide trend. With industrialization comes more food, better public health practices (especially a purer water supply), and more effective ways of fighting the diseases that kill children. Consequently, when a country industrializes, more of its people live longer and reach older ages. The Social Map on the next page illustrates this principle.

You can see that the industrialized countries have the highest percentage of elderly. The range among nations is broad, from just 1 of 45 citizens in nonindustrialized Sudan to *nine* times higher than this, to almost 1 of 5 in postindustrial Italy (*Statistical Abstract* 2005:Table 1322).

In just two decades, *half* the population of Italy and Japan will be older than 50 (Kinsella and Phillips 2005). The graying of the globe is so new that *two-thirds of all people who have ever passed age 50 in the history of the world are alive today* (Zaslow 2003).

As a nation's elderly population increases, so, too, does the bill its younger citizens pay to provide for their needs. This expense has become a major social issue. Although Americans complain that Social Security taxes are too high, the U.S. rate of 15.3 percent is comparatively low. French workers are hit the hardest; they pay 39 percent of their wages into social security. Only a percentage or two less is paid by citizens in Poland, Austria, and Holland (*Statistical Abstract* 2005:Tables 517, 1347). People in the Least Industrialized Nations pay no social security taxes. There, families are expected to take care of their own elderly, with no help from the government.

With industrialization continuing without letup and with the proportion of the elderly population continuing to increase, future liabilities for care of the elderly have alarmed analysts. An outstanding case is Germany. By the year 2020, about 30 percent of Germans will be over the age of 60. To continue to furnish them the high level of care that they now receive, Germany's future workers would have to pay nearly *all* their income in taxes (Wessel 1995). Obviously, this is impossible, but no one has yet come up with a workable solution to the problem.

The Graying of America

As Figure 10.9 illustrates, the United States is part of this global trend. This figure shows how U.S. **life expectancy,** the number of years people can expect to live, has increased since 1900. To me, and perhaps to you, it is startling to realize that a hundred years ago, the average American could not even expect to see age 50. Since then, we've added about 30 years to our life expectancy, and Americans born today can expect to live into their 70s or 80s.

The term **graying of America** refers to this increasing proportion of older people in the U.S. population. Look at Figure 10.10 on page 280. In 1900, only 4 percent of Americans were age 65 and over. Today about 13 percent are. The average 65-year-old can expect to live another eighteen years (*Statistical Abstract* 2005:Table 94). U.S. society has become so "gray" that, as Figure 10.11 shows, the median age has almost *doubled* since 1850. Today, there are seven million *more* elderly Americans than there are teenagers (*Statistical Abstract* 2005:Table 11). Despite this change, on a global scale Americans rank below the top ten in life expectancy.

Figure 10.8 **The Graying of the Globe**

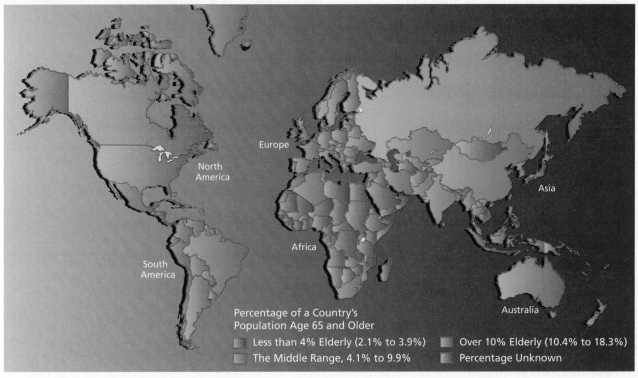

Percentage of a Country's
Population Age 65 and Older

- Less than 4% Elderly (2.1% to 3.9%)
- The Middle Range, 4.1% to 9.9%
- Over 10% Elderly (10.4% to 18.3%)
- Percentage Unknown

Source: By the author. Based on *Statistical Abstract* 2005:Table 1322.

Figure 10.9 **U.S. Life Expectancy by Year of Birth**

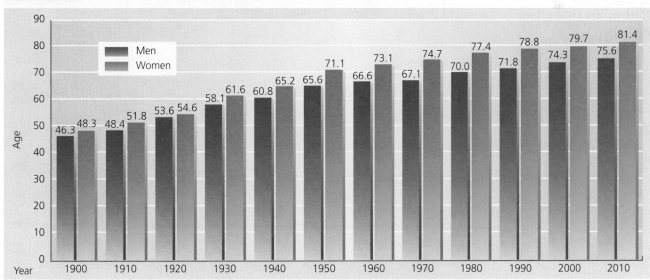

Sources: By the author. Based on *Historical Statistics of the United States, Colonial Times to 1970,* Bicentennial Edition, Part I, Series B, 107–115; *Statistical Abstract* 2005:Table 92.

Figure 10.10 The Graying of America: Americans Age 65 and Older

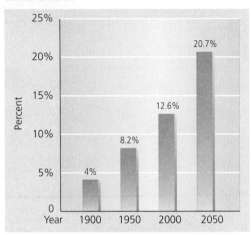

Source: By the author. Based on *Statistical Abstract* 2005: Table 12, and earlier years.

Figure 10.11 The Median Age of the U.S. Population

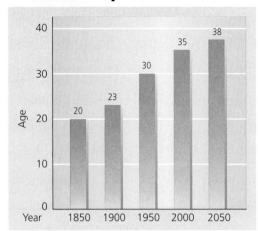

Source: By the author. Based on *Statistical Abstract* 2000: Table 14; 2005:Table 12, and earlier years.

As anyone who has ever visited Florida has noticed, the elderly population is not evenly distributed around the country. (As Jerry Seinfeld sardonically noted, "There's a law that when you get old you've got to move to Florida.") The Social Map below shows how uneven this distribution is.

Although more people are living to old age, the maximum length of life possible, the **life span,** has not increased.

Experts disagree, however, on what that maximum is. It is at least 122, for this was the well-documented age of Jeanne Louise Calment of France at her death in 1998. If the reports on the Abkhasians are correct (and this is a matter of controversy), the human life span may exceed even this number by a comfortable margin. It is also likely that advances in genetics will extend the human life span, a topic we will return

Figure 10.12 As Florida Goes, So Goes the Nation

Source: By the author. Based on *Statistical Abstract* 2005:Table 20.

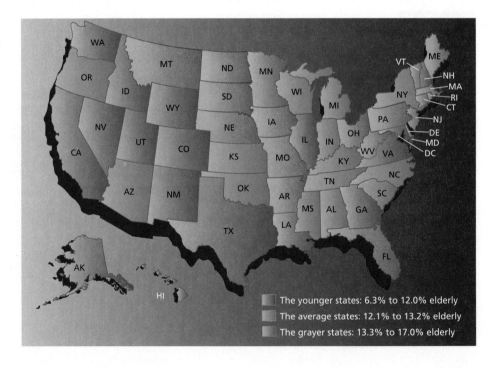

to later. For now, let's see the different pictures of aging that emerge when we apply the three theoretical perspectives.

The Symbolic Interactionist Perspective

To apply symbolic interactionism, let's consider ageism and how negative stereotypes of the elderly developed.

Ageism: The Concept

At first, the audience sat quietly as the developers explained their plans to build a high-rise apartment building. After a while, people began to shift uncomfortably in their seats. Then they began to show open hostility.

"That's too much money to spend on those people," said one.

"You even want them to have a swimming pool?" asked another incredulously.

Finally, one young woman put their attitudes in a nutshell when she asked, "Who wants all those old people around?"

When physician Robert Butler (1975, 1980) heard these responses to plans to build apartments for senior citizens, he began to realize how deeply antagonistic feelings against the elderly can run. He coined the term **ageism** to refer to prejudice, discrimination, and hostility directed against people because of their age. Let's see how ageism developed in U.S. society.

Shifting Meanings of Growing Old

As we have seen, there is nothing inherent in old age to summon forth any particular attitude, negative or not. Old age may even have been positively regarded in early U.S. society (Cottin 1979; Kart 1990; Clair et al. 1993). In Colonial times, growing old was seen as an accomplishment because so few people made it to old age. With no pensions, the elderly continued to work at jobs that changed little over time. They were viewed as storehouses of knowledge about work skills and sources of wisdom about how to live a long life.

The coming of industrialization, however, eroded these bases of respect. With better sanitation and medical care, more people reached old age. No longer was being elderly an honorable distinction. The new forms of mass production made young workers as productive as the elderly. Coupled with mass education, this stripped away the elderly's superior knowledge (Cowgill 1974; Hunt 2005).

A basic principle of symbolic interactionism is that people perceive both themselves and others according to the symbols of their culture. Thus, as the meaning of old age was transformed—when it changed from an asset to a liability—not only did younger people come to view the elderly differently but also the elderly began to perceive themselves in a new light. This shift in meaning is demonstrated in the way people lie about their age: They used to claim that they were older than they were, but now they say that they are younger than they are (Clair et al. 1993).

The meaning of old age is shifting once again. Today, most U.S. elderly can take care of themselves financially, and many are well-off. In addition, members of the baby boom generation have entered their 50s. With their vast numbers, better health, and financial strength, they also are destined to positively affect our images of the elderly. The next step in this symbolic shift, now in process, is to celebrate old age as a time of renewal—not simply as a period that precedes death, but, rather, a new stage of growth.

Influence of the Mass Media

In Chapter 3 (pages 70–72), we noted that the mass media help to shape our ideas about both gender and relationships between men and women. As a powerful source of symbols, the media also influence our ideas of the elderly, the topic of the Mass Media box on the next page.

PEANUTS® by Charles M. Schulz

Stereotypes, which play such a profound role in social life, are a basic area of sociological investigation. In contemporary society, the mass media are a major source of stereotypes.

mass Media in social life

Shaping Our Perceptions of the Elderly

The mass media profoundly influence our lives. What we hear and see on television and in the movies, the songs we listen to, the books and magazines we read—all become part of our world view. Without our knowing it, the media shape our images of people. They influence how we view minorities and dominant groups; men, women, and children; people with disabilities; people from other cultures—and the elderly.

The shaping is subtle, so much so that it usually occurs without our awareness. The elderly, for example, are underrepresented on television and in most popular magazines. The covert message is that the elderly are of little consequence and can be safely ignored. Consider how the media reflect and reinforce stereotypes of *gender age*. Older male news anchors are likely to

be retained, while female anchors who turn the same age are more likely to be transferred to less visible positions. Similarly, in movies older men are more likely to play romantic leads—and to play them opposite much younger rising stars.

Then there is advertising. The American Association of Retired Persons (AARP) points out that television ads often depict the elderly as being feeble or foolish (Goldman 1993). The AARP claims this happens because younger people dominate advertising firms, and their ads reflect their negative images of older people. They pick out the "worst traits of the group, making everyone believe that old is something you don't want to be."

The message is not lost. As we add years, we go to great lengths to deny that we are growing old. This plays into the hands of advertisers, who exploit our fears of losing our youth so that they can sell us their hair dyes, skin creams, Botox injections, and other products that supposedly

Age is more than biology. In some cultures, Demi Moore, 42, would be considered elderly. Moore is shown here with her husband, Ashton Kutcher, 27. Almost inevitably, when there is a large age gap between a husband and wife, it is the husband who is the older one. The marriage of Kutcher and Moore is a reversal of the typical pattern.

conceal even the appearance of old age. For the same reason, Americans visit plastic surgeons to remove telltale signs of aging.

The elderly's growing numbers and affluence translate into economic clout and political power. It is inevitable, then, that the media's images of the elderly will change. An indication of that change is shown in the photo on the next page.

The Functionalist Perspective

Functionalists analyze how the parts of society work together. Among the components of society are **age cohorts**—people who were born at roughly the same time and who pass through the life course together. Although not visible to us, age cohorts have major effects on our lives. For example, if the age cohort nearing retirement is large (a "baby boom" generation), many jobs open up at roughly the same time. In contrast, if it is small (a "baby bust" generation), fewer jobs open up. Let's look at three theories that focus on how people adjust to retirement.

Disengagement Theory

Elaine Cumming and William Henry (1961) analyzed how society prevents disruption when the elderly leave their po-

sitions of responsibility. In what is called **disengagement theory,** they explained how it would be disruptive if the elderly left their positions only when they died or became incompetent. To avoid this, pensions are offered to entice the elderly to hand over their positions to younger people. Retirement (or disengagement), then, is a mutually beneficial arrangement between two parts of society. It helps to smooth the transition between the generations.

Cumming (1976) also examined disengagement from the individual's perspective. She pointed out that people start to disengage during middle age, long before retirement, when they sense that the end of life is closer than its start. They do not immediately disengage, however, but begin to assign priority to goals and tasks, realizing that time is limited. Disengagement begins in earnest when children leave home, then increases with retirement and eventually widowhood.

Evaluation of the Theory.   Almost from the time it was formulated, disengagement theory came under attack (Hatch 2000). Anthropologist Dorothy Jerrome (1992) pointed out that it contains an implicit bias against older people—assumptions that the elderly disengage from productive social roles and then sort of slink into oblivion. Her own research shows that instead of disengaging, the elderly *exchange* one set of roles for another. The new roles, which often center on friendship, are no less satisfying than the earlier roles. They are less visible to researchers, however, who tend to have a youthful orientation—and who show their bias by assuming that productivity is the measure of self-worth.

The concept of retirement is changing as well. Computers, the Internet, and new types of work have blurred the dividing line between work and retirement. Less and less does retirement mean to abruptly stop working. Many workers just slow down. Some continue at their jobs, but put in fewer hours, or work occasionally as consultants. Others switch careers, even though they are in their 60s. Some move to a warmer climate, but take their work with them. Many never "retire"—at least not in the sense of sinking into a recliner or being forever on the golf course. If disengagement theory is ever resurrected, it must come to grips with this fundamental change.

Activity Theory

Are retired people more satisfied with life? Are intimate activities more satisfying than formal ones? Such questions are the focus of **activity theory,** which assumes that the more activities elderly people engage in, the more they find life satisfying. Although we could consider this theory from other perspectives, we are examining it from the functionalist perspective because its focus is how disengagement is functional or dysfunctional.

Evaluation of the Theory.   The results are mixed. In general, researchers have found that more active people are more satisfied. But not always. A study of retired people in France found that some people are happier when they are more active, others when they are less involved (Keith 1982). Similarly, most people find informal, intimate activities, such as spending time with friends, to be more satisfying than formal activities. But not everyone does. In one study, 2,000 retired U.S. men reported formal activities to be as important as informal ones. Even solitary activities, such as doing home repairs, had about the same impact as intimate activities on these men's life satisfaction (Beck and Page 1988). It is similarly the case with spending time with adult children. The amount of interaction with adult children that increases satisfaction with life differs for each person—when, in their words, they see their children "frequently enough" (Hatch 2000).

In short, just counting the amount of interaction or number of activities of elderly people is simplistic, and this theory, too, has been rejected. If it is ever resurrected, researchers must take into account what activities *mean* to people.

As the numbers of U.S. elderly grow, a new emphasis is being placed on their well-being. Researchers are exploring the elderly's mental and social development, as well as the causes of physical and emotional well-being. As research progresses, do you think we will reach the point where the average old person will be in this woman's physical condition?

Continuity Theory

Another theory of how people adjust to growing old is **continuity theory.** As its name implies, the focus of this theory is how people adjust to old age by continuing ties with their past (Kinsella and Phillips 2005). When they retire, many people take on new roles that are similar to the ones they gave up. For example, a former CEO might serve as a consultant, a retired electrician might do small electrical repairs, or a pensioned banker might volunteer to direct the finances of her church. Researchers have found that people who have multiple roles (wife, author, mother, intimate friend, church member, etc.) are better equipped to handle the changes that growing old entails. They have also found that with their greater resources to meet the challenges of old age, people from higher social classes adjust better to aging.

Evaluation of the Theory. The basic criticism of continuity theory is that it is too broad (Hatch 2000). We all have anchor points based on our experiences, and we all rely on them to make adjustments to the changes we encounter in life. This applies to people of all ages beyond infancy. This theory is really a collection of loosely connected ideas, with no specific application to the elderly.

IN SUM The *broader* perspective of the functionalists is how society's parts work together to keep society functioning smoothly. Although it is inevitable that younger workers replace the elderly, this transition could be disruptive. To entice the elderly out of their positions so that younger people can take over, the elderly are offered pensions. Functionalists also use a *narrower* perspective to focus on how the elderly adjust to their retirement. The findings of this narrower perspective are too mixed to be of much value—except that people with better resources (including multiple roles) adjust better to old age.

The theories discussed here were developed when retirement at age 65 was required by law. Today, people can keep their jobs if they want to. Choice, then, needs to be a factor in any theory—especially how people reconstruct their identities and come to terms with the new life they choose.

The Conflict Perspective

From the conflict perspective, the guiding principle of social life is the struggle of social groups for power and resources. How does this apply to

society's age groups? Regardless of whether the young and old recognize it, they are part of a basic struggle that threatens to throw society into turmoil. The passage of Social Security legislation is an example of this struggle.

Social Security Legislation

In the 1920s, before Social Security provided an income for the aged, two-thirds of all citizens over 65 had no savings and could not support themselves (Holtzman 1963; Crossen 2004a). The fate of workers worsened during the Great Depression, and in 1930, Francis Townsend, a physician, started a movement to rally older citizens. He soon had one-third of all Americans over age 65 enrolled in his Townsend clubs. They demanded that the federal government impose a national sales tax of 2 percent to provide $200 a month for every person over 65 (about $2,100 a month in today's money). In 1934, the Townsend Plan went before Congress. Because it called for such high payments and many were afraid that it would destroy people's incentive to save for the future, Congress looked for a way to reject the plan without appearing to oppose the elderly. When President Roosevelt announced his own, more modest Social Security plan in 1934, Congress embraced it (Schottland 1963; Amenta et al. 1999).

To provide jobs for younger people, this legislation required that workers retire at 65. It did not matter how well people did their work or how much they needed the pay. For decades, the elderly protested. Finally, in 1986, Congress eliminated mandatory retirement. Today, almost 90 percent of Americans retire by age 65, but most do so voluntarily. No longer can they be forced out of their jobs simply because of their age.

Conflict theorists point out that Social Security did not come about because the members of Congress had generous hearts. Rather, Social Security emerged from a struggle between competing interest groups. As conflict theorists stress, equilibrium is only a temporary balancing of social forces, one that can be upset at any time. Perhaps, more direct conflict may emerge. Let's consider this possibility.

Intergenerational Conflict

Will the future bring conflict between the elderly and the young? Although violence is not likely, if you listen closely, you can hear ripples of grumbling—complaints that the elderly are getting more than their fair share of society's resources. The huge costs of Social Security and Medicare have become a national concern. These two programs alone account for *one of every three* (35 percent) tax dollars (*Statistical Abstract* 2005:Table 465). As Figure 10.13

Figure 10.13 Social Security Payments to Beneficiaries

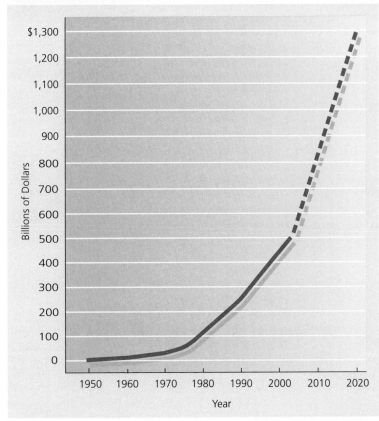

Source: By the author. Based on *Statistical Abstract* 1997:Table 518; 2005:Table 465. Broken line indicates the author's projections.

Figure 10.14 Fewer Workers Supporting a Larger Number of Retirees and Disabled Workers

Source: By the author. Based on Social Security Administration; *Statistical Abstract* 2005:Tables 523, 527.

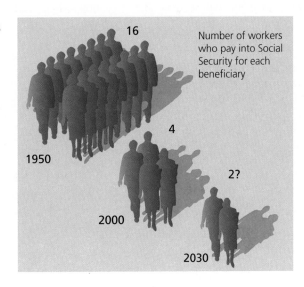

shows, Social Security payments were $781 million in 1950; now they run about *600 times* higher.

Some form of conflict seems inevitable. The graying of the United States leaves fewer workers to pay for the benefits received by the increasing millions who collect Social Security. Some see this shift in the **dependency ratio**—the number of people who collect Social Security compared with the number of workers who contribute to it—as especially troubling. As Figure 10.14 shows, sixteen workers used to support each person who was collecting Social Security. Now the dependency ratio has dropped to four to one. As this ratio continues to shrink, will younger workers be willing to pay the huge sums it will take to support the older generation? How will they be able to pay for the soaring costs of health care shown in Figure 10.15 on the next page?

As the government transferred resources to the elderly, their condition improved drastically. On Figure 10.16 on the next page, you can trace their declining rate of poverty. As you do so, look also at how the poverty rate of U.S. children increased from 1967 until the early 1990s. Some analysts suggested that the decline in the elderlys' rate of poverty might have come at the expense of the nation's children. But did it? Conflict sociologists Meredith

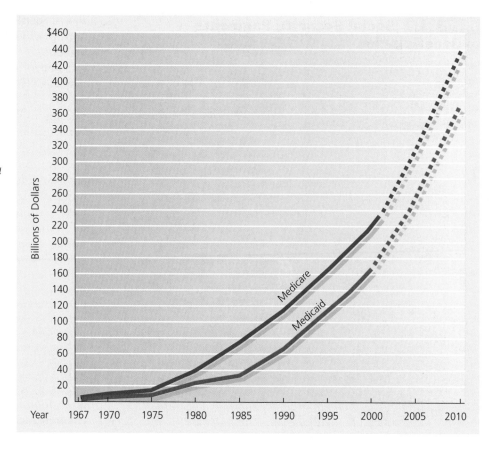

Figure 10.15 **Health Care Costs for the Elderly and Disabled**

Medicare is intended for the elderly and disabled, Medicaid for the poor. About 29 percent of Medicaid payments ($41 billion) goes to the elderly. (*Statistical Abstract* 2005:Table 133).

Source: By the author. Based on *Statistical Abstract,* various years, and 2005:Tables 130, 139. *Note:* Broken lines indicate the author's projections.

Minkler and Ann Robertson (1991) point out that such a comparison is misleading. The money that went to the elderly did *not* come from the children. Would anyone say that the money the government gives to flood victims comes from the children? Of course not. Politicians make choices about where to spend taxes, and they can very well decide to increase spending to relieve the poverty of *both* the elderly and children.

This is no longer such an issue for, as Figure 10.16 shows, the poverty rate of children has fallen in recent years.

Figure 10.16 **Trends in Poverty**

Sources: By the author. *Statistical Abstract,* various years, and 2005:Table 686. *Note:* Broken lines indicate the author's projections.

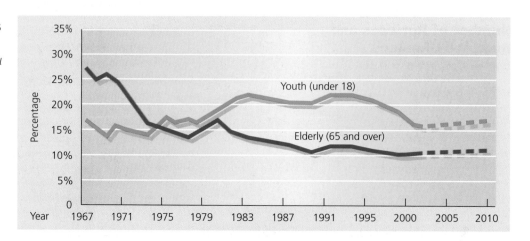

But as conflict theorists point out, framing the issue as a case of money going to one group at the expense of another group can divide the working class. To get working-class people to think that they must choose between pathetic children and suffering old folks can splinter them into opposing groups, breaking their power to work together to improve society.

Looking Toward the Future

Throughout this text, we have examined some of the deep impacts that technology is having on our lives. To close this chapter, I would like you to reflect on how technological breakthroughs might affect your own life as you grow older.

Thinking Critically

How Long Do You Want to Live? Approaching Methuselah

Would you like to live to 200? To 500? To 1,000?

Such a question may strike you as absurd. But with our new and still developing technology, science may stretch the life span to limits unheard of since biblical days.

We are just at the beginning stages of genetic engineering, and ahead of us may lie a brave new world. Predictions are that technicians will be able to snip out our bad DNA and replace it with more compliant bits. The caps at the ends of our chromosomes, the telomeres, shrink as we age, causing the cells to die. An enzyme called telomerase may be able to modify this process, allowing cells to reproduce many more times than they currently are able to (Demidov 2005).

By manipulating genes, scientists have already been able to extend the life span of worms by six times. Humans have these same genes. A human life span six times longer than what we now have would take the longest living people to over 500 (Chase 2003). We are only peering over the edge of the future, glimpsing what might be possible. Some optimistic geneticists predict that some people currently alive will live 1,000 years or longer (Gorman 2003).

Some geneticists say that we should think of our body as being like a house (Gorman 2003). A house keeps standing, not because it is built to last forever, but because people keep repairing it. This is what science will allow us to do with our bodies. In the future, we will grow spare body parts.

From the same stem cells will come livers, hearts, kidneys, fingers. As parts of our body wear out, we'll simply replace them with new ones.

In grade school, many of us heard stories about Ponce de Leon, an explorer from Spain who searched for the fountain of youth. He eventually "discovered" Florida, but the fountain of youth eluded him. In our perpetual search for immortality, could we be discovering what eluded Ponce de Leon?

for your Consideration

Let's assume that biomedical science does stretch the human life span, that living to be 150 or 200 becomes common. If people retire at age 65, how could society afford to support them for 100 years or so? People can't work much past 70, for—and this may be the basic flaw in this brave new world scenario—even with new body parts, the world would not be filled with 200-year-olds who functioned as though they were 25. They would be very old people, subject to the diseases and debilities that come with advanced age. If Medicare costs are bulging at the seams now, what would they be like in such a world?

Finally, how would you answer this question: Is the real issue how we can live longer, or how we can live better?

Because of medical advances, public health and better nutrition, millions of the elderly enjoy good health. Rather than being considered a sequel to ill health and death, older age is being redefined as a period of opportunity to pursue interests and develop talents that provide new perspectives and a continued sense of satisfaction with life.

Summary *and* Review

ISSUES OF SEX AND GENDER

What is gender stratification?

The term **gender stratification** refers to unequal access to property, power, and prestige on the basis of sex. Each society establishes a structure that, on the basis of sex and gender, opens and closes doors to its privileges. P. 256.

How do sex and gender differ?

Sex refers to biological distinctions between males and females. It consists of both primary and secondary sex characteristics. **Gender,** in contrast, is what a society considers proper behaviors and attitudes for its male and female members. Sex physically distinguishes males from females; gender defines what is "masculine" and "feminine." P. 256.

Why do the behaviors of males and females differ?

The "nature versus nurture" debate refers to whether differences in the behaviors of males and females are caused by inherited (biological) or learned (cultural) characteristics. Almost all sociologists take the side of nurture. In recent years, however, sociologists have begun to cautiously open the door to biology. Pp. 256–261.

How Females Became a Minority Group

How did females become a minority group?

Patriarchy, or male dominance, appears to be universal. The origin of discrimination against females is lost in history, but the primary theory of how females became a minority group in their own societies focuses on the physical limitations imposed by childbirth. Pp. 261–263.

Gender Inequality in the United States

Is the feminist movement new?

In what is called the "first wave," feminists made demands for social change in the early 1900s—and were met with hostility and even violence. The "second wave" began in the 1960s and continues today. A "third wave" is emerging. P. 264.

What forms does gender inequality in education take?

Although more women than men attend college, each tends to select "feminine" or "masculine" fields. Women are underrepresented in most doctoral programs in science, and they are less likely to complete these programs. Fundamental change is indicated by the growing numbers of women in law and medicine. Pp. 264–267.

How are women discriminated against in health care?

Women are referred for heart surgery later than men, resulting in higher rates of surgical death. Exploiting women's fears, surgeons also perform unnecessary hysterectomies. Pp. 267–268.

How does gender inequality show up in the workplace?

Over the last century, women have made up an increasing proportion of the work force. Nonetheless, all occupations show a gender gap in pay. For college graduates, the lifetime pay gap runs about $600,000 in favor of men. **Sexual harassment** also continues to be part of the workplace. Pp. 268–272.

What is the relationship between gender and violence?

Overwhelmingly, the victims of rape and murder are females. Female circumcision and "honor killings" are special cases of violence against females. Conflict theorists point out that men use violence to maintain their power and privilege. Pp. 272–274.

The Changing Face of Politics

What is the trend in gender inequality in politics?

A traditional division of gender roles—women as child care providers and homemakers, men as workers outside the home—used to keep women out of politics. Women continue to be underrepresented in politics, but the trend toward greater political equality is firmly in place. Pp. 274–276.

INEQUALITIES OF AGING

How are the elderly treated around the world?

No single set of attitudes, beliefs, or policies regarding the aged characterizes the world's nations. Rather, they vary from exclusion and killing to integration and honor. The global trend is for more people to live longer. P. 277.

How does industrialization affect aging?

Because industrialization brings a higher standard of living, people live longer. One result is the graying of the globe. Pp. 278–280.

The Symbolic Interactionist Perspective

What does the social construction of aging mean?

Nothing in the nature of aging summons forth any particular set of attitudes. Rather, attitudes toward the elderly are rooted in culture and differ from one social group to another. **Ageism,** negative reactions to the elderly, is based on stereotypes. Pp. 277, 281–282.

The Functionalist Perspective

How is retirement functional for society?

Functionalists focus on how the withdrawal of the elderly from positions of responsibility benefits society. **Disengagement theory** examines retirement as a device for ensuring that a society's positions of responsibility will be passed smoothly from one generation to the next.

Activity theory examines how people adjust when they disengage from productive roles. **Continuity theory** focuses on how people adjust to growing old by continuing their roles and using coping techniques. Pp. 282–284.

The Conflict Perspective

Is there conflict among different age groups?

Social Security legislation is an example of one generation making demands on another generation for limited resources. As the number of retired people grows, there are relatively fewer workers to support them. The argument that benefits to the elderly come at the cost of benefits to children is fallacious. Pp. 284–287.

Looking Toward the Future

What technological developments can be a wild card in social planning for the aged?

Technological breakthroughs may stretch the human **life span.** If so, it is difficult to see how younger workers would be able to support retired people for 100 years or so. P. 287.

Thinking Critically
about Chapter 10

1. What is your position on the "nature versus nurture" (biology or culture) debate? What materials in this chapter support your position?
2. What do you think can be done to reduce gender inequality?
3. If you were appointed to head the U.S. Department of Health and Human Services, how would you improve our nursing homes?

Additional Resources

Companion Website www.ablongman.com/henslin

- Content Select Research Database for Sociology, with suggested key terms and annotated references
- Link to 2000 Census, with activities
- Flashcards of key terms and concepts
- Practice Tests
- Weblinks
- Interactive Maps

Where Can I Read More on This Topic?

Suggested readings for this chapter are listed at the back of this book.

Politics and the Economy

Fred Otnes, *We The People* 1978

POLITICS: ESTABLISHING LEADERSHIP

Power, Authority, and Violence
Authority and Legitimate Violence
Traditional Authority
Rational-Legal Authority
Charismatic Authority
The Transfer of Authority

Types of Government
Monarchies
Democracies
Dictatorships and Oligarchies

The U.S. Political System
Political Parties and Elections
Voting Patterns
Lobbyists and Special-Interest Groups

Who Rules the United States?
The Functionalist Perspective
The Conflict Perspective
Which View Is Right?

War and Terrorism: Ways of Implementing Political Objectives
War
Terrorism

THE ECONOMY: WORK IN THE GLOBAL VILLAGE

The Transformation of Economic Systems
Preindustrial Societies
Industrial Societies
Postindustrial Societies
Biotech Societies
Implications for Your Life
Ominous Trends in the United States

World Economic Systems
Capitalism
Socialism
Ideologies of Capitalism
   and Socialism
Criticisms of Capitalism
   and Socialism
The Convergence of Capitalism
   and Socialism

Capitalism in a Global Economy
Corporate Capitalism
Multinational Corporations
A New World Order?

Summary and Review

In 1949, George Orwell wrote *1984,* a book about a time in the future in which the government, known as "Big Brother," dominates society, dictating almost every aspect of each individual's life. Even loving someone is considered sinister—a betrayal of the supreme love and total allegiance that all citizens owe Big Brother.

Despite the danger, Winston and Julia fall in love. They meet furtively, always with the threat of discovery hanging over their heads. When informers turn them in, interrogators separate Julia and Winston and proceed swiftly to quash their affection and restore their loyalty to Big Brother.

Then follows a remarkable account of Winston and his tormentor, O'Brien. Winston is strapped into a chair so tightly that he can't even move his head. O'Brien explains that although inflicting pain is not always enough to break a person's will, everyone has a breaking point. There is some worst fear that will push anyone over the edge.

O'Brien tells Winston that he has discovered his worst fear. Then he sets a cage with two giant, starving sewer rats on the table next to Winston. O'Brien picks up a hood connected to the door of the cage and places it over Winston's head. He then explains that when he presses the lever, the door of the cage will slide up, and the rats will shoot out like bullets and bore straight into Winston's face. Winston's eyes, the only part of his body that he can move, dart back and forth, revealing his terror. Speaking so quietly that Winston has to strain to

> ### Even loving someone is considered sinister— a betrayal of the supreme love and total allegiance that all citizens owe Big Brother.

hear him, O'Brien adds that the rats sometimes attack the eyes first, but sometimes they burrow through the cheeks and devour the tongue. When O'Brien places his hand on the lever, Winston realizes that the only way out is for someone else to take his place. But who? Then he hears his own voice screaming, "Do it to Julia! . . . Tear her face off. Strip her to the bones. Not me! Julia! Not me!"

Orwell does not describe Julia's interrogation, but when Julia and Winston see each other later, they realize that each has betrayed the other. Their love is gone. Big Brother has won.

Winston's and Julia's misplaced loyalty had made them political heretics, for every citizen had the duty to place the state above all else in life. To preserve the state's dominance over the individual, their allegiance to one another had to be stripped from them. As you see, it was.

Although seldom this dramatic, politics is always about power and authority.

POLITICS: ESTABLISHING LEADERSHIP

To exist, every society must have a system of leadership. Some people must have power over others. Let's explore this topic that is so significant for our lives.

Power, Authority, and Violence

As Max Weber (1913/1947) pointed out, we perceive power as either legitimate or illegitimate. *Legitimate* power is called **authority.** This is power that people accept as right. In contrast, *illegitimate* power—called **coercion**—is power that people do not accept as just.

> Imagine that you are on your way to buy a digital TV that is on sale for $250. As you approach the store, a man jumps out of an alley and shoves a gun in your face. He demands your money. Frightened for your life, you hand over your $250. After filing a police report, you head back to college to take a sociology exam. You are running late, so you step on the gas. As the speedometer needle hits 85, you see flashing blue and red lights in your rear-view mirror. Your explanation about the robbery doesn't faze the officer—or the judge who hears your case a few weeks later. She first lectures you on safety and then orders you to pay $50 in court costs plus $10 for every mile an hour over 65. You pay the $250.

The mugger, the police officer, and the judge—each has power, and in each case you part with $250. What, then, is the difference? The difference is that the mugger has no authority. His power is *illegitimate*—he has no *right* to do what he did. In contrast, you acknowledge that the officer has the right to stop you and that the judge has the right to fine you. They have authority, or *legitimate* power.

Authority and Legitimate Violence

As sociologist Peter Berger observed, it makes little difference whether you willingly pay the fine that the judge levies against you or refuse to pay it. The court will get its money one way or another.

> There may be innumerable steps before its application [of violence], in the way of warnings and reprimands. But if all the warnings are disregarded, even in so slight a matter as paying a traffic ticket, the last thing that will happen is that a couple of cops show up at the door with handcuffs and a Black Maria [billy club]. Even the moderately courteous cop who hands out the initial traffic ticket is likely to wear a gun—just in case. (Berger 1963)

The *government,* then, also called the **state,** claims a monopoly on legitimate force or violence. This point, made by Max Weber (1946, 1922/1968)—that the state claims both the exclusive right to use violence and the right to punish everyone else who uses violence—is crucial to our understanding of politics. If someone owes you a debt, you cannot take the money by force, much less imprison that person. The state, however, can. The ultimate proof of the state's authority is that you cannot kill someone because he or she has done something that you consider absolutely horrible—but the state can. As Berger (1963) summarized this matter, *"Violence is the ultimate foundation of any political order."*

Why do people accept power as legitimate? Max Weber (1922/1968) identified three sources of authority: traditional, rational-legal, and charismatic. Let's examine each.

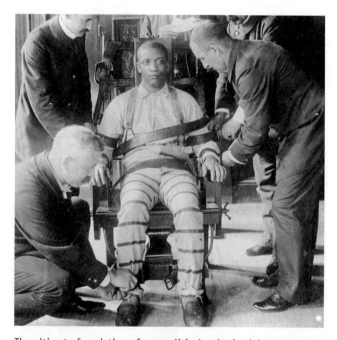

The ultimate foundation of any political order is violence. At no time is this more starkly demonstrated than when a government takes a human life. Shown in this 1910 photo from New York's Sing Sing Prison is a man who is about to be executed.

Traditional Authority

Throughout history, the most common basis for authority has been tradition. **Traditional authority,** which is based on custom, is the hallmark of tribal groups. In these societies, custom dictates basic relationships. For example, birth into a particular family makes an individual the chief, king, or queen. As far as members of that society are concerned, this is the right way to determine who shall rule, because "we've always done it this way."

Traditional authority declines with industrialization, but it never dies out. Although we live in a postindustrial society, parents continue to exercise authority over their children *because* parents always have had such authority. From generations past, we inherit the idea that parents have the right to discipline their children, choose their children's doctors and schools, and teach their children religion and morality.

Rational-Legal Authority

The second type of authority, **rational-legal authority,** is based not on custom but on written rules. *Rational* means reasonable, and *legal* means part of law. Thus, *rational-legal* refers to matters that have been agreed to by reasonable people and written into law (or regulations of some sort). The matters that are agreed to may be as broad as a constitution that specifies the rights of all members of a society or as narrow as a contract between two individuals. Because bureaucracies are based on written rules, rational-legal authority is sometimes called *bureaucratic authority.*

Rational-legal authority comes from the *position* that someone holds, not from the person who holds that position. In a democracy, for example, the president's authority comes from the legal power assigned to that office, as specified in a written constitution—not from custom or the individual's personal characteristics. In rational-legal authority, everyone—no matter how high the office—is subject to the organization's written rules. In governments based on traditional authority, the ruler's word may be law, but in those based on rational-legal authority, the ruler's word is subject to the law.

Charismatic Authority

A few centuries back, in 1429, the English controlled large parts of France. When they prevented the coronation of a new French king, a farmer's daughter heard a voice telling her that God had a special assignment for her—that she should put on men's clothing, recruit an army, and go to war against the English. Inspired, Joan of Arc raised an army, conquered cities, and defeated the English. Later that year, her visions were fulfilled as she stood next to Charles VII while he was crowned king of France. (Bridgwater 1953)

Joan of Arc is an example of **charismatic authority,** the third type of authority Weber identified. (*Charisma* is a Greek word that means a gift freely and graciously given [Arndt and Gingrich 1957].) People are drawn to a charismatic individual because they believe that individual has been touched by God or has been endowed by nature with exceptional qualities (Lipset 1993). The armies did not follow Joan of Arc because it was the custom to do so, as in traditional authority. Nor did they risk their lives alongside her because she held a position defined by written rules, as in rational-legal authority. Instead, people followed her because they were attracted by her outstanding

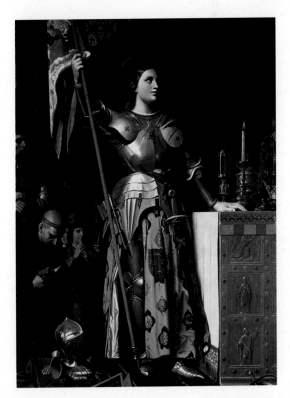

One of the best examples of *charismatic authority* is Joan of Arc, shown here at the coronation of Charles VII, whom she was instrumental in making king. Uncomfortable at portraying Joan of Arc wearing only a man's coat of armor, the artist has made certain she is wearing plenty of makeup, and also has added a ludicrous skirt.

Charismatic authorities can be of any morality, from the saintly to the most bitterly evil. Like Joan of Arc, Adolf Hitler attracted throngs of people, providing the stuff of dreams and arousing them from disillusionment to hope. This poster from the 1930s, titled *Es Lebe Deutschland* ("Long Live Germany"), illustrates the qualities of leadership that Germans of that period saw in Hitler.

traits. They saw her as a messenger of God, fighting on the side of justice, and they accepted her leadership because of these appealing qualities.

The Threat Posed by Charismatic Leaders. Kings and queens owe allegiance to tradition, and presidents to written laws. To what, however, do charismatic leaders owe allegiance? Their authority resides in their ability to attract followers, which is often based on their sense of a special mission or calling. Not tied to tradition or the regulation of law, charismatic leaders pose a threat to the established political order. Following their personal inclination, charismatic leaders can inspire followers to disregard—or even to overthrow—traditional and rational-legal authorities.

This threat does not go unnoticed, and traditional and rational-legal authorities often oppose charismatic leaders. If they are not careful, however, their opposition may arouse even more sentiment in favor of the charismatic leader, with him or her being viewed as an underdog per-

secuted by the powerful. Occasionally the Roman Catholic Church faces such a threat, as when a priest claims miraculous powers that appear to be accompanied by amazing healings. As people flock to this individual, they bypass parish priests and the formal ecclesiastical structure. This transfer of allegiance from the organization to an individual threatens the church hierarchy. Consequently, church officials may encourage the priest to withdraw from the public eye, perhaps to a monastery, to rethink matters. Thus the threat is defused, rational-legal authority is reasserted, and the stability of the organization is maintained.

The Transfer of Authority

The orderly transfer of authority from one leader to another is crucial for social stability. Under traditional authority, people know who is next in line. Under rational-legal authority, people might not know who the next leader will be, but they do know how that person will be selected. In both traditional and rational-legal systems of authority, the rules of succession are firm.

Charismatic authority has no such rules of succession, however. This makes it less stable than either traditional or rational-legal authority. Because charismatic authority is built around a single individual, the death or incapacitation of a charismatic leader can mean a bitter struggle for succession. To avoid this, some charismatic leaders make arrangements for an orderly transition of power by appointing a successor. This does not guarantee orderly succession, of course, for the followers may not perceive the designated heir in the same way as they did the charismatic leader, reducing or eliminating their commitment to the appointed successor. A second strategy is for the charismatic leader to build an organization. As the organization develops a system of rules or regulations, it transforms itself into a rational-legal organization. Weber used the term the **routinization of charisma** to refer to the transition of authority from a charismatic leader to either traditional or rational-legal authority.

Types of Government

How do the various types of government—monarchies, democracies, dictatorships, and oligarchies—differ? As we compare them, let's also look at how the institution of the state arose, and why the concept of citizenship was revolutionary.

Monarchies: The Rise of the State

Early societies were small and needed no extensive political system. They operated more like an extended family. As surpluses developed and societies grew larger, cities evolved—perhaps around 3500 B.C. (Fischer 1976). **City-states** then came into being, with power radiating outward from a city like a spider's web. Although the city controlled the immediate area around it, the areas between cities remained in dispute. Each city-state had its own **monarchy,** a king or queen whose right to rule was passed on to their children.

City-states often quarreled, and wars were common. The victors extended their rule, and eventually, a single city-state was able to wield power over an entire region. As the size of these regions grew, the people slowly began to identify with the larger region. That is, they began to see distant inhabitants as "we" instead of "they." What we call the **state**—the political entity that claims a monopoly on the use of violence within a territory—came into being.

Democracies: Citizenship as a Revolutionary Idea

The United States had no city-states. Each colony, however, was small and independent like a city-state. After the American Revolution, the colonies united. With the greater strength and resources that came from political unity, they conquered almost all of North America, bringing it under the power of a central government.

The government formed in this new country was called a **democracy.** (Derived from two Greek words—*demos* [common people] and *kratos* [power]—*democracy* literally means "power to the people.") Because of the bitter antagonisms associated with the revolution against the British king, the founders of the new country were distrustful of monarchies. They wanted to put political decisions into the hands of the people.

This was not the first democracy the world had seen, but such a system had been tried before only with smaller groups. Athens, a city-state of Greece, practiced democracy two thousand years ago, with each free male above a certain age having the right to be heard and to vote. Members of some Native American tribes, such as the Iroquois, also elected their chiefs, and in some, women were able to vote and to hold the office of chief. (The Incas and Aztecs of Mexico and Central America had monarchies.)

Because of their small size, tribes and cities were able to practice **direct democracy.** That is, they were small enough for the eligible voters to meet together, express their opinions, and then vote publicly—much like a town hall meeting today. As populous and spread out as the United States was, however, direct democracy was impossible, and the founders invented **representative democracy.** Certain citizens (at first only white male landowners) voted for men to represent them in Washington. Later, the vote was extended to men who didn't own property, to African American men, then to women, and to others. Our new communications technologies, which make "electronic town meetings" possible, could even allow a new form of direct democracy to develop.

Today we take the concept of citizenship for granted. What is not evident to us is that this idea had to be envisioned in the first place. There is nothing natural about citizenship; it is simply one way in which people choose to define themselves. Throughout most of human history, people were thought to *belong* to a clan, to a tribe, or even to a ruler. The idea of **citizenship**—that by virtue of birth and residence people have basic rights—is quite new to the human scene (Eisenstadt 1999).

The concept of representative democracy based on citizenship—perhaps the greatest gift the United States has given to the world—was revolutionary. Power was to be vested in the people themselves, and government was to flow from the people. That this concept was revolutionary is generally forgotten, but its implementation meant *the reversal of traditional ideas. It made the government responsive to the people's will, not the people responsive to the government's will.* To keep the government responsive to the needs of its citizens, people were expected to express dissent. In a widely quoted statement, Thomas Jefferson observed that

> A little rebellion now and then is a good thing. . . . It is a medicine necessary for the sound health of government . . . . God forbid that we should ever be twenty years without such a rebellion. . . . The tree of liberty must be refreshed from time to time with the blood of patriots and tyrants. (In Hellinger and Judd 1991)

The idea of **universal citizenship**—of *everyone* having the same basic rights by virtue of being born in a country (or by immigrating and becoming a naturalized citizen)—flowered slowly, and came into practice only through fierce struggle. When the United States was founded, for example, this idea was still in its infancy. Today it seems inconceivable to Americans that gender or race-ethnicity should be the basis to deny anyone the right to vote, hold office, make a contract, testify in court, or own property. For earlier generations of property-owning white

American men, however, it seemed just as inconceivable that women, racial–ethnic minorities, and the poor should be *allowed* such rights.

Dictatorships and Oligarchies: The Seizure of Power

If an individual seizes power and then dictates his will onto the people, the government is known as a **dictatorship.** If a small group seizes power, the government is called an **oligarchy.** The occasional coups in Central and South America, in which military leaders seize control of a country, are examples of oligarchies. Although one individual may be named president, often it is military officers, working behind the scenes, who make the decisions. If their designated president becomes uncooperative, they remove him from office and appoint another.

Monarchies, dictatorships, and oligarchies vary in the amount of control they wield over their citizens. **Totalitarianism** is almost *total* control of a people by the government. In Nazi Germany, Hitler organized a ruthless secret police force, the Gestapo, which searched for any sign of dissent. Spies even watched how moviegoers reacted to newsreels, reporting those who did not respond "appropriately" (Hipler 1987). Saddam Hussein acted just as ruthlessly toward Iraqis. The lucky ones who opposed Hussein were shot; the unlucky ones had their eyes gouged out, were bled to death, or were buried alive (Amnesty International 2005). To even tell a joke about Hussein could result in death at the hands of his security forces.

People around the world find great appeal in the freedom that is inherent in citizenship and representative democracy. Those who have no say in their government's decisions, or who face prison or even death for expressing dissent, find in these ideas the hope for a brighter future. With today's electronic communications, people no longer remain ignorant of whether they are more or less politically privileged than others. This knowledge produces pressure for greater citizen participation in government. As electronic communications develop further, this pressure will increase.

The U.S. Political System

With this global background, let's examine the U.S. political system. We shall consider the two major political parties, voting patterns, and the role of lobbyists and PACs.

Political Parties and Elections

After the founding of the United States, numerous political parties emerged, but by the time of the Civil War, two parties dominated U.S. politics (Burnham 1983): the Democrats, who in the public mind are associated with the working class, and the Republicans, who are associated with wealthier people. Each party nominates candidates, and in pre-elections, called *primaries,* the voters decide which candidates will represent their party. Each candidate then campaigns, trying to appeal to the most voters. The Social Map on the next page shows how Americans align themselves with political parties.

Although the Democrats and Republicans represent somewhat different philosophical principles, each party appeals to a broad membership, and it is difficult to distinguish a conservative Democrat from a liberal Republican. The extremes are easy to discern, however. Deeply committed Democrats support legislation that transfers income from those who are richer to those who are poorer, or that controls wages, working conditions, and competition. Deeply committed Republicans, in contrast, oppose such legislation.

Those who are elected to Congress may cross party lines. That is, some Democrats vote for legislation proposed by Republicans, and vice versa. This happens because officeholders support their party's philosophy, but not necessarily its specific proposals. When it comes to a particular bill, such as raising the minimum wage, some conservative Democrats may view the measure as unfair to small employers and vote against the bill along with the Republicans. At the same time, liberal Republicans—feeling that the proposal is just, or sensing a dominant sentiment in voters back home—may side with the bill's Democratic backers.

Regardless of their differences and their public quarrels, the Democrats and Republicans represent *different slices of the center.* Although each party may ridicule the opposing party and promote different legislation, they both firmly support such fundamentals of U.S. political philosophy as free public education; a strong military; freedom of religion, speech, and assembly; and, of course, capitalism—especially the private ownership of property.

Third parties also play a role in U.S. politics, but to gain power, they must also support these centrist themes. Any party that advocates radical change is doomed to a short life. Because most Americans consider a vote for a third party a waste, third parties do notoriously poorly at the polls. Two exceptions are the Bull Moose party, whose candidate, Theodore Roosevelt, won more votes in 1912 than

Figure 11.1 Which Political Party Dominates?

Note: Domination by a political party does *not* refer to votes for President or Congress. This social map is based on the composition of the states' upper and lower houses. When different parties dominate a state's houses, the total number of legislators was used. In case of ties (or, as with Nebraska, which has no party designation), the percentage vote for President was used.

Source: By the author. Based on *Statistical Abstract* 2005:Tables 387, 401.

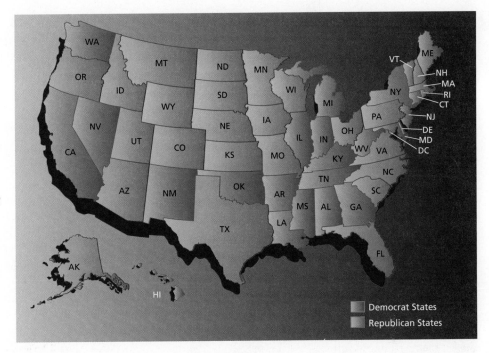

Democrat States
Republican States

Robert Taft, the Republican presidential candidate, and the United We Stand (Reform) party, founded by billionaire Ross Perot, which won 19 percent of the vote in 1992. Amidst internal bickering, the Reform Party declined rapidly, dropping to 8 percent of the presidential vote in 1996, less than 1 percent in 2000, and then off the political map (Bridgwater 1953; *Statistical Abstract* 1995:Table 437; 2005:Table 385).

Voting Patterns

Year after year, Americans show consistent voting patterns. From Table 11.1 (on the next page), you can see that the percentage of people who vote increases with age. This table also shows how significant race-ethnicity is. Non-Hispanic whites are more likely to vote than are African Americans, while Latinos are the least likely to vote. The significance of race-ethnicity is so great that Latinos are only half as likely to vote as are African Americans and non-Hispanic whites.

From Table 11.1 you can also see how voting increases with education—that college graduates are twice as likely to vote as are those who don't complete high school. From this table, you can also see how significant employment and income are. People who make more than $50,000 a year are twice as likely to vote as are those who make less than $10,000. Finally, note that women are slightly more likely than men to vote.

Social Integration. How can we explain the voting patterns shown in Table 11.1? Look at the extremes. Those who are most likely to vote are whites who are older, more educated, affluent, and employed. Those who are least likely to vote are Latinos who are younger, less educated, poor, and unemployed. From these extremes, we can draw this principle: *The more that people feel they have a stake in the political system, the more likely they are to vote.* They have more to protect, and they feel that voting can make a difference. In effect, people who have been rewarded more by the political and economic system feel more socially integrated. They vote because they perceive that elections make a difference in their lives, including the type of society in which they and their children live.

Alienation and Apathy. In contrast, those who gain less from the system—in terms of education, income, and jobs—are more likely to feel alienated from politics. Viewing themselves as outsiders, many feel hostile toward the government. Some feel betrayed, believing that politicians have sold out to special-interest groups. They are convinced that all politicians are liars. Minorities who feel that the U.S. political system is a "white" system are less likely to vote.

From Table 11.1 on page 298, we see that many highly educated people with good incomes also stay away from the

Table 11.1 Who Votes for President?

	1980	1984	1988	1992	1996	2000	2004
Overall							
Americans Who Vote	59%	60%	57%	61%	54%	55%	58%
Age							
18–20	36	37	33	39	31	28	42[d]
21–24	43	44	46	46	33	35	42[d]
25–34	55	58	48	53	43	44	47
35–44	64	64	61	64	55	55	57
45–64	69	70	68	70	64	64	67
65 and older	65	68	69	70	67	68	71
Sex							
Male	59	59	56	60	53	53	62
Female	59	61	58	62	56	56	65
Race/Ethnicity[a]							
Whites	61	61	59	64	56	56	66
African Americans	51	56	52	54	51	54	56
Latinos	30	33	29	29	27	28	28
Education							
Grade school only	43	43	37	35	28	27	24
High school dropout	46	44	41	41	34	34	35
High school graduate	59	59	55	58	49	49	52
College dropout	67	68	65	69	61	60	66
College graduate	80	79	78	81	73	72	73
Advanced degree	NA	NA	NA	NA	NA	77	—
Marital Status							
Married	NA	NA	NA	NA	NA	50	NA
Divorced	NA	NA	NA	NA	NA	38	NA
Labor Force							
Employed	62	62	58	64	55	56	66
Unemployed	41	44	39	46	37	35	51
Income[c]							
Under $5,000	38	39	35	NA	NA	21[b]	NA
$5,000 to $9,999	46	49	41	NA	NA	24	NA
$10,000 to $19,999	54	55	48	NA	NA	30	NA
$15,000 to $24,999	59	63	56	NA	NA	35	NA
$25,000 to $34,999	67	74	64	NA	NA	40	NA
$35,000 to $49,999	74	74	70	NA	NA	44	NA
$50,000 to $74,999	NA	NA	NA	NA	NA	50	NA
$75,000 and over	NA	NA	NA	NA	NA	57	NA

Notes
[a]Only these racial-ethnic groups are listed in all sources.
[b]Because the breakdown of voting by income for the year 2002 is not contained in the 2002 source, data for 1998 from U.S. Census Bureau, *Current Population Report*, P. 20–523, 2000:Tables 1, 5, 7, 8, 9 are used.
[c]For years preceding 1998, the category $35,000 to $49,999 is $35,000 and over, except for 1998, which is an average of $35,000 to $49,900 and over $50,000.
[d]The 2005 source lists 42 percent for age category 18–24. I assume that those aged 18–20 had a lower percentage.

Sources: As listed above and *Statistical Abstract* 1991:Table 450; 1997:Table 462; *Statistical Abstract* 2002:Table 393. U.S. Census Bureau 2005:Table 1.

polls. Many people do not vote because of **voter apathy,** or indifference. Their view is that "next year will just bring more of the same, regardless of who is in office." A common attitude of those who are apathetic is "What difference will my one vote make when there are millions of voters?" Many also see little difference between the two major political parties.

Alienation and apathy are so common that *half* of the nation's eligible voters do not vote for president, and even more fail to vote for candidates for Congress (*Statistical Abstract* 2005:Table 410).

The Gender and Racial-Ethnic Gaps in Voting. Historically, men and women have voted the same way, but we now have a *political gender gap.* That is, when they go to the ballot box, men and women are somewhat more likely to vote for different presidential candidates. As you can see from Table 11.2, men are more likely to favor the Republican candidate, while women are more likely to vote for the Democratic candidate. This table also illustrates the much larger racial-ethnic gap in politics. Note how few African Americans vote for a Republican presidential candidate.

As we saw in Table 11.1, voting patterns reflect life experiences, especially people's economic conditions. On average, women earn less than men, and African Americans earn less than whites. As a result, at this point in history, women and African Americans tend to look more favorably on government programs that redistribute income, and they are more likely to vote for Democrats.

Lobbyists and Special-Interest Groups

Suppose that you are president of the United States, and you want to make milk and bread more affordable for the poor. As you check into the matter, you find that part of the reason that prices are high is because the government is paying farmers billions of dollars a year in price supports. You propose to eliminate these subsidies.

Immediately, large numbers of people leap into action. They contact their senators and representatives and hold news conferences. Your office is flooded with calls, faxes, and e-mail. Reuters and the Associated Press distribute pictures of farm families—their Holsteins grazing contentedly in the background—and inform readers that your harsh proposal will destroy these hard-working, healthy, happy, good Americans who are struggling to make a living. President or not, you have little chance of getting your legislation passed.

What happened? The dairy industry went to work to protect its special interests. A **special-interest group** consists of people who think alike on a particular issue and who can be mobilized for political action. The

| Table 11.2 | How the Two-Party Presidential Vote Is Split |

	1988	1992	1996	2000	2004
Women					
Democrat	50%	61%	65%	56%	50%
Republican	50%	39%	35%	44%	49%
Men					
Democrat	44%	55%	51%	47%	46%
Republican	56%	45%	49%	53%	53%
African Americans					
Democrat	92%	94%	99%	92%	92%
Republican	8%	6%	1%	8%	8%
Whites					
Democrat	41%	53%	54%	46%	40%
Republican	59%	47%	46%	54%	59%
Latinos					
Democrat	NA	NA	NA	61%	58%
Republican	NA	NA	NA	39%	42%
Asian Americans					
Democrat	NA	NA	NA	62%	77%
Republican	NA	NA	NA	38%	23%

Source: Gallup Poll 2000, *Los Angeles Times Exit Poll*, November 7, 2001; *Statistical Abstract* 1999:Table 464; 2002: Table 372; Zogby 2004.

dairy industry is just one of thousands of such groups that employ **lobbyists,** people who are paid to influence legislation on behalf of their clients. Special-interest groups and lobbyists have become a powerful force in U.S. politics. Members of Congress who want to be re-elected must pay attention to them, for they represent blocs of voters who share a vital interest in the outcome of specific bills. Well financed and able to contribute huge sums, lobbyists can deliver votes to you—or to your opponent.

Some members of Congress who lose an election step into a pot of gold. So do people who have served on the president's cabinet. Because their former position opens doors to them that are closed to others, they are sought after as lobbyists. Some can demand $2 million a year (Shane 2004). *Half* of the top one hundred White House officials go to work for or advise the very companies that they regulated while they worked for the President (Ismail 2003).

To prevent special-interest groups from unduly influencing legislation, Congress passed a law that limits the amount of money that any individual, corporation, or special-interest group can donate to a candidate. This law also requires all contributions over $1,000 to be reported. To get around this law, special-interest groups form **political action committees (PACs).** These organizations solicit contributions from many donors—each contribution being within the legal limit—and then use the large total to influence legislation.

PACs are powerful, for they bankroll lobbyists and legislators. To influence politics, about 4,000 PACs shell out $280 million a year directly to their candidates (*Statistical Abstract* 2005:Tables 411, 412). PACs also contribute millions in indirect ways. Some give "honoraria" to senators who agree to say a few words at a breakfast. A few PACs represent broad social interests such as environmental protection. Most, however, stand for the financial interests of specific groups, such as the dairy, oil, banking, and construction industries.

Criticism of Lobbyists and PACs. The major criticism leveled against lobbyists and PACs is that their money, in effect, buys votes. Rather than representing the people who elected them, legislators support the special interests of groups that have the ability to help them stay in power. The PACs that have the most clout in terms of money and votes gain the ear of Congress. To politicians, the sound of money talking apparently sounds like the voice of the people.

Even if the United States were to outlaw PACs, special-interest groups would not disappear from U.S. politics.

Lobbyists walked the corridors of the Senate long before PACs, and for good or ill, they play an essential role in the U.S. political system.

Who Rules the United States?

With lobbyists and PACs wielding such influence, just whom do U.S. senators and representatives really represent? This question has led to a lively debate among sociologists.

The Functionalist Perspective: Pluralism

Functionalists view the state as having arisen out of the basic needs of the social group. To protect themselves from oppressors, people formed a government and gave it the monopoly on violence. The risk is that the state can turn that force against its own citizens. Thus, people must find a balance between having no government—which would lead to **anarchy,** a condition of disorder and violence—and having a government that protects them from violence, but that also may itself turn against them. When functioning well, then, the state is a balanced system that protects its citizens from both one another *and* government.

What keeps the U.S. government from turning against its citizens? Functionalists say that **pluralism,** a diffusion of power among many special-interest groups, prevents any one group from gaining control of the government and using it to oppress the people (Polsby 1959; Dahl 1961, 1982; Safran 2003). To keep the government from coming under the control of any one group, the founders of the United States set up three branches of government: the executive branch (the president), the judiciary branch (the courts), and the legislative branch (the Senate and House of Representatives). Each is sworn to uphold the Constitution, which guarantees rights to citizens, and each can nullify the actions of the other two. This system, known as **checks and balances,** was designed to ensure that power remains distributed and that no one branch of government dominates.

Our pluralist society has many parts—women, men, racial-ethnic groups, farmers, factory and office workers, religious organizations, bankers, bosses, the unemployed, the retired—as well as such broad categories as the rich, middle class, and poor. No group dominates. Rather, as each group pursues its own interests, it is balanced by other groups that are pursuing theirs. To attain their goals, groups must negotiate and compromise with one another.

This minimizes conflict. Because these groups have political muscle to flex at the polls, politicians try to design policies that please as many groups as they can. This, say functionalists, makes the political system responsive to the people, and no one group rules.

The Conflict Perspective: The Power Elite

Conflict theorists disagree (Hofacker 2005). If you focus on the lobbyists scurrying around Washington, they say, you get a blurred image of superficial activities. What really counts is the big picture, not its fragments. The important question is who holds the power that determines the country's overarching policies. For example, who determines interest rates—and their impact on the price of our homes? Who sets policies that transfer jobs from the United States to countries where labor costs less? And the ultimate question of power: Who is behind the decision to go to war?

Sociologist C. Wright Mills (1956) took the position that the country's most important matters are not decided by lobbyists or even by Congress. Rather, the decisions that have the greatest impact on the lives of Americans—and people across the globe—are made by a **power elite.** As depicted in Figure 11.2, the power elite consists of the top leaders of the largest corporations, the most powerful generals and admirals of the armed forces, and certain elite politicians—the president, his cabinet, and senior members of Congress who chair the major committees. It is they who wield power, who make the decisions that direct the country and shake the world.

Are the three groups that make up the power elite—the top business, military, and political leaders—equal in power? Mills said that they were not, but he didn't point to the president and his staff or even to the generals and admirals as the most powerful. The most powerful, he said, are the corporate leaders. Because all three segments of the power elite view capitalism as essential to the welfare of the country, Mills said that business interests take center stage in setting national policy.

Sociologist William Domhoff (1990, 1999b) uses the term *ruling class* to refer to the power elite. He focuses on the 1 percent of Americans who belong to the super-rich, the powerful capitalist class analyzed in Chapter 8 (pp. 202–204). Members of this class control our top corporations and foundations, even the boards that oversee our major universities. It is no accident, says Domhoff, that from this group the president chooses most members of

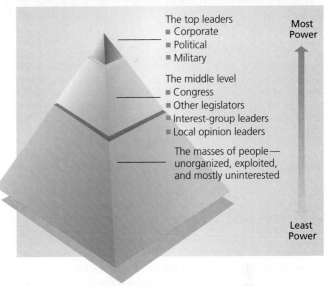

Figure 11.2 **Power in the United States: The Model Proposed by C. Wright Mills**

The top leaders
- Corporate
- Political
- Military

The middle level
- Congress
- Other legislators
- Interest-group leaders
- Local opinion leaders

The masses of people—unorganized, exploited, and mostly uninterested

Most Power

Least Power

Source: Based on Mills 1956.

his cabinet and appoints ambassadors to the most powerful countries of the world.

Conflict theorists point out that we should not think of the power elite (or ruling class) as some secret group that meets together to agree on specific matters. Rather, their unity springs from the similarity of their backgrounds and orientations to life. All have attended prestigious private schools, they belong to exclusive clubs, and they are millionaires many times over. Their behavior stems not from some grand conspiracy to control the country but from a mutual interest in solving the problems that face big business (Useem 1984). With their political connections extending to the highest centers of power, this elite determines the economic and political conditions under which the rest of the country operates (Domhoff 1990, 1998).

Which View Is Right?

The functionalist and conflict views of power in U.S. society cannot be reconciled. Either competing interests block any single group from being dominant, as functionalists assert, or a power elite oversees the major decisions of the United States, as conflict theorists maintain. The answer may have to do with the level you look at. Perhaps at the middle level of power depicted in Figure 11.2, the competing groups do keep each other at bay, and none is able to dominate. If so, the functionalist view would apply to this level. But which level holds the key to U.S. power? Perhaps the functionalists have not looked high enough, and activities at the peak remain invisible to them. On that level, does an elite dominate? To protect its mutual interests, does a small group make the major decisions of the United States?

The answer is not yet conclusive. For this, we must await more research.

War and Terrorism: Ways of Implementing Political Objectives

As we have noted, an essential characteristic of the state is that it claims a monopoly on violence. At times, a state may direct that violence against other nations. **War,** armed conflict between nations (or politically distinct groups), is often part of national policy. Let's look at this aspect of politics.

War

War is common in human history. In just the last century, war cost over 50 million lives, as well as countless billions of dollars. Back in the 1960s, sociologist Nicholas Timasheff (1965) wanted to find out why nations go to war, even though it is so costly. As he studied war, he identified three essential conditions of war. The first is an antagonistic situation in which two or more states confront incompatible objectives. For example, each may want the same land or resources. The second is a cultural tradition of war. Because their nation has fought wars in the past, the leaders of a group see war as an option for dealing with serious disputes with other nations. The third is a "fuel" that heats the antagonistic situation to a boiling point, so that politicians cross the line from thinking about war to actually waging it.

Timasheff identified seven such "fuels." He found that war is likely if a country's leaders see the antagonistic situation as an opportunity to achieve one or more of these objectives:

1. *Revenge:* settling "old scores" from earlier conflicts
2. *Power:* dictating their will to a weaker nation
3. *Prestige:* saving the nation's "honor"
4. *Unity:* uniting rival groups within their country

5. *Position:* the leaders protecting or exalting their own position
6. *Ethnicity:* bringing under their rule "our people" who are living in another country
7. *Beliefs:* forcibly converting others to religious or political beliefs

Timasheff's analysis is excellent, and you can use these three essential conditions and seven fuels to analyze any war. They will help you understand why the politicians at that time chose this political action.

War and Dehumanization

Proud of his techniques, the U.S. trainer was demonstrating to the South American soldiers how to torture a prisoner. As the victim screamed in anguish, the trainer was interrupted by a phone call from his wife. His students could hear him say, "A dinner and a movie sound nice. I'll see you right after work." Hanging up the phone, he then continued the lesson. (Stockwell 1989)

War exacts many costs in addition to killing people and destroying property. One is its effect on morality. Exposure to brutality and killing often causes **dehumanization,** the process of reducing people to objects that do not deserve to be treated as humans. As soldiers come to view their enemy as things, not people, they no longer identify with them emotionally. This breeds callousness and cruelty, and even "good people" can torture political prisoners. Brutality and killing, though regrettable, come to be seen as tools that help to get a job done—and someone has to do the "dirty work" (Hughes 1962/2005).

As sociologist Tamotsu Shibutani (1970) stressed, dehumanization is aided by the tendency for prolonged conflicts to be transformed into a struggle between good and evil. The enemy, of course, represents evil in the equation. As discussed in the Down-to-Earth Sociology box on the next page, the prisoner abuse at Abu Ghraib occurred within such a context. The thinking goes like this: To defeat absolute evil requires the suspension of moral standards—for we are fighting for the precarious survival of good. As soldiers participate in acts that they, too, would normally condemn, they try to protect their self-concept and mental adjustment. To dehumanize prisoners helps to insulate the soldiers from acknowledging their behaviors as wrong—for these types of people don't deserve normal treatment. In World War II, for example, German surgeons thought of Jews as "lower people

Down-to-Earth Sociology

Prisoner Abuse at Abu Ghraib: A Normal Event

To understand the prisoner abuse at Abu Ghraib, we need to place it within its social context. When we do, we will see that this abuse was a normal event—so much so that it would have been *abnormal* for prisoner abuse not to occur.

The social context begins before U.S. forces took over the Abu Ghraib prison. The watershed event is 9/11.

After 9/11, U.S. officials expected other attacks. The next one could be a conventional bomb detonated at a sports event or a mall—or it could be a weapon of mass destruction unleashed in a major city. Officials needed to find out where the next attack was going to take place. They decided that soft interrogation techniques would be inadequate. To get the information immediately, they needed to use harsh methods to interrogate prisoners. The Geneva Accords that specify humane treatment for prisoners of war stood in the way—but not for long. U.S. officials decided that Al-Qaeda prisoners were not prisoners of war: They had not worn uniforms, and they did not represent a country.

The next obstacle to harsh treatment came from international treaties that ban torture. U.S. officials had to find some way to get around these agreements. But how? The answer lay in the definition of torture: No one had actually defined torture. After long discussions, U.S. officials decided that they could come up with their own definition of torture. The CIA then determined that *water boarding* is not an act of torture (Risen, Johnston, and Lewis 2004). In water boarding, a prisoner is made to believe that his captors are going to drown him. They strap the prisoner to a board and forcibly push him under water. When they raise the prisoner out of the water, they again ask their questions. If they don't get an answer, they continue to repeat this procedure.

This is not torture? That is quite a definition that U.S. officials used. In fact, water boarding and other forms of treatment of prisoners that were determined to be "not torture" were so severe that the FBI ordered its agents to stay out of these interrogations.

The abuse of Iraqi prisoners at Abu Ghraib prison in Baghdad is not a surprise to sociologists. Set up the right conditions—absolute power over an enemy accompanied by secrecy and lack of accountability —and such events are the logical outcome.

This, then, is the first context for what happened at Abu Ghraib. To this, we must add what the soldiers had been told—that they were on the side of good, protecting democracy and freedom. The enemy was evil, threatening the very foundations of good. In addition, there was an urgent need to get prisoners to talk. U.S. soldiers were dying from roadside bombs and artillery attacks, and the prisoners might have information to protect fellow soldiers. Now combine these factors with utter control over the prisoners, secrecy, and the tacit approval of your superiors.

Within this social context, the abuse of prisoners was normal. That is, how could anyone expect a different outcome? If the attention of the world had not been directed to the events at Abu Ghraib, the inevitable result would have been a torture machine. Like the many torture machines that came before it, this one would have been run by "good" people—soldiers and civilians—who were convinced that they had to suspend "normal" standards of right and wrong so they could do the "dirty work" necessary to maintain "goodness."

Something else about Abu Ghraib caught the media's attention: The abusers took trophy photographs, which they proudly shared with one another. These photos, such as the one in this box, shocked the world. They provided clear evidence of abuse, and no longer could convoluted definitions of torture rule the dark.

for your Consideration

1. How can good people do such things as abuse or even torture and kill prisoners?
2. What system would you set up to prevent the abuse of prisoners?
3. Isn't the abuse of prisoners, or even their torture, justified if it prevents the deaths of others, perhaps even hundreds or thousands of other people?

(*Untermenschen*) who are going to die anyway." This enabled them to mutilate Jews just to study the results.

Terrorism

Terrorism, too, has been common in world history, although it has only recently become a fact of life for Americans. **Terrorism,** the use of violence to create fear in an effort to bring about political objectives, is most often used by a group that is weaker politically than its opponent. Because it is weaker and cannot meet its enemy on the battlefield, the group chooses terror as a weapon. You can also use Timasheff's findings (on page 302) to analyze terrorism. Just substitute the word *terrorism* for *war* as you review his main points.

Hatred between groups can span generations, sometimes centuries. Some groups nurture their bitterness by endlessly chronicling the atrocities committed by their archenemy. This encourages terrorism, for if a weaker group seeks to attack a more powerful group, terrorism is one of its few options. *Suicide terrorism* is sometimes chosen, a tactic that shocks the world and captures headlines, as it has done time after time when Palestinians have used it against Israelis. The most dramatic example of suicide terrorism, of course, was the attack on the World Trade Center and the Pentagon under the direction of Osama

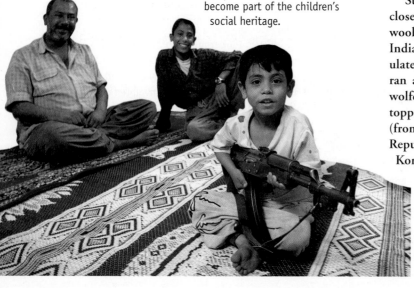

Viewed from the outside, it is difficult to fathom the depth and complexity of the mutual hatreds that enmesh some groups. From their perspective, however, nourishing the hatreds and planning revenge makes sense. Hatred and vengeance become part of the children's social heritage.

bin Laden. These acts have led to a major civil rights issue, the topic of the Down-to-Earth Sociology boxes on pages 306 and 307.

The suicide attacks on New York and Washington were tiny in comparison with the real danger: the threat of nuclear, chemical, and biological weapons. Unleashed against a civilian population, such weapons could cause millions of deaths. In 2001, Americans caught a glimpse of how easily such weapons can be unleashed when anthrax was mailed to a few select victims. The availability of nuclear, chemical, and biological weapons circulating on the black market since the breakup of the Soviet empire—combined with an extensive al–Queda network—makes further terrorism on U.S. soil a chilling possibility.

THE ECONOMY: WORK IN THE GLOBAL VILLAGE

If you are like most students, you are wondering how changes in the economy are going to affect your chances of getting a good job. Let's see if we can shed some light on this question. We will begin with this story:

The sound of her alarm rang in Kim's ears. "Not Monday already," she groaned. "There must be a better way of starting the week." She pressed the snooze button on her alarm clock (from Germany) to sneak another ten minutes' sleep. In what seemed like just thirty seconds, the alarm shrilly insisted that she get up and face the week.

Still bleary-eyed after her shower, Kim peered into her closet and picked out a silk blouse (from China), a plaid wool skirt (from Scotland), and leather shoes (from India). She nodded, satisfied, as she added a pair of simulated pearls (from Taiwan). Running late, she hurriedly ran a brush (from Mexico) through her hair. As Kim wolfed down a bowl of cereal (from the United States) topped with milk (from the United States), bananas (from Costa Rica), and sugar (from the Dominican Republic), she turned on her kitchen television (from Korea) to listen to the weather forecast.

Gulping the last of her coffee (from Brazil), Kim grabbed her briefcase (from Wales), purse (from Spain), and jacket (from Malaysia), left her house, and quickly climbed into her car (from Japan). As she glanced at her watch (from Switzerland), she hoped that the traffic would be in her favor. She muttered to herself as she pulled up at a stoplight (from Great Britain) and eyed her gas gauge. She muttered again when she pulled into a station and paid for gas (from Saudi Arabia), for the price had risen over the weekend. "My paycheck never keeps up with prices," she moaned.

When Kim arrived at work, she found the office abuzz. Six months ago, New York headquarters had put the company up for sale, but there had been no takers. The big news this Monday was that both a German and a Canadian company had put in bids over the weekend. No one got much work done that day, as the whole office speculated about how things might change.

As Kim walked to the parking lot after work, she saw a tattered "Buy American" bumper sticker on the car next to hers. "That's right," she said to herself. "If people were more like me, this country would be in better shape."

The Transformation of Economic Systems

Although this vignette may be slightly exaggerated, many of us are like Kim: We use a multitude of products from around the world, and yet we're concerned about our country's ability to compete in global markets. Our **economy** today—our system of producing and distributing goods and services—differs radically from those in all but our most recent past. The products that Kim uses make it apparent that today's economy knows no national boundaries. To better understand how global forces affect the U.S. economy—and your life—let's begin with an overview of sweeping historical changes.

Preindustrial Societies: The Birth of Inequality

The earliest human groups, *hunting and gathering societies,* had a **subsistence economy.** In small groups of about twenty-five to forty, people lived off the land. They gathered plants and hunted animals in one place, and then moved to another as these sources of food ran low. Because these people had few possessions, they did little trading with one another. With no excess to accumulate, as was mentioned in Chapter 4, everybody owned as much (or, really, as little) as everyone else.

Then people discovered how to breed animals and cultivate plants. The more dependable food supply in what became *pastoral and horticultural societies* allowed humans to settle down in a single place. Human groups grew larger, and for the first time in history, it was no longer necessary

for everyone to work at producing food. Some people became leather workers, others weapon makers, and so on. This new division of labor produced a surplus, and groups traded items with one another. The primary sociological significance of surplus and trade is this: They fostered *social inequality,* for some people accumulated more possessions than others. The effects of that change remain with us today.

The plow brought the next major change, ushering in *agricultural societies.* Plowed land was much more productive, allowing even more people to specialize in activities other than producing food. More specialized divisions of labor followed, and trade expanded. Trading centers then developed, which turned into cities. As power passed from the heads of families and clans to a ruling elite, social, political, and economic inequality grew.

Industrial Societies: The Birth of the Machine

The steam engine, invented in 1765, ushered in *industrial societies.* Based on machines powered by fuels, these societies created a surplus unlike anything the world had seen. This, too, stimulated trade among nations and brought even greater social inequality. A handful of individuals opened factories and exploited the labor of many.

Then came more efficient machines. As the surpluses grew even greater, the emphasis changed from producing goods to consuming them. In 1912, sociologist Thorstein Veblen coined the term **conspicuous consumption** to describe this fundamental change in people's orientations. By this term, Veblen meant that the Protestant ethic identified by Weber—an emphasis on hard work, savings, and a concern for salvation (discussed in Chapter 13)—was being replaced by an eagerness to show off wealth by the "elaborate consumption of goods."

Postindustrial Societies: The Birth of the Information Age

In 1973, sociologist Daniel Bell noted that *a new type of society was emerging.* This new society, which he called the *postindustrial society,* has six characteristics: (1) a service sector so large that *most* people work in it; (2) a vast surplus of goods; (3) even more extensive trade among nations; (4) a wider variety and quantity of goods available to the average person; (5) an information explosion; and (6) a "global village"—that is, the world's nations are linked by fast communications, transportation, and trade.

Down-to-Earth Sociology

Is Big Brother Knocking on the Door? Civil Liberties and Homeland Security

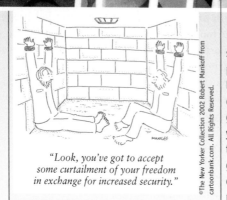

"Look, you've got to accept some curtailment of your freedom in exchange for increased security."

SEE IF YOU CAN GUESS WHICH country this is. Government agents can break into your home while you are at work, copy the files on your computer, and leave a "bug" that records every keystroke from then on—without a search warrant. Government agents can also check with your local library and make a list of every book, record, or movie that you've ever checked out.

What country is this? It is the United States.

Things have changed since 9/11. There is no question that we must have security. Our nation cannot be at risk, and we cannot live in peril. But does security have to come at the price of our civil liberties?

Balancing security and civil liberties has always been a sensitive issue in the history of the United States. In times of war, the U.S. government has curtailed freedoms. During the War Between the States, as the Civil War is called in the South, Abraham Lincoln even banned the right of habeas corpus (Neely 1992). This took away people's right to appear in court and ask judges to determine whether they had been unlawfully arrested and imprisoned.

After the terrorist attacks on New York and Washington in 2001, Congress authorized the formation of the Department of Homeland Security. Other than beefed-up security at airports, few citizens noticed a difference. People who were suspected of terrorism, however, felt a major impact. They were imprisoned without charges being lodged against them in a court, and they were denied the right to consult lawyers or to have a hearing in court.

People shrugged this off. "Terrorists deserve whatever they get," they said. What ordinary citizens didn't realize, however, was that behind the scenes their own liberties were being curtailed. FBI agents placed listening devices on cars, in buildings, and on streets. They then used Nightstalkers (aircraft outfitted with electronic surveillance equipment) to listen to conversations. This was done without warrants (Hentoff 2003).

Then there is the "no-fly list" of the Transportation Security Agency. Anyone who *might* have some kind of connection with some kind of terrorist is not allowed to board an airplane. This agency has also developed CAPPS II (Computer Assisted Passenger Pre-Screening System). Each traveler is labeled as a "green," "yellow," or "red" security risk. Green means you're fine, and red is reserved for known terrorists.

But what about those who are stamped with the yellow code? These people are suspect. As the American Civil Liberties Union says, anyone could get caught up in this system, with no way to get out. (For all I know, I could be coded yellow for criticizing Homeland Security in this box.) Agents in government intelligence—an oxymoron, if ever there was one—are known for being humorless, suspicious, and almost downright paranoid.

You might get stamped yellow simply for reading the wrong books—because agents of the Department of Homeland Security now have the right to track the books we buy or those we check out at libraries. They can even record the Internet sites we visit at libraries. This is all done in secret. When librarians receive orders to reveal who has checked out certain books, they can be arrested if they even tell anyone that they received such an order (Lichtblau 2005).

If such surveillance continues, the government will eventually maintain an intelligence file on almost all of us. If you get coded yellow, that information could be shared with other government agencies. This, in turn, could affect your chances of getting a job, government benefits, or even a college scholarship.

How far do government officials want to go? The Homeland Security Bill passed by Congress comes with TIA (Total Information Awareness). TIA allows officials to track our telephone conversations, credit card purchases, e-mails, medical histories, and travel history (O'Malley 2003). Congress refused to approve TIPS (Terrorism Information and Prevention System), in which mail carriers, truck drivers, cable installers, and utility employees would have served as voluntary spies, searching our neighborhoods for suspicious behavior.

Security we must have. But at what cost? A dossier on each of us? Government watchdogs looking over our shoulders, writing down the names of our friends and associates, even the books and magazines we read? Microphones planted to eavesdrop on our conversations? Will they eventually install a computer chip in our right hand or in our forehead?

for your Consideration

What civil liberties do you think we should give up to help our nation be secure from terrorist attacks? Are you willing to have the government keep track of your everyday affairs in the name of homeland security? What is your opinion of the government keeping a list of the books you check out at the library? Listening to your conversations? Keeping track of people you associate with?

Down-to-Earth Sociology

Your Author Is a Suspect!?

During a recent trip to India, I changed planes in Frankfurt, Germany. German security opened my carry-on bag and camera and rubbed them with what appeared to be a swatch of cloth. When I asked what they were doing, they explained that they were testing for the residue of explosives.

Upon my arrival in India, one of my bags was missing. When I reported it at the lost luggage desk, a woman pulled out a printed list that had my bag number recorded on it. She said that my bag would arrive later. I chalked this up to some unusual Indian efficiency, unmatched by anything I had ever seen in that country—or anywhere else. I was impressed. When my missing bag turned up several days later, it contained a "Notice of Baggage Inspection" by the U.S. Transportation Security Administration.

The next month, I flew to Minneapolis. Again, a security guard opened my luggage, and, wearing plastic gloves, ran a swatch of cloth around my camera and computer, and then inside my carry-on. His boss explained to me that this was "for practice" because he was a new employee.

Two weeks later, I flew to Las Vegas. On my return flight to Florida, a uniformed woman asked me to step out of the line. I asked why, and she pointed to a special code on my ticket. After my luggage was searched, I walked over to her supervisor and asked, nicely, if he knew why I had been picked out. He said that he had no idea, and then handed me a form and an envelope in case I wanted to complain.

A month later, I flew to Latvia, with passage through London. I thought it strange that of all the passengers on my plane, the inspector selected only me to pat down. After ordering me to take off my belt, which he carefully inspected, he told me to stretch out my arms. He then began to feel all areas of my jacket, which I was still wearing. As I stood there, arms outstretched, I saw my billfold, camera, and computer go by on the adjacent conveyer belt. This made me nervous, but I did not dare grab them.

Finishing the inspection, the man ordered me to go back through the line and to place my jacket on the conveyer belt so it would go through the X-ray machine. I asked why,

since he had already inspected my jacket so carefully, and he said, "Your jacket feels thick."

When I arrived in Latvia, only one of my two checked bags made it. "What a coincidence," was my first thought. As in India, the Latvian airport personnel found my missing bag on a computerized list. They assured me that my bag would arrive the next day.

When the missing duffel bag was delivered, I noticed that it had been opened. The photo in this box shows what I found as I unpacked the bag—another little greeting from the Transportation Security Administration—as well as my cut padlock. Inside, the corners of a box containing a chess set had been peeled back—an indication of the thoroughness of their search.

On my return to Florida from Lativia, I waited at the baggage carousel. As I watched the luggage go round and round, with mine not appearing, I didn't feel surprise. This time, too, my bags were delivered to my home the day after I arrived.

All of this is pushing the envelope of coincidence a little too far. Have I joined that Yellow List—or some other kind of "suspect" list? If so, what put me on it? Arab looking? No. Male? Yes, but that's not enough. Beard? Yes, but not enough. Burqua? Not in public, at least. Author of the box on the facing page, in which I criticize Homeland Security? Hmmm.

All guesswork. The rules for getting on The Yellow List are secret. And once on The List, there is no way to get your name removed. Sort of reminds me of *Catch 22*. If you are sane enough to know you're crazy, then you are sane enough to stay in the Army. If somehow you get on the Yellow or Red List and you are a loyal citizen, you shouldn't mind because the whole purpose of The List is to protect loyal citizens.

Ah, social life today. But, hey! I should relax and be happy. This is how I get data! As I live life, I do participant observation—even when I don't intend to.

Figure 11.3 illustrates our transition to this new society, a change without parallel in human history. In the 1800s, most U.S. workers were farmers. Today, farmers make up only about 2 percent of the work force. To see why this transition came about, we can note that with the technology of the 1800s, a typical farmer produced enough food for only five people. With powerful machinery and hybrid seeds, a typical farmer now feeds about eighty. In 1940, about half of U.S. workers wore a blue collar. Then changing technology shrank the market for blue-collar jobs, while white-collar work continued its ascent, reaching the dominant position it holds today. Figure 11.3 illustrates nothing less than the transition to a new society.

Biotech Societies: The Merger of Biology and Economics

We may be on the verge of yet another new type of society. This one is being ushered in by advances in biology, especially the deciphering of the human genome system. While the specifics of this new society have yet to unfold, the marriage of biology and economics should yield even greater surpluses and more extensive trade. The global village will continue to expand. The technological advances that will emerge in this new society may also allow us to live longer and healthier lives. As history is our guide, it also may create even greater inequality between the rich and poor nations.

Implications for Your Life

The broad changes in societies that I have just sketched may seem to be abstract matters, but they are far from irrelevant to your life. Whenever society changes, so do our lives. Consider the information explosion. After you graduate from college, you will most likely do some form of "knowledge work." Instead of working in a factory, you will manage information or design, sell, or service products. The type of work you do has profound implications for your life. It produces social networks, nurtures attitudes, and even affects how you view yourself and the world.

It is the same with the global village. Think of the globe as being divided into three neighborhoods—the three worlds of industrialization and postindustrialization that we reviewed in Chapter 7 (pages 180–186). Some nations are located in the poor part of the village. Their citizens barely eke out a living from menial work. Some even starve to death. In contrast, their fellow villagers in the rich neighborhood feast on the best that the globe has to offer. It's the same village, but what a difference the neighborhood makes.

Now visualize any one of the three neighborhoods. Again you will see gross inequalities. Not everyone who lives in the poor neighborhood is poor, and some areas of the rich neighborhood are packed with poor people. Because the United States is the global economic leader, occupying the most luxurious mansion in the best neighborhood and spearheading the developing biotech society, let's look at U.S. trends.

Ominous Trends in the United States

Reduction in Jobs and Benefits.   The global village also means fierce global competition. Nike soccer balls and sports shoes can be made by U.S. workers who are paid $20 an hour or by workers in a Least Industrialized Nation who earn $2 a day. To remain competitive in the global marketplace, U.S. multinational firms assign work where it is the cheapest (or most "cost effective," as they put it).

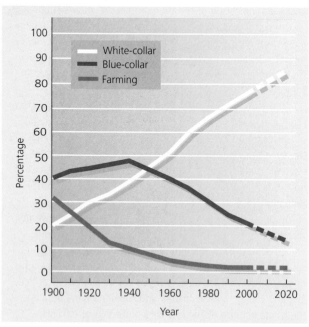

Figure 11.3   The Revolutionary Change in the U.S. Work Force

Note: From 1900 to 1940, "workers" refers to people age 14 and over; from 1970 to people age 16 and over. Broken lines are the author's projections. The totals shown here are broadly accurate only, as there is disagreement on how to classify some jobs. Agriculture, for example, includes forestry, fishing, and hunting.

Source: By the author. Based on *Statistical Abstract,* various years, and 2005:Tables 597, 1354.

Sometimes this means using child labor in India, but other times powerful U.S. machinery can spew out those same products even more cheaply.

The implications for U.S. workers (and those of Canada, Germany, France, and so on) are ominous. Waiting impatiently on the sidelines are millions upon millions of men, women, and children who are ready to work for a pittance. To reduce costs, U.S. firms are "*downsizing*" (a nice word for firing workers). In their place, they hire temporary workers, who can be released at will. This allows firms to bypass costly "frills," such as health insurance, vacation pay, and retirement benefits. Some analysts are concerned that these patterns may be permanent, that they foreshadow an era of easily discharged workers who will always live with insecurity, low pay, and few benefits.

The globalization of capitalism, accompanied by the transfer of jobs and the closing of plants, has brought a special challenge to small towns, which were already suffering severe losses because of urbanization. We explore this consequence in the photo essay on the next two pages.

With cost, not education, their chief concern, even colleges and universities are following this pattern. When their full-time, better-paid teachers retire, they are replaced with part-timers. Hired only to teach specific courses one semester at a time, these instructors are exempt from tenure, promotion, sick leave, and retirement benefits. Some of them are not even given offices where they can meet with their students. This might interfere with education, but it certainly cuts down on the utility bill.

Stagnant Paychecks. U.S. workers are some of the most productive in the world (*Statistical Abstract* 2005:Table 1337). One might think, therefore, that their pay would be increasing. This brings us to a disturbing trend.

Look at Figure 11.4 on page 312. The gold bars show current dollars. These are the dollars the average worker finds in his or her paycheck. You can see that since 1970 the average pay of U.S. workers has soared from just over $3 an hour to almost $16 an hour. Workers today are bringing home almost *five* times as many dollars as workers used to.

One of the negative consequences of early industrialization in the West was the use of child labor. In the photo on the left, of the U.S. textile industry in the 1800s, you can see spindle boys at work in a Georgia cotton mill. Today's Least Industrialized Nations are experiencing the same negative consequence as they industrialize. The photo on the right shows boys at work in a contemporary textile factory in Varanas, India. About the only improvement is that the child workers in India are able to sit down as they exhaust their childhood.

Small Town USA
Struggling to Survive

all across the nation, small towns are struggling to survive. Parents and town officials are concerned because so few young adults remain in their home town. There is little to keep them there, and when they graduate from high school, most move to the city. With young people leaving and old ones dying, the small towns are shriveling.

How can small towns contend with cutthroat global competition when workers in some countries are paid a couple of dollars a day? Even if you open a store,

down the road, Wal-Mart sells the same products for about what you pay for them—and offers much greater variety.

There are exceptions: Some small towns are located close to a city, and they receive the city's spillover. A few possess a rare treasure—some unique historical event or a natural attraction—that draws visitors with money to spend. Most of the others, though, are drying up, left in a time warp as history shifts around them. This photo essay tells the story.

I was struck by the grandiosity of people's dreams, at least as reflected in the names that some small-towners give their businesses. Donut Palace has a nice ring to it inspiring thoughts of wealth and royalty (note the crowns). Unfortunately, like so many others, this business didn't make it.

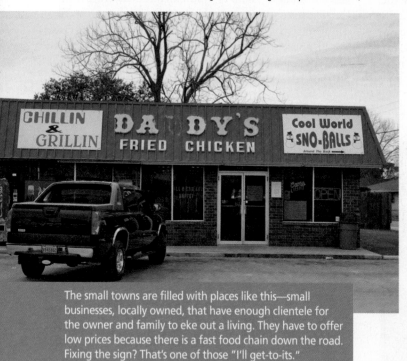

The small towns are filled with places like this—small businesses, locally owned, that have enough clientele for the owner and family to eke out a living. They have to offer low prices because there is a fast food chain down the road. Fixing the sign? That's one of those "I'll get-to-its."

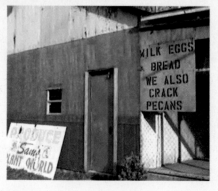

People do whatever they can to survive. This enterprising proprietor uses the building for an unusual combination of purposes: a "plant world," along with the sale of milk, eggs, bread, and, in a quaint southern touch, cracking pecans.

In striking contrast to the grandiosity of some small town business names is the utter simplicity of others. Cafe tells everyone that some type of food and drinks are served here. Everyone in this small town knows the details.

©James M. Henslin, all photos

One of the few buildings consistently in good repair in the small towns is the U.S. Post Office. Although its importance has declined in the face of telecommunications, for "small towners" the post office still provides a vital link with the outside world.

With little work available, it is difficult to afford adequate housing. This house, although cobbled together and in disrepair, is a family's residence.

There is no global competition for this home-grown business. This enterprising individual has located her sign on a main highway in a litttle town just outside New Orleans.

This is a successful business. The store goes back to the early 1900s, and the proprietors have capitalized on the "old timey" atmosphere.

This general store used to be the main business in the area; it even has a walk-in safe. It has been owned by the same family since the 1920s, but is no longer successful. To get into the building, I had to find out where the owner (shown here) lived, knock on her door, and then wait while she called around to find out who had the keys.

Figure 11.4 Average Hourly Earnings of U.S. Workers in Current and Constant (1982) Dollars

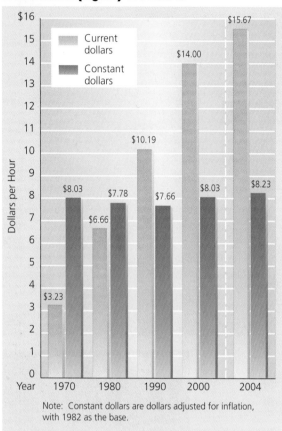

Note: Constant dollars are dollars adjusted for inflation, with 1982 as the base.

Source: By the author. Based on *Statistical Abstract* 1992:Table 650; 1999: Table 698; 2006:Table 628.

But let's strip away the illusion. Look at the green bars, which show constant dollars, the *buying power* of those paychecks. These bars show how inflation has whittled away the value of the dollars that workers earn. Today's workers can buy only a little more with their $16 an hour than workers in 1970 could with their "measly" $3 an hour. The question is not "How could workers live on just $3 an hour back then?" but, rather, "How can workers get by on a 20-cent-an-hour raise that it took 34 years to get?" Incredibly, despite increased education, technical training, computers, and productivity, this is how much the average worker's purchasing power increased from 1970 to 2004.

Income Inequalities. The inverted pyramid shown in Figure 11.5 provides a snapshot of how the nation's income is divided. Each rectangle on the left represents a fifth of the U.S. population, about 60 million people. The rectangles on the right represent the proportion of the nation's income that goes to each of these fifths. From this inverted pyramid, you can see that *48 percent* of the entire country's income goes to the richest fifth of Americans, while only *4 percent* goes to the poorest fifth. This gap is now greater than it has been in generations. Rather than bringing equality, then, the postindustrial economy has perpetuated and enlarged the income inequalities of the industrial economy.

Figure 11.5 The Inverted Income Pyramid: The Proportion of Income Received by Each Fifth of the U.S. Population

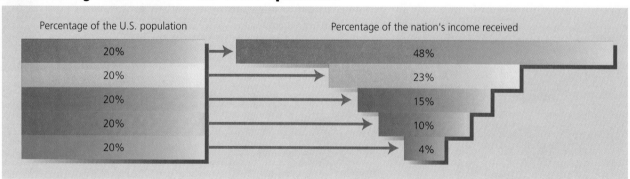

Source: By the author. Based on *Statistical Abstract* 2005:Table 672.

World Economic Systems

To understand where the United States stands in the world economic order, let's compare capitalism and socialism, the two main economic systems in force today.

Capitalism

People who live in a capitalist society may not understand its basic tenets, even though they see them reflected in their local shopping malls and fast-food chains. Table 11.3 distills the many businesses of the United States down to their basic components. As you can see, **capitalism** has three essential features: (1) *private ownership of the means of production* (individuals own the land, machines, and factories and decide what they will produce); (2) *market competition* (an exchange of items between willing buyers and sellers); and (3) the pursuit of *profit* (selling something for more than it costs).

Some people believe that the United States is an example of pure capitalism. Pure capitalism, however, known as **laissez-faire capitalism** (literally, "hands off" capitalism), means that the government doesn't interfere in the market. Such is not the case in the United States. The current form of U.S. capitalism is **welfare** or **state capitalism.** Private citizens own the means of production and pursue profits, but they do so within a vast system of laws designed to protect the welfare of the population.

Table 11.3 Comparing Capitalism and Socialism

Capitalism	Socialism
1. Individuals own the means means of production	1. The public owns the means of production
2. The owners determine production, based on competition	2. Central committees plan production; no competition
3. The pursuit of profit is the reason for distributing goods and services	3. No profit motive in the distribution of goods and services

Suppose that you discover what you think is a miracle tonic: It will grow hair, erase wrinkles, and dissolve excess fat. If your product works, you will become an overnight sensation—not only a millionaire but also the toast of television talk shows and the darling of Hollywood.

But don't count your money or broadcast your fame yet. You still have to reckon with *market restraints,* the laws and regulations of welfare capitalism that limit your capacity to produce and sell. First, you must comply with local and state rules. You must obtain a business license and a state tax number that allows you to buy your ingredients without paying sales taxes. Then come the federal regulations. You cannot simply take your product to local stores and ask them to sell it; you first must seek approval from federal agencies that monitor compliance with the Pure Food and Drug Act. This means that you must prove that your product will not cause harm to the public. In addition, you must be able to substantiate your claims—or else face being shut down by state and federal agencies that monitor the market for fraud. Your manufacturing process is also subject to federal, state, and local laws concerning hygiene and the disposal of hazardous wastes.

Suppose that you overcome these obstacles, and your business prospers. Other federal agencies will monitor your compliance with laws concerning racial, sexual, and disability discrimination; minimum wages; and Social Security taxes. State agencies will examine your records to see whether you have paid unemployment taxes and sales taxes. Finally, the Internal Revenue Service will look over your shoulder and demand a share of your profits (about 35 percent).

In short, the U.S. economic system is highly regulated and is far from an example of laissez-faire capitalism.

Socialism

As Table 11.3 shows, **socialism** also has three essential components: (1) public ownership of the means of production, (2) central planning, and (3) the distribution of goods without a profit motive.

In socialist countries, the government owns the means of production—not only the factories but also the land, railroads, oil wells, and gold mines. Unlike capitalism, in which **market forces**—supply and demand—determine both what will be produced and the prices that will be charged, a central committee determines that the country needs X number of toothbrushes, Y toilets,

This advertisement from 1885 represents an early stage of capitalism when individuals were free to manufacture and market products with little or no interference from the government. Today, the production and marketing of goods take place under detailed, complicated government laws and regulations.

In their search for profits, companies seek markets wherever they can find them. Mattel's stunning success with Barbie, bringing in over a billion dollars a year, spawned numerous imitators. The Bratz dolls, hipper and cooler than Barbie, with such names as Cloe, Jade, Sasha, and Yasmin, proved such a success that Mattel came out with its own "street smart" Flava dolls. These two lines of dolls reflect fundamental changes in U.S. culture. What changes do you think that they reflect?

and Z shoes. The committee decides how many of each will be produced, which factories will produce them, what price will be charged for the items, and where they will be distributed.

Socialism is designed to eliminate competition, for goods are sold at predetermined prices regardless of the demand for an item or the cost of producing it. Profit is not the goal, nor is encouraging consumption of goods that are in low demand (by lowering the price), nor is limiting the consumption of hard-to-get goods (by raising the price). Rather, the goal is to produce goods for the general welfare and to distribute them according to people's needs, not their ability to pay.

In a socialist economy, *everyone* in the economic chain works for the government. The members of the central committee who determine production goals are government employees, as are the supervisors who implement their plans, the factory workers who produce the merchandise, the truck drivers who move it, and the clerks who sell it. Those who buy the items may work at different jobs—in offices, on farms, in schools, or in day care centers—but they, too, are government employees.

Just as capitalism does not exist in a pure form, neither does socialism. Although the ideology of socialism calls for resources to be distributed according to need and not the ability to pay, in line with the functionalist argument of social stratification presented in Chapter 7, socialist countries found it necessary to offer higher salaries for some jobs in order to entice people to take on greater responsibilities. For example, in socialist countries, factory managers always earned more than factory workers. By narrowing the huge pay gaps that characterize capitalist nations, however, socialist nations established considerably greater equality of income.

Dissatisfied with the greed and exploitation of capitalism and the lack of freedom and individuality of socialism, Sweden and Denmark developed **democratic socialism** (also called *welfare socialism*). In this form of socialism, both the state and individuals produce and distribute goods and services. The government owns and runs the steel, mining, forestry, and energy concerns as well as the country's telephones, television stations, and airlines. Remaining in private hands are the retail stores, farms, manufacturing concerns, and most service industries.

Ideologies of Capitalism and Socialism

Not only do capitalism and socialism have different approaches to producing and distributing goods but also they represent opposing belief systems. *Capitalists* believe that market forces should determine both products and prices. They also believe that profits are good for humanity. If people strive for profits, it stimulates them to produce and distribute goods efficiently as well as to develop new products. This benefits society, bringing a more abundant supply of goods at cheaper prices.

Socialists, in contrast, consider profits to be immoral. Karl Marx said that an item's value is based on the work that goes into it. The only way there can be profit, he stressed, is by paying workers less than the value of their labor. Profit, then, is the *excess value* that has been withheld from workers. Socialists believe that the government should protect workers from this exploitation. To do so, the government should own the means of production, using them not to generate profit but to produce items that match people's needs, not their ability to pay.

Adherents to these ideologies paint each other in such stark colors that *each perceives the other system as one of exploitation.* Capitalists believe that socialists violate the basic human rights of freedom of decision and opportunity. Socialists believe that capitalists violate the basic human right of freedom from poverty. With each side claiming moral superiority while viewing the other as a threat to its very existence, the last century witnessed the world split into two main blocs. In what was known as the *Cold War,* the West armed itself to defend and promote capitalism, the East to defend and promote socialism.

Criticisms of Capitalism and Socialism

The primary criticism leveled against capitalism is that it leads to social inequality. Capitalism, say its critics, produces a tiny top layer of wealthy, powerful people who exploit a vast bottom layer of poorly paid workers. Another criticism is that the tiny top layer wields vast political power. Those few who own the means of production reap huge profits, accrue power, and get legislation passed that goes against the public good.

The primary criticism leveled against socialism is that it does not respect individual rights (Berger 1991). Others (in the form of some government body) decide where people will work, live, and go to school. In China, they even decide how many children women may bear (Mosher 1983). Critics also argue that central planning is grossly inefficient and that socialism is not capable of producing much wealth. They say that its greater equality really amounts to giving almost everyone an equal chance to be poor.

The Convergence of Capitalism and Socialism

Regardless of the validity of these mutual criticisms, as nations industrialize, they come to resemble one another. They urbanize, produce similar divisions of labor (such as professionals and skilled technicians), and encourage higher education. Even similar values emerge (Kerr 1983). By itself, this tendency would make capitalist and socialist nations grow more alike, but another factor also brings them closer to one another (Form 1979): Despite their incompatible ideologies, both capitalist and socialist systems have adopted features of each other.

That capitalism and socialism are growing similar is known as **convergence theory.** This view points to an impending hybrid or mixed economy. Fundamental changes in socialist countries in the last few decades give evidence for convergence theory. Russia and China suffered from the production of shoddy goods, they were plagued by shortages, and their standard of living severely lagged behind that of the West. To try to catch up, in the 1980s and 1990s, Russia and China reinstated market forces. They made the private ownership of property legal, and they auctioned off many of their state-owned industries. Making a profit—which had been a crime—was encouraged. In China, leaders even invited capitalists to join the Communist Party (Kahn 2002). Even Vietnam, whose communism the United States was so concerned about, has embraced capitalism (Lamb 2004).

Changes in capitalism also support this theory. The United States has adopted many socialist practices. One of the most obvious is extracting money from some individuals to pay for the benefits it gives to others. Examples include unemployment compensation (taxes paid by workers are distributed to those who no longer produce a profit); subsidized housing (shelter, paid for by the many, is given to the poor and elderly, with no motive of profit); welfare (taxes from the many are distributed to the needy); a minimum wage (the government, not the employer, determines the minimum that workers receive); and Social Security (the retired do not receive what they paid into the system but, rather, money that the government collects from current workers). Such embracing of socialist principles indicates that the United States has produced its own version of a mixed type of economy.

Perhaps, then, convergence is unfolding before our very eyes. On the one hand, capitalists now assume that their system should provide workers with at least minimal support during unemployment, extended illness, and old age. On the other hand, socialist leaders have reluctantly admitted that profit does motivate people to work harder.

Capitalism in a Global Economy

To understand today's capitalism, we need to consider the corporation within the context of a global economy.

Corporate Capitalism

Capitalism is driving today's global interdependence. Its triumph as the world's dominant economic force can be traced to a social invention called the corporation. A **corporation** is a business that is treated legally as a person. A corporation can make contracts, incur debts, sue and be sued. Its liabilities and obligations, however, are separate from those of its owners. For example, each shareholder of Ford Motor Company—whether he or she has 1 or 100,000 shares—owns a portion of the company. However, Ford, not its individual owners, is responsible for fulfilling its contracts and paying its debts. To indicate how corporations now dominate the economy, sociologists use the term **corporate capitalism.**

One of the most surprising, but functional, aspects of corporations is their *separation of ownership and management.* Unlike most businesses, it is not the owners, those who own the company's stock, who run the day-to-day affairs of the company (Walters 1995; Sklair 2001). Instead, managers run the corporation, and they are able to treat it *as though it were their own.* The result is the "ownership of wealth without appreciable control, and control

of wealth without appreciable ownership" (Berle and Means 1932). Sociologist Michael Useem (1984) put it this way:

> When few owners held all or most of a corporation's stock, they readily dominated its board of directors, which in turn selected top management and ran the corporation. Now that a firm's stock [is] dispersed among many unrelated owners, each holding a tiny fraction of the total equity, the resulting power vacuum allow[s] management to select the board of directors; thus management [becomes] self-perpetuating and thereby acquire[s] de facto control over the corporation.

Because of this power vacuum, at their annual meeting, stockholders ordinarily rubber-stamp management's recommendations. It is so unusual for this *not* to happen that these rare cases are called **stockholders' revolts.** The irony of this term is generally lost, but remember that in such cases it is not the workers who are rebelling against the control of the owners but the owners who are rebelling at the control of the workers!

Interlocking Directorates. The wealthy expand their power through **interlocking directorates;** that is, they serve on the board of directors of several companies. Their fellow members on those boards also sit on the boards of other companies, and so on. Like a spider's web that starts at the center and then fans out in all directions, the top companies are interlocked into a network (Mintz and Schwartz 1985; Davis 2003). The chief executive officer of a firm in England, who sits on the board of directors of half a dozen other companies, noted,

> If you serve on, say, six outside boards, each of which has, say, ten directors, and let's say out of the ten directors, five are experts in one or another subject, you have a built-in panel of thirty friends who are experts whom you meet regularly, automatically each month, and you really have great access to ideas and information. You're joining a club—a very good club. (Useem 1984)

Multinational Corporations

The two Social Maps on pages 317 and 318 illustrate how corporations have outgrown their national boundaries. The world map shows the investments that U.S. corporations have made in other countries. Cross-border investments are not a one-way street, however, as the U.S. map on the next page shows: About 1 of every 20 U.S. businesses is owned by people in other countries.

As **multinational corporations**—corporations that operate across national borders—do business, they become more and more detached from the interests and values of their country of origin. A U.S. executive made this revealing statement, "The United States does not have an automatic call on our resources. There is no mind-set that puts the country first" (Greidner 2001). These global giants move investments and production from one part of the globe to another—with no concern for consequences other than profits. How adding—or withdrawing—investments affects workers is of no concern to them. With profit as their moral guide, the conscience of multinational corporations is dominated by dollar signs. As they soar past geographical barriers in the attempt to conquer markets, the road is not without bumps. As discussed in the Cultural Diversity box on page 319, this leads to some humorous situations.

Multinational corporations have become a powerful political force, one that is reshaping the globe as no army has ever been able to do. Although we take the presence of multinational corporations for granted—as well as their cornucopia of products—their power and presence are new to the world scene. It is possible that an unintended consequence of the globalization of capitalism will be a New World Order. Let's consider this possibility.

A New World Order?

Today we see the world's nations almost frantically embracing capitalism. Underlying this fury is the worldwide flow of information, capital, and goods that we have been discussing. Perhaps the most significant consequence of this frenzied pursuit of profits, however, will be an unintended bonus: world peace.

Let's consider some significant trends. The United States, Canada, and Mexico have formed the North American Free Trade Association (NAFTA), to which all of South America may eventually belong. Some South American countries have adopted the dollar as an official currency, even as their national currency coexists alongside it. Transcending their national boundaries, twenty-five

Figure 11.6 **The Globalization of Capitalism: U.S. Ownership in Other Countries**

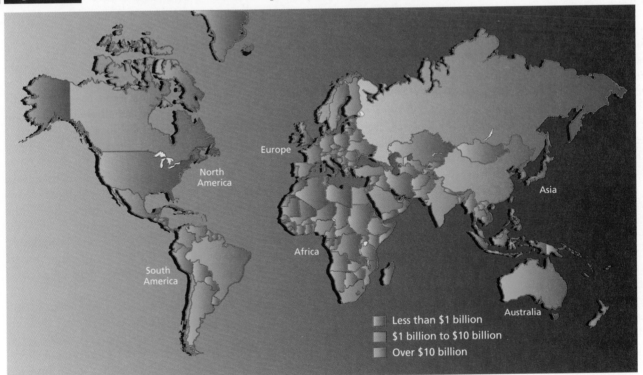

Less than $1 billion
$1 billion to $10 billion
Over $10 billion

Source: By the author. Based on *Statistical Abstract* 2005:Table 1288.

Figure 11.7 The Globalization of Capitalism: Foreign Ownership of U.S. Business

Businesses in which at least 10 percent of the voting interest is controlled by a non-U.S. owner.

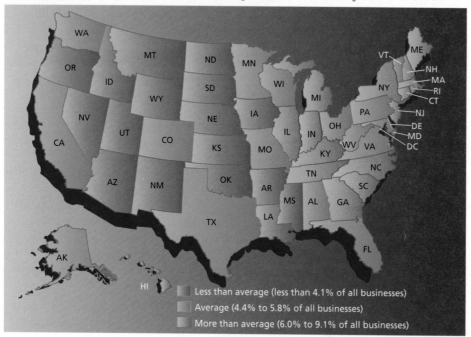

Less than average (less than 4.1% of all businesses)

Average (4.4% to 5.8% of all businesses)

More than average (6.0% to 9.1% of all businesses)

Source: By the author. Based on *Statistical Abstract* 2005:Table 1285.

European countries have formed an economic and political unit (the European Union, or EU). These nations have produced a cross-national currency, the Euro, which has replaced their marks, francs, liras, and pesetas. The EU has established a "rapid reaction force" of 60,000 troops under a unified command (Cohen 2001). The rejection of the proposed EU constitution by France and Holland in 2005 presented an obstacle that these nations have to overcome. Ten Asian countries with an even larger population (a half billion people) have formed a regional trading partnership called ASEAN (Association of South East Nations). On the global level is the fledgling World Trade Organization, with a membership of 149 nations.

Will this process of economic and political consolidation continue until there is just one state or empire that envelops the earth itself? In light of these historical trends, we can see that this is a distinct possibility. Even Russia, now that it has joined the global capitalist club, is calling for a worldwide system. When Russia was accepted into NATO, the country's prime minister made this remarkable statement: "We must now together build the New World Order" (Purdum 2002).

Underlying these economic and political events is the triumph of capitalism. As the multinational corporations expand, the pressure for profits will stimulate more trade agreements. To forge them, and to solidify their interlocking interests, the corporate elites court national elites, those who wield power within a country. In exchange for access to a country's workers, natural resources, and markets, the corporate elites give the national elites cash, credit, and armaments that help them to stay in power. This process of mutual back-scratching may ultimately interconnect the business and political elites of the world's nations into a single cooperative system. If so, far removed from the tribal loyalties of national boundaries, the regional—and eventually global—trade agreements forged by the multinational corporations may well become a force for peace.

With the world yearning for peace, such economic and political unity carries strong, seductive appeal. It is likely to come at a high price, however. If our new world order is dominated by a handful of corporate leaders, our everyday life with Big Brother could be like that of Winston and Julia in our opening vignette.

Cultural Diversity *around the* World

Doing Business in the Global Village

The World

The globalization of capitalism means that businesspeople face cultural hurdles as they sell products in other cultures. Some of the cultural mistakes they make as they try to clear these hurdles are downright humorous.

Spanish-speaking Americans and Mexico's growing middle class make up a large market for new products. In trying to reach this audience, some companies have stumbled over their Spanish. Parker Pen was using a slogan "It won't leak in your pocket and embarrass you." The translation, however, came out as "It won't leak in your pocket and make you pregnant." Frank Perdue's cute chicken slogan "It takes a strong man to make a tender chicken" didn't fare any better. It came out as "It takes an aroused man to make a chicken affectionate." And when American Airlines launched a "Fly in Leather" campaign to promote its leather seats in first class, the Mexican campaign stumbled just a bit. "Fly in Leather" (*vuela en cuero*), while literally correct, came out as "Fly Naked." I suppose that slogan did appeal to some (Archbold and Harmon 2001).

The Spanish market is so huge that it keeps enticing more companies to run marketing campaigns to reach it. The American Dairy Association made a hit in the United States with its humorous campaign, "Got Milk?" In Mexico, though, the Spanish translation read "Are you lactating?" All those mouths with white milk on them suddenly took on new meaning. Coors didn't fare any better. Their slogan, "Turn It Loose," was a hit in the United States, but in Spanish it came out as "Get Diarrhea."

A device that makes the sound of a flushing toilet? Apparently useless in the United States, but popular in Japan, this product illustrates cultural differences in marketing.

It isn't only Spanish that has given U.S. companies problems. Vicks decided to sell its cough drops in Germany. In German, the "v" is pronounced "f." Unfortunately, this made Vicks sound like the "f" word in English, which is just what ficks means in German.

Cultural mistakes are a two-way street, of course. Electrolux is a vacuum cleaner made in Sweden. Their cute slogan reads just fine in Swedish, but the translation for their U.S. ads came out as "Nothing sucks like an Electrolux."

Some businesspeople have managed to avoid such problems. They have seized profit opportunities in cultural differences. For example, Japanese women are embarrassed by the sounds they make in public toilets. To drown out the offensive sounds, they flush the toilet an average of 2.7 times a visit (Iori 1988). This wastes a lot of water, of course. Seeing this cultural trait as an opportunity, a U.S. entrepreneur developed a battery-powered device that is mounted in the toilet stall. When a woman activates the device, it emits a 25-second flushing sound. A toilet-sound duplicator may be useless in our culture, but the Japanese have bought thousands of them.

for your Consideration

1. Why do you think that it is often difficult to do business across cultures?
2. How can businesspeople avoid cross-cultural mistakes?
3. If a company offends a culture in which it is trying to do business, what should it do?

Summary *and* Review

Power, Authority, and Violence

How are authority and coercion related to power?

Authority is **power** that people view as legitimately exercised over them, while **coercion** is power they consider unjust. The **state** is a political entity that claims a monopoly on violence over some territory. P. 292.

What kinds of authority are there?

Max Weber identified three types of authority. In **traditional authority,** power derives from custom—patterns set down in the past serve as rules for the present. Power in **rational-legal authority** (also called *bureaucratic authority*) is based on law and written procedures. In **charismatic authority,** power is based on loyalty to an individual to whom people are attracted. Charismatic authority, which undermines traditional and rational-legal authority, has built-in problems in transferring authority to a new leader. Pp. 293–294.

Types of Government

How are the types of government related to power?

In a **monarchy,** power is based on hereditary rule; in a **democracy,** power is given to the ruler by citizens; and in a **dictatorship,** power is seized by an individual or small group. Pp. 294–296.

The U.S. Political System

What are the main characteristics of the U.S. political system?

The United States has two main political parties, each trying to win the center of the political spectrum. Voter turnout is higher among people who are more socially integrated, those who sense a greater stake in the outcome of elections, such as the more educated and well-to-do. **Lobbyists** and **special-interest groups,** such as **political action committees (PACs),** play a significant role in U.S. politics. Pp. 296–300.

Who Rules the United States?

Is the United States controlled by a ruling class?

In a view known as **pluralism,** functionalists say that no one group holds power, that the country's many competing interest groups balance one another. Conflict theorists, who focus on the top level of power, say that the United States is governed by a **power elite,** a ruling class made up of the top corporate, military, and political leaders. At this point, the matter is not settled. Pp. 300–302.

War and Terrorism: Ways of Implementing Political Objectives

How are war and terrorism related to politics?

War and **terrorism** are both means of attempting to accomplish political objectives. Timasheff identified three essential conditions of war and seven fuels that bring about war. His analysis can be applied to terrorism as well. Nuclear, biological, and chemical terrorism are major threats. One of the chief costs of war and terrorism is **dehumanization.** Pp. 302–304.

The Transformation of Economic Systems

How are economic systems linked to types of societies?

In the earliest societies (hunting and gathering), small groups lived off the land and produced little or no surplus. Economic systems grew more complex as people discovered how to domesticate animals and cultivate crops (pastoral and horticultural societies), farm (agricultural societies), and manufacture (industrial societies). As people produced a surplus, trade developed. Trade, in turn, brought social inequality as some people accumulated more than others. Service industries dominate the postindustrial societies. If a biotech society is emerging, it is too early to know its consequences. Pp. 304–312.

World Economic Systems

How do the major economic systems differ?

The world's two major economic systems are capitalism and socialism. In **capitalism,** private citizens own the means of production and pursue profits. In **socialism,** the state owns the means of production and has no goal of profit. Adherents of each have developed ideologies that defend their own system and portray the other as harmful. As expected from **convergence theory,** each system has adopted features of the other. Pp. 312–316.

Capitalism in a Global Economy

What is the role of the corporation in global capitalism?

The term **corporate capitalism** indicates that giant corporations dominate capitalism. The profit goal of **multinational corporations** removes their allegiance from any particular nation. The global expansion of capitalism due to new technology, accompanied by the trend toward larger economic and political unions, may indicate that a world political order is developing. This may bring world peace but perhaps at a high cost of personal freedom. Pp. 316–319.

Thinking Critically
about Chapter 11

1. What are the three sources of authority, and how do they differ from one another?
2. What global forces are affecting the U.S. economy? What consequences are they having? How might they affect your own life?
3. How can anyone say that the average U.S. worker hasn't gotten ahead in recent years, when the average hourly wage is so much larger than it used to be? What implications does this have for your own future?

Additional Resources

Companion Website www.ablongman.com/henslin

- Content Select Research Database for Sociology, with suggested key terms and annotated references
- Link to 2000 Census, with activities
- Flashcards of key terms and concepts

- Practice Tests
- Weblinks
- Interactive Maps

Where Can I Read More on This Topic?

Suggested readings for this chapter are listed at the back of this book.

Marriage and Family

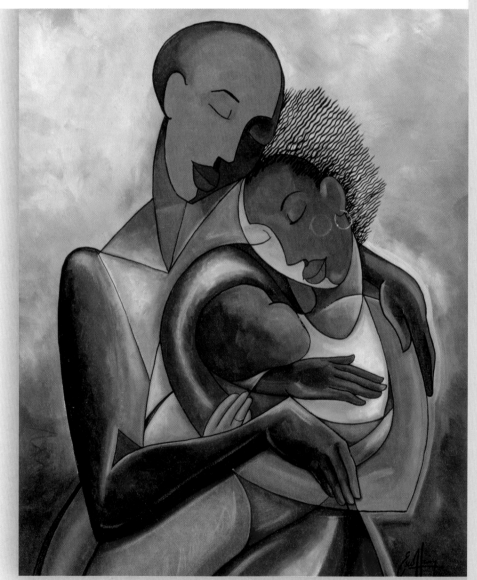

Michael Escoffery, *Circle of Love*, 1996

Marriage and Family in Global Perspective
What Is a Family?
Common Cultural Themes

Marriage and Family in Theoretical Perspective
The Functionalist Perspective
The Conflict Perspective
The Symbolic Interactionist
    Perspective

The Family Life Cycle
Love and Courtship in Global
    Perspective
Marriage
Childbirth and Child Rearing
Family Transitions in Later Life

Diversity in U.S. Families
African American Families
Latino Families
Asian American Families
Native American Families
Single-Parent Families
Families Without Children
Blended Families
Gay and Lesbian Families

Trends in U.S. Families
Postponing Marriage and Childbirth
Cohabitation
Unmarried Mothers
Grandparents as Parents
The Sandwich Generation and
    Elder Care

Divorce and Remarriage
Problems in Measuring Divorce
Children of Divorce
Grandchildren of Divorce
The Absent Father and Serial
    Fatherhood
The Ex-Spouses
Remarriage

Two Sides of Family Life
The Dark Side of Family Life:
    Battering, Child Abuse, and
    Incest
The Bright Side of Family Life:
    Successful Marriages

The Future of Marriage and Family

Summary and Review

"Hold still. We're going to be late," said Sharon as she tried to put shoes on 2-year-old Michael, who kept squirming away.

Finally succeeding with the shoes, Sharon turned to 4-year-old Brittany, who was trying to pull a brush through her hair. "It's stuck, Mom," Brittany said.

"Well, no wonder. Just how did you get gum in your hair? I don't have time for this, Brittany. We've got to leave."

Getting to the van fifteen minutes behind schedule, Sharon strapped the kids in and then herself. Just as she was about to pull away, she remembered that she had not checked the fridge for messages.

"Just a minute, kids. I'll be right back."

Running into the house, she frantically searched for a note from Tom. She vaguely remembered his mumbling something about being held over at work. She grabbed the Post-it and ran back to the van.

"He's picking on me," complained Brittany when her mother climbed back in.

"Oh, shut up, Brittany. He's only 2. He can't pick on you."

"Yes, he did," Brittany said, crossing her arms defiantly, as she stretched out her foot to kick her brother's seat.

"Oh, no! How did Mikey get that smudge on his face? Did you do that, Brit?"

> **"Yes, he did," Brittany said, crossing her arms defiantly as she stretched out her foot to kick her brother's seat.**

Brittany crossed her arms again, pushing out her lips in her classic pouting pose.

As Sharon drove to the day care center, she tried to calm herself. "Only two more days of work this week, and then the weekend. Then I can catch up on house-work and have a little relaxed time with the kids. And Tom can finally cut the lawn and buy the gro-ceries," she thought. "And maybe we'll even have time to make love. Boy, that's been a long time."

At a traffic light, Sharon found time to read Tom's note.

"Oh, no. That's what he meant. He has to work Saturday. Well, there go those plans."

What Sharon didn't know was that her boss had also made plans for Sharon's Saturday. And that their emergency Saturday babysitter wouldn't be available. And that Michael was coming down with the flu. And that Brittany would get it next. And that . . .

Marriage and Family in Global Perspective

To better understand U.S. patterns of marriage and family, let's first look at how customs differ around the world. This will give us a context for interpreting our own experiences in this vital social institution.

What Is a Family?

"What is a family, anyway?" asked William Sayres at the beginning of an article on this topic. In posing this question, Sayres (1992) meant that although the family is so significant to humanity that it is universal—every human group in the world organizes its members in families—the world's cultures display so much variety that the term *family* is difficult to define. For example, although the Western world regards a family as a husband, wife, and children, other groups have family forms in which men have more than one wife (**polygyny**) or women more than one husband (**polyandry**). How about the obvious? Can we define the family as the approved group into which children are born? Then we would be overlooking the Banaro of New Guinea. In this group, a young woman must give birth before she can marry—and she *cannot* marry the father of her child (Murdock 1949).

And so it goes. For just about every element you might regard as essential to marriage or family, some group has a different custom. Consider the sex of the bride and groom. Although in almost every instance the bride and groom are female and male, there are exceptions. In some Native American tribes, a man or woman who wanted to be a member of the opposite sex went through a ceremony (*berdache*) that officially *declared* their change in sex. Not only did the "new" man or woman do the tasks associated with his or her new sex but also the individual was allowed to marry. In this instance, the husband and wife were of the same biological sex. In the 1980s, several European countries legalized same-sex marriages. In 2003, so did Canada, followed by the state of Massachusetts in 2004.

Such remarkable variety means that we have to settle for a broad definition. A **family** consists of people who consider themselves related by blood, marriage, or adoption. A **household,** in contrast, consists of people who occupy the same housing unit—a house, apartment, or other living quarters.

We can classify families as **nuclear** (husband, wife, and children) and **extended** (including people such as grandparents, aunts, uncles, and cousins in addition to the nuclear

Often one of the strongest family bonds is that of mother–daughter. The young artist, an eleventh grader, wrote: "This painting expresses the way I feel about my future with my child. I want my child to be happy and I want her to love me the same way I love her. In that way we will have a good relationship so that nobody will be able to take us apart. I wanted this picture to be alive; that is why I used a lot of bright colors."

unit). Sociologists also refer to the **family of orientation** (the family in which an individual grows up) and the **family of procreation** (the family that is formed when a couple have their first child). Finally, regardless of its form, **marriage** can be viewed as a group's approved mating arrangements—usually marked by a ritual of some sort (the wedding) to indicate the couple's new public status.

Common Cultural Themes

Despite this diversity, several common themes run through the concepts of marriage and family. As Table 12.1 illustrates, all societies use marriage and family to establish patterns of mate selection, descent, inheritance, and authority. Let's look at these patterns.

Mate Selection. Each human group establishes norms to govern who marries whom. If a group has norms of **endogamy,** it specifies that its members must marry *within*

Table 12.1 **Common Cultural Themes: Marriage in Traditional and Industrialized Societies**

Characteristic	Traditional Societies	Industrial (and Postindustrial) Societies
What is the structure of marriage?	*Extended* (marriage embeds spouses in a large kinship network of explicit obligations)	*Nuclear* (marriage brings fewer obligations toward the spouse's relatives)
What are the functions of marriage?	Encompassing (see the six functions listed on p. 326)	More limited (many functions are fulfilled by other social institutions)
Who holds authority?	*Patriarchal* (authority is held by males)	Although some patriarchal features remain, authority is divided more equally
How many spouses at one time?	Most have one spouse (*monogamy*), while some have several (*polygamy*)	One spouse
Who selects the spouse?	Parents, usually the father, select the spouse	Individuals choose their own spouse
Where does the couple live?	Couples usually reside with the groom's family (*patrilocal residence*), less commonly with the bride's family (*matrilocal residence*)	Couples establish a new home (*neolocal residence*)
How is descent figured?	Usually figured from male ancestors (*patrilineal kinship*), less commonly from female ancestors (*matrilineal kinship*)	Figured from male and female ancestors equally (*bilineal kinship*)
How is inheritance figured?	Rigid system of rules; usually patrilineal, but can be matrilineal	Highly individualistic; usually bilineal

their group. For example, some groups prohibit interracial marriage. In some societies, these norms are written into law, but in most cases they are informal. In the United States most whites marry whites and most African Americans marry African Americans—not because of any laws but because of informal norms. In contrast, norms of **exogamy** specify that people must marry *outside* their group. The best example of exogamy is the **incest taboo,** which prohibits sex and marriage among designated relatives.

Descent.   How are you related to your father's father or to your mother's mother? The answer to this question is not the same all over the world. Each society has a **system of descent,** the way people trace kinship over generations. We use a **bilineal system,** for we think of ourselves as related to *both* our mother's and our father's sides of the family. "Doesn't everyone?" you might ask. Ours, however, is only one logical way to reckon descent. Some groups use a **patrilineal system,** tracing descent only on the father's side; they don't think of children as being related to their mother's relatives. Others follow a **matrilineal system,** tracing descent only on the mother's side, and not considering children to be related to their

father's relatives. The Naxi of China, for example, don't even have a word for father (Hong 1999).

Inheritance.   Marriage and family—in whatever form is customary in a society—are also used to compute rights of inheritance. In a bilineal system, property is passed to both males and females; in a patrilineal system, only to males; and in a matrilineal system (the rarest form), only to females. No system is natural. Rather, each matches a group's ideas of what is reasonable and just.

Authority.   Historically, some form of **patriarchy,** a social system in which men dominate women, has formed a thread that runs through all societies. Contrary to what some think, there are no historical records of a true **matriarchy,** a social system in which women as a group dominate men as a group. Our marriage and family customs, then, developed within a framework of patriarchy. Although U.S. family patterns are becoming more **egalitarian,** or equal, many of today's customs still reflect their patriarchal origin. One of the most obvious examples is U.S. naming patterns. Despite some changes, the typical bride still takes the groom's last name, and children usually receive the father's last name.

Marriage and Family in Theoretical Perspective

Around the world human groups have chosen many forms of mate selection, numerous ways to trace descent, and a variety of ways to view the parent's responsibility. Although these patterns are arbitrary, each group perceives its own forms of marriage and family as natural. Now let's see what picture emerges when we apply the three sociological perspectives.

The Functionalist Perspective: Functions and Dysfunctions

Functionalists stress that to survive, a society must fulfill basic functions (that is, meet its basic needs). When functionalists look at marriage and family, they examine how they are related to other parts of society, especially the ways they contribute to the well-being of society.

Why the Family Is Universal. Although the form of marriage and family varies from one group to another, the family is universal. The reason for this, say functionalists, is that the family fulfills six needs that are basic to the survival of every society. These needs, or functions, are (1) economic production, (2) socialization of children, (3) care of the sick and aged, (4) recreation, (5) sexual control, and (6) reproduction. To make certain that these functions are performed, every human group has adopted some form of the family.

Functions of the Incest Taboo. Functionalists note that the incest taboo helps families to avoid *role confusion*. This, in turn, facilitates the socialization of children. For example, if father-daughter incest were allowed, how should a wife treat her daughter—as a daughter, as a subservient second wife, or even as a rival? Should the daughter consider her mother as a mother, as the first wife, or as a rival? Would her father be a father or a lover? And would the wife be the husband's main wife, a secondary wife—or even the "mother of the other wife" (whatever role that might be)? And if the daughter had a child by her father, what relationships would everyone have? Maternal incest would lead to complications every bit as confusing as these.

The incest taboo also forces people to look outside the family for marriage partners. Anthropologists theorize that *exogamy* was especially functional in tribal societies, for it forged alliances between tribes that otherwise might have killed each other off. Today, exogamy still extends a bride's

This January 1937 photo from Sneedville, Tennesse, shows Eunice Johns, age 9, and her husband, Charlie Johns, age 22. The groom gave his wife a doll as a wedding gift. The new husband and wife planned to build a cabin and, as Charlie Johns phrased it, "go to housekeepin.'" Is this an example of gender age as symbolic interactionists might say? Or, as conflict theorists would say, of gender exploitation?

and groom's social networks beyond their nuclear family by adding and building relationships with their spouse's family and friends.

Isolation and Emotional Overload. As you know, functionalists also analyze dysfunctions. One of those dysfunctions comes from the relative isolation of today's nuclear family. Because extended families are enmeshed in large kinship networks, their members can count on many people for material and emotional support. In nuclear families, in contrast, the stresses that come with crises such as the loss of a job—or even the routine pressures of a harried life, as depicted in our opening vignette—are spread among fewer people. This places greater strain on each family member, creating *emotional overload*. In addition, the relative isolation of the nuclear family makes it vulnerable to a "dark side"—incest and various other forms of abuse, matters that we examine later in this chapter.

The Conflict Perspective: Gender and Power

As you recall, central to conflict theory is the struggle over power. In marriage, the power of wives has been increasing. Wives are contributing more of the income *and* making more of the marital decisions than they used to (Rogers and Amato 2000). Husbands and wives maneuver for power in many areas, but owing to space limitations, let's focus on housework.

The Power Struggle over Housework. Most men resist doing housework, and fairly successfully so. Even wives who work outside the home full time do considerably more housework than their husbands (Lee and Waite 2005). As you can see from Figure 12.1, wives who spend 40 hours a week working for wages put in an average of 7-1/2 more hours doing housework each week than their husbands. If we include child care, the total may come closer to 11 hours a week (Bianchi and Spain 1996). *Incredibly, this is the equivalent of seventy-two 8-hour days a year.*

Sociologist Arlie Hochschild (1989) calls this the working wife's "second shift." To stress the one-sided nature of the second shift, she quotes this satire by Garry Trudeau in the *Doonesbury* comic strip:

> **A "liberated" father is sitting at his word processor writing a book about raising his child. He types, "Today I wake up with a heavy day of work ahead of me. As Joanie gets Jeffrey ready for day care, I ask her if I can be relieved of my usual household responsibilities for the day. Joanie says, 'Sure, I'll make up the five minutes somewhere.'"**

Not surprisingly, the burden of the second shift creates discontent among wives (Amato et al. 2003). These problems, as well as how wives and husbands cope with them, are discussed in the following Thinking Critically section.

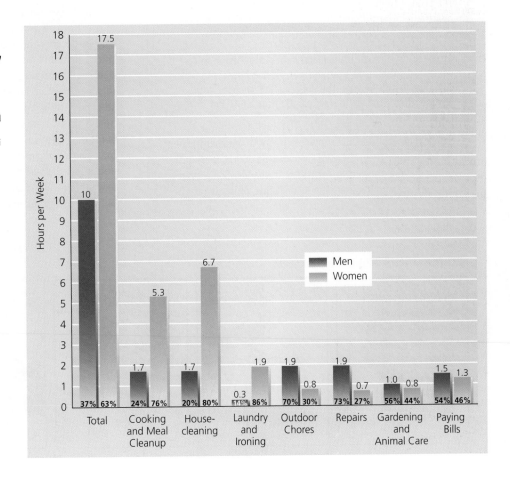

Figure 12.1 In Two-Paycheck Marriages, Who Does the Housework?

Note: Based on a national sample. Cooking and meal cleanup are combined from the original data.
Source: By the author. Based on Bianchi et al. 2000:Table 1.

Thinking Critically

The Second Shift—Strains and Strategies

To find out what life is like in two-paycheck marriages, sociologist Arlie Hochschild (1989) and her research associates interviewed and reinterviewed over fifty families over the span of nine years. Hochschild also did participant observation with a dozen of them. She "shopped with them, visited friends, watched television, ate with them, and came along when they took their children to day care."

Although men are doing more housework today than they did just a few years ago (Bianchi et al. 2000), most men feel that the *second shift*—the household duties that follow the day's work for pay—is the wife's responsibility. They tend to see themselves as "helping out." But as the wives cook, clean, and take care of the children after their job at the office or factory, many feel tired, emotionally drained, and resentful. Not uncommonly, these feelings show up in the bedroom, where the wives show a lack of interest in sex.

The strains from working the second shift affect not only the marital relationship but also the wife's self-concept. Here is how one woman tried to lift her flagging self-esteem:

> After taking time off for her first baby, Carol Alston felt depressed, "fat," and that she was "just a housewife." For a while she became the supermarket shopper who wanted to call down the aisles, "I'm an MBA! I'm an MBA!"

Some wives feel that it is hopeless to try to get their husbands to change. They work the second shift, but they resent it. Others have a showdown with their husbands. Some even give an ultimatum: "It's share the second shift, or it's divorce." Still others try to be the "supermom" who can do it all.

Some men cooperate and cut down on their commitment to a career. Others cut back on movies, seeing friends, doing hobbies. Most men, however, engage in what Hochschild describes as *strategies of resistance*. She identified the following:

- *Waiting it out.* Many men never volunteer to do housework. Since many wives dislike asking, because it feels like "begging," this strategy often works. Some men make this strategy even more effective by showing irritation or becoming glum when they are asked, which discourages the wife from asking again.
- *Playing dumb.* When they do housework, some men become incompetent. They can't cook rice without burning it; when they go to the store, they forget grocery lists; they never can remember where the broiler pan is. Hochschild did not claim that husbands do these things on purpose, but, rather, by withdrawing their mental attention from the task, they "get credit for trying and being a good sport"—but in such a way that they are not chosen next time.
- *Needs reduction.* An example of this strategy is the father of two who explained that he never shopped because he didn't "need anything." He didn't need to iron his clothes because he "[didn't] mind wearing a wrinkled shirt." He didn't need to cook because "cereal is fine." As Hochschild observed, "Through his reduction of needs, this man created a great void into which his wife stepped with her 'greater need' to see him wear an ironed shirt . . . and cook his dinner."
- *Substitute offerings.* Expressing appreciation to the wife for being so organized that she can handle both work for wages and the second shift at home can be a substitute for helping—and a subtle encouragement for her to keep on working the second shift.

ARLO & JANIS ® by Jimmy Johnson

The cartoonist has beautifully captured the reduction of needs strategy discussed by Hochschild.

The Symbolic Interactionist Perspective: Gender and Housework

As was noted in Chapter 1, symbolic interactionists focus on the meanings that people give their experiences. Let's apply this perspective to some surprising findings about husbands and housework.

The first finding is probably what you expect: The closer a husband and wife's earnings, the more likely they are to share housework. Although husbands in such marriages don't share housework equally, they share more than other husbands. This finding, however, may be surprising:

In Hindu marriages, the roles of husband and wife are firmly established. Neither this woman, whom I photographed in Chittoor, India, nor her husband question whether she should carry the family wash to the village pump. Women here have done this task for millennia. As India industrializes, as happened in the West, who does the wash will be questioned—and may eventually become a source of strain in marriage.

When husbands get laid off, most do *less* housework than before. *And husbands who earn less than their wives do the least housework.*

How can we explain this? It would seem that husbands who get laid off or who earn less than their wives would want to balance things out by doing more around the house, not less. Researchers suggest that the key is gender role. If a wife earns more than her husband, it threatens his masculinity—he takes it as a sign that he is failing in his traditional gender role of provider. To do housework—"women's work" in his eyes—threatens it even further. By avoiding housework, he "reclaims" his masculinity (Hochschild 1989; Brines 1994).

The Family Life Cycle

We have seen how the forms of marriage and family vary widely, and we have examined marriage and family from the three sociological perspectives. Now let's discuss love, courtship, and the family life cycle.

Love and Courtship in Global Perspective

Until recently, social scientists thought that romantic love originated in western Europe during the medieval period (Mount 1992). When anthropologists William Jankowiak and Edward Fischer (1992) surveyed the data available on 166 societies around the world, however, they found that this was not so. **Romantic love**—people being sexually attracted to one another and idealizing each other—showed up in 88 percent (147) of these groups. The role of love, however, differs sharply from one society to another. As the Cultural Diversity box on the next page details, for example, Indians don't expect love to occur until *after* marriage.

Because love plays such a significant role in Western life—and often is regarded as the *only* proper basis for marriage—social scientists have probed this concept with the tools of the trade: experiments, questionnaires, interviews, and observations. In a fascinating experiment, psychologists Donald Dutton and Arthur Aron discovered that fear breeds romantic love (Rubin 1985). Here's what they did.

About 230 feet above the Capilano River in North Vancouver, British Columbia, a rickety footbridge sways in the wind. It makes you feel like you won't make it across, that you might fall into the rocky gorge below. A more solid

Cultural Diversity *around the* World

East Is East and West Is West: Love and Arranged Marriage in India

AFTER ARUN BHARAT RAM RETURNED to India with a degree from the University of Michigan, his mother announced that she wanted to find him a wife. Arun would be a good catch anywhere: 27 years old, educated, well mannered, intelligent, handsome—and, not incidentally, heir to a huge fortune.

Arun's mother already had someone in mind. Manju came from a middle-class family and was a college graduate. Arun and Manju met in a coffee shop at a luxury hotel—along with both sets of parents. He found her pretty and quiet. He liked that. She was impressed that he didn't boast about his background.

After four more meetings, including one at which the two young people met by themselves, the parents asked their children whether they were willing to marry. Neither had any major objections.

The Prime Minister of India and fifteen hundred other guests came to the wedding.

"I didn't love him," Manju says. "But when we talked, we had a lot in common." She then adds, "But now I couldn't live without him. I've never thought of another man since I met him."

This billboard in Chennai, India, caught my attention. As the text indicates, even though India is industrializing, most of its people still follow traditional customs. This billboard is a sign of changing times.

Although India has undergone extensive social change, Indian sociologists estimate that parents still arrange 90 to 95 percent of marriages. Today, however, as with Arun and Manju, couples have veto power over their parents' selection. Another innovation is that the prospective bride and groom are allowed to talk to each other before the wedding—unheard of just a generation ago.

Why do Indians have arranged marriages? And why does this practice persist today, even among the educated and upper classes? We can also ask why the United States has such an individualistic approach to marriage.

The answers to these questions take us to two sociological principles. First, *a group's marriage practices match its values*. Individual mate selection matches U.S. values of individuality and independence, while arranged marriages match the Indian value of children deferring to parental authority. To Indians, allowing unrestricted dating would mean entrusting important matters to inexperienced young people.

Second, *a group's marriage practices match its patterns of social stratification*. Arranged marriages in India affirm caste lines by channeling marriage within the same caste. Unchaperoned dating would encourage premarital sex, which, in turn, would break down family lines. Virginity at marriage, in contrast, assures the upper castes that they know the fatherhood of the children. Consequently, Indians socialize their children to think that parents have superior wisdom in these matters. In the United States, where family lines are less important and caste is an alien concept, the practice of young people choosing their own dating partners mirrors the relative openness of our social class system.

These different backgrounds have produced contrasting ideas of love. Americans idealize love as being mysterious, a passion that suddenly seizes an individual. Indians view love as a peaceful feeling that develops when a man and a woman are united in intimacy and share common interests and goals in life. For Americans, love just "happens," while Indians think of love as something that can be created between two people by arranging the right conditions. Marriage is one of those right conditions.

The end result is this startling difference: *For Americans, love produces marriage—while for Indians, marriage produces love.*

Sources: Based on Gupta 1979; Bumiller 1992; Sprecher and Chandak 1992; Dugger 1998; Gautham 2002; Derne 2003; Easley 2003, Berger 2004.

for your Consideration

What advantages do you see to the Indian approach to love and marriage? Do you think that the Indian system could work in the United States? Why or why not? Do you think that love can be created? Or does love suddenly "seize" people? What do you think love is?

footbridge crosses only ten feet above a shallow stream. The experimenters had an attractive woman approach men who were crossing these bridges. She told them she was studying "the effects of exposure to scenic attractions on creative expression." She showed them a picture, and they wrote down their associations. The sexual imagery in their stories showed that the men on the unsteady, frightening bridge were more sexually aroused than were the men on the solid bridge. More of these men also called the young woman afterward—supposedly to get information about the study.

You may have noticed that this research was really about sexual attraction, not love. The point, however, is that romantic love usually begins with sexual attraction. Finding ourselves sexually attracted to someone, we spend time with that person. If we discover mutual interests, we may label our feelings "love." Apparently, then, *romantic love has two components.* The first is emotional, a feeling of sexual attraction. The second is cognitive, a label that we attach to our feelings. If we attach this label, we describe ourselves as being "in love."

Marriage

In the typical case, marriage in the United States is preceded by "love," but contrary to folklore, whatever love is, it certainly is not blind. That is, love does not hit anyone willy-nilly, as if Cupid had shot darts blindly into a crowd. If it did, marital patterns would be unpredictable. An examination of who marries whom, however, reveals that love is socially channeled.

The Social Channels of Love and Marriage. The most highly predictable social channels are age, education, social class, and race-ethnicity. For example, a Latina with a college degree whose parents are both physicians is likely to fall in love with and marry a Latino slightly older than herself who has graduated from college. Similarly, a female high school dropout whose parents are on welfare is likely to fall in love with and marry a man who comes from a background similar to hers.

Sociologists use the term **homogamy** to refer to the tendency of people who have similar characteristics to marry one another. Homogamy occurs largely as a result of *propinquity,* or spatial nearness. That is, we tend to "fall in love" with and marry people who live near us or whom we meet at school, church, or work. The people with whom we associate are far from a random sample of the population, for social filters produce neighborhoods, schools, and places of worship that follow racial-ethnic and social class lines.

As with all social patterns, there are exceptions. Although 93 percent of Americans who marry choose someone of their same racial-ethnic background, 7 percent do not. Because there are 60 million married couples in the United States, those 7 percent add up, totaling 4 million couples (*Statistical Abstract* 2005:Table 52).

One of the more dramatic changes in U.S. marriage patterns is a sharp increase in marriages between African Americans and whites. Today it is difficult to realize how norm shattering such marriages are, but in some states they used to be illegal and carry a jail sentence. In Mississippi, the penalty for interracial marriage was life in prison (Crossen 2004b). There always have been a few couples who crossed the "color line," but the social upheaval of the 1960s broke this barrier permanently.

Figure 12.2 illustrates this increase. The consistent pattern in the background of the husbands and wives illustrates that here, too, Cupid's arrows are far from random. If you look closely, you can see a change that has begun to emerge in this pattern: Marriages between African American women and white men are now increasing faster than those between African American men and white women.

Figure 12.2 Marriages Between Whites and African Americans: The Race-Ethnicity of the Husbands and Wives

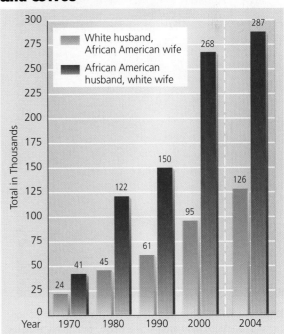

Source: By the author. Based on *Statistical Abstract* 1990:Table 53; 2006:Table 54.

Childbirth and Child Rearing

Contrary to what you might expect, today's parents are spending *more* time with their children than parents did in the 1970s and 1980s. This is true of both mothers and fathers (Sayer, Cohen, and Casper 2004). How can this be, especially since more mothers are working outside the home? Since there are still only 24 hours in a day, you might assume that the parents are giving something up—either sleep or something else. This, it turns out, is exactly right—and it isn't sleep. The parents are doing less cooking and housework than they used to. They are buying more "instant" foods and prepared meals, and some are hiring cleaning services. It is also possible that they have become less fussy about how the house looks.

Despite this new trend, with mothers and fathers spending so many hours away from home at work, we must ask: Who's minding the kids while the parents are at work?

Married Couples and Single Mothers.   Figure 12.3 on the next page compares the child care arrangements of married couples and single mothers. As you can see, their overall arrangements are similar. A main difference is the

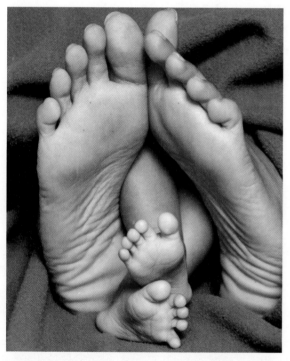

No adequate substitute has been found for the family. Although its form and functions vary around the world, the family remains the primary socializer of children.

role of the child's father while the mother is at work. For married couples, about one of five children is cared for by the father, while for single mothers, care by the father drops to one of ten. As you can see, grandparents help to fill the gap left by the absent father. Single mothers also rely more on organized day care.

Day Care.   Figure 12.3 also shows that about one of four children is in day care. The broad conclusions of research on day care were reported in Chapter 3 (page 73). Apparently only a minority of U.S. day care centers offer high-quality care as measured by stimulating learning activities, safety, and emotional warmth (Bergmann 1995; Blau 2000). A primary reason for this dismal situation is the low salaries paid to day care workers, who average only about $15,000 a year (*Statistical Abstract* 2005:Table 556, adjusted for inflation).

It is difficult for parents to judge the quality of day care, since they don't know what takes place when they are not there. If you ever look for day care, however, these two factors best predict that children will receive quality care: staff who have taken courses in early childhood development and a low ratio of children per staff member (Blau 2000). If you have nagging fears that your children might be neglected or even abused, choose a center that streams live Web cam images on the Internet. While at work, you can "visit" each room of the day care center via cyberspace, and monitor your toddler's activities and care.

Nannies.   For upper-middle-class parents, nannies have become a popular alternative to day care centers. Parents love the one-on-one care. They also like the convenience of in-home care, which eliminates the need to transport the child to an unfamiliar environment, reduces the chances of their child catching illnesses, and eliminates the hardship of parents having to take time off from work when their child becomes ill. A recurring problem, however, is tensions between the parents and the nanny: jealousy that the nanny might see the first step, hear the first word, or—worse yet—be called "mommy." There are also tensions over different discipline styles; disdain on the part of the nanny that the mother isn't staying home with her child; and feelings of guilt or envy as the child cries when the nanny leaves but not when the mother goes to work.

Social Class.   Social class makes a huge difference in child rearing. If you thought about it, you'd probably guess that people's views on how children develop would affect their child-rearing practices. Sociologists have found this to be true—and that the working and middle classes hold different views of how children develop (Lareau 2002). Working-class parents think of children as wild flowers

Figure 12.3 **Who Takes Care of Preschoolers While Their Mothers Are at Work?**

Source: *America's Children* 2005: Table POP8.B.

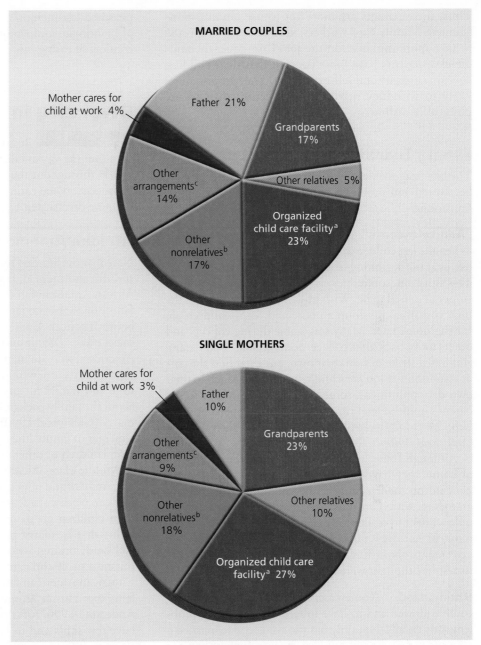

MARRIED COUPLES

Mother cares for child at work 4%

Father 21%

Grandparents 17%

Other relatives 5%

Other arrangements[c] 14%

Organized child care facility[a] 23%

Other nonrelatives[b] 17%

SINGLE MOTHERS

Mother cares for child at work 3%

Father 10%

Grandparents 23%

Other arrangements[c] 9%

Other relatives 10%

Other nonrelatives[b] 18%

Organized child care facility[a] 27%

[a]Includes in-home babysitters and other non-relatives providing care in either the child's or the provider's home.
[b]Includes self-care and no regular arrangements
[c]Includes daycare center, nursery schools, preschools, and Head start programs.

that develop naturally, while middle-class parents think of children as garden flowers that need a lot of nurturing if they are to bloom. Consequently, working-class parents set limits on their children and then let them choose their own activities. Middle-class parents, in contrast, try to involve their children in leisure activities that they think will develop the children's thinking and social skills.

Sociologist Melvin Kohn (1963, 1977; Kohn and Schooler 1969) also found that the type of work that parents do has an impact on how they rear their children. Because members of the working class are closely supervised on their jobs, where they are expected to follow explicit rules, their concern is less with their children's motivation and more with their outward conformity.

Thus, these parents are more apt to use physical punishment. Middle-class workers, in contrast, are expected to take more initiative on the job. Consequently, middle-class parents have more concern that their children develop curiosity and self-expression. They are also more likely to withdraw privileges or affection than to use physical punishment.

Family Transitions in Later Life

The later stages of family life bring their own pleasures to be savored and problems to be solved. Let's look at two transitions.

"Adultolescents" and the Not-So-Empty Nest. When the last child leaves home, the husband and wife are left, as at the beginning of their marriage, "alone together." This situation, sometimes called the empty nest, is not as empty as it used to be. With prolonged education and the high cost of establishing a household, U.S. children are leaving home later. Many stay home during college, and others move back after college. Some (called "boomerang children") strike out on their own, but then find the cost or responsibility too great and return home. Much to their own disappointment, some even leave and return to the parent's home several times. As a result, 42 percent of all U.S. 24- to 29-year-olds are living with their parents (*Statistical Abstract* 2000:Tables 12, 70).

Although these "adultolescents" enjoy the protection of home, they have to work out issues of remaining dependent on their parents at the same time that they are grappling with concerns and fears about establishing independent lives. For the parents, "boomerang children" result in not only a disruption of routines but also disagreements about turf, authority, and responsibilities—issues they thought were long ago resolved.

Widowhood. Women are more likely than men to become widowed and to have to face the wrenching problems this entails. Not only has the average wife married a man older than herself but also she lives longer than her husband. The death of a spouse tears at the self, clawing at identities that had merged through the years. When the one who had become an essential part of the self is gone, the survivor is forced to wrestle with the perplexing question "Who am I?"

When death is unexpected, the adjustment is more difficult (Hiltz 1989). Survivors who know that death is impending make preparations that smooth the transition—from arranging finances to psychologically preparing themselves for being alone. Saying goodbye and cultivating treasured last memories help them to adjust to the death of an intimate companion. Sudden death does not offer the comfort of easing into the loss.

Diversity in U.S. Families

It is important to note that there is no such thing as *the* American family. Rather, family life varies widely throughout the United States. The significance of social class, noted earlier, will continue to be evident as we examine diversity in U.S. families.

African American Families

Note that the heading reads African American *families,* not *the* African American family. There is no such thing as *the* African American family any more than there is *the* white family or *the* Latino family. The primary distinction is not between African Americans and other groups, but between social classes (Willie and Reddick 2003). Because African Americans who are members of the upper class follow the class interests reviewed in Chapter 8—preservation of privilege and family fortune—they are especially concerned about the family background of those whom their children marry (Gatewood 1990). To them, marriage is viewed as a merger of family lines. Children of this class marry later than children of other classes.

Middle-class African American families focus on achievement and respectability. Both husband and wife are likely to work outside the home. A central concern is that their children go to college, get good jobs, and marry well—that is, marry people like themselves, respectable and hardworking, who want to get ahead in school and pursue a successful career.

African American families in poverty face all the problems that cluster around poverty (Wilson 1987, 1996; Anderson 1990/2006). Because the men are likely to have few skills and to be unemployed, it is difficult for them to fulfill the cultural roles of husband and father. Consequently, these families are likely to be headed by a woman and also to have a high rate of births to single women. Divorce and desertion are also more common than among other classes. Sharing scarce resources and "stretching kinship" are primary survival mechanisms. That is, people who have helped out in hard times are considered brothers, sisters, or cousins to whom one owes obligations as though they were blood relatives (Stack 1974). Sociologists use the term *fictive kin* to refer to this stretching of kinship.

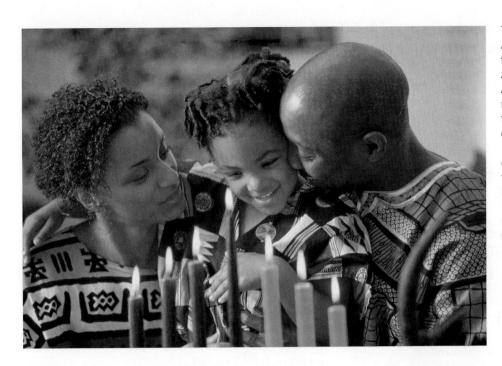

There is no such thing as *the* African American family, any more than there is *the* Native American, Asian American, Latino, or Irish American family. Rather, each racial-ethnic group has different types of families, the primary determinant being social class.

This African American family is observing Kwanzaa, a relatively new festival, that celebrates African heritage. Can you explain how Kwanzaa is an example of *ethnic work*, a concept introduced in Chapter 9?

From Figure 12.4, (on the next page) you can see that, compared with other groups, African American families are the least likely to be headed by married couples and the most likely to be headed by women. Because African American women tend to go farther in school than African American men, they are more likely than women in other racial-ethnic groups to marry men who are less educated than themselves (South 1991; Eshleman 2000).

Latino Families

As Figure 12.4 shows, the proportion of Latino families headed by married couples and women falls in between that of whites and African Americans. The effects of social class on families, which I just sketched, also apply to Latinos. In addition, families differ by country of origin. Families from Mexico, for example, are more likely to be headed by a married couple than are families from Puerto Rico (*Statistical Abstract* 2005: Table 40). The longer that Latinos have lived in the United States, the more their families resemble those of middle-class Americans (Saenz 2004).

Although there is no such thing as *the* Latino family, in general, Latinos place high emphasis on extended family relationships.

With such a wide variety, experts disagree on what distinguishes Latino families. Some point to the Spanish language, the Roman Catholic religion, and a strong family orientation coupled with a disapproval of divorce. Others add that Latinos emphasize loyalty to the extended family, with an obligation to support the extended family in times of need (Cauce and Domenech-Rodriguez 2002). Descriptions of Latino families used to include **machismo**—an emphasis on male strength, sexual vigor, and dominance—but current studies show that *machismo* now characterizes only a small proportion of

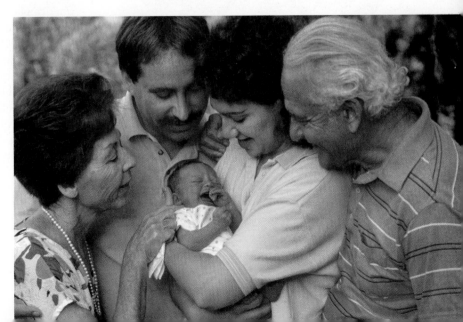

Latino husband-fathers (Torres, Solberg, and Carlstrom 2002). *Machismo* apparently decreases with each generation in the United States (Hurtado et al. 1992; Wood 2001). Some researchers have found that the husband-father plays a stronger role than in either white or African American families (Vega 1990; Torres et al. 2002). Apparently, the wife-mother is usually more family-centered than her husband, displaying more warmth and affection for her children

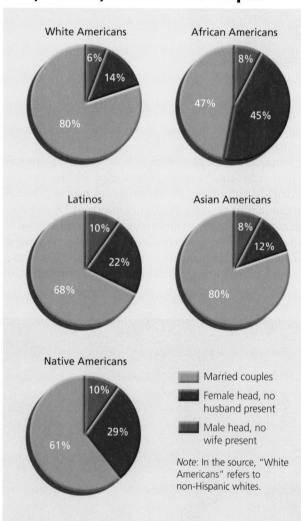

Figure 12.4 **Family Structure: The Percentage of U.S. Families Headed by Men, Women, and Married Couples**

White Americans
6%
14%
80%

African Americans
8%
45%
47%

Latinos
10%
22%
68%

Asian Americans
8%
12%
80%

Native Americans
10%
29%
61%

■ Married couples
■ Female head, no husband present
■ Male head, no wife present

Note: In the source, "White Americans" refers to non-Hispanic whites.

Sources: By the author. Based on "American Community . . ." 2004; *Statistical Abstract* 2005:Tables 33, 38, 40.

It is difficult to draw generalizations because, as with other racial-ethnic groups, individual Latino families vary considerably (Contreras, Kerns, and Neal-Barnett 2002). Some Latino families, for example, have acculturated to such an extent that they are Protestants who do not speak Spanish.

Asian American Families

As you can see from Figure 12.4, the structure of Asian American families is almost identical to that of white families. As with other racial-ethnic groups, family life also reflects social class. In addition, because Asian Americans emigrated from many different countries, their family life reflects those many cultures. As with Latino families, the more recent their immigration, the more closely their family life reflects the patterns in their country of origin (Kibria 1993; Glenn 1994).

Despite such differences, sociologist Bob Suzuki (1985), who studied Chinese American and Japanese American families, identified several distinctive characteristics of Asian American families. Although Asian Americans have adopted the nuclear family structure, they have retained Confucian values that provide a distinct framework for family life: humanism, collectivity, self-discipline, hierarchy, respect for the elderly, moderation, and obligation. Obligation means that each member of a family owes respect to other family members and is responsible never to bring shame on the family. Asian Americans tend to be more permissive than Anglos in child rearing. To control their children, they are more likely to use shame and guilt rather than physical punishment.

Native American Families

Perhaps the single most significant issue that Native American families face is whether to follow traditional values or to assimilate into the dominant culture (Yellowbird and Snipp 1994). This primary distinction creates vast differences among families. The traditionals speak native languages and emphasize distinctive Native American values and beliefs. Those who have assimilated into the broader culture do not.

Figure 12.4 depicts the structure of Native American families. You can see how it is almost identical to that of Latinos. In general, Native American parents are permissive with their children and avoid physical punishment. Elders play a much more active role in their children's families than they do in most U.S. families: Elders, especially grandparents, not only provide child care but also teach and discipline children. Like others, Native American families differ by social class.

To search for *the* Native American family would be fruitless. There are rural, urban, single-parent, extended, nuclear, rich, poor, traditional, and assimilated Native American families, to name just a few. Shown here is a traditional Navaho family in Utah.

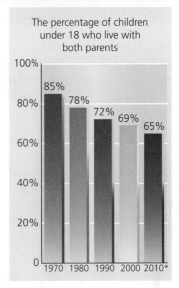

Figure 12.5 **The Decline of Two-Parent Families**

The percentage of children under 18 who live with both parents

Year	Percentage
1970	85%
1980	78%
1990	72%
2000	69%
2010*	65%

*Author's estimate

Source: By the author. Based on *Statistical Abstract* 1995:Table 79; 2005:Table 59.

IN SUM From this brief review, you can see that race-ethnicity signifies little for understanding family life. Rather, social class and culture hold the keys. The more resources a family has, the more it assumes the characteristics of a middle-class nuclear family. Compared with the poor, middle-class families have fewer children and fewer unmarried mothers. They also place greater emphasis on educational achievement and deferred gratification.

Single-Parent Families

Another indication of how extensively the U.S. family is changing is the increase in single-parent families. As you can see from Figure 12.5, the percentage of U.S. children who live with two parents (not necessarily their biological parents) has dropped from 85 percent in 1970 to about 65 percent today. The concerns that are often expressed about single-parent families may have more to do with their poverty than with children being reared by one parent. Because women head most single-parent families, these families tend to be poor. Most divorced women earn less than their former husbands, yet about 85 percent of children of divorce live with their mothers ("Child Support . . ." 1995; Aulette 2002).

To understand the typical single-parent family, then, we need to view it through the lens of poverty, for that is its primary source of strain. The results are serious, not just for these parents and their children but for society as a whole. Children from single-parent families are more likely to drop out of school, to get arrested, to have emotional problems, and to get divorced (McLanahan and Sandefur 1994; Menaghan et al. 1997; McLanahan and Schwartz 2002). If female, they are more likely to become sexually active at a younger age and to bear children while still unmarried teenagers.

Families Without Children

While most married women give birth, about one of five (19 percent) do not (DeOilos and Kapinus 2003). The number of childless couples has *doubled* from what it was 20 years ago. Some couples are infertile, but most childless couples have made a *choice* to not have children. Why do they make this choice? Some women believe they would be stuck at home—bored, lonely, with dwindling career opportunities. Other couples see their marriage as too fragile to withstand the strains that a child would bring (Gerson 1985). A common reason is to attain a sense of freedom—to pursue a career, to be able to change jobs, and to have less stress (Lunneborg 1999; Letherby 2002). Many couples see the cost of rearing a child as too expensive. Consider this statement from a newsletter:

> We are DINKS (Dual Incomes, No Kids). We are happily married. I am 43; my wife is 42. We have been married for almost twenty years. . . . Our investment strategy has a lot to do with our personal philosophy. "You can have kids—or you can have everything else."

With trends firmly in place—more education and careers for women; legal abortion; advances in contraception; the high cost of rearing children; and an emphasis on possessing more material things—the proportion of women who never bear children is likely to increase.

Blended Families

The **blended family,** one whose members once were part of other families, is an increasingly significant type of family in the United States. Two divorced people who marry and each bring their children into a new family unit become a blended family. With divorce common, millions of children spend some of their childhood in blended families. One result is more complicated family relationships. Consider this description written by one of my students:

> I live with my dad. I should say that I live with my dad, my brother (whose mother and father are also my mother and father), my half sister (whose father is my dad, but whose mother is my father's last wife), and two stepbrothers and stepsisters (children of my father's current wife). My father's wife (my current stepmother, not to be confused with his second wife, who, I guess, is no longer my stepmother) is pregnant, and soon we all will have a new brother or sister. Or will it be a half brother or half sister?
>
> If you can't figure this out, I don't blame you. I have trouble myself. It gets very complicated around Christmas. Should we all stay together? Split up and go to several other homes? Who do we buy gifts for, anyway?

Gay and Lesbian Families

In 1989, Denmark became the first country to legalize marriage between people of the same sex. Since then, several European countries and Canada have made same-sex marriages legal. You are familiar with the controversy—accompanied by debates and protests—that occurred as a result of Massachusetts becoming, in 2004, the first state to legalize same-sex marriages.

Even without the benefit of legal marriage, gay and lesbian couples are located throughout the United States.

They are far from evenly distributed, and about half are concentrated in just twenty cities. The greatest concentrations are in San Francisco, Los Angeles, Atlanta, New York City, and Washington, D.C. About one-fifth of gay and lesbian couples were previously married to heterosexuals. Twenty-two percent of female couples and 5 percent of male couples have children from their earlier heterosexual marriages (Bianchi and Casper 2000).

What are same-sex relationships like? Like everything else in life, these couples cannot be painted with a single brush stroke. As with opposite-sex couples, social class is significant, and orientations to life differ according to education, occupation, and income. Sociologists Philip Blumstein and Pepper Schwartz (1985) interviewed same-sex couples and found their main struggles to be housework, money, careers, problems with relatives, and sexual adjustment—the same problems that face heterosexual couples. Same-sex couples are more likely to break up, however, and one argument for legalizing gay marriages is that these relationships will become more stable: If they were surrounded by laws, same-sex marriages would be like opposite-sex marriages—they would require not just a license but also personal commitment, and to break them would necessitate negotiating around legal obstacles.

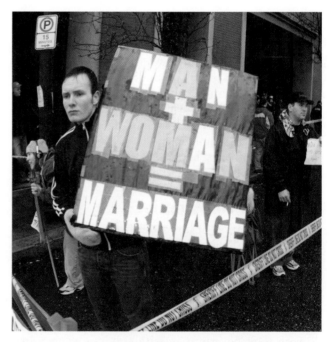

A major issue that has caught the public's attention is whether same-sex couples should have the right of legal marriage. This issue will be decided not by public protest but by legislation and the courts.

Trends in U.S. Families

As is apparent from this discussion, marriage and family life in the United States is undergoing a fundamental shift. Let's examine other indicators of this change.

Postponing Marriage and Childbirth

Figure 12.6 illustrates one of the most significant changes in U.S. marriages. As you can see, the average age of first-time brides and grooms declined from 1890 to about 1950. In 1890, the typical first-time bride was 22, but by 1950, she had just left her teens. For about twenty years, there was little change. Then in 1970, the average age started to increase sharply. *Today's average first-time bride and groom are older than at any other time in U.S. history.*

Since postponing marriage is today's norm, it may come as a surprise to many readers to learn that *most* U.S. women used to be married by the time they reached 24. To see this remarkable change, look at Figure 12.7 on the next page. Postponing marriage has become so extensive that the percentage of women of this age who are unmarried is now more than *double* what it was in

1970. Another consequence of postponing marriage is that the average age at which U.S. women have their first child is also the highest in U.S. history (Mathews and Hamilton 2002).

Why have these changes occurred? The primary reason is cohabitation (Michael et al. 2004). Although Americans have postponed the age at which they first marry, they have *not* postponed the age at which they first set up housekeeping with someone of the opposite sex. Let's look at this trend.

Cohabitation

Figure 12.8 on the next page shows the increase in **cohabitation,** adults living together in a sexual relationship without being married. This figure is one of the most remarkable in sociology. Hardly ever do we have totals that rise this steeply and consistently. Cohabitation is *almost ten times* more common today than it was 30 years ago. Today, sixty percent of the couples who marry for the first time have lived together before marriage. A generation ago, it was just 8 percent (Bianchi and Casper 2000; Batalova and Cohen 2002). Cohabitation has become so common that about 40 percent of U.S. children will spend some time in a cohabiting family (Scommegna 2002).

Figure 12.6 **The Median Age at Which Americans Marry for the First Time**

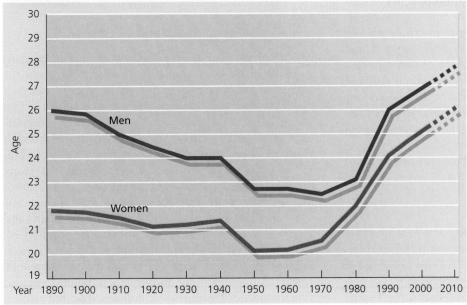

Note: The broken lines indicate the author's estimate.
Source: By the author. Based on *Statistical Abstract* 1999:Table 158; U.S. Bureau of the Census 2003; Fields 2004.

Figure 12.7 Americans Ages 20–24 Who Have Never Married

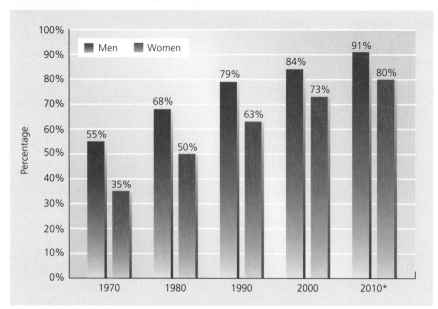

*Author's estimate.

Source: By the author. Based on *Statistical Abstract* 1993:Table 60; 2002:Table 48; 2005:Table 54.

Figure 12.8 Cohabitation in the United States

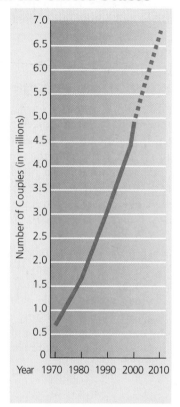

Note: Broken line indicates author's estimate.
Source: By the author. Based on *Statistical Abstract* 1995:Table 60; 2005: Table 55.

Commitment is the essential difference between cohabitation and marriage. In marriage, the assumption is permanence; in cohabitation, couples agree to remain together for "as long as it works out." For marriage, individuals make public vows that legally bind them as a couple; for cohabitation, they simply move in together. Marriage requires a judge to authorize its termination; if a cohabiting relationship sours, the partners separate and tell their friends that it didn't work out. Perhaps the single statement that pinpoints the difference in commitment is this: Cohabiting couples are less likely than married couples to have a joint bank account (Brines and Joyner 1999). As you know, some cohabiting couples do marry. But do you know how this is related to what cohabitation means to them? This is the subject of our Down-to-Earth Sociology box on the next page.

Unmarried Mothers

Births to single women in the United States have increased steadily during the past decades, going from 10 percent in 1970 to 34 percent today (*Statistical Abstract* 1995:Table 94; 2005:Table 79). Let's place these births in global perspective. As Figure 12.9 on page 342 shows, the United States is not alone in its increase. Of the twelve nations for which we have data, all except Japan have experienced sharp increases in births to unmarried mothers. Far from the highest, the U.S. rate lies in the middle of these nations.

From this figure, it would seem fair to conclude that industrialization sets in motion social forces that encourage out-of-wedlock births. There are several problems with this conclusion, however. Why was the rate so low in 1960? Industrialization had been in process for many decades before that time. Why are the rates in the bottom four nations only a fraction of those in the top two nations? Why does Japan's rate remain low? Why are Sweden's and Denmark's rates so high? With only a couple of minor exceptions, the ranking of these nations today is the same as in 1960. By itself, then, industrialization is too simple an answer. A fuller explanation must focus on customs and values embedded within these cultures. For that answer, we will have to await further research.

Down-to-Earth Sociology

"You Want Us to Live Together? What Do You Mean By That?"

WHAT HAS LED TO the surge of cohabitation in the United States? Let's consider two fundamental changes in U.S. culture.

The first is changed ideas of sexual morality. It is difficult for today's college students to grasp the sexual morality that prevailed before the 1960s sexual revolution. Almost everyone used to consider sex before marriage to be immoral. Premarital sex existed, to be sure, but it took place furtively and often with guilt. To live together before marriage was called "shacking up," and the couple was thought to be "living in sin." A double standard prevailed. It was the woman's responsibility to say no to sex before marriage. Consequently, she was considered to be the especially sinful one in cohabitation.

Although the divorce rate has declined since 1980, today's young adults have seen more divorce than any prior generation. This makes marriage seem fragile, something that is not likely to last regardless of how much you devote yourself to it. This is scary. Cohabitation reduces the threat by offering intimacy without the long-term commitment of marriage, in a relationship in which divorce is impossible. You can break up, but you can't get divorced.

From the outside, all cohabitation may look the same, but not to people who are living together. As you can see from Table 12.2, for about 10 percent of couples, cohabitation is a substitute for marriage. These couples consider themselves married but for some reason don't want a marriage certificate. Some object to marriage on philosophical grounds ("What difference does a piece of paper make?"); others do not yet have a legal divorce from a spouse. Almost half of cohabitants (46 percent) view cohabitation as a step on the path to marriage. For them, cohabitation is more than "going steady" but less than engagement. Another 15 percent of couples are simply "giving it a try." They want to see what marriage to one another might be like. For the least committed, about 29 percent, cohabitation is a form of dating. It provides a dependable source of sex and emotional support.

Do these distinctions make a difference in whether couples marry? Let's look at these couples a half dozen years after they began to live together. As you can see from Table 12.2, couples who view cohabitation as a substitute for marriage are the least likely to marry and the most likely to continue to cohabit. For couples who see cohabitation as a step toward marriage, the outcome is just the opposite: They are the most likely to marry and the least likely to still be cohabiting. Couples who are the most likely to break up are those who "tried" cohabitation and those for whom cohabitation was a form of dating.

for your Consideration

Can you explain why the meaning of cohabitation makes a difference in whether couples marry? Can you classify cohabiting couples you know into these four types? Do you think there are other types? If so, what would they be?

Table 12.2 Commitment in Cohabitation: Does It Make a Difference?

Level of Commitment	Percent of Couples	Split Up	Still Together	After 5 to 7 years	
				Of those still together	
				Married	Cohabiting
Substitute for marriage	10%	35%	65%	37%	63%
Step toward marriage	46%	31%	69%	73%	27%
Trial marriage	15%	51%	49%	66%	34%
Coresidential dating	29%	46%	54%	61%	39%

Source: Recomputed from Bianchi and Casper 2000.

Figure 12.9 **Births to Unmarried Women in Ten Industrialized Nations**

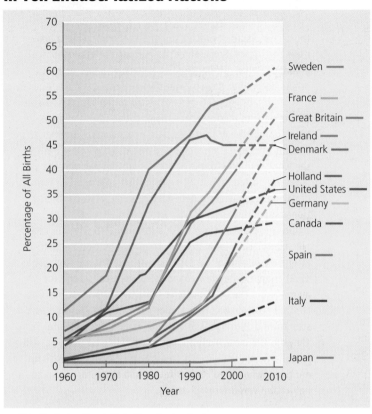

Note: The broken lines indicate the author's estimates.
Source: By the author. Based on *Statistical Abstract* 1993:Table 1380; 2001:Table 1331; 2005:Table 1326.

Grandparents as Parents

It is becoming more common for grandparents to rear their grandchildren. About 4 percent of white children, 7 percent of Latino children, and 14 percent of African American children are being reared by their grandparents (Waldrop and Weber 2001). The main reason for these *skipped-generation families* is that the parents are incapable of caring for their children (Goldberg-Glen et al. 1998). Some of the parents have died, but the most common reasons are that the parents are ill, homeless, addicted to drugs, or in prison. In other instances, they have neglected and abused their children, and the grandparents have taken the children in.

Caring for grandchildren can bring great satisfaction. The grandparents know that their grandchildren are in loving hands, they build strong emotional bonds with them, and they are able to transmit their family values. But taking over as parents also brings stress: additional financial costs, the need to continue working when they were anticipating retirement, and conflict with the parents of the children (Waldrop and Weber 2001). This added wear and tear takes its toll, and these grandmothers are 55 percent more likely to have heart disease (Lee et al. 2003). (We don't have these data for the grandfathers.)

The Sandwich Generation and Elder Care

The *"sandwich generation"* refers to people who find themselves sandwiched between two generations, responsible for both their children and their own aging parents. Typically between the ages of 40 and 55, these people find themselves pulled in two compelling directions. Overwhelmed by two sets of competing responsibilities, they are plagued with guilt and anger because they can be only in one place at a time and have so little time to pursue personal interests.

Concerns about elder care have gained the attention of the corporate world, and half of the 1,000 largest U.S. companies offer elder care assistance to their employees (Hewitt Associates 2004). This assistance includes seminars, referral services, and flexible work schedules designed to help employees meet their responsibilities without missing so much work. Why are companies responding more positively to the issue of elder care than to child day care? Most CEOs are older men whose wives stayed home to take care of their children, so they don't understand the stresses of balancing work and child care. In contrast, nearly all have aging parents, and many have faced the turmoil of trying to cope with both their parents' needs and those of work and their own family.

With people living longer, this issue is likely to become increasingly urgent.

Divorce and Remarriage

The topic of family life would not be complete without considering divorce. Let's first try to determine how much divorce there really is.

Problems in Measuring Divorce

You probably have heard that the U.S. divorce rate is 50 percent, a figure that is popular with reporters. The statistic is true in the sense that each year about half as many divorces are granted as there are marriages performed. The totals are 2.2 million marriages and about 1 million divorces (Munson and Sutton 2005).

What is wrong, then, with saying that the divorce rate is 50 percent? The real question is why we should compare the number of divorces and marriages that take place during the same year. The couples who divorced do not—with rare exceptions—come from the group that married that year. The one number has *nothing* to do with the other, so these statistics in no way establish the divorce rate.

What figures should we compare, then? Couples who divorce are drawn from the entire group of married people in the country. Since the United States has 60,000,000 married couples, and only about 1 million of them obtain divorces in a year, the divorce rate is slightly less than 2

percent, not 50 percent. A couple's chances of still being married at the end of a year are 98 percent—not bad odds—and certainly much better odds than the mass media would have us believe. As the Social Map below shows, however, the "odds"—if we want to call them that—change depending on where you live.

Over time, of course, those 2 percent a year add up. A third way of measuring divorce, then, is to ask, "Of all U.S. adults, what percentage are divorced?" Figure 12.11 on page 345 answers this question. You can see how divorce has increased over the years and how race-ethnicity makes a difference for the likelihood that couples will divorce. If you look closely, you can also see that the rate of divorce has slowed down.

What most of us want to know is what *our* chances of divorce are. It is one thing to know that a certain percentage of Americans are divorced, but have sociologists found out anything that will tell me about *my* chances of divorce? This is the topic of the Down-to-Earth Sociology box on the next page.

Figure 12.10 The "Where" of U.S. Divorce

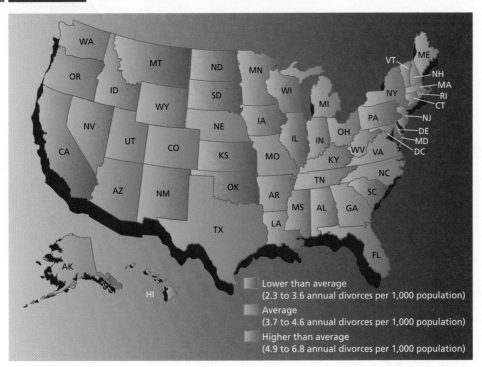

Note: Data for California, Colorado, Indiana, and Louisiana, based on earlier editions, have been decreased by the average decrease in U.S. divorce.
Source: By the author. Based on *Statistical Abstract* 2005:Table 113, and earlier editions.

Down-to-Earth Sociology

"What Are Your Chances of Getting Divorced?"

IT IS PROBABLY TRUE that *over a lifetime* about half of all marriages fail (Whitehead and Popenoe 2004). If you have that 50 percent figure dancing in your head, you might as well make sure that you have an escape door open even while you're saying "I do."

Not every group carries the same risk of divorce. Some have a much higher risk, and some much lower. Let's look at some factors that reduce people's risk. As Table 12.3 shows, sociologists have worked out percentages that you might find useful (Whitehead and Popenoe 2004).

Table 12.3 What Reduces the Risk of Divorce?

Factors that Reduce People's Chances of Divorce	How Much Does This Decrease the Risk of Divorce?
Some college (vs. high-school dropout)	–13%
Affiliated with a religion (vs. none)	–14%
Parents not divorced	–14%
Age 25 or over at marriage (vs. under 18)	–24%
Having a baby 7 months or longer after marriage (vs. before marriage)	–24%
Annual income over $50,000 (vs. under $25,000)	–30%

Note: These percentages apply to the first ten years of marriage.

As you can see, people who go to college, participate in a religion, wait to get married to have children, and so on, have a much better chance of having a lasting marriage. You can also reverse these factors and see how the likelihood of divorce increases for people who have a baby before they marry, who marry in their teens, and so on. It is important to note, however, that these factors reduce the risk of divorce for *groups* of people, not for any certain individual.

Here are two other factors that *increase* the risk for divorce (Aberg 2003). For these, sociologists have not computed percentages. Working with co-workers who are of the opposite sex (I'm sure you can figure out why) and working with people who are recently divorced increase a person's risk. Apparently divorce is "contagious," following a pattern like measles. Perhaps being around divorced people makes divorce more acceptable. This would increase the likelihood that married people will act on their inevitable dissatisfactions and attractions. Or it could be that divorced people are more likely to "hit" on their fellow workers—and human nature being what it is . . .

for your Consideration

Why do you think that people who go to college have a lower risk of divorce? How would you explain the other factors shown in Table 12.3? What other factors discussed in this chapter indicate a greater or lesser risk of divorce?

Why can't you figure your own chances of divorce by starting with some percentage (say 30 percent likelihood of divorce for the first 10 years of marriage) and then reducing it according to the table above (subtracting 13 percent of the 30 percent for going to college, and so on)? To better understand this, you might want to read the section on the misuse of statistics on page 349.

Children of Divorce

Each year, more than 1 million U.S. children learn that their parents are divorcing (Cherlin 2002). These children are more likely than children reared by both parents to experience emotional problems, both during childhood and after they grow up (Amato and Sobolewski 2001; Weitoft et al. 2003). They are also more likely to become juvenile delinquents (Wallerstein et al. 2001), and less likely to complete high school, to attend college, and to graduate from college (McLanahan and Schwartz 2002). Finally, the children of divorce are themselves more likely to divorce (Wolfinger 2003), thus perpetuating a marriage-divorce cycle.

Is the greater maladjustment of the children of divorce a serious problem? This question initiated a lively debate between two researchers, both psychologists. Judith Wallerstein claims that divorce scars children,

Figure 12.11 What Percentage of Americans Are Divorced?

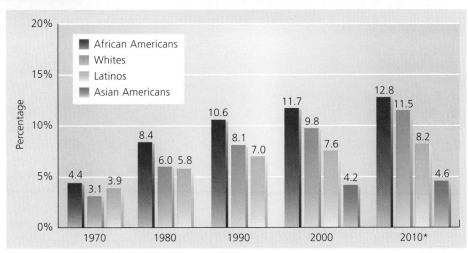

Note: This figure shows the percentage who are divorced and have not remarried, not the percentage who have *ever* divorced. Only these racial-ethnic groups are listed in the source. *Author's estimate
Source: By the author. Based on Kreider and Simmons 2003; *Statistical Abstract* 1995:Table 58; 2005:Table 51.

making them depressed and leaving them with insecurities that follow them into adulthood (Wallerstein et al. 2001). Mavis Hetherington replies that 75 to 80 percent of children of divorce function as well as children who are reared by both of their parents (Hetherington and Kelly 2003).

Without meaning to weigh in on either side of this debate, it doesn't seem to be a simple case of the glass being half empty or half full. If 75 to 80 percent of children of divorce don't suffer long-term harm, this leaves one-fourth to one-fifth who do. Any way you look at it, one-fourth or one-fifth of a million children each year is a lot of kids who are having a lot of problems.

What helps children adjust to divorce? Children of divorce who feel close to both parents make the best adjustment; those who feel close to one parent make the next best adjustment. Those who don't feel close to either parent make the worst adjustment (Richardson and McCabe 2001). Other studies show that children adjust well if they experience little conflict, feel loved, live with a parent who is making a good adjustment, and have consistent routines. It also helps if their family has adequate money to meet its needs. Children also adjust better if a second adult can be counted on for support (Hayashi and Strickland 1998). Urie Bronfenbrenner (1992) says this person is like the third leg of a stool, giving stability to the smaller family unit. Any adult can be the third leg, he says—a relative, friend, mother-in-law,

or even co-worker—but the most powerful stabilizing third leg is the father, the ex-husband.

As mentioned, when the children of divorce grow up and marry, they are more likely to divorce than are adults who grew up in intact families. Have researchers found any factors that increase the likelihood that the children of divorce will have successful marriages? Actually, they have. These individuals' chances increase if they marry someone whose parents did not divorce. This increases the level of trust and reduces the level of conflict. If both husband and wife come from broken families, however, it is not good news. Those marriages are likely to be marked by high distrust and conflict, leading to a higher chance of divorce (Wolfinger 2003).

Grandchildren of Divorce

Paul Amato and Jacob Cheadle (2005), the first sociologists to study the grandchildren of divorced parents, found that the effects of divorce continue across generations. Using a national sample, they compared children whose grandparents divorced with those whose grandparents did not divorce. Their findings are astounding. The grandchildren of divorce have weaker ties to their parents, they don't go as far in school, and they don't get along as well with their spouses. As these researchers put it, when parents divorce, the consequences ripple through the lives of children who are not yet born.

It is difficult to capture the anguish of the children of divorce, but when I read
these lines by the fourth-grader who drew these two pictures, my heart was touched:

Me alone in the park . . .
All alone in the park.
My Dad and Mom are divorced
that's why I'm all alone.

This is me in the picture with my son
We are taking a walk in the park.
I will never be like my father.
I will never divorce my wife and kid.

The Absent Father and Serial Fatherhood

With divorce common and mothers usually granted custody of the children, a new fathering pattern has emerged. In this pattern, known as **serial fatherhood,** a divorced father maintains high contact with his children during the first year or two after the divorce. As the man develops a relationship with another woman, he begins to play a fathering role with the woman's children and reduces contact with his own children. With another breakup, this pattern may repeat. Only about one-sixth of children who live apart from their fathers see their dad as often as every week. Actually, *most* divorced fathers stop seeing their children altogether (Ahlburg and De Vita 1992; Furstenberg and Harris 1992; Seltzer 1994). Apparently, for many men, fatherhood has become a short-term commitment.

The Ex-Spouses

Anger, depression, and anxiety are common feelings at divorce. But so is relief. Women are more likely than men to feel that the divorce is giving them a "new chance" in life. A few couples manage to remain friends through it all—but they are the exception. The spouse who initiates the divorce usually gets over it sooner (Kelly 1992; Wang and Amato 2000). This spouse also usually remarries sooner (Sweeney 2002).

After divorce, the ex-spouses' cost of living increases—two homes, two utility bills, and so forth. But men and women feel a different financial impact. Divorce often spells economic hardship for women (Smock et al. 1999). This is especially true for mothers of small children, whose standard of living drops about a third (Seltzer 1994). The more education a woman has, the better prepared she is to survive financially after divorce (Dixon and Rettig 1994).

Remarriage

Despite the number of people who emerge from divorce court swearing "Never again!" many do remarry. The rate at which they remarry, however, has dropped, and today only half of women who divorce remarry (Bramlett and Mosher 2002). The women who are most likely to remarry are young mothers and those with less education (Glick and Lin 1986; Schmiege et al. 2001). Apparently, women who are more educated and more independent (no children) can afford to be more selective. Figure 12.12 shows how significant race-ethnicity is in determining whether women remarry. Comparable data are not available for men.

How do remarriages work out? The divorce rate of remarried people *without* children is the same as that of first marriages. Those who bring children into a new marriage, however, are more likely to divorce again (MacDonald and DeMaris 1995). Certainly those relationships are more

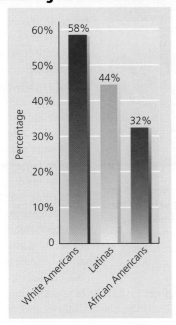

Figure 12.12 The Probability that Divorced Women Will Remarry in Five Years

Note: Only these groups are listed in the source.
Source: By the author. Based on Bramlett and Mosher 2002.

complicated and stressful. A lack of clear norms to follow may also play a role (Coleman et al. 2000). As sociologist Andrew Cherlin (1989) noted, we lack satisfactory names for stepmothers, stepfathers, stepbrothers, stepsisters, stepaunts, stepuncles, stepcousins, and stepgrandparents. At the very least, these are awkward terms to use, but they also represent ill-defined relationships.

Two Sides of Family Life

Let's first look at situations in which marriage and family have gone seriously wrong and then try to answer the question of what makes marriage work.

The Dark Side of Family Life: Battering, Child Abuse, and Incest

The dark side of family life involves events that people would rather keep in the dark. We shall look at spouse battering, child abuse, and incest.

Spouse Battering. To study spouse abuse, some sociologists have studied just a few victims in depth (Goetting 2001), while others have interviewed nationally representative samples of U.S. couples (Straus and Gelles 1988; Straus 1992). Although not all sociologists agree (Dobash et al. 1992, 1993; Pagelow 1992), Murray Straus concludes that husbands and wives are about equally likely to attack one another. If gender equality exists here, however, it certainly vanishes when it comes to the effects of violence—85 percent of the injured are women (Rennison 2003). A good part of the reason, of course, is that most husbands are bigger and stronger than their wives, putting women at a physical disadvantage in this literal battle of the sexes. The Down-to-Earth Sociology box on the next page discusses why some women remain with their abusive husbands.

Violence against women is related to the sexist structure of society, which we reviewed in Chapter 8, and to the socialization that we analyzed in Chapter 3. Because they grew up with norms that encourage aggression and the use of violence, some men feel that it is their right to control women. When frustrated in a relationship—or even by events outside it—some men become violent. The basic sociological question is how to socialize males to handle frustration and disagreements without resorting to violence (Rieker et al. 1997). We do not yet have this answer.

Child Abuse

I answered an ad about a lakeside house in a middle-class neighborhood that was for sale by owner. As the woman showed me through her immaculate house, I was surprised to see a plywood box in the youngest child's bedroom. About 3 feet high, 3 feet wide, and 6 feet long, the box was perforated with holes and had a little door with a padlock. Curious, I asked what it was. The woman replied matter-of-factly that her son had a behavior problem, and this was where they locked him for "time out." She added that other times they would tie him to a float, attach a line to the dock, and put him in the lake.

I left as soon as I could. With thoughts of a terrorized child filling my head, I called the state child abuse hot line.

As you can tell, what I saw upset me. Most of us are bothered by child abuse—helpless children being victimized by their parents and other adults who are supposed to love, protect, and nurture them. The most gruesome of these cases make the evening news: The 4-year-old girl who was beaten and raped by her mother's boyfriend, who passed into a coma and then three days later passed

Down-to-Earth Sociology

"Why Doesn't She Just Leave?" The Dilemma of Abused Women

"WHY WOULD SHE EVER PUT UP WITH violence?" is a question on everyone's mind. From the outside, it looks so easy. Just pack up and leave. "I know I wouldn't put up with anything like that."

Yet this is not what typically happens. Women tend to stay with their men after they are abused. Some stay only a short while, to be sure, but others remain in abusive situations for years. Why?

Sociologist Ann Goetting (2001) asked this question, too. To learn the answer, she interviewed women who had made the break. She wanted to find out what it was that set them apart. How were they able to leave, when so many women couldn't seem to? She found that

1. They had a positive self-concept.
   Simply put, they believed that they deserved better.
2. They broke with traditional values.
   They did not believe that a wife had to stay with her husband no matter what.
3. They found adequate finances.
   For some, this was easy to accumulate enough money to move out, others saved for years, putting away just a dollar or two a week.
4. They had supportive family and friends.
   A support network served as a source of encouragement to help them rescue themselves.

If you take the opposite of these four characteristics, you can understand why some women put up with abuse: They don't think they deserve anything better, they believe it is their duty to stay, they don't think they can make it financially, and they lack a supportive network. These four factors are not of equal importance to all women, of course.

Domestic abuse is one of the most common forms of violence. Until recently, it was treated by the police as a private family matter. Shown here are police pulling a woman from her bathroom window, where she had fled from her husband, who was threatening to shoot her.

For some, the lack of finances is the most important, while for others, it is their low self-concept. The lack of a supportive network is also significant.

There are two additional factors: The woman must define what her husband is doing as abuse that warrants her leaving, and she must decide that he is not going to change. If she defines her husband's acts as normal, or perhaps as deserved in some way, she does not have a motive to leave. If she defines his acts as temporary, thinking that her husband will change, she is likely to stick around to try to change her husband.

Sociologist Kathleen Ferraro (2006) reports that when she was a graduate student, her husband "monitored my movements, eating, clothing, friends, money, make-up, and language. If I challenged his commands, he slapped or kicked me or pushed me down." Ferraro was able to leave only after she defined her husband's acts as intolerable abuse—not simply that she was caught up in an unappealing situation that she had to put up with—and after she decided that her husband was not going to change. Fellow students formed the supportive network that Ferraro needed to act on her definition. Her graduate mentor even hid her from her husband after she left him.

for your Consideration

On the basis of these findings, what would you say to a woman whose husband is abusing her? How do you think battered women's shelters fit into this explanation? What other parts of this puzzle can you think of—such as the role of love?

out of this life; the 6- to 10-year-old children whose stepfather videotaped them engaging in sex acts. Unlike these cases, which made headlines in my area, most child abuse is never brought to our attention: the children who live in filth, who are neglected—left alone for hours or even days at a time—or who are beaten with extension cords—cases like the little boy I learned about when I went house hunting.

Child abuse is extensive. Each year, about 3 million U.S. children are reported to the authorities as victims of abuse or neglect. About 900,000 of these cases are confirmed as abuse (*Statistical Abstract* 2005:Table 332). The excuses that parents make are incredible. Of those I have read, one I can only describe as fantastic is this statement, made by a mother to a Manhattan judge, "I slipped in a moment of anger, and my hands accidentally wrapped around my daughter's windpipe" (LeDuff 2003).

Incest.   Sexual relations between certain relatives (for example, between brothers and sisters or between parents and children) constitute **incest.** Incest is most likely to occur in families that are socially isolated (Smith 1992). Sociologist Diana Russell (n.d.), who interviewed women in San Francisco, found that incest victims who experience the greatest trauma are those who were victimized the most often, whose assaults occurred over longer periods of time, and whose incest was "more intrusive"—for example, sexual intercourse as opposed to sexual touching.

Who are the offenders? Russell found that uncles are the most common offenders, followed by first cousins, fathers (stepfathers especially), brothers, and, finally, relatives ranging from brothers-in-law to stepgrandfathers. Other researchers report that brother–sister incest is several times more common than father–daughter incest (Canavan et al. 1992). Incest between mothers and sons is rare.

The Bright Side of Family Life: Successful Marriages

Successful Marriages.   After examining divorce and family abuse, one could easily conclude that marriages seldom work out. This would be far from the truth, however, for about three of every five married Americans report that they are "very happy" with their marriages (Whitehead and Popenoe 2004). Husbands are consistently somewhat more happy with their marriages, likely because on average they get more out of them. To find out what makes marriage successful, sociologists Jeanette and Robert Lauer (1992) interviewed 351 couples who had been married fifteen years or longer. Fifty-one of these marriages were unhappy, but the couples stayed together for religious reasons, because of family tradition, or "for the sake of the children."

Of the others, the 300 happy couples, all:

1. Think of their spouse as their best friend
2. Like their spouse as a person
3. Think of marriage as a long-term commitment
4. Believe that marriage is sacred

5. Agree with their spouse on aims and goals
6. Believe that their spouse has grown more interesting over the years
7. Strongly want the relationship to succeed
8. Laugh together

Sociologist Nicholas Stinnett (1992) used interviews and questionnaires to study 660 families from all regions of the United States and parts of South America. He found that happy families:

1. Spend a lot of time together
2. Are quick to express appreciation
3. Are committed to promoting one another's welfare
4. Do a lot of talking and listening to one another
5. Are religious
6. Deal with crises in a positive manner

Sociologists have uncovered two other factors: Marriages are happier when a couple get along with their in-laws (Bryant et al. 2001) and when they do leisure activities that they both enjoy (Crawford et al. 2002).

Symbolic Interactionism and the Misuse of Statistics.   Many students express concerns about their own marital future, a wariness born out of the divorce of their parents, friends, neighbors, relatives—even their pastors and rabbis. They wonder about their chances of having a successful marriage. Because sociology is not just about abstract ideas but is really about our lives, it is important to stress that you are an individual, not a statistic. That is, if the divorce rate were 33 percent or 50 percent, this would *not* mean that if you marry, your chances of getting divorced are 33 percent or 50 percent. That is a misuse of statistics—and a common one at that. Divorce statistics represent all marriages and have absolutely *nothing* to do with any individual marriage. Our own chances depend on our own situations—and especially the way we approach marriage.

To make this point clearer, let's apply symbolic interactionism. From a symbolic interactionist perspective, we create our own worlds. That is, because our experiences don't come with built-in meanings, we interpret our experiences, and act accordingly. As we do so, we create a sort of self-fulfilling prophecy. For example, if we think that our marriage might fail, we are more likely to run when things become difficult. If we think that our marriage is going to work out, we are more likely to stick around and to do things to make the marriage successful. The folk saying "There are no guarantees in life" is certainly true, but it does help to have a vision that a good marriage is possible and that it is worth the effort to achieve.

The Future of Marriage and Family

What can we expect of marriage and family in the future? Despite its many problems, marriage is in no danger of becoming a relic of the past. Marriage is so functional that it exists in every society. Consequently, the vast majority of Americans will continue to find marriage vital to their welfare.

Certain trends are firmly in place. Cohabitation, births to single women, age at first marriage, and parenting by grandparents will increase. More married women will join the work force, and they will continue to gain marital power. Equality in marriage, however, is not yet on the horizon. As the number of elderly increase, more couples will find themselves sandwiched between caring for their parents and rearing their own children.

Our culture will continue to be haunted by distorted images of marriage and family: the bleak ones portrayed in the mass media and the rosy ones perpetuated by cultural myths. Sociological research can help to correct these distortions and allow us to see how our own family experiences fit into the patterns of our culture. Sociological research can also help to answer the big question: how to formulate social policy that will support and enhance family life.

Summary *and* Review

Marriage and Family in Global Perspective

What is a family—and what themes are universal?

Family is difficult to define. There are exceptions to every element that one might consider essential. Consequently, **family** is defined broadly: as people who consider themselves related by blood, marriage, or adoption. Universally, **marriage** and family are mechanisms for governing mate selection, reckoning descent, and establishing inheritance and authority. Pp. 324–325.

Marriage and Family in Theoretical Perspective

What is the functionalist perspective on marriage and family?

Functionalists examine the functions and dysfunctions of family life. Examples include the **incest taboo** and how weakened family functions increase divorce. P. 326.

What is the conflict perspective on marriage and family?

Conflict theorists examine inequalities in marriage and family, especially inequalities between husbands and wives. An example is marital struggles over housework. Pp. 327–329.

What is a symbolic interactionist perspective on marriage and family?

Symbolic interactionists examine the contrasting experiences and perspectives of men and women in marriage. They stress that only by grasping the perspectives of wives and husbands can we understand their behavior. P. 329.

The Family Life Cycle

What are major elements of the family life cycle?

The major elements are love and courtship, marriage, childbirth, child rearing, and the family in later life. Most mate selection follows predictable patterns of age, race-ethnicity, religion, and social class. Childbirth and child-rearing patterns also vary by social class. Pp. 329–334.

Diversity in U.S. Families

How significant is race-ethnicity in family life?

The primary distinction is social class, not race-ethnicity. Families of the same social class are likely to be similar, regardless of their race-ethnicity. Pp. 334–337.

What other diversity in U.S. families is there?

Also discussed are single-parent, childless, **blended,** and gay families. Each has its unique characteristics, but social class is significant in determining their primary characteristics. Poverty is especially significant for one-parent families, most of which are headed by women. Pp. 337–338.

Trends in U.S. Families

What changes characterize U.S. families?

Three changes are postponement of first marriage, an increase in **cohabitation,** and more grandparents serving as parents to their grandchildren. With more people living longer, many middle-aged couples find themselves sandwiched between rearing their children and taking care of their parents. Pp. 339–342.

Divorce and Remarriage

What is the current divorce rate?

Depending on what numbers you choose to compare, you can produce almost any rate you wish, from 50 percent to less than 2 percent. Pp. 342–344.

How do children and their parents adjust to divorce?

Divorce is difficult for children, whose adjustment problems often continue into adulthood. Most divorced fathers do not maintain ongoing relationships with their children. Financial problems are usually greater for the former wives. Although most divorced people remarry, their rate of remarriage has slowed. Pp. 344–347.

Two Sides of Family Life

What are the two sides of family life?

The dark side is abuse—spouse battering, child abuse, and **incest.** These acts involve the misuse of family power. The bright side is that most people find marriage and family to be rewarding. Pp. 347–349.

The Future of Marriage and Family

What is the likely future of marriage and family?

We can expect cohabitation, births to unmarried women, age at first marriage, and parenting by grandparents to increase. The growing numbers of women in the work force are likely to continue to shift the balance of marital power. P. 350.

Thinking Critically
about Chapter 12

1. Functionalists stress that the family is universal because it provides basic functions for individuals and society. What functions does your family provide? Hint: In addition to the section "The Functionalist Perspective," also consider the section "Common Cultural Themes."

2. Explain why social class is more important than race-ethnicity in determining a family's characteristics.

3. Apply this chapter's contents to your own experience with marriage and family. What social factors affect your family life? In what ways is your family life different from that of your grandparents when they were your age?

Additional Resources

Companion Website www.ablongman.com/henslin

- Content Select Research Database for Sociology, with suggested key terms and annotated references
- Link to 2000 Census, with activities
- Flashcards of key terms and concepts

- Practice Tests
- Weblinks
- Interactive Maps

Where Can I Read More on This Topic?

Suggested readings for this chapter are listed at the back of this book.

CHAPTER

13

Education and Religion

Pascale Carrivaul, *Students/Literacy*

OUTLINE

EDUCATION
Education in Global Perspective
Education and Industrialization
Education in Japan
Education in Russia
Education in Egypt
The Functionalist Perspective
Teaching Knowledge and Skills
Cultural Transmission of Values
Social Integration
Gatekeeping
The Conflict Perspective
The Hidden Curriculum
Discrimination by IQ
Unequal Funding
The Symbolic Interactionist Perspective
The Rist Research
How Do Teacher Expectations Work?
Problems and Solutions
Problems: Mediocrity and Violence
Solutions: Safety and Standards
RELIGION
What Is Religion?
The Functionalist Perspective
Functions of Religion
Dysfunctions of Religion
The Symbolic Interactionist Perspective
Religious Symbols
Rituals and Beliefs
Religious Experience
The Conflict Perspective
Opium of the People
A Legitimation of Social Inequalities
Religion and Capitalism
Types of Religious Groups
Cult
Sect
Church
Ecclesia
Variations in Patterns
Religion in the United States
Characteristics of Members
Characteristics of Religious Groups
Secularization and the Splintering of
    U.S. Churches
The Future of Religion
Summary and Review

Kathy Spiegel was upset. Horace Mann, the school principal in her hometown in Oregon, had asked her to come into his office. He explained that Kathy's 11-year-old twins had been acting up in class. They were disturbing both the other children and the teacher—and what was Kathy going to do about this?

Kathy didn't want to tell Mr. Mann what he could do with the situation. *That* would have gotten her kicked out of the office. Instead, she bit her tongue and said she would talk to her daughters.

. . . .

On the other side of the country, Jim and Julia Attaway were pondering their own problem. When they visited their son's school in the Bronx, they didn't like what they saw. The boys looked like they were gang members, and the girls dressed and acted in sexually provocative ways. Their own 13-year-old son had started using street language at home, and it was becoming increasingly difficult to communicate with him.

. . . .

In Minneapolis, Denzil and Tamika Jefferson were facing a much quieter crisis. They found life frantic as they rushed from one school activity to another. Their 13-year-old son attended a private school, and the demands were so intense that it felt like junior year in high school. They no longer seemed to have any relaxed family time together.

. . . .

In Atlanta, Jaime and Maria Morelos were upset at the language that their 8-year-old daughter had begun to use at home. As devout first-generation Protestants, Jaime and Maria felt moral issues were a top priority, and they didn't like what they were hearing.

. . . .

Kathy talked the matter over with her husband, Bob. Jim and Julia discussed their problem, as did Denzil and Tamika and Jaime and Maria. They all came to the same conclusion: The problem was not their children. The problem was the school their children attended. All four sets of parents also came to the same solution: home schooling for their children.

Home schooling might seem to be a radical solution to today's education problems, but it is one that the parents of almost a million U.S. children have chosen. We'll come back to this topic, but, first, let's take a broad look at education.

They all came to the same conclusion: The problem was the school their children attended.

EDUCATION: TRANSFERRING KNOWLEDGE AND SKILLS

Education in Global Perspective

Have you ever wondered why you need a high school diploma to sell cars or to join the U.S. Marines? You will learn what you need to know on the job. Why, then, do employers insist on diplomas and degrees? Why don't they simply use on-the-job training?

In some cases, of course, specific job skills must be mastered before you are allowed to do the work. In these instances, colleges and specialized schools provide that training. This is precisely why doctors display their credentials so prominently. Their framed degrees declare that an institution of higher learning has certified them as capable of caring for your body.

But testing in algebra or paragraph construction to sell cars? Sociologist Randall Collins (1979) observed that industrialized nations have become **credential societies.** By this, he means that employers use diplomas and degrees as *sorting devices* to determine who is eligible for a job. Because employers don't know potential workers, they depend on schools to weed out the capable from the incapable. For example, when you graduate from college, potential employers will presume that you are a responsible person—that you have shown up on time for numerous classes, have turned in scores of assignments, and have demonstrated basic writing and thinking skills. They will then graft their particular job skills onto this foundation, which has been certified by your college.

Education and Industrialization

In the early years of the United States, there was no free public education. The average family could not afford to send its children to grade school. As the country industrialized during the 1800s, political and civic leaders recognized the need for an educated work force. They also feared the influx of foreign values, for this was a period of high immigration. They saw public schools as a means to accomplish two major goals: producing more educated workers and "Americanizing" immigrants (Hellinger and Judd 1991).

As industrialization progressed and as fewer people made their living from farming, formal education came

This 1893 photo of a school in Hecla, Montana, taught by Miss Blanche Lamont, provides a glimpse into the past, when free public education, pioneered in the United States, was still in its infancy. In these one-room rural schools, a single teacher had charge of grades 1 to 8. Children were assigned a grade not by age but by mastery of subject matter. Occasionally, adults who wished to learn to read, to write, or to add and subtract would join the class. Attendance was sporadic, for the family's economic survival came first.

to be regarded as essential to the well-being of society. With the distance to the nearest college too far and the cost of tuition and lodging too great, many high school graduates were unable to attend college. As is discussed in the Down-to-Earth Sociology box on the next page, this predicament gave birth to community colleges. As you can see from Figure 13.1 on page 356, receiving a bachelor's degree in the United States is now *twice* as common as completing high school used to be.

To further place our own educational system in perspective, let's look at education in three countries at different levels of industrialization. This will help us see how education is directly related to a nation's culture and its economy.

Education in the Most Industrialized Nations: Japan

A central sociological principle of education is that a nation's education reflects its culture. Because a core Japanese value is solidarity with the group, the Japanese discourage

Down-to-Earth Sociology

Community Colleges: Challenges Old and New

I ATTENDED A JUNIOR COLLEGE IN OAKLAND, California. From there, with fresh diploma in hand, I transferred to a senior college—a college in Ft. Wayne, Indiana, that had no freshmen or sophomores.

I didn't realize that my experimental college matched the vision of some of the founders of the community college movement. In the early 1900s, they foresaw a system of local colleges that would be accessible to the average high school graduate—a system so extensive that it would be unnecessary for universities to offer courses at the freshman and sophomore levels (Manzo 2001).

A group with an equally strong opinion questioned whether preparing high school graduates for entry to four-year colleges and universities should be the goal of junior colleges. They insisted that the purpose of junior colleges should be vocational preparation, to equip people for the job market as electricians and other technicians. In some regions, where the proponents of transfer dominated, the admissions requirements for junior colleges were higher than those of Yale (Pedersen 2001). This debate was never won by either side, and you can still hear its echoes today.

The name *junior* college also became a problem. Some felt that the word *junior* made their institution sound as though it weren't quite a real college. A struggle to change the name ensued, and about three decades ago *community* college won out.

The name change didn't settle the debate about whether the purpose was preparing students to transfer to universi-

Community colleges have opened higher education to millions of students who would not otherwise have access to college because of cost or distance.

ties or training them for jobs, however. Community colleges continue to serve this dual purpose.

Community colleges have become such an essential part of the U.S. educational system that two of every five of all undergraduates in the United States are enrolled in them (*Statistical Abstract* 2005:Table 262). Most students are *nontraditional* students: Many are age 25 or older, are from the working class, have jobs, and attend college part time (Bryant 2001).

To help their students transfer to four-year colleges and universities, many community colleges work closely with top-tier public and private universities (Chaker 2003). Some provide admissions guidance on how to enter flagship state schools. Others coordinate courses, making sure that they match the university's title and numbering system, as well as its rigor of instruction and grading. More than a third offer honors programs that prepare talented students to transfer with ease into these schools (Padgett 2005).

The challenges that community colleges face are the usual ones of securing adequate budgets in the face of declining resources, continuing an open-door policy, meeting changing job markets, and maintaining quality instruction. New challenges include meeting the shifting needs of students, such as the growing need to teach immigrants English as a second language and to provide on-campus day care for parents who no longer enjoy an extensive familial support system.

---

competition among individuals. In the work force, people who are hired together work as a team. They are not expected to compete with one another for promotions; instead, they are promoted as a group (Ouchi 1993). Japanese education reflects this group-centered approach to life. Children in grade school work as a group, all mastering the same skills and materials. On any one day, children all over Japan study the same page from the same textbook ("Less Rote . . ." 2000).

In a fascinating cultural contradiction, college admissions in Japan are highly competitive. Just as most U.S. college-bound high school juniors and seniors take the Scholastic Assessment Test (SAT), Japanese seniors who want to attend college must also take a national test.

Figure 13.1 **Educational Achievement in the United States**

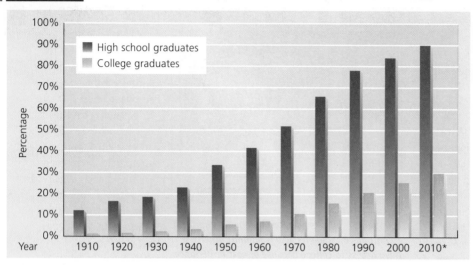

Note: Americans 25 years and over. Asterisk indicates author's estimate.
Sources: By the author. Based on National Center for Education Statistics 1991:Table 8; *Statistical Abstract* 2005:Table 212.

U.S. high school graduates who perform poorly on the SAT can usually find some college to attend—as long as their parents can pay the tuition. In Japan, however, only the top scorers—rich and poor alike—are admitted to college. Japanese sociologists have found that even though the tests are open to all, children from the richer families are more likely to be admitted to college. The reason is not favoritism on the part of college officials but, rather, that the richer parents apparently spend more for tutors and intensive training classes to prepare their children for the college entrance exams (Ono 2001).

Education in the Industrializing Nations: Russia

After the Russian Revolution of 1917, the Soviet Communist party changed the nation's educational system. At that time, as in most countries, education was limited to children of the elite. The communists expanded the educational system until eventually it encompassed all children. Following the sociological principle that education reflects culture, the new government made certain that socialist values dominated its schools, for it saw education as a means to undergird the new political system. As a result, schoolchildren were taught that capitalism was evil and that communism was the salvation of the world. Every classroom was required to prominently display a photograph of Stalin.

Education, including college, was free. Schools stressed mathematics and the natural sciences, and few courses in the social sciences were taught. Just as the economy was directed from central headquarters in Moscow, so was education. Schools throughout the country followed the state-prescribed curriculum, and all students in the same grade used the same textbooks. To prevent critical thinking, which might lead to criticisms of communism, students memorized course materials and were taught to repeat lectures on oral exams (Deaver 2001).

Russia's switch from communism to capitalism brought a change in culture—especially new ideas about profit, private property, and personal freedoms. This, in turn, meant that the educational system had to adjust its values and teaching methods to match the country's changing views of the world. Not only did the photos of Stalin come down, but, for the first time, private, religious, and even foreign-run schools were allowed. For the first time also, teachers were able to encourage students to think for themselves.

The problems that Russia confronted in "reinventing" its educational system are mind-boggling. Tens of thousands of teachers who were used to teaching rote political answers had to learn new methods of instruction. As the economy shrank during Russia's faltering transition to capitalism, so did school budgets. Some teachers went unpaid for months; teachers at one school were even paid in toilet paper and vodka (Deaver 2001). Abysmal salaries have encouraged corruption, and students know which professors can be bribed for good grades (MacWilliams 2001b; "Russia . . ." 2004).

Because it is true of education everywhere, we can confidently predict that Russia's educational system will continue to reflect its culture. Its educational system will glorify Russia's historical exploits and reinforce its values and world views—no matter how they might change.

Education in the Least Industrialized Nations: Egypt

Education in the Least Industrialized Nations stands in sharp contrast to that in the industrialized world. Because most of the citizens of these nations work the land or take care of families, there is little emphasis on formal schooling. Even if a Least Industrialized Nation has mandatory attendance laws, they are not enforced. Formal education is expensive and most of these nations cannot afford it. As we saw in Figure 7.2 (pages 182–183), many people in the Least Industrialized Nations live on less than $1,000 a year. Consequently, in some of these nations few children go to school beyond the first couple of grades. Figure 13.2 contrasts education in China with that in the United States. As was once common around the globe, it is primarily the wealthy in the Least Industrialized Nations who have the means and the leisure for formal education—especially anything beyond the basics. As an example, let's look at education in Egypt.

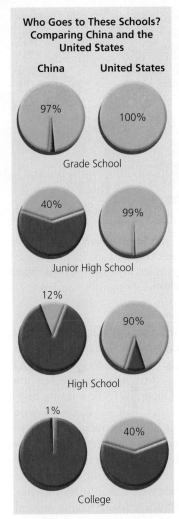

Figure 13.2 Education in a Most Industrialized (Postindustrial) Nation and a Least Industrialized Nation

Who Goes to These Schools? Comparing China and the United States

China | United States

97% | 100%
Grade School

40% | 99%
Junior High School

12% | 90%
High School

1% | 40%
College

Note: These are initial attendance rates, not completion rates. The U.S. junior high school total is the author's estimate.
Sources: Brauchli 1994; Kahn 2002; *Statistical Abstract* 2005:Tables 212, 256.

In hunting and gathering societies, there is no separate social institution called *education*. As with these boys of the Vedda tribe in Sri Lanka, children learn from their parents and other kin. This is likely the last generation of Vedda hunters and gatherers, as they are running out of game. Some are now becoming farmers.

Within the Least Industrialized Nations are pockets of high quality schools taught by and for Westerners. This bicycle-powered school bus in Nepal transports children to the English Boarding School.

Although the Egyptian constitution guarantees five years of free grade school for all children, many poor children receive no education at all. For those who do attend school, qualified teachers are few and classrooms are crowded (Cook 2001). As a result, one-third of Egyptian men and over half of Egyptian women are illiterate (UNESCO 2005). Those who go beyond the five years of grade school attend a preparatory school for three years. High school also lasts for three years. During the first two years, all students take the same courses, but during the third year they specialize in arts, science, or mathematics. All high school students take a monthly examination as well as a national exam at the end of the senior year.

The Functionalist Perspective: Providing Social Benefits

A central position of functionalism is that when the parts of society are working properly, each contributes to the well-being or stability of that society. The positive things that people intend their actions to accomplish are known as **manifest functions.** The positive consequences they did not intend are called **latent functions.** Let's look at the functions of education.

Teaching Knowledge and Skills

Education's most obvious manifest function is to teach knowledge and skills—whether the traditional three R's or their more contemporary counterparts, such as computer literacy. Each generation must train the next to fulfill the group's significant positions. Because our postindustrial society needs highly educated people, the schools supply them.

Over the years, the functions of U.S. schools have expanded, and they now rival some family functions. Child care is an example. Grade schools do double duty as babysitters for working parents. Child care has always been a latent function of formal education, for it was an unintended consequence. Now, however, because most families have two wage earners, child care has become a manifest function. Some schools even offer child care both before and after formal classes. Another function that schools are performing is providing sex education and birth control advice. This has stirred controversy, for some families resent this function being taken from them. Disagreement over values has fueled the social movement for home schooling, featured in our opening vignette and in the Down-to-Earth Sociology box on the next page.

Cultural Transmission of Values

Another manifest function of education is the **cultural transmission of values,** a process by which schools pass a society's core values from one generation to the next. Consequently, schools in a socialist society stress values of socialism, while schools in a capitalist society teach values that support capitalism. U.S. schools, for example, stress respect for private property, individualism, and competition.

Regardless of a country's economic system, loyalty to the state is a cultural value, and schools around the world teach patriotism. U.S. schools teach that the United States is the best country in the world; Russians learn that no country is better than Russia; and French, Japanese, and Afghani students all learn the same about their respective countries. Grade school teachers in every country extol the virtues of the society's founders, their struggle for freedom from oppression, and the goodness of the country's basic social institutions.

Social Integration

Schools also bring about *social integration;* that is, they help to mold students into a more cohesive unit. They promote

Down-to-Earth Sociology

Home Schooling: The Search for Quality and Values

"YOU'RE DOING WHAT? YOU'RE GOING TO teach your kids at home?" is the typical, incredulous response to parents who decide to home school their children.

The unspoken questions are, "How can you teach? You're not trained. And taking your kids out of the public schools—do you want them to become social misfits?"

The home schooling movement was small at first, just a trickle of parents who were dissatisfied with the rigidity of the school bureaucracy, lax discipline, incompetent teachers, low standards, lack of focus on individual needs, and, in some instances, of hostility to their religion.

The trickle has grown. While not yet a raging river, the number of children who are being taught at home is more than twice the size of the public school system of Chicago. About one million children are being home schooled (Princiotta et al. 2004; *Statistical Abstract* 2005:Table 229).

Home schooling seems to have burst onto the U.S. scene, but, surprisingly, it is not new. In the colonial era, home schooling was the *typical* form of education (Carper 2000). Today's home-schooling movement is restoring this earlier pattern, but it also reflects a fascinating shift in U.S. politics. Political and religious *liberals* began the contemporary home schooling movement in the 1950s and 1960s. Their objection was that the schools were too conservative. Then the schools changed, and in the 1970s and 1980s, political and religious *conservatives* embraced home schooling (Lines 2000; Stevens 2001). Their objection was that the schools were too liberal.

Does home schooling work? Can parents who are not trained as teachers actually teach? The early results of testing home schoolers were promising, but they were limited to small groups or to single states. Then in 1990, a national sample of 2,000 home schoolers showed that these students did better than students who were in public schools. Could this really be true?

To find out, researchers tested 21,000 home schoolers across the nation (Rudner 1999). The results are astounding. The median scores for every test at every grade were in the 70th to 80th percentiles. The home schoolers outscored students in both public and Catholic schools.

The basic reason for the stunning success of home schooling appears to be the parents' involvement in their children's edu-

As the home schooling social movement has grown, it has become increasingly institutionalized. Home schoolers now have their own class rings.

cation. Home schoolers receive an intense, one-on-one education. Their curriculum—although it includes the subjects that are required by the state—is designed around the student's interests and needs. Ninety percent of students are taught by their mothers, 10 percent by their fathers (Lines 2000). Ninety-eight percent of the fathers of home schoolers are in the labor force, but only 22 percent of the mothers. The parents' income is also above average.

What we do not know is what these home schoolers' test scores would have been if they had been taught in public schools. With their parents' involvement in their education, they likely would have done very well there, too. In addition, although the Rudner study was large, about 21,000 students, it was not a random sample, and we cannot say how the *average* home schooler is doing. But, then, we have no random sample of all public school students, either.

What about the children's social skills? Since they don't attend school with dozens and even hundreds of other students, do they become social misfits? The studies show that they do just fine on this level, too. They actually have fewer behavior problems than children who attend conventional schools (Lines 2000). Contrary to stereotypes, home-schooled children are not isolated. As part of their educational experience, their parents take them to libraries, museums, factories, and nursing homes (Medlin 2000). Some home schoolers participate in the physical education and sports programs of the public schools. For social activities, many of the children meet with other children who are being home schooled. There are even home-schooling associations, which run conferences for parents and children, and hold sporting events. As the photo shows, the same companies that sell class rings to public high schools also sell class rings to home schoolers (McGinn and McLure 2003).

for your Consideration

Two of every 100 students across the country are being taught at home. Why do you think that home schooling is turning out to be so popular? Do you think this social movement could eventually become a threat to U.S. public schools? Would you consider home schooling your children? Why or why not?

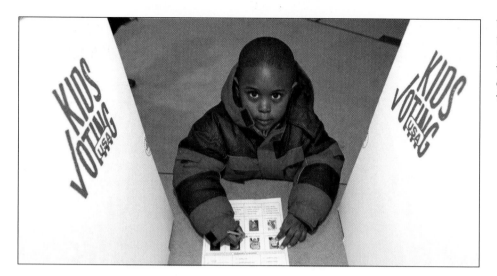

This student in New Hampshire, who is voting in a mock presidential primary, is learning that the identity of "American" overrides individual identities—and that it is a citizen's duty to vote.

a sense of national identity by having students salute the flag, sing the national anthem, and, as in the photo above, participate in mock elections. One of the best examples of how schools promote political integration is the education of millions of immigrants, who have learned mainstream ideas and values in U.S. schools. Coming to regard themselves as Americans, they gave up their earlier national and cultural identities (Rodriguez 1995; Carper 2000).

This integrative function of education goes far beyond making people similar in their appearance or speech. *To forge a national identity is to stabilize the political system.* If people identify with a society's social institutions and *perceive them as the basis of their welfare,* they have no reason to rebel. This function is especially significant when it comes to the lower social classes, from which most social revolutionaries emerge. The wealthy already have a vested interest in maintaining the status quo, but getting the lower classes to identify with a social system *as it is* goes a long way toward preserving the system in its current state.

People with disabilities often have found themselves left out of the mainstream of society. To overcome this, U.S. schools have added a manifest function, **mainstreaming,** or inclusion. This means that schools try to incorporate students with disabilities into regular social activities. As a matter of routine policy, students with disabilities used to be placed in special schools. There, however, they learned to adjust to a specialized world; this left them ill prepared to cope with the dominant world. Educational philosophy then shifted to encourage or even to require students with disabilities to attend regular schools. For people who cannot walk, wheelchair ramps are provided; for those who

cannot hear, interpreters who use sign language may attend classes with them. Most students who are blind attend special schools, as do people with severe learning disabilities. Overall, one half of students with disabilities now attend school in regular classrooms ("State of American Education," 2000).

Gatekeeping

Gatekeeping, or determining which people will enter what occupations, is another function of education. One type of gatekeeping is *credentialing*—using diplomas and degrees to determine who is eligible for a job—which opens the door of opportunity for some and closes it to others. Gatekeeping is often accomplished by **tracking,** sorting students into different educational programs on the basis of their perceived abilities. Some U.S. high schools funnel students into one of three tracks: general, college prep, or honors. Students on the lowest track are likely to go to work after high school, or to take vocational courses. Those on the highest track usually attend prestigious colleges. Those in between usually attend a local college or regional state university. The impact is lifelong, affecting opportunities for jobs, income, and lifestyle. Although schools have retreated from formal tracking, placing students in "ability groups" serves the same purpose (Lucas 1999; Tach and Farkas 2003).

Gatekeeping sorts people on the basis of merit, said functionalists Talcott Parsons (1940), Kingsley Davis, and Wilbert Moore (1945). They pioneered a view known as **social placement,** arguing that some jobs require few skills and can be performed by people of lesser intelligence.

Other jobs, however, such as that of physician, require high intelligence and advanced education. To motivate capable people to postpone gratification and put up with years of rigorous education, rewards of high income and prestige are offered. Thus, functionalists look at education as a system that, to benefit society, sorts people according to their abilities and ambitions.

The Conflict Perspective: Perpetuating Social Inequality

Unlike functionalists, who look at the benefits of education, conflict theorists examine how *the educational system reproduces the social structure.* By this, they mean that schools perpetuate the social divisions of society and help members of the elite to maintain their dominance.

To illustrate this principle, conflict theorists point to social class. In predicting which children will attend college, for example, family background is more important than children's abilities. If you rank families from the poorest to the richest, as a family's income increases so does the likelihood that their children will attend college (Bowles 1977; Manski 1992–1993). As conflict theorists stress, this means that children inherit the life opportunities that were laid down for them before they were born.

Conflict theorists also point out how education helps to reproduce the racial-ethnic structure for the next generation. Look at Figure 13.3. You can see that, compared to whites, African Americans and Latinos are less likely to complete high school and less likely to go to college. The difference is the greatest for Latinos. People without college degrees, of course, are more apt to end up with low-paying, dead-end jobs.

How does the educational system reproduce the social structure? Let's look at three ways.

The Hidden Curriculum

The term **hidden curriculum** refers to the attitudes and the unwritten rules of behavior that schools teach in addition to the formal curriculum. Examples are obedience to authority and conformity to mainstream norms. Conflict theorists stress that the hidden curriculum helps to perpetuate social inequalities.

To understand this central point, consider the way English is taught. Middle-class schools—whose teachers know where their students are headed—stress "proper"

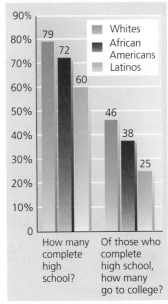

Figure 13.3 The Funneling Effects of Eucation: Race-Ethnicity

Typo!

Note: The source gives totals only for these three groups.
Source: By the author. Based on *Statistical Abstract* 2005:Table 256.

English and "good" manners. In contrast, the teachers in inner-city schools—who also know where *their* students are headed—allow ethnic and street language in the classroom. Each type of school is helping to reproduce the social structure. That is, each is preparing students to work in positions similar to those of their parents. The social class of some children destines them for higher positions. For these jobs, they need "refined" speech and manners. The social destiny of others is low-status jobs. For this work, they need only to obey rules (Bowles and Gintis 1976; 2002). Teaching these students "refined" speech and manners would be a wasted effort.

How schools approach language and manners, then, is significant. It is a way in which education prepares children for positions similar to those of their parents. In other words, even the teaching of English and manners helps to keep the social classes intact across generations.

Tilting the Tests: Discrimination by IQ

Even intelligence tests play a part in keeping the social class system intact. For example, how would you answer the following question?

A symphony is to a composer as a book is to
a(n) _____

_____ paper _____ sculptor _____ musician
_____ author _____ man

You probably had no difficulty coming up with "author" as your choice. Wouldn't any intelligent person have done so?

In point of fact, this question raises a central issue in intelligence testing. Not all intelligent people would know the answer. This question contains *cultural biases.* Children from some backgrounds are more familiar with the concepts of symphonies, composers, and sculptors than are other children. Consequently, the test is tilted in their favor.

Perhaps asking a different question will make the bias clearer. How would you answer this question?

If you throw two dice and "7" is showing on the top, what is facing down?

_____ seven _____ snake eyes _____ box cars
_____ little Joes _____ eleven

This question, suggested by Adrian Dove (n.d.), a social worker in Watts, a poor area of Los Angeles, is slanted toward a lower-class experience. It surely is obvious that this *particular* cultural bias tilts the test so that children from certain social backgrounds will perform better than others.

It is no different with IQ (intelligence quotient) tests that use such words as *composer* and *symphony.* A lower-class child may have heard about rap, rock, hip hop, or jazz but not about symphonies. In other words, IQ tests measure not only intelligence but also acquired knowledge. Whatever else we can say, the cultural bias that is built into IQ tests is clearly *not* tilted in favor of the lower classes. One consequence is that the children of the poor who score lower on these tests are assigned less demanding courses to match their supposedly inferior intelligence. This destines them for lower-paying jobs in adult life. Thus, conflict theorists view IQ tests as another weapon in an arsenal designed to maintain the social class structure across the generations.

Stacking the Deck: Unequal Funding

The way that U.S. schools are funded also helps education reproduce the social structure. Conflict theorists stress that in *all* states the deck is stacked against the poor. Because public schools are supported largely by local property taxes, the richer communities (where property values are higher) have more to spend on their children, and the poorer communities have less to spend on theirs. Consequently, the richer communities can offer higher salaries and take their pick of the more qualified and motivated teachers. They can also afford to buy the latest textbooks, computers, and software, as well as to offer courses in foreign language, music, and the arts.

IN SUM It is no accident that education's doors of opportunity swing wide open for some but have to be pried open by others. U.S. schools are designed to reflect and reproduce the U.S. social class system. They equip the children of the elite with the tools they need to maintain their dominance, while they prepare the children of the poor for lower-status positions. By doing this, they also reproduce society's racial-ethnic divisions. In short, the educational system perpetuates social inequality across generations. In fact, conflict theorists add, this is one of its primary purposes.

The Symbolic Interactionist Perspective: Fulfilling Teacher Expectations

Functionalists look at how education benefits society, and conflict theorists examine how education perpetuates social inequality. Symbolic interactionists, in contrast, study face-to-face interaction in the classroom. They have found that the expectations of teachers have profound consequences for their students.

The Rist Research

Why do some people get tracked into college prep courses and others into vocational ones? There is no single answer, but in what has become a classic study, sociologist Ray Rist came up with some intriguing findings. Rist (1970) did participant observation in an African American grade school with an African American faculty. He found that after only eight days in the classroom, the kindergarten teacher felt that she knew the children's abilities well enough to assign them to three separate work tables. To Table 1, Mrs. Caplow assigned those she considered to be "fast learners." They sat at the front of the room, closest to her. Those whom she saw as "slow learners," she assigned to Table 3, located at the back of the classroom. She placed "average" students at Table 2, in between the other tables.

This seemed strange to Rist. He knew that the children had not been tested for ability, yet their teacher was certain that she could identify the bright and slow children. Investigating further, Rist found that social class was the underlying basis for assigning the children to the different tables. Middle-class students were separated out for Table 1, children from poorer homes to Tables 2 and 3. The teacher paid the most attention to the children at Table 1, who were closest to her, less to Table 2, and the least to Table 3. As the year went on, children from Table 1 perceived that they were treated better and came to see themselves as smarter. They became the leaders in class activities and even ridiculed children at the other tables, calling them "dumb." Eventually, the children at Table 3 disengaged themselves from many classroom activities. At the end of the year, only the children at Table 1 had completed the lessons that prepared them for reading.

This early tracking stuck. Their first-grade teacher looked at the work these students had done, and she placed students from Table 1 at her Table 1. She treated her tables much as the kindergarten teacher had, and the children at Table 1 again led the class.

The children's reputations continued to follow them. The second-grade teacher reviewed their scores and also divided her class into three groups. The first she named the "Tigers" and, befitting their name, gave them challenging readers. Not surprisingly, the Tigers came from the original Table 1 in kindergarten. The second group she called the "Cardinals." They came from the original Tables 2 and 3. Her third group consisted of children she had failed the previous year, whom she called the "Clowns." The Cardinals and Clowns were given less advanced readers.

Rist concluded that *each child's journey through school was determined by the eighth day of kindergarten!* This research, like that done on the Saints and Roughnecks (reported in Chapter 6), demonstrates the power of labels: They can set people on courses of action that affect the rest of their lives.

What occurred was a **self-fulfilling prophecy.** This term, coined by sociologist Robert Merton (1949), refers to a false assumption that something is going to happen that then comes true simply because it was predicted. For example, if people believe an unfounded rumor that a credit union is going to fail, they all rush to the credit union to demand their money. The prediction—although originally false—is now likely to come true.

How Do Teacher Expectations Work?

Sociologist George Farkas (1990a, 1990b, 1996) became interested in how teacher expectations affect grades. Using a stratified sample of students in a large school district in Texas, he found that teacher expectations produced gender and racial–ethnic bias. On the gender level: *even though boys and girls had the same test scores,* girls, on average, were given higher course grades. On the racial–ethnic level: Asian Americans received higher grades than did African Americans, Latinos, and whites who had the same test scores.

At first, this may sound like more of the same old news—another case of discrimination. But this explanation doesn't fit, which is what makes the finding fascinating. Look at who the victims are. It is most unlikely that the teachers would be prejudiced against boys and whites. To interpret these unexpected results, Farkas used symbolic interactionism. He observed that some students "signal" to their teachers that they are "good students." They show an eagerness to cooperate, and they quickly agree with what the teacher says. They also show that they are "trying hard." The teachers pick up these signals and reward these "good students" with better grades. Girls and Asian Americans, the researcher concluded, are better at displaying these characteristics so coveted by teachers.

We do not have enough information on how teachers communicate their expectations to students. Nor do we know much about how students "signal" messages to teachers. Perhaps you will become the educational sociologist who will shed more light on this significant area of human behavior.

Problems in U.S. Education— and Their Solutions

To conclude this section, let's examine two problems facing U.S. education—and consider their potential solutions.

Problems: Mediocrity and Violence

The Rising Tide of Mediocrity.   All Arizona high school sophomores took a math test. It covered the math that sophomores should know. *One of ten passed.* Meanwhile, to enable its students to graduate, New York state had to drop its passing grade to 55 out of 100 (Steinberg 2000). Some New York City schools are so bad that the city and state have given up and turned them over to private, for-profit companies (Wyatt 2000). When test results showed that 1,500 of Michigan's high schools "needed improvement," officials lowered the percentage needed to pass. Overnight, 1,300 schools improved, leaving only 200 schools that still "needed improvement" (Dillon 2003). If the officials had lowered the passing score to the point that no schools "needed improvement," then all Michigan teachers would have been "good" and all their students "smart."

Perhaps nothing so captures what is wrong with U.S. schools as this event, reported by sociologist Thomas Sowell (1993):

> [A]n international study of 13-year-olds . . . found that Koreans ranked first in mathematics and Americans last. When asked if they thought they were "good at mathematics," only 23 percent of the Korean youngsters said "yes"—compared to 68 percent of American 13-year-olds. The American educational dogma that students should "feel good about themselves" was a success in its own terms—though not in any other terms.

Figure 13.4, which summarizes the scores on the SAT, indicates how sharply student achievement declined from the 1960s to 1980. At that point, educators—and even Congress—expressed concern and demanded greater accountability. Schools raised their standards, and math scores started to climb. The recovery in math has been excellent, and, as you can see, today's high school seniors score higher in math than seniors did in the 1960s. Administrators are requiring more of teachers, and teachers are requiring more of students. Each is performing according to the higher expectations.

The verbal score has not recovered, however. Compared with students of the past, today's students perform so poorly that the makers of the SAT eliminated the analogy part of the verbal test. Analogies demand penetrating thinking, and, unfortunately, today's students just couldn't handle it. No one knows exactly why, although the culprits are often identified as "dummied down" textbooks, less rigorous teaching, and less reading because of the hours that children spend watching television and playing video and computer games.

How to Cheat on the SATs. If you receive poor grades this semester, wouldn't you like to use a magic marker to—presto!—change them into higher grades? I suppose every student would. Now imagine that you had that power. Would you use it?

Some people in authority apparently have found such a magic marker, and they are using it to raise our embarrassingly low verbal scores. Table 274 of the 1996 edition of the *Statistical Abstract of the United States* reports that in 1995, only 8.3 percent of students earned 600 or more (of a maximum 800) on the verbal portion of the SAT test. The very next edition, in 1997, however, holds a pleasant surprise. Table 276 tells us that it was really 21.9 percent of students who scored 600 or higher in 1995. Later editions of this source retain the higher figure. What a magic marker!

In the twinkle of an eye, we get another bonus. Somehow, between 1996 and 1997, the scores of *everyone* who took the test in previous years improved. Now that's the kind of power we all would like to have. Students, grab your report cards. Workers, change those numbers on your paycheck.

It certainly is easier to give simpler tests than to teach more effectively. And this is what has happened to the SAT. The test is now shorter, and students have more time to answer fewer questions. To make the verbal part easier, the test on antonyms was also dropped (Manno 1995; Stecklow 1995). Results of previous years were then "rescored" to match the easier test. This "dummying down" of the SAT is yet another form of grade inflation, the topic to which we shall now turn.

Grade Inflation, Social Promotion, and Functional Illiteracy. High school teachers used to give about twice as many *C*'s as *A*'s, but now they give more *A*'s than *C*'s. Grades are so inflated that some of today's *A*'s are the *C*'s of years past. Another sign of grade inflation is that *47 percent* of all college freshmen have an

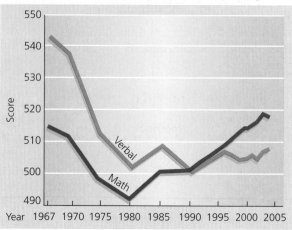

Figure 13.4 **National Results of the Scholastic Assessment Test (SAT)**

Sources: By the author. Based on Pope 2004; *Statistical Abstract* 2005:Table 248.

overall high school grade point average of *A*. This is more than *twice* what it was in 1970 (*Statistical Abstract* 2005:Table 268). Grade inflation has also hit the Ivy League. At Harvard University, *half* of the course grades are *A*'s and *A*–'s. *Ninety* percent of Harvard students graduate with honors. To rein in the "honor inflation," the Harvard faculty voted to limit the number of students who graduate with honors to 60 percent of a class (Hartocollis 2002; Douthat 2005).

Grade inflation in the face of declining standards has been accompanied by **social promotion,** the practice of passing students from one grade to the next even though they have not mastered the basic materials. One result is **functional illiteracy,** high school graduates having difficulty with reading and writing. Some high school graduates cannot even fill out job applications; others can't figure out whether they got the right change at the grocery store.

The Influence of Peer Groups.   What do you think is the most important factor in how teenagers do in school? Two psychologists and a sociologist, who studied 20,000 high school students in California and Wisconsin, found that it is the student's peer group (Steinberg et al. 1996). Simply put: Teens who hang out with good students tend to do well; those who hang out with friends who do poorly in school do poorly themselves. Student subcultures include informal norms about grades. Some groups have norms of classroom excellence, while others sneer at good grades. The applied question that arises from this research, of course, is how to build educational achievement into student culture.

Violence in Schools.   Some U.S. schools have deteriorated to the point that safety is an issue. In these schools, uniformed guards and metal detectors have become permanent fixtures. Some grade schools even supplement their traditional fire drills with "drive-by shooting drills." Because they might be targeted by terrorists, other schools hold "Code Blue" drills: The classrooms—each equipped with a phone—are locked, the windows are locked, and the shades are drawn. Whether these measures create feelings of security or produce fear is yet to be studied by sociologists.

Solutions: Safety and Standards

It is one thing to identify problems, quite another to find solutions for them. Let's consider solutions to the problems we just reviewed.

A Secure Learning Environment.   The first step in offering a good education is to ensure that students are safe and free from fear. With the high rate of violence in U.S. society, we can expect some violence to spill over into the schools. To minimize this spillover, school administrators can expel all students who threaten the welfare of others. They also can refuse to tolerate threats, violence, and weapons. The zero tolerance policy for guns and other weapons on school property that school boards and administrators have adopted help to make schools safer.

Higher Standards.   What else can we do to improve the quality of education? A study by sociologists James Coleman and Thomas Hoffer (1987) provides helpful guidelines. They wanted to see why the test scores of students in Roman Catholic schools average 15 to 20 percent higher than those of students in public schools. Is it because Catholic schools attract better students, while public schools have to put up with everyone? To find out, Coleman and Hoffer tested 15,000 students in public and Catholic high schools.

Their findings? From the sophomore through senior years, students at Catholic schools pull ahead of public school students by a full grade in verbal and math skills. The superior test performance of students in Catholic schools, they concluded, is due not to better students but to higher standards. Catholic schools have not watered down their curricula as have public schools. The researchers also underscored the importance of parental involvement. Parents and teachers in Catholic schools reinforce each other's commitment to learning.

These findings support the basic principle reviewed earlier about teacher expectations. Students perform better when they are expected to meet higher standards. This principle also means that we must expect (and require) more of teachers. These two expectations are combined in the following Thinking Critically section.

Thinking Critically

Breaking Through the Barriers: Restructuring the Classroom

Jaime Escalante taught in an East Los Angeles inner-city school that was plagued with poverty, crime, drugs, and gangs. In this self-defeating environment, he taught calculus. His students scored so highly on national tests that officials suspected cheating. They asked his students to retake the test. They did. This time, they earned even higher scores.

How did Escalante do it?

First, Escalante had to open his students' minds to the possibility of success: They had to believe that they *could* excel. Most Latino students were being tracked into craft classes, where they made jewelry and birdhouses. "Our kids are just as talented as anyone else. They just need the opportunity to show it," Escalante said. "They just don't think about becoming scientists or engineers."

Students also need to see learning as a way out of the inner city, as the path to good jobs. Escalante arranged for foundations to provide money for students to attend the colleges of their choice. Students learned that if they did well, their poverty wouldn't stop them.

Escalante also changed the system of instruction. He had his students think of themselves as a team, of him as the coach, and of the national math exams as a sort of Olympics for which they were preparing. To foster team identity, students wore team jackets, caps, and T-shirts with logos that identified them as part of the math team. Before class, his students did "warm-ups" (hand clapping and foot stomping to a rock song).

Escalante's team had practice schedules as rigorous as those of a championship football team. Students had to sign a contract that bound them to participate in a summer program, to complete the daily homework, and to attend Saturday morning and after-school study sessions. To remind students that self-discipline pays off, Escalante covered his walls with posters of sports figures.

The sociological point is this: The problem was not the ability of the students. Their failure to do well in school was not

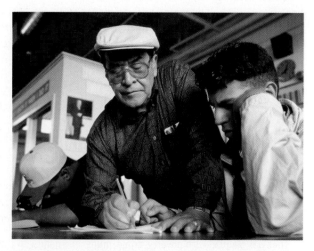

To say that today's schoolchildren can't learn as well as those in previous generations is a case of blaming the victim. As discussed in the text, Jaime Escalante (shown here) demonstrated that teachers can motivate even highly deprived students to study hard and to excel in learning. His experience challenges us to rethink our approach to education.

due to something *within* them. The problem was the *system,* the way classroom instruction was designed. When Escalante changed the system of instruction—*and* brought in hope—both attitudes and performance changed.

Sources: Based on Barry 1989; Meek 1989; Escalante and Dirmann 1990; Hilliard 1991.

for your Consideration

What principles discussed in this or earlier chapters did Escalante apply? What changes do you think we can make in education to bring about similar results all over the country?

RELIGION: ESTABLISHING MEANING

Let's look at the main characteristics of a second significant social institution.

What Is Religion?

Sociologists who do research on religion analyze the relationship between society and religion and study the role that religion plays in people's lives. They do not seek to prove that one religion is better than another. Nor is their goal to verify or disprove anyone's faith. As was mentioned in Chapter 1, sociologists have no tools for deciding that one course of action is more moral than another, much less for determining that one religion is "the" correct one. Religion is a matter of faith—and sociologists deal with empirical matters, things they can observe or measure. Thus, sociologists study the effects of religious beliefs and practices on people's lives. They also analyze how religion is related to stratification systems. Unlike theologians, however, sociologists cannot evaluate the truth of a religion's teachings.

In 1912, Emile Durkheim published an influential book, *The Elementary Forms of the Religious Life,* in which he tried to identify the elements that are common to all religions. After surveying religions around the world, Durkheim could find no specific belief or practice that all religions share. He did find, however, that all religions develop a community around their practices and beliefs. All religions also separate the sacred from the profane. By **sacred,** Durkheim referred to aspects of life having to do with the supernatural that inspire awe, reverence, deep respect, even fear. By **profane,** he meant aspects of life that

When I visited a Hindu temple in Chattisgargh, India, I was impressed by the colorful and expressive statues on its roof. Here is a close-up of some of those figures, which represent some of the millions of gods that Hindus worship.

are not concerned with religion or religious purposes but, instead, are part of ordinary, everyday life. Durkheim (1912/1965) concluded:

> A religion is a unified system of beliefs and practices relative to sacred things, that is to say, things set apart and forbidden—beliefs and practices which unite into one single moral community called a Church, all those who adhere to them.

Thus, Durkheim said, **religion** is defined by three elements:

1. *Beliefs* that some things are sacred (forbidden, set apart from the profane)
2. *Practices* (rituals) centering on the things considered sacred
3. *A moral community* (a church) resulting from a group's beliefs and practices

Durkheim used the word **church** in an unusual sense, to refer to any "moral community" centered on beliefs and practices regarding the sacred. In Durkheim's sense, *church* refers to Buddhists bowing before a shrine, Hindus dipping in the Ganges River, and Confucians offering food to their ancestors. Similarly, the term *moral community* does not imply morality in the sense familiar to most of us—of ethical conduct. Rather, a moral community is simply a group of people who are united by their religious practices—and that would include sixteenth-century

Aztec priests who each day gathered around an altar to pluck out the beating heart of a virgin.

To better understand the sociological approach to religion, let's see what pictures emerge when we apply the three theoretical perspectives.

The Functionalist Perspective

Functionalists stress that religion is universal because it meets basic human needs. Let's look at some of the functions—and dysfunctions—of religion.

Functions of Religion

Around the world, religions provide answers to perplexing questions about ultimate meaning—such as the purpose of life, why people suffer, and the existence of an afterlife. Religion fosters social solidarity by uniting believers into a community that shares values and perspectives ("we Jews," "we Christians," "we Muslims"). The religious rituals that surround marriage, for example, link the bride and groom with a broader community that wishes them well. So do other religious rituals, such as those that celebrate birth and mourn death.

The teachings of religion help people adjust to life's problems and provide guidelines for daily life. Six of the Ten Commandments, for example, contain practical instructions—from how to get along with parents, employers, and neighbors to warnings about lying, stealing, and having affairs. One consequence is that people who attend church are less likely to abuse alcohol and illegal drugs than are people who don't go to church (Ostling 2001). This holds true for both adults and teens. In general, churchgoers follow a healthier lifestyle, and they live longer than those who don't go to church. The effects of religion on health, however, go deeper than this, a topic we explore in the Down-to-Earth Sociology box on the next page.

Just as education instills the value of patriotism, so do most religions. The most obvious example is the way some churches prominently display the U.S. flag and hold special Memorial Day and 4th of July services. The U.S. government reciprocates by supporting God—as witnessed by the inaugural speeches of U.S. presidents, who, believers or not, invariably ask God to bless the nation.

Although religion is often so bound up with the prevailing social order that it resists social change, religion occasionally spearheads change. In the 1960s, for example, the civil rights movement, which sought to desegregate public facilities and abolish racial discrimination at southern polls, was led by religious leaders, especially leaders of

Down-to-Earth Sociology

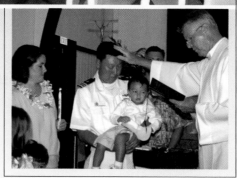

Religion and Health: What We Know and Don't Know

Does religion make a difference in people's health? Although scientists cannot pass judgment on the truth of any religion, they can study the effects of religion on people's lives—and this is one of those areas.

"After seeing the data, I think I should go to church," said Lynda Powell, an epidemiologist at Rush University Medical Center in Chicago (Helliker 2005). What would ever prompt such a response?

Powell, along with two colleagues, evaluated the research articles that had been published on the effects of religion on health. They evaluated only research that met solid scientific criteria. For example, they threw out studies that didn't control for age, gender, or race-ethnicity, significant variables in health (Powell, Shahabi, and Thoresen 2003). Their most outstanding finding is this: People who attend religious services at least once a week have 25 percent fewer deaths than people who don't go to church. Think about it: For every hundred deaths among people who don't attend church, there are only 75 deaths of people who attend church weekly.

How could this possibly be? You might think that the churchgoers were already healthier. This wasn't the reason, though, for the researchers compared people who were at the same levels of health or illness.

How about healthier lifestyles? Perhaps this is the reason. After all, churchgoers are less likely to smoke, to get drunk, and so on. Not this either. The researchers also controlled for lifestyles. Actually, the weekly churchgoers had 30 percent less mortality. When the researchers adjusted for lifestyle and social class, the difference in mortality dropped to 25 percent (Powell, Shahabi, and Thoresen 2003).

What explanation could there be, then? Remember that the researchers are scientists, so they aren't going to say "God." Here are three mechanisms that they suggest might account for the lower mortality of churchgoers: involvement in social roles that produce a sense of self-worth and purpose in life; experiencing positive emotions from worship and interacting with like-minded people; and learning calming ways of coping with crises from compassionate role models. (These mechanisms are related to the sense of community that I suggested might help to explain the possible longer life of the Abkhasians. You might want to review page 277.)

The explanations suggested by the researchers could be correct, but we need research to find out.

Is there anything about religion itself that could account for this remarkable reduction in mortality? Some researchers think they've put their finger on it: prayer. Apparently, prayer (or meditation) changes people's brain activity and improves their immune response. Scientists are investigating this hypothesis (Kalb 2003).

One researcher points to something else about religion—the practice of forgiveness. It turns out that people who forgive easily are more likely to be in good psychological health. They are especially less likely to be depressed (Krause and Ellison 2003). Forgiving people who have done you wrong apparently brings release from resentment, bitterness, and hatred—but holding on to grudges rips you apart inside.

What have researchers found about praying for people who are sick? Does this help them to get better? So far, most researchers haven't found any difference between people who are prayed for and those who are not. But researchers have encountered a problem. How do they find a control group of people who are not being prayed for? There is so much prayer—from parents, siblings, aunts and uncles, friends and neighbors—that some people don't even know they are being prayed for. I'm sure that researchers will solve this.

We are just at the initial stages of research on religion and health. At this point, we have hardly any answers, but we do have this astounding statistic about death and weekly attendance at religious services.

So, if you want to live longer . . .

Religion can promote social change, as was evident in the U.S. civil rights movement. Dr. Martin Luther King, Jr., a Baptist minister, shown here in his famous "I have a dream" speech, was the foremost leader of this movement.

African American churches, such as Dr. Martin Luther King, Jr. Churches also served as centers at which demonstrators were trained and rallies were organized.

Dysfunctions of Religion

Functionalists also examine ways in which religion is *dysfunctional,* that is, how it can bring about harmful results. Two dysfunctions are religious persecution and war and terrorism.

Religion as Justification for Persecution. Beginning in the 1200s and continuing into the 1800s, in what has become known as the Inquisition, special commissions of the Roman Catholic Church tortured women to make them confess that they were witches and then burned them at the stake. In 1692, Protestant leaders in Salem, Massachusetts, executed twenty-one women and men who were accused of being witches. In 2001, in the Democratic Republic of the Congo, about 1,000 alleged witches were hacked to death in a single "purge" (Jenkins 2002). Similarly, it seems fair to say that the Aztec religion had its dysfunctions—at least for the virgins who were offered to appease angry gods. In short, religion has been used to justify oppression and any number of brutal acts.

War and Terrorism.   History is filled with wars based on religion—commingled with politics. Between the eleventh and fourteenth centuries, for example, Christian monarchs conducted nine bloody Crusades in an attempt to wrest control of the region they called the Holy Land

from the Muslims. As discussed in the Down-to-Earth Sociology box on the next page, some terrorists also use religion to justify their acts.

The Symbolic Interactionist Perspective

Symbolic interactionists focus on the meanings that people give their experiences, especially how they use symbols. Let's apply this perspective to religious symbols, rituals, and beliefs to see how they help forge a community of like-minded people.

Religious Symbols

Suppose that it is about two thousand years ago, and you have just joined a new religion. You have come to believe that a recently crucified Jew named Jesus is the Messiah, the Lamb of God offered for your sins. The Roman leaders are persecuting the followers of Jesus. They hate your religion because you and your fellow believers will not acknowledge Caesar as God.

Christians are few in number, and you are eager to have fellowship with other believers. But how can you tell who is a believer? Spies are everywhere. The government has sworn to destroy this new religion, and you do not relish the thought of being fed to the lions in the Coliseum.

Down-to-Earth Sociology

Terrorism and the Mind of God

WARNING: The "equal time" contents of this box are likely to offend just about everyone.

AFTER 9/11, THE QUESTION ON MANY people's minds was some form of, "How can people do such evil in the name of God?"

To answer this question, we need to broaden the context. The question is fine, but it cannot be directed solely at Islamic terrorists. If it is, it misses the point.

We need to consider other religions, too. For Christians, we don't have to go back centuries to the Inquisition or to the Children's Crusades. We only have to look at Ireland, and the bombings in Belfast. There, Protestants and Catholics slaughtered each other in the name of God.

In the United States, we can consider the killing of abortion doctors. Paul Hill, a minister who was executed for killing a doctor in Florida, was convinced that his act was good, that he had saved the lives of unborn babies. Before his execution, he said that he was looking forward to heaven. His friend, Reverend Michael Bray, took no lives; instead, he burned abortion clinics.

Since I want to give equal time to the major religions, we can't forget the Jews. Dr. Baruch Goldstein was convinced that Yahweh wanted him to take a Galil assault rifle, go to the Tomb of the Patriarchs, and shoot into a crowd of praying Palestinian men and boys. His admirers built a monument on his grave (Juergensmeyer 2000).

Finally, for the sake of equality, let's not let the Hindus, Buddhists, and Sikhs off the hook. In India, these groups continue to slaughter one another. In the name of their gods, they attack the houses of worship of the others and blow one another up. (The Hindus are actually equal opportunists—they kill Christians, too. I visited a state in India where Hindus had doused a jeep with gasoline and burned alive an Australian missionary and his two sons.)

None of these terrorists—Islamic, Christian, Jew, Sikh, Buddhist, or Hindu—represent the mainstream of their religion, but they do commit violence for religious reasons. How can they do so? Here are five elements that religious terrorists seem to have in common. (I have extrapolated these principles from the acts of individuals and small groups. Terrorism by the state is another matter.)

First, the individuals believe that they are under attack. Evil forces are bent on destroying the good of their world—whether that be their religion, their way of life, or unborn babies.

Second, they become convinced that God wants the evil destroyed.

Third, they conclude that it will take violence to resolve the situation, and that this turns violence into good.

Fourth, they become convinced that God has chosen them for this task. They don't necessarily want to kill or to die, but they accept their fate. Dying for God's cause is a greater calling than living as a coward who won't stand up for what is right.

Fifth, these perspectives are nurtured by a community, a group in which the individuals find identity. This group may realize that most members of their faith do not support their views, but that is because the others are uninformed, even brainwashed by the enemy or by the liberal, secularized media. The smaller community holds the truth.

For those groups that have scriptures, there are enough references to violence that they are able to interpret selective passages as "God's mandated" solution to the threat they feel.

If these orientations are accompanied by the view that we are in a final confrontation between good and evil, they become even more powerful. If we are in the end times and this is the final battle, there is no retreat. Some Christians, Jews, Muslims, and Sikhs hold such a view (Juergensmeyer 2000).

Under these conditions, morality is turned upside down. Killing becomes a moral act, a good done for a greater cause. This greater good may require self-sacrifice—the most notable example being suicide bombers.

There is just enough truth in these points of view to keep the delusion alive. After all, wouldn't it have been better for the millions of Jews and the millions of other victims if someone had had the nerve and foresight to kill Hitler? Wouldn't his death and one's own self-sacrifice have been a greater good? Today, there are those bad Protestants, those bad Catholics, those bad Jews, those bad Palestinians, those bad abortionists, those bad Americans—an endless list. And the violence is for the Greater Good: what God wants.

Once people buy into this closed system of thought, discussion in which contrasting views are shared and considered flies out the window. The individuals become convinced that they have access to the mind of God.

This analysis would not be complete without stressing that religious violence is often a political instrument. There are those who exploit the conditions analyzed here to enforce their political agenda. Religious riots in India, for example, are usually not spontaneous, but, rather, are "produced" by leaders who benefit from them (Brass 2003). Similarly, the violent demonstrations that occurred after Danish newspapers published cartoons of Muhammad in 2006 seem to have been orchestrated by political and religious leaders.

You use a simple technique. While talking with a stranger, as though doodling absentmindedly in the sand or dust, you casually trace out the outline of a fish. Only fellow believers know the meaning—that, taken together, the first letter of each word in the Greek sentence "Jesus (is) Christ the Son of God" spell the Greek word for fish. If the other person gives no response, you rub out the outline and continue the interaction as usual. If there is a response, you eagerly talk about your new faith.

All religions use symbols to provide identity and social solidarity for their members. For Muslims, the primary symbol is the crescent moon and star; for Jews, the Star of David; for Christians, the cross. For members, these are not ordinary symbols but sacred emblems that evoke feelings of awe and reverence. In Durkheim's terms, religions use symbols to represent what the group considers sacred and to separate the sacred from the profane.

A symbol is a condensed way of communicating. Worn by a fundamentalist Christian, for example, the cross says, "I am a follower of Jesus Christ. I believe that He is the Messiah, the promised Son of God, that He loves me, that He died to take away my sins, that He rose from the dead and is going to return to earth, and that through Him I will receive eternal life."

That is a lot to pack into one symbol—and it is only part of what the symbol means to a fundamentalist believer. To people in other traditions of Christianity, the cross conveys somewhat different meanings—but to all Christians, the cross is a shorthand way of expressing many meanings. So it is with the Star of David, the crescent moon and star, the cow (expressing to Hindus the unity of all living things), and the various symbols of the world's many other religions.

Symbolic interactionists stress that a basic characteristic of humans is that they attach meaning to objects and events and then use representations of those objects or events to communicate with one another. Some religious symbols are used to communicate feelings of awe and reverence. Michaelangelo's *Pietà*, depicting Mary tenderly holding her son, Jesus, after his crucifixion, is one of the most acclaimed symbols in the Western world. It is admired for its beauty by believers and nonbelievers alike.

Rituals and Beliefs

Rituals, ceremonies or repetitive practices, are also symbols that help to unite people into a moral community. Some rituals, such as the bar mitzvah of Jewish boys and the Holy Communion of Christians, are designed to create in devout believers a feeling of closeness with God and unity with one another. Rituals include kneeling and praying at set times; bowing; crossing oneself; singing; lighting candles and incense; reading scripture; and following prescribed traditions at processions, baptisms, weddings, and funerals.

Symbols, including rituals, develop from beliefs. The belief may be vague ("God is") or highly specific ("God wants us to prostrate ourselves and face Mecca five times each day"). Religious beliefs include not only *values* (what is considered good and desirable in life—how we ought to live) but also a **cosmology,** a unified picture of the world. For example, the Jewish, Christian, and Muslim belief that there is only one God, the Creator of the universe, who is concerned about the actions of humans and who will hold us accountable for what we do, is a cosmology. It presents a unifying picture of the universe.

Religious Experience

The term **religious experience** refers to a sudden awareness of the supernatural or a feeling of coming into contact with God. Some people undergo a mild version, such as feeling closer to God when they look at a mountain or listen to a certain piece of music. Others report a life-transforming experience. St. Francis of Assisi, for example, said that he became aware of God's presence in every living thing.

Some Protestants use the term **born again** to describe people who have undergone such a life-transforming religious experience. These people say that they have come to the realization that they have sinned, that Jesus died for their sins, and that God wants them to live a new life. Their worlds become transformed. They look forward to the Resurrection and to a new life in heaven, and they see relationships with spouses, parents, children, and even bosses in a new light. They also report a need to make changes in how they interact with others so that their lives reflect their new, personal commitment to Jesus as their "Savior and Lord." They describe a feeling of beginning life anew; hence the term *born again.*

The Conflict Perspective

In general, conflict theorists are highly critical of religion. They stress that religion is used to support the status quo, that it is a means to perpetuate social inequality. Let's look at some of their analyses.

Opium of the People

Karl Marx, an avowed atheist who believed that the existence of God was impossible, set the tone for conflict theorists with his most famous statement on this subject: "Religion is the sigh of the oppressed creature, the sentiment of a heartless world. . . . It is the opium of the people" (Marx 1844/1964). By this statement, Marx meant that oppressed workers find escape in religion. For them, religion is like a drug that helps them to forget their misery. By diverting their thoughts toward future happiness in an afterlife, religion takes their eyes off their suffering in this world, thereby reducing the possibility that they will rebel against their oppressors.

A Legitimation of Social Inequalities

Just as they do with education, conflict theorists examine how religion legitimates the social inequalities of society. By this, they mean that religion teaches that the existing social arrangements of a society represent what God desires. For example, during the Middle Ages, Christian theologians decreed the "divine right of kings." This doctrine meant that God determined who would become king and set him on the throne. The king ruled in God's place, and it was the duty of a king's subjects to be loyal to him (and to pay their taxes). To disobey the king was to disobey God.

In what was perhaps the supreme technique of legitimating the social order (and one that went even a step farther than the "divine right of kings"), the religion of ancient Egypt held that the Pharaoh was a god. The Emperor of Japan was similarly declared divine. If this were so, who could even question his decisions? Today's politicians would give their right arm for such a religious teaching!

Conflict theorists point to many other examples of how religion legitimates the social order. In India, Hinduism supports the caste system by teaching that an individual who tries to change caste will come back in the next life as a member of a lower caste—or even as an animal. In the decades before the American Civil War, Southern ministers used Scripture to defend slavery, saying that it was God's will—while Northern ministers legitimated *their* region's social structure by using Scripture to denounce slavery as evil (Ernst 1988; Nauta 1993; White 1995).

Religion and the Spirit of Capitalism

For sociologist Max Weber, to discover the origin of capitalism was as intriguing as an unsolved murder is to a detective. Weber found the clue that unraveled the mystery when he noted that capitalism thrived only in certain parts of Europe. "There has be a reason for this," he mused. As Weber pursued the matter, he noted that capitalism flourished in Protestant countries, while Roman Catholic countries held on to tradition and were relatively untouched by capitalism. "Somehow, then, religion holds the key," he thought.

To explain how religion brought about capitalism, Weber wrote *The Protestant Ethic and the Spirit of Capitalism* (1904–1905/1958). He said that

1. Capitalism is not just a superficial change. Rather, capitalism represents a fundamentally different way of thinking about work and money. *Traditionally, people worked just enough to meet their basic needs, not so they would have a surplus to invest.* To accumulate money (capital) as an end in itself, not just to spend it, was a radical departure from traditional thinking. People even came to consider it a duty to invest money in order to make profits, which, in turn, they reinvested to make more profits. Weber called this new approach to work and money the **spirit of capitalism.**

2. Why did the spirit of capitalism develop in Europe and not, for example, in China or India, where the people had similar material resources and education? According to Weber, *religion was the key.* The religions of China and India, and indeed Roman Catholicism in Europe, encouraged a traditional approach to life, not thrift and investment. Capitalism appeared when Protestantism came on the scene.

3. What was different about Protestantism, especially Calvinism? John Calvin, a Protestant theologian, taught that God had predestined some people to go to heaven, others to hell. People could depend neither on church membership nor on feelings about their relationship with God to know they were saved. You wouldn't know your fate until after you died.

4. This doctrine made people anxious. "Am I predestined to hell or to heaven?" Calvinists wondered. As they wrestled with this question, they concluded that church members have a duty to prove that they are God's elect and to live as though they are predestined to heaven—for good works are a demonstration of salvation.

5. This conclusion motivated Calvinists to lead moral lives *and* to work hard, to not waste time, and to be frugal—for idleness and needless spending were signs of worldliness. Weber called this self-denying approach to life the **Protestant ethic.**

6. As people worked hard and spent money only on necessities (a pair of earrings or a second pair of dress shoes would have been defined as sinful luxuries), they had money left over. Because it couldn't be spent, this capital was invested, which led to a surge in production.

7. Ironically, a change in religion (from Catholicism to Protestantism, especially Calvinism) led to a fundamental change in thought and behavior (the *Protestant ethic*). The result was the *spirit of capitalism.* Thus, capitalism originated in Europe and not in places where religion did not encourage capitalism's essential elements: the accumulation of capital and its investment and reinvestment.

At this point in history, the Protestant ethic and the spirit of capitalism are not confined to any specific religion or even to any one part of the world. Rather, they have become cultural traits that have spread to societies around the globe (Greeley 1964; Yinger 1970). U.S. Catholics have about the same approach to life as do U.S. Protestants. In addition, Hong Kong, Japan, Malaysia, Singapore, South Korea, and Taiwan—not exactly Protestant countries—have embraced capitalism (Levy 1992).

Types of Religious Groups

Sociologists have identified four types of religious groups: cult, sect, church, and ecclesia. The summary presented here is a modification of analyses by sociologists Ernst Troeltsch (1931), Liston Pope (1942), and Benton Johnson (1963). Figure 13.5 illustrates the relationship between each of these four types of groups.

Cult

The word *cult* conjures up bizarre images: shaven heads, weird music, brainwashing—even ritual suicide may come to mind. Cults, however, are not necessarily weird, and few

---

Figure 13.5 **Religious Groups: From Hostility to Acceptance**

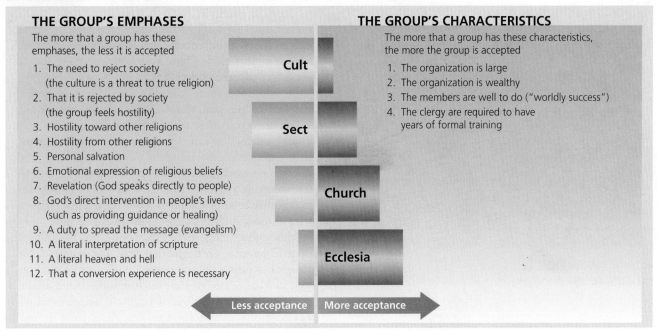

THE GROUP'S EMPHASES

The more that a group has these emphases, the less it is accepted

1. The need to reject society (the culture is a threat to true religion)
2. That it is rejected by society (the group feels hostility)
3. Hostility toward other religions
4. Hostility from other religions
5. Personal salvation
6. Emotional expression of religious beliefs
7. Revelation (God speaks directly to people)
8. God's direct intervention in people's lives (such as providing guidance or healing)
9. A duty to spread the message (evangelism)
10. A literal interpretation of scripture
11. A literal heaven and hell
12. That a conversion experience is necessary

THE GROUP'S CHARACTERISTICS

The more that a group has these characteristics, the more the group is accepted

1. The organization is large
2. The organization is wealthy
3. The members are well to do ("worldly success")
4. The clergy are required to have years of formal training

Cult

Sect

Church

Ecclesia

← Less acceptance | More acceptance →

Note: Any religious organization can be placed somewhere on this continuum, based on its having "more" or "less" of these characteristics and emphases. The varying proportions of the rectangles are intended to represent the group's relative characteristics and emphases.

Sources: By the author. Based on Troeltsch 1931; Pope 1942; and Johnson 1963.

practice "brainwashing" or bizarre rituals. In fact, *all religions began as cults* (Stark 1989). A **cult** is simply a new or different religion, whose teachings and practices put it at odds with the dominant culture and religion. Because the term cult arouses such negative meanings in the public mind, however, some scholars prefer to use *new religion* instead.

Cults originate with the appearance of a **charismatic leader,** an individual who inspires people because he or she seems to have extraordinary qualities. **Charisma** refers to an outstanding gift or some exceptional quality. People feel drawn to both the person and the message because they find something highly appealing about the individual—in some instances, almost a magnetic charm.

The most popular religion in the world began as a cult. Its handful of followers believed that an unschooled carpenter who preached in remote villages in a backwater country was the Son of God, that he was killed and came back to life. Those beliefs made the early Christians a cult, setting them apart from the rest of their society. Persecuted by both religious and political authorities, these early believers clung to one another for support. Many cut off associations with their unbelieving families and friends. To others, the early Christians must have seemed deluded and brainwashed.

Most cults fail. Although cults stress *evangelism*, the active recruitment of new members, not many people believe the new message, and most cults fade into obscurity. If the group recruits large numbers of people, however, the new religion changes from a cult to a sect.

Sect

A **sect** is larger than a cult. Its members still feel tension between their views and the prevailing beliefs and values of the broader society, but if a sect grows, that tension fades. To appeal to a broader base, the sect shifts some of its doctrines, redefining matters to remove some of the rough edges that created tension between it and the rest of society. As the members become more respectable in the eyes of society, they feel less hostility and little, if any, isolation. If a sect follows this course, as it grows and becomes more integrated into society, it changes into a church.

Church

At this point, the religious group is highly bureaucratized—probably with national and international headquarters that direct the local congregations. The relationship with God has grown less intense. Worship services are likely to be more sedate, with less emphasis on personal salvation and emotional expression. Sermons become more formal, and

written prayers may be read before the congregation. Most new members have not joined through conversion—after seeing the "new truth"—but are children born to existing members. To affirm their group's beliefs, the children, when older, may be asked to go through a ceremony such as a confirmation or bar mitzvah.

Ecclesia

Finally, some groups become so well integrated into a culture, and so strongly allied with their government, that it is difficult to tell where one leaves off and the other takes over. In these *state religions,* also called **ecclesia,** the government and religion work together to try to shape society. There is no recruitment of members, for citizenship makes everyone a member. For most people in the society, the religion provides little meaning: The religion is part of a cultural identity, not an eye-opening experience. How extensively religion and government intertwine in an ecclesia is illustrated by Sweden. In the 1860s, all citizens had to memorize Luther's *Small Catechism* and be tested on it yearly (Anderson 1995). Today, Lutheranism is still the state religion, but most Swedes come to church only for baptisms, marriages, and funerals.

Variations in Patterns

Obviously, not all religious groups go through all these stages—from cult to sect to church to ecclesia. Some die out because they fail to attract enough members. Others, such as the Amish, remain sects. And, as is evident from the few countries that have state religions, very few religions ever become ecclesias.

In addition, these classifications are not perfectly matched in the real world. For example, although the Amish are a sect, they place little or no emphasis on recruiting others. The early Quakers, another sect, shied away from emotional expressions of their beliefs. They would quietly meditate in church, with no one speaking until God gave someone a message to share with others. Finally, some groups that become churches may retain a few characteristics of sects, such as an emphasis on evangelism.

Although all religions began as cults, not all varieties of a particular religion begin that way. For example, some **denominations**—"brand names" within a major religion, such as Methodism or Reform Judaism—begin as splinter groups. Some members of a church disagree with *particular* aspects of the church's teachings (not its major message), and they break away to form their own organization. An example is the Southern Baptist Convention, which was formed in 1845 to defend the right to own slaves (Ernst 1988; Nauta 1993; White 1995).

Religion in the United States

▮▮ ▮◢▮ Although many people think that religion is less important to Americans than it used to be, the growth in religious membership does not support such an assumption. As Table 13.1 shows, the proportion of Americans who belong to a church or synagogue is now *four* times higher than it was when the country was founded. Ninety-four percent of Americans believe that there is a God, and 82 percent believe that there is a life after death. On any given weekend, two of every five Americans report that they attend a church or synagogue (Woodward 1989; Gallup 1990; Greeley and Hout 1999; *Statistical Abstract* 2002:Table 64).

Characteristics of Members

Let's look at the characteristics of the 65 percent of Americans who hold formal membership in a religion.

Social Class Religion in the United States is stratified by social class. As you can see from Figure 13.6, some religious groups are "top-heavy," and others are "bottom-heavy." The most top-heavy are Jews and Episcopalians; the most bottom-heavy are Assembly of

Table 13.1 Growth in Religious Membership	
The Percentage of Americans who Belong to a Church or Synagogue	
Year	**Percentage Who Claim Membership**
1776	17%
1860	37%
1890	45%
1926	58%
1975	71%
2000	68%
2005	65%

Note: The sources do not contain data on mosque membership.
Sources: Finke and Stark 1992; *Statistical Abstract* 2002:Table 64; Gallup Poll 2005.

God, Southern Baptists, and Jehovah's Witnesses. This figure provides further confirmation that churchlike groups tend to appeal to people who are more economically

Figure 13.6 Social Class and Religious Affiliation

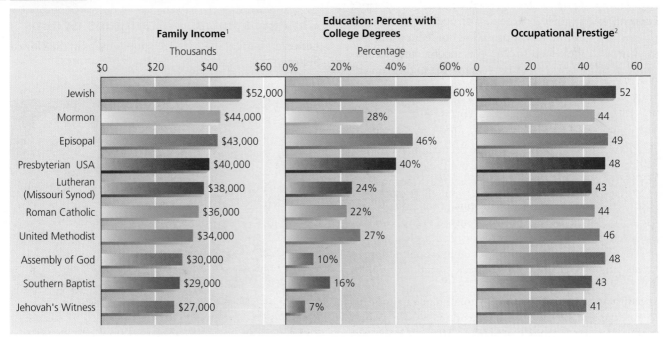

[1]Inflation since the income data were reported is approximately 24 percent.
[2]Higher numbers mean that more of the group's members work at occupations that have higher prestige, generally those that require more education and pay more. For more information on occupational prestige, see Table 8.2 on page 199.
Source: By the author. Based on Smith and Faris 2005.

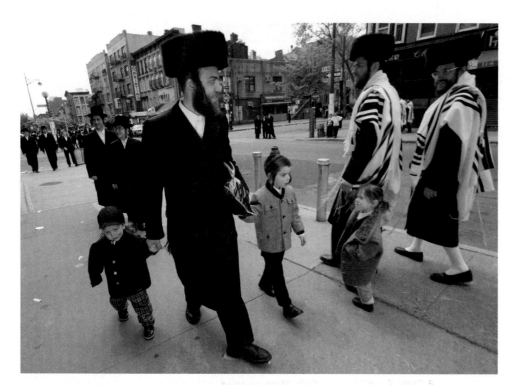

Religion, which provides community and identity, is often passed from the older to the younger. Shown here are Hasidic Jews in Brooklyn. Differences among religious groups are often incomprehensible to outsiders. The man on the left is carrying a pouch under his left arm, considered by the men on the right to be a violation of the Sabbath.

successful, while the more sectlike groups attract the less successful.

From this figure, you can see how *status consistency* (a concept you studied in Chapter 4) applies to religious groups. If a group ranks high (or low) on education, it is also likely to rank high (or low) on income and occupational prestige. Jews, for example, rank the highest on education, income, and occupational prestige, while Jehovah's Witnesses rank the lowest on these three measures of social class. The most glaring exception to this pattern is Assembly of God, whose members rank 8th in income and 9th in education, but tie for third in occupational prestige. I don't have an explanation for this, but the exception is so jarring that there could be a problem with the sample.

Race-Ethnicity All major religious groups draw from the nation's many racial-ethnic groups. Like social class, however, race-ethnicity tends to cluster. People of Latino or Irish descent are likely to be Roman Catholics, those of Greek origin to belong to the Greek Orthodox church. African Americans are likely to be Protestants—more specifically, Baptists—or to belong to fundamentalist sects.

Although many churches are integrated, it is with good reason that Sunday morning between 10 and 11 A.M. has been called "the most segregated hour in the United States." African Americans tend to belong to African American churches, while most whites see only whites in

their churches. The segregation of churches is based on custom, not law.

Characteristics of Religious Groups

Let's examine features of the religious groups in the United States.

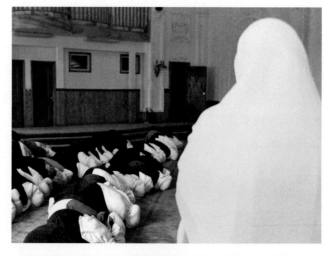

Universally, children are socialized into the religion of their group. The students shown here at the Al-Ghazaly Islamic school in Jersey City, New Jersey, are learning how to pray.

Diversity.   With its 300,000 congregations and hundreds of denominations, no religious group even comes close to being a dominant religion in the United States (*Statistical Abstract* 2005:Tables 67, 68). Table 13.2 illustrates some of this remarkable diversity.

Competition and Recruitment.   The many religious groups of the United States compete for clients. They even advertise in the Yellow Pages of the telephone directory and insert appealing advertising—under the guise of news—in the religion section of the Saturday or Sunday edition of the local newspapers.

Fundamentalist Revival.   The fundamentalist Christian churches are undergoing a revival. They teach that the Bible is literally true and that salvation comes only through a personal relationship with Jesus Christ. They also denounce what they see as the degeneration of U.S. culture: flagrant sex on television and in movies, abortion, corruption in public office, premarital sex, cohabitation, and drug use. Their answer to these problems is firm, simple, and direct: People whose hearts are changed through religious conversion will change their lives.

The mainstream churches, which offer a more remote God and a corresponding reduction in emotional involvement, fail to meet the religious needs of large numbers of Americans. Consequently, as Figure 13.7 on the next page shows, the mainstream churches are losing members, while the fundamentalists are gaining. The exception is the Roman Catholics, whose growth is due primarily to immigration from Mexico and other Roman Catholic countries.

The Electronic Church.   What began as a ministry to shut-ins and those who do not belong to a church has blossomed into its own type of church. Its preachers, called "televangelists," reach millions of viewers and raise millions of dollars. Some of its most famous ministries are those of Robert Schuller (the "Crystal Cathedral") and Pat Robertson (the 700 Club).

Many local ministers view the electronic church as a competitor. They complain that it competes for the attention and dollars of their members. The electronic church replies that its money goes to good causes and that through its conversions, it feeds members into the local churches, strengthening, not weakening them.

Secularization and the Splintering of U.S. Churches

As the model, fashionably slender, paused before the head table of African American community leaders, her gold necklace glimmering above the low-cut bodice of her

Table 13.2 How U.S. Adults Identify with Religion[a]	
Christian	162,000,000
Protestant	110,000,000
Baptist	34,000,000
No denomination	21,300,000
Methodist	14,000,000
Lutheran	9,600,000
Pentecostal	7,600,000
Presbyterian	5,600,000
Churches of Christ	4,000,000
Episcopalian/Anglican	3,500,000
Mormon	2,800,000
United Church of Christ	1,400,000
Jehovah's Witness	1,300,000
Evangelical Church	1,000,000
Seventh Day Adventist	700,000
Church of the Nazarene	550,000
Disciples of Christ	500,000
Reformed Churches	500,000
Church of the Brethren	360,000
Mennonite	350,000
Quakers	200,000
Other	350,000
Roman Catholic	51,000,000
Eastern Orthodox	650,000
Other Religions	8,000,000
Jews	2,800,000
Buddhist	1,100,000
Islamic	1,100,000
Hindu	800,000
Unitarian/Universalist	600,000
Pagan	150,000
Wican	150,000
Native American	100,000
Spiritualist	100,000
Other and unclassified	850,000
No Religion	30,000,000
Refused to answer	11,000,000

[a]All totals must be taken as approximate. Some groups ignore reporting forms. Totals are rounded to the nearest 100,000.
Sources: Niebuhr 2001 (for Muslim total); *Statistical Abstract* 2000:Table 74; 2005:Table 67.

emerald-green dress, the hostess, a member of the Church of God in Christ, said, "It's now OK to wear more revealing clothes—as long as it's done in good taste." Then she

Figure 13.7 U.S. Churches: Gains and Losses in Ten Years

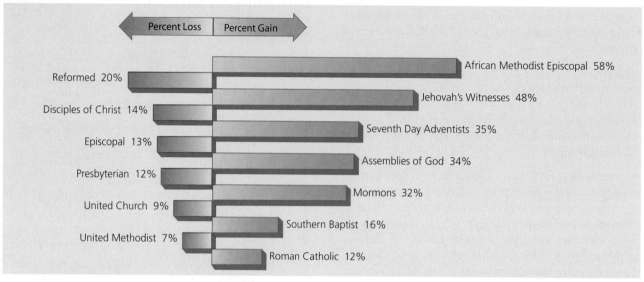

Note: Mergers are excluded. Inconsistent reporting and classification make it difficult to compare membership over time, making these totals only approximate.
Source: By the author. Recomputed from Jones et al. 2002.

added, "You couldn't do this when I was a girl, but now it's OK—and you can still worship God." (Author's files)

When I heard these words, I grabbed a napkin and quickly jotted them down, my sociological imagination stirred at their deep implication. As strange as it may seem, this simple event pinpoints the essence of why the Christian churches in the United States have splintered. Let's see how this could possibly be.

The simplest explanation for why Christians don't have just one church, or at most several, instead of the hundreds of sects and denominations that dot the U.S. landscape, is disagreements about doctrine (church teaching). As theologian and sociologist Richard Niebuhr pointed out, however, there are many ways of settling doctrinal disputes besides splintering off and forming other religious organizations. Niebuhr (1929) suggested that the answer lies more in *social* change than it does in *religious* conflict.

The explanation goes like this. As was noted earlier, when a sect becomes more churchlike, there is less tension between it and the mainstream culture. Quite likely, when a sect is first established, its founders and first members are poor, or at least not very successful in worldly pursuits. Feeling like strangers in the dominant culture, they derive a good part of their identity from their religion. In their church services and lifestyle, they stress how different their values are from those of the dominant culture. They are also likely to emphasize the joys of the coming afterlife, when they will be able to escape from their present pain.

As time passes, the group's values—such as frugality and the avoidance of gambling, alcohol, and drugs—help later generations become successful. As these later generations attain more education and become more middle class, they grow more respectable in the eyes of society. They no longer experience the alienation that was felt by the founders of their group. Life's burdens don't seem as heavy, and the need for relief through an afterlife becomes less pressing. Similarly, the pleasures of the world no longer appear as threatening to the "true" belief. As is illustrated by the woman at the fashion show, people then attempt to harmonize their religious beliefs with their changing ideas about the culture. This process is called the **secularization of religion**—shifting the focus from spiritual matters to the affairs of this world. (*Secular* means "belonging to the world and its affairs.")

Accommodation with the secular culture, however, displeases some of the group's members, especially those who have had less worldly success. They still feel a gulf between themselves and the broader culture. For them, tension and hostility continue to be real. They see secularization as a desertion of the group's fundamental truths, a "selling out" to the secular world.

After futile attempts by die-hards to bring the group back to its senses, the group splinters. Those who protested the secularization of Methodism, for example, were kicked out—even though they represented the values around which the group had organized in the first place. The dissatisfied—who have come to be viewed as complainers—

then form a sect that once again stresses its differences from the world, the need for more personal, emotional religious experience, and salvation from the pain of living in this world. As time passes, the cycle repeats: adjustment to the dominant culture by some, continued dissatisfaction by others, and more splintering.

The Future of Religion

Religion thrives in even the most scientifically advanced nations—and, as Soviet authorities of communist Russia were disheartened to learn, in even the most ideologically hostile climate. Humans are inquiring creatures. As they reflect on life, they ask: What is the purpose of it all? Why are we born? Is there an afterlife? If so, where are we going? Out of these concerns arises this question: If there is a God, what does God want of us in this life? Does God have a preference about how we should live?

Science, including sociology, cannot answer such questions. By its very nature, science cannot tell us about four main concerns that many people have:

1. *The existence of God.* About this, science has nothing to say. No test tube has either isolated God or refuted God's existence.
2. *The purpose of life.* Although science can provide a definition of life and describe the characteristics of living organisms, it has nothing to say about ultimate purpose.
3. *An afterlife.* Science can offer no information on this at all, for it has no tests to prove or disprove a "hereafter."
4. *Morality.* Science can demonstrate the consequences of behavior but not the moral superiority of one action compared with another. This means that science cannot even prove that loving your family and neighbor is superior to hurting and killing them. Science can describe death and measure consequences, but it cannot determine the moral superiority of any action, even in such an extreme example.

There is no doubt that religion will last as long as humanity lasts—for what could replace it? And if something did, and answered such questions, would it not be religion under another name?

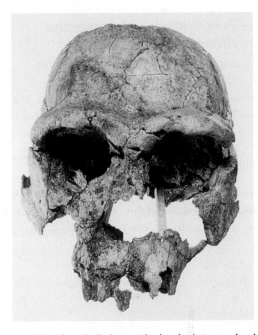

A basic principle of symbolic interactionism is that meaning is not inherent in an object or event, but is determined by people as they interpret the object or event. Old bones and fossils are an excellent illustration of this principle. Does this skull of homo erectus "prove" evolution? Does it "disprove" creation? Such "proof" and "disproof" lie in the eye of the beholder, as evidenced by "scientific creationism" and "intelligent design," which are gaining adherents at U.S. universities.

Summary *and* Review

Education in Global Perspective

What is a credential society, and how did it develop?

A **credential society** is one in which employers use diplomas and degrees to determine who is eligible for a job. One reason that credentialism developed is that large, anonymous societies lack the personal knowledge common to smaller groups; educational certification provides evidence of a person's ability. P. 354.

How does education compare among the Most Industrialized, Industrializing, and Least Industrialized Nations?

In general, formal education reflects a nation's economy. Education is extensive in the Most Industrialized Nations, undergoing vast change in the Industrializing Nations, and spotty in the Least Industrialized Nations. Japan, Russia, and Egypt provide examples of education in countries at three levels of industrialization. Pp. 354–358.

The Functionalist Perspective: Providing Social Benefits

What is the functionalist perspective on education?

Among the functions of education are the teaching of knowledge and skills, **cultural transmission** of values, social integration, **gatekeeping,** and **mainstreaming.** Functionalists also note that education has replaced some traditional family functions. Pp. 358–361.

The Conflict Perspective: Perpetuating Social Inequality

What is the conflict perspective on education?

The basic view of conflict theorists is that *education reproduces the social class structure;* that is, through such mechanisms as unequal funding, education perpetuates a society's basic social inequalities from one generation to the next. Pp. 361–362.

The Symbolic Interactionist Perspective: Fulfilling Teacher Expectations

What is the symbolic interactionist perspective on education?

Symbolic interactionists focus on face-to-face interaction. In examining what occurs in the classroom, they have found that student performance tends to conform to teacher expectations, whether they are high or low. Pp. 362–363.

Problems in U.S. Education—and Their Solutions

What are the chief problems that face U.S. education?

In addition to violence, the major problems are low achievement as shown by SAT scores, **grade inflation, social promotion,** and **functional illiteracy.** Pp. 363–365.

What are the potential solutions to these problems?

The primary solution is to restore high educational standards, which can be done only after providing basic security for students. Any solution for improving quality must be based on expecting more of *both* students and teachers. Pp. 365–366.

What Is Religion?

Durkheim identified three essential characteristics of **religion:** beliefs that set the **sacred** apart from the **profane, rituals,** and a moral community (a **church**). Pp. 366–367.

The Functionalist Perspective

What are the functions and dysfunctions of religion?

Among the functions of religion are answering questions about ultimate meaning; providing social solidarity, guidelines for everyday life, adaptation, and support for the government; and fostering social change. Among the dysfunctions of religion are religious persecution, war, and terrorism. Pp. 367–369.

The Symbolic Interactionist Perspective

What aspects of religion do symbolic interactionists study?

Symbolic interactionists focus on the meanings of religion for its followers. They examine religious symbols, rituals, beliefs, **religious experiences,** and the sense of community that religion provides. Pp. 369–371.

The Conflict Perspective

What aspects of religion do conflict theorists study?

Conflict theorists examine the relationship of religion to social inequalities, especially how religion reinforces a society's stratification system. P. 372.

Religion and the Spirit of Capitalism

What does the spirit of capitalism have to do with religion?

Max Weber saw religion as a primary source of social change. He analyzed how Protestantism gave rise to the **Protestant ethic,** which stimulated what he called the

spirit of capitalism. The result was capitalism, which transformed society. Pp. 372–373.

Types of Religious Groups

What types of religious groups are there?

Sociologists divide religious groups into cults, sects, churches, and ecclesias. All religions began as **cults.** Those that survive tend to develop into **sects** and eventually into **churches.** Sects, often led by **charismatic leaders,** are unstable. Some are perceived as threats and are persecuted by the state. **Ecclesias,** or state religions, are rare. Pp. 373–374.

Religion in the United States

What are the main characteristics of religion in the United States?

Membership varies by social class, age, and race-ethnicity. Among the major characteristics are diversity, competition, a fundamentalist revival, and the electronic church. Pp. 375–377.

What is the connection between secularization of religion and the splintering of churches?

Secularization of religion, a change in a religious group's focus from spiritual matters to concerns of "this world," is the key to understanding why churches divide. Basically, as a cult or sect changes to accommodate its members' upward social class mobility, it changes into a church. Left dissatisfied are members who are not upwardly mobile. They tend to splinter off and form a new cult or sect, and the cycle repeats itself. Pp. 377–379.

The Future of Religion

What is the future of religion?

Although industrialization led to the secularization of religion, this did not spell the end of religion. Because science cannot answer questions about ultimate meaning, the existence of God or an afterlife, or provide guidelines for morality, the need for religion will remain. In any foreseeable future, religion will prosper. P. 379.

Thinking Critically
about Chapter 13

1. How have your experiences in education (including teachers and assignments) influenced your goals, attitudes, and values? How have your classmates influenced you? Be specific.

2. How do you think that U.S. schools can be improved?

3. Since 9/11, many people have wondered how religion can be used to defend or promote terrorism. How does the Down-to-Earth Sociology box on terrorism and the mind of God on page 370 help to answer this question? How do the concepts of groupthink (in Chapter 5, page 135) and dehumanization (in Chapter 11, page 302) fit into your analysis?

Additional Resources

Companion Website www.ablongman.com/henslin

- Content Select Research Database for Sociology, with suggested key terms and annotated references
- Link to 2000 Census, with activities
- Flashcards of key terms and concepts

- Practice Tests
- Weblinks
- Interactive Maps

Where Can I Read More on This Topic?

Suggested readings for this chapter are listed at the back of this book.

Population and Urbanization

Sharon Florin, *Feast of San Gennaro*, 1998

OUTLINE

POPULATION IN GLOBAL PERSPECTIVE

A Planet with no Space to Enjoy Life?
The New Malthusians
The Anti-Malthusians
Who Is Correct?
Why Are People Starving?

Population Growth
Why Do the Least Industrialized Nations Have So Many Children?
Implications of Different Rates of Growth
The Three Demographic Variables
Problems in Forecasting Population Growth

URBANIZATION

The Development of Cities
The Process of Urbanization
U.S. Urban Patterns
The Rural Rebound
Models of Urban Growth

City Life
Alienation and Community
Who Lives in the City?
Urban Sentiment: Finding a Familiar World
The Norm of Noninvolvement and the Diffusion of Responsibility

Urban Problems and Social Policy
Suburbanization
Disinvestment and Deindustrialization
The Potential of Urban Revitalization

Summary and Review

The image still haunts me. There stood Celia, age 30, her distended stomach visible proof that her thirteenth child was on the way. Her oldest was only 14 years old! A mere boy by our standards, he had already gone as far in school as he ever would. Each morning, he joined the men to work in the fields. Each evening around twilight, I saw him return home, exhausted from hard labor in the subtropical sun.

I was living in Colima, Mexico, and Celia and Angel had invited me for dinner. Their home clearly reflected the family's poverty. A thatched hut consisting of only a single room served as home for all fourteen members of the family. At night, the parents and younger children crowded into a double bed, while the eldest boy slept in a hammock. As in many homes in the village, despite the crawling scorpions, the other children slept on mats spread on the dirt floor.

The home was meagerly furnished. It had only a gas stove, a table, and a cabinet where Celia stored her few cooking utensils and clay dishes. There were no closets; their few clothes were hung on pegs in the walls. There also were no chairs, not even one. I was used to poverty in this village, but this really startled me. The family was so poor that they could not afford even a single chair.

Celia beamed as she told me how much she looked forward to the birth of her next child. Could she really mean it? It was hard to imagine that any woman would want to be in her situation.

Yet Celia meant every word. She was as full of delighted anticipation as she had been with her first child—and with all the others in between.

How could Celia have wanted so many children, especially when she lived in such poverty? That question bothered me. I couldn't let it go until I understood why.

This chapter helps to provide an answer.

> **There stood Celia, age 30, her distended stomach visible proof that her thirteenth child was on the way.**

POPULATION IN GLOBAL PERSPECTIVE

Celia's story takes us into the heart of **demography,** the study of the size, composition, growth, and distribution of human populations. It brings us face to face with the question of whether we are doomed to live in a world so filled with people that there will be very little space for anybody. Will our planet be able to support its growing population? Or are chronic famine and mass starvation the sorry fate of most earthlings?

Let's look at how concern about population growth began.

A Planet with No Space to Enjoy Life?

The story begins with the lowly potato. When the Spanish *conquistadores* found that people in the Andes Mountains ate this vegetable, which was unknown in Europe, they brought some home to cultivate. At first, Europeans viewed the potato with suspicion, but gradually it became the main food of the lower classes. With a greater abundance of food, fertility increased, and the death rate dropped. Europe's population soared, almost doubling during the 1700s (McKeown 1977; McNeill 1999).

Thomas Malthus (1766–1834), an English economist, viewed this surging growth as a sign of doom. In 1798, he wrote a book that became world famous, *First Essay on Population 1798.* In it, Malthus proposed what became

known as the **Malthus theorem.** He argued that although population grows geometrically (from 2 to 4 to 8 to 16 and so forth), the food supply increases only arithmetically (from 1 to 2 to 3 to 4 and so on). This meant, he claimed, that if births go unchecked, the population of a country, or even of the world, will outstrip its food supply.

The New Malthusians

Was Malthus right? This question has become a matter of heated debate among demographers. One group, which can be called the *New Malthusians,* is convinced that today's situation is at least as grim as, if not grimmer than, Malthus ever imagined. For example, *the world's population is growing so fast that in just the time it takes you to read this chapter, another twenty to forty thousand babies will be born!* By this time tomorrow, the earth will have over 200,000 more people to feed. This increase goes on hour after hour, day after day, without letup. For an illustration of this growth, see Figure 14.1.

The New Malthusians point out that the world's population is following an **exponential growth curve.** This means that if growth doubles during approximately equal intervals of time, it suddenly accelerates. To illustrate the far-reaching implications of exponential growth, sociologist William Faunce (1981) retold an old parable about a poor man who saved a rich man's life. The rich man was grateful and said that he wanted to reward the man for his heroic deed.

The man replied that he would like his reward to be spread out over a four-week period, with each day's amount being

Figure 14.1   How Fast Is the World's Population Growing?

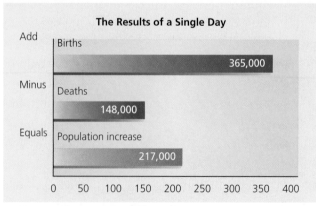

The Results of a Single Day

Add — Births — 365,000
Minus — Deaths — 148,000
Equals — Population increase — 217,000

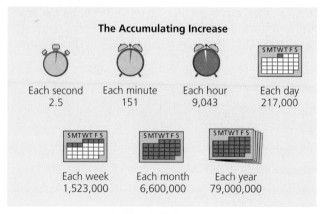

The Accumulating Increase

Each second 2.5
Each minute 151
Each hour 9,043
Each day 217,000
Each week 1,523,000
Each month 6,600,000
Each year 79,000,000

Source: By the author. Based on Haub 2002.

twice what he received on the preceding day. He also said he would be happy to receive only one penny on the first day. The rich man immediately handed over the penny and congratulated himself on how cheaply he had gotten by. At the end of the first week, the rich man checked to see how much he owed and was pleased to find that the total was only $1.27. By the end of the second week, he owed only $163.83. On the twenty-first day, however, the rich man was surprised to find that the total had grown to $20,971.51. When the twenty-eighth day arrived, the rich man was shocked to discover that he owed $1,342,177.28 for that day alone and that the total reward had jumped to $2,684,354.56!

This is precisely what alarms the New Malthusians. They claim that humanity has just entered the "fourth week" of an exponential growth curve. Figure 14.2 shows why they think the day of reckoning is just around the corner. It took from the beginning of time until 1800 for the world's population to reach its first billion. It then took only 130 years (1930) to add the second billion. Just thirty years later (1960), the world population hit 3 billion. The time it took to reach the fourth billion was cut in half, to only fifteen years (1975). Then just twelve years later (in 1987), the total reached 5 billion, and in another twelve years (in 1999) it hit 6 billion.

On average, every minute of every day, 253 babies are born. As Figure 14.1 shows, at sunset the world has 217,000 more people than it did the day before. In one year, this amounts to an increase of 79 million people. In just four years, the population of the world increases by an amount greater than the entire U.S. population (Haub 2005; *Statistical Abstract* 2005:Table 1321). You might think of it this way: *In just the next twelve years the world's population will increase as much as it did during the first 1,800 years after the birth of Christ.*

These totals terrify the New Malthusians. They are convinced that we are headed toward a showdown between population and food. In the year 2025, the population of just India, Pakistan, and Bangladesh is expected to be more than the entire world's population was 100 years ago (Haub 2002). It is obvious that we will run out of food if we don't curtail population growth. Soon we are going to see more pitiful, starving Pakistani and Bangladeshi children on television.

The Anti-Malthusians

All of this seems obvious, and no one wants to live shoulder-to-shoulder and fight for scraps. How, then, can anyone argue with the New Malthusians?

An optimistic group of demographers, which we can call the *Anti-Malthusians,* paint a far different picture. They believe that Europe's **demographic transition** provides a more accurate picture of the future. This transition is diagrammed in Figure 14.3 on the next page. During most of its history, Europe was in Stage 1. Its population remained about the same from year to year, for high death rates offset the high birth rates. Then came Stage 2, the "population explosion" that so upset Malthus. Europe's population surged because birth rates remained high while death rates went down. Finally, Europe made the transition to Stage 3: The population stabilized as people brought their birth rates into line with their lower death rates.

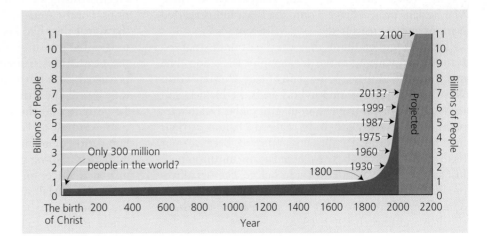

Figure 14.2 World Population Growth Over 2,000 Years

Sources: Modified from Piotrow 1973; McFalls 2003.

Figure 14.3 **The Demographic Transition**

Note: The standard demographic transition is depicted by Stages 1–3. Stage 4 has been suggested by some Anti-Malthusians.

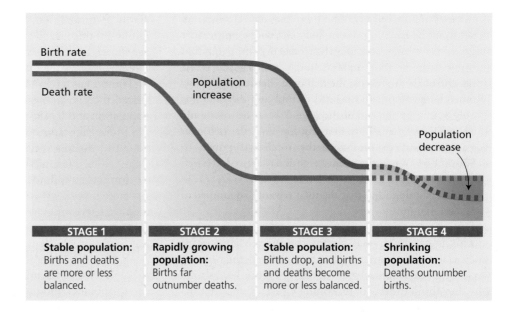

Birth rate

Death rate

Population increase

Population decrease

STAGE 1	STAGE 2	STAGE 3	STAGE 4
Stable population: Births and deaths are more or less balanced.	**Rapidly growing population:** Births far outnumber deaths.	**Stable population:** Births drop, and births and deaths become more or less balanced.	**Shrinking population:** Deaths outnumber births.

This, say the Anti-Malthusians, will also happen in the Least Industrialized Nations. Their current surge in population growth simply indicates that they have reached Stage 2 of the demographic transition. Hybrid seeds and medicine imported from the Most Industrialized Nations have cut their death rates, but their birth rates remain high. When they move into Stage 3, as surely they will, we will wonder what all the fuss was about. In fact, their growth is already slowing.

Who Is Correct?

As you can see, both the New Malthusians and the Anti-Malthusians have looked at historical trends and projected them onto the future. The New Malthusians project continued world growth and are alarmed. The Anti-Malthusians project Stage 3 onto the Least Industrialized Nations and are reassured.

There is no question that the Least Industrialized Nations are in Stage 2 of the demographic transition. The question is: Will these nations enter Stage 3? After World War II, the West exported hybrid seeds, herbicides, and techniques of public hygiene around the globe. Death rates plummeted in the Least Industrialized Nations as their food supply increased and health improved. Because their birth rates stayed high, their populations mushroomed. Just as Malthus had done 200 years before, demographers predicted worldwide catastrophe if something were not done immediately to halt the population explosion (Ehrlich and Ehrlich 1972, 1978).

We can use the conflict perspective to understand what happened when this message reached the leaders of the industrialized world. They saw the mushrooming populations of the Least Industrialized Nations as a threat to the global balance of power they had so carefully worked out. With swollen populations, the poorer countries might demand a larger share of the earth's resources. The leaders found the United Nations to be a willing tool, and they used it to spearhead efforts to reduce world population growth. The results have been remarkable. The birth rates of the Most Industrialized Nations have dropped from an average of 2.1 percent a year in the 1960s to 1.5 percent today (Haub and Yinger 1994; Haub 2005).

The New Malthusians and Anti-Malthusians have greeted this news with significantly different interpretations. For the Anti-Malthusians, this slowing of growth is the signal they had been waiting for: Stage 3 of the demographic transition has begun. First the death rates in the Least Industrialized Nations fell—now, just as they predicted, their birth rates are also falling. Did you notice, they would say, if they looked at Figure 14.2, that it took 12 years to add the fifth billion to the world's population—and also 12 years to add the sixth billion? Population momentum is slowing. The New Malthusians reply that a slower growth rate still spells catastrophe—it just takes longer for it to hit (Ehrlich and Ehrlich 1997).

The Anti-Malthusians also argue that our future will be the opposite of what the New Malthusians worry about: There are going to be too few children in the world, not too many. The world's problem will not be a population explosion, but **population shrinkage**—populations getting smaller. They point out that births in sixty-five countries have already dropped so low that those countries no longer produce enough children to maintain their populations. Of the forty-two countries of Europe, *all* of them fill more coffins than cradles (Haub 2005).

Some Anti-Malthusians even predict a "demographic free fall" (Mosher 1997). As more nations enter Stage 4 of the demographic transition, the world's population will peak at about 8 or 9 billion, then begin to grow smaller. Two hundred years from now, they say, we will have a lot fewer people on earth.

Who is right? It simply is too early to tell. Like the proverbial pessimists who see the glass of water half empty, the New Malthusians interpret changes in world population growth negatively. And like the eternal optimists who see the same glass half full, the Anti-Malthusians view the figures positively. Sometime during our lifetimes, we should know the answer.

Why Are People Starving?

Pictures of starving children gnaw at our conscience. We live in such abundance, while these children and their parents starve before our very eyes. Why don't they have enough food? Is it because there are too many of them, or simply because the abundant food produced around the world does not reach them?

The Anti-Malthusians make a point that seems irrefutable. As Figure 14.4 shows, *there is now more food for each person in the world than there was in 1950.* Although the world's population has more than doubled since 1950, improved seeds and fertilizers have made more food available for *each* person on earth. Even more food may be on the way, for bioengineers are making breakthroughs in agriculture. The United Nations estimates that even without agricultural gains through bioengineering, there will be ample food to keep up with the world's growing population for at least the next 30 years (United Nations 2000).

Then why do people die of hunger? From Figure 14.4, we can conclude that starvation occurs not because the earth produces too little food but because particular places lack food. Droughts and wars are the main reasons. Just as droughts slow or stop food production, so does war. In nations ravaged by civil war, opposing sides either confiscate or burn crops, and farmers flee to the cities, leaving their fields unplanted (Thurow 2005). While some countries have their food supply disrupted, others are producing more food than their people can consume. At the same time that countries of Africa are hit by drought and civil wars—and millions starve to death—the U.S. government pays farmers to *reduce* their output of crops. The United States' problem is too much food; West Africa's is too little.

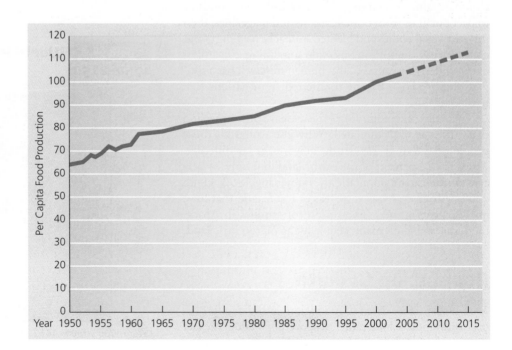

Figure 14.4 How Much Food Does the World Produce Per Person?

Note: Julian Simon provided the stimulus for producing this figure. I used to reproduce a figure that he had developed, but since his death in 1998 inconsistencies in data have made it difficult to update his work. Based on UN data, this figure overcomes that limitation.

Source: By the author. Based on Simon 1981; Food and Agriculture Organization of the United Nations 2005.

Photos of starving people, such as this mother and her child, haunt Americans and other members of the Most Industrialized Nations. Many of us wonder why, when some are starving, we should live in the midst of such abundance, often overeating and even casually scraping excess food into the garbage. We even have eating contests to see who can eat the most food in the least time. The text discusses reasons for such unconscionable disparities.

The New Malthusians counter with the argument that the world's population is still growing and that we do not know how long the earth will continue to produce enough food. They remind us of the penny doubling each day. It is only a matter of time, they insist, until the earth no longer produces enough food—not "if," but "when."

Both the New Malthusians and the Anti-Malthusians have contributed significant ideas, but theories will not eliminate famines. Starving children are going to continue to peer out at us from our televisions and magazines, their tiny, shriveled bodies and bloated stomachs nagging at our conscience and imploring us to do something. Regardless of the underlying causes of this human misery, it has a simple solution: Food can be transferred from nations that have a surplus.

These pictures of starving Africans leave the impression that Africa is overpopulated. Why else would all those people be starving? The truth, however, is far different. Africa has 22 percent of the earth's land, but only 14 percent of the earth's population (Nsamenang 1992; Haub 2005). Africa even has vast areas of fertile land that have not yet been farmed. The reason for famines in Africa, then, *cannot* be too many people living on too little land.

Population Growth

Even if starvation is the result of a maldistribution of food rather than overpopulation, the fact remains that the Least Industrialized Nations are growing *fifteen times faster* than the Most Industrialized Nations—

1.5 percent a year compared with 0.1 percent (Haub 2005). At these rates, it will take 1,000 years for the average Most Industrialized Nation to double its population, but just 48 years for the average Least Industrialized Nation to do so. Figure 14.5 puts the matter in stark perspective. So does the Down-to-Earth Sociology box on the next page. Why do the nations that can least afford it have so many children?

Figure 14.5 **World Population Growth, 1750–2150**

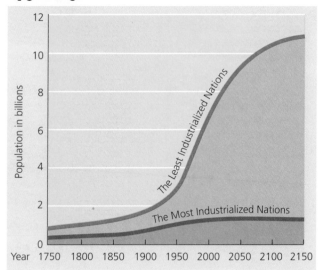

Source: "The World of the Child 6 Billion," 2000.

Down-to-Earth Sociology

How the Tsunami Can Help Us to Understand Population Growth

On December 26, 2004, the world witnessed the worst tsunami in modern history. As the giant waves rolled over the shores of unsuspecting countries, they swept away people from all walks of life—from lowly sellers of fish to wealthy tourists visiting the fleshpots of Sri Lanka. Over the next several days, as the government reports came in, the media kept increasing the death toll. When those reports were tallied two months later, the total stood at 286,000 people.

In terms of lives lost, this was not the worst single disaster the world had seen. Several hundred thousand people had been killed in China's Tangshan earthquake in 1976. And then there was the 1945 firebombing of Dresden, Germany, by U.S. and British forces, where the loss of lives came to between 35,000 and a half million (lower estimates by U.S. sources and higher ones by German sources).

In terms of geography, however, this was the broadest. It involved more countries than any other disaster in modern history. And, unlike, its predecessors, this tsunami occurred during a period of instantaneous, global reporting of events.

As news of the tsunami was transmitted around the globe, the world went into shock. The response was almost immediate, and aid poured in—in unprecedented amounts. Governments gave over $3 billion. Citizens pitched in, too, from Little Leaguers and religious groups to the "regulars" at the local bars.

I want to use the tsunami disaster to illustrate the incredible population growth that is taking place in the Least Industrialized Nations. My intention is not to dismiss the tragedy of the deaths, for they were horrible—as were the maiming of so many, the sufferings of families, the lost livelihoods, and the many children who were left without parents.

This photo was snapped at Koh Raya in Thailand, just as the tsunami wave of December 26, 2004, landed.

Let's consider Indonesia first. With 233,000 deaths, this country was hit the hardest. Indonesia has an annual growth rate of 1.6 percent (its "rate of natural increase," as demographers call it). With a population of 220 million, Indonesia is growing by 3,300,000 people each year (Haub 2005). This increase, coming to 9,041 people each day, means that it took Indonesia just under four weeks (26 days) to replace the huge number of people it lost to the tsunami.

The next greatest loss of lives took place in Sri Lanka. With its lower rate of natural increase of 1.3 and its smaller population of 19 million, it took Sri Lanka a little longer to replace the 31,000 people it lost: 46 days.

India was the third hardest hit. With India's 1 billion people and its 1.7 rate of natural increase, India is adding 17 million people to its population each year. This comes to 46,575 people each day. At an increase of 1,940 people per hour, India took just 8 or 9 hours to replace the 16,000 people it lost to the tsunami.

The next hardest hit was Thailand. It took Thailand 4 or 5 days to replace the 5,000 people that it lost.

For the other countries, the losses were small: 298 for Somalia, 82 for the Maldives, 68 for Malaysia, 61 for Myanmar, 10 for Tanzania, 2 for Bangladesh, and 1 for Kenya ("Tsunami deaths..." 2005).

Again, I don't want to detract from the horrifying tragedy of the 2004 tsunami. But by using this event as a comparative backdrop, we can gain a better grasp of the unprecedented population growth that is taking place in the Least Industrialized Nations.

Why the Least Industrialized Nations Have So Many Children

Why do people in the countries that can least afford it have so many children? To understand this, let's figure out why Celia is so happy about having her thirteenth child. Here, we need to apply the symbolic interactionist perspective. We must take the role of the other so that we can understand the world of Celia and Angel as *they* see it. As our culture does for us, their culture provides a perspective on life that guides their choices. Celia and Angel's culture tells them that twelve children are *not* enough, that they ought to have a thirteenth—as well as a fourteenth and fifteenth. How can this be? Let's consider three reasons why bearing many children plays a central role in their lives—and in the lives of millions upon millions of poor people around the world.

First is the status of parenthood. In the Least Industrialized Nations, motherhood is the most prized status a woman can achieve. The more children a woman bears, the more she is thought to have achieved the purpose for which she was born. Similarly, a man proves his manhood by fathering children. The more children he fathers, especially sons, the better—for through them, his name lives on.

Second, the community supports this view. Celia and those like her live in *Gemeinschaft* communities, where people identify closely with one another and share similar views of life. To them, children are a sign of God's blessing. By producing children, people reflect the values of their community, achieve status, and are assured that they are blessed by God. It is the barren woman, not the woman with a dozen children, who is to be pitied.

These factors certainly provide strong motivations for bearing many children. Yet there is also another powerful incentive: For poor people in the Least Industrialized Nations, children are economic assets. Like Celia and Angel's eldest son, children begin contributing to the family income at a young age. (See Figure 14.6.) But even more than this: Children are also the equivalent of our Social Security. Their government does not provide social security or medical and unemployment insurance. This motivates people to bear *more* children, for when parents become too old to work, or when no work is to be found, their children take care of them. The more children they have, the broader their base of support.

To those of us who live in the Most Industrialized Nations, it seems irrational to have many children. And *for us, it would be.* Understanding life from the framework of the people who are living it, however—the essence of the symbolic interactionist perspective—reveals how it makes perfect sense to have many children. Consider this report by a government worker in India:

Large families on U.S. farms used to be common. Children helped plant and harvest crops, take care of animals, and prepare food. As the country industrialized and urbanized, children became nonproducers, making them expensive to have around. Consequently, the size of families shrank as we entered Stage 3 of the demographic transition, and today U.S. families of this size are practically nonexistent. (Note the trousers that the boy on the far left is wearing. They used to be his father's.)

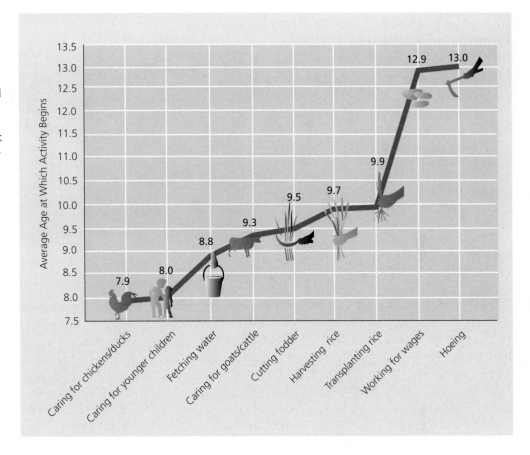

Figure 14.6 **Why the Poor Need Children**

Children are an economic asset in the Least Industrialized Nations. Based on a survey in Indonesia, this figure shows that boys and girls can be net income earners for their families by the age of 9 or 10.

Source: U.N. Fund for Population Activities.

Thaman Singh (a very poor man, a water carrier) welcomed me inside his home, gave me a cup of tea (with milk and "market" sugar, as he proudly pointed out later), and said: "You were trying to convince me that I shouldn't have any more sons. Now, you see, I have six sons and two daughters and I sit at home in leisure. They are grown up and they bring me money. One even works outside the village as a laborer. You told me I was a poor man and couldn't support a large family. Now, you see, because of my large family I am a rich man." (Mamdani 1973)

Conflict theorists offer a different view of why women in the Least Industrialized Nations bear so many children. Feminists argue that women like Celia have internalized values that support male dominance. In Latin America, *machismo*—an emphasis on male virility and dominance—is common. To father many children, especially sons, shows that a man is sexually potent, giving him higher status in the community. From a conflict perspective, then, the reason poor people have so many children is that men control women's reproductive choices.

Implications of Different Rates of Growth

The result of Celia and Angel's desire for many children—and of the millions of Celias and Angels like them—is that Mexico's population will double in thirty-five years. In contrast, women in the United States are having so few children that if it weren't for immigration, the U.S. population would begin to shrink. To illustrate population dynamics, demographers use **population pyramids.** These depict a country's population by age and sex. Look at Figure 14.7 on the next page, which shows the population pyramids of the United States, Mexico, and the world.

To see why population pyramids are important, I would like you to imagine a miracle. Imagine that, overnight, Mexico is transformed into a nation as industrialized as the United States. Imagine also that overnight the average number of children per woman drops to 2.0, the same as in the United States. If this happened, it would seem that Mexico's population would grow at the same rate as that of the United States, right?

Figure 14.7 **Three Population Pyramids**

Source: Population Today, 26, 9, September 1998:4, 5.

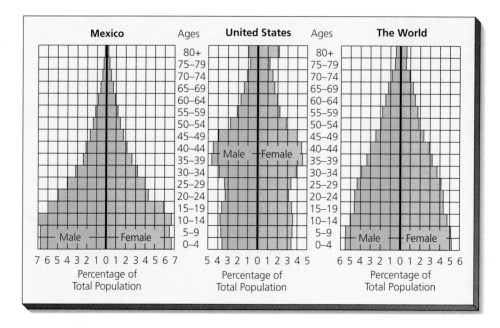

But this isn't at all what would happen. Instead, the population of Mexico would continue to grow much faster. As you can see from Figure 14.7, a much higher percentage of Mexican women are in their childbearing years. Even if Mexico and the United States had the same birth rate (2.0 children per woman), a larger percentage of women in Mexico would be giving birth, and Mexico's population would grow faster. As demographers like to phrase this, *Mexico's age structure gives it greater population momentum.*

Mexico's population momentum is so strong that, as we saw earlier, its population will double in thirty-five years. The implications of a doubling population are mind-boggling. *Just to stay even,* within thirty-five years Mexico must double the number of available jobs and housing facilities; its food production; its transportation and communication facilities; all water, gas, sewer, and electrical systems; and the number of schools, hospitals, churches, civic buildings, theaters, stores, and parks. If Mexico fails to double them, its already meager standard of living will drop even further.

Conflict theorists point out that a declining standard of living poses the threat of political instability—protests, riots, even revolution—and, in response, repression by the government. Political instability in one country can spill into others, threatening an entire region's balance of power. Fearing such disruptions, leaders of the Most Industrialized Nations are using the United Nations to direct a campaign of worldwide birth control. With one hand, they give agricultural aid, IUDs, and condoms to the masses in the Least

Industrialized Nations—while, with the other, they sell weapons to the elites in these countries. Both actions, say conflict theorists, serve the same purpose: that of promoting political stability in order to maintain the dominance of the Most Industrialized Nations in global stratification.

The Three Demographic Variables

How many people will live in the United States fifty years from now? What will the world's population be then? These are important questions. Educators want to know how many schools to build. Manufacturers want to anticipate changes in the market for their products. The government needs to know how many doctors, engineers, and executives to train. Politicians want to know how many people will be paying taxes—and how many young people will be available to fight a war.

To project future populations, demographers use three **demographic variables:** fertility, mortality, and migration. Let's look at each.

Fertility. The number of children that the average woman bears is called the **fertility rate.** The world's overall fertility rate is 2.8, which means that during her lifetime the average woman in the world bears 2.8 children. At 2.0, the fertility rate of U.S. women is considerably less (Haub 2004). A term that is sometimes confused with fertility is **fecundity,** the number of children that women are *capable* of bearing. This number is rather high, as some women have given birth to 30 children (McFalls 2003).

The region of the world that has the highest fertility rate is Middle Africa, where the average woman gives birth to 6.4 children; the lowest is Eastern and Southern Europe, where the average woman bears 1.3 children (Haub 2005). As you can see from Table 14.1, Macao has the world's lowest fertility rate. There, the average woman gives birth to only 0.8 children. With the exception of Macao and Hong Kong, these low-birth-rate countries are located in Europe. The countries with the highest birth rate are also clustered. With the exception of Afghanistan and Yemen, all of them are in Africa. Niger in West Africa holds the record for the world's highest birth rate. There, the average woman gives birth to eight children, *ten* times as many children as the average woman in Macao.

To compute the fertility rate of a country, demographers analyze the government's records of births. From these, they figure the country's **crude birth rate,** the annual number of live births per 1,000 population. There may be considerable inaccuracies here, of course. The birth records in many of the Least Industrialized Nations are haphazard at best.

Mortality.   The second demographic variable is measured by the **crude death rate,** the annual number of deaths per 1,000 population. It, too, varies widely around the world. The highest death rate is 28, a record held by Mozambique in East Africa. Two oil-rich countries in the Middle East—Kuwait and United Arab Emirates—tie for the world's lowest death rate of 2 (Haub 2005).

Migration.   The third demographic variable is the **net migration rate,** the difference between the number of *immigrants* (people moving into a country) and *emigrants* (people moving out of a country) per 1,000 population. Unlike fertility and mortality, this rate does not affect the global population, for people are simply shifting their residence from one country or region to another.

As you know, immigrants are seeking a better life. They are willing to give up the security of their family and friends to move to a country with a strange language and unfamiliar customs. What motivates people to embark on such a venture? To understand migration, we need to look at both push and pull factors. The *push* factors are what people want to escape: poverty or persecution for their religious and political ideas. The *pull* factors are the magnets that draw people to a new land, such as opportunities for education, higher wages, better jobs, the freedom to worship or to discuss political ideas, and a more promising future for their children.

Around the world, the flow of migration is from the Least Industrialized Nations to the industrialized countries. After "migrant paths" are established, immigration often accelerates as networks of kin and friends become additional magnets that attract more people from the same nation—and even from the same villages.

By far, the United States is the world's number one choice of immigrants. The United States admits more immigrants each year than all the other nations of the world combined. Thirty-three million residents—one of every nine Americans—were born in other countries (*Statistical Abstract* 2005:Table 45). Table 14.2 shows where recent U.S. immigrants were born. To escape grinding poverty, such as that which surrounds Celia and Angel, millions of people also enter the United States illegally, most of them from Mexico and many others from Central and South America.

Experts cannot agree whether immigrants are a net contributor to the U.S. economy or a drain on it. Economist Julian Simon (1986, 1993) claimed that immigrants benefit the economy. After subtracting what immigrants collect in welfare and adding what they produce in jobs and taxes, he concluded that immigrants produce more than they cost. Other economists (Huddle 1993; Davis and Weinstein 2002) conclude that immigrants drain taxpayers of billions of dollars a year. The fairest conclusion seems to be that the more educated immigrants produce more than they cost, while the less educated cost more than they produce.

Table 14.1   Extremes in Childbirth

Where Do Women Give Birth to the Fewest Children?		Where Do Women Give Birth to the Most Children?	
Country	Number of Children	Country	Number of Children
1. Macao	0.8	1. Niger	8.0
2. Hong Kong	0.9	2. Guinea-Bissau	7.1
3. Armenia	1.2	3. Somalia	7.1
4. Czech Republic	1.2	4. Mali	7.0
5. Poland	1.2	5. Yemen	7.0
6. Romania	1.2	6. Uganda	6.9
7. Slovakia	1.2	7. Afghanistan	6.8
8. South Korea	1.2	8. Angola	6.8
9. Taiwan	1.2	9. Comoros	6.8
10. Ukraine	1.2	10. Congo, Democratic Republic of	6.8

Note: Other countries with 1.2 children per woman are Belarus, Bosnia-Herzegovina, Bulgaria, Moldova, San Marino, and Slovenia.

Source: Haub 2004.

Table 14.2   Country of Origin of Immigrants to the United States, 1981–2002

North America	7,855,000	Lebanon	94,000	**Europe**	**2,367,000**
Mexico	4,331,000*	Bangladesh	94,000	Great Britain	313,000
Dominican Republic	637,000	Jordan	81,000	Poland	292,000
Jamaica	418,000	Israel	76,000	Ukraine	184,000
Cuba	396,000	Iraq	71,000	Russia	169,000
Haiti	369,000	Turkey	54,000	Germany	157,000
Canada	298,000	Syria	53,000	Romania	108,000
Trinidad and Tobago	115,000	Afghanistan	47,000	Ireland	95,000
Asia	**6,402,000**	**Central and South America**	**2,275,000**	Bosnia-Herzegovina	88,000
Philippines	1,005,000	El Salvador	495,000	Portugal	66,000
China	931,000	Columbia	291,000	Yugoslavia	62,000
Vietnam	892,000	Guatemala	221,000	Italy	61,000
India	787,000	Peru	193,000	France	59,000
Korea	552,000	Guyana	188,000	Greece	45,000
Iran	291,000	Nicaragua	173,000	**Africa**	**690,000**
Pakistan	216,000	Ecuador	153,000	Nigeria	119,000
Laos	192,000	Honduras	129,000	Ethiopia	89,000
Hong Kong	151,000	Brazil	95,000	Egypt	88,000
Cambodia	140,000	Venezuela	58,000	Ghana	59,000
Taiwan	128,000	Panama	57,000	South Africa	46,000
Japan	123,000	Argentina	57,000		
Thailand	121,000	Chile	44,000		

*This total does not include the estimated 7 million to 10 million illegal immigrants in the United States, about 70 percent of whom are from Mexico (Martin and Midgley 2003).

Note: Because only the countries with the largest immigration to the United States are listed, the total for each region is larger than the total of the countries listed from that region.

Source: By the author. Based on *Statistical Abstract* 2005:Table 8.

Problems in Forecasting Population Growth

The total of the three demographic variables—fertility, mortality, and net migration—gives us a country's **growth rate,** the net change after people have been added to and subtracted from a population. What demographers call the **basic demographic equation** is quite simple:

Growth rate = births − deaths + net migration

If population increase depended only on biology, the demographer's job would be easy. But social factors—wars, economic booms and busts, plagues, and famines—push rates of birth and death and migration up or down. As is shown in the Cultural Diversity box on the next page, even infanticide can affect population growth. Politicians also complicate projections. Some governments try to persuade women to bear fewer—or more—children. When Hitler

decided that Germany needed more "Aryans," the German government outlawed abortion and offered cash bonuses to women who gave birth. The population increased. Today, European leaders are alarmed that their birth rates have dropped so low that their populations will shrink without immigration. The commissioner of social affairs for the European Union declared that "Europeans must have more children" (*Population Today* 2002). Declarations, however, are unlikely to accomplish anything.

In China, we find the opposite situation. Many people know that China tries to limit population growth with its "One couple, one child" policy, but few know how ruthlessly officials have enforced this policy. Steven Mosher, an anthropologist who did fieldwork in China, revealed that—whether she wants it or not—after the birth of her first child, each woman is fitted with an IUD (intrauterine device). If a woman has a second child, she is sterilized. If a woman gets pregnant without government permission

Cultural Diversity *around the* World

Killing Little Girls: An Ancient and Thriving Practice

"The Mysterious Case of the Missing Girls" could have been the title of this box. Around the globe, for every 100 girls born, about 105 boys are born. In China, however, for every 100 baby girls, there are 120 baby boys. Given China's huge population, this means that China has several million fewer baby girls than it should have. Why?

The answer is *female infanticide,* the killing of baby girls. When a Chinese woman goes into labor, the village midwife sometimes grabs a bucket of water. If the newborn is a girl, she is plunged into the water before she can draw her first breath.

At the root of China's sexist infanticide is economics. The people are poor, and they have no pensions. When parents can no longer work, sons support them. In contrast, a daughter must be married off, at great expense, and at that point, her obligations transfer to her husband and his family.

In the past few years, the percentage of boy babies has grown. The reason, again, is economics, but this time it has a new twist. As China

This lithograph of baby girls being buried in China was published in 1855. The men at the upper left represent Western opposition to this practice.

opened the door to capitalism, travel and trade opened up—but primarily to men, for it is not thought appropriate for women to travel alone. Thus, men find themselves in a better position to bring profits home to the family, giving parents one more reason to want male children.

The gender ratio is so lop-sided that for people in their 20s there are six bachelors for every five potential brides. Concerned about this gender imbalance, officials have begun a campaign to stop the drowning of girl babies. They are also trying to crack down on the abortions of girl fetuses.

In India, female infanticide is also common. Many Indian women use ultrasound to learn the sex of their child and then abort the fetus if it is a girl. Doctors take portable ultrasound machines from village to village, charging $11 for the test and $44 for the abortion. Although the use of ultrasound for this purpose is illegal, this practice accounts for the abortion of about 3 million girls a year.

One abortion led to a public outcry in India. The outrage was not about female infanticide, however, nor was it due to an antiabortion movement. Rather, the public became incensed when a physician mistakenly gave the parents wrong information and aborted a *male* baby!

It is likely that the preference for boys, and the resulting female infanticide, will not disappear until the social structures that perpetuate sexism are dismantled. This is unlikely to take place until women hold as much power as men, a development that, should it ever occur, apparently lies far in the future.

In the meantime, politicians have become concerned about a primary sociological implication of female infanticide—that large numbers of young men who cannot marry pose a political threat. These "bare branches," as they are referred to in China, disgruntled and lacking the stabilizing influences of marriage and children, could become a breeding ground for political dissent. This threat could motivate the national elites to take steps against female infanticide.

Sources: Lagaipa 1990; Renteln 1992; Greenhalgh and Li 1995; Jordan 2000; Dugger 2001; Eckholm 2002; Raghunathan 2003; French 2004; Hudson and den Boer 2004; Riley 2004.

(yes, you read that right), the fetus is aborted. If she does not consent to an abortion, one is performed on her anyway—even if she is nine months pregnant (Erik 1982). In some provinces government agents even checked sanitary napkins to make sure that women were having their menstrual periods and were not pregnant.

In the face of Western disapproval and wanting to present a better image to accompany its new role on the world political stage, Chinese leaders have relented somewhat. They have kept their "One couple, one child" policy, but they have begun to make exceptions to it. In some rural areas, authorities allow a woman to bear a second child—

The government uses billboards to remind people of its "one couple, one child" policy. The fat on the child's face on this billboard in Shanghai carries an additional message—that curtailing childbirth brings prosperity, abundant food for all.

if the first child is a girl. This improves the couple's chances of getting a son (Riley 2004). In Shanghai, officials now allow two divorced people who marry to have a child even if both partners already have a child from their previous marriages (Watts 2004).

Government actions can change a country's growth rate, but the main factor is not the government, but industrialization. *In every country that industrializes, the birth rate declines.* Not only does industrialization open up economic opportunities but also it makes rearing children more expensive. Children require more education and remain dependent longer. Significantly, the basis for conferring status also changes—from having many children to attaining education and displaying material wealth. People like Celia and Angel begin to see life differently, and their motivation to have many children drops sharply. Not knowing how rapidly industrialization will progress or how quickly changes in values and reproductive behavior will follow adds to the difficulty of making accurate projections.

Because of these many complications, demographers play it safe by making several projections of population growth. For example, what will the U.S. population be in the year 2050? Between now and then, will we have **zero population growth,** with every 1,000 women giving birth to 2,100 children? (The extra 100 children make up for those who do not survive or reproduce.) Will a larger proportion of women go to college? (The more education women have, the fewer children they bear [Sutton and Matthews 2004].) How will immigration change? Will some devastating disease appear? With such huge variables, it is easy to see why demographers make the three projections of the U.S. population shown in Figure 14.8.

Figure 14.8 Population Projections of the United States

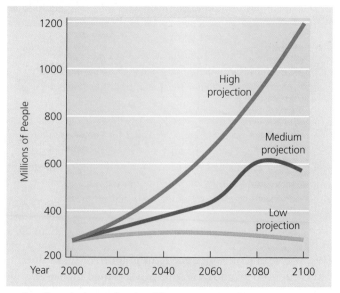

Note: The projections are based on different assumptions of fertility, mortality, and, especially, immigration.

Source: By the author. Based on *Statistical Abstract* 2002:Table 3.

Let's look at a different aspect of population: where people live. Because more and more people around the world are living in cities, we will concentrate on urban trends and urban life.

URBANIZATION

As I was climbing a steep hill in Medellin, Colombia, in a district called El Tiro, my informant, Jaro, said, "This used to be a garbage heap." I stopped to peer through the vegetation alongside the path we were on, and sure enough, I could see bits of refuse still sticking out of the dirt. The "town" had been built on top of garbage.

This was but the first of my many revelations that day. The second was that El Tiro was so dangerous that the Medellin police refused to enter it. I shuddered for a moment, but I had good reason to trust Jaro. He had been a pastor in this town for several years, and he knew the people well. I knew that if I stayed close to him I would be safe.

Actually, El Tiro was safer now than it had been. A group of young men had banded together to make it so, Jaro told me. A sort of frontier justice prevailed. This group told the prostitutes and drug dealers that there would be no prostitution or drug dealing in El Tiro, and to "take it elsewhere." They killed anyone who robbed or killed someone. And they even made families safer—they would beat up any man who got drunk and beat "his" woman. With the threat of instant justice, the area had become much safer.

Jaro then added that each household had to pay the group a monthly fee, which turned out to be just a few cents in U.S. money. Each business had to pay a little more. For this, they received security.

As we wandered the streets of El Tiro, it did look safe—but I still stayed close to Jaro. And I wondered about this

group of men who had made the area safe. What kept them from turning on the residents? Jaro had no answer. When Jaro pointed to two young men, who he said were part of the ruling group, I asked if I could take their picture. They refused. I did not try to snap one on the sly.

My final revelation was El Tiro itself. On the next two pages, you can see some of the things I saw that day.

In this second part of the chapter, I will try to lay the context for understanding urban life—and El Tiro. Let's begin by first finding out how the city itself came about.

The Development of Cities

Cities are not new to the world scene. Perhaps as early as seven thousand years ago, people built small cities with massive defensive walls, such as biblically famous Jericho (Homblin 1973). Cities on a larger scale originated about 3500 B.C., about the same time that writing was invented (Chandler and Fox 1974; Hawley 1981). At that time, cities appeared in several parts of the world— first in Mesopotamia (Iran) and later in the Nile, Indus, and Yellow River valleys, in West Africa, around the shores of the Mediterranean, in Central America, and in the Andes (Fischer 1976; Flanagan 1990). In the Americas, the first city was Caral, in what is now Peru (Fountain 2001).

The key to the origin of cities is the development of more efficient agriculture (Lenski and Lenski 1987). Only when farming produces a surplus can some people stop producing food and gather in cities to spend time in other economic pursuits. A **city,** in fact, can be defined as a place in which a large number of people are permanently based and do not produce their own food. The invention of the plow about five thousand years ago created widespread agricultural surpluses, stimulating the development of towns and cities.

Early cities were small economic centers surrounded by walls to keep out enemies. These cities had to be fortresses, for they were threatened by armed, roving tribesmen and by leaders of nearby city-states who raised armies to enlarge their domain and enrich their coffers by sacking neighboring cities. Pictured here is Carcasonne, a restored medieval city in southern France. Note that it has a double wall, each with towers for archers.

A Walk Through El Tiro in
Medellin, Colombia

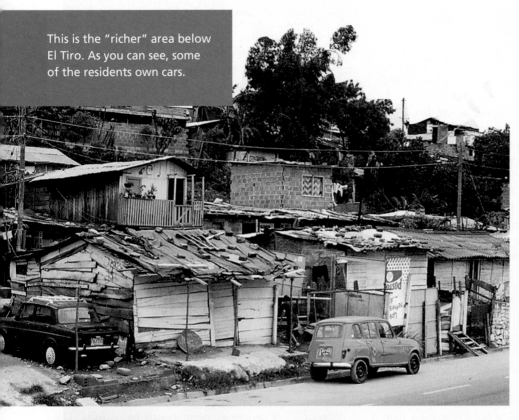

This is the "richer" area below El Tiro. As you can see, some of the residents own cars.

Kids are kids the world over. These children don't know they are poor. They are having a great time playing on a pile of dirt in the street.

This is one of my favorite photos. The woman is happy that she has a home—and proud of what she has done with it. What I find remarkable is the flower garden she so carefully tends, and has taken great effort to protect from children and dogs. I can see the care she would take of a little suburban home.

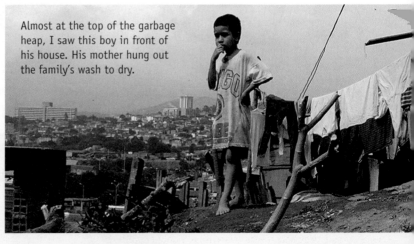

Almost at the top of the garbage heap, I saw this boy in front of his house. His mother hung out the family's wash to dry.

© James M. Henslin, all photos

It doesn't take much skill to build your own house in El Tiro. A hammer and saw, some nails and used lumber will provide most of what you need. This man is building his house on top of another house.

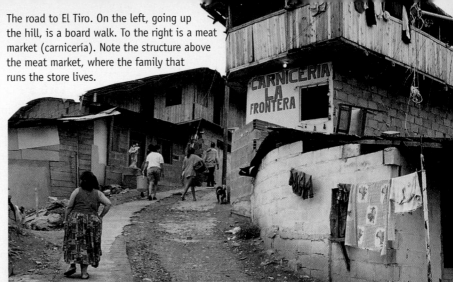

The road to El Tiro. On the left, going up the hill, is a board walk. To the right is a meat market (carnicería). Note the structure above the meat market, where the family that runs the store lives.

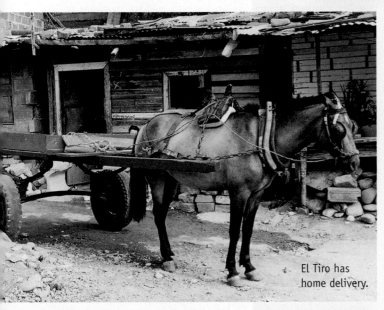

El Tiro has home delivery.

An infrastructure has developed to serve El Tiro. This woman is waiting in line to use the only public telephone.

What do the people do to make a living in El Tiro? Anything they can. This man is sharpening a saw in front of his home.

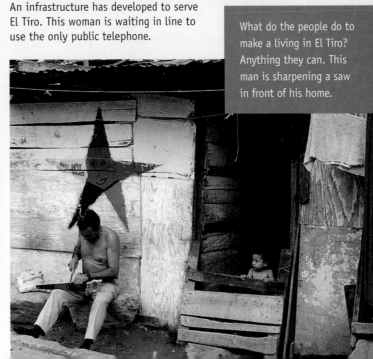

"What does an El Tiro home look like inside?" I kept wondering. Then Jaro, my guide at the left, took me inside the home of one of his parishioners. Amelia keeps a neat house with everything highly organized.

Most early cities were tiny in comparison with those of today, merely a collection of a few thousand people in agricultural centers or on major trade routes. The most notable exceptions are two cities that reached one million residents for a brief period of time before they declined—Changan in China about A.D. 800 and Baghdad in Persia (Iraq) about A.D. 900 (Chandler and Fox 1974). Even Athens at the peak of its power in the fifth century B.C. had about 250,000 inhabitants. Rome, at its peak, may have had a million people or more, but as it declined, its population fell to just 35,000 (Palen 2005).

Even 200 years ago, the only city in the world that had a population of more than a million was Peking (now Beijing), China (Chandler and Fox 1974). Then in just 100 years, by 1900, the number of such cities jumped to sixteen. The reason was the Industrial Revolution, which drew people to cities by providing work. The Industrial Revolution also stimulated rapid transportation and communication and allowed people, resources, and products to be moved efficiently—all essential factors (called *infrastructure*) on which large cities depend. Figure 14.9 shows the global growth in the number of cities that have a million or more people.

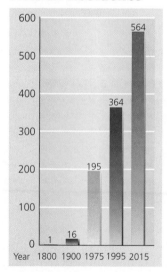

Figure 14.9 **The Global Growth of Cities over One Million Residents**

Sources: By the author. Based on Chandler and Fox 1974; Brockerhoff 2000.

The Process of Urbanization

Although cities are not new to the world scene, urbanization is. **Urbanization** refers to masses of people moving to cities and these cities having a growing influence on society. Urbanization is taking place all over the world. In 1800, only 3 percent of the world's population lived in cities (Hauser and Schnore 1965). Today the number is 48 percent: 76 percent of people in the industrialized world and 41 percent of those who live in the Least Industrialized Nations (Haub 2005). The year 2007 is expected to mark the historic moment when more than half of all humanity will live in cities (Massey 2001). Without the Industrial Revolution, this remarkable growth could not have taken place, for an extensive infrastructure is needed to support hundreds of thousands and even millions of people in a relatively small area.

To understand what attracts people to the city, we need to consider the pulls of urban life. Because of its exquisite division of labor, the city offers incredible variety—music ranging from rap and salsa to country and classical, shops that feature imported delicacies from around the world and those that sell special foods for vegetarians and diabetics. Cities also offer anonymity, which so many find refreshing in light of the tighter controls of village and small town life. And, of course, the city offers work.

Some cities have grown so large and have so much influence over a region that the term *city* is no longer adequate to describe them. The term **metropolis** is used instead. This term refers to a central city surrounded by smaller cities and their suburbs. They are linked by transportation and communication and connected economically, and sometimes politically, through county boards and regional governing bodies. St. Louis is an example.

Although this name, St. Louis, properly refers to a city of fewer than 350,000 people in Missouri, it also refers to another 2 million people who live in more than a hundred separate towns in both Missouri and Illinois. Altogether, the region is known as the "St. Louis or Bi-State Area." Although these towns are independent politically, they form an economic unit. They are linked by work (many people in the smaller towns work in St. Louis or are served by industries from St. Louis), by communications (they share the same area newspaper and radio and television stations), and by transportation (they use the same interstate highways, the Bi-State Bus system, and international airport). As symbolic interactionists would note, shared symbols (the Arch, the Mississippi River, Busch Brewery, the Cardinals, the Rams, the Blues—both the hockey team and the music) provide the residents a common identity.

Most of the towns run into one another, and if you were to drive through this metropolis, you would not know that you were leaving one town and entering another—unless you had lived there for some time and were aware of the fierce small town identifications and rivalries that coexist within this overarching identity.

Some metropolises have grown so large and influential that the term **megalopolis** is used to describe them. This term refers to an overlapping area consisting of at least two metropolises and their many suburbs. Of the twenty or so megalopolises in the United States, the three largest are the Eastern seaboard running from Maine to Virginia; the area in Florida between Miami, Orlando, and Tampa; and California's coastal area between San Francisco and San Diego. This California megalopolis extends into Mexico and includes Tijuana and its suburbs.

This process of urban areas turning into a metropolis, and a metropolis developing into a megalopolis, occurs worldwide. When a city's population hits 10 million, it is called a **megacity.** In 1950, New York City was the only megacity in the world. Today there are 19. Figure 14.10 shows the world's ten largest megacities. Note that most megacities are located in the Least Industrialized Nations.

U.S. Urban Patterns

From Country to City   In its early years, the United States was almost exclusively rural. In 1790, only about 5 percent of Americans lived in cities. By 1920, this figure had jumped to 50 percent. Urbanization has continued without letup, and today 79 percent of Americans live in cities.

The U.S. Census Bureau divides the country into 274 **metropolitan statistical areas (MSAs).** Each MSA consists of a central city of at least 50,000 people and the urbanized areas linked to it. About three of five Americans live in just fifty or so MSAs. As you can see from the Social Map on the next page, like our other social patterns, urbanization is uneven across the United States.

From City to City.   As Americans migrate in search of work and better lifestyles, some cities gain population while others shrink. Table 14.3 on the next page compares the fastest-growing U.S. cities with those that are losing people. This table reflects a major shift of people, resources, and power that is occurring between regions of the United States. As you can see, six of the nine fastest-growing cities are in the West, and three are in the South. Of the nine declining cities, eight are in the Northeast, while one is in the Midwest.

Figure 14.10 The Population of the World's Largest Megacities (in millions)

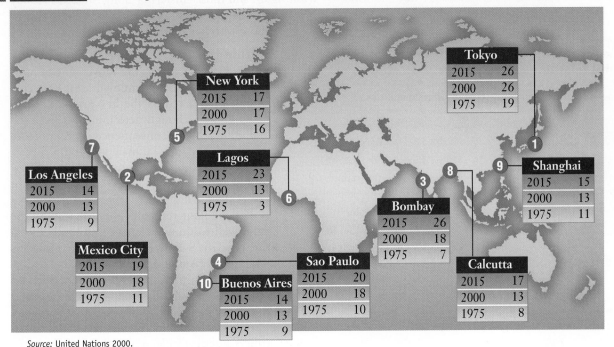

Source: United Nations 2000.

Figure 14.11 **How Urban Is Your State? The Rural-Urban Makeup of the United States**

Note: The most rural state is Vermont (38% urban). The most urban states are California and New Jersey (94% urban).

Source: By the author. Based on *Statistical Abstract* 2005:Table 25.

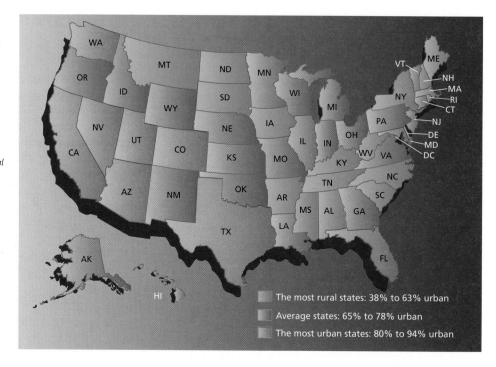

The most rural states: 38% to 63% urban

Average states: 65% to 78% urban

The most urban states: 80% to 94% urban

Between Cities. As Americans migrate, **edge cities** have developed to meet their needs. This term refers to clusters of buildings and services near the intersection of major highways. These areas of shopping malls, hotels, office parks, and apartment complexes are not cities in the traditional sense. Rather than being political units with their own mayor or city manager, they overlap political boundaries and can include parts of several cities or towns. Yet, edge cities—such as Tysons Corner in Washington and those clustering along the LBJ Freeway in Dallas, Texas—provide a sense of place to those who live or work there.

Within the City. Another U.S. urban pattern is **gentrification,** the movement of middle-class people into rundown areas of a city. They are attracted by the low prices for large houses that, although deteriorated, can be restored. A positive consequence is an improvement in the appearance of some urban neighborhoods—freshly painted buildings, well-groomed lawns, and the absence of boarded-up windows. A negative consequence is that the poor residents are displaced by the more well-to-do newcomers. Tension between the gentrifiers and those being displaced is widespread (Anderson 1990, 2006).

A common pattern is for the gentrifiers to be whites and the displaced to be minorities. As is discussed in the Down-to-Earth Sociology box, in Harlem, New York City, both the gentrifiers and the displaced are African Americans.

Table 14.3 **The Shrinking and Fastest-Growing Cities**

The Fastest Growning Cities			The Shrinking Cities		
1.	100%	Las Vegas, NV	1.	−5.9%	Utica, NY
2.	79%	Naples, FL	2.	−5.1%	Binghamton, NY
3.	60%	McCallen, TX	3.	−4.1%	Scranton, PA
4.	58%	Austin, TX	4.	−3.3%	Youngstown, OH
5.	57%	Raleigh, NC	5.	−2.4%	Pittsburgh, PA
6.	56%	Phoenix, AZ	6.	−2.1%	Buffalo, NY
7.	55%	Boise City, ID	7.	−0.9%	Syracuse, NY
8.	54%	Fayetteville, AR	8.	−0.5%	Huntington, WV
9.	48%	Provo, UT	9.	−0.3%	Charleston, WV

Note: The totals indicate the percentage of population change from 1990–2003. A minus sign indicates a loss of population.

Source: By the author. Based on *Statistical Abstract* 2005:Table 24.

Down-to-Earth Sociology

Reclaiming Harlem: "It Feeds My Soul"

The story is well known. The inner city is filled with crack, crime, and corruption. It stinks from foul, festering filth strewn on the streets and piled up around burned-out buildings. Only those who have no choice live in this desolate, despairing environment where danger lurks around every corner.

What is not so well known is that affluent African Americans are reclaiming some of these areas.

Howard Sanders was living the American Dream. After earning a degree from Harvard Business School, he took a position with a Manhattan investment firm. He lived in an exclusive apartment on Central Park West, but he missed Harlem, where he had grown up. He moved back, along with his wife and daughter.

African American lawyers, doctors, professors, and bankers are doing the same.

What's the attraction? The first is nostalgia, a cultural identification with the Harlem of legend and folklore. It was here that black writers and artists lived in the 1920s, here that the blues and jazz attracted young and accomplished musicians.

The second reason is a more practical one. Harlem offers housing value. Five-bedroom homes with 6,000 square feet are available. Some feature Honduran mahogany. Some brownstones are only shells and have to be completely renovated; others are in good condition.

What is happening is the rebuilding of a community. Some people who "made" it want to be role models. They want children in the community to see them going to and returning from work.

When the middle class moved out of Harlem, so did its amenities. Now that young professionals are moving back in, the amenities are returning, too. There were no coffee shops, restaurants, jazz clubs, florists, copy centers, dentist and optometrist offices, or art galleries—the types of things urbanites take for granted. Now there are.

The same thing is happening on Chicago's West Side and in other U.S. cities.

The drive to find community—to connect with others and with one's roots—is strong. As an investment banker who migrated to Harlem said, "It feeds my soul."

Source: Based on Cose 1999; McCormick 1999b; Waldman 2000; Scott 2001; Taylor 2002; Leland 2003; Freeman 2004.

As middle-class and professional African Americans reclaim this area, an infrastructure—which includes everything from Starbucks coffee houses to dentists—follows. So do soaring real estate prices.

From City to Suburb. **Suburbanization** refers to people moving from cities to suburbs, the communities located just outside a city. Suburbanization is not new. Archaeologists recently found that the Mayan city of Caracol (in what is now Belize) had suburbs, perhaps even with specialized subcenters, the equivalent of today's strip malls (Wilford 2000). The extent to which people have left U.S. cities in search of their dreams is remarkable. Fifty years ago, about 20 percent of Americans lived in the suburbs (Karp et al. 1991). Today, over half of all Americans live in them (Palen 2005).

The automobile was a major impetus for suburbanization. Beginning about one hundred years ago, whites began to move to small towns near the cities where they worked. After the racial integration of U.S. schools in the 1950s and 1960s, suburbanization picked up pace as whites fled the cities. Minorities began to move to the suburbs about 1970. In some of today's suburbs, minorities are the majority.

Smaller Centers. The most recent urban trend is the development of *micropolitan areas.* A *micropolis* is a city of 10,000 to 50,000 residents that is not a suburb (McCarthy 2004). Most micropolises are located "next to nowhere." They are fairly self-contained in terms of providing work, housing, schools, shopping, and entertainment, and few of their residents commute to urban centers for work. Micropolises are growing, as residents of both rural and urban areas find their cultural attractions and conveniences appealing, especially in the absence of the city's crime and pollution.

The Rural Rebound

The desire to retreat to a safe haven has led to a migration to rural areas that is without precedent in the history of the United States. Some little farming towns are making a comeback, their boarded-up stores and schools once again open for business and learning.

The "push" factor for this fundamental shift is fear of urban crime and violence. The "pull" factors are safety, lower cost of living, and more living space. Interstate highways have made airports—and the city itself—accessible from longer distances. With satellite communications, cell phones, fax machines, and the Internet, people can be "plugged in"—connected with people around the world—even though they live in what just a short time ago were remote areas.

Listen to the wife of one of my former students as she explains why she and her husband moved to a rural area, three hours from the international airport that they fly out of each week:

> I work for a Canadian company. Paul works for a French company, with headquarters in Paris. He flies around the country doing computer consulting. I give motivational seminars to businesses. When we can, we drive to the airport together, but we often leave on different days. I try to go with my husband to Paris once a year.
>
> We almost always are home together on the weekends. We often arrange three- and four-day weekends, because I can plan seminars at home, and Paul does some of his consulting from here.
>
> Sometimes shopping is inconvenient, but we don't have to lock our car doors when we drive, and the new Wal-Mart superstore has most of what we need. E-commerce is a big part of it. I just type in www—whatever, and they ship it right to my door. I get make-up and books online. I even bought a part for my stove.
>
> Why do we live here? Look at the lake. It's beautiful. We enjoy boating and swimming. We love to walk in this park-like setting. We see deer and wild turkeys. We love the sunsets over the lake. (author's files)

Models of Urban Growth

In the 1920s, Chicago was a vivid mosaic of immigrants, gangsters, prostitutes, the homeless, the rich, and the poor—much as it is today. Sociologists at the University of Chicago studied these contrasting ways of life. One of these sociologists, Robert Park, coined the term **human ecology** to describe how people adapt to their environment (Park and Burgess 1921; Park 1936). (This concept is also known as *urban ecology*.) The process of urban growth is of special interest to sociologists. Let's look at the three main models they developed.

The Concentric Zone Model.   To explain how cities expand, sociologist Ernest Burgess (1925) proposed a *concentric zone model*. As shown in part A of Figure 14.12 on the next page, Burgess noted that a city expands outward from its center. Zone 1 is the central business district. Zone 2, which encircles this downtown area, is in transition. It contains rooming houses and deteriorating housing, which Burgess said breed poverty, disease, and vice. Zone 3 is the area to which thrifty workers have moved to escape the zone in transition and yet maintain easy access to their work. Zone 4 contains more expensive apartments, residential hotels, single-family houses, and exclusive areas where the wealthy live. Commuters live in Zone 5, which consists of suburbs or satellite cities that have grown up around transportation routes.

Burgess intended this model to represent "the tendencies of any town or city to expand radially from its central business district." He noted, however, that no "city fits perfectly this ideal scheme." Some cities have physical obstacles, such as a lake, river, or railroad, that cause their expansion to depart from the model. Burgess also noted that businesses had begun to deviate from the model by locating in outlying zones (see Zone 10). That was in 1925. He didn't know it, but Burgess was seeing the beginning of a major shift that led businesses away from downtown areas and toward suburban shopping malls. Today, these malls account for most of the country's retail sales.

The Sector Model.   Sociologist Homer Hoyt (1939, 1971) noted that a city's concentric zones do not form a complete circle, and he modified Burgess' model of urban growth. As shown in part B of Figure 14.12, a concentric zone can contain several sectors—one of working-class housing, another of expensive homes, a third of businesses, and so on, all competing for the same land.

An example of this dynamic competition is what sociologists call an **invasion-succession cycle.** Poor immigrants and rural migrants settle in low-rent areas. As their numbers swell, they spill over into adjacent areas. Upset by their presence, the middle class moves out, which expands the sector of low-cost housing. The invasion-succession cycle is never complete, for later another group will replace this earlier one. The cycle, in fact, can go full circle, for as discussed in the Down-to-Earth Sociology box

Figure 14.12 How Cities Develop: Models of Urban Growth

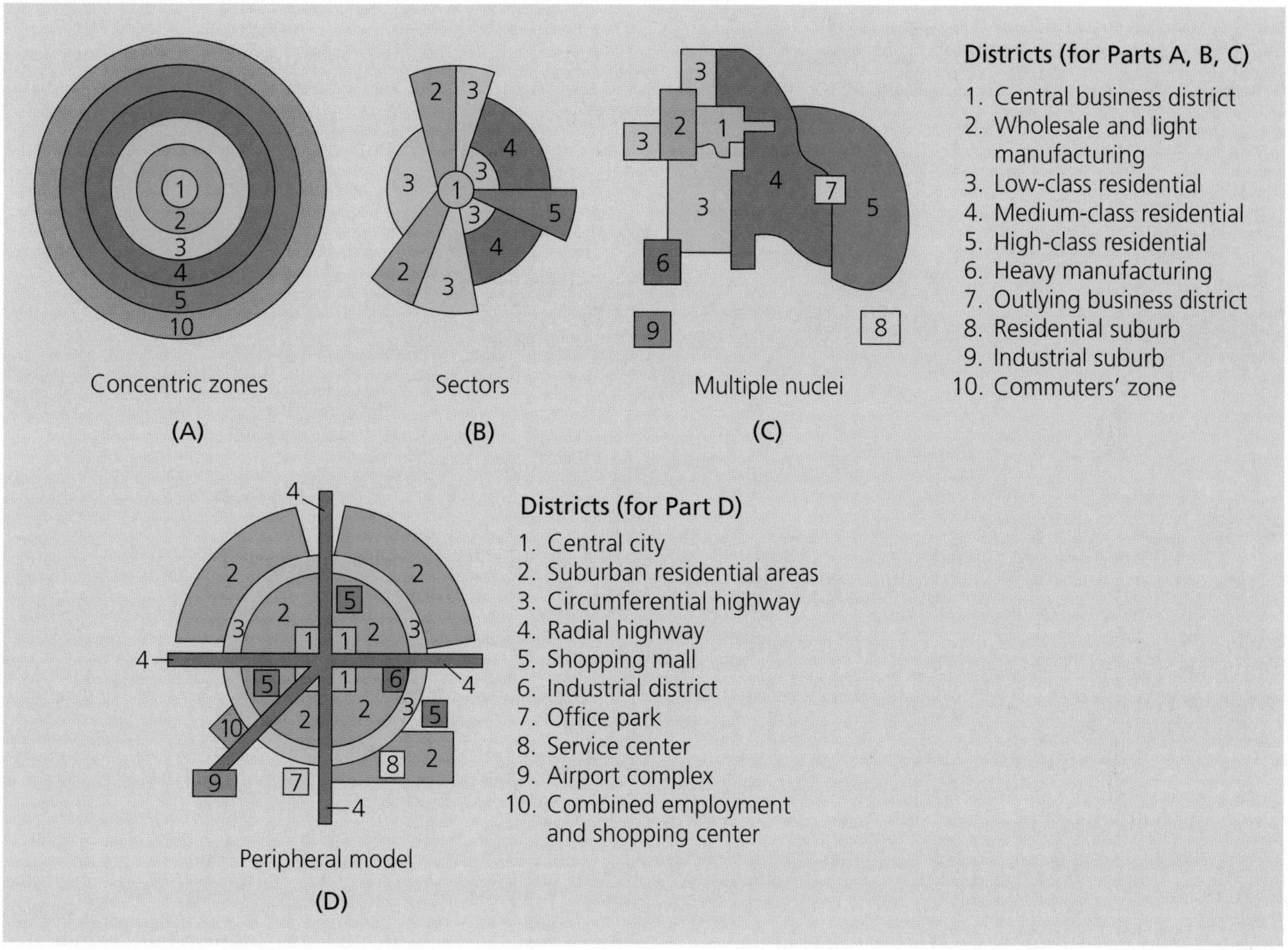
Concentric zones
(A)
Sectors
(B)
Multiple nuclei
(C)
Districts (for Parts A, B, C)
1. Central business district
2. Wholesale and light manufacturing
3. Low-class residential
4. Medium-class residential
5. High-class residential
6. Heavy manufacturing
7. Outlying business district
8. Residential suburb
9. Industrial suburb
10. Commuters' zone
Peripheral model
(D)
Districts (for Part D)
1. Central city
2. Suburban residential areas
3. Circumferential highway
4. Radial highway
5. Shopping mall
6. Industrial district
7. Office park
8. Service center
9. Airport complex
10. Combined employment and shopping center

Source: Cousins and Nagpaul 1970; Harris 1997.

on Harlem (page 403), the "invaders" can be the middle and upper-middle classes.

The Multiple-Nuclei Model. Geographers Chauncey Harris and Edward Ullman noted that some cities have several centers or nuclei (Harris and Ullman 1945; Ullman and Harris 1970). As shown in part C of Figure 14.12, each nucleus contains some specialized activity. A familiar example is the clustering of fast-food restaurants in one area and automobile dealerships in another. Sometimes similar activities are grouped together because they profit from cohesion; retail districts, for example, draw more customers if there are more stores. Other clustering occurs because some types of land use, such as factories and expensive homes, are incompatible with one another. One result is that services are not spread evenly throughout the city.

The Peripheral Model. Chauncey Harris (1997) also developed the peripheral model shown in part D of Figure 14.12. This model portrays the impact of radial highways on the movement of people and services away from the central city and toward the city's periphery, or outskirts. It also shows the development of industrial and office parks.

Critique of the Models. These models tell only part of the story. They are time bound, for medieval cities didn't follow these patterns (see the photo on page 397). In addition, they do not account for urban planning policies. England, for example, has planning laws that preserve green belts (trees and farmlands) around the city. This prevents urban sprawl: Wal-Mart cannot buy land outside the city and put up a store; instead, it must locate in the downtown area with the other stores. Norwich has 250,000 people—

yet the city ends abruptly, and on its green belt, pheasants skitter across plowed fields while sheep graze in verdant meadows (Milbank 1995).

If you were to depend on these models, you would be surprised if you visited the cities of the Least Industrialized Nations. There, the wealthy often claim the inner city, where fine restaurants and other services are readily accessible. Tucked behind walls and protected from public scrutiny, they enjoy luxurious homes and gardens. The poor, in contrast, especially rural migrants, settle in areas outside the city—or, as in the case of El Tiro, featured in the photo essay on pages 398–399, on top of piles of garbage in what used to be the outskirts of a city.

City Life

Just as cities provide opportunities, they also create problems. Let's look at some of these problems.

Alienation and Community

We humans are complex beings. Certainly, we have physical needs of food, shelter, and safety, and satisfying them is important. But this is only part of who we are. We also have a deep need for community, a feeling that we belong—the sense that others care about what happens to us and that we can depend on the people around us. Some people find this sense of community in the city; others experience its opposite, **alienation,** a sense of not belonging and a feeling that no one cares what happens to you.

> Twenty-eight-year-old Catherine Genovese, who was called Kitty by almost everyone in her Queens neighborhood, was returning home from work. After she parked her car, a man grabbed her. She screamed, "Oh, my God, he stabbed me! Help me! Please help me!"
>
> For more than half an hour, thirty-eight respectable, law-abiding citizens looked out their windows and watched as the killer stalked and stabbed Kitty in three separate attacks. Twice the sudden glow from their bedroom lights interrupted him and frightened him off. Each time he returned, sought her out, and stabbed her again. Not one person telephoned the police during the assault.
>
> When the police interviewed them, some witnesses said, "I didn't want to get involved." Others said, "We thought it was a lovers' quarrel." Some simply said, "I don't know." (Gansberg 1964)

People throughout the country were shocked. It was as though Americans awoke one morning to discover that the country had changed overnight. They took this event as a sign that the city was a cold, lonely place. Some, however, dispute this account of Kitty's murder. They say that only a few people saw part of what happened, and that due to darkness, distance, and obstructions, these people didn't understand that Kitty was being attacked (De May 2005).

Regardless of who is right, the city often alienates people from one another. Why? In a classic essay, "Urbanism as a Way of Life," sociologist Louis Wirth (1938) argued that the city undermines kinship and neighborhood relationships, which are the traditional sources of social control and social solidarity. Urban dwellers live in anonymity. As they go from one superficial encounter with strangers to another, they grow aloof and indifferent to other people's problems. In short, the price of the personal freedom that the city offers is alienation.

But this is only part of the story. The city is more than a mosaic of strangers who feel disconnected and distrustful of one another. It also consists of a series of smaller worlds, within which people find community. People become familiar with the smaller areas of the city where they live, work, shop, and play. Even slums, which to outsiders seem so threatening, can provide a sense of belonging. In a classic study, sociologist Herbert Gans (1962:12) noted,

> After a few weeks of living in the West End (of Boston), my observations—and my perceptions of the area—changed drastically. The search for an apartment quickly indicated that the individual units were usually in much better condition than the outside or the hallways of the buildings. Subsequently, in wandering through the West End, and in using it as a resident, I developed a kind of selective perception, in which my eye focused only on those parts of the area that were actually being used by people. Vacant buildings and boarded-up stores were no longer so visible, and the totally deserted alleys or streets were outside the set of paths normally traversed, either by myself or by the West Enders . . .
>
> Since much of the area's life took place on the street, faces became familiar very quickly. I met my neighbors on the stairs and in front of my building. And, once a shopping pattern developed, I saw the same storekeepers frequently, as well as the area's "characters" who wandered through the streets every day on a fairly regular route and schedule. In short, the exotic quality of the stores and the residents also wore off as I became used to seeing them.

As he lived in the West End, Gans gradually gained an insider's perspective of the area. Despite the narrow streets, substandard buildings, and even piled-up garbage, most West Enders had chosen to live there: *To them, the West End was a low-rent district, not a slum.* Within this deteriorated area was a community, people who visited back and forth with relatives and were involved in networks of friendships and acquaintances. Gans therefore titled his book *The Urban Villagers* (1962).

Then came well-intentioned urban planners, who drew up plans to get rid of the "slum." The residents of the West End were upset when they heard about the coming urban renewal and distrustful that the improvements would benefit them. Their distrust proved well founded, for the urban renewal brought with it another invasion-succession cycle. Along with the gleaming new buildings came people with more money who took over the area. The former residents were dispossessed, their intimate patterns ripped apart.

Who Lives in the City?

Among the factors that influence people's reactions to city life is the "type" of resident they are. Consider the five types that Gans (1962, 1968, 1991) identified. Which type are you? How does this affect your chances of finding alienation or community in the city?

The first three types live in the city by choice; they find a sense of community.

The Cosmopolites. The cosmopolites are the city's students, intellectuals, professionals, musicians, artists, writers, and entertainers. They have been drawn to the city because of its conveniences and cultural benefits.

The Singles. Young, unmarried people come to the city seeking jobs and entertainment. Businesses and services such as singles bars, singles apartment complexes, and computer dating companies cater to their needs. Their stay in the city is often temporary, for most move to the suburbs after they marry and have children.

The Ethnic Villagers. United by race-ethnicity and social class, these people live in tightly knit neighborhoods that resemble villages and small towns. Their close circle of family and friends helps to insulate them from what they perceive as the harmful effects of city life.

The next two groups, the deprived and the trapped, have little choice about where they live. As alienated outcasts of the information society, they are always skirting the edge of disaster.

The Deprived. The deprived live in blighted neighborhoods that are more like urban jungles than urban villages. Poor and emotionally disturbed, the deprived represent the bottom of society in terms of income, education, prestige, and work skills. Some of them stalk their

The city dwellers who Gans identified as ethnic villagers find community in the city. Living in tightly knit neighborhoods, they know many other residents. Some first-generation immigrants have even come from the same village in the "old country."

jungle in search of prey, their victims usually deprived people like themselves. Their future holds practically no chance for anything better in life.

The Trapped.   The trapped can find no escape either. Some could not afford to move when their neighborhood was "invaded" by another ethnic group. Others in this group are the elderly who are not wanted elsewhere, alcoholics and other drug addicts, and the downwardly mobile. Like the deprived, the trapped suffer high rates of assault, mugging, robbery, and rape.

Urban Sentiment: Finding a Familiar World

If the city were simply a single massive area, it could not meet people's need for community, for a feeling of belonging and identifying with something larger than themselves. To provide this sense of belonging, *people divide the city into little worlds* that they come to know down to their smallest details. For example, people create a sense of intimacy by *personalizing* their shopping (Stone 1954; Gans 1970). They shop in the same stores, and after a period of time, customers and clerks greet each other by name. The shops, restaurants, and bars that urban dwellers patronize are more than just buildings in which they make purchases or stop for a drink. These places provide an anchor to their identity. Here they build social relationships and share informal news, commonly called gossip.

Spectator sports also help urban dwellers to find a familiar world. When Mark McGwire of the Cardinals hit the sixty-first home run that broke Roger Maris' longstanding record, fans around the country celebrated, but for the St. Louis area, the celebration was special: It was for "our" man on "our" team—even though fewer than one in seven of the area's 2.5 million people live in the city. Sociologists David Karp and William Yoels (1990) note that identifying with sports teams is so intense that long after moving to other parts of the country, people maintain an emotional allegiance to the team of the city in which they grew up.

The Norm of Noninvolvement and the Diffusion of Responsibility

Urban dwellers try to avoid intrusions from strangers. As they go about their everyday lives in the city, they follow a *norm of noninvolvement.* They avoid eye contact or "stare through" one another. Even though they are in public spaces, they use devices such as iPods to retreat into private worlds. On subways, they look vacantly into space, lean back and close their eyes, or immerse themselves in

newspapers and magazines or work they've brought from the office. The message is, "I'm here, but not with you. We just happen to be occupying the same space for a while."

Recall Kitty Genovese, whose story was recounted on page 406. Her death so troubled social psychologists John Darley and Bibb Latané (1968) that they ran the series of experiments featured in Chapter 5, page 130. In their experiments, Darley and Latané uncovered the *diffusion of responsibility*—the more bystanders there are, the less likely people are to help. As a group grows, people's sense of responsibility becomes diffused, with each person assuming that *another* will do the responsible thing. "With these other people here, it is not *my* responsibility," they reason.

The diffusion of responsibility, along with the norm of noninvolvement, helps to explain why people can ignore the plight of others. If there really were witnesses to the death of Kitty Genovese (as I indicated, there is some question about this), the bystanders were *not* uncaring people. They simply were following an urban norm, one that is helpful for getting them through everyday city life but, unfortunately, that is dysfunctional in some crucial situations. This norm, combined with the fears nurtured by urban killings, rapes, and muggings, makes many people want to retreat to a safe haven. This topic is discussed in the Down-to-Earth Sociology box on the next page.

Urban Problems and Social Policy

To close this chapter, let's look at the primary reasons that U.S. cities have declined, and then consider the potential of urban revitalization.

Suburbanization

The U.S. city has been the loser in the transition to suburbs. As people moved out of the city, businesses and jobs followed. White-collar corporations, such as insurance companies, first moved their offices to the suburbs, followed by manufacturing firms. This process has continued so relentlessly that today, twice as many manufacturing jobs are located in the suburbs as in the city (Palen 2005). As the city's tax base shrank, it left a budget squeeze that affected not only parks, zoos, libraries, and museums, but also the city's basic services—its schools, streets, sewer and water systems, and police and fire departments.

This shift in population and resources left behind people who had no choice but to stay in the city. As we

Down-to-Earth Sociology

Urban Fear and the Gated Fortress

GATED NEIGHBORHOODS—WHERE GATES open and close to allow or prevent access to a neighborhood—are not new. They always have been available to the rich. What is new is the rush of the upper middle class to towns where they pay high taxes to keep all of the town's facilities, including its streets, private.

Towns cannot discriminate on the basis of religion or race-ethnicity, but they can—and do—discriminate on the basis of social class. Klahanie, Washington, is an excellent example. Begun in 1985, it was supposed to take twenty years to develop. With its winding streets, pavilions, gardens, swimming pools, parks, private libraries, infant-toddler playcourt, and 25 miles of hiking-bicycling-running trails on 300 acres of open space, demand for the $300,000 to $500,000 homes nestled by a lake in this private community exceeded supply (Egan 1995; Klahanie Association Web site 2005).

As the upper middle class flees urban areas and tries to build a bucolic dream, we will see many more private towns. A sign of the future is Celebration, a town of 20,000 people planned and built by the Walt Disney Company just five minutes from Disney World. Celebration boasts the usual serv-

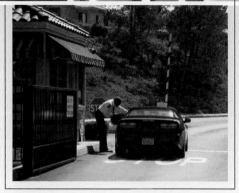

To protect themselves, primarily from the poor, the upper middle class increasingly seeks sanctuary behind gated residential enclaves like this one in California.

ices of schools, restaurants, and state-of-the-art hospital. In addition, Celebration offers a Robert Trent Jones golf course, walking and bicycling paths, a hotel with a lighthouse tower and bird sanctuary, a health and fitness center with a rock-climbing wall, and its own cable TV channel. With fiber-optic technology, the residents of private communities can communicate with the outside world while remaining securely locked within their sanctuaries.

for your Consideration

Community involves a sense of togetherness, a sense of identity with one another. Can you explain how this concept also contains the idea of separation from others (not just in the example of gated communities)? What will our future be if we become a nation of gated communities, where middle-class homeowners withdraw into private domains, separating themselves from the rest of the nation?

reviewed in Chapter 9, sociologist William Julius Wilson (1987) says that this exodus transformed the inner city into a ghetto. Left behind were families and individuals who, lacking skills and jobs, were trapped by poverty and welfare dependency. Also left behind were people who prey on others through street crime. The term *ghetto,* says Wilson, "suggests that a fundamental social transformation has taken place . . . that groups represented by this term are collectively different from and much more socially isolated from those that lived in these communities in earlier years" (quoted in Karp et al. 1991).

City Versus Suburb.   Having made the move out of the city—or having been born in a suburb and preferring

to stay there—suburbanites want the city to keep its problems to itself. They reject proposals to share suburbia's revenues with the city and oppose measures that would allow urban and suburban governments joint control over what has become a contiguous mass of people and businesses. Suburban leaders generally believe that it is in their best interests to remain politically, economically, and socially separate from the nearby city. They do not mind going to the city to work or venturing there on weekends for the diversions it offers, but they do not want to help pay the city's expenses.

It is likely that the mounting bill will come due ultimately, however, and that suburbanites will have to pay for their uncaring attitude toward the urban disadvantaged. Karp et al. (1991) put it this way:

It may be that suburbs can insulate themselves from the problems of central cities, at least for the time being. In the long run, though, there will be a steep price to pay for the failure of those better off to care compassionately for those at the bottom of society.

The violence of our inner cities and our occasional urban riots may be part of that bill—perhaps just the down payment.

Suburban Flight. In some places, the bill is coming due quickly. As they age, some suburbs are becoming mirror images of the city that their residents so despise. Suburban crime, the flight of the middle class, a shrinking tax base, and eroding services create a spiraling sense of insecurity, stimulating more middle-class flight. Figure 14.13 illustrates this process, which is new to the urban-suburban scene.

Disinvestment and Deindustrialization

As the cities' tax base shrank and their services declined, neighborhoods deteriorated, and banks began **redlining:** Afraid of loans going bad, bankers drew a line around a problem area on a map and refused to make loans for housing or businesses there. This **disinvestment** (withdrawal of investment) pushed these areas into further decline. Youth gangs, muggings, and murders are common in these areas, while good jobs are not—all woven into this process of disinvestment.

The globalization of capitalism has also left a heavy mark on U.S. cities. As we reviewed in Chapter 11, to compete in the global market, many U.S. industries

As suburbs age, some are reflecting the problems that previously plagued cities. Shown here is deteriorated housing on Main Street in Hempstead, New York.

Figure 14.13 **Urban Growth and Urban Flight**

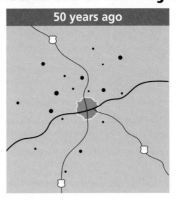

50 years ago

At first, the city and surrounding villages grew independently.

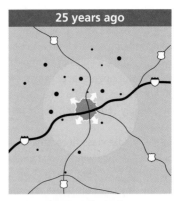

25 years ago

As city dwellers fled urban decay, they created a ring of suburbs.

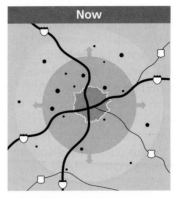

Now

As middle-class flight continues outward, urban problems are arriving in the outer rings.

abandoned local communities and moved their factories to countries where labor costs are lower. This process, called **deindustrialization,** made U.S. industries more competitive, but it eliminated millions of U.S. manufacturing jobs. Lacking training in the new information technologies, many poor people are locked out of the benefits of the postindustrial economy that is engulfing the United States. Left behind in the inner cities, many live in despair.

The Potential of Urban Revitalization

Social policy usually takes one of two forms. The first is to tear down and rebuild—something that is fancifully termed **urban renewal.** The result is the renewal of an area—but *not* for the benefit of its inhabitants. Stadiums, high-rise condos, luxury hotels, and boutiques replace rundown, cheap housing. Outpriced, the area's inhabitants are displaced into adjacent areas.

The second is some sort of **enterprise zone,** a designated area of the city that offers economic incentives, such as reduced taxes, to businesses that move into it. Although the intention is good, failure is usually the result. Most businesses refuse to locate in high-crime areas. Those that do relocate pay a high price for security and losses from crime, which can eat up the tax savings. If workers are hired from within the problem area and the jobs pay a decent wage, which most do not, the workers move to better neighborhoods—which doesn't help the area (Lemann 1994). After all, who chooses to live with the fear of violence?

A form of the enterprise zone, called *Federal Empowerment Zones,* has brought some success. In addition to tax breaks, this program offers low-interest loans targeted for redeveloping an area. It is, in effect, the opposite of disinvestment, which devastates areas. The Down-to-Earth Sociology box on page 403 featured the renaissance of Harlem. Stimulating this change was the designation of Harlem as a Federal Empowerment Zone. The economic incentives lured grocery stores, dry cleaners, and video stores, attracting urbanites who expect such services. As middle class people moved back in, the demand for more specialty shops followed. A self-feeding cycle of development has begun, replacing the self-feeding cycle of despair, crime, and drug use that accompanies disinvestment.

U.S. cities can be revitalized and made into safe and decent places to live, but replacing old buildings with new ones is certainly not the answer. Instead, sociological principles of building community need to be followed. Here are guiding principles suggested by sociologist William Flanagan (1990):

> *Scale.* Regional and national planning is necessary. Local jurisdictions, with their many rivalries, competing goals, and limited resources, end up with a hodgepodge of mostly unworkable solutions.
>
> *Livability.* Cities must be appealing and meet human needs, especially the need of community. This will attract the middle classes into the city, which will increase its tax base. In turn, this will help finance the services that make the city more livable.
>
> *Social justice.* In the final analysis, social policy must be evaluated by how it affects people. "Urban renewal" programs that displace the poor for the benefit of the middle class and wealthy do not pass this standard. The same would apply to solutions that create "livability" for select groups but neglect the poor and the homeless.

Finally, unless we address the *root* causes of urban problems—poverty, poor schools, and lack of jobs—any solutions that we try will be only Band-Aids that cover them up. Such fixes will be window dressings for politicians who want to *appear* as though they are doing something constructive about the problems that affect our quality of life.

Urban renewal is occurring in many places across the globe. As the globalization of capitalism makes urban spaces more valuable, buildings, still usable for decades, are replaced with other structures. This photo was taken in Shenzhen, China.

Summary *and* Review

A Planet with No Space to Enjoy Life?

What debate did Thomas Malthus initiate?

In 1798, Thomas Malthus analyzed the surge in Europe's population. He concluded that the world's population will outstrip its food supply. The debate between today's New Malthusians and those who disagree, the Anti-Malthusians, continues. Pp. 383–387.

Why are people starving?

Starvation is not due to a lack of food in the world, for there is now more food for each person in the entire world than there was fifty years ago. Rather, starvation is due to a maldistribution of food, which is primarily due to drought and war. Pp. 387–388.

Population Growth

Why do the poor nations have so many children?

In the Least Industrialized Nations, children often are viewed as gifts from God, they cost little to rear, they contribute to the family's income at an early age, and they provide the parents' social security. Consequently, people are motivated to have large families. Pp. 388–392.

What are the three demographic variables?

To compute population growth, demographers use *fertility, mortality,* and *migration.* The **basic demographic equation** is births minus deaths plus net migration equals growth rate. Pp. 392–393.

Why is forecasting population growth difficult?

A nation's growth rate is affected by unanticipated variables—from economic cycles, wars, and famines to industrialization and government policies. Pp. 394–396.

The Development of Cities

What factors underlie the growth of cities?

Cities can develop only if there is a large agricultural surplus, which frees people from food production. The primary impetus to the development of cities was the invention of the plow. After the Industrial Revolution stimulated an infrastructure of rapid transportation and communication, cities grew quickly and became much larger. Today, **urbanization** is so extensive that some cities have become **metropolises,** dominating the area adjacent to them. The areas of influence of some metropolises have merged, forming a **megalopolis.** Pp. 397–404.

What models of urban growth have been proposed?

The primary models are concentric zone, sector, multiple-nuclei, and peripheral. These models fail to account for ancient and medieval cities, many European cities, cities in the Least Industrialized Nations, and urban planning. Pp. 404–406.

City Life

Who lives in the city?

Some people experience **alienation** in the city; others find **community** in it. What people find depends largely on their background and urban networks. Five major types of people who live in cities are cosmopolites, singles, ethnic villagers, the deprived, and the trapped. Pp. 406–408.

Urban Problems and Social Policy

Why have U.S. cities declined?

Three primary reasons for the decline of U.S. cities are **suburbanization** (as people moved to the suburbs, the tax base of cities eroded and services deteriorated), **disinvestment** (banks withdrawing their financing), and **deindustrialization** (which caused a loss of jobs). Pp. 408–411.

What social policy can salvage U.S. cities?

Three guiding principles for developing social policy are scale, livability, and social justice. P. 411.

Thinking Critically

about Chapter 14

1. Do you think that the world is threatened by a population explosion? Use data from this chapter to support your position.

2. Why is it difficult for demographers to make accurate predictions about the future of a country's population?

3. What are the causes of urban problems, and what can we do to solve those problems?

Additional Resources

Companion Website www.ablongman.com/henslin

- Content Select Research Database for Sociology, with suggested key terms and annotated references
- Link to 2000 Census, with activities
- Flashcards of key terms and concepts

- Practice Tests
- Weblinks
- Interactive Maps

Where Can I Read More on This Topic?

Suggested readings for this chapter are listed at the back of this book.

Social Change: Technology, Social Movements, and the Environment

How Social Change Transforms Social Life
The Four Social Revolutions
From *Gemeinschaft* to *Gesellschaft*
Capitalism, Modernization, and
   Industrialization
Conflict, Power, and Global Politics

Theories and Processes of Social Change
Cultural Evolution
Natural Cycles
Conflict over Power
Ogburn's Theory

How Technology Changes Society
The Cutting Edge of Change:
   The Computer
Cyberspace and Social Inequality

Social Movements as a Source of Social Change
Types of Social Movements
Propaganda and the Mass Media
The Stages of Social Movements

The Growth Machine Versus the Earth
Environmental Problems in the
   Most Industrialized Nations
Environmental Problems in the
   Industrializing and Least
   Industrialized Nations
The Environmental Movement
Environmental Sociology

Summary and Review

Jose Ortega, *People With Globe and Computer*, 1998

The morning of January 28, 1986, dawned clear but near freezing—strange weather for subtropical Florida. At the Kennedy Space Center, icicles 6 to 12 inches long hung like stalactites from launch pad 39B. Shortly after 8 A.M., the crew entered the crew module. By 8:36 A.M., the seven members of the crew were strapped in their seats. They were understandably disappointed when liftoff, scheduled for 9:38 A.M., was delayed because of the ice.

Screams of horror arose from the crowd . . . and bits of debris began to fall from the sky.

Public interest in the flight ran high. Attention focused on Christa McAuliffe, a 37-year-old high school teacher from Concord, New Hampshire, the first private citizen to fly aboard a space shuttle. Mrs. McAuliffe had been selected from thousands of applicants (including the author of this text). She was to give a televised lesson during the flight about life aboard a spacecraft, and across the nation, schoolchildren watched with anticipation.

Eagerly awaiting the launch at the viewing site were the families and friends of the crew, as well as thousands of spectators. After two hours of delays, they were delighted to see *Challenger*'s two solid-fuel boosters ignite, and they broke into cheers as this product of technological innovation thundered majestically into space. The time was 11:38 A.M.

Seventy-three seconds later, the *Challenger* was 7 miles from the launch site, racing skyward at 2,900 feet per second. Suddenly, a brilliant glow appeared on one side of the external tank. In seconds, the glow blossomed into a gigantic fireball. Screams of horror arose from the crowd as the *Challenger,* now 19 miles away, exploded, and bits of debris began to fall from the sky.

In classrooms across the country, children burst into tears. Adults stared at their televisions in stunned disbelief.

— *Sources:* Based on Broad 1986; Magnuson 1986; Lewis 1988; Maier 1993.

If any characteristic describes social life today, it is rapid social change. As we shall see in this chapter, technology, such as that which made the *Challenger* both a reality and a disaster, is a driving force behind this change. To understand social change is to better understand today's society—and our own lives.

How Social Change Transforms Social Life

 **Social change,** a shift in the characteristics of culture and society, is such a vital part of social life that it has been a recurring theme throughout this book. To make this theme more explicit, let's review the main points about social change that were made in the preceding chapters.

The Four Social Revolutions

The rapid social change that the world is currently experiencing did not "just happen." Rather, today's social change is the result of forces that were set in motion thousands of years ago, beginning with the domestication of plants and animals. This first social revolution allowed hunting and gathering societies to develop into horticultural and pastoral societies (see pages 89–95). The plow

Social change comes in many forms. Shown here is a Chinese peasant in 1911, whose pigtail is being cut off by the revolutionary army. To retain the custom of never cutting one's hair was considered a sign of allegiance to warlords and of resistance to the new regime.

brought about the second social revolution, from which agricultural societies emerged. The third social revolution, prompted by the invention of the steam engine, ushered in the Industrial Revolution. Now we are in the midst of the fourth social revolution, stimulated by the invention of the microchip. The process of change has accelerated so greatly that the mapping of the human genome system may have pushed us into yet another new type of society, one based on biotechnology.

From *Gemeinschaft* to *Gesellschaft*

Although so many aspects of our lives have already changed, we have seen only the tip of the iceberg. By the time this fourth—and perhaps fifth—social revolution is full-blown, little of our current way of life will remain. We can assume this because that is how it was with the earlier social revolutions. For example, the change from agricultural to industrial society meant not only that people moved from villages to cities but also that many intimate, lifelong relationships were replaced by impersonal, short-term associations. Paid work, contracts, and money replaced the reciprocal obligations (such as exchanging favors) that were essential to relationships based on kinship, social status, and friendship. As reviewed on page 95, sociologists use the terms *Gemeinschaft* and *Gesellschaft* to indicate this fundamental shift in society.

Capitalism, Modernization, and Industrialization

Just why did societies change from *Gemeinschaft* to *Gesellschaft*? Karl Marx pointed to a social invention called *capitalism.* He analyzed how the breakup of feudal society threw people off the land, creating a surplus of labor. These masses moved to cities, where they were exploited by the owners of the means of production (factories, machinery, tools). This set in motion antagonistic relationships between capitalists and workers that remain today.

Max Weber, in contrast, traced capitalism to the Protestant Reformation (see pages 372–373). He noted that the Reformation stripped Protestants of the assurance that church membership saved them. As they agonized over heaven and hell, they concluded that God did not want the elect to live in uncertainty. Surely God would give a sign to assure them that they were predestined to heaven. That sign, they decided, was prosperity. An unexpected consequence of the Reformation, then, was to make Protestants work hard and be thrifty. This created an economic surplus, which stimulated capitalism. In this way, Protestantism laid the groundwork for the Industrial Revolution that transformed the world.

The Protestant Reformation ushered in not only religious change but also, as Max Weber analyzed, fundamental social-economic change. This painting by Hans Holbein, the Younger, shows the new prosperity of the merchant class. Previously, only the nobility and higher clergy could afford such possessions.

Table 15.1 **Comparing Traditional and Modern Societies**		
Characteristics	Traditional Societies	Modern Societies
General Characteristics		
Social change	Slow	Rapid
Size of group	Small	Large
Religious orientation	More	Less
Formal education	No	Yes
Place of residence	Rural	Urban
Family size	Larger	Smaller
Infant mortality	High	Low
Life expectancy	Short	Long
Health care	Home	Hospital
Temporal orientation	Past	Future
Demographic transition	First stage	Third stage (or Fourth)
Material Relations		
Industrialized	No	Yes
Technology	Simple	Complex
Division of labor	Simple	Complex
Income	Low	High
Material possessions	Few	Many
Social Relationship		
Basic organization	*Gemeinschaft*	*Gesellschaft*
Families	Extended	Nuclear
Respect for elders	More	Less
Social stratification	Rigid	More open
Statuses	More ascribed	More achieved
Gender equality	Less	More
Norms		
View of life and morals	Absolute	Relativistic
Social control	Informal	Formal
Tolerance of differences	Less	More

Source: By the author.

The sweeping changes ushered in by the Industrial Revolution are called **modernization.** Table 15.1 summarizes these changes. The traits listed on this table are *ideal types* in Weber's sense of the term, for no society exemplifies all of them to the maximum degree. Our new technology has also brought about a remarkable unevenness in the characteristics of societies. For example, in Uganda, a traditional society, the elite have computers. Thus, the characteristics shown in Table 15.1 should be interpreted as "more" or "less" rather than "either-or."

When technology changes, societies change. Consider how the technology from the industrialized world is transforming traditional societies. When the West exported medicine to the Least Industrialized Nations, for example, death rates dropped while birth rates remained high. As a result, the population exploded. This second stage of the demographic transition upset traditional balances of family and property. It brought hunger and led to mass migration to cities that have little industrialization to support the masses of people moving into them.

Conflict, Power, and Global Politics

In our fast-paced world, our attention goes to the changes that have an immediate impact on our own lives. Usually going unnoticed is one of the most signficant changes of all, the arrangement of power among nations. By the sixteenth century, global divisions had begun to emerge. Those nations that had the most advanced technology (at that time, the swiftest ships and the most powerful cannons) became wealthy by conquering other nations and taking control of their resources. Then, as capitalism emerged, some nations industrialized. The newly industrialized nations then exploited the resources of those countries that had not yet industrialized. According to *world system theory,* this made the nonindustrialized nations dependent and unable to develop their own resources (see page 186).

Since World War II, a realignment of the world's powers (called *geopolitics*) has resulted in a triadic division of the globe: a Japan-centered East (soon to be dominated by China), a Germany-centered Europe, and a United States-centered western hemisphere. These three powers, along with five lesser ones—Canada, France, Great Britain, Italy, and Russia—dominate the globe today. They first called themselves G-7, meaning the "Group of 7." Fear of Russia's nuclear arsenal and an attempt to gain Russia's cooperation in global affairs prompted the G-7 nations to let Russia join its elite club. It is now known as G-8.

These industrial giants hold annual meetings at which they decide how to divide up the world's markets and set policies to guide global economic matters such as interest rates, tariffs, and currency exchanges. Their goal is to perpetuate their global dominance, which includes trying to maintain low prices on the raw materials they buy from the Least Industrialized Nations. Access to abundant oil is essential for this goal, which requires that they dominate the Middle East, not letting it become an independent power. If those countries were to set prices and policies according to their own interests, it would undermine the world order being orchestrated by G-8.

Threatening the global divisions that G-8 has so carefully constructed is the resurgence of ethnic conflicts. The breakup of the Soviet empire unleashed the centuries-old hatreds and frustrated nationalistic ambitions of many ethnic groups. With the Soviet military and the KGB in disarray, these groups turned violently against one another. Ethnic violence in the former Yugoslavia was so severe that this country split into five separate nations. The situation in Africa is similar. When European powers controlled Africa with armed forces, they drew arbitrary political boundaries that lumped ethnic groups and tribal territories together. Every now and then, ethnic rivalries in these African countries turn violent. Ethnic conflicts also threaten to erupt in Germany, France, Italy, the United States, and Mexico. We do not know how long the lid can be kept on these seemingly bottomless resentments and hatreds, or if they will ever play themselves out.

The growing wealth and power of China poses another threat to G-8. China wants to recapture its glory of centuries past, and as it expands its domain of influence it infringes on the interests of G-8. Bowing to the inevitable and attempting to reduce the likelihood of conflict, G-8 has allowed China to become an observer at its annual summits. If China follows G-8's rules, the next step will be to incorporate China into the organization.

Despite the globe's vast social change, people all over the world continue to make race a fundamental distinction. Shown here is a Ukrainian being measured to see if he is really "full lipped" enough to be called a Tartar.

For global control, G-8 must be able to depend on political and economic stability, both in its own back yard and in those countries that provide the raw materials essential for G-8's industrial machine. This explains why the Most Industrialized Nations have cared little when African nations self-destruct in ethnic slaughter but have refused to tolerate interethnic warfare in their own neighborhoods. For example, to let interethnic warfare in Bosnia or Kosovo go unchecked would be to tolerate conflict that could spread and engulf Europe. In contrast, the deaths of hundreds of thousands of Tutsis in Rwanda had little or no political significance for G-8.

The Most Industrialized Nations have begun to perceive connections between Africa and their own interests, however, and their attitudes and actions have begun to change. They are realizing that African poverty, and the discontent it breeds, can provide fertile ground for political unrest and for recruiting terrorists. In addition, as the world's last largely untapped market, Africa could provide a huge outlet for their underutilized economic machinery. Then, too, there are Africa's oil reserves, which could counterbalance those of the unstable Middle East. As a result, the United States has raised funds for African AIDS victims and, as in the case of armed conflict in Liberia and Somalia, has begun to intervene in African politics.

Just as the development of armaments in the fourteenth and fifteenth centuries had an impact on global stratification, so, too, today's information revolution is destined to have similar far-reaching consequences. Those nations that make the most significant advances in information technology will dominate in the coming generation. Which nations will this be? The forecast points to an inevitable conclusion—a continuation of the dominance of the Most Industrialized Nations, and those nations that join this group.

Theories and Processes of Social Change

Social change has always fascinated theorists. Of the many attempts to explain why societies change, we shall consider just four: cultural evolution, cycles, conflict, and the pioneering views of sociologist William Ogburn.

Cultural Evolution

Evolutionary theories of how societies change are of two types, unilinear and multilinear. *Unilinear* theories assume that all societies follow the same path: Each evolves from simpler to more complex forms. This journey takes each society through uniform sequences (Barnes 1935). Of the many versions of this theory, the one proposed by Lewis Morgan (1877) once dominated Western thought. Morgan said that all societies go through three stages: savagery, barbarism, and civilization. In Morgan's eyes, England, his own society, was the epitome of civilization. All others societies were destined to follow the same path.

Multilinear views of evolution replaced unilinear theories. Instead of assuming that all societies follow the same sequence, multilinear theorists proposed that different routes lead to the same stage of development. Although the paths all lead to industrialization, societies need not pass through the same sequence of stages on their journey (Sahlins and Service 1960; Lenski and Lenski 1987).

Central to all evolutionary theories, whether unilinear or multilinear, is the assumption of *cultural progress.* Tribal societies are assumed to have a primitive form of human culture. As these societies evolve, they will reach a higher state—the supposedly advanced and superior form that characterizes the Western world. Growing appreciation of the rich diversity—and complexity—of tribal cultures discredited this idea. In addition, Western

culture is now in crisis (poverty, racism, war, terrorism, sexual assaults, unsafe streets) and is no longer regarded as the apex of human civilization. Consequently, the idea of cultural progress has been cast aside, and evolutionary theories have been rejected (Eder 1990; Smart 1990).

Natural Cycles

Cyclical theories attempt to account for the rise of entire civilizations. Why, for example, did Egypt, Greece, and Rome wield such power and influence, only to crest and fall into a decline? Cyclical theories assume that civilizations are like organisms: They are born, see an exuberant youth, come to maturity, then decline as they reach old age, and finally die (Hughes 1962).

Why do civilizations go through this cycle? Historian Arnold Toynbee (1946) said that each civilization faces challenges to its existence. The solutions to these challenges are not accepted by all, and oppositional forces remain. The ruling elite manages to keep these forces under control, but at a civilization's peak, when it has become an empire, the ruling elite loses its capacity to keep the masses in line "by charm rather than by force." The fabric of society eventually rips apart. Force may hold the empire together for hundreds of years, but the civilization is doomed.

In a book that provoked widespread controversy, *The Decline of the West* (1926–1928), Oswald Spengler, a high school teacher in Germany, proposed that Western civilization had passed its peak and was in decline. Although the West succeeded in overcoming the crises provoked by Hitler and Mussolini, as Toynbee noted, civilizations don't end in sudden collapse. Because the decline can last hundreds of years, perhaps the crisis in Western civilization mentioned earlier (poverty, rape, murder, and so on) indicates that Spengler was right, and we are now in decline. If so, it appears that China is waiting on the horizon to be the next global power and to forge a new civilization.

Conflict over Power

Long before Toynbee, Karl Marx identified a recurring process of social change. He said that each *thesis* (a current arrangement of power) contains its own *antithesis* (contradiction or opposition). A struggle develops between the thesis and its antithesis, leading to a *synthesis* (a new arrangement of power). This new social order, in turn, becomes a thesis that will be challenged by its own antithesis, and so on. Figure 15.1 on the next page gives a visual summary of this process.

According to Marx's view (called a **dialectical process** of history), each ruling group sows the seeds of its own

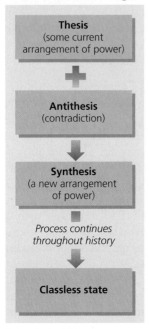

Figure 15.1 Marx's Model of Historical Change

Thesis
(some current arrangement of power)

+

Antithesis
(contradiction)

↓

Synthesis
(a new arrangement of power)

Process continues throughout history

↓

Classless state

Source: By the author.

destruction. Consider capitalism. Marx said that capitalism (the thesis) is built on the exploitation of workers (an antithesis, or built-in opposition). With workers and owners on a collision course, the dialectical process will not stop until workers establish a classless state (the synthesis).

The analysis of G-8 in the previous section follows conflict theory. G-8's current division of the globe's resources and markets is a thesis. Resentment on the part of have-not nations is an antithesis. If one of the Least Industrialized Nations gains in military power, that nation will press for a redistribution of resources. China, India, Pakistan, and soon, North Korea and Iran, with their nuclear weapons, fit this scenario. So do the efforts of al-Qaeda to change the balance of power between the Middle East and the industrialized West. Any new arrangement, a new synthesis, will contain its own antitheses. These may be ethnic hostilities, or leaders feeling that their country has been denied its fair share of resources. These antitheses will haunt the arrangement of power and must at some point be resolved into a synthesis. The process repeats itself.

Ogburn's Theory

Sociologist William Ogburn (1922/1938, 1961, 1964) proposed a view of social change that is based largely on technology. Technology, he said, changes society by three

processes: invention, discovery, and diffusion. Let's consider each.

Invention.   Ogburn defined **invention** as a combining of existing elements and materials to form new ones. We usually think of inventions as being only material items, such as computers, but there also are *social inventions*. We have considered several social inventions in this text including democracy and citizenship (pages 295–296), capitalism (pages 312–313, 372–373), socialism (pages 314–315), bureaucracy (pages 121–126), the corporation (pages 126–127, 316–317), and in Chapter 10, gender equality. As we saw in these instances, social inventions can have far-reaching consequences on society and on people's relationships to one another. So can material inventions, and in this chapter we will examine how the computer has transformed society.

Discovery.   Ogburn identified **discovery,** a new way of seeing reality, as a second process of change. The reality is already present, but people see it for the first time. An example is Columbus' "discovery" of North America, which had consequences so huge that they altered the course of human history. This example also illustrates another principle: A discovery brings extensive change only when it comes at the right time. Other groups, such as the Vikings, had already "discovered" North America in the sense of learning that a new land existed—obviously no discovery to the Native Americans already living in it. Viking settlements disappeared into history, however, and Norse culture was untouched by the discovery.

Diffusion.   Ogburn stressed how **diffusion,** the spread of an invention or discovery from one area to another, can have extensive effects on people's lives. Consider an object as simple as the axe. When missionaries introduced steel axes to the Aborigines of Australia, it upset their whole society. Before this, the men controlled axe-making. They used a special stone that was available only in a remote region, and fathers passed axe-making skills on to their sons. Women had to request permission to use the axe. When steel axes became common, women also possessed them, and the men lost both status and power (Sharp 1995).

Diffusion also includes the spread of ideas. As we saw in Chapter 11, the idea of citizenship changed political structures around the world. It removed monarchs as an unquestioned source of authority. The concept of gender equality is now circling the globe. Although taken for granted in a few parts of the world, the idea that it is wrong to withhold rights on the basis of someone's sex is revolu-

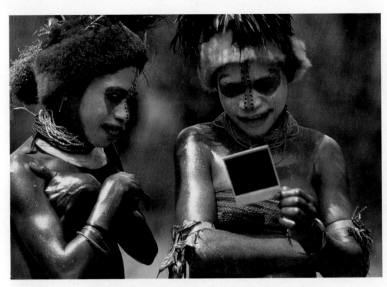

Culture contact is the source of *diffusion*, the spread of an *invention* or *discovery* from one area to another. Shown here are two children of the Huli tribe in Papua New Guinea. They are amused by a photo of themselves.

tionary. Like citizenship, this idea is destined to transform basic human relationships and entire societies.

Cultural Lag. Ogburn coined the term **cultural lag** to refer to how some elements of a culture lag behind the changes that come from invention, discovery, and diffusion. Technology, he suggested, usually changes first, with culture lagging behind. In other words, we play catch-up with changing technology, adapting our customs and ways of life to meet its needs.

Technology underlies the rapid change that is engulfing us today. As we consider technology, let's focus on the computer, that powerful machine, which, for good or ill, is transforming society and, with it, our way of life.

How Technology Changes Society

As you may recall from Chapter 2, *technology* has a double meaning. It refers to both the *tools,* the items used to accomplish tasks, and the skills or procedures needed to make and use those tools. Technology refers to tools as simple as a comb and as complicated as a computer. Technology's second meaning—the skills or procedures needed to make and use tools—refers in this case not only to the procedures used to manufacture combs and computers but also to those that are required to "produce" an acceptable hairdo or to go online. Apart from its par-

ticulars, technology always refers to *artificial means of extending human abilities.*

All human groups make and use technology, but the chief characteristic of technology in postindustrial societies (also called **postmodern societies**) is that it greatly extends our abilities to communicate, to travel, and to analyze information. These *new technologies,* as they are called, allow us to do what had never been done before: to communicate almost instantaneously anywhere on the globe; to probe space; to travel greater distances faster; and to store, retrieve, and analyze vast amounts of information.

This level of accomplishment, although impressive, is really superficial. Of much greater sociological significance is a deeper issue: how technology changes our way of life. *Technology is much more than the apparatus.* It is obvious, for example, that without automobiles, telephones, and televisions, our entire way of life would be strikingly different. The computer is bringing about changes that are every bit as drastic as these.

The Cutting Edge of Change: The Computer

The ominous wail seemed too close for comfort. Angela looked in her rear-view mirror and realized that the flashing lights and screaming siren might be for her. She felt confused. "I'm just on my way to Soc," she thought. "I'm not speeding or anything." After she pulled over, an angry voice over a loudspeaker ordered her out of the car.

As she got out, someone barked the command, "Back up with your hands in the air!" Bewildered, Angela stood frozen for a moment. "Put 'em up now! Right now!" She did as she was told.

The officer crouched behind his open door, his gun drawn. When Angela reached the police car—still backing up—the officer grabbed her, threw her to the ground, and handcuffed her hands behind her back. She heard words she would never forget, "You are under arrest for murder. You have the right to remain silent. Anything you say can and will be used against you in a court of law. You have the right to an attorney. If you cannot afford one, one will be provided for you."

Traces of alarm still flicker across Angela's face when she recalls her arrest. She had never even had a traffic ticket, much less been arrested for anything. Angela's nightmare was due to a "computer error." With the inversion of two numbers, her car's license plate number had been entered into the police database instead of the number belonging to a woman wanted for a brutal killing earlier that day.

In the photo on the left, Henry Ford proudly displays his 1905 car, the latest in automobile technology. As is apparent, especially from the spokes on the car's wheels, new technology builds on existing technology. At the time this photo was taken, who could have imagined that this vehicle would transform society?

The photo on the right illustrates future technology. Toyota's I-Unit, a "personal car," is not expected to go into production until 2030.

None of us is untouched by the computer, but it is unlikely that many of us have felt its power as directly and dramatically as Angela did. For most of us, the computer's control lies quietly in the background. Although the computer has intruded into our daily lives, most of us never think about it. Our grades are computerized, as are our paychecks. When we buy groceries, a computer scans our purchases and presents a printout of the name, price, and quantity of each item.

Most of us are pleased with the computer's capacity to improve our quality of life. We welcome the higher quality of manufactured goods and the reduction of drudgery. With e-mail, we can type just one letter, and with the press of a button, that letter will be delivered in seconds to everyone in our address book.

Some people, however, have deep reservations about our computerized society. They worry about errors that can creep into computerized records, fearing that something similar to Angela's misfortune could happen to them. For others, identity theft and privacy are the issues. Then there is the matter of political control. Proposals have been made to inject into our bodies an identity chip the size of a grain of rice ("Microchips Under . . . " 2001). The chip could store not only our name, address, age, weight, height, hair and skin color, race-ethnicity, where we went to school, our grades, and our work and medical history but also the names and addresses of our friends and associates, even any suspected acts of disloyalty. The chip could be activated by radio, without any of us knowing that we were under surveillance. Such computerized techniques could help usher in Orwell's Big Brother society.

At this point, let's consider how the computer is changing education, medicine, business, and war. We'll then consider its likely effects on social inequality.

Computers in Education.   Computers are having a major impact on education. Students who attend schools that have no teachers who are knowledgeable in foreign languages are able to take courses in Russian, German, and Spanish. Even though they have no sociology instructors, they can take courses in the sociology of gender, race, social class, or even sex, and sports. (The comma is important. It isn't sex and sports. That course isn't offered—yet.).

We've barely begun to harness the power of computers, but I imagine that the day will come when you will be able to key in the terms *social interaction* and *gender,* select your preference of historical period, geographical area, age, and ethnic group—and the computer will spew out text, maps, moving images, and sounds. You will be able to compare sexual discrimination in the military in 1985 and today or compare the prices of marijuana and cocaine in Los

Technology, which drives much social change, is at the forefront of our information revolution. This revolution, based on the computer chip, allows reality to cross with fantasy, a merging that sometimes makes it difficult to tell where one ends and the other begins. A computer projects an image onto the front of the coat, making its wearer "invisible."

Angeles and Miami. If you wish, the computer will give you a test—geared to the level of difficulty you choose—so that you can check your mastery of the material.

Distance learning, courses taught to students who are not physically present with their instructor, will become such a part of mainstream education that most students will take at least some of their high school, college, and graduate courses through this arrangement. Web cameras on their computers allow everyone in the "class" to see everyone else simultaneously, even though the students live in different countries. Imagine this—and likely it soon will be a reality for you: Your fellow students in a course on diversity in human culture will be living in Thailand, Latvia, South Africa, Egypt, China, and Australia. You will be able to compare your customs on eating, dating, marriage, family, or burial—whatever is of interest to you. You can then write a joint paper in which you compare your experiences with one another, applying the theories taught in the text, and then submit your paper to your mutual instructor.

Computers in Medicine.

The patient's symptoms were mystifying. After exercise, one side of his face and part of his body turned deep red, the other chalky white. He looked as though someone had taken a ruler and drawn a line down the middle of his body.

Stumped, the patient's physician consulted a medical librarian who punched a few words into a computer to search for clues in the world's medical literature. Soon, the likely answer flashed on the screen: Harlequin's disease. (Winslow 1994)

The computer was right, and a surgeon was able to correct a defect in the patient's nervous system. With computers, physicians can peer within the body's hidden recesses to determine how its parts are functioning or to see if surgery is necessary. Surgeons can operate on previously inaccessible parts of the brain—even on unborn babies. In a few years, tiny devices—smaller than the diameter of a single human hair—will be inserted into the bloodstream to detect cancer cells (Kalb 2000). In what is called *telemedicine,* data transmitted by fiber-optic cable allow doctors to use stethoscopes to check the hearts and lungs of patients who are hundreds of miles away. Remote-controlled robots and images relayed via satellite will allow surgeons in Boston or San Francisco to operate on wounded soldiers in battlefield hospitals on the other side of the world.

Will the computer lead to "doctorless" medical offices? Will we perhaps one day feed vital information about ourselves into a computer and receive a printout of what is wrong with us (and, of course, a prescription)? Many patients are likely to resist, for they would miss interacting with their doctors, especially the assurances and other emotional support that good physicians provide. Somehow "Take two aspirins and click on me in the morning" doesn't sound comforting. Physicians, of course, will vigorously repel such an onslaught on their expertise. It is likely, then, that the computer will remain a diagnostic tool for physicians, not a replacement for them.

Computers in Business and Finance. Not long ago, the advanced technology of businesses consisted of cash registers and adding machines. Connection to the outside world was managed by telephone. Today, those same businesses are electronically "wired" to suppliers, salespeople, and clients around the country—and around the world. Computers record changes in inventory and set in motion the process of reordering and restocking. They produce detailed reports of sales that alert managers to changes in their customers' tastes or preferences.

National borders have become meaningless as computers instantaneously transfer billions of dollars from one country to another. No "cash" changes hands in these transactions. The money consists of digits in computer memory banks. In the same day, this digitized money can be transferred from the United States to Switzerland, from there to the Grand Cayman Islands, and then to the Isle of Man. Its zigzag, instantaneous path leaves few traces for sleuths to follow. "Where's my share?" governments around the world are grumbling as they consider how to control—and tax—this new technology.

Computers are also having a major impact on the way war is fought, the topic of the Down-to-Earth Sociology box on the next page.

Cyberspace and Social Inequality

We've already stepped into our future. The Net gives us access to libraries of electronic information. We can utilize software that sifts, sorts, and transmits images, sound, and video. We use e-mail to zap messages and images to people on the other side of the globe—or even in our own dorm or office. Our world has become linked by almost instantaneous communications, with information readily accessible around the globe. Few places can still be called "remote."

This new technology carries severe implications for national and global stratification. On the national level, this technology could perpetuate present inequalities: We could end up with information have-nots, primarily inner-city residents cut off from the flow of information on which prosperity depends. Or this technology could provide an opportunity to break out of the inner city and the rural centers of poverty. On the global level, the question is similar, but on a grander scale, taking us to one of the more profound issues of this century: Will unequal access to advanced technology destine the Least Industrialized Nations to a perpetual pauper status? Or will access to this new technology be their passport to affluence?

Social Movements as a Source of Social Change

The contradictions (such as social inequality) that are built into arrangements of power create discontent. One result is **social movements,** large numbers of people who organize to promote or resist social change. Members of social movements hold strong ideas about what is wrong with the world—or some part of it—and how to make things right. Examples include the civil rights movement, the white supremacist movement, the women's movement, the animal rights crusade, and the environmental movement.

At the heart of social movements lies a sense of injustice (Klandemans 1997). Some find a particular condition of society intolerable, and their goal is to promote social change. Theirs is called a **proactive social movement.** Others, in contrast, feel threatened because some condition of society is changing, and they *react* to resist that change. Theirs is a **reactive social movement.**

To further their goals, people develop **social movement organizations.** Those whose goal is to promote social change develop such organizations as the National Association for the Advancement of Colored People (NAACP). In contrast, those who are trying to resist these particular changes form organizations such as the Ku Klux Klan. To recruit followers and publicize their grievances, leaders of social movements use attention-getting devices, from marches and rallies to sit-ins and boycotts. Some stage "media events," sometimes quite effectively.

Social movements are like a rolling sea, observed sociologist Mayer Zald (1992). During one period, few social movements may appear, but shortly afterward, a wave of them rolls in, each competing for the public's attention.

Social movements involve large numbers of people who, upset about some condition in society, organize to do something about it. Shown here is Carrie Nation, a temperance leader who in 1900 began to break up saloons with a hatchet. Her social movement eventually became so popular and powerful that it resulted in Prohibition.

Down-to-Earth Sociology

The Coming Star Wars

STAR WARS IS ON ITS WAY.

We already have the Predator, an un-manned plane that flies thousands of feet above enemy lines and beams streaming video back to the base. Sensors from the Global Positioning System report the Predator's precise location. When operators at the base see a target they want to hit, they press a button, the Predator beams a laser onto the target, and the operators launch guided bombs (Barry and Thomas 2001).

The enemy doesn't know what hit them. They see neither the Predator nor the laser. Perhaps, however, just before they are blown to bits, they do hear the sound of an incoming bomb (Barry 2001).

On its way is War Fighter I, a camera that uses hyper-spectral imaging, a way of identifying objects by detecting their "light signatures." This camera is so precise that it can report from space whether a field of grain contains natural or genetically altered grain—and whether the grain has adequate nitrogen. The military use of this camera? It can also locate tanks that are camouflaged or even hiding under trees (Hitt 2001).

Robot soldiers are on their way, too. In a project called Future Combat Systems, the Pentagon is developing robots that will see and react like humans. They might not look like humans. In fact, they might look like hummingbirds—or tractors, or cockroaches. They will gather intelligence, search buildings, and fire weapons (Weiner 2005).

The first robots are already being used in Iraq. These are primitive versions, however, simply remote-controlled devices that dispose of bombs. The next ones are likely to have the capacity to drive vehicles.

The Pentagon is also building its own Internet called the Global Information Grid (GIG). The goal of GIG, encircling the globe, is grandiose: to give the Pentagon a "God's eye view" of every enemy everywhere (Weiner 2004).

All this is but a prelude. The U.S. Defense Department is planning to "weaponize" space. Concerned that other nations will also launch intelligence-gathering devices and space weapons, the United States is set to launch microsatellites the size of a suitcase. These satellites will be able to pull alongside an enemy satellite and, using a microwave gun, fry its electronic system.

Coming also is a laser whose beam will bounce off a mirror in space, making the night battlefield visible to ground soldiers who are wearing special goggles. Also on its way is a series of Star Wars weapons: kinetic energy rods, space-based lasers, pyrotechnic electromagnetic pulsers, holographic decoys, suppression clouds, oxygen suckers, robo-bugs—and whatever else the feverish imaginations of military planners can devise.

We are on the edge of a surrealistic world. Politicians and the military assume that it is normal both to dominate the world and to weaponize space. The chilling reality is reflected in a report by a congressional commission: "Every medium—air, land and sea—has seen conflict. Reality indicates that space will be no different" (Hitt 2001).

We watch war and the campaign against terrorism from the comfort of our living rooms, as though the battles and bombings were video games. It is one thing, however, to fight an enemy that is using outdated technology, but quite another to face an enemy that possesses similar technology. When this happens, as is inevitable, no longer will war seem like a remote, bloodless game.

Zald suggests that a *cultural crisis* can give birth to a wave of social movements. By this, he means that there are times when a society's institutions fail to keep up with social change. During these times, many people's needs go unfulfilled, massive unrest follows, and social movements spring into action to bridge the gap.

Let's see what types of social movements there are, how they use propaganda, and the stages they go through.

Types of Social Movements

Since social change is their goal, we can classify social movements according to their *target* and the *amount of change* they seek. Look at Figure 15.2 on the next page. If you read across, you will see that the target of the first two types of social movements is *individuals*. **Alterative social movements** seek only to *alter* some specific behavior. An example is the Women's Christian Temperance Union, a

Figure 15.2 **Types of Social Movements**

Sources: The first four types are from Aberle 1966; the last two are by the author.

powerful social movement of the early 1900s. Its goal was to get people to stop drinking alcohol. Its members were convinced that if they could shut down the saloons, such problems as poverty and wife abuse would go away. **Redemptive social movements** also target individuals, but their goal is *total* change. An example is a religious social movement that stresses conversion. In fundamentalist Christianity, for example, when someone converts to Christ, the entire person is supposed to change, not just some specific behavior. Self-centered acts are to be replaced by loving behaviors toward others as the convert becomes, in their terms, a "new creation."

The target of the next two types of social movements is *society*. **Reformative social movements** seek to *reform* some specific aspect of society. The animal rights movement, for example, seeks to reform the ways in which society views and treats animals. **Transformative social movements,** in contrast, seek to *transform* the social order itself. Its members want to replace the current social order with their vision of the good society. Revolutions, such as those in the American colonies, France, Russia, and Cuba, are examples.

As Figure 15.2 indicates, some social movements have a global orientation. Participants of **transnational social movements** (also called *new social movements*) want to change some condition that exists not just in their society, but also throughout the world. (See Cell 5 of Figure 15.2.) These social movements often center on improving the

quality of life (Melucci 1989). Examples are the women's movement, labor movement, and the environmental movement (McAdam et al. 1988; Smith et al. 1997; Walter 2001). As you can see from these examples, transnational social movements still focus on some specific condition, but that condition cuts across societies.

Cell 6 in Figure 15.2 represents a rare type of social movement. The goal of **metaformative social movements** is to change the social order itself—not just of a specific country, but an entire civilization, or even the whole world. The objective is to change concepts and practices of race-ethnicity, class, gender, family, religion, government, and the global stratification of nations. These were the aims of the communist social movement of the early to middle parts of the twentieth century and the fascist social movement of the 1920s to 1940s. (The fascists consisted of the Nazis in Germany, the Black Shirts of Italy, and other groups throughout Europe and the United States.)

Today, we are witnessing another metaformative social movement, that of Islamic fundamentalism. Like other social movements before it, this movement is not united, but consists of many separate groups with differing goals and tactics. Al-Qaeda, for example, would not only cleanse Islamic societies of Western influences—which they contend are demonic and degrading to men, women, and morality—but also replace Western civilization with an extremist form of Islam. This frightens both Muslims and non-Muslims, who hold sharply differing views of what constitutes quality of life. If the Islamic fundamentalists—or the communists or fascists before them—have their way, they will usher in a New World Order fashioned after their particular views of the good life.

Propaganda and the Mass Media

The leaders of social movements try to manipulate the mass media to influence **public opinion,** how people think about some issue. The right kind of publicity enables the leaders to arouse sympathy and to lay the groundwork for recruiting more members. Pictures of bloodied, dead baby seals, for example, go a long way toward getting a group's message across.

A key to understanding social movements, then, is **propaganda.** Although this word often evokes negative images, it actually is a neutral term. Propaganda is simply the presentation of information in the attempt to influence people. Its original meaning was positive. *Propaganda* referred to a committee of cardinals of the Roman Catholic church whose assignment was the care of foreign missions. (They were to *propagate*—multiply or spread—the faith.) The term has traveled a long way since then, however, and

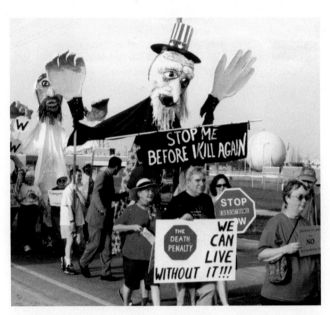

Giving one-sided information on some topic, including a social issue, is one definition of *propaganda*. What propaganda do you see in this photo that I took of a demonstration at the execution of a mass murderer?

today it usually refers to a presentation of information so one-sided that it distorts reality.

Propaganda, in the sense of organized attempts to influence public opinion, is a part of everyday life. Our news is filled with propaganda, as various interest groups—from retailers to the government—try to manipulate our perceptions of the world. Our movies, too, although seemingly intended as simply entertainment devices, are actually propaganda vehicles. The basic techniques that underlie propaganda are discussed in the Down-to-Earth Sociology box on the next page. Perhaps by understanding these techniques, you will be able to resist one-sided appeals—whether they come from social movements or from hawkers of jeans, running shoes, or perfumes.

The mass media play such a crucial role that we can say they are the gatekeepers to social movements. If those who control and work in the mass media—from owners to reporters—are sympathetic to some particular "cause," you can be sure that it will receive sympathetic treatment. If the social movement goes against their views, however, it likely will be ignored or will receive unfavorable treatment. If you ever get the impression that the media are trying to manipulate your opinions and attitudes—even your feelings—on some particular issue or social movement, you probably are right. Far from doing unbiased reporting, the media are under the control and influence of people who have an agenda to get across. To the materials in the Down-to-Earth

Sociology box on propaganda, then, we need to add the biases of the media establishment—the issues it chooses to publicize, those it chooses to ignore, and its favorable and unfavorable treatment of issues and movements.

Sociology can be a liberating discipline (Berger 1963/2005). Sociology sensitizes us to *multiple realities;* that is, for any single point of view on some topic, there are competing points of view. Each represents reality as people see it, their distinct experiences having led them to different perceptions. Consequently, different people find each point of view equally compelling. Although the committed members of a social movement are sincere—and perhaps even make sacrifices for "the cause"—theirs is but one view of the world. If other sides were presented, the issue would look quite different.

The Stages of Social Movements

Sociologists have identified five stages in the growth and maturity of social movements (Lang and Lang 1961; Mauss 1975; Spector and Kitsuse 1977; Jasper 1991; Tilly 2004):

1. *Initial unrest and agitation.* During this first stage, people are upset about some condition in society and want to change it. Leaders emerge who verbalize people's feelings and crystallize issues. Most social movements fail at this stage. Unable to gain enough support, after a brief flurry of activity, they quietly die.

2. *Resource mobilization.* A crucial factor that enables social movements to make it past the first stage is **resource mobilization.** By this term, sociologists mean the mobilization of resources—time, money, information, people's skills, and the ability to get the attention of the mass media. Those resources may also include access to churches to organize protests (Mirola 2003). Another key resource is communications technology such as cell phones, Internet sites, and blogs. Also important is access to mailing lists for direct mailing, faxing, and e-mailing.

   In some cases, an indigenous leadership arises to mobilize resources. Other groups, lacking capable leadership, turn to "guns for hire," outside specialists who sell their services. As sociologists John McCarthy and Mayer Zald (1977; Zald and McCarthy 1987) point out, even though large numbers of people may be upset over some condition of society, without resource mobilization they are only upset people, perhaps even agitators, but they do not constitute a social movement.

3. *Organization.* A division of labor is set up. The leadership makes policy decisions, and the rank and file

Down-to-Earth Sociology

"Tricks of the Trade"— Deception and Persuasion in Propaganda

SOCIOLOGISTS ALFRED AND ELIZABETH LEE (1939) found that propaganda relies on seven basic techniques, which they termed "tricks of the trade." To be effective, the techniques should be subtle, with the audience unaware that their minds and emotions are being manipulated. If propaganda is effective, people will not know why they support something, but they'll fervently defend it. Becoming familiar with these techniques can help you keep your mind and emotions from being manipulated.

- *Name calling.* This technique aims to arouse opposition to the competing product, candidate, or policy by associating it with a negative image. By comparison, one's own product, candidate, or policy is attractive. Republicans who call Democrats "soft on crime" and Democrats who call Republicans "insensitive to the poor" are using this technique.

- *Glittering generality.* Essentially the opposite of the first technique, this one surrounds the product, candidate, or policy with images that arouse positive feelings. "She's a real Democrat" has little meaning, but it makes the audience feel that something substantive has been said. "This Republican stands for individual rights" is so general that it is meaningless; yet the audience thinks that it has heard a specific message about the candidate.

- *Transfer.* In its positive form, this technique associates the product, candidate, or policy with something the public approves of or respects. You might not be able to get by with saying "Coors is patriotic," but surround a beer with images of the country's flag, and beer drinkers will get the idea that it is more patriotic to drink this brand of beer than some other kind. In its negative form, this technique associates the product, candidate, or policy with something generally disapproved of by the public.

- *Testimonials.* Famous individuals endorse a product, candidate, or policy. Serena Williams lends her name to Nike products, Lindsay Lohan touts the merits of drinking milk, and Tiger Woods tells you that Buicks make fine SUVs. Candidates for political office solicit the endorsement of movie stars who may know next to nothing about the candidate or even about politics. In the negative form of this technique, a despised person is associated with the competing product. If propagandists (called "spin doctors" in politics) could get away with it, they would show Osama bin Laden announcing support for an opposing candidate.

- *Plain folks.* Sometimes it pays to associate the product, candidate, or policy with "just plain folks." "If Mary or John Q. Public likes it, you will, too." A political candidate who kisses babies, puts on a hard hat, and has lunch at McDonald's while photographers "catch him (or her) in the act" is using the "plain folks" strategy. "I'm just a regular person" is the message of the presidential candidate who poses for photographers in jeans and work shirt—while making certain that the chauffeur-driven Mercedes does not show up in the background.

- *Card stacking.* The aim of this technique is to present only positive information about what you support, and only negative information about what you oppose. The intent is to make it sound as though there is only one conclusion a rational person can draw. Falsehoods, distortions, and illogical statements are often used.

- *Bandwagon.* "Everyone is doing it" is the idea behind this technique. Emphasizing how many other people buy the product or support the candidate or policy conveys the message that anyone who doesn't join in is on the wrong track.

The Lees (1939) added, "Once we know that a speaker or writer is using one of these propaganda devices in an attempt to convince us of an idea, we can separate the device from the idea and see what the idea amounts to on its own merits."

for your Consideration

What propaganda techniques have you seen or heard recently? Recall TV ads, political ads, movies, and newspaper reports. Explain why it was not simply information, but a technique of propaganda.

carry out the day–to–day tasks necessary to keep the movement going. There is still much collective excitement about the issue, the movement's focal point of concern.

4. *Institutionalization.* At this stage, the movement has developed a bureaucracy, the type of formal hierarchy that was described in Chapter 5. Control lies in the hands of career officers, who may care more about their own position in the organization than the movement for which the organization's initial leaders made sacrifices. The collective excitement diminishes.

5. *Organizational decline and possible resurgence.* During this phase, the management of the day-to-day affairs of the organization dominates the leadership. A change in public sentiment may even have occurred, and there may no longer be a group of committed people who share a common cause. The movement is likely to wither away.

Decline is not inevitable, however. More idealistic and committed leaders can emerge who reinvigorate the movement. Or, as in the case of abortion, conflict between groups on opposing sides of the issue may invigorate each side and prevent the movement's decline. The following Thinking Critically section contrasts abortion activists.

Thinking Critically

Which Side of the Barricades? Prochoice and Prolife as a Social Movement

No issue so divides Americans as abortion. Although most Americans take a more moderate view, on one side are some who believe that abortion should be permitted under any circumstance, even during the last month of pregnancy. They are matched by individuals on the other side who are convinced that abortion should never be allowed under any circumstance, not even during the first month of pregnancy. This polarization constantly breathes new life into the movement.

When the U.S. Supreme Court made its 1973 decision, *Roe v. Wade,* that states could not prohibit abortion, the prochoice side relaxed. Victory was theirs, and they thought their opponents would quietly disappear. Instead, large numbers of Americans were disturbed by what they saw as the legal right to murder unborn children.

The views of the two sides could not be more incompatible. Those who favor choice view the 1.3 million abortions that are performed annually in the United States as examples of women exercising their basic reproductive rights. Those who gather under the prolife banner see these abortions as legal-

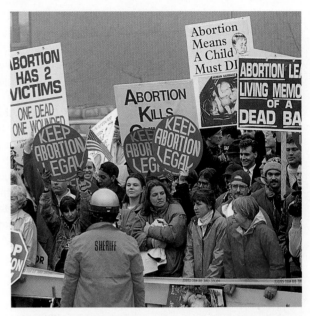

Activists in social movements become committed to "the cause." The social movement around abortion, which has split Americans, is highly visible and has articulate spokespeople on both sides.

ized murder. To the prochoice side, those who oppose abortion are blocking women's rights—they would force women to continue pregnancies they want to terminate. To the prolife side, those who advocate choice are perceived as condoning murder—they would sacrifice their unborn children for the sake of school, career, or convenience.

There is no way to reconcile these contrary views. Each sees the other as unreasonable and extremist. And each uses propaganda by focusing on worst-case scenarios: prochoice images of young women raped at gunpoint, forced to bear the children of rapists; prolife images of women who are eight months pregnant killing their babies instead of nurturing them.

With no middle ground, these views remain in perpetual conflict. As each side fights for what it considers basic rights, it reinvigorates the other. When in 1989, the U.S. Supreme Court decided in *Webster* v. *Reproductive Services* that states could restrict abortion, one side mourned it as a defeat, and the other hailed it as a victory. Seeing the political battle going against them, the prochoice side regrouped for a determined struggle. The prolife side, sensing judicial victory within its grasp, gathered forces for a push to complete the overthrow of *Roe* v. *Wade*.

This goal of the prolife side almost became reality in *Casey* v. *Planned Parenthood*. On June 30, 1992, in a 6-to-3 decision, the Supreme Court upheld the right of states to require women to wait 24 hours between the confirmation of pregnancy and abortion, to require girls under 18 to obtain the consent of one parent, and to require that women be informed about alternatives to abortion and that they be given materials that describe the fetus. In the same case, however, in a 5-to-4 decision, the Court ruled that a wife does not have to inform her husband if she intends to have an abortion. This legal part of the battle comes to the forefront each time the Senate holds hearings on a nominee to the U.S. Supreme Court.

Because the two sides do not share the same reality, this social movement cannot end unless the vast majority of Americans commit to one side or the other. Every legislative and judicial outcome—including the extremes of a constitutional amendment that declares abortion to be either murder or a woman's right—is a victory to one and a defeat to the other. To committed activists, then, no battle is ever complete. Rather, each action is only one small part of a long, hard-fought, moral struggle.

Sources: Neikirk and Elsasser 1992; McKenna 1995; Williams 1995; *Statistical Abstract* 2003:Table 104; Henslin 2006.

for your Consideration

Typically, the last stage of a social movement is decline. Why hasn't this social movement declined? Under what conditions will it decline?

The longer the duration of the pregnancy, the fewer the Americans who approve of abortion. How do you feel about abortion during the second month versus the eighth month? Or partial-birth abortion (also known as *late-term abortion*)? What do you think about abortion in cases of rape and incest? Can you identify some of the *social* reasons that underlie your opinions?

The Growth Machine Versus the Earth

Of all the changes swirling around us, those that affect the natural environment appear to hold the most serious implications for human life.

Underlying today's environmental decay is the globalization of capitalism, which I have stressed throughout this text. To maintain their dominance and increase their wealth, the Most Industrialized Nations, spurred by multinational corporations, continue to push for economic growth. At the same time, the Industrializing Nations, playing catch-up, are striving to develop their economies. Meanwhile, the Least Industrialized Nations are anxious to enter the race: Because they start from even farther behind, they have to strive for even faster growth.

Many people are convinced that the earth cannot withstand such an onslaught. Global economic production creates extensive pollution, and faster-paced production

means faster-paced destruction of our environment. If the goal is a **sustainable environment,** a world system in which we use our physical environment to meet our needs without destroying humanity's future, we cannot continue to trash the earth. In short, the ecological message is incompatible with an economic message that implies it is OK to rape the earth for the sake of profits.

Before looking at the social movement that has emerged about this issue, let's examine major environmental problems.

Environmental Problems in the Most Industrialized Nations

Although even tribal groups produced pollution, the frontal assault on the natural environment did not begin in earnest until nations industrialized. The more extensive its industrialization, the better it was considered for a nation's welfare. For the Most Industrialized Nations, the slogan has been "Growth at any cost."

Industrial growth did come, but at a high cost to the natural environment. Today, for example, formerly pristine streams are polluted sewers, and the water supply of some cities is unfit to drink. When Los Angeles announces "smog days," schoolchildren are kept inside during recess and everyone is warned to stay indoors. Nuclear wastes, which we knew would remain lethal for thousands of years, have been stored in rusting containers (Wald 2002). We simply don't know what to do with this deadly garbage. Hazardous wastes are a special problem. Despite the danger to people and the environment, much toxic waste has simply been dumped. The Social Map on the next page shows the locations of the worst hazardous waste sites in the United States. These sites represent corporate garbage, some of it subsidized by corporate welfare, the topic of the Down-to-Earth Sociology box on the next page.

The major polluters are the Most Industrialized Nations. Our follies include harming the ozone layer in order to have the convenience of aerosol spray bottles and air conditioners. With limited space to address this issue, I would like to focus on an overarching aspect of the pollution of our environment: the burning of fossil fuels.

Fossil Fuels and the Environment.   Burning fossil fuels to run factories, motorized vehicles, and power plants has been especially harmful. Fish can no longer survive in some lakes in Canada and the northeastern United States because of **acid rain.** As Figure 15.4 on page 432 illustrates, the burning of fossil fuels releases sulfur dioxide and nitrogen oxide, which react with moisture in the air to become sulfuric and nitric acids.

Figure 15.3 **How Does Your State Rank?**

The Location of the Worst Hazardous Waste Sites

Source: By the author. Based on *Statistical Abstract* 2005:Table 369.

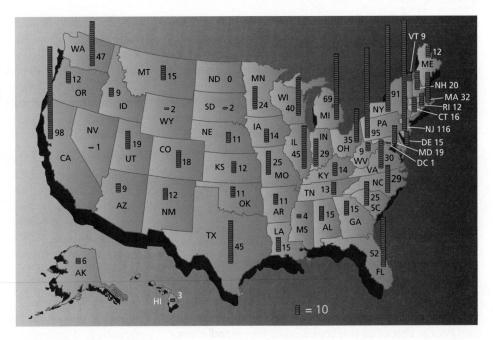

Down-to-Earth Sociology

Corporations and Big Welfare Bucks: How to Get Paid to Pollute

WELFARE IS ONE OF THE MOST CONTROVERSIAL topics in the United States. It arouses the ire of many wealthy and middle-class Americans, who view the poor who collect welfare as parasites. But have you heard about *corporate welfare*?

Corporate welfare refers to handouts that are given to corporations. Some states will reduce a company's taxes if it locates within the state, or remains if it has threatened to leave. Some states provide land and buildings at bargain prices. The reason: jobs.

Corporate welfare even goes to companies that foul the land, water, and air. Borden Chemicals in Louisiana has buried hazardous wastes without a permit and released clouds of hazardous chemicals so thick that to protect drivers, sometimes the police have had to shut down the highway that runs near the plant. Borden even contaminated the groundwater beneath its plant, threatening the aquifer that provides drinking water for residents of Louisiana and Texas.

Borden's pollution has cost the company dearly: $3.6 million in fines, $3 million to clean up the groundwater, and $400,000 for local emergency response units. That's a hefty $7 million. But if we add corporate welfare, the company

didn't make out so badly. With $15 million in reduced and cancelled property taxes, Borden has enjoyed a net gain of $8 million (Bartlett and Steele 1998). And that's not counting the savings the company racked up by not having to properly dispose of its toxic wastes in the first place.

Louisiana has added a novel twist to corporate welfare. It offers an incentive to help start-up companies. This itself isn't novel; the owners of that little "mom and pop" grocery store on your corner may have received some benefits when they first opened. Louisiana's twist is what it counts as a start-up company. One of these little start-ups is called Exxon Corp. Although Exxon opened for business about 125 years ago, it had $213 million in property taxes canceled under this start-up program. Another little company that the state figured could use a nudge to help it get started was Shell Oil Co., which had $140 million slashed from its taxes (Bartlett and Steele 1998). Then there were International Paper, Dow Chemical, Union Carbide, Boise Cascade, Georgia Pacific, and another tiny one called Procter & Gamble.

for your Consideration

Apply the functionalist, symbolic interactionist, and conflict perspectives to corporate welfare. Which do you think provides the best explanation of corporate welfare? Why?

An invisible but infinitely more serious consequence is the **greenhouse effect.** Burning fossil fuels releases gases that, like the glass of a greenhouse, allow sunlight to enter the earth's atmosphere freely but inhibit the release of heat. It is as though the gases have smudged the windows of our earth's greenhouse, and our planet can no longer breathe the way it should. The buildup of heat is causing **global warming:** Glaciers are melting and the seas are rising, threatening to flood the world's shorelines. The climate boundaries may move north several hundred miles, and many animal and plant species are likely to become extinct (Parmesan and Yohe 2003; Glick 2004). Although scientists disagree about the specific causes of global warming—since the earth does go through cycles—most agree that the increase in the earth's temperature has been extraordinarily rapid, the consequences are likely to be catastrophic, and we should reduce the burning of fossil fuels.

The Energy Shortage and Multinational Corporations.   If you ever read about an energy shortage, you can be sure that what you read is false. There is no energy shortage, nor can there ever be. We can produce unlimited low-cost power, which can help to raise the living standards of humans across the globe. The sun, for example, produces more energy than humanity could ever use. Boundless energy is also available from the tides and the winds. In some cases, we need better technology to harness these sources of energy; in others, we need only apply technology we already have.

Burning fossil fuels in internal combustion engines is the main source of pollution in the Most Industrialized Nations.

Of the technologies being developed to use alternative sources of energy in vehicles, the most prominent is the gas-electric hybrid. Some of these cars are expected to eventually get several hundred miles per gallon of gasoline (Hakim 2005). The hybrid, however, is simply a bridge until vehicles powered by fuel cells become practical. Fuel cells convert hydrogen into electricity; water, instead of carbon monoxide, will come out of a car's exhaust pipe.

Environmental Injustice.   Unequal power has led to **environmental injustice,** minorities and the poor being the ones who suffer the most from the effects of pollution (Dunlap and Michelson 2002). Polluting industries locate where land is cheap, which is *not* where the wealthy live. Nor will the rich allow factories to spew pollution near their homes. As a result, low-income communities, which are often inhabited by minorities, are more likely to be exposed to pollution. Sociologists have studied, formed, and joined *environmental justice* groups that fight to close polluting plants and block construction of polluting industries.

Environmental Problems in the Industrializing and Least Industrialized Nations

Consequences of industrialization such as ozone depletion, the greenhouse effect, and global warming cannot be laid solely at the feet of the Most Industrialized Nations. With their rush to be contenders in the global competition, along with a lack of funds to pay for pollution controls and few antipollution laws, the Industrializing Nations have made enormous contributions to this problem. The air of Mexico City, for example, is so bad that the lungs of *most* children living there have been harmed ("Study . . ." 2001).

The former Soviet Union is a special case. Until this empire broke up, pollution had been treated as a state secret. Scientists and journalists were forbidden to mention pollution in public. Even peaceful demonstrations to call attention to pollution could net participants two years in prison (Feshbach 1992). With protest stifled and no environmental protection laws, pollution was rampant: Almost half of Russia's arable land has been made unsuitable for farming, about a third of Russians live in cities where air pollution is *ten* times greater than levels permitted in the United States, and half of Russia's tap water is unfit to drink. Pollution is so severe that it may be partially responsible for the drop in the life expectancy of Russians. If so, it is a lesson that should not be lost on the rest of us as we make decisions about how to treat our environment.

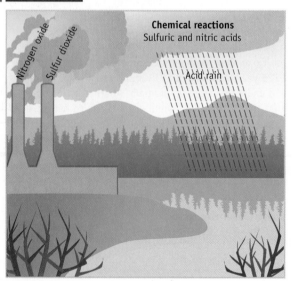

■ **Figure 15.4**   **Acid Rain**

Nitrogen oxide

Sulfur dioxide

Chemical reactions
Sulfuric and nitric acids

Acid rain

THE GROWTH MACHINE VERSUS THE EARTH **433**

The greater poverty and swelling populations of the Least Industrialized Nations give them an even greater incentive to industrialize at any cost. With these pressures, combined with almost nonexistent environmental regulations, the Least Industrialized Nations have become major sources of pollution (Fialka 2003).

Their lack of environmental protection laws has not gone unnoticed by opportunists in the Most Industrialized Nations, who export their dirty industries to these countries and produce there chemicals that are outlawed in their own countries (Smith 1995; Mol 2001). Alarmed at the growing environmental destruction, the World Bank, the monetary arm of G-8, has pressured the Least Industrialized Nations to reduce pollution and soil erosion. When New Delhi officials tried to comply, workers blocked traffic and set fires, closing down the city for several days (Freund 2001). Understandably, the basic concern of workers is to provide food for their families first, and to worry about the environment later.

Although the rain forests cover just 7 percent of the earth's land area, they are home to *one-third to one-half* of all the earth's plant and animal species. Despite our knowledge that the rain forests are essential for humanity's welfare, we seem bent on destroying them for the sake of timber and farms. In the process, we extinguish plant and animal species, perhaps thousands a year (Durning 1990; Wolfensohn and Fuller 1998). As biologists remind us, once a species is lost, it is gone forever.

As the rain forests disappear, so do the Indian tribes who live in them. With their extinction goes their knowledge of the environment, the topic of the Cultural Diversity box on the next page. Like Esau who traded his birthright for a bowl of porridge, we are exchanging our future for some lumber, farms, and pastures.

The Environmental Movement

Concern about environmental problems has produced a worldwide social movement. One result is *green parties,* political parties whose central issue is the environment. In some European countries, these parties have made a political impact. In Germany, for example, the Green Party has won seats in the national legislature. Green parties have had little success in the United States, but in the 2000 election, a green party headed by Ralph Nader arguably tipped the balance and gave the presidential election to George W. Bush.

Activists in the environmental movement generally seek solutions in politics, education, and legislation. Despairing that pollution continues, that the rain forests are still being cleared, and that species are becoming extinct, some activists are convinced that the planet is doomed unless urgent steps are taken. Choosing a more radical course, they use extreme tactics to try to arouse indignation among the public and force the government to act. Convinced that they stand for true morality, many are willing to break the law and go to jail for their actions. Such activists are featured in the following Thinking Critically section.

Thinking Critically

Ecosabotage

Chaining oneself to a giant Douglas fir that is slated for cutting; tearing down power lines and ripping up survey stakes; driving spikes into redwood trees, sinking whaling vessels, and torching SUVs and Hummers—are these the acts of dangerous punks who are intent on vandalizing and who have little understanding of the needs of modern society? Or are they the acts of brave men and women who are willing to risk their freedom, and even their lives, on behalf of the earth itself?

To understand why **ecosabotage**—actions taken to sabotage the efforts of people who are thought to be legally harming the environment—is taking place, consider the Medicine Tree, a 3,000-year-old redwood in the Sally Bell Grove near the northern California coast. Georgia Pacific, a lumber company, was determined to cut down the Medicine Tree, the oldest and largest of the region's redwoods, which rests on a sacred site of the Sinkyone Indians. Members of Earth First! chained themselves to the tree. After they were arrested, the sawing began. Other protesters jumped over the police-lined barricade and stood defiantly in the path of men wielding axes and chain saws. A logger swung an axe and barely missed a demonstrator. At that moment, the sheriff radioed a restraining order, and the cutting stopped.

Twenty-four-year-old David Chain's dedication cost him his life. The federal government and the state of California were trying to purchase 10,000 acres of pristine redwoods for half a billion dollars. As last-minute negotiations dragged on, loggers from the Pacific Lumber Company kept felling trees, and Earth First! activists kept trying to stop them. David Chain died of a crushed skull when a felled tree struck him.

How many 3,000-year-old trees remain on this planet? Does our desire for fences and picnic tables for backyard barbecues justify cutting them down? Issues like these—as well as the slaughter of seals, the destruction of the rain forests, and the drowning of dolphins in mile-long drift nets—spawned Earth First! and other organizations devoted to preserving the environment, such as Greenpeace, Rainforest Action Network, the Ruckus Society, and the Sea Shepherds.

Cultural Diversity *around the* World

The Rain Forests: Lost Tribes, Lost Knowledge

Since 1900, ninety of Brazil's 270 Indian tribes have disappeared. Other tribes have moved to villages as settlers have taken over their lands. Tribal knowledge is lost as group members adapt to village life.

Tribal groups are not just "wild" people who barely survive despite their ignorance. On the contrary, they have intricate forms of social organization and possess knowledge that has accumulated over thousands of years. The 2,500 Kayapo Indians, for example, belong to one of the Amazon's endangered tribes. The Kayapo use 250 types of wild fruit and hundreds of nut and tuber species. They cultivate thirteen types of bananas, eleven kinds of manioc (cassava), sixteen strains of sweet potato, and seventeen kinds of yams. Many of these varieties are unknown to non-Indians. The Kayapo also use thousands of medicinal plants, one of which contains a drug that is effective against intestinal parasites.

Until recently, Western scientists dismissed tribal knowledge as superstitious and worthless. Now, however, some have come to realize that to lose tribes is to lose valuable knowledge. In the Central African Republic, a man whose chest was being eaten away by an amoeboid infection lay dying because his infection did not respond to drugs. Out of desperation, the Roman Catholic nuns who were treating him sought the advice of a native doctor. He applied crushed termites to the open wounds. To the amazement of the nuns, the man made a remarkable recovery.

With their way of life threatened, the Yaguas of Peru are among the last rainforest nomads in the world. Shown here is the tribal chief.

The disappearance of the rain forests means the destruction of plant species that may have healing properties. Some of the discoveries from the rain forests have been astounding. The needles from a Himalayan tree in India contain taxol, a drug that is effective against ovarian and breast cancer. A flower from Madagascar is used in the treatment of leukemia. A frog in Peru produces a painkiller that is more powerful, but less addictive, than morphine (Wolfensohn and Fuller 1998).

On average, one tribe of Amazonian Indians has been lost each year for the past century—because of violence, greed for their lands, and exposure to infectious diseases against which they have little resistance. Ethnocentrism underlies much of this assault. Perhaps the extreme is represented by the cattle ranchers in Colombia who killed eighteen Cueva Indians. The cattle ranchers were perplexed when they were put on trial for murder. They asked why they should be charged with a crime, since everyone knew that the Cuevas were animals, not people. They pointed out that there was even a verb in Colombian Spanish, *cuevar,* which means "to hunt Cueva Indians." So what was their crime, they asked? The jury found them innocent because of "cultural ignorance."

Sources: Durning 1990; Gorman 1991; Linden 1991; Stipp 1992; Nabhan 1998; Simons 2006.

"We feel like there are insane people who are consciously destroying our environment, and we are compelled to fight back," explains a member of one of the militant groups. "No compromise in defense of Mother Earth!" says another. "With famine and death approaching, we're in the early stages of World War III," adds another.

Radical environmentalists represent a broad range of activities and purposes. They are united neither on tactics nor on

goals. Most espouse a simpler lifestyle that will consume less energy and reduce pressure on the earth's resources. Some want to stop a specific action, such as the killing of whales. Others want to destroy all nuclear weapons and dismantle nuclear power plants. Some want everyone to become vegetarians. Still others want the earth's population to drop to one billion, roughly what it was in 1800. Some even want humans to return to hunting and gathering societies. These groups are so splintered that the founder of Earth First!, Dave Foreman, quit his own organization when it became too confrontational for his taste.

Radical groups have had some successes. They have brought a halt to the killing of dolphins off Japan's Iki Island, achieved a ban on whaling, established trash recycling programs, and saved hundreds of thousands of acres of trees, including, of course, the Medicine Tree.

Sources: Carpenter 1990; Eder 1990; Foote 1990; Parfit 1990; Reed and Benet 1990; Knickerbocker 2003; Gunther 2004.

for your Consideration

Should we applaud ecosaboteurs or jail them? As symbolic interactionists stress, it all depends on how you view their actions. And as conflict theorists emphasize, your view likely depends on your location in the economy. That is, if you own a lumber company, you will see ecosaboteurs differently from the way a camping enthusiast will. How does your own view of ecosaboteurs depend on your life situation? What effective alternatives to ecosabotage are there for people who are convinced that we are destroying the very life support system of our planet?

Environmental Sociology

About 1970, **environmental sociology** emerged. The focus of this subdiscipline of sociology is the relationship between human societies and the environment (Dunlap and Catton 1979, 1983; Casper 2003). Its main assumptions are:

1. The physical environment should be a significant variable in sociological investigation.
2. Human beings are but one species among many that depend on the natural environment.

3. Because of feedback to nature, human actions have many unintended consequences.
4. The world is finite, so there are physical limits to economic growth.
5. Economic expansion requires increased extraction of resources from the environment.
6. Increased extraction of resources leads to ecological problems.
7. These ecological problems place restrictions on economic expansion.
8. Governments create environmental problems by encouraging the accumulation of capital.

The goal of environmental sociology is not to stop pollution or nuclear power, but, rather, to study how humans (their cultures, values, and behavior) affect the physical environment and how the physical environment affects human activities. Environmental sociologists, however, generally are also environmental activists, and the Section on Environment and Technology of the American Sociological Association tries to influence social policies (American Sociological Association n.d.).

Technology and the Environment: The Goal of Harmony. It is inevitable that humans will continue to develop new technologies. But the abuse of our environment by those technologies is not inevitable. To understate the matter, the destruction of our planet is an unwise choice.

If we are to live in a world that is worth passing on to coming generations, we must seek harmony between technology and the natural environment. This will not be easy. At one extreme are people who claim that to protect the environment, we must eliminate industrialization and go back to a tribal way of life. At the other

The social movement that centers on the environment has become global. In all nations, people are concerned about the destruction of the earth's resources. This photo is a sign of changing times. Instead of jumping on this beached whale and carving it into pieces, these Brazilians are doing their best to save its life.

extreme are people who are blind to the harm being done to the natural environment, who want the entire world to industrialize at full speed. Somewhere, there must be a middle ground, one that recognizes not only that industrialization is here to stay but also that we *can* control it, for it is our creation. Industrialization, controlled, can enhance our quality of life; uncontrolled, it will destroy us.

It is essential, then, that we develop ways to reduce or eliminate the harm that technology does to the environment. This includes mechanisms to monitor the production, use, and disposal of technology. The question, of course, is whether we have the resolve to take the steps necessary to preserve the environment for future generations. What is at stake is nothing less than the welfare of planet Earth. Surely that is enough to motivate us to make wise choices.

Summary and Review

How Social Change Transforms Social Life

What major trends have transformed the course of human history?

The primary changes in human history are the four social revolutions (domestication, agriculture, industrialization, and information); the change from *Gemeinschaft* to *Gesellschaft* societies; capitalism and industrialization; **modernization;** and global stratification. Social movements indicate cutting edges of social change. Ethnic conflicts threaten the global divisions G-8 is working out. We may also be on the cutting edge of a new biotech society. Pp. 415–419.

Theories and Processes of Social Change

Besides technology, capitalism, modernization, and so on, what other theories of social change are there?

Evolutionary theories presuppose that societies move from the same starting point to some similar ending point. *Unilinear* theories, which assume the same evolutionary path for every society, were replaced by *multilinear* theories, which assume that different paths lead to the same stage of development. *Cyclical* theories view civilizations as going through a process of birth, youth, maturity, decline, and death. Conflict theorists view social change as inevitable, for each *thesis* (basically an arrangement of power) contains an *antithesis* (contradictions). A new *synthesis* develops to resolve these contradictions, but it, too, contains contradictions that must be resolved, and so on. This is called a **dialectical process.** Pp. 419–420.

What is Ogburn's theory of social change?

William Ogburn identified technology as the basic cause of social change, which comes through three processes: **invention, discovery,** and **diffusion.** The term **cultural lag** refers to symbolic culture lagging behind changes in technology. Pp. 420–421.

How Technology Changes Society

How does new technology affect society?

Because **technology** is an organizing force of social life, changes in technology can have profound effects. The computer was used as an extended example. It is changing the way we learn, receive health care, do business, and fight wars. We don't yet know whether information technologies will help to perpetuate or to reduce social inequalities on both a national and a global level. Pp. 421–424.

Social Movements as a Source of Social Change

What types of social movements are there?

Social movements consist of large numbers of people who organize to promote or resist social change. Depending on their target (individuals or society) and the amount of social change that is desired (partial or complete), social movements can be classified as **alterative, redemptive, reformative, transformative, transnational,** and **metaformative.** Pp. 424–426.

How are the mass media related to social movements?

The mass media are gatekeepers for social movements. Leaders of social movements use **propaganda** to influence **public opinion.** Pp. 426–427.

What stages do social movements go through?

Sociologists have identified five stages of social movements: initial unrest and agitation, mobilization, organization, institutionalization, and, finally, decline. Resurgence is also possible, if, as in the case of abortion, opposing sides revitalize one another. Pp. 427–430.

The Growth Machine Versus the Earth

What are the environmental problems of the Most Industrialized Nations?

The environmental problems of the Most Industrialized Nations range from smog and **acid rain** to the **greenhouse effect. Global warming** will fundamentally affect our lives. Burning fossil fuels in internal combustion engines lies at the root of many environmental problems. The location of factories and hazardous waste sites creates **environmental injustice,** with environmental problems having a greater impact on minorities and the poor. Pp. 430–432.

What are the environmental problems of the Industrializing and Least Industrialized Nations?

The worst environmental problems are found in the former Soviet Union, a legacy of the unrestrained exploitation of resources by the Communist party. The rush of the Least Industrialized Nations to industrialize is adding to our environmental decay. The world is facing a basic conflict between the lust for profits through the exploitation of the earth's resources and the need to produce a **sustainable environment.** Pp. 432–433.

What is the environmental movement?

The environmental movement is an attempt to restore a healthy environment for the world's people. This global social movement takes many forms, from a peaceful attempt to influence the political process to **ecosabotage.** Pp. 433–435.

What is environmental sociology?

Environmental sociology is not an attempt to change the environment but a study of the relationship between humans and the environment. Environmental sociologists are generally also environmental activists. Pp. 435–436.

Thinking Critically
about Chapter 15

1. Pick a social movement and analyze it according to the sociological principles and findings reviewed in this chapter.
2. In what ways does technology change society? How has social change affected your life? Be specific—what changes, how? Does Ogburn's theory help to explain your experiences? Why or why not?
3. What practical steps do you think we can take to produce a sustainable environment?

Additional Resources

Companion Website www.ablongman.com/henslin

- Content Select Research Database for Sociology, with suggested key terms and annotated references
- Link to 2000 Census, with activities
- Flashcards of key terms and concepts

- Practice Tests
- Weblinks
- Interactive Maps

Where Can I Read More on This Topic?

Suggested readings for this chapter are listed at the back of this book.

EPILOGUE: WHY MAJOR IN SOCIOLOGY?

As you explored social life in this textbook, I hope that you found yourself thinking along with me. If so, you should have gained a greater understanding of why people think, feel, and act as they do—as well as insights into why *you* view life the way you do. Developing your sociological imagination was my intention in writing this book. I have sincerely wanted to make sociology come alive for you.

Majoring in Sociology

If you feel a passion for peering beneath the surface—for seeking out the social influences in people's lives, and for seeing these influences in your own life—this is the best reason to major in sociology. As you take more courses in sociology, you will continue this enlightening process of social discovery. As your sociological imagination grows, you will become increasingly aware of how social factors underlie human behavior.

In addition to people who have a strong desire to continue this fascinating process of social discovery, there is a second type of person whom I also urge to major in sociology. Let's suppose that you have a strong, almost unbridled sense of wanting to explore many aspects of life. Let's also assume that because you have so many interests, you can't make up your mind about what you want to do with your life. You can think of so many things you'd like to try, but for each one there are other possibilities that you find equally as compelling. Let me share what one student who read this text wrote me:

> I'd love to say what my current major is—if only I truly knew. I know that the major you choose to study in college isn't necessarily the field of work you'll be going into. I've heard enough stories of grads who get jobs in fields that are not even related to their majors to believe it to a certain extent. My only problem is that I'm not even sure what it is I want to study, or what I truly want to be in the future for that matter.
>
> The variety of choices I have left open for myself are very wide, which creates a big problem, because I know I have to narrow it down to just one, which isn't something easy at all for me. It's like I want to be the best and do the best (medical doctor), yet I also wanna do other things (such as being a paramedic, or a cop, or firefighter, or a pilot), but I also realize I've only got one life to live. So the big question is: What's it gonna be?

This note reminded me of myself. In my reply, I said:

> You sound so much like myself when I was in college. In my senior year, I was plagued with uncertainty about what would be the right course for my life. I went to a counselor and took a vocational aptitude test. I still remember the day when I went in for the test results. I expected my future to be laid out for me, and I hung on every word. But then I heard the counselor say, "Your tests show that mortician should be one of your vocational choices."
>
> Mortician! I almost fell off my chair. That choice was so far removed from anything that I wanted that I immediately gave up on such tests.
>
> I like your list of possibilities: physician, cop, firefighter, and paramedic. In addition to these, mine included cowboy, hobo, and beach bum. One day, I was at the dry cleaners (end of my sophomore year in college), and the guy standing next to me was a cop. We talked about his job, and when I left the dry cleaners, I immediately went to the police station to get an application. I found out that I had to be 21, and I was just 20. I went back to college.
>
> I'm very happy with my choice. As a sociologist, I am able to follow my interests. I was able to become a hobo (or at least a traveler and able to experience different cultural settings). As far as being a cop, I developed and taught a course in the sociology of law.
>
> One of the many things I always wanted to be was an author. I almost skipped graduate school to move to Greenwich Village and become a novelist. The problem was that I was too timid, too scared of the unknown—and I had no support at all—to give it a try. My ultimate choice of sociologist has allowed me to fulfill this early dream.

It is sociology's breadth that is so satisfying to those of us who can't seem to find the limit to our interests, who can't pin ourselves down to just one thing in life. Sociology covers *all* of social life. Anything and everything that people do is part of sociology. For those of us who feel such broad, and perhaps changing interests, sociology is a perfect major.

But what if you already have a major picked out, yet you really like thinking sociologically? You can *minor* in sociology. Take sociology courses that strike your interest. Then after college, continue to stimulate your sociological interests through your reading, including novels. This ongoing development of your sociological imagination will serve you well as you go through life.

But What Can You Do With a Major in Sociology?

I can just hear someone say: "That's fine for you, since you became a sociologist. I don't want to go to graduate school, though. I just want to get my bachelor's degree and get out of college and get on with life. So, how can a bachelor's in sociology help me?"

This is a fair question. Just what can you do with a bachelor's degree in sociology?

A few years ago, in my sociology department we began to develop a concentration in applied sociology. At that time, since this would be a bachelor's degree, I explored this very question. I was surprised at the answer: *Almost anything!*

It turns out that most employers don't care what you major in. (Exceptions are some highly specialized fields such as nursing, computers, and engineering.) *Most* employers just want to make certain that you have completed college, and for most of them one degree is the same as another. *College provides the base on which the employer builds.*

Because you have your bachelor's degree—no matter what it is in—employers assume that you are a responsible person. This credential implies that you have proven yourself: You were able to stick with a four-year course of studies, you showed up for classes, listened to lectures, took notes, passed tests, and carried out whatever assignments you were given. On top of this base of presumed responsibility, employers will add the specifics necessary for you to do their particular work, whether that be in sales or service, in insurance, banking, retailing, marketing, product development, or whatever.

If you major in sociology, then, you don't have to look for a job as a sociologist. If you ever decide to go on for an advanced degree, that's fine. But such plans are *not* necessary. The bachelor's in sociology can be your passport to most types of work in society.

Final Note

I want to conclude by stressing the reason to major in sociology that goes far beyond how you are going to make a living. It is the *sociological perspective* itself, the way of thinking and understanding that sociology provides. Wherever your path in life may lead, the sociological perspective will accompany you.

You are going to live in a fast-paced, rapidly-changing society that, with all its conflicting crosscurrents, is going to be in turmoil. The sociological perspective will cast a different light on life's events, allowing you to perceive them in more insightful ways. As you watch television, attend a concert, converse with a friend, listen to a boss or co-worker—you will be more aware of the contexts that underlie such behavior. The sociological perspective that you develop as you major in sociology will equip you to view what happens to you in life differently from someone who does not have your sociological background. Even events in the news will look different to you.

The final question that I want to leave you with, then, is, "If you enjoy sociology, why not major in it?"

With my best wishes for your success in life,

Jim Henslin

Glossary

achieved statuses positions that are earned, accomplished, or involve at least some effort or activity on the individual's part

acid rain rain containing sulfuric and nitric acids (burning fossil fuels release sulfur dioxide and nitrogen oxide that become sulfuric and nitric acids when they react with moisture in the air)

activity theory the view that satisfaction during old age is related to a person's amount and quality of activity

age cohort people born at roughly the same time who pass through the life course together

ageism prejudice, discrimination, and hostility directed against people because of their age; can be directed against any age group, including youth

agents of socialization people or groups that affect our self-concept, attitudes, behaviors, or other orientations toward life

aggregate individuals who temporarily share the same physical space but who do not see themselves as belonging together

agricultural society a society based on large-scale agriculture; plows drawn by animals are the source of food production

alienation Marx's term for workers' lack of connection to the product of their labor; caused by their being assigned repetitive tasks on a small part of a product—this leads to a sense of powerlessness and normlessness; others use the term in the general sense of not feeling a part of something

alterative social movement a social movement that seeks to alter only some specific aspects of people

anarchy a condition of lawlessness or political disorder caused by the absence or collapse of governmental authority

anomie Durkheim's term for a condition of society in which people become detached from the norms that usually guide their behavior

anticipatory socialization because one anticipates a future role, one learns parts of it now

applied sociology the use of sociology to solve problems—from the micro level of family relationships to the macro level of crime and pollution

ascribed statuses positions an individual either inherits at birth or receives involuntarily later in life

assimilation the process of being absorbed into the mainstream culture

authoritarian leader an individual who leads by giving orders

authoritarian personality Theodor Adorno's term for people who are prejudiced and rank high on scales of conformity, intolerance, insecurity, respect for authority, and submissiveness to superiors

authority power that people consider legitimate, as rightly exercised over them; also called *legitimate power*

background assumptions deeply embedded common understandings of how the world operates and of how people ought to act

basic demographic equation growth rate equals births minus deaths plus net migration

bilineal (system of descent) a system of reckoning descent that counts both the mother's and the father's side

bioetech society a society whose economy increasingly centers around the application of genetics—human genetics for medicine, and plant and animal genetics for the production of food and materials

blended family a family whose members were once part of other families

born again a term describing Christians who have undergone a life-transforming religious experience so radical that they feel they have become new persons

bourgeoisie Marx's term for capitalists, those who own the means of production

bureaucracy a formal organization with a hierarchy of authority and a clear division of labor; emphasis on written rules, communications, and records; and impersonality of positions

capital punishment the death penalty

capitalism an economic system characterized by the private ownership of the means of production, the pursuit of profit, and market competition

capitalist class the wealthy who own the means of production and buy the labor of the working class

caste system a form of social stratification in which one's status is determined by birth and is lifelong

category people who have similar characteristics

charisma literally, an extraordinary gift from God; more commonly, an outstanding, "magnetic" personality

charismatic authority authority based on an individual's outstanding traits, which attract followers

charismatic leader literally, someone to whom God has given a gift; more commonly, someone who exerts extraordinary appeal to a group of followers

checks and balances the separation of powers among the three branches of U.S. government—legislative, executive, and judicial—so that each is able to nullify the actions of the other two, thus preventing the domination of any single branch

church according to Durkheim, one of the three essential elements of religion—a moral community of believers; also refers to a type of religious organization, to a large, highly organized group with formal, sedate worship services and little emphasis on personal conversion

citizenship the concept that birth (and residence) in a country impart basic rights

city a place in which a large number of people are permanently based and do not produce their own food

city-state an independent city whose power radiates outward, bringing the adjacent area under its rule

class conflict Marx's term for the struggle between capitalists and workers

class consciousness Marx's term for awareness of a common identity based on one's position in the means of production

class system a form of social stratification based primarily on the possession of money or material possessions

clique a cluster of people within a larger group who choose to interact with one another; an internal faction

closed-ended questions questions that are followed by a list of possible answers to be selected by the respondent

coalition the alignment of some members of a group against others

coalition government a government in which a country's largest party aligns itself with one or more smaller parties

coercion power that people do not accept as rightly exercised over them; also called *illegitimate power*

cohabitation unmarried couples living together in a sexual relationship

colonialism the process by which one nation takes over another nation, usually for the purpose of exploiting its labor and natural resources

compartmentalize to separate acts from feelings or attitudes

conflict theory a theoretical framework in which society is viewed as composed of groups that are competing for scarce resources

conspicuous consumption Thorstein Veblen's term for a change from the Protestant ethic to an eagerness to show off wealth by the consumption of goods

continuity theory the focus of this theory is how people adjust to retirement by continuing aspects of their earlier lives

contradictory class locations Erik Wright's term for a position in the class structure that generates contradictory interests

control group the group of subjects who are not exposed to the independent variable

control theory the idea that two control systems—inner controls and outer controls—work against our tendencies to deviate

convergence theory the view that as capitalist and socialist economic systems each adopt features of the other, a hybrid (or mixed) economic system will emerge

corporate capitalism the domination of the economic system by giant corporations

corporate crime crimes committed by executives in order to benefit their corporation

corporate culture the orientations that characterize corporate work settings

corporate welfare the financial incentives (tax breaks, subsidies, and even land and stadiums) given to corporations in order to attract them to an area or induce them to remain

corporation the joint ownership of a business enterprise, whose liabilities and obligations are separate from those of its owners

cosmology teachings or ideas that provide a unified picture of the world

counterculture a group whose values, beliefs, and related behaviors place its members in opposition to the broader culture

credential society the use of diplomas and degrees to determine who is eligible for jobs, even though the diploma or degree may be irrelevant to the actual work

crime the violation of norms written into law

criminal justice system the system of police, courts, and prisons set up to deal with people who are accused of having committed a crime

crude birth rate the annual number of live births per 1,000 population

crude death rate the annual number of deaths per 1,000 population

cult a new religion with few followers, whose teachings and practices put it at odds with the dominant culture and religion

cultural diffusion the spread of cultural characteristics from one group to another

cultural goals the legitimate objectives held out to the members of a society

cultural lag Ogburn's term for human behavior lagging behind technological innovations

cultural leveling the process by which cultures become similar to one another; refers especially to the process by which U.S. culture is being exported and diffused into other nations

cultural relativism not judging a culture but trying to understand it on its own terms

cultural transmission of values in reference to education, the ways in which schools transmit a society's culture, especially its core values

culture the language, beliefs, values, norms, behaviors, and even material objects that are passed from one generation to the next

culture of poverty the assumption that the values and behaviors of the poor make them fundamentally different from other people, that these factors are largely responsible for their poverty, and that parents perpetuate poverty across generations by passing these characteristics to their children

culture shock the disorientation that people experience when they come in contact with a fundamentally different culture and can no longer depend on their taken-for-granted assumptions about life

degradation ceremony a term coined by Harold Garfinkel to describe an attempt to remake the self by stripping away an individual's self-identity and stamping a new identity in its place

dehumanization the act or process of reducing people to objects that do not deserve the treatment accorded humans

deindustrialization industries moving out of a country or region

democracy a system of government in which authority derives from the people; the term comes from two Greek words that translate literally as "power to the people"

democratic leader an individual who leads by trying to reach a consensus

democratic socialism a hybrid economic system in which capitalism is mixed with state ownership

demographic transition a three-stage historical process of population growth: first, high birth rates and high death rates; second, high birth rates and low death rates; and third, low birth rates and low death rates; a fourth stage has begun to appear in the Most Industrialized Nations, as depicted in Figure 14.3

demographic variables the three factors that influence population growth: fertility, mortality, and net migration

demography the study of the size, composition, growth, and distribution of human populations

denomination a "brand name" within a major religion, for example, Methodist or Baptist

dependency ratio the number of workers who are required to support each dependent person—those 65 and older and those 15 and under

dependent variable a factor that is changed by an independent variable

deviance the violation of rules or norms

dialectical process (of history) each arrangement, or thesis, contains contradictions, or antitheses, which must be resolved; the new arrangement, or synthesis, contains its own contradictions, and so on

dictatorship a form of government in which an individual has seized power

differential association Edwin Sutherland's term to indicate that associating with some groups results in learning an "excess of definitions" of deviance, and, by extension, in a greater likelihood that one will become deviant

diffusion the spread of an invention or a discovery from one area to another; identified by William Ogburn as one of three processes of social change

direct democracy a form of democracy in which the eligible voters meet together to discuss issues and make their decisions

discovery a new way of seeing reality; identified by William Ogburn as one of three processes of social change

discrimination an act of unfair treatment directed against an individual or a group

disengagement theory the view that society prevents disruption by having the elderly vacate (or disengage from) their positions of responsibility so the younger generation can step into their shoes

disinvestment the withdrawal of investments by financial institutions, which seals the fate of an urban area

divine right of kings the idea that the king's authority comes directly from God

division of labor the splitting of a group's or a society's tasks into specialties

documents in its narrow sense, written sources that provide data; in its extended sense, archival material of any sort, including photographs, movies, CDs, DVDs, and so on

dominant group the group with the most power, greatest privileges, and highest social status

downward social mobility movement down the social class ladder

dramaturgy an approach, pioneered by Erving Goffman, in which social life is analyzed in terms of drama or the stage; also called *dramaturgical analysis*

dyad the smallest possible group, consisting of two persons

ecclesia a religious group so integrated into the dominant culture that it is difficult to tell where the one begins and the other leaves off; also called a *state religion*

economy a system of producing and distributing goods and services

ecosabotage actions taken to sabotage the efforts of people who are thought to be legally harming the environment

edge city a large clustering of service facilities and residential areas near highway intersections that provides a sense of place to people who live, shop, and work there

egalitarian authority more or less equally divided between people or groups, in this instance between husband and wife

ego Freud's term for a balancing force between the id and the demands of society

electronic community individuals who regularly interact with one another on the Internet and who think of themselves as belonging together

endogamy the practice of marrying within one's own group

enterprise zone the use of economic incentives in a designated area to encourage investment

environmental injustice refers to the pollution of our environment affecting minorities and the poor the most

environmental sociology a specialty within sociology where the focus is the relationship between human societies and the environment

ethnic cleansing a policy of population elimination, including forcible expulsion and genocide

ethnic work activities designed to discover, enhance, or maintain ethnic and racial identification

ethnicity (and **ethnic**) having distinctive cultural characteristics

ethnocentrism the use of one's own culture as a yardstick for judging the ways of other individuals or societies, generally leading to a negative evaluation of their values, norms, and behaviors

ethnomethodology the study of how people use background assumptions to make sense out of life

exchange mobility about the same numbers of people moving up and down the social class ladder, such that, on balance, the social class system shows little change

exogamy the practice of marrying outside one's group

experiment the use of control and experimental groups and dependent and independent variables to test causation

experimental group the group of subjects who are exposed to the independent variable

exponential growth curve a pattern of growth in which numbers double during approximately equal intervals, thus accelerating in the latter stages

expressive leader an individual who increases harmony and minimizes conflict in a group; also known as a *socioemotional leader*

extended family a nuclear family plus other relatives, such as grandparents, uncles, and aunts

face-saving behavior techniques used to salvage a performance that is going sour

false class consciousness Marx's term to refer to workers identifying with the interests of capitalists

family two or more people who consider themselves related by blood, marriage, or adoption

family of orientation the family in which a person grows up

family of procreation the family formed when a couple's first child is born

fecundity the number of children that women are capable of bearing

feminism the philosophy that men and women should be politically, economically, and socially equal; organized activities on behalf of this principle

fertility rate the number of children that the average woman bears

folkways norms that are not strictly enforced

functional analysis a theoretical framework in which society is viewed as composed of various parts, each with a function that, when fulfilled, contributes to society's equilibrium; also known as *functionalism* and *structural functionalism*

functional illiterate a high school graduate who has difficulty with basic reading and math

gatekeeping the process by which education opens and closes doors of opportunity; another term for the *social placement* function of education

Gemeinschaft a type of society in which life is intimate; a community in which everyone knows everyone else and people share a sense of togetherness

gender the behaviors and attitudes that a society considers proper for its males and females; masculinity or femininity

gender socialization the ways in which society sets children onto different courses in life *because* they are male or female

gender stratification males' and females' unequal access to power, prestige, and property on the basis of their sex

generalized other the norms, values, attitudes, and expectations of people "in general"; the child's ability to take the role of the generalized other is a significant step in the development of a self

genetic predisposition inborn tendencies; in this context, to commit deviant acts

genocide the systematic annihilation or attempted annihilation of a people because of their presumed race or ethnic group

gentrification middle class people moving into a rundown area of a city, displacing the poor as they buy and restore homes

Gesellschaft a type of society that is dominated by impersonal relationships, individual accomplishments, and self-interest

gestures the ways in which people use their bodies to communicate with one another

glass ceiling the mostly invisible barrier that keeps women from advancing to the top levels at work

glass escalator the mostly invisible accelerators that push men into higher-level positions, more desirable work assignments, and higher salaries

global warming an increase in the earth's temperature due to the greenhouse effect

globalization of capitalism capitalism (investing to make profits within a rational system) becoming the globe's dominant economic system

goal displacement the adoption of new goals by an organization; also known as *goal replacement*

graying of America refers to the growing percentage of older people in the U.S. population

greenhouse effect the buildup of carbon dioxide in the earth's atmosphere that allows light to enter but inhibits the release of heat; believed to cause global warming

gross domestic product (GDP) the amount of goods and services produced by a nation

group people who have something in common and who believe that what they have in common is significant; also called a *social group*

group dynamics the ways in which individuals affect groups and the ways in which groups influence individuals

groupthink a narrowing of thought by a group of people, leading to the perception that there is only one correct answer, in which to even suggest alternatives becomes a sign of disloyalty

growth rate the net change in a population after adding births, subtracting deaths, and either adding or subtracting net migration

hate crime crimes to which more severe penalties are attached because they are motivated by hatred (dislike, animosity) of someone's race-ethnicity, religion, sexual orientation, disability, or national origin

hidden curriculum the unwritten goals of schools, such as teaching obedience to authority and conformity to cultural norms

homogamy the tendency of people with similar characteristics to marry one another

Horatio Alger myth the belief that due to limitless possibilities anyone can get ahead if he or she tries hard enough

horticultural society a society based on cultivating plants by the use of hand tools

household people who occupy the same housing unit

human ecology Robert Park's term for the relationship between people and their environment (such as land and structures); also known as *urban ecology*

hunting and gathering society a human group that depends on hunting and gathering for its survival

hypothesis a statement of how variables are expected to be related to one another, often according to predictions from a theory

id Freud's term for our inborn basic drives

ideal culture the ideal values and norms of a people; the goals held out for them

ideology beliefs about the way things ought to be that justify social arrangements

illegitimate opportunity structure opportunities for crimes that are woven into the texture of life

impression management people's efforts to control the impressions that others receive of them

incest sexual relations between specified relatives, such as brothers and sisters or parents and children

incest taboo the rule that prohibits sex and marriage among designated relatives

income money received, usually from a job, business, or assets

independent variable a factor that causes a change in another variable, called the dependent variable

individual discrimination the negative treatment of one person by another on the basis of that person's perceived characteristics

Industrial Revolution the third social revolution, occurring when machines powered by fuels replaced most animal and human power

industrial society a society based on the harnessing of machines powered by fuels

in-groups groups toward which one feels loyalty

institutional discrimination negative treatment of a minority group that is built into a society's institutions; also called *systemic discrimination*

institutionalized means approved ways of reaching cultural goals

instrumental leader an individual who tries to keep the group moving toward its goals; also known as a *task-oriented leader*

intergenerational mobility the change that family members make in social class from one generation to the next

interlocking directorates the same people serving on the board of directors of several companies

internal colonialism the policy of economically exploiting minority groups

invasion-succession cycle the process of one group of people displacing a group whose racial-ethnic or social class characteristics differ from their own

invention the combination of existing elements and materials to form new ones; identified by William Ogburn as one of three processes of social change

[the] iron law of oligarchy Robert Michels' term for the tendency of formal organizations to be dominated by a small, self-perpetuating elite

labeling theory the view that the labels people are given affect their own and others' perceptions of them, thus channeling their behavior either into deviance or into conformity

laissez-faire capitalism unrestrained manufacture and trade (literally "hands off" capitalism)

laissez-faire leader an individual who leads by being highly permissive

language a system of symbols that can be combined in an infinite number of ways and can represent not only objects but also abstract thought

latent functions unintended beneficial consequences of people's actions

leader someone who influences other people

leadership styles ways in which people express their leadership

life course the stages of our life as we go from birth to death

life expectancy the number of years that an average person at any age, including newborns, can expect to live

life span the maximum length of life of a species; for humans, the longest that a human has lived

lobbyists people who influence legislation on behalf of their clients

looking-glass self a term coined by Charles Horton Cooley to refer to the process by which our self develops through internalizing others' reactions to us

machismo an emphasis on male strength and dominance

macro-level analysis an examination of large-scale patterns of society

macrosociology analysis of social life that focuses on broad features of society, such as social class and the relationships of groups to one another; usually used by functionalists and conflict theorists

mainstreaming helping people to become part of the mainstream of society

Malthus theorem an observation by Thomas Malthus that although the food supply increases arithmetically (from 1 to 2 to 3 to 4 and so on), population grows geometrically (from 2 to 4 to 8 to 16 and so forth)

manifest functions the intended beneficial consequences of people's actions

marginal working class the most desperate members of the working class, who have few skills, little job security, and are often unemployed

market forces the law of supply and demand

market restraints laws and regulations that limit the capacity to manufacture and sell products

marriage a group's approved mating arrangements, usually marked by a ritual of some sort

mass media forms of communication, such as radio, newspapers, and television that are directed to mass audiences

master status a status that cuts across the other statuses that an individual occupies

material culture the material objects that distinguish a group of people, such as their art, buildings, weapons, utensils, machines, hairstyles, clothing, and jewelry

matriarchy a society in which women as a group dominate men as a group

matrilineal (system of descent) a system of reckoning descent that counts only the mother's side

[the] McDonaldization of society the process by which ordinary aspects of life become rationalized and efficiency comes to rule them, including such things as food preparation

means of production the tools, factories, land, and investment capital used to produce wealth

mechanical solidarity Durkheim's term for the unity (a shared consciousness) that people feel as a result of performing the same or similar tasks

medicalization of deviance to make deviance a medical matter, a symptom of some underlying illness that needs to be treated by physicians

megacity a city of 10 million or more residents

megalopolis an urban area consisting of at least two metropolises and their many suburbs

melting pot the view that Americans of various backgrounds would blend into a sort of ethnic stew

meritocracy a form of social stratification in which all positions are awarded on the basis of merit

metaformative social movement a social movement that has the goal to change the social order not just of a country or two, but of a civilization, or even of the entire world

metropolis a central city surrounded by smaller cities and their suburbs

metropolitan statistical area (MSA) a central city and the urbanized counties adjacent to it

micro-level analysis an examination of small-scale patterns of society

microsociology analysis of social life that focuses on social interaction; typically used by symbolic interactionists

minority group people who are singled out for unequal treatment and who regard themselves as objects of collective discrimination

modernization the transformation of traditional societies into industrial societies

monarchy a form of government headed by a king or queen

mores norms that are strictly enforced because they are thought essential to core values or the well-being of the group

multiculturalism (also called *pluralism*) a philosophy or political policy that permits or encourages ethnic difference

multinational corporations companies that operate across national boundaries; also called *transnational corporations*

negative sanction an expression of disapproval for breaking a norm, ranging from a mild, informal reaction such as a frown to a formal reaction such as a prison sentence or an execution

neocolonialism the economic and political dominance of the Least Industrialized Nations by the Most Industrialized Nations

net migration rate the difference between the number of immigrants and emigrants per 1,000 population

networking using one's social networks for some gain

new technology the emerging technologies of an era that have a significant impact on social life

nonmaterial culture (also called *symbolic culture*) a group's ways of thinking (including its beliefs, values, and other assumptions about the world) and doing (its common patterns of behavior, including language and other forms of interaction)

nonverbal interaction communication without words through gestures, use of space, silence, and so on

norms expectations, or rules of behavior, that reflect and enforce values

nuclear family a family consisting of a husband, wife, and child(ren)

oligarchy a form of government in which a small group of individuals holds power; the rule of the many by the few

open-ended questions questions that respondents answer in their own words

operational definition the way in which a researcher measures a variable

organic solidarity Durkheim's term for the interdependence that results from the division of labor; people depending on others to fulfill their jobs

out-groups groups toward which one feels antagonism

pan-Indianism a movement that focuses on common elements in the cultures of Native Americans in order to develop a cross-tribal self-identity and to work toward the welfare of all Native Americans

participant observation (or **fieldwork**) research in which the researcher participates in a research setting while observing what is happening in that setting

pastoral society a society based on the pasturing of animals

patriarchy a society or group in which men dominate women; authority is vested in males

patrilineal (system of descent) a system of reckoning descent that counts only the father's side

peer group a group of individuals of roughly the same age who are linked by common interests

personality disorders the view that a personality disturbance of some sort causes an individual to violate social norms

pluralism the diffusion of power among many interest groups that prevents any single group from gaining control of the government

pluralistic society a society made up of many different groups

political action committee (PAC) an organization formed by one or more special-interest groups to solicit and spend funds for the purpose of influencing legislation

polyandry a form of marriage in which women have more than one husband

polygyny a form of marriage in which men have more than one wife

population the target group to be studied

population pyramid a graphic representation of a population, divided into age and sex

population shrinkage the process by which a country's population becomes smaller because its birth rate and immigration are too low to replace those who die and emigrate

population transfer forcing a minority group to move

positive sanction a reward or positive reaction for following norms, ranging from a smile to a prize

positivism the application of the scientific approach to the social world

postindustrial (information) society a society based on information, services, and high technology, rather than on raw materials and manufacturing

postmodern society another term for postindustrial society; a chief characteristic is the use of tools that extend human abilities to gather and analyze information, to communicate, and to travel

poverty line the official measure of poverty; calculated to include incomes that are less than three times a low-cost food budget

power the ability to carry out your will, even over the resistance of others

power elite C. Wright Mills' term for the top people in U.S. corporations, military, and politics who make the nation's major decisions

prejudice an attitude or prejudging, usually in a negative way

prestige respect or regard

primary group a group characterized by intimate, long-term, face-to-face association and cooperation

proactive social movement a social movement that promotes some social change

profane Durkheim's term for common elements of everyday life

proletariat Marx's term for the exploited class, the mass of workers who do not own the means of production

propaganda in its broad sense, the presentation of information in the attempt to influence people; in its narrow sense, one-sided information used to try to influence people

Protestant ethic Weber's term to describe the ideal of a self-denying, highly moral life accompanied by hard work and frugality

public opinion how people think about some issue

race physical characteristics that distinguish one group from another

racism prejudice and discrimination on the basis of race

random sample a sample in which everyone in the target population has the same chance of being included in the study

rapport (ruh-POUR) a feeling of trust between researchers and the people they are studying

[the] rationalization of society a widespread acceptance of rationality and social organizations that are built largely around this idea

rational-legal authority authority based on law or written rules and regulations; also called *bureaucratic authority*

reactive social movement a social movement that resists some social change

real culture the norms and values that people actually follow

recidivism rate the proportion of released convicts who are rearrested

redemptive social movement a social movement that seeks to change people totally, to redeem them

redlining the officers of a financial institution deciding not to make loans in a particular area

reference group a group that we use as a standard to evaluate ourselves

reformative social movement a social movement that seeks to reform some specific aspects of society

reliability the extent to which research produces consistent or dependable results

religion according to Durkheim, beliefs and practices that separate the profane from the sacred and unite its adherents into a moral community

religious experience a sudden awareness of the supernatural or a feeling of coming in contact with God

replication repeating a study in order to test its findings

representative democracy a form of democracy in which voters elect representatives to meet together to discuss issues and make decisions on their behalf

research method (or **research design**) one of six procedures that sociologists use to collect data: surveys, participant observation, secondary analysis, documents, experiments, and unobtrusive measures

reserve labor force the unemployed; unemployed workers are thought of as being "in reserve"—capitalists take them "out of reserve" (put them back to work) during times of high production and then lay them off (put them back in reserve) when they are no longer needed

resocialization the process of learning new norms, values, attitudes, and behaviors

resource mobilization a theory that social movements succeed or fail based on their ability to mobilize resources such as time, money, and people's skills

respondents people who respond to a survey, either in interviews or by self-administered questionnaires

rising expectations the sense that better conditions are soon to follow, which, if unfulfilled, increases frustration

rituals ceremonies or repetitive practices; in this context, religious observances or rites, often intended to evoke a sense of awe of the sacred

role the behaviors, obligations, and privileges attached to a status

role conflict conflicts that someone feels *between* roles because the expectations attached to one role are incompatible with the expectations of another role

role performance the ways in which someone performs a role within the limits that the role provides; showing a particular "style" or "personality"

role strain conflicts that someone feels *within* a role

romantic love feelings of erotic attraction accompanied by an idealization of the other

routinization of charisma the transfer of authority from a charismatic figure to either a traditional or a rational-legal form of authority

sacred Durkheim's term for things set apart or forbidden, that inspire fear, awe, reverence, or deep respect

sample the individuals intended to represent the population to be studied

sanctions expressions of approval or disapproval given to people for upholding or violating norms

Sapir-Whorf hypothesis Edward Sapir's and Benjamin Whorf's hypothesis that language creates ways of thinking and perceiving

science the application of systematic methods to obtain knowledge and the knowledge obtained by those methods

secondary analysis the analysis of data that have been collected by other researchers

secondary group compared with a primary group, a larger, relatively temporary, more anonymous, formal, and impersonal group based on some interest or activity. Its members are likely to interact on the basis of specific statuses

sect a religious group larger than a cult that still feels substantial hostility from and toward society

secularization of religion the replacement of a religion's spiritual or "other worldly" concerns with concerns about "this world"

segregation the policy of keeping racial–ethnic groups apart

selective perception seeing certain features of an object or situation, but remaining blind to others

self the unique human capacity of being able to see ourselves "from the outside"; the views we internalize of how others see us

self-fulfilling prophecy Robert Merton's term for an originally false assertion that becomes true simply because it was predicted

serial fatherhood a pattern of parenting in which a father, after divorce, reduces contact with his own children, serves as a father to the children of the woman he marries or lives with, then ignores these children, too, after moving in with or marrying another woman

serial murder the killing of several victims in three or more separate events

sex biological characteristics that distinguish females and males, consisting of primary and secondary sex characteristics

sexual harassment the abuse of one's position of authority to force unwanted sexual demands on someone

significant other an individual who significantly influences someone else's life

slavery a form of social stratification in which some people own other people

small group a group small enough for everyone to interact directly with all the other members

social change the alteration of culture and societies over time

social class according to Weber, a large group of people who rank close to one another in wealth, prestige, and power; according to Marx, one of two groups: capitalists who own the means of production or workers who sell their labor

social construction of reality the use of background assumptions and life experiences to define what is real

social control a group's formal and informal means of enforcing its norms

social environment the entire human environment, including direct contact with others

social inequality a social condition in which privileges and obligations are given to some but denied to others

social institution the organized, usual, or standard ways by which society meets its basic needs

social integration the degree to which members of a group or a society feel united by shared values and other social bonds; also known as social cohesion

social interaction what people do when they are in one another's presence

social location the group memberships that people have because of their location in history and society

social mobility movement up or down the social class ladder

social movement a large group of people who are organized to promote or resist some social change

social movement organization an organization to promote the goals of a social movement

social network the social ties radiating outward from the self that link people together

social order a group's usual and customary social arrangements, on which its members depend and on which they base their lives

social placement a function of education—funneling people into a society's various positions

social promotion passing students on to the next level even though they have not mastered basic materials

social stratification the division of large numbers of people into layers according to their relative power, property, and prestige; applies to both nations and to people within a nation, society, or other group

social structure the framework that surrounds us, consisting of the relationships of people and groups to one another, which gives direction to and sets limits on behavior

socialism an economic system characterized by the public ownership of the means of production, central planning, and the distribution of goods without a profit motive

socialization the process by which people learn the characteristics of their group—the knowledge, skills, attitudes, values, and actions thought appropriate for them

society people who share a culture and a territory

sociological perspective understanding human behavior by placing it within its broader social context

sociology the scientific study of society and human behavior

special-interest group a group of people who support a particular issue and who can be mobilized for political action

spirit of capitalism Weber's term for the desire to accumulate capital as a duty—not to spend it, but as an end in itself—and to constantly reinvest it

split labor market workers split along racial, ethnic, gender, age, or any other lines; this split is exploited by owners to weaken the bargaining power of workers

state a political entity that claims monopoly on the use of violence in some particular territory; commonly known as a country

status the position that someone occupies in society or in a social group

status consistency ranking high or low on all three dimensions of social class

status inconsistency ranking high on some dimensions of social class and low on others, also called *status discrepancy*

status set all the statuses or positions that an individual occupies

status symbols items used to identify a status

stereotype assumptions of what people are like, whether true or false

stigma "blemishes" that discredit a person's claim to a "normal" identity

stockholders' revolt the refusal of a corporation's stockholders to rubber-stamp decisions made by its managers

strain theory Robert Merton's term for the strain engendered when a society socializes large numbers of people to desire a cultural goal (such as success), but withholds from many the approved means of reaching that goal; one adaptation to the strain is crime, the choice of an innovative means (one outside the approved system) to attain the cultural goal

stratified random sample a sample from selected subgroups of the target population in which everyone in those subgroups has an equal chance of being included in the research

street crime crimes such as mugging, rape, and burglary

structural mobility movement up or down the social class ladder that is due to changes in the structure of society, not to individual efforts

subculture the values and related behaviors of a group that distinguish its members from the larger culture; a world within a world

subsistence economy a type of economy in which human groups live off the land and have little or no surplus

suburbanization the movement from the city to the suburbs

superego Freud's term for the conscience, the internalized norms and values of our social groups

survey the collection of data by having people answer a series of questions

sustainable environment a world system that takes into account the limits of the environment, produces enough material goods for everyone's needs, and leaves a heritage of a sound environment for the next generation

symbol something to which people attach meanings and then use to communicate with others

symbolic culture another term for nonmaterial culture

symbolic interactionism a theoretical perspective in which society is viewed as composed of symbols that people use to establish meaning, develop their views of the world, and communicate with one another

system of descent how kinship is traced over the generations

taboo a norm so strong that it often brings revulsion if violated

taking the role of the other putting oneself in someone else's shoes; understanding how someone else feels and thinks and thus anticipating how that person will act

teamwork the collaboration of two or more people to manage impressions jointly

techniques of neutralization ways of thinking or rationalizing that help people deflect (or neutralize) society's norms

technology in its narrow sense, tools; its broader sense includes the skills or procedures necessary to make and use those tools

terrorism the use of violence or the threat of violence to produce fear in order to attain political objectives

theory a general statement about how some parts of the world fit together and how they work; an explanation of how two or more facts are related to one another

Thomas theorem William I. and Dorothy S. Thomas' classic formulation of the definition of the situation: "If people define situations as real, they are real in their consequences."

total institution a place in which people are cut off from the rest of society and are almost totally controlled by the officials who run the place

totalitarianism a form of government that exerts almost total control over people

tracking the sorting of students into different educational programs on the basis of real or perceived abilities

traditional authority authority based on custom

transformative social movement a social movement that seeks to change society totally, to transform it

transitional adulthood a term that refers to a period following high school when young adults have not yet taken on the responsibilities ordinarily associated with adulthood; also called *adultolescence*

transnational social movement a social movement whose emphasis is on some condition around the world, instead of on a condition in a specific country; also known as *new social movements*

triad a group of three people

underclass a group of people for whom poverty persists year after year and across generations

universal citizenship the idea that everyone has the same basic rights by virtue of being born in a country (or by immigrating and becoming a naturalized citizen)

unobtrusive measures ways of observing people who do not know they are being studied

upward social mobility movement up the social class ladder

urban renewal the rehabilitation of a rundown area, which usually results in the displacement of the poor who are living in that area

urbanization the process by which an increasing proportion of a population lives in cities and has a growing influence on the culture

validity the extent to which an operational definition measures what it was intended to measure

value cluster values that together form a larger whole

value contradiction values that contradict one another; to follow the one means to come into conflict with the other

value free the view that a sociologist's personal values or biases should not influence social research

values the standards by which people define what is desirable or undesirable, good or bad, beautiful or ugly

variable a factor thought to be significant for human behavior, which can *vary* (or change) from one case to another

voluntary association a group made up of people who voluntarily organize on the basis of some mutual interest; also known as *voluntary memberships* and *voluntary organizations*

voter apathy indifference and inaction on the part of individuals or groups with respect to the political process

war armed conflict between nations or politically distinct groups

WASP White Anglo-Saxon Protestant; narrowly, an American of English descent; broadly, an American of western European ancestry

wealth the total value of everything someone owns, minus the debts

welfare (or state) capitalism an economic system in which individuals own the means of production but the state regulates many economic activities for the welfare of the population

white ethnics white immigrants to the United States whose cultures differ from that of WASPs

white-collar crime Edwin Sutherland's term for crimes committed by people of respectable and high social status in the course of their occupations; for example, bribery of public officials, securities violations, embezzlement, false advertising, and price fixing

working class those people who sell their labor to the capitalist class

world system theory economic and political connections that tie the world's countries together

zero population growth a demographic condition in which women bear only enough children to reproduce the population

SUGGESTED READINGS

CHAPTER 1   The Sociological Perspective

Bartos, Otomar J., and Paul Wehr. *Using Conflict Theory.* New York: Cambridge University Press, 2003. In this application of the conflict perspective, the author's primary concerns are the causes of social conflicts and how to manage or resolve conflict.

Berger, Peter L. *Invitation to Sociology: A Humanistic Perspective.* New York: Doubleday, 1972. This analysis of how sociology applies to everyday life has become a classic in sociology.

Best, Joel. *More Damned Lies and Statistics: How Numbers Confuse Public Issues.* Berkeley: University of California Press, 2004. The author shows how special-interest groups manipulate and misrepresent statistics in order to promote their agendas.

Charon, Joel M. *Symbolic Interactionism: An Introduction, an Interpretation, an Integration,* 8th ed. Upper Saddle River, N.J.: Prentice Hall, 2005. The author lays out the main points of symbolic interactionism, providing an understanding of why this perspective is important in sociology.

Henslin, James M., ed. *Down to Earth Sociology: Introductory Readings,* 14th ed. New York: Free Press, 2007. This collection of readings about everyday life and social structure is designed to broaden the reader's understanding of society, and of the individual's place within it.

Mills, C. Wright. *The Sociological Imagination.* New York: Oxford University Press, 2000. First published in 1960, this classic analysis provides an overview of sociology from the framework of the conflict perspective.

Ritzer, George. *Classic Sociological Theory,* 3rd ed. New York: McGraw-Hill, 2004. To help readers understand the personal and historical context of how theory develops, the author includes biographical sketches of the theorists.

Ruane, Janet M., and Karen A. Cerulo. *Second Thoughts: Seeing Conventional Wisdom Through the Sociological Eye,* 3rd ed. Thousand Oaks, Calif.: Sage Publications, 2004. As the authors explode common stereotypes and myths, the relevance of sociology becomes apparent.

How Sociologists Do Research

Bryman, Alan. *Social Research Methods,* 2nd ed. Oxford, U.K.: Oxford University Press, 2005. The author provides an overview of the research methods used by sociologists, with an emphasis on the logic that underlies these methods.

Creswell, John W. *Research Design: Qualitative, Quantitative, and Mixed Methods Approaches.* Beverly Hills, Calif.: Sage, 2003. This introduction to research methods walks you through the research experience and helps you to understand when to use a particular method.

Gosselin, Denise Kindschi. *Heavy Hands: An Introduction to the Crimes of Family Violence,* 2nd ed. Upper Saddle River, N.J.: Prentice Hall, 2003. This book explores causes, consequences, and prevalence of domestic violence; and also has an emphasis on law enforcement.

Lee, Raymond M. *Unobtrusive Methods in Social Research.* Philadelphia: Open University Press, 2000. This overview of unobtrusive ways of doing social research summarizes many interesting studies.

Lomand, Turner C. *Social Science Research: A Cross Section of Journal Articles for Discussion and Evaluation,* 4th ed. Los Angeles: Pyrczak Publishing, 2005. This overview of the methods of research used by sociologists includes articles on current topics.

Neuman, W. Lawrence. *Social Research Methods: Qualitative and Quantitative Approaches,* 6th ed. Boston: Allyn and Bacon, 2006. This "how-to" book of sociological research describes how sociologists gather data and the logic that underlies each method.

Whyte, William Foote. *Creative Problem Solving in the Field: Reflections on a Career.* Lanham, Md.: AltaMira Press, 1997. Focusing on his extensive field experiences, the author provides insight into the researcher's role in participant observation.

Wysocki Diane Kholos, ed. *Readings in Social Research Methods,* 2nd ed. Belmont, Calif.: Wadsworth, 2004. The authors of these articles provide an overview of research methods.

Journals

Applied Behavioral Science Review; Clinical Sociology Review; International Clinical Sociology; Journal of Applied Sociology; The Practicing Sociologist; Sociological Practice: A Journal of Clinical and Applied Sociology; and *Sociological Practice Review* report the experiences of sociologists who work in applied settings, from peer group counseling and suicide prevention to recommending changes to school boards.

Contexts, published by the American Sociological Association, uses a magazine format to present sociological research in a down-to-earth fashion.

Humanity & Society, the official journal of the Association for Humanist Sociology, publishes articles intended "to advance the quality of life of the world's people."

Electronic Journals

Electronic Journal of Sociology (http://www.sociology.org) and *Sociological Research Online* (http://www.socresonline.org.uk) publish articles on various sociological topics. Access is free.

Writing Papers for Sociology

Cuba, Lee J. *A Short Guide to Writing about Social Science,* 4th ed. Boston: Pearson Longman, 2002. The author summarizes the types of social science literature, presents guidelines on how to organize and write a research paper, and explains how to prepare an oral presentation.

Richlin-Klonsky, Judith, and Ellen Strenski, eds. The Sociology Writing Group. *A Guide to Writing Sociology Papers,* 5th ed. New York: St. Martin's Press, 2001. This guide walks students through the steps in writing a sociology paper, from choosing the initial assignment to doing the research and turning in a finished paper. It also explains how to manage time and correctly cite sources.

About Majoring in Sociology

You like sociology and perhaps are thinking about majoring in it, but what can you do with a sociology major? Be sure to check the epilogue of this book (pages 439–440). Also check out the resources that are available from the American Sociological Association. Go to www.asanet.org. This will bring you to the ASA's home page. Here, you can click around and get familiar with what this professional association offers students.

On the menu at the top of ASA's home page, click *Students.* This will bring you to a page that has links to resources for students. You may be interested in *The Student Sociologist,* a newsletter for students. The link, *Careers,* will take you to several free online publications, including those that feature information on careers in both basic and applied sociology. You will also see such links as the student forum, student involvement, and funding.

If you want to contact the ASA by snail mail or by telephone or fax, here is that information: American Sociological Association 1307 New York Avenue NW, Suite 700, Washington, D.C. 20005-4701. Tel. (202) 383-9005. Fax (202) 638-0882. E-mail: Executive.Office@ asanet.org

You might also be interested in the following book. If your library doesn't have it, I'm sure they'll order it if you request it.

Stephens, W. Richard, Jr. *Careers in Sociology,* 4th ed. Boston: Pearson Education, 2004. How can you make a living with a major in sociology? The author explores careers in sociology, from business and government to health care and the law.

CHAPTER 2   Culture

Berger, Peter L., and Samuel P. Huntington, eds. *Many Globalizations: Cultural Diversity in the Contemporary World.* New York: Oxford University Press, 2002. One of the recurring themes of this book is how globalization is changing cultures.

Borofsky, Robert, and Bruce Albert. *Yanomani: The Fierce Controversy and What We Can Learn from It.* Berkeley: University of California Press, 2006. The authors criticize the research on the Yanomani, including that by Chagnon in the next book, with an emphasis on anthropologists' lack of consideration of human rights.

Chagnon, Napoleon A. *Yanomamö: The Fierce People,* 5th ed. New York: Harcourt, Brace, Jovanovich, 1997. This account of a tribal

people whose customs are extraordinarily different from ours will help you to see how arbitrary the choices are that underlie human culture.

Edgerton, Robert B. *Sick Societies: Challenging the Myth of Primitive Harmony.* New York: Free Press, 1993. The author's thesis is that cultural relativism is misinformed, that we have the obligation to judge cultures that harm its members as inferior to those that do not.

Jacobs, Mark D., and Nancy Weiss Hanrahan, eds. *The Blackwell Companion to the Sociology of Culture.* Malden, Mass.: Blackwell Publishing, 2005. The authors of these articles explore cultural systems, everyday life, identity, collective memory, and citizenship in a global economy.

Sullivan, Nikki. *Tattooed Bodies: Subjectivity, Textuality, Ethics, and Pleasure.* Westport, Conn.: Praeger, 2001. A sociological analysis of this very old and very new custom.

Wolf, Mark J. P., and Bernard Perron, eds. *The Video Game: Theory Reader.* New York: Routledge, 2003. The authors of these articles on gamers and games examine sociological and economic issues that surround gaming.

Zellner, William W. *Countercultures: A Sociological Analysis.* New York: St. Martin's Press, 1995. The author's analysis of skinheads, the Ku Klux Klan, survivalists, satanists, the Church of Scientology, and the Unification Church (Moonies) helps us understand why people join countercultures.

CHAPTER 3   Socialization

Ariès, Philippe. *Centuries of Childhood: A Social History of Family Life.* New York: Vintage Books, 1972. The author analyzes how childhood in Europe during the Middle Ages differs from childhood today.

Blumer, Herbert. *George Herbert Mead and Human Conduct.* Lanham, Md.: AltaMira Press, 2004. An overview of symbolic interactionism by a sociologist who studied and lectured on Mead's teachings all of his life.

Heywood, Colin. *A History of Childhood: Children and Childhood in the West from Medieval to Modern Times.* Cambridge, U.K.: Polity Press, 2001. Critical of the Ariès book listed above, the author explores the changing experiences and perceptions of childhood from the early Middle Ages to the beginning of the twentieth century.

Hunt, Stephen J. *The Life Course: A Sociological Introduction.* New York: Palgrave McMillan, 2006. This book gives an overview of the life course while considering what is distinct about a sociological approach to this topic.

Lareau, Annette. *Unequal Childhoods: Class, Race, and Family Life.* Berkeley: University of California Press, 2003. The author documents differences in child rearing in poor, working-class, and middle-class U.S. families.

Rymer, Russ. *Genie: A Scientific Tragedy.* New York: HarperPerennial Library, 1994. This account of Genie includes the battles to oversee Genie among linguists, psychologists, and social workers, all of whom claimed to have Genie's best interests at heart.

Segal, Nancy L. *Entwined Lives: Twins and What They Tell Us About Human Behavior.* New York: Plume, 2001. This summary of research on twins and human behavior is thorough, but, unfortunately, provides little basis from which to draw firm conclusions.

Settersten, Richard A., Jr., and Timothy J. Owens, eds. *New Frontiers in Socialization.* Greenwich, Conn.: JAI Press, 2003. The authors of these articles focus on the adult years in the life course, examining the influence of families, neighborhoods, communities, friendship, education, work, volunteer associations, medical institutions, and the media.

Sociological Studies of Child Development: A Research Annual. Greenwich, Conn.: JAI Press, published annually. Along with theoretical articles, this publication reports on sociological research on the socialization of children.

CHAPTER 4 Social Structure and Social Interaction

Goffman, Erving. *The Presentation of Self in Everyday Life.* New York: Peter Smith, Publisher, 1999. First published in 1959, this classic statement of dramaturgical analysis provides a different way of looking at everyday life. This was one of the best books I read as a student.

Johnson, Kim K. P., and Sharron J. Lennon, eds. *Appearance and Power.* Oxford, U.K.: Berg Publishers, 2000. The authors of these articles analyze how significant appearance, especially clothing, is for what happens to us in social life.

LeBesco, Kathleen. *Revolting Bodies: The Struggle to Redefine Fat Identity.* Amherst, Mass.: University of Massachusetts Press, 2004. This analysis of the political struggle over the cultural meaning of fatness examines oppression and negative stereotypes.

Schauer, Frederick. *Profiles, Probabilities, and Stereotypes.* Cambridge, Mass: Belknap Press, 2004. The focus of this book is the question of whether we can generalize about members of a group on the basis of the statistical tendencies of that group.

Schmidt, Kimberly D., Diane Zimmerman Umble, and Steven D. Reschly, eds. *Strangers at Home: Amish and Mennonite Women in History.* Baltimore: Johns Hopkins University Press, 2002. These accounts of the experiences of Amish and Mennonite women provide a window onto history, as well as insight into how social structure influences social interaction.

Seidman, Steven. *The Social Construction of Sexuality.* New York: W.W. Norton, 2004. The author explores how society influences our sexual choices, our beliefs about sexuality, and our sexual standards.

Tönnies, Ferdinand. *Community and Society (Gemeinschaft und Gesellschaft).* New York: Dover Publications, 2003. Originally published in 1887, this classic work, focusing on social change, provides insight into how society influences personality. It is rather challenging reading.

Whyte, William Foote. *Street Corner Society: The Social Structure of an Italian Slum,* 4th ed. Chicago: University of Chicago Press, 1993. Originally published in 1943. The author's analysis of interaction in a U.S. Italian slum demonstrates how social structure affects personal relationships.

Journals

Qualitative Sociology, Symbolic Interaction, and *Urban Life* feature articles on symbolic interactionism and analyses of everyday life.

CHAPTER 5 Social Groups and Formal Organizations

Ackoff, Russell L., and Sheldon Rovin. *Beating the System: Using Creativity to Outsmart Bureaucracies.* San Francisco: Berrett-Koehler, Publishers, 2005. This analysis can be applied to everyday situations, such as avoiding getting lost in a maze as you try to solve a problem with the phone company or some other bureaucracy.

Bakan, Joel. *The Corporation: The Pathological Pursuit of Profit and Power.* New York: The Free Press, 2004. The author's thesis is that the corporation's lust for power undermines democracy, social justice, equality, and compassion.

Cross, Robert, and Andrew Parker. *The Hidden Power of Social Networks: Understanding How Work Really Gets Done in Organizations.* Cambridge, Mass: Harvard Business School Press, 2004. Based on their research and experience in organizations, the authors explain how understanding networks can improve communication and productivity.

Fineman, Stephen, Gabriel Yiannis, and David P. Sims. *Organizing and Organizations,* 3rd ed. Beverly Hills, Calif.: Sage Publications, 2006. The authors draw on many first-hand accounts to help enliven the study of formal organizations.

Hall, Richard H., and Pamela S. Tolbert. *Organizations: Structures, Processes, and Outcomes,* 9th ed. Upper Saddle River, N.J.: 2005. The focus of this review of the literature on social organizations is on the impacts that organizations have upon individuals and society.

Homans, George C. *The Human Group.* New Brunswick, N.J.: Transaction Publishers, 2001. First published in 1950. In this classic work, the author develops the idea that all human groups share common activities, interactions, and sentiments.

Hughes, Richard L., Robert C. Ginnett, and Gordon J. Curphy. *Leadership: Enhancing the Lessons of Experience,* 5th ed. New York: McGraw-Hill, 2005. Supplementing empirical studies with illustrative anecdotes, the authors focus on what makes effective leaders.

Janis, Irving L. *Groupthink: Psychological Studies of Policy Decisions and Fiascoes,* 2nd ed. New York: Houghton Mifflin, 1982. Janis analyzes how groups can become cut off from alternatives, interpret evidence in light of their preconceptions, and embark on courses of action that they should have seen as obviously incorrect.

Parkinson, C. Northcote. *Parkinson's Law.* Boston: Buccaneer Books, 1997. Although this exposé of the inner workings of bureaucracies is delightfully satirical, if what Parkinson analyzes were generally true, bureaucracies would always fail.

Putnam, Robert D., and Lewis M. Feldstein. *Better Together.* New York: Simon and Schuster, 2003. The authors' premise is that Americans' sense of community has deteriorated over the past two generations; they provide case studies on what some communities have done to develop networks of mutual support.

Ritzer, George. *The McDonaldization of Society: An Investigation into the Changing Character of Contemporary Life,* 4th ed. Thousand Oaks, Calif.: Pine Forge Press, 2004. The author examines how Durkheim's predictions about the rationalization of society are coming true in everyday life.

Wilson, Gerald L. *Groups in Context: Leadership and Participation in Small Groups,* 7th ed. New York: McGraw-Hill, 2005. The book provides an overview of principles and processes of interaction in small groups, with an emphasis on how to exercise leadership.

CHAPTER 6 Deviance and Social Control

Girshick, Lori B. *No Safe Haven: Stories of Women in Prison.* Boston: Northeastern University Press, 2001. Do women occupy a special status in the criminal justice system? The author analyzes the life stories of forty imprisoned women to help find the answer.

Goffman, Erving. *Stigma: Notes on the Management of Spoiled Identity.* New York: Simon & Schuster, 1986. First published in 1968. The author outlines the social and personal reactions to "spoiled identity," appearances that—due to disability, weight, ethnicity, birth marks, and so on—do not match dominant expectations.

Goode, Erich. *Deviance in Everyday Life: Personal Accounts of Unconventional Lives.* Prospect Heights, Il.: Waveland Press, 2002. The author provides insight into the process of becoming deviant and an understanding of how people justify their norm violations.

Hendershott, Anne. *The Politics of Deviance.* San Francisco: Encounter Books, 2002. The author protests the medicalization of deviance, the mainstreaming of deviance, and social reactions to deviance that replace personal accountability.

Jankowski, Martín Sánchez. *Islands in the Street: Gangs and American Urban Society.* Berkeley: University of California Press, 1992. The author's report on his participant observation of street gangs provides insightful understanding into the gang members' lives.

Lintner, Bert. *Blood Brothers: The Criminal Underworld of Asia.* New York: Palgrave MacMillan, 2004. This book maps out the topography of organized crime in East Asia.

Lombroso, Cesare, Guglielmo Ferrero, Nicole Hahn Rafter, and Mary Gibson. *Criminal Woman, the Prostitute, and the Normal Woman.* Durham, N.C.: Duke University Press, 2005. This translation of a classic work from the 1800s on women and crime is put into current social context by two researchers on female criminals.

Lott, John R., Jr. *More Guns, Less Crime.* Chicago: University of Chicago Press, 2000. After reviewing state data on crime and right-to-carry gun laws, the author comes to the surprising conclusion that more guns mean less crime.

Rathbone, Cristina. *A World Apart: Women, Prison, and Life Behind Bars.* New York: Random House, 2006. A journalist's account of the four years she spent investigating MCI Framingham, the oldest women's prison in the United States.

Reiman, Jeffrey. *The Rich Get Richer and the Poor Get Prison: Ideology, Class, and Criminal Justice,* 7th ed. Boston: Allyn and Bacon, 2004. An analysis of how social class works to produce different types of criminals and different types of justice.

Rodriguez, Luis J. *The Republic of East L.A.: Stories.* Los Angeles: Rayo, 2003. These hard-hitting vignettes let the reader know what life is like in this poverty-plagued section of Los Angeles.

Scott, Kody (Sanyika Shakur). *Monster: The Autobiography of an L.A. Gang Member.* New York: Addison Wesley, 1998. This intriguing insider's view of gang life provides a rare glimpse of the power of countercultural norms.

Silberman, Matthew, ed. *Violence and Society: A Reader.* Upper Saddle River, N.J.: Prentice Hall, 2003. As the authors of these articles analyze the social factors that underlie violence, they focus on social inequality, culture, and family, sexual, and criminal violence.

Journals

Criminal Justice Review: Issues in Criminal, Social, and Restorative Justice and *Journal of Law and Society* examine the social forces that shape law and justice.

CHAPTER 7 Global Stratification

Deliege, Robert. *The Untouchables of India.* Oxford, U.K.: Berg, 2001. The author provides an overview of India's caste system, with an emphasis on the *Dalits,* or untouchables.

Friedman, Thomas L. *The World Is Flat.* New York: Farrar, Straus, and Giroux, 2005. The author envisions a global economy where, in addition to powerful transnational corporations, individuals use inexpensive technology to compete for international business.

Held, David, and Anthony McGrew, eds. *Global Transformations Reader: An Introduction to the Globalization Debate.* Cambridge, U.K.: Polity Press, 2003. The authors of these articles analyze how globalization is transforming state power, national cultures, the world economy, global inequality, and environmental challenges.

Huggins, Martha K., Mika Haritos-Fatouros, and Philip G. Zimbardo. *Violence Workers: Police Torturers and Murderers Reconstruct Brazilian Atrocities.* Berkeley: University of California Press, 2002. If you want an insider's perspective in order to understand how ordinary people can rape, torture, and kill, this book will provide it.

Ritzer, George. *The Globalization of Nothing.* Thousand Oaks, Calif: Pine Forge Press, 2004. The author expresses concerns about the short- and long-term effects of globalization.

Sachs, Jeffrey D. *The End of Poverty: Economic Possibilities for Our Time.* East Rutherford, N.J.: Penguin Press, 2005. After visiting 100 countries, representing 90% of the world's population, the author suggests ways that we can end global poverty.

Sernau, Scott. *Worlds Apart: Social Inequalities in a Global Economy,* 2nd ed. Thousand Oaks, Calif.: Pine Forge Press, 2005. The author's thesis is that the market-driven global economy contributes to rather than reduces social inequality.

Sklair, Leslie. *Globalization: Capitalism and its Alternatives,* 3rd ed. Oxford, U.K.: Oxford University Press, 2003. The author identifies positive aspects of globalization, along with limitations of capitalism.

Wilkins, David E., and K. Tsianina Lomawaima. *Uneven Ground: American Indian Sovereignty and Federal Law.* Norman: University of Oklahoma Press, 2002. The author traces the relationship of Native Americans and the U.S. government.

Zakaria, Fareed. *The Future of Freedom: Illiberal Democracy at Home and Abroad.* New York: W.W. Norton, 2004. The author considers whether democracy is the best alternative in different parts of the world, and suggests that democracy requires strong limits to function properly.

CHAPTER 8 Social Class in the United States

Beeghley, Leonard. *The Structure of Social Stratification in the United States,* 4th ed. Boston: Pearson, 2005. In this brief book, the author presents an overview of the U.S. social classes.

Bowles, Samuel, Herbert Gintis, and Melissa Osborne Groves, eds. *Unequal Chances: Family Background and Economic Success.* New York: Russell Sage, 2005. The authors of these articles focus on how our economic origins affect our social destination as adults.

Ehrenreich, Barbara. *Nickel and Dimed: On (Not) Getting By in America.* New York: Metropolitan Books, 2001. The author, a sociologist, takes a series of unskilled, minimum-wage jobs—and tries to live on her earnings.

Florida, Richard. *The Rise of the Creative Class: And How It's Transforming Work, Leisure, Community and Everyday Life.* New York: Basic Books, 2004. The author's thesis is that a new social class has evolved, consisting of scientists, engineers, architects, educators, writers, artists, and entertainers, and that this class needs to become cohesive and work for the common good.

Gatewood, Willard B. *Aristocrats of Color: The Black Elite, 1880–1920.* Fayetteville: University of Arkansas Press, 2000. Analyzing the rise and decline of the African American upper class that developed after the Civil War, the author focuses on marriage, occupations, education, religion, clubs, and relationships with whites and with African Americans of lower classes.

Liebow, Elliot. *Tally's Corner: A Study of Negro Streetcorner Men.* Boston: Little, Brown, 1999. First published in 1968. The author's participant observation with a group of Washington, D.C., African American men provides insight into the dynamics of their decision making and relationships.

Moscowitz, Marina. *Standard of Living: The Measure of the Middle Class in Modern America.* Baltimore, Md: Johns Hopkins University Press, 2005. The author focuses on the relationship between middle class identity and material culture.

Neckerman, Kathryn. *Social Inequality.* New York: Russell Sage, 2004. The author examines implications of the increasing economic inequality analyzed in this chapter for the quality of family and neighborhood life, access to education and health care, job satisfaction, and political participation.

Perucci, Robert, and Earl Wyson. *The New Class Society,* 2nd ed. Lanham, Md.: Rowman and Littlefield, 2003. An overview of the U.S. social class structure, with the suggestion that no longer is there a middle class.

Schram, Sanford F. *Praxis for the Poor: Piven and Cloward and the Future of Social Science in Social Welfare.* Albany: New York University Press, 2003. The author's thesis is that politically engaged scholarship can contribute to the struggle for social justice.

Wilson, William Julius. *When Work Disappears: The World of the New Urban Poor.* New York: Knopf, 1997. The author analyzes consequences of the disappearance of unskilled jobs near the inner city: the destruction of inner-city businesses, the flight of the middle class, and the stranding of poor people who have few alternatives.

Zweig, Michael. *What's Class Got to Do With It?: American Society in the Twenty-First Century.* Ithaca, N.Y.: ILR Press, 2004. The author explains how social class is central to our everyday lives, how it shapes our life chances both as children and as adults.

Journals

Journal of Children and Poverty and *Journal of Poverty* analyze issues that affect the quality of life of people who live in poverty.

Race, Gender, and Class publishes interdisciplinary articles on the topics listed in its title.

CHAPTER 9 Race and Ethnicity

Acosta, Teresa Palomo, and Ruthe Winegarten. *Los Tejanas: 300 Years of History.* Austin: University of Texas Press, 2003. This account traces how Tejanas in the colonial period and from the Republic of Texas up to 1900 overcame obstacles to their success.

Blee, Kathleen M. *Inside Organized Racism: Women in the Hate Movement.* Berkeley: University of California Press, 2002. Why and how do people join hate groups? The author's research provides answers to this troubling question.

Deutscher, Irwin, and Linda Lindsey. *Preventing Ethnic Conflict: Successful Cross-National Strategies.* Lanham, Md.: Lexington Books, 2005. Instead of focusing on what doesn't work, the authors examine positive ethnic relationships around the world.

Dray, Phillip. *At the Hands of Persons Unknown: The Lynching of Black America.* New York: The Modern Library, 2004. The author examines the history of the lynching of African Americans and the social background behind these acts.

Du Bois, W. E. B. *Black Reconstruction in America: An Essay Toward a History of the Part Which Black Folk Played in the Attempt to Reconstruct Democracy in America, 1860–1880.* New York: Harcourt, Brace 1935; New York: The Free Press, 2000. This analysis of the role of African Americans in the Civil War and during the years immediately following provides a glimpse into a neglected part of U.S. history.

Hilberg, Raul. *The Destruction of the European Jews,* 3rd ed. New Haven: Yale University Press, 2003. The focus of this book is the machinery of death that the Nazis put together to annihilate the Jewish community of Europe.

Mander, Jerry. *In the Absence of the Sacred: The Failure of Technology and the Survival of the Indian Nations.* New York: Pete Smith, Publisher, 1999. With a focus on the impact of technology, the author analyzes past and present relations of Native Americans and the U.S. government.

Mueller, Timothy, and Sarah Sue Goldsmith. *Nations Within: The Four Sovereign Tribes of Louisiana.* Baton Rouge: University of Louisiana Press, 2004. Analyzes the relationship of four sovereign nations to the dominant, colonizing governmental power.

Parrillo, Vincent, N. *Strangers to these Shores: Race and Ethnic Relations in the United States,* 8th ed. Boston: Allyn and Bacon, 2006. This text reviews the experiences of more than 50 racial-ethnic groups.

Ryan, Nick. *Into a World of Hate.* New York: Routledge, 2005. The author spent six years exploring the underworld of hatred in Europe and the United States.

Smith, Andrea. *Conquest: Sexual Violence and American Indian Genocide.* Cambridge, Mass.: South End Press, 2005. The author's thesis is that almost all acts that negatively impact Native Americans can be interpreted as a form of sexual violence and genocide.

Sowell, Thomas. *Black Rednecks and White Liberals.* San Francisco: Encounter Books, 2005. In this provocative and controversial analysis, the author places ghetto culture, slavery, the education of African Americans, and the exportation of democracy in socio-historical context.

Walker, Samuel, Cassia Spohn, and Miriam Delone. *The Color of Justice: Race, Ethnicity, and Crime in America,* 4th ed. Belmont, Calif.: Wadsworth, 2007. The authors analyze racial, ethnic, and gender discrimination in the criminal justice system.

Wilson, William Julius. *The Bridge over the Racial Divide: Rising Inequality and Coalition Politics.* Berkeley: University of California Press, 2000. The author analyzes how monetary, trade, and tax policies increase social inequality; he includes recommendations to increase multiracial political cooperation.

CHAPTER 10 Inequalities of Gender and Age

Inequalities of Gender

Anderson, Margaret L. *Thinking about Women: Sociological Perspectives on Sex and Gender,* 7th ed. Boston: Allyn and Bacon, 2006. An overview of the main issues of sex and gender in contemporary society, ranging from sexism and socialization to work and health.

Beynon, John. *Masculinities and Culture.* Philadelphia: Open University Press, 2002. The author's thesis is that because masculinity is shaped by society and culture, differing from place to place and time to time, the term "masculinities" is more appropriate.

Brettell, Caroline B., and Carolyn F. Sargent, eds. *Gender in Cross-Cultural Perspective,* 4th ed. Upper Saddle River, N.J.: Prentice Hall, 2005. The net is spread wide as the authors examine gender and biology, in prehistory, at home, and the divi-

sion of labor, and the body, property, kinship, religion, politics, and the global economy.

Colapinto, John. *As Nature Made Him: The Boy Who Was Raised as a Girl.* New York: HarperCollins, 2001. This is a detailed account of the event summarized in this chapter of the boy whose penis was accidentally burned off.

Gilbert, Paula Ruth, and Kimberly K. Eby, eds. *Violence and Gender: An Interdisciplinary Reader.* Upper Saddle River:, N.J. Prentice Hall, 2004. The authors of these articles examine violence and youth, the human body, war, intimacy, sports, the media, and how to prevent violence.

Gilman, Charlotte Perkins. *The Man-Made World or, Our Androcentric Culture.* New York: Charlton, 1911. Reprinted in 1971 by Johnson Reprint. This early book on women's liberation provides an excellent view of female-male relations at the beginning of the last century.

Goldberg, Steven. *Why Men Rule: A Theory of Male Dominance.* Chicago: Open Court, 1994. A detailed explanation of the author's theory of male dominance featured in this chapter.

Johnson, Allan G. *Privilege, Power, and Difference.* New York: McGraw-Hill, 2003. The author helps us see the nature and consequences of privilege and our connection to it.

Kimmel, Michael S., ed. *The Gendered Society Reader,* 2nd ed. New York: Oxford University Press, 2004. The authors of these articles examine the relationship of gender and violence in the contexts of culture, family, classroom, workplace, and intimacy.

Kimmel, Michael S., and Michael A. Messner, eds. *Men's Lives,* 7th ed. Boston: Allyn and Bacon, 2007. The authors of these articles examine issues of sex and gender as they affect men. The articles often provide different views from those presented in the Anderson book.

Lorber, Judith, and Lisa Jean Moore. *Gender and the Social Construction of Illness,* 2nd ed. Lanham, Md.: Rowman and Littlefield, 2003. Taking the position that both gender and medicine are social institutions, the authors examine their interrelationships.

Renzetti, Claire, and Daniel J. Curran. *Women, Men, and Society,* 6th ed. Boston: Allyn and Bacon, 2007. This basic text summarizes major issues in the sociology of gender.

Wharton, Amy S. *The Sociology of Gender: An Introduction to Theory and Research.* Medford, Mass.: Blackwell Publishers, 2005. Research on gender is viewed through three frameworks: the individual, the interactional, and the institutional.

Wolf, Naomi. *The Beauty Myth: How Images of Beauty Are Used Against Women.* New York: Harper Perennial, 2003. The author analyzes the unrealistic images of female beauty portrayed in the media.

Journals

These journals focus on the role of gender in social life: *Feminist Studies; Gender and Behavior; Gender and Society; Forum in Women's and Gender Studies; Gender and History; Gender, Place and Culture: A Journal of Feminist Geography; Journal of Gender, Culture, and Health; Journal of Interdisciplinary Gender Studies; Journal of Men's Health and Gender; Sex Roles;* and *Signs: Journal of Women in Culture and Society.*

Inequalities of Age

Dychtwald, Ken. *Age Power: How the 21st Century Will Be Ruled by the New Old.* Los Angeles: J.P. Tarcher, 2001. The author speculates on how the growing numbers of elderly will affect society, and suggests how we should prepare for the coming change.

Gass, Thomas Edward, and Bruce C. Vladeck. *Nobody's Home: Candid Reflections of a Nursing Home Aide.* Ithaca, N.Y.: ILR Press, 2004. A first-hand account of the reality of life in a nursing home.

Gubrium, Jaber F., and James A. Holstein, eds. *Ways of Aging.* Malden, Mass.: Blackwell Publishers, 2003. The authors of these articles examine how people construct their self definitions as they adjust to the realities of aging bodies.

Hatch, Laurie Russell. *Beyond Gender Differences: Adaptation to Aging in Life Course Perspective.* Amityville, N.Y.: Baywood Publishing Company, 2000. The author reviews the research on how men and women adapt to growing old.

Hooyman, Nancy, and H. Asuman Kiyak. *Social Gerontology: A Multidisciplinary Perspective,* 7th ed. Boston: Allyn and Bacon, 2005. As the authors consider factors that influence how people experience old age, they cover differences by age and cohort, gender, race-ethnicity, sexual orientation, and socioeconomic status.

Quadagno, Jill S. *Aging and the Life Course: An Introduction to Social Gerontology,* 3rd ed. New York: McGraw-Hill, 2004. In this review of major issues in gerontology, the author examines how the quality of life that people experience in old age is the result of earlier choices, opportunities, and constraints.

Roszak, Theodore. *The Longevity Revolution: As Boomers Become Elders.* Berkeley, Calif.: Berkeley Hills Books, 2001. The author's thesis is that the elderly are not a burden to society, but a great resource.

Rubin, Lillian B. *Tangled Lives: Daughters, Mothers, and the Crucible of Aging.* Boston: Beacon Press, 2002. The author reflects on her own experiences with illness and death to try to come to grips with the meaning of growing old—and of life.

Stoller, Eleanor Palo, and Rose Campbell Gibson. *Worlds of Difference: Inequality in the Aging Experience,* 3rd ed. Thousand Oaks, Calif.: Pine Forge Press, 2002. The authors document inequalities borne by the U.S. elderly and explain the social conditions that create those inequalities.

Journals

Elderly Latinos; The Gerontologist, Journal of Aging and Identity; Journal of Aging and Social Policy; Journal of Aging Studies; Journal of Cross-Cultural Gerontology; Journal of Elder Abuse and Neglect; Journal of Gerontology; and *Journal of Women and Aging* focus on issues of aging, while *Youth and Society* and *Journal of Youth Studies* examine adolescent culture.

CHAPTER 11   Politics and the Economy

Politics

Amnesty International. *Amnesty International Report.* London: Amnesty International Publications, published annually. This report summarizes human rights violations around the world, listing specific instances, including names, country by country.

Barstow, Anne Llewellyn, ed. *War's Dirty Secret: Rape, Prostitution, and Other Crimes Against Women.* New York: Pilgrim Press, 2003. The authors of these articles document how sexual violence against women accompanies war in Africa, Asia, Europe, and the Americas.

Byman, Daniel. *Deadly Connections: States that Sponsor Terrorism.* Cambridge, U.K.: Cambridge University Press, 2005. The author examines the different types of support that states provide terrorists, their motivations for doing so, and the impact of their sponsorship.

Domhoff, G. William. *Who Rules America?: Power and Politics,* 5th ed. New York: McGraw-Hill, 2006. An analysis of how the multinational corporations dominate the U.S. government.

Ferguson, Charles D., and William C. Potter. *The Four Faces of Nuclear Terrorism.* New York: Routledge, 2005. The authors examine the motivations and capabilities of terrorist organizations to acquire and use nuclear weapons and recommend ways to prevent nuclear terrorism and to reduce the consequences of the most likely nuclear terror attacks.

Ginzburg, Eugenia Semyonovna. *Journey into the Whirlwind.* New York: Harvest Books, 2003. The autobiographical and moving account of a woman who spent 18 years in Stalin's prison camps.

McFaul, Michael, Nikolai Petrov, and Andrei Ryabov. *Between Dictatorship and Democracy: Russian Post-Communist Political Reform.* Washington, D.C.: Carnegie Endowment for International Peace, 2004. An account of Russia's transition to capitalism, including the modification of its social institutions.

Mills, C. Wright. *The Power Elite,* 2nd ed. New York: Textbook Publishers, 2003. First published in 1956. This classic analysis elaborates the conflict thesis summarized in this chapter—that U.S. society is ruled by the nation's top corporate leaders, together with an elite from the military and political institutions.

Research in Political Sociology: A Research Annual. Greenwich, Conn.: JAI Press. This annual publication is not recommended for beginners, as the findings and theories are often difficult and abstract. It does, however, analyze political topics of vital concern to our well-being.

Journals

Many sociology journals publish articles on politics. Four that focus on this area of social life are *American Political Science Review, Journal of Political and Military Sociology, Social Policy,* and *Social Politics.*

The Economy

Amott, Teresa. *Caught in the Crisis: Women and the U.S. Economy Today,* 2nd ed. New York: Monthly Review Press, 2004. The author provides an analysis of how the transformation of the economy is affecting women.

Bales, Kevin. *Disposable People: New Slavery in the Global Economy,* revised edition. Berkeley: University of California Press, 2005. The author documents the relationship between the globalization of capitalism and current slavery in Brazil, India, Mauritania, Pakistan, and Thailand.

Bergsten, C. Fred. *The United States and the World Economy.* Washington, D.C.: Institute for International Economics, 2005. This analysis of the globalization of capitalism focuses on how the prosperity of the United States is related to the world economy.

Chua, Amy. *World on Fire: How Exporting Free Market Democracy Breeds Ethnic Hatred and Global Instability.* New York: Doubleday, 2003. The author's thesis is that the globalization of capitalism has brought economic devastation, ethnic hatreds, and genocidal violence throughout the Least Industrialized Nations.

Katz, Richard. *Japanese Phoenix: The Long Road to Economic Revival.* New York: M. E. Sharpe, 2003. The author explains why the Japanese economy faltered and suggests reforms to restore economic growth.

Konecny, Peter. *Gogol's Ghost: Life in St. Petersburg Between Communism and Capitalism.* Lincoln, Nebr: Writer's Club Press, 2003. Examines life in St. Petersburg in the early years of Russia's transformation from communism to capitalism.

Lenin, Vladimir Ilyich. *The Development of Capitalism in Russia.* Honolulu, Hawaii: University Press of the Pacific, 2004. This is an English translation of Lenin's 1899 book.

Lucarelli, Bill. *Monopoly Capitalism in Crisis.* New York: Palgrave Macmillan, 2005. Is U.S. prosperity about to end? The author argues that the global economy is about to deflate owing to excess global production capacity.

Stiglitz, Joseph E. *Globalization and Its Discontents.* New York: W.W. Norton, 2003. The author, who served as Chair of the President's Council of Economic Advisors, documents how politicians put the interests of Wall Street ahead of the needs of the Least Industrialized Nations.

CHAPTER 12   Marriage and Family

Contreras, Josefina M., Kathryn A. Kerns, and Angela M. Neal-Barnett. *Latino Children and Families in the United States: Current Research and Future Directions.* New York: Praeger, 2003. The authors consider how parenting beliefs and practices of Latinos differ by socioeconomic and cultural backgrounds and try to identify family values that can be considered "Latino."

Coontz, Stephanie. *Marriage, a History: From Obedience to Intimacy or How Love Conquered Marriage.* New York: Viking, 2005. This analysis of how the fundamental orientations to marriage have changed contains enlightening excerpts from the past.

Edin, Kathryn, and Maria Kefalas. *Promises I Can Keep: Why Poor Women Put Motherhood Before Marriage.* Berkeley: University of California Press, 2005. The author's interviews provide insight into how low-income single mothers think about marriage and family.

Epstein, Cynthia Fuchs, and Arne L Kalleberg, eds. *Fighting for Time: Shifting Boundaries of Work and Social Life.* New York: Russell Sage, 2005. The authors explore changes in the time people spend at work and the consequences of those changes for individuals and families.

Hochschild, Arlie Russell. *The Time Bind: When Work Becomes Home and Home Becomes Work.* New York: Owl Books, 2001. Do parents really want to spend more time with their families and less at work? Or do parents flee families, finding work a respite from family pressures? The author presents some surprising answers.

Johnson, Leonor Boulin, and Robert Staples. *Black Families at the Crossroads: Challenges and Prospects.* New York: Jossey-Bass, 2005. After placing today's black families in historical context, the authors analyze the impact of economic policies and social change.

Plane, Ann Marie. *Colonial Intimacies: Indian Marriage in Early New England.* Ithaca, N.Y.: Cornell University Press, 2000. Based on legal records, travel narratives, and missionary tracts, the author analyzes Native American–white marriages during the first century and a half of Native American contact with Europeans.

Romano, Renee Christine. *Race Mixing: Black-White Marriage in Postwar America.* Cambridge, Mass.: Harvard University Press, 2003. The author provides the legislative background on these marriages, plus social trends, accompanied by first person accounts.

Wallace, Harvey. *Family Violence,* 4th ed. Boston: Allyn and Bacon, 2005. This overview examines family violence through three perspectives: legal, medical, and social.

Journals

Family Relations; The History of the Family; International Journal of Sociology of the Family; Journal of Comparative Family Studies; Journal of Divorce; Journal of Divorce and Remarriage; Journal of Family and Economic Issues; Journal of Family Issues; Journal of Family Violence; Journal of Marriage and the Family; and *Marriage and Family Review* publish articles on almost every aspect of marriage and family life.

CHAPTER 13   Education and Religion

Education

Corwin, Miles. *And Still We Rise: The Trials and Triumphs of 12 Gifted Inner City Students.* New York: HarperPerennial Library, 2001. The author, a journalist who spent a year in a South Los Angeles high school, details the lives of twelve students in an advanced placement program.

Hess, Frederick M. *Common Sense School Reform.* New York: Palgrave Macmillan, 2005. Critical of current efforts to reform U.S. education, the author makes the case that reform needs to be based around accountability, competition, and leadership.

Kozol, Jonathan. *Ordinary Resurrections: Children in the Years of Hope.* New York: Crown Publishers, 2001. To listen as these children from a dismal neighborhood in South Bronx talk about life is to become aware of the potential that schools have to transform the lives of children in poverty.

Lee, Valerie E., and David T. Burkam. *Inequality at the Starting Gate: Social Background Differences in Achievement as Children Begin School.* Washington, D.C.: Economic Policy Institute, 2002. This short book gives a crisp analysis that documents social class and racial-ethnic advantage and disadvantage at kindergarten.

Lopez, Nancy. *Hopeful Girls, Troubled Boys: Race and Gender Disparity in Urban Education.* New York: Rutledge, 2003. Building on her thesis that education is failing boys of color, the author suggests ways to improve education.

Rothstein, Richard. *Class and Schools: Using Social, Economic, and Educational Reform to Close the Black-White Achievement Gap.* Washington, D.C.: Economic Policy Institute, 2004. The author's thesis is that because social class influences learning in school, public policy must address the social and economic conditions of children's lives.

Spring, Joel H. *Deculturalization and the Struggle for Equality: A Brief History of the Education of Dominated Cultures in the United States,* 4th ed, New York: McGraw-Hill 2004. The author examines how Anglos have used their control of schools to strip away the cultures of minorities and replace them with Anglo culture.

Stevens, Michael L. *Kingdom of Children: Culture and Controversy in the Homeschooling Movement.* Princeton: Princeton University Press, 2003. This analysis of the home schooling movement, based on interviews and participant observation, contains numerous quotations that provide insight into why parents home school their children.

Weiler, Jeanne Drysdale. *Codes and Contradictions: Race, Gender Identity, and Schooling.* New York: State University of New York Press, 2000. After studying girls of African American, Latina, Puerto Rican, and European backgrounds who are at risk of failing in school, the author concludes that schools are able to reorient young women so they perceive educational success as crucial to their future well-being.

Journals

The following journals contain articles that examine almost every aspect of education: *Education and Urban Society, Harvard Educational Review, Sociology and Education,* and *Sociology of Education.*

Religion

Cateura, Linda Brandi, and Omid Safi. *Voices of American Muslims.* New York: Hippocrene Books, 2006. U.S. Muslims describe their religion, experiences with suspicion and misunderstandings, and, in this heated period of terrorist attacks by Muslims, their devotion to the United States.

Gilman, Sander. *Jewish Frontiers: Essays on Bodies, Histories, and Identities.* New York: Macmillan, 2003. The author analyzes Jewish identity from the framework of living on a frontier, and the representation of this identity in the mass media.

Juergensmeyer, Mark. *Terror in the Mind of God: The Global Rise of Religious Violence,* 3rd ed. Berkeley: University of California Press, 2003. The author's summaries of religious violence provide a rich background for understanding this behavior.

Mazur, Eric Michael. *The Americanization of Religious Minorities: Confronting the Constitutional Order.* Baltimore: Johns Hopkins University Press, 2000. What happens when religious beliefs conflict with U.S. law? The author analyzes the experiences of Jehovah's Witnesses, Mormons, and Native Americans.

McRoberts, Omar M. *Streets of Glory: Church and Community in a Black Urban Neighborhood.* Chicago: University of Chicago Press, 2003. Four Corners, one of the toughest areas of Boston, contains twenty-nine mostly storefront churches. The author finds most of them are attended and run by people who do not live in the neighborhood and who have little or no attachment to the surrounding area.

Smith, Christian, and Melinda Denton. *Soul Searching: The Religious and Spiritual Life of American Teenagers.* Oxford, U.K.: Oxford University Press, 2006. The authors survey the spiritual life of U.S. teenagers.

Thibodeau, David, and Leon Whiteson. *A Place Called Waco: A Survivor's Story.* New York: Public Affairs, 2000. A first-person account of life inside the Branch Davidian compound, written by one of only four survivors of the fire who were not sentenced to prison.

Wolfe, Alan. *The Transformation of American Religion: How We Actually Live Our Faith.* New York: The Free Press, 2004. The author's thesis is that individualism is changing the shape and substance of religion in the United States, minimizing doctrine and maximizing feelings and personal satisfactions.

Zellner, William W., and William M. Kephart. *Extraordinary Groups: An Examination of Unconventional Lifestyles,* 7th ed. New York: Worth, 2001. This sketch of the history and characteristics of eight groups (the Old Order Amish, Oneida Community, Gypsies, Church of Christ Scientist, Hasidim, Father Divine Movement, Mormons, and Jehovah's Witnesses) illustrates how groups can maintain unconventional beliefs and practices.

Journals

These journals publish articles that focus on the sociology of religion: *Journal for the Scientific Study of Religion, Review of Religious Research,* and *Sociological Analysis: A Journal in the Sociology of Religion.*

CHAPTER 14　Population and Urbanization

Department of Agriculture. *Yearbook of Agriculture.* Washington, D.C.: Department of Agriculture, published annually. This yearbook focuses on specific aspects of U.S. agribusiness, especially international economies and trade.

Duneier, Mitchell. *Sidewalk.* New York: Farrar, Straus, Giroux, 2000. This analysis of city streets provides insight into how the urban mosaic works.

Jacobs, Jane. *Dark Age Ahead.* New York: Random House, 2004. The author's thesis is that there are severe indications that the West is headed for another Dark Age, unless we take steps to prevent it.

Lin, Jan, and Christopher Mele, eds. *The Urban Sociology Reader.* New York: Routledge, 2006. The authors of these articles review the major issues in urban change and development.

Mosher, Steven W. *A Mother's Ordeal: One Woman's Fight Against One-Child China.* New York: HarperCollins, 1994. This book puts a human face on China's coercive family planning policies.

Orfield, Myron. *American Metropolitics: The New Suburban Reality.* Washington, D.C.: Brookings Institution Press, 2002. The author explains why regionalism is needed in order to meet the needs of urban areas.

Palen, John J. *The Urban World,* 7th ed. New York: McGraw-Hill, 2005. A short, basic text that summarizes major issues in urban sociology.

Taylor, Monique M. *Harlem: Between Heaven and Hell.* Minneapolis: University of Minnesota Press, 2002. This book provides a history and analysis of contemporary Harlem, with many quotes from current residents.

Tobin, Kathleen A. *Politics and Population Control: A Documentary History.* Westport, Conn.: Greenwood Press, 2005. From the past to the present, the author analyzes how population issues have concerned authorities for centuries.

Tilly, Charles. *The Politics of Collective Violence.* New York: Cambridge University Press, 2003. The author analyzes causes, combinations, and settings that underlie collective violence and tries to identify ways to reduce violence.

Journals

City and Community, Journal of Rural Studies, Journal of Urban Affairs, Review of Regional and Urban Development Studies, Rural Sociology, and *Urban Studies* publish articles whose focus is the city, community, immigration, migration, rural life, and suburbs. *Social Movement Studies* examines the origins, development, organization, context, and impact of social movements.

CHAPTER 15   Social Change: Technology, Social Movements, and the Environment

Brown, Lester R., ed. *State of the World.* New York: Norton, published annually. Experts on environmental issues analyze environmental problems throughout the world; a New Malthusian perspective.

Council on Environmental Quality. *Environmental Quality.* Washington, D.C.: U.S. Government Printing Office, published annually. Each report evaluates the condition of some aspect of the environment.

DuPuis, E. Melanie, ed. *Smoke and Mirrors: The Politics and Culture of Air Pollution.* New York: New York University Press, 2004. The 15 articles in this book review the emergence of air pollution as a social problem and the status of air pollution today.

Fox, Nicols. *Against the Machine: The Hidden Luddite Tradition in Literature, Art, and Individual Lives.* Washington, D.C.: Island Press, 2004. The author covers broad historical ground as he analyzes reactions against modernization in the West.

Gottlieb, Robert. *Environmentalism Unbound: Exploring New Pathways for Change.* Cambridge, Mass.: MIT Press, 2001. The main emphases of this book are food politics or eco-farming and controlling chemical pollution.

Homer-Dixon, Thomas F. *Environment, Scarcity, and Violence.* Princeton: Princeton University Press, 2002. The author argues that the growth in population and production will create environmental scarcities, which, in turn, will lead to insurrections, ethnic clashes, urban unrest, and other forms of violence.

Howard, Russell D., and Reid L. Sawyer, eds. *Terrorism and Counterterrorism: Understanding the New Security Environment, Readings and Interpretations.* New York: McGraw-Hill, 2003. These analyses stress causes of terrorism and suggest steps to take to combat terrorism; a militaristic emphasis runs through the articles.

Inglehart, Ronald L., ed. *Human Values and Social Change: Findings from the World Values Surveys.* Boston: Brill Academic Publishers, 2003. This book provides an overview of how values are changing around the world.

Luker, Kristin. *Abortion and the Politics of Motherhood.* Berkeley: University of California Press, 2000. Based on documents and interviews with pro-choice and pro-life advocates, the author demonstrates how people's moral positions on abortion are related to their views on sexual behavior, the care of children, and family life.

Markell, David L. *Greening NAFTA: The North American Commission for Environmental Cooperation.* Stanford, Calif: Stanford University Press, 2003. As this book makes evident, without winning elections, green politics is having tremendous influence in international affairs and on our lives.

Meyer, David S., Nancy Whittier, and Belinda Robnett, eds. *Social Movements: Identity, Culture, and the State.* New York: Oxford University Press, 2002. Examining wide-ranging social movements, the authors analyze mobilization, organization, strategies, identities, and the culture of social movements.

Naco, Brigitte Lebens. *Terrorism and Counterterrorism: Understanding Threats and Responses in the Post 9/11 World.* New York: Longman, 2006. This overview of terrorism includes both new terror in the post–Cold War world and historical acts of terror.

Rogers, Everett M. *Diffusion of Innovations,* 5th ed. New York: The Free Press, 2003. The author takes you on a tour of the world, examining the acceptance and rejection of innovations, and the success and failure of each.

Journals

Earth First! Journal and *Sierra,* magazines published by Earth First! and the Sierra Club respectively, are excellent sources for keeping informed of major developments in the environmental movement.

REFERENCES

Aberg, Yvonne. *Social Interactions: Studies of Contextual Effects and Endogenous Processes.* Doctoral Dissertation, Department of Sociology, Stockholm University, 2003.

Aberle, David. *The Peyote Religion among the Navaho.* Chicago: Aldine, 1966.

Addams, Jane. *Twenty Years at Hull-House.* New York: Signet, 1981. First published in 1910.

Adler, Patricia A., and Peter Adler. *Peer Power: Preadolescent Culture and Identity.* New Brunswick, N.J.: Rutgers University Press, 1998.

Adorno, Theodor W., Else Frenkel-Brunswick, D. J. Levinson, and R. N. Sanford. *The Authoritarian Personality.* New York: Harper & Row, 1950.

Aeppel, Timothy. "More Amish Women Are Tending to Business." *Wall Street Journal,* February 8, 1996:B1, B2.

Ahlburg, Dennis A., and Carol J. De Vita. "New Realities of the American Family." *Population Bulletin, 47,* 2, August 1992:1–44.

Akol, Jacob. "Slavery in Sudan." *New African,* September 1998.

Alarid, Leanne Fiftal, Velmer S. Burton, Jr., and Francis T. Cullen. "Gender and Crime among Felony Offenders: Assessing the Generality of Social Control and Differential Association Theories." *Journal of Research in Crime and Delinquency, 37,* 2, May 2000:171–199.

Alba, Richard, and Victor Nee. *Remaking the American Mainstream: Assimilation and Contemporary Immigration.* Cambridge, Mass.: Harvard University Press, 2003.

Aldrich, Nelson W., Jr. *Old Money: The Mythology of America's Upper Class.* New York: Vintage Books, 1989.

Alexander, Gerianne M., and Melissa Hines. "Sex Differences in Response to Children's Toys in Nonhuman Primates." *Evolution and Human Behavior, 23,* 2002:467–479.

Allport, Floyd. *Social Psychology.* Boston: Houghton Mifflin, 1954.

Amato, Paul R., and Jacob Cheadle. "The Long Reach of Divorce: Divorce and Child Well-Being Across Three Generations." *Journal of Marriage and Family, 67,* February 2005:191–206.

Amato, Paul R., and Juliana M. Sobolewski. "The Effects of Divorce and Marital Discord on Adult Children's Psychological Well-Being." *American Sociological Review, 66,* 6, December 2001:900–921.

Amato, Paul R., David R. Johnson, Alan Booth, and Stacy J. Rogers, "Continuity and Change in Marital Quality Between 1980 and 2000." *Journal of Marriage and Family, 65,* February 2003:1–22.

Amenta, Edwin, Drew Halfmann, and Michael P. Young. "The Strategies and Contexts of Social Protest: Political Mediation and the Impact of the Townsend Movement in California." *Mobilization, 4,* 1, April 1999:1–23.

America's Children: Key National Indicators of Well-Being 2005. Washington, D.C.: Federal Interagency Forum on Child and Family Statistics, 2005.

"American Community Survey 2003." Washington, D.C.: U.S. Census Bureau, 2004.

American Sociological Association. "Code of Ethics." Washington, D.C.: American Sociological Association, August 14, 1989; Spring 1997.

American Sociological Association. "Section on Environment and Technology." Pamphlet, no date.

Amnesty International. "Decades of Human Rights Abuse in Iraq." Online, 2005.

Anderson, Elijah. "Streetwise." In *Exploring Social Life: Readings to Accompany Essentials of Sociology, Sixth Edition,* 2nd ed., James M. Henslin, ed. Boston: Allyn and Bacon, 2006:147–156.

Anderson, Elijah. *Streetwise.* Chicago: University of Chicago Press, 1990.

Anderson, Elijah. *A Place on the Corner.* Chicago: University of Chicago Press, 1978.

Anderson, Nels. *Desert Saints: The Mormon Frontier in Utah.* Chicago: University of Chicago Press, 1966. First published in 1942.

Anderson, Philip. "God and the Swedish Immigrants." *Sweden and America,* Autumn 1995:17–20.

Andersson, Hilary. "Born to Be a Slave in Niger." BBC News, World Edition, February 11, 2005.

Angler, Natalie. "Do Races Differ? Not Really, DNA Shows." *New York Times,* August 22, 2000.

Annin, Peter. "Big Money, Big Trouble." *Newsweek,* April 19, 1999:59.

Annin, Peter, and Kendall Hamilton. "Marriage or Rape?" *Newsweek,* December 16, 1996:78.

Ansberry, Clare. "Despite Federal Law, Hospitals Still Reject Sick Who Can't Pay." *Wall Street Journal,* November 29, 1988:A1, A4.

Aptheker, Herbert. "W.E.B. Du Bois: Struggle Not Despair." *Clinical Sociology Review, 8,* 1990:58–68.

Archbold, Ronna, and Mary Harmon. "International Success: Acceptance." Online: The Five O'clock Club, 2001.

Ariès, Philippe. *Centuries of Childhood.* R. Baldick, trans. New York: Vintage Books, 1965.

Arlacchi, P. *Peasants and Great Estates: Society in Traditional Calabria.* Cambridge, England: Cambridge University Press, 1980.

Arndt, William F., and F. Wilbur Gingrich. *A Greek-English Lexicon of the New Testament and Other Early Christian Literature.* Chicago: University of Chicago Press, 1957.

R

"ASA Council Statement on the Causes of Gender Differences in Science and Math Career Achievement." *Footnotes,* March 2005:10.

Asch, Solomon. "Effects of Group Pressure Upon the Modification and Distortion of Judgments." In *Readings in Social Psychology,* Guy Swanson, Theodore M. Newcomb, and Eugene L. Hartley, eds. New York: Holt, Rinehart and Winston, 1952.

"Ask America: 2004 Nationwide Policy Survey." National Republican Congressional Committee, 2004.

Aulette, Judy Root. *Changing American Families.* Boston: Allyn and Bacon, 2002.

Avery, Robert B., Glenn B. Canner, and Robert E. Cook. "New Information Reported Under FMDA and Its Application in Fair Lending Enforcement." *Federal Reserve Bulletin,* Summer 2005:344–394.

Ayittey, George B. N. "Black Africans Are Enraged at Arabs." *Wall Street Journal,* September 4, 1998.

Bales, Robert F. "The Equilibrium Problem in Small Groups." In *Working Papers in the Theory of Action,* Talcott Parsons et al., eds. New York: Free Press, 1953:111–115.

Bales, Robert F. *Interaction Process Analysis.* Reading, Mass.: Addison-Wesley, 1950.

Baltzell, E. Digby. *Puritan Boston and Quaker Philadelphia.* New York: Free Press, 1979.

Baltzell, E. Digby, and Howard G. Schneiderman. "Social Class in the Oval Office." *Society,* September–October 1988:42–49.

Banerjee, Neela. "Rape (and Silence About It) Haunts Baghdad." *New York Times,* July 16, 2003.

Barbalet, Jack, ed. *Emotions and Sociology.* Oxford: Blackwell Publishing, 2002.

Barlett, Donald L., and James B. Steele. "Wheel of Misfortune." *Time,* December 16, 2002:44–58.

Barlett, Donald L., and James B. Steele. "Paying a Price for Polluters." *Time,* November 23, 1998:72–80.

Barnes, Fred. "How to Rig a Poll." *Wall Street Journal,* June 14, 1995:A14.

Barnes, Harry Elmer. *The History of Western Civilization,* Vol. 1. New York: Harcourt, Brace, 1935.

Barnes, Helen. "A Comment on Stroud and Pritchard: Child Homicide, Psychiatric Disorder and Dangerousness." *British Journal of Social Work, 31,* 3, June 2001.

Baron, Stephen W. "Street Youth: Labour Market Experiences and Crime." *Canadian Review of Sociology and Anthropology, 38,* 2, May 2001:189–215.

Barro, Robert J., and Rachel M. McCleary. "Religion and Economic Growth Across Countries." *American Sociological Review, 68,* October 2003:760–781.

Barry, John. "A New Breed of Soldier." *Newsweek,* December 10, 2001:24–31.

Barry, John, and Evan Thomas. "Dropping the Bomb." *Newsweek,* June 25, 2001.

Barry, Paul. "Strong Medicine: A Talk with Former Principal Henry Gradillas." *College Board Review,* Fall 1989:2–13.

Barstow, David, and Lowell Bergman. "Death on the Job, Slaps on the Wrist." *Wall Street Journal,* January 10, 2003.

Bartos, Otomar J., and Paul Wehr. *Using Conflict Theory.* New York: Cambridge University Press, 2002.

Baskin, D. R., and I. B. Sommers. *Casualties of Community Disorder: Women's Careers in Violent Crime.* Boulder: Westview Press, 1998.

Batalova, Jeanne A., and Philip N. Cohen. "Premarital Cohabitation and Housework: Couples in Cross-National Perspectives." *Journal of Marriage and the Family, 64,* 3, August 2002:743–755.

Bates, Marston. *Gluttons and Libertines: Human Problems of Being Natural.* New York: Vintage Books, 1967. Quoted in Crapo, Richley H. *Cultural Anthropology: Understanding Ourselves and Others,* 5th ed. Boston: McGraw Hill, 2002.

Bean, Frank D., Jennifer Lee, Jeanne Batalova, and Mark Leach. "Immigration and Fading Color Lines in America." Washington, D.C.: Population Reference Bureau, 2004.

Beck, Scott H., and Joe W. Page. "Involvement in Activities and the Psychological Well-Being of Retired Men." *Activities, Adaptation, & Aging, 11,* 1, 1988:31–47.

Becker, Howard S. *Outsiders: Studies in the Sociology of Deviance.* New York: Free Press, 1966.

Beckett, Paul. "Even Piñatas Sold in Mexico Seem to Originate in Hollywood Now." *Wall Street Journal,* September 11, 1996:B1.

Beeghley, Leonard. *The Structure of Social Stratification in the United States,* 4th ed. Boston: Allyn and Bacon, 2005.

Begley, Sharon. "Twins: Nazi and Jew." *Newsweek, 94,* December 3, 1979:139.

Bell, Daniel. *The Coming of Post-Industrial Society: A Venture in Social Forecasting.* New York: Basic Books, 1973.

Bell, David A. "An American Success Story: The Triumph of Asian-Americans." In *Sociological Footprints: Introductory Readings in Sociology,* 5th ed., Leonard Cargan and Jeanne H. Ballantine, eds. Belmont, Calif.: Wadsworth, 1991:308–316.

Benet, Sula. "Why They Live to Be 100, or Even Older, in Abkhasia." *New York Times Magazine, 26,* December 1971.

Berger, Arthur Asa. *Video Games: A Popular Culture Phenomenon.* New Brunswick, N.J.: Transaction Publishers, 2002.

Berger, Joseph. "Family Ties and the Entanglements of Caste." *New York Times,* October 24, 2004.

Berger, Peter L. *The Capitalist Revolution: Fifty Propositions about Prosperity, Equality, and Liberty.* New York: Basic Books, 1991.

Berger, Peter L. "Invitation to Sociology." In *Down to Earth Sociology: Introductory Readings,* 13th ed., James M. Henslin, ed. New York: The Free Press, 2005:3–7. Originally published in 1963.

Berger, Peter L. *Invitation to Sociology: A Humanistic Perspective.* New York: Doubleday, 1963.

Bergmann, Barbara R. "The Future of Child Care." Paper presented at the 1995 meetings of the American Sociological Association.

Berle, Adolf, Jr., and Gardiner C. Means. *The Modern Corporation and Private Property.* New York: Harcourt, Brace and World, 1932. As cited in Useem 1980:44.

Bernard, Viola W., Perry Ottenberg, and Fritz Redl. "Dehumanization: A Composite Psychological Defense in Relation to Modern War." In *The Triple Revolution Emerging: Social Problems in Depth,* Robert Perucci and Marc Pilisuk, eds. Boston: Little, Brown, 1971:17–34.

Bernstein, Robert, and Mike Bergman. "Hispanic Population Reaches All-Time High of 38.8 Million, New Census Bureau Estimates Show." *U.S. Department of Commerce News,* June 18, 2003.

Bertrand, Marianne, and Sendhil Mullainathan. "Are Emily and Brendan More Employable than Lakish and Jamal? A Field Experiment on Labor Market Discrimination." Unpublished paper, November 18, 2002.

Bianchi, Suzanne M., and Daphne Spain. "Women Work, and Family in America." *Population Bulletin, 51,* 3, December 1996: 1–47.

Bianchi, Suzanne M., and Lynne M. Casper. "American Families." *Population Bulletin, 55,* 4, December 2000:1–42.

Bianchi, Suzanne M., Melissa A. Milkie, Liana C. Sayer, and John P. Robinson. "Is Anyone Doing the Housework? Trends in the Gender Division of Household Labor." *Social Forces, 79,* 1, September 2000:191–228.

Bishop, Jerry E. "Study Finds Doctors Tend to Postpone Heart Surgery for Women, Raising Risk." *Wall Street Journal,* April 16, 1990:B4.

Bjerklie, David, Andrea Dorfman, Wendy Cole, Jeanne DeQuine, Helen Gibson, David S. Jackson, Leora Moldofsky, Timothy Roche, Chris Taylor, Cathy Booth Thomas, and Dick Thompson. "Baby, It's You: And You, and You, . . ." *Time,* February 19, 2001:47–57.

Blau, David M. "The Production of Quality in Child-Care Centers: Another Look." *Applied Developmental Science, 4,* 3, 2000:136–148.

Blau, Peter M., and Otis Dudley Duncan. The *American Occupational Structure.* New York: Wiley, 1967.

Blee, Kathleen M. "Inside Organized Racism." In *Life in Society: Readings to Accompany Sociology A Down-to-Earth Approach, Seventh Edition,* James M. Henslin, ed. Boston: Allyn and Bacon, 2005:46–57.

Blumstein, Philip, and Pepper Schwartz. *American Couples: Money, Work, Sex.* New York: Pocket Books, 1985.

Booth, Alan, David R. Johnson, and Douglas A. Granger. "Testosterone, Marital Quality, and Role Overload." Paper presented at the 2004 meetings of the American Sociological Association.

Booth, Alan, and James M. Dabbs, Jr. "Testosterone and Men's Marriages." *Social Forces, 72,* 2, December 1993:463–477.

Bosman, Ciska M., et al. "Business Success and Businesses' Beauty Capital." National Bureau of Economic Research Working Paper: 6083, July 1997.

"The Boss's Pay." The WSJ/Mercer 2004 CEO Compensation Survey, May 11, 2005.

Bourgois, Philippe. "Crack in Spanish Harlem." In *Haves and Have-Nots: An International Reader on Social Inequality,* James Curtis and Lorne Tepperman, eds. Englewood Cliffs, N.J.: Prentice Hall, 1994:131–136.

Bowles, Samuel. "Unequal Education and the Reproduction of the Social Division of Labor." In *Power and Ideology in Education,* J. Karabel and A. H. Halsey, eds. New York: Oxford University Press, 1977.

Bowles, Samuel, and Herbert Gintis. "*Schooling in Capitalist America* Revisited." *Sociology of Education, 75,* 2002:1–18.

Bowles, Samuel, and Herbert Gintis. *Schooling in Capitalist America.* New York: Basic Books, 1976.

Boyle, Elizabeth Heger, Fortunata Songora, and Gail Foss. "International Discourse and Local Politics: Anti-Female-Genital-Cutting Laws in Egypt, Tanzania, and the United States," *Social Problems, 48,* 4, November 2001:524–544.

Brajuha, Mario, and Lyle Hallowell. "Legal Intrusion and the Politics of Fieldwork: The Impact of the Brajuha Case." *Urban Life, 14,* 4, January 1986:454–478.

Bramlett, M. D., and W. D. Mosher. "Cohabitation, Marriage, Divorce, and Remarriage in the United States." Hyattsville, Md.: National Center for Health Statistics, Vital Health Statistics, Series 23, Number 22, July 2002.

Brannigan, Augustine. *The Rise and Fall of Social Psychology: The Use and Misuse of the Experimental Method.* New York: Aldine de Gruyter, 2004.

Brass, Paul R. *The Production of Hindu-Muslim Violence in Contemporary India.* Seattle: University of Washington Press, 2003.

Brauchli, Marcus W. "Wary of Education But Needing Brains, China Faces a Dilemma." *Wall Street Journal,* November 15, 1994:A1, A10.

Bray, Rosemary L. "Rosa Parks: A Legendary Moment, a Lifetime of Activism. *Ms., 6,* 3, November-December 1995:45–47.

"Brazil Arrests U.S. Pilot Over Obscene Gesture." Associated Press, January 15, 2004.

Bretos, Miguel A. "Hispanics Face Institutional Exclusion." *Miami Herald,* May 22, 1994.

Bridgwater, William, ed. *The Columbia Viking Desk Encyclopedia.* New York: Viking Press, 1953.

Brines, Julie. "Economic Dependency, Gender, and the Division of Labor at Home." *American Journal of Sociology, 100,* 3, November 1994:652–688.

Brines, Julie, and Kara Joyner. "The Ties That Bind. Principles of Cohesion in Cohabitation and Marriage." *American Sociological Review, 64,* June 1999:333–355.

Broad, William J. "The Shuttle Explodes." *New York Times,* January 29, 1986, A1, A5.

Brockerhoff, Martin P. "An Urbanizing World." *Population Bulletin, 55,* 3, September 2000:1–44.

Broder, Michael S., David E. Kanouse, Brian S. Mittman, and Steven J. Bernstein. "The Appropriateness of Recommendations for Hysterectomy." *Obstetrics and Gynecology, 95,* 2, February 2000:199–205.

Bronfenbrenner, Urie, as quoted in Diane Fassel. "Divorce May Not Harm Children." In *Family in America: Opposing Viewpoints,* Viqi Wagner, ed. San Diego, Calif.: Greenhaven Press, 1992: 115–119.

Brooks-Gunn, Jeanne, Greg. J. Duncan, and Lawrence Aber, eds. *Neighborhood Poverty, Volume 1: Context and Consequences for Children.* New York: Russell Sage Foundation, 1997.

Browning, Christopher R. *Ordinary Men: Reserve Police Battalion 101 and the Final Solution in Poland.* New York: HarperPerennial, 1993.

Bryant, Alyssa N. "Community College Students: Recent Findings and Trends." *Community College Review, 29,* 3, 2001:77–93.

Bryant, Chalandra M., Rand D. Conger, and Jennifer M. Meehan. "The Influence of In-Laws on Changes in Marital Success." *Journal of Marriage and the Family, 63,* 3, August 2001:614–626.

Budrys, Grace. *Unequal Health: How Inequality Contributes to Health or Illness.* Lanham, Md.: Rowman and Littlefield, 2003.

Bumiller, Elisabeth. "First Comes Marriage—Then, Maybe, Love." In *Marriage and Family in a Changing Society,* 4th ed., James M. Henslin, ed. New York: Free Press, 1992:120–125.

Buraway, Michael. "Public Sociologies: Reply to Hausknecht." *Footnotes,* January 2003:8.

Burgess, Ernest W. "The Growth of the City: An Introduction to a Research Project." In *The City,* Robert E. Park, Ernest W. Burgess, and Roderick D. McKenzie, eds. Chicago: University of Chicago Press, 1925:47–62.

Burgess, Ernest W., and Harvey J. Locke. *The Family: From Institution to Companionship.* New York: American Books, 1945.

Burnham, Walter Dean. *Democracy in the Making: American Government and Politics.* Englewood Cliffs, N.J.: Prentice Hall, 1983.

Burris, Val. "Interlocking Directorates and Political Cohesion Among Corporate Elites." *American Journal of Sociology, 111,* 1, 2005:249–283.

Burris, Val. "The Myth of Old Money Liberalism: The Politics of the Forbes 400 Richest Americans." *Social Problems, 47,* 3, August 2000:360–378.

Bush, Diane Mitsch, and Robert G. Simmons. "Socialization Processes over the Life Course." In *Social Psychology: Sociological Perspectives,* Morris Rosenberg and Ralph H. Turner, eds. New Brunswick, N.J.: Transaction Books, 1990:133–164.

Butler, Robert N. "Ageism: Another Form of Bigotry." *Gerontologist, 9,* Winter 1980:243–246.

Butler, Robert N. *Why Survive? Being Old in America.* New York: Harper & Row, 1975.

Butterfield, Fox. "Indians' Wish List: Big-City Sites for Casinos." *New York Times,* April 8, 2005.

Butterfield, Fox. "With Cash Tight, States Reassess Long Jail Terms." *New York Times,* November 10, 2003.

Canavan, Margaret M., Walter J. Meyer III, and Deborah C. Higgs. "The Female Experience of Sibling Incest." *Journal of Marital and Family Therapy, 18,* 2, 1992:129–142.

Cancian, Maria, Marieka M. Klawitter, Daniel R. Meyer, Ann Rangarajan, Geoffrey Wallace, and Robert G. Wood. "Income and Program Participation Among Early TRANF Recipients: The Evidence from New Jersey, Washington, and Wisconsin." *Focus, 22,* 3, Summer 2003:2–10.

Carlson, Lewis H., and George A. Colburn. *In Their Place: White America Defines Her Minorities, 1850–1950.* New York: Wiley, 1972.

Carpenito, Lynda Juall. "The Myths of Acquaintance Rape." *Nursing Forum, 34,* 4, October-December 1999:3.

Carpenter, Betsy. "Redwood Radicals." *U.S. News & World Report, 109,* 11, September 17, 1990:50–51.

Carper, James C. "Pluralism to Establishment to Dissent: The Religious and Educational Context of Home Schooling." *Peabody Journal of Education, 75,* ¹/₂, 2000:8–19.

Carr, Deborah, Carol D. Ryff, Burton Singer, and William J. Magee. "Bringing the 'Life' Back into Life Course Research: A 'Person-Centered' Approach to Studying the Life Course." Paper presented at the 1995 meetings of the American Sociological Association.

Carrington, Tim. "Developed Nations Want Poor Countries to Succeed on Trade, But Not Too Much." *Wall Street Journal,* September 20, 1993:A10.

Cartwright, Dorwin, and Alvin Zander, eds. *Group Dynamics,* 3rd ed. Evanston, Ill.: Peterson, 1968.

Casper, Monica J., ed. *Synthetic Planet: Chemical Politics and the Hazards of Modern Life.* New York: Taylor and Francis, 2003.

Cassel, Russell N. "Examining the Basic Principles for Effective Leadership." *College Student Journal, 33,* 2, June 1999:288–301.

Cauce, Ana Mari, and Melanie Domenech-Rodriguez. "Latino Families: Myths and Realities." In *Latino Children and Families in the United States: Current Research and Future Directions,* Josefina M. Contreras, Kathryn A. Kerns, and Angela M. Neal-Barnett, eds. Westport, Conn.: Praeger, 2002:3–25.

Central Intelligence Agency. *The World Fact Book,* Washington, D.C.: Office of Public Affairs, 2005.

Chafetz, Janet Saltzman. *Gender Equity: An Integrated Theory of Stability and Change.* Newbury Park, Calif.: Sage, 1990.

Chafetz, Janet Saltzman, and Anthony Gary Dworkin. *Female Revolt: Women's Movements in World and Historical Perspective.* Totowa, N.J.: Rowman & Allanheld, 1986.

Chagnon, Napoleon A. *Yanomamo: The Fierce People,* 2nd ed. New York: Holt, Rinehart and Winston, 1977.

Chaker, Anne Marie. "A Backdoor Route to a College Dream." *Wall Street Journal,* June 26, 2003.

Chaker, Anne Marie, and Hilary Stout. "After Years off, Women Struggle to Revive Careers." *Wall Street Journal,* May 6, 2004.

Chalkley, Kate. "Female Genital Mutilation: New Laws, Programs Try to End Practice." *Population Today, 25,* 10, October 1997:4–5.

Chamberlain, Claudine. "Implicit Association Test." ABCNews Online, September 30, 1998.

Chambliss, Daniel F. "The World of the Hospital." In *Down to Earth Sociology: Introductory Readings,* 12th ed., James M. Henslin, ed. New York: The Free Press, 2003:434–446.

Chambliss, William J., "My Personal Journey Into Sociology." In *Social Problems,* 7th ed., by James M. Henslin. Upper Saddle River, N.J.: Prentice Hall, 2006:175.

Chambliss, William J. "The Saints and the Roughnecks." In *Down to Earth Sociology: Introductory Readings,* 13th ed. James M. Henslin, ed. New York: Free Press, 2005. First published in *Society,* 11, 1973.

Chandler, Tertius, and Gerald Fox. *3000 Years of Urban Growth.* New York: Academic Press, 1974.

Chandra, Vibha P. "Fragmented Identities: The Social Construction of Ethnicity, 1885–1947." Unpublished paper, 1993a.

Chase, Marilyn. "Scientists Extend Life Span of Worms by Altering Genes." *Wall Street Journal,* October 24, 2003.

Chen, Edwin. "Twins Reared Apart: A Living Lab." *New York Times Magazine,* December 9, 1979:112.

Chen, Kathy. "China's Women Face Obstacles in Workplace." *Wall Street Journal,* August 28, 1995:B1, B5.

Cherlin, Andrew J. "A 'Quieting' of Change." *Contexts, 1,* 1, Spring 2002:67–68.

Cherlin, Andrew J. "Remarriage as an Incomplete Institution." In *Marriage and Family in a Changing Society,* 3rd ed., James M. Henslin, ed. New York: Free Press, 1989:492–501.

"Child Support for Custodial Mothers and Fathers." *Current Population Reports,* Series P60-187. Washington, D.C.: U.S. Bureau of the Census, 1995.

Chin, Nancy P., Alicia Monroe, and Kevin Fiscella. "Social Determinants of (Un)Healthy Behaviors." *Education for Health: Change in Learning and Practice, 13,* 3, November 2000: 317–328.

Chodorow, Nancy J. "What Is the Relation between Psychoanalytic Feminism and the Psychoanalytic Psychology of Women?" In *Theoretical Perspectives on Sexual Difference,* Deborah L. Rhode, ed. New Haven, Conn.: Yale University Press, 1990:114–130.

Churchill, Ward. *A Little Matter of Genocide: Holocaust and Denial in the Americas, 1492 to the Present.* San Francisco: City Lights Books, 1997.

Clair, Jeffrey Michael, David A. Karp, and William C. Yoels. *Experiencing the Life Cycle: A Social Psychology of Aging,* 2nd ed. Springfield, Ill.: Thomas, 1993.

Clark, Candace. *Misery and Company: Sympathy in Everyday Life.* Chicago: University of Chicago Press, 1997.

Cloud, John. "For Better or Worse." *Time,* October 26, 1998:43–44.

Cloward, Richard A., and Lloyd E. Ohlin. *Delinquency and Opportunity: A Theory of Delinquent Gangs.* New York: Free Press, 1960.

Cnaan, Ram A. "Neighborhood-Representing Organizations: How Democratic Are They?" *Social Science Review,* December 1991:614–634.

Cohen, Patricia. "Forget Lonely. Life Is Healthy at the Top." *New York Times,* May 15, 2004.

Cohen, Roger. "Europe's Shifting Role Poses Challenge to U.S." *New York Times,* Feburary 11, 2001.

Colapinto, John. *As Nature Made Him: The Boy Who Was Raised as a Girl.* New York: HarperCollins, 2001.

Cole, Elizabeth R., and Safiya R. Omari. "Race, Class and the Dilemmas of Upward Mobility for African Americans." *Journal of Social Issues, 59,* 4, 2003:785–802.

Coleman, James, and Thomas Hoffer. *Public and Private Schools: The Impact of Communities.* New York: Basic Books, 1987.

Coleman, Marilyn, Lawrence Ganong, and Mark Fine. "Reinvestigating Remarriage: Another Decade of Progress." *Journal of Marriage and the Family, 62,* 4, November 2000: 1288–1307.

Collins, Randall. "Socially Unrecognized Cumulation." *American Sociologist, 30,* 2, Summer 1999:41–61.

Collins, Randall. *Theoretical Sociology.* San Diego, Calif.: Harcourt Brace Jovanovich, 1988.

Collins, Randall. *The Credential Society: An Historical Sociology of Education.* New York: Academic Press, 1979.

Collymore, Yvette. "Conveying Concerns: Women Report on Gender-Based Violence." Washington, D.C.: Population Reference Bureau, 2000.

Conklin, John E. *Why Crime Rates Fell.* Boston: Allyn and Bacon, 2003.

Conley, Dalton. "Forty Acres and a Mule: What If America Pays Reparations?" *Contexts,* Fall 2002:13–20.

Connors, L. "Gender of Infant Differences in Attachment: Associations with Temperament and Caregiving Experiences." Paper presented at the Annual Conference of the British Psychological Society, Oxford, England, 1996.

Contreras, Josefina M., Kathryn A. Kerns, and Angela M. Neal-Barnett, eds. *Latino Children and Families in the United States: Current Research and Future Directions.* Westport, Conn.: Praeger, 2002.

Cook, Bradley J. "Islam and Egyptian Higher Education: Student Attitudes." *Comparative Education Review, 45,* 3, August 2001: 379–403.

Cookson, Peter W., Jr., and Caroline Hodges Persell. "Preparing for Power: Cultural Capital and Elite Boarding Schools." In *Life in Society: Readings to Accompany Sociology A Down-to-Earth Approach, Seventh Edition,* James M. Henslin, ed. Boston: Allyn and Bacon, 2005:175–185.

Cooley, Charles Horton. *Social Organization.* New York: Scribner's, 1909.

Cooley, Charles Horton. *Human Nature and the Social Order.* New York: Scribner's, 1902.

Copeland, Libby. "Click Clique: Facebook's Online College Community." *Washington Post,* December 28, 2004.

Corcoran, Mary. "Mobility, Persistence, and Consequences of Poverty for Children: Child and Adult Outcomes." In *Understanding Poverty,* Sheldon H. Danziger and Robert H. Haveman, eds. New York: Russell Sage, 2001:127–161.

Cortese, Anthony. *Provocateur: Images of Women and Minorities in Advertising,* 2nd ed. Boulder, Colo: Rowman and Littlefield Publishers, 2003.

Cose, Ellis. "What's White Anyway?" *Newsweek,* September 18, 2000:64–65.

Cose, Ellis. "The Good News About Black America." *Newsweek,* June 7, 1999:29–40.

Coser, Lewis A. *Masters of Sociological Thought: Ideas in Historical and Social Context,* 2nd ed. New York: Harcourt Brace Jovanovich, 1977.

Cottin, Lou. *Elders in Rebellion: A Guide to Senior Activism.* Garden City, N. Y.: Anchor Doubleday, 1979.

Cousins, Albert N., and Hans Nagpaul. *Urban Man and Society: A Reader in Urban Sociology.* New York: McGraw-Hill, 1970.

Cowen, Emory L., Judah Landes, and Donald E. Schaet. "The Effects of Mild Frustration on the Expression of Prejudiced Attitudes." *Journal of Abnormal and Social Psychology,* January 1959:33–38.

Cowgill, Donald. "The Aging of Populations and Societies." *Annals of the American Academy of Political and Social Science, 415,* 1974:1–18.

Cowley, Geoffrey. "Attention: Aging Men." *Newsweek,* November 16, 1996:66–75.

Cowley, Joyce. *Pioneers of Women's Liberation.* New York: Merit, 1969.

Crawford, Duane W., Renate M. Houts, Ted L. Huston, and Laura J. George. "Compatibility, Leisure, and Satisfaction in Marital Relationships." *Journal of Marriage and Family, 64,* May 2002:433–449.

Crosette, Barbara. "Caste May Be India's Moral Achilles' Heel." *New York Times,* October 20, 1996, electronic version.

Crossen, Cynthia. "Before Social Security, Most Americans Faced Very Bleak Retirement." *Wall Street Journal,* September 15, 2004a.

Crossen, Cynthia. "Déjà Vu." *New York Times,* February 25, 2004b.

Crossen, Cynthia. "Deja Vu." *Wall Street Journal,* March 5, 2003.

Crossen, Cynthia. *Wall Street Journal,* November 14, 1991:A1, A7.

Cumming, Elaine. "Further Thoughts on the Theory of Disengagement." In *Aging in America: Readings in Social Gerontology,* Cary S. Kart and Barbara B. Manard, eds. Sherman Oaks, Calif.: Alfred Publishing, 1976:19–41.

Cumming, Elaine, and William E. Henry. *Growing Old: The Process of Disengagement.* New York: Basic Books, 1961.

Dabbs, James M., Jr., Marian F. Hargrove, and Colleen Heusel. "Testosterone Differences Among College Fraternities: Well-Behaved vs. Rambunctious." *Personality and Individual Differences, 20,* 1996:157–161.

Dabbs, James M., Jr., and Robin Morris. "Testosterone, Social Class, and Antisocial Behavior in a Sample of 4,462 Men." *Psychological Science, 1,* 3, May 1990:209–211.

Dahl, Robert A. *Dilemmas of Pluralist Democracy: Autonomy vs. Control.* New Haven, Conn.: Yale University Press, 1982.

Dahl, Robert A. *Who Governs?* New Haven, Conn.: Yale University Press, 1961.

Darley, John M., and Bibb Latané. "Bystander Intervention in Emergencies: Diffusion of Responsibility." *Journal of Personality and Social Psychology, 8,* 4, 1968:377–383.

Darweesh, Suzanne. "Use Your Buying Power to Promote Ethics." *Los Angeles Times,* November 5, 2000.

Dasgupta, Nilanjana, Debbie E. McGhee, Anthony G. Greenwald, and Mahzarin R. Banaji. "Automatic Preference for White Americans: Eliminating the Familiarity Explanation." *Journal of Experimental Social Psychology, 36,* 3, May 2000:316–328.

Davis, Donald R., and David E. Weinstein. "Technological Superiority and the Losses From Migration." Working Paper. National Bureau of Economic Research. June 2002.

Davis, Gerald F. "American Cronyism: How Executive Networks Inflated the Corporate Bubble." *Contexts, 2,* 3, Summer 2003: 34–40.

Davis, Kingsley. "Extreme Isolation." In *Down to Earth Sociology: Introductory Readings,* 13th ed., James M. Henslin, ed. New York: The Free Press, 2005.

Davis, Kingsley. "Extreme Social Isolation of a Child." *American Journal of Sociology, 45,* 4, January 1940:554–565.

Davis, Kingsley, and Wilbert E. Moore. "Reply to Tumin." *American Sociological Review, 18,* 1953:394–396.

Davis, Kingsley, and Wilbert E. Moore. "Some Principles of Stratification." *American Sociological Review, 10,* 1945:242–249.

Davis, Nancy J., and Robert V. Robinson. "Class Identification of Men and Women in the 1970s and 1980s." *American Sociological Review, 53,* February 1988:103–112.

Davis, Stan. *Lessons From the Future: Making Sense of a Blurred World.* New York: Capstone Publishers, 2001.

Dawley, Richard Lee. *Amish in Wisconsin.* New Berlin, Wis.: Amish Insight, 2003.

De May, J. "A Picture History of Kew Gardens, N. Y.—Kitty Genovese." Online. April 15, 2005.

Deaver, Michael V. "Democratizing Russian Higher Education." *Demokratizatsiya, 9,* 3, Summer 2001:350–366.

Deck, Leland P. "Buying Brains by the Inch." *Journal of the College and University Personnel Association, 19,* 1968:33–37.

DeCrow, Karen. Foreword to *Why Men Earn More* by Warren Farrell. New York: AMACOM, 2005:xi–xii.

Deegan, Mary Jo. "W. E. B. Du Bois and the Women of Hull-House, 1895–1899." *American Sociologist,* Winter 1988: 301–311.

Deliege, Robert. *The Untouchables of India.* New York: Berg Publishers, 2001.

DeMartini, Joseph R. "Basic and Applied Sociological Work: Divergence, Convergence, or Peaceful Co-existence?" *The Journal of Applied Behavioral Science, 18,* 2, 1982:203–215.

DeMause, Lloyd. "Our Forebears Made Childhood a Nightmare." *Psychology Today, 8,* 11, April 1975:85–88.

Demidov, Vadim. "Ten Years of Rolling the Minicircles: RCA Assays in DNA Diagnostics." *Expert Review of Molecular Diagnostics, 5,* 4, July 2005:477–478. <http://www.future-drugs.com/loi/erm;jsessionid=o_3C1_i2Jnr-mGoATO>

DeNavas-Walt, Carmen, Bernadette D. Proctor, and Robert J. Mills. "Income, Poverty, and Health Insurance Coverage in the United States: 2003." U.S. Census Bureau, *Current Population Reports,* August 2004.

Denney, Nancy W., and David Quadagno. *Human Sexuality,* 2nd ed. St. Louis: Mosby Year Book, 1992.

DeOilos, Ione Y., and Carolyn A. Kapinus. "Aging Childless Individuals and Couples: Suggestions for New Directions in Research." *Sociological Inquiry, 72,* 1, Winter 2002:72–80.

Derne, Steve. "Arnold Schwarzenegger, Ally McBeal and Arranged Marriages: Globalization on the Ground in India." *Contexts,* Summer 2003:12–18.

Diamond, Milton, and Keith Sigmundson. "Sex Reassignment at Birth: Long-Term Review and Clinical Implications." *Archives of Pediatric and Adolescent Medicine, 151,* March 1997:298–304.

Dietz, Tracy L. "An Examination of Violence and Gender Role Portrayals in Video Games." *Women and Language, 23,* 2, Fall 2000:64–77.

Dillon, Sam. "States Cut Test Standards to Avoid Sanctions." *New York Times,* May 21, 2003.

Dixon, Celvia Stovall, and Kathryn D. Rettig. "An Examination of Income Adequacy for Single Women Two Years after Divorce." *Journal of Divorce and Remarriage, 22,* 1–2, 1994:55–71.

Doane, Ashley W., Jr. "Dominant Group Ethnic Identity in the United States: The Role of 'Hidden' Ethnicity in Intergroup Relations." *The Sociological Quarterly, 38,* 3, Summer 1997: 375–397.

Dobash, Russell P., R. Emerson Dobash, Margo Wilson, and Martin Daly. "Marital Violence Is Not Symmetrical: A Response to Campbell." *SSSP Newsletter, 24,* 3, Fall 1993:26–30.

Dobash, Russell P., R. Emerson Dobash, Margo Wilson, and Martin Daly. "The Myth of Sexual Symmetry in Marital Violence." *Social Problems, 39,* 1, February 1992:71–91.

Dobriner, William M. "The Football Team as Social Structure and Social System." In *Social Structures and Systems: A Sociological Overview.* Pacific Palisades, Calif.: Goodyear, 1969a:116–120.

Dobriner, William M. *Social Structures and Systems.* Pacific Palisades, California: Goodyear, 1969b.

Dobyns, Henry F. *Their Numbers Became Thinned: Native American Population Dynamics in Eastern North America.* Knoxville: University of Tennessee Press, 1983.

Dodds, Peter Sheridan, Roby Muhamad, and Duncan J. Watts. "An Experimental Study of Search in Global Social Networks." *Science, 301,* August 8, 2003:827–830.

Dollard, John, et al. *Frustration and Aggression.* New Haven, Conn.: Yale University Press, 1939.

Domhoff, G. William. *Changing the Powers That Be: How the Left Can Stop Losing and Win.* New York: Rowman and Littlefield, 2003.

Domhoff, G. William. *Who Rules America? Power and Politics,* 4th ed. New York: McGraw-Hill, 2002.

Domhoff, G. William. "The Bohemian Grove and Other Retreats." In *Down to Earth Sociology: Introductory Readings,* 10th ed., James M. Henslin, ed. New York: Free Press, 1999a:391–403.

Domhoff, G. William. "State and Ruling Class in Corporate America (1974): Reflections, Corrections, and New Directions." *Critical Sociology, 25,* 2–3, July 1999b:260–265.

Domhoff, G. William. *Who Rules America?: Power and Politics in the Year 2000,* 3rd ed. Mountain View, Calif.: Mayfield Publishing, 1998.

Domhoff, G. William. *The Power Elite and the State: How Policy Is Made in America.* New York: Aldine de Gruyter, 1990.

Donaldson, Stephen. "A Million Jockers, Punks, and Queens: Sex Among American Male Prisoners and Its Implications for Concepts of Sexual Orientation." February 4, 1993. Online.

Dottridge, Mike. "Dollars and Sense." *New Internationalist, 337,* August 2001:16–17.

Douglas, Carol Anne, et al. "Kenya: FGM Increasingly Occurring in Hospitals." *Off Our Backs, 35,* January–February 2005:5.

Douthat, Ross. "The Truth About Harvard." *Atlantic Monthly,* March 2005.

Dove, Adrian. "Soul Folk 'Chitling' Test or the Dove Counterbalance Intelligence Test." no date. (mimeo)

Dowd, Maureen. "The Knife Under the Tree." *New York Times,* December 5, 2002.

Du Bois, W. E. B. *Black Reconstruction in America: An Essay Toward a History of the Part Which Black Folk Played in the Attempt to Reconstruct Democracy in America, 1860–1880.* New York: Atheneum, 1992. First published in 1935.

Du Bois, W. E. B. *The Autobiography of W. E. B. Du Bois: A Soliloquy on Viewing My Life from the Last Decade of Its First Century.* New York: International Press, 1968.

Du Bois, W. E. B. *The Souls of Black Folk: Essays and Sketches.* Chicago: McClurg, 1903.

Dudenhefer, Paul. "Poverty in the Rural United States." *Focus, 15,* 1, Spring 1993:37–46.

Duff, Christina. "Superrich's Share of After-Tax Income Stopped Rising in Early '90s, Data Show." *Wall Street Journal,* November 22, 1995:A2.

Dugger, Celia W. "Abortion in India Is Tipping Scales Sharply Against Girls." *New York Times,* April 22, 2001.

Dugger, Celia W. "Wedding Vows Bind Old World and New." *New York Times,* July 20, 1998.

Duneier, Mitchell. *Sidewalk.* New York: Farrar, Straus and Giroux, 1999.

Dunlap, Riley, and William Michelson, eds. *Handbook of Environmental Sociology.* Westport, Conn.: Greenwood Press, 2002.

Dunlap, Riley E., and William R. Catton, Jr. "What Environmental Sociologists Have in Common Whether Concerned with 'Built' or 'Natural' Environments." *Sociological Inquiry, 53,* 2/3, 1983:113–135.

Dunlap, Riley E., and William R. Catton, Jr. "Environmental Sociology." *Annual Review of Sociology, 5,* 1979:243–273.

Durkheim, Emile. *Suicide: A Study in Sociology.* John A. Spaulding and George Simpson, trans. New York: Free Press, 1966. First published in 1897.

Durkheim, Emile. *The Elementary Forms of the Religious Life.* New York: Free Press, 1965. First published in 1912.

Durkheim, Emile. *The Rules of Sociological Method.* Sarah A. Solovay and John H. Mueller, trans. New York: Free Press, 1938, 1958, 1964. First published in 1895.

Durkheim, Emile. *The Division of Labor in Society.* George Simpson, trans. New York: Free Press, 1933. First published in 1893.

Durning, Alan. "Cradles of Life." In *Social Problems 90/91,* LeRoy W. Barnes, ed. Guilford, Conn.: Dushkin, 1990:231–241.

Dush, Claire M. Kamp, Catherine L. Cohan, and Paul R. Amato. "The Relationship Between Cohabitation and Marital Quality and Stability: Change Across Cohorts?" *Journal of Marriage and Family, 65,* 3, August 2003:539–549.

Dyer, Gwynne. "Anybody's Son Will Do." In *Life in Society: Readings to Accompany Sociology A Down-to-Earth Approach, Seventh Edition,* James M. Henslin, ed. Boston: Allyn and Bacon, 2005:26–36.

Easley, Hema. "Indian Families Continue to Have Arranged Marriages." *The Journal News,* June 9, 2003.

Ebner, Johanna. "Fighting International Terrorism with Social Science Knowledge." *Footnotes,* February 2005.

Ebomoyi, Ehigie. "The Prevalence of Female Circumcision in Two Nigerian Communities." *Sex Roles, 17,* 3/4, 1987:139–151.

Eckholm, Erik. "Desire for Sons Drives Use of Prenatal Scans in China." *New York Times,* June 21, 2002.

Eder, Donna. "On Becoming Female: Lessons Learned in School." In *Down to Earth Sociology: Introductory Readings,* 13th ed., James M. Henslin, ed. New York: The Free Press, 2005:155–161.

Eder, Klaus. "The Rise of Counter-Culture Movements Against Modernity: Nature as a New Field of Class Struggle." *Theory, Culture & Society, 7,* 1990:21–47.

Edgerton, Robert B. *Sick Societies: Challenging the Myth of Primitive Harmony.* New York: Free Press, 1992.

Edgerton, Robert B. *Deviance: A Cross-Cultural Perspective.* Menlo Park, Calif.: Benjamin/Cummings, 1976.

Egan, Timothy. "Many Seek Security in Private Communities." *New York Times,* September 3, 1995:1, 22.

Ehrlich, Paul R., and Anne H. Ehrlich. *Betrayal of Science and Reason: How Anti-Environmental Rhetoric Threatens Our Future.* Washington, D.C.: Island Press, 1997.

Ehrlich, Paul R., and Anne H. Ehrlich. "Humanity at the Crossroads." *Stanford Magazine,* Spring–Summer 1978:20–23.

Ehrlich, Paul R., and Anne H. Ehrlich. *Population, Resources, and Environment: Issues in Human Ecology,* 2nd ed. San Francisco: Freeman, 1972.

Eisenstadt, Shmuel Noah. *Paradoxes of Democracy: Fragility, Continuity, and Change.* Washington, D.C.: Woodrow Wilson Center Press, 1999.

Ekman, Paul. *Faces of Man: Universal Expression in a New Guinea Village.* New York: Garland Press, 1980.

Ekman, Paul, Wallace V. Friesen, and John Bear. "The International Language of Gestures." *Psychology Today,* May 1984:64.

Elder, Glen H., Jr. *Children of the Great Depression: Social Change in Life Experience.* Boulder: Westview Press, 1999.

Elder, Glen H., Jr. "Age Differentiation and Life Course." *Annual Review of Sociology, 1,* 1975:165–190.

Elias, Paul. " 'Molecular Pharmers' Hope to Raise Human Proteins in Crop Plants." *St. Louis Post-Dispatch,* October 28, 2001:F7.

Elson, Jean. *Am I Still a Woman? Hysterectomy and Gender Identity.* Philadelphia: Temple University Press, 2004.

England, Paula. "The Impact of Feminist Thought on Sociology." *Contemporary Sociology: A Journal of Reviews,* 2000:263–267.

Epstein, Cynthia Fuchs. *Deceptive Distinctions: Sex, Gender, and the Social Order.* New Haven, Conn.: Yale University Press, 1988.

Erik, John. "China's Policy on Births." *New York Times,* January 3, 1982: IV, 19.

Ernst, Eldon G. "The Baptists." In *Encyclopedia of the American Religious Experience: Studies of Traditions and Movements,* Vol. 1, Charles H. Lippy and Peter W. Williams, eds. New York: Scribner's, 1988:555–577.

Escalante, Jaime, and Jack Dirmann. "The Jaime Escalante Math Program." *Journal of Negro Education, 59,* 3, Summer 1990:407–423.

Eshleman, J. Ross. *The Family,* 9th ed. Boston: Allyn and Bacon, 2000.

"Ethiopia: Fighting Female Circumcision at Local Level." African News Service, February 16, 2005.

"Executive Pay." *Wall Street Journal,* April 14, 2003.

Fabrikant, Geraldine. "Old Nantucket Warily Meets the New." *New York Times,* June 5, 2005.

Fagot, Beverly I., Richard Hagan, Mary Driver Leinbach, and Sandra Kronsberg. "Differential Reactions to Assertive and Communicative Acts of Toddler Boys and Girls." *Child Development, 56,* 1985:1499–1505.

Faris, Robert E. L., and Warren Dunham. *Mental Disorders in Urban Areas.* Chicago: University of Chicago Press, 1939.

Farkas, George. *Human Capital or Cultural Capital?: Ethnicity and Poverty Groups in an Urban School District.* New York: Walter DeGruyter, 1996.

Farkas, George, Daniel Sheehan, and Robert P. Grobe. "Coursework Mastery and School Success: Gender, Ethnicity, and Poverty Groups within an Urban School District." *American Educational Research Journal, 27,* 4, Winter 1990b:807–827.

Farkas, George, Robert P. Grobe, Daniel Sheehan, and Yuan Shuan. "Cultural Resources and School Success: Gender, Ethnicity, and Poverty Groups within an Urban School District." *American Sociological Review, 55,* February 1990a:127–142.

"Fat Is a Financial Issue." *Economist, 357,* 8198, November 25, 2000:93.

Faunce, William A. *Problems of an Industrial Society,* 2nd ed. New York: McGraw-Hill, 1981.

FBI Uniform Crime Reports. Washington, D.C.: U.S. Government Printing Office, published annually.

Feagin, Joe R. "The Continuing Significance of Race: Antiblack Discrimination in Public Places." In *Majority and Minority: The Dynamics of Race and Ethnicity in American Life,* 6th ed., Norman R. Yetman, ed. Boston: Allyn and Bacon, 1999: 384–399.

Featherman, David L. "Opportunities Are Expanding." *Society, 13,* 1979:4–11.

Featherman, David L., and Robert M. Hauser. *Opportunity and Change.* New York: Academic Press, 1978.

Feldman, Saul D. "The Presentation of Shortness in Everyday Life—Height and Heightism in American Society: Toward a Sociology of Stature." Paper presented at the 1972 meetings of the American Sociological Association.

Felsenthal, Edward. "Justices' Ruling Further Defines Sex Harassment." *Wall Street Journal,* March 5, 1998:B1, B2.

Felton, Lee Ann, Andrea Gumm, and David J. Pittenger. "The Recipients of Unwanted Sexual Encounters Among College Students." *College Student Journal, 35,* 1, March 2001: 135–143.

Fernandez-Kelly, Patricia. "The Moral Monster: Public Sociology in a Maximum Security Prison." In "An Invitation to Public Sociology," *American Sociological Association,* 2004:46–50.

Ferraro, Kathleen J. "Intimate Partner Violence." In *Social Problems,* 7th ed., by James M. Henslin. Upper Saddle River, N.J.: Prentice Hall, 2006:373.

Feshbach, Murray. "Russia's Farms, Too Poisoned for the Plow." *Wall Street Journal,* May 14, 1992:A14.

Fialka, John J. "A Dirty Discovery Over Indian Ocean Sets Off a Fight." *Wall Street Journal,* May 6, 2003:A1, A6.

Fields, Jason. "America's Families and Living Arrangements: 2003." *Current Population Reports,* November 2004.

Filkins, Dexter. "61 Slain as Violence Rocks the Caste System in India." *Seattle Times,* December 3, 1997.

Finer, Jonathan. "Faculty Group Rebukes Harvard President With Vote." *Washington Post,* March 16, 2005.

Finke, Roger, and Roger Stark. *The Churching of America, 1776–1990: Winners and Losers in Our Religious Economy.* New Brunswick, N.J.: Rutgers University Press, 1992.

Fischer, Claude S. *The Urban Experience.* New York: Harcourt, 1976.

Fish, Jefferson M. "Mixed Blood." *Psychology Today, 28,* 6, November–December 1995:55–58, 60, 61, 76, 80.

Fisher, Sue. *In the Patient's Best Interest: Women and the Politics of Medical Decisions.* New Brunswick, N.J.: Rutgers University Press, 1986.

Flanagan, William G. *Urban Sociology: Images and Structure.* Boston: Allyn and Bacon, 1990.

Flavel, John H., et al. *The Development of Role-Taking and Communication Skills in Children.* New York: Wiley, 1968.

Flavel, John, Patricia H. Miller, and Scott A. Miller. *Cognitive Development,* 4th ed. Upper Saddle River, N.J.: Prentice Hall, 2002.

Fletcher, June. "Address Envy: Fudging to Get the Best." *Wall Street Journal*, April 25, 1997:B10.

Flippen, Annette R. "Understanding Groupthink From a Self-Regulatory Perspective." *Small Group Research, 30*, 2, April 1999: 139–165.

Food and Agriculture Organization of the United Nations. FAO Statistical Databases. February, 2005.

Foote, Jennifer. "Trying to Take Back the Planet." *Newsweek, 115*, 6, February 5, 1990:20–25.

Form, William. "Comparative Industrial Sociology and the Convergence Hypothesis." In *Annual Review of Sociology, 5*, 1, 1979, Alex Inkeles, James Coleman, and Ralph H. Turner, eds.

Fountain, Henry. "Archaeological Site in Peru Is Called Oldest City in Americas." *New York Times*, April 27, 2001.

Fox, Elaine, and George E. Arquitt. "The VFW and the 'Iron Law of Oligarchy.'" In *Down to Earth Sociology: Introductory Readings*, 4th ed., James M. Henslin, ed. New York: Free Press, 1985: 147–155.

Fraser, Graham. "Fox Denies Free Trade Exploiting the Poor in Mexico." *Toronto Star*, April 20, 2001.

Freedman, Jane. *Feminism*. Philadelphia: Open University Press, 2001.

Freeman, Lance. "There Goes the 'Hood:' the Meaning of Gentrification to Long-Term Residents." Paper presented at the 2004 meetings of the American Sociological Association.

French, Howard W. "As Girls 'Vanish,' Chinese City Battles Tide of Abortions." *New York Times*, April 14, 2004.

Freund, Charles Paul. "A Riot of Our Own." *Reason, 32*, 10, March 2001:10.

Friedl, Ernestine. "Society and Sex Roles." In *Conformity and Conflict: Readings in Cultural Anthropology*. James P. Spradley and David W. McCurdy, eds. Glenview, Ill.: Scott, Foresman, 1990:229–238.

Friedman, Thomas. *The World Is Flat: A Brief History of the Twenty-First Century*. New York: Farrar, Straus, and Giroux, 2005.

Fuller, Rex, and Richard Schoenberger. "The Gender Salary Gap: Do Academic Achievement, Internship Experience, and College Major Make a Difference?" *Social Science Quarterly, 72*, 4, December 1991:715–726.

Furstenberg, Frank F., Jr., and Kathleen Mullan Harris. "The Disappearing American Father? Divorce and the Waning Significance of Biological Fatherhood." In The *Changing American Family: Sociological and Demographic Perspectives*, Scott J. South and Stewart E. Tolnay, eds. Boulder, Colo.: Westview Press, 1992: 197–223.

Furstenberg, Frank F., Jr., Sheela Kennedy, Vonnie C. McLoyd, Ruben G. Rumbaut, and Richard A. Settersten, Jr. "Growing Up Is Harder to Do." *Contexts, 3*, 3, Summer 2004:33–41.

Galbraith, John Kenneth. *The Nature of Mass Poverty*. Cambridge, Mass.: Harvard University Press, 1979.

Gallup, George, Jr. The *Gallup Poll: Public Opinion 1989*. Wilmington, Del.: Scholarly Resources, 1990.

Gallup Poll 2000, *Los Angeles Times Exit Poll*, November 7, 2001; *Statistical Abstract* 1999:Table 464; 2002: Table 372; Zogby 2004.

Gallup Poll. "Religion and Social Trends." Princeton, N.J.: The Gallup Organization, 2005.

Gans, Herbert. J., "Public Sociologies: Reply to Hausknecht." *Footnotes*, January 2003:8.

Gans, Herbert J. *People, Plans, and Policies: Essays on Poverty, Racism, and Other National Urban Problems*. New York: Columbia University Press, 1991.

Gans, Herbert J. "Urbanism and Suburbanism." In *Urban Man and Society: A Reader in Urban Ecology*, Albert N. Cousins and Hans Nagpaul, eds. New York: Knopf, 1970:157–164.

Gans, Herbert J. *People and Plans: Essays on Urban Problems and Solutions*. New York: Basic Books, 1968.

Gans, Herbert J. *The Urban Villagers*. New York: Free Press, 1962.

Gansberg, Martin. "37 Who Saw Murder Didn't Call the Police." *New York Times*, March 27, 1964.

Garfinkel, Harold. "Conditions of Successful Degradation Ceremonies." *American Journal of Sociology, 61*, 2, March 1956: 420–424.

Garfinkel, Harold. *Studies in Ethnomethodology*. Englewood Cliffs, N.J.: Prentice Hall, 1967.

Gatewood, Willard B. *Aristocrats of Color: The Black Elite, 1880–1920*. Bloomington: Indiana University Press, 1990.

Gautham, S. "Coming Next: The Monsoon Divorce." *New Statesman, 131*, 4574, February 18, 2002:32–33.

Gaviak, Dale. "In Sudan, Childhoods of Slavery." *Christian Science Monitor*, August 22, 2000:6.

Gerhard, Jane. "Revisiting 'The Myth of the Vaginal Orgasm': The Female Orgasm in American Sexual Thought and Second Wave Feminism." *Feminist Studies, 26*, 2, Fall 2000:449–477.

Gerson, Kathleen. *Hard Choices: How Women Decide about Work, Career, and Motherhood*. Berkeley: University of California Press, 1985.

Gerth, H. H., and C. Wright Mills. *From Max Weber: Essays in Sociology*. New York: Galaxy, 1958.

Gerth, Jeff. "Two Companies Pay Penalties for Improving China Rockets." *New York Times*, March 3, 2003.

Gilbert, Dennis L. *The American Class Structure in an Age of Growing Inequality*, 6th ed. Belmont, Calif.: Wadsworth Publishing, 2003.

Gilbert, Dennis, and Joseph A. Kahl. *The American Class Structure: A New Synthesis*. 4th ed. Belmont, Calif.: Wadsworth Publishing, 1998.

Gilligan, Carol. *The Birth of Pleasure*. New York: Knopf, 2002.

Gilman, Charlotte Perkins. *The Man-Made World or, Our Androcentric Culture*. New York: Johnson Reprint, 1971. First published in 1911.

Gitlin, Todd. *The Twilight of Common Dreams: Why America Is Wracked by Culture Wars*. New York: Metropolitan Books, 1997.

Glascock, Jack. "Gender Roles on Prime-Time Network Television: Demographics and Behaviors." *Journal of Broadcasting and Electronic Media, 45*, Fall 2001:656–669.

Glenn, Evelyn Nakano. "Chinese American Families." In *Minority Families in the United States: A Multicultural Perspective*, Ronald L. Taylor, ed. Englewood Cliffs, N.J.: Prentice Hall, 1994:115–145.

Glick, Daniel. "The Big Thaw." *National Geographic*, September 2004:13–33.

Glick, Paul C., and S. Lin. "More Young Adults Are Living with Their Parents: Who Are They?" *Journal of Marriage and Family, 48,* 1986:107–112.

Goetting, Ann. *Getting Out: Life Stories of Women Who Left Abusive Men.* New York: Columbia University Press, 2001.

Goffman, Erving. *Stigma.* Englewood Cliffs, N.J.: Prentice Hall, 1963.

Goffman, Erving. *Asylums: Essays on the Social Situation of Mental Patients and Other Inmates.* Chicago: Aldine, 1961.

Gold, Ray. "Janitors versus Tenants: A Status–Income Dilemma." *American Journal of Sociology, 58,* 1952:486–493.

Goldberg, Susan, and Michael Lewis. "Play Behavior in the Year-Old Infant: Early Sex Differences." *Child Development, 40,* March 1969:21–31.

Goldberg-Glen, Robin, Roberta G. Sands, Ralph D. Cole, and Carolyn Cristofalo. "Multigenerational Patterns and Internal Structures in Families in Which Grandparents Raise Grandchildren." *Families in Society: The Journal of Contemporary Human Services, 79,* 5, September 1998:477–489.

Goldman, Kevin. "Seniors Get Little Respect on Madison Avenue." *Wall Street Journal,* September 20, 1993:B6.

Goleman, Daniel. "Pollsters Enlist Psychologists in Quest for Unbiased Results." *New York Times,* September 7, 1993:C1, C11.

Goode, Erica. "Study Says 20% of Girls Reported Abuse by a Date." *New York Times,* August 1, 2001.

Gorman, James. "High-Tech Daydreamers Investing in Immortality." *Wall Street Journal,* November 1, 2003.

Gorman, Peter. "A People at Risk: Vanishing Tribes of South America." *The World & I,* December 1991:678–689.

Gorman, Thomas J. "Cross-Class Perceptions of Social Class." *Sociological Spectrum, 20,* 2000:93–120.

Gottfredson, Michael R., and Travis Hirschi. *A General Theory of Crime.* Stanford, Calif.: Stanford University Press, 1990.

Gottschalk, Peter, Sara McLanahan, and Gary Sandefur, "The Dynamics and Intergenerational Transmission of Poverty and Welfare Participation." In *Confronting Poverty: Prescriptions for Change,* Sheldon H. Danziger, Gary D. Sandefur, and Daniel H. Weinberg, eds. Cambridge, Mass.: Harvard University Press, 1994.

Gourevitch, Philip. "After the Genocide." *New Yorker,* December 18, 1995:78–94.

Greeley, Andrew M. "The Protestant Ethic: Time for a Moratorium." *Sociological Analysis, 25,* Spring 1964:20–33.

Greeley, Andrew M., and Michael Hout. "Americans' Increasing Belief in Life After Death: Religious Competition and Acculturation." *American Sociological Review, 64,* December 1999:813–835.

Greenhalgh, Susan, and Jiali Li. "Engendering Reproductive Policy and Practice in Peasant China: For a Feminist Demography of Reproduction." *Signs, 20,* 3, Spring 1995:601–640.

Greenhouse, Linda. "Justices Uphold Long Prison Terms in Repeat Crimes." *New York Times,* March 6, 2003.

Greider, William. "Pro Patria, Pro Mundus." *Nation, 273,* 15, November 12, 2001:22–24.

Gross, Jan T. *Neighbors.* New Haven, Conn.: Yale University Press, 2001.

Gross, Jane. "Right School for a 4-Year-Old? Find an Adviser." *New York Times,* May 28, 2003.

Gross, Jane. "In the Quest for the Perfect Look, More Girls Choose the Scalpel." *New York Times,* November 29, 1998.

Guensburg, Carol. "Bully Factories." *American Journalism Review, 23,* 6, 2001:51–59.

Guice, Jon. "Sociologists Go to Work in High Technology." *Footnotes,* November 1999:8.

"Guide to the New Congress." *Congressional Quarterly Today,* November 4, 2004.

Gunther, Marc. "The Mosquito in the Tent." *Fortune, 149,* 11, May 31, 2004:158.

Gupta, Giri Raj. "Love, Arranged Marriage, and the Indian Social Structure." In *Cross-Cultural Perspectives of Mate Selection and Marriage,* George Kurian, ed. Westport, Conn.: Greenwood Press, 1979.

Haas, Jack. "Binging: Educational Control Among High-Steel Iron Workers." *American Behavioral Scientist, 16,* 1972:27–34.

Hacker, Helen Mayer. "Women as a Minority Group." *Social Forces, 30,* October 1951:60–69.

Hage, Dave. *Reforming Welfare by Rewarding Work.* Minneapolis: University of Minnesota Press, 2004.

Hakim, Danny. "Hybrid-Car Tinkerers Scoff at No-Plug-In Rule." *New York Times,* April 2, 2005.

Hall, Edward T. *The Hidden Dimension.* Garden City, N.Y.: Anchor Books, 1969.

Hall, Edward T. *The Silent Language.* New York: Doubleday, 1959.

Hall, Edward T., and Mildred R. Hall. "The Sounds of Silence." In *Down to Earth Sociology: Introductory Readings,* 13th ed., James M. Henslin, ed. New York: The Free Press, 2005.

Hall, G. Stanley. *Adolescence: Its Psychology and Its Relations to Physiology, Anthropology, Sociology, Sex, Crime, Religion, and Education.* New York: Appleton, 1904.

Hall, Ronald E. "The Tiger Woods Phenomenon: A Note on Biracial Identity." *The Social Science Journal, 38,* 2, April 2001: 333–337.

Hamermesh, Daniel S., and Jeff E. Biddle. "Beauty and the Labor Market." *American Economic Review, 84,* 5, December 1994: 1174–1195.

Harlow, Harry F., and Margaret K. Harlow. "The Affectional Systems." In *Behavior of Nonhuman Primates: Modern Research Trends,* Vol. 2, Allan M. Schrier, Harry F. Harlow, and Fred Stollnitz, eds. New York: Academic Press, 1965:287–334.

Harlow, Harry F., and Margaret K. Harlow. "Social Deprivation in Monkeys." *Scientific American, 207,* 1962:137–147.

Harrington, Michael. *The Vast Majority: A Journey to the World's Poor.* New York: Simon & Schuster, 1977.

Harrington, Michael. *The Other America: Poverty in the United States.* New York: Macmillan, 1962.

Harris, Chauncey D. "The Nature of Cities and Urban Geography in the Last Half Century." *Urban Geography, 18,* 1997:15–35.

Harris, Chauncey D., and Edward Ullman. "The Nature of Cities." *Annals of the American Academy of Political and Social Science, 242,* 1945:7–17.

Harris, Diana K. *The Sociology of Aging.* New York: Harper, 1990.

Harris, Kim, Dwight R. Sanders, Shaun Gress, and Nick Kuhns. "Starting Salaries for Agribusiness Graduates From an AASCARR Institution: The Case of Southern Illinois University." *Agribusiness, 21,* 1, 2005:65–80.

Harris, Marvin. "Why Men Dominate Women." *New York Times Magazine,* November 13, 1977:46, 115, 117–123.

Harrison, Paige M., and Allen J. Beck. "Prison and Jail Inmates at Midyear 2004." Bureau of Justice Statistics. April 2005.

Harrison, Paul. *Inside the Third World: The Anatomy of Poverty,* 3rd ed. London: Penguin Books, 1993.

Hart, C. W. M., and Arnold R. Pilling. *The Tiwi of North Australia,* Fieldwork Edition. New York: Holt, Rinehart and Winston, 1979.

Hart, Paul. "Groupthink, Risk-Taking and Recklessness: Quality of Process and Outcome in Policy Decision Making." *Politics and the Individual, 1,* 1, 1991:67–90.

Hartley, Eugene. *Problems in Prejudice.* New York: King's Crown Press, 1946.

Hartocollis, Anemona. "Harvard Faculty Votes to Put the Excellence Back in the A." *New York Times,* May 22, 2002.

Haslick, Leonard. *Gerontologist, 14,* 1974:37–45.

Hatch, Laurie Russell. *Beyond Gender Differences: Adaptation to Aging in Life Course Perspective.* Amityville, N.Y.: Baywood Publishing Company, 2000.

Haub, Carl. "World Population Data Sheet." Washington, D.C.: Population Reference Bureau, 2005.

Haub, Carl. "World Population Data Sheet." Washington, D.C.: Population Reference Bureau, 2004.

Haub, Carl. "World Population Data Sheet." Washington, D.C.: Population Reference Bureau, 2003.

Haub, Carl. "Has Global Growth Reached Its Peak?" *Population Today, 30,* 6, August–September 2002:6.

Haub, Carl, and Nancy Yinger. "The U.N. Long-Range Population Projections: What They Tell Us." Washington, D.C.: Population Reference Bureau, 1994.

Hauser, Philip, and Leo Schnore, eds. *The Study of Urbanization.* New York: Wiley, 1965.

Hawley, Amos H. *Urban Society: An Ecological Approach.* New York: Wiley, 1981.

Hayashi, Gina M., and Bonnie R. Strickland. "Long-Term Effects of Parental Divorce on Love Relationships: Divorce as Attachment Disruption." *Journal of Social and Personal Relationships, 15,* 1, February 1998, 23–38.

Haynes, Richard M., and Donald M. Chalker. "World Class Schools." *American School Board Journal,* May 1997:20, 22–25.

Heilbrun, Alfred B. "Differentiation of Death-Row Murderers and Life-Sentence Murderers by Antisociality and Intelligence Measures." *Journal of Personality Assessment, 64,* 1990: 617–627.

Heilman, Madeline E. "Description and Prescription: How Gender Stereotypes Prevent Women's Ascent Up the Organizational Ladder." *Journal of Social Issues, 57,* 4, Winter 2001:657–674.

Helliker, Kevin. "Body and Spirit: Why Attending Religious Services May Benefit Health." *Wall Street Journal,* May 3, 2005.

Hellinger, Daniel, and Dennis R. Judd. The Democratic Façade. Pacific Grove, Calif.: Brooks/Cole, 1991.

Henley, Nancy, Mykol Hamilton, and Barrie Thorne. "Womanspeak and Manspeak." In *Beyond Sex Roles,* Alice G. Sargent, ed. St. Paul, Minn.: West, 1985.

Henslin, James M. *Social Problems,* 7th ed. Upper Saddle River, N.J.: Prentice Hall, 2006.

Henslin, James M. "On Becoming Male: Reflections of a Sociologist on Childhood and Early Socialization." In *Down to Earth Sociology: Introductory Readings,* 13th ed., James M. Henslin, ed. New York: The Free Press, 2005:143–154.

Henslin, James M., and Mae A. Biggs. "Behavior in Pubic Places: The Sociology of the Vaginal Examination." In *Down to Earth Sociology: Introductory Readings,* 13th ed., James M. Henslin, ed. New York: Free Press, 2005. Original version published as "Dramaturgical Desexualization: The Sociology of the Vaginal Examination." In *Studies in the Sociology of Sex,* James M. Henslin, ed. New York: Appleton-Century-Crofts, 1971:243–272.

Hentoff, Nat. "Bush-Ashcroft Versus Homeland Security." *The Village Voice,* April 18, 2003.

Herring, Cedric. "Is Job Discrimination Dead?" *Contexts.* Summer 2002:13–18.

Hetherington, Mavis, and John Kelly. *For Better or For Worse: Divorce Reconsidered.* New York: W. W. Norton, 2003.

Hewitt Associates. *Worklife Benefits Provided by Major U.S. Employers, 2003–2004.* Lincolnshire, Ill.: Hewitt Associates, 2004.

Higginbotham, Elizabeth, and Lynn Weber. "Moving with Kin and Community: Upward Social Mobility for Black and White Women." *Gender and Society, 6,* 3, September 1992:416–440.

Higley, Stephen. "The U.S. Upper Class." In *Down to Earth Sociology: Introductory Readings,* 12th ed., James M. Henslin, ed. New York: The Free Press, 2003:347–359.

Hill, Mark E. "Skin Color and the Perception of Attractiveness Among African Americans: Does Gender Make a Difference?" *Social Psychology Quarterly, 65,* 1, 2002:77–91.

Hilliard, Asa, III. "Do We Have the Will to Educate All Children?" *Educational Leadership, 49,* September 1991:31–36.

Hiltz, Starr Roxanne. "Widowhood." In *Marriage and Family in a Changing Society,* 3rd ed., James M. Henslin, ed. New York: Free Press, 1989:521–531.

Hippler, Fritz. Interview in a television documentary with Bill Moyers in *Propaganda,* in the series "Walk through the 20th Century," 1987.

Hirschi, Travis. *Causes of Delinquency.* Berkeley: University of California Press, 1969.

Hitt, Jack. "The Next Battlefield May Be in Outer Space." *New York Times,* August 5, 2001.

Hochschild, Arlie Russell. *The Second Shift: Working Parents and the Revolution at Home.* New York: Viking, 1989.

Hochschild, Arlie Russell. *The Managed Heart: Commercialization of Human Feeling.* Chicago: University of Chicago Press, 1983.

Hochschild, Arlie Russell. "The Sociology of Feeling and Emotion: Selected Possibilities." In *Another Voice: Feminist Perspectives on Social Life and Social Science,* Marcia Millman and Rosabeth Moss Kanter, eds. Garden City, N.Y.: Anchor Books, 1975.

Hofacker, Paul W. "The Elevation of the Elite: Historical Trends and Complicity of the Masses." *Public Organization Review: A Global Journal, 5,* 2005:3–33.

Hofferth, Sandra. "Did Welfare Reform Work? Implications for 2002 and Beyond." *Contexts,* Spring 2002:45–51.

Holloway, Andy. "Welcome to the Bioeconomy." *Canadian Business. Com,* September 2, 2002.

Holtzman, Abraham. *The Townsend Movement: A Political Study.* New York: Bookman, 1963.

Homblin, Dora Jane. *The First Cities.* Boston: Time-Life Books, 1973.

Honeycutt, Karen. "Disgusting, Pathetic, Bizarrely Beautiful: Representations of Weight in Popular Culture." Paper presented at the 1995 meetings of the American Sociological Association.

Hong, Lawrence. "Marriage in China." In *Til Death Do Us Part: A Multicultural Anthology on Marriage,* Sandra Lee Browning and R. Robin Miller, eds. Stamford, Conn.: JAI Press, 1999.

hooks, bell. *Where We Stand: Class Matters.* New York: Routledge, 2000.

Horowitz, Ruth. "Studying Violence Among the 'Lions.'" In James M. Henslin, *Social Problems.* Upper Saddle River, N.J.: Prentice Hall, 2005:135.

Horowitz, Ruth. "Community Tolerance of Gang Violence." *Social Problems, 34,* 5, December 1987:437–450.

Horowitz, Ruth. *Honor and the American Dream: Culture and Identity in a Chicano Community.* New Brunswick, N.J.: Rutgers University Press, 1983.

Hostetler, John A. *Amish Society,* 3rd ed. Baltimore: Johns Hopkins University Press, 1980.

"House Divided." *People Weekly,* May 24, 1999:126.

Houtman, Dick. "What Exactly Is a 'Social Class'?: On the Economic Liberalism and Cultural Conservatism of the 'Working Class.'" Paper presented at the 1995 meetings of the American Sociological Association.

Howells, Lloyd T., and Selwyn W. Becker. "Seating Arrangement and Leadership Emergence." *Journal of Abnormal and Social Psychology, 64,* February 1962:148–150.

Hoyt, Homer. "Recent Distortions of the Classical Models of Urban Structure." In *Internal Structure of the City: Readings on Space and Environment,* Larry S. Bourne, ed. New York: Oxford University Press, 1971:84–96.

Hoyt, Homer. *The Structure and Growth of Residential Neighborhoods in American Cities.* Washington, D.C.: Federal Housing Administration, 1939.

Hsu, Francis L. K. *The Challenge of the American Dream: The Chinese in the United States.* Belmont, Calif.: Wadsworth, 1971.

Huber, Joan. "Micro-Macro Links in Gender Stratification." *American Sociological Review, 55,* February 1990:1–10.

Huddle, Donald. "The Net National Cost of Immigration." Washington, D.C.: Carrying Capacity Network, 1993.

Hudson, Valerie M., and Andrea M. den Boer. *Bare Branches: The Security Implications of Asia's Surplus Male Population.* Cambridge, Mass.: MIT Press, 2004.

Huggins, Martha K., Mika Haritos-Fatouros, and Philip G. Zimbardo. *Violence Workers: Police Torturers and Murderers Reconstruct Brazilian Atrocities.* Berkeley: University of California Press, 2002.

Hughes, Everett C. "Good People and Dirty Work." In *Life in Society: Readings to Accompany Sociology: A Down-to-Earth Approach, Seventh Edition,* James M. Henslin, ed. Boston: Allyn and Bacon, 2005:125–134. Article originally published in 1962.

Hughes, H. Stuart. *Oswald Spengler: A Critical Estimate,* rev. ed. New York: Scribner's, 1962.

Hughes, Kathleen A. "Even Tiki Torches Don't Guarantee a Perfect Wedding." *Wall Street Journal,* February 20, 1990:A1, A16.

Humphreys, Laud. "Impersonal Sex and Perceived Satisfaction." In *Studies in the Sociology of Sex,* James M. Henslin, ed. New York: Appleton-Century-Crofts, 1971:351–374.

Humphreys, Laud. *Tearoom Trade: Impersonal Sex in Public Places,* enlarged ed. Chicago: Aldine, 1970, 1975.

Hundley, Greg. "Why Women Earn Less Than Men in Self-Employment." *Journal of Labor Research, 22,* 4, Fall 2001:817–827.

Hunt, Stephen. *The Life Course: A Sociological Introduction.* London: Palgrave Macmillan, 2005.

Hurtado, Aída, David E. Hayes-Bautista, R. Burciaga Valdez, and Anthony C. R. Hernández. *Redefining California: Latino Social Engagement in a Multicultural Society.* Los Angeles: UCLA Chicano Studies Research Center, 1992.

Huttenbach, Henry R. "*The Roman Porajmos:* The Nazi Genocide of Europe's Gypsies." *Nationalities Papers, 19,* 3, Winter 1991:373–394.

Hymowitz, Carol. "Through the Glass Ceiling." *Wall Street Journal,* November 8, 2004.

Iori, Ron. "The Good, the Bad and the Useless." *Wall Street Journal,* June 10, 1988:18R.

Ismail, M. Asif. "The Clinton Top 100: Where Are They Now?" Washington, D.C.: The Center for Public Integrity, 2003.

Itard, Jean Marc Gospard. *The Wild Boy of Aveyron.* Translated by George and Muriel Humphrey. New York: Appleton-Century-Crofts, 1962.

Jacobs, Charles. "Money Talks." *The Boston Globe,* February 19, 1999.

Jacobs, Jerry A. "Detours on the Road to Equality: Women, Work and Higher Education." *Contexts,* Winter 2003:32–41.

Jacobs, Margaret A. "'New Girl' Network Is Boon for Women Lawyers." *Wall Street Journal,* March 4, 1997:B1, B7.

Jaggar, Alison M. "Sexual Difference and Sexual Equality." In *Theoretical Perspectives on Sexual Difference,* Deborah L. Rhode, ed. New Haven, Conn.: Yale University Press, 1990:239–254.

Janis, Irving. L. *Groupthink: Psychological Studies of Policy Decisions and Fiascoes.* Boston: Houghton Mifflin, 1982.

Janis, Irving L. *Victims of Groupthink.* Boston: Houghton Mifflin, 1972.

Jankowiak, William R., and Edward F. Fischer. "A Cross-Cultural Perspective on Romantic Love." *Journal of Ethnology, 31,* 2, April 1992:149–155.

Jankowski, Martín Sánchez. *Islands in the Street: Gangs and American Urban Society.* Berkeley: University of California Press, 1991.

Jaspar, James M. "Moral Dimensions of Social Movements." Paper presented at the annual meetings of the American Sociological Association, 1991.

Jenkins, Philip. "The Next Christianity." *Atlantic Monthly,* October 2002:53–68.

Jerrome, Dorothy. *Good Company: An Anthropological Study of Old People in Groups.* Edinburgh, England: Edinburgh University Press, 1992.

Johansson, Perry. "Consuming the Other: The Fetish of the Western Woman in Chinese Advertising and Popular Culture." *Postcolonial Studies, 2,* 3, November 1999.

Johnson, Benton. "On Church and Sect." *American Sociological Review, 28,* 1963:539–549.

Johnson, Paul. *A History of the American People.* New York: HarperCollins, 1998.

Jones, Dale E., et al. "Religious Congregations and Membership in the United States 2000: An Enumeration by Region, State and County. Based on Data Reported by 149 Religious Bodies." Nashville, Tenn.: Glenmary Research Center, 2002.

Jones, Del. "Female CEOs Struggle in '04." *Money Magazine,* January 4, 2005.

Jones, James H. *Bad Blood: The Tuskegee Syphilis Experiment,* 2nd ed. New York: Free Press, 1993.

Jones, Steve. "Let the Games Begin: Gaming Technology and Entertainment Among College Students." Washington, D.C.: PEW Internet and American Life Project, 2003.

Jordan, Miriam. "Blacks vs. Latinos at Work." *Wall Street Journal,* January 24, 2006.

Jordan, Miriam. "New Ethnic Bloc Emerges in Race for L. A. Mayor." *Wall Street Journal,* April 13, 2005.

Jordan, Miriam. "Among Poor Villagers, Female Infanticide Still Flourishes in India." *Wall Street Journal,* May 9, 2000:A1, A12.

Judge, Timothy A., and Daniel M. Cable. "The Effect of Physical Height on Workplace Success and Income: Preliminary Test of a Theoretical Model." Unpublished paper, 2004.

"Judge Rules Against Ford in Discrimination Lawsuit." *New York Times,* March 17, 2005.

Juergensmeyer, Mark. *Terror in the Mind of God: The Global Rise of Religious Violence.* Berkeley: University of California Press, 2000.

Kaebnick, Gregory E. "On the Sanctity of Nature." *Hastings Center Report, 30,* 5, September–October 2000:16–23.

Kagan, Jerome. "The Idea of Emotions in Human Development." In *Emotions, Cognition, and Behavior,* Carroll E. Izard, Jerome Kagan, and Robert B. Zajonc, eds. New York: Cambridge University Press, 1984:38–72.

Kahn, Joseph. "Some Chinese See the Future, and It's Capitalist." *New York Times,* May 4, 2002.

Kalb, Claudia. "Faith and Healing." *Newsweek,* November 10, 2003:44–56.

Kalb, Claudia. "The War on Disease Goes Miniature." *Newsweek,* January 1, 2000:89.

Kalof, Linda. "Vulnerability to Sexual Coercion Among College Women: A Longitudinal Study." *Gender Issues, 18,* 4, Fall 2000:47–58.

Kanter, Rosabeth Moss. *The Change Masters: Innovation and Entrepreneurship in the American Corporation.* New York: Simon & Schuster, 1983.

Kanter, Rosabeth Moss. *Men and Women of the Corporation.* New York: Basic Books, 1977.

Karp, David A., Gregory P. Stone, and William C. Yoels. *Being Urban: A Sociology of City Life,* 2nd ed. New York: Praeger, 1991.

Karp, David A., and William C. Yoels. "Sport and Urban Life." *Journal of Sport and Social Issues, 14,* 2, 1990:77–102.

Kart, Cary S. *The Realities of Aging: An Introduction to Gerontology,* 3rd ed. Boston: Allyn and Bacon, 1990.

Katz, Sidney. "The Importance of Being Beautiful." In *Down to Earth Sociology: Introductory Readings,* 13th ed., James M. Henslin, ed. New York: The Free Press, 2005:323–330.

Kaufman, Joanne. "Married Maidens and Dilatory Domiciles." *Wall Street Journal,* May 7, 1996:A16.

Keith, Jennie. *Old People, New Lives: Community Creation in a Retirement Residence,* 2nd ed. Chicago: University of Chicago Press, 1982.

Kelly, Joan B. "How Adults React to Divorce." In *Marriage and Family in a Changing Society,* 4th ed., James M. Henslin, ed. New York: Free Press, 1992:410–423.

Keniston, Kenneth. *Youth and Dissent: The Rise of a New Opposition.* New York: Harcourt Brace Jovanovich, 1971.

"Kenya: Girls Score Court Victory Against Genital Mutilation." *Women's International Network News, 27,* 2, Spring 2001:64.

Kephart, William M., and William W. Zellner. *Extraordinary Groups: An Examination of Unconventional Life-Styles,* 7th ed. New York: Worth Publishing, 2001.

Kerr, Clark. *The Future of Industrialized Societies.* Cambridge, Mass.: Harvard University Press, 1983.

Kibria, Nazli. *Family Tightrope: The Changing Lives of Vietnamese Americans.* Princeton, N.J.: Princeton University Press, 1993.

Kifner, John. "Building Modernity on Desert Mirages." *New York Times,* February 7, 1999.

Kingston, Maxine Hong. *The Woman Warrior.* New York: Vintage Books, 1975:108. Quoted in Frank J. Zulke, and Jacqueline P. Kirley. *Through the Eyes of Social Science,* 6th ed. Prospect Heights, Ill.: Waveland Press, 2002.

Kinsella, Kevin, and David R. Phillips. "Global Aging: The Challenge of Success." Washington, D.C.: Population Reference Bureau, 2005.

Klahanie Association Web site. http://www.klahanie.com/

Klandermans, Bert. *The Social Psychology of Protest.* Cambridge, Mass.: Blackwell, 1997.

Kleinfeld, Judith S. "Gender and Myth: Data About Student Performance." In *Through the Eyes of Social Science,* 6th ed., Frank J. Zulke and Jacqueline P. Kirley, eds. Prospect Heights, Ill.: Waveland Press, 2002a:380–393.

Kleinfeld, Judith S. "The Small World Problem." *Society,* January–February, 2002b:61–66.

Kluegel, James R., and Eliot R. Smith. *Beliefs About Inequality: America's Views of What Is and What Ought to Be.* Hawthorne, N.Y.: Aldine de Gruyter, 1986.

Knickerbocker, Brad. "Firebrands of 'Ecoterrorism' Set Sights on Urban Sprawl." *Christian Science Monitor,* August 6, 2003.

Kohlberg, Lawrence, and Carol Gilligan. "The Adolescent as a Philosopher: The Discovery of the Self in a Postconventional World." *Daedalus, 100,* 1971:1051–1086.

Kohn, Melvin L. *Class and Conformity: A Study in Values,* 2nd ed. Homewood, Ill.: Dorsey Press, 1977.

Kohn, Melvin L. "Occupational Structure and Alienation." *American Journal of Sociology, 82,* 1976:111–130.

Kohn, Melvin L. "Social Class and Parent–Child Relationships: An Interpretation." *American Journal of Sociology, 68,* 1963:471–480.

Kohn, Melvin L. "Social Class and Parental Values." *American Journal of Sociology, 64,* 1959:337–351.

Kohn, Melvin L., and Carmi Schooler. *Work and Personality: An Inquiry into the Impact of Social Stratification.* New York: Ablex Press, 1983.

Kohn, Melvin L., and Carmi Schooler. "Class, Occupation, and Orientation." *American Sociological Review, 34,* 1969:659–678.

Kohn, Melvin L., Kazimierz M. Slomczynski, and Carrie Schoenbach. "Social Stratification and the Transmission of Values in the Family: A Cross-National Assessment." *Sociological Forum, 1,* 1, 1986:73–102.

Kontos, Louis, David Brotherton, and Luis Barrios, eds. *Gangs and Society: Alternative Perspectives.* New York: Columbia University Press, 2003.

Krane, Vikki, Julie A. Stiles-Shipley, Jennifer Waldron, and Jennifer Michalenok. "Relationships Among Body Satisfaction, Social Physique Anxiety, and Eating Behaviors in Female Athletes and Exercisers." *Journal of Sport Behavior, 24,* 3, September 2001: 247–264.

Krause, Neal, and Christopher G. Ellison. "Forgiveness by God, Forgiveness of Others, and Psychological Well-Being in Late Life." *Journal for the Scientific Study of Religion, 42,* 1, 2003: 77–93.

Kraybill, Donald B. *The Riddle of Amish Culture.* Revised edition. Baltimore, Md.: Johns Hopkins University Press, 2002.

Kreider, Rose M., and Tavia Simmons. "Marital Status 2000." U.S. Bureau of the Census, October 2003.

Kristoff, Nicholas D. "Interview With a Humanoid." *New York Times,* July 23, 2002.

Kronholz, June. "Immigration Costs Move to Fore." *Wall Street Journal,* May 24, 2006.

KRT News Services. "U.S. Nearly Had bin Laden, Omar." December 23, 2003.

Krugman, Paul. "White Man's Burden." *New York Times,* September 24, 2002.

Kubrin, Charis E., and Ronald Weitzer. "Retaliatory Homicide: Concentrated Disadvantage and Neighborhood Culture." *Social Problems, 50,* 2, May 2003:157–180.

Kurian, George Thomas. *Encyclopedia of the Third World,* Vols. 1, 2, 3. New York: Facts on File, 1992.

Kurian, George Thomas. *Encyclopedia of the Second World.* New York: Facts on File, 1991.

Kurian, George Thomas. *Encyclopedia of the First World,* Vols. 1, 2. New York: Facts on File, 1990.

Lacayo, Richard. "The 'Cultural' Defense." *Time,* Fall 1993:61.

Lachica, Eduardo. "Third World Told to Spend More on Environment." *Wall Street Journal,* May 18, 1992:A2.

Lagaipa, Susan J. "Suffer the Little Children: The Ancient Practice of Infanticide as a Modern Moral Dilemma." *Issues in Comprehensive Pediatric Nursing, 13,* 1990:241–251.

Lalumiere, Martin L., and Vernon Quinsey. "Good Genes, Mating Effort, and Delinquency." *Behavioral and Brain Sciences, 23,* 4, August 2000:608–609.

Lamb, David. "Hanoi: Shedding the Ghosts of War." *National Geographic,* May 2004:80–97.

Landtman, Gunnar. *The Origin of the Inequality of the Social Classes.* New York: Greenwood Press, 1968. First published in 1938.

Lang, Kurt, and Gladys E. Lang. *Collective Dynamics.* New York: Crowell, 1961.

Lareau, Annette. "Invisible Inequality: Social Class and Childrearing in Black Families and White Families." *American Sociological Review, 67,* October 2002:747–776.

Larson, Jeffry H. "The Marriage Quiz: College Students' Beliefs in Selected Myths about Marriage." *Family Relations,* January 1988:3–11.

Laub, John H., and Robert J. Sampson. *Shared Beginnings, Divergent Lives: Delinquent Boys to Age 70.* Cambridge, Mass.: Harvard University Press, 2004.

Lauer, Jeanette, and Robert Lauer. "Marriages Made to Last." In *Marriage and Family in a Changing Society,* 4th ed., James M. Henslin, ed. New York: Free Press, 1992:481–486.

LeDuff, Charlie. "Handling the Meltdowns of the Nuclear Family." *New York Times,* May 28, 2003.

Lee, Alfred McClung, and Elizabeth Briant Lee. *The Fine Art of Propaganda: A Study of Father Coughlin's Speeches.* New York: Harcourt Brace, 1939.

Lee, Nick. *Childhood and Society: Growing Up in an Age of Uncertainty.* New York: Open University Press, 2001.

Lee, Raymond M. *Unobtrusive Methods in Social Research.* Philadelphia: Open University Press, 2000.

Lee, Sharon M. "Asian Americans: Diverse and Growing." *Population Bulletin, 53,* 2, June 1998:1–39.

Lee, Sunmin, Graham Colditz, Lisa Berkman, and Ichiro Kawachi. "Caregiving to Children and Grandchildren and Risk of Coronary Heart Disease in Women." *American Journal of Public Health, 93,* November 2003:1939–1944.

Lee, Yun-Suk, and Linda J. Waite. "Husbands' and Wives' Time Spent on Housework: A Comparison of Measures." *Journal of Marriage and Family, 67,* May 2005:325–336.

Leland, John. "A New Harlem Gentry in Search of Its Latte." *New York Times,* August 7, 2003.

Leland, John, and Gregory Beals. "In Living Colors." *Newsweek,* May 5, 1997:58–60.

Lemann, Nicholas. "The Myth of Community Development." *New York Times Magazine,* January 9, 1994:27.

Lenski, Gerhard. *Power and Privilege: A Theory of Social Stratification.* New York: McGraw-Hill, 1966.

Lenski, Gerhard. "Status Crystallization: A Nonvertical Dimension of Social Status." *American Sociological Review, 19,* 1954:405–413.

Lenski, Gerhard, and Jean Lenski. *Human Societies: An Introduction to Macrosociology,* 5th ed. New York: McGraw-Hill, 1987.

Lerner, Gerda. *The Creation of Patriarchy.* New York: Oxford University Press, 1986.

Lerner, Gerda. *Black Women in White America: A Documentary History.* New York: Pantheon Books, 1972.

"Less Rote, More Variety: Reforming Japan's Schools." *The Economist,* December 16, 2000:8.

Lester, David. *Suicide in American Indians.* New York: Nova Science Publishers, 1997.

Letherby, Gayle. "Childless and Bereft? Stereotypes and Realities in Relation to 'Voluntary' and'Involuntary' Childlessness and Womanhood." *Sociological Inquiry, 72,* 1, Winter 2002:7–20.

Levine, John M. "Solomon Asch's Legacy for Group Research." *Personality and Social Psychology Review, 3,* 4, 1999:358–364.

Levinson, D. J. *The Seasons of a Man's Life.* New York: Knopf, 1978.

Levy, Marion J., Jr. "Confucianism and Modernization." *Society, 24,* 4, May–June 1992:15–18.

Lewin, Tamar. "Little Sympathy or Remedy for Inmates Who Are Raped." *New York Times,* April 15, 2001b.

Lewis, Neil A. "Justice Dept. Toughens Rules on Torture." *New York Times,* January 1, 2005.

Lewis, Oscar. "The Culture of Poverty." *Scientific American, 113,* October 1966a:19–25.

Lewis, Oscar. *La Vida.* New York: Random House, 1966b.

Lewis, Richard S. *Challenger: The Final Voyage.* New York: Columbia University Press, 1988.

Lichtblau, Eric. "Librarians Say Yes, Officials Do Quiz Them About Users." *New York Times,* June 20, 2005.

Lichter, Daniel T., and Martha L. Crowley. "Poverty in America: Beyond Welfare Reform." *Population Bulletin, 57,* 2, June 2002: 1–36.

Liebow, Elliott. *Tally's Corner: A Study of Negro Streetcorner Men.* Boston: Little, Brown, 1999. Originally published in 1967.

Liebow, Elliot. "Tally's Corner." In *Down to Earth Sociology: Introductory Readings,* 9th ed., James M. Henslin, ed. New York: Free Press, 1997:330–339.

Lightfoot-Klein, A. "Rites of Purification and Their Effects: Some Psychological Aspects of Female Genital Circumcision and Infibulation (Pharaonic Circumcision) in an Afro-Arab Society (Sudan)." *Journal of Psychological Human Sexuality, 2,* 1989:61–78.

Lind, Michael. *The Next American Nation: The New Nationalism and the Fourth American Revolution.* New York: Free Press, 1995.

Linden, Eugene. "Lost Tribes, Lost Knowledge." *Time,* September 23, 1991:46, 48, 50, 52, 54, 56.

Lines, Patricia M. "Homeschooling Comes of Age." *Public Interest,* Summer 2000:74–85.

Linton, Ralph. *The Study of Man.* New York: Appleton-Century-Crofts, 1936.

Lippitt, Ronald, and Ralph K. White. "An Experimental Study of Leadership and Group Life." In *Readings in Social Psychology,* 3rd ed., Eleanor E. Maccoby, Theodore M. Newcomb, and Eugene L. Hartley, eds. New York: Holt, Rinehart and Winston, 1958:340–365. (As summarized in Olmsted and Hare 1978: 28–31.)

Lipset, Seymour Martin. "The Social Requisites of Democracy Revisited." Presidential address to the American Sociological Association, Boston, Massachusetts, 1993.

Lipset, Seymour Martin, ed. *The Third Century: America as a Post-Industrial Society.* Stanford, Calif.: Hoover Institution Press, 1979.

Lipset, Seymour Martin. "Democracy and Working-Class Authoritarianism." *American Sociological Review, 24,* 1959:482–502.

Lombroso, Cesare. *Crime: Its Causes and Remedies,* H. P. Horton, trans. Boston: Little, Brown, 1911.

Lublin, Joann S. "Who Made the Biggest Bucks." *Wall Street Journal,* April 12, 2004.

Lublin, Joann S. "Living Well." *Wall Street Journal,* April 8, 1999.

Lublin, Joann S. "Women at Top Still Are Distant from CEO Jobs." *Wall Street Journal,* February 28, 1996:B1.

Lucas, Samuel Roundfield. *Tracking Inequality: Stratification and Mobility in American High Schools.* New York: Teachers College Press, 1999.

Luhnow, David. "As Jobs Move East, Plants in Mexico Retool to Compete." *Wall Street Journal,* March 5, 2004.

Lunneborg, Patricia. *Chosen Lives of Childfree Men.* Westport, Conn.: Bergin and Garvey, 1999.

Lurie, Nicole, Jonathan Slater, Paul McGovern, Jacqueline Ekstrum, Lois Quam, and Karen Margolis. "Preventive Care for Women: Does the Sex of the Physician Matter?" *New England Journal of Medicine, 329,* August 12, 1993:478–482.

Mabry, Marcus. "The Price Tag on Freedom." *Newsweek,* May 3, 1999:50–51.

MacDonald, William L., and Alfred DeMaris. "Remarriage, Stepchildren, and Marital Conflict: Challenges to the Incomplete Institutionalization Hypothesis." *Journal of Marriage and the Family, 57,* May 1995:387–398.

MacWilliams, Bryon. "For Russia's Universities, a Decade of More Freedom and Less Money." *The Chronicle of Higher Education,* December 14, 2001:A42–44.

Magnuson, E. "A Cold Soak, a Plume, a Fireball." *Time,* February 17, 1986:25.

Mahoney, John S., Jr., and Paul G. Kooistra. "Policing the Races: Structural Factors Enforcing Racial Purity in Virginia (1630–1930)." Paper presented at the 1995 meetings of the American Sociological Association.

Mahran, M. "Medical Dangers of Female Circumcision." *International Planned Parenthood Federation Medical Bulletin, 2,* 1981:1–2.

Mahran, M. *Proceedings of the Third International Congress of Medical Sexology.* Littleton, Mass.: PSG Publishing, 1978.

Maier, Mark. "Teaching from Tragedy: An Interdisciplinary Module on the Space Shuttle *Challenger.*" *T. H. E. Journal,* September 1993:91–94.

Malthus, Thomas Robert. *First Essay on Population 1798.* London: Macmillan, 1926. Originally published in 1798.

Mamdani, Mahmood. "The Myth of Population Control: Family, Caste, and Class in an Urban Village." New York: Monthly Review Press, 1973.

Mander, Jerry. *In the Absence of the Sacred: The Failure of Technology and the Survival of the Indian Nations.* San Francisco, Calif.: Sierra Club Books, 1992.

Manno, Bruno V. "The Real Score on the SATs." *Wall Street Journal,* September 13, 1995:A14.

Manski, Charles F. "Income and Higher Education." *Focus, 14,* 3, Winter 1992–1993:14–19.

Manzo, Kathleen Kennedy. "History in the Making." *Community College Week, 13,* 15, March 5, 2001:6–8.

Marable, Manning. "Whites Have an Obligation to Recognize Slavery's Legacy." *Newsweek,* August 27, 2001:22.

Marshall, Samantha. "It's So Simple: Just Lather Up, Watch the Fat Go down the Drain." *Wall Street Journal,* November 2, 1995:B1.

Marshall, Samantha. "Vietnamese Women Are Kidnapped and Later Sold in China as Brides." *Wall Street Journal,* August 3, 1999.

Martin, Philip, and Elizabeth Midgley. "Immigration: Shaping and Reshaping America." *Population Bulletin, 58,* 2, June 2003:1–44.

Martineau, Harriet. *Society in America.* Garden City, N.Y.: Doubleday 1962. First published in 1837.

Marx, Karl. "Contribution to the Critique of Hegel's Philosophy of Right." In *Karl Marx: Early Writings,* T. B. Bottomore, ed. New York: McGraw-Hill, 1964:45. First published in 1844.

Marx, Karl, and Friedrich Engels. *Communist Manifesto.* New York: Pantheon, 1967. First published in 1848.

Massey, Douglas S., and Garvey Lundy. "Use of Black English and Racial Discrimination in Urban Housing Markets: New Methods and Findings." *Urban Affairs Review, 36,* 2001: 451–468.

Mathews, T. J., and Brady E. Hamilton. "Mean Age of Mother, 1970–2000." *National Vital Statistics Report, 51,* 1, December 11, 2002.

Mauss, Armand. *Social Problems as Social Movements.* Philadelphia: Lippincott, 1975.

McAdam, Doug, John D. McCarthy, and Mayer N. Zald. "Social Movements." In *Handbook of Sociology,* Neil J. Smelser, ed. Newbury Park, Calif.: Sage, 1988:695–737.

McCall, Michael. "Who and Where Are the Artists?" In *Fieldwork Experience: Qualitative Approaches to Social Research,* William B. Shaffir, Robert A. Stebbins, and Allan Turowetz, eds. New York: St. Martin's, 1980:145–158.

McCarthy, John D., and Mayer N. Zald. "Resource Mobilization and Social Movements: A Partial Theory." *American Journal of Sociology, 82,* 6, 1977:1212–1241.

McCarthy, Michael J., "Granbury, Texas, Isn't a Rural Town: It's a 'Micropolis.'" *Wall Street Journal,* June 3, 2004.

McCarthy, Michael J. "James Bond Hits the Supermarket: Stores Snoop on Shoppers' Habits to Boost Sales." *Wall Street Journal,* August 25, 1993:B1, B8.

McCormick, John. "The Sorry Side of Sears." *Newsweek,* February 22, 1999a:36–39.

McCormick, John. "Change Has Taken Place." *Newsweek,* June 7, 1999b:34.

McFalls, Joseph A., Jr. "Population: A Lively Introduction," 4th ed. *Population Bulletin, 58,* 1, December 2003:1–40.

McGee, Glenn. "Cloning, Sex, and New Kinds of Families." *Journal of Sex Research, 37,* 3, August 2000:266–272.

McGinn, Daniel, and Jason McLure. "Home School: The Ring." *Newsweek,* November 10, 2003:12.

McIntosh, Peggy. "White Privilege and Male Privilege: A Personal Account of Coming to See Correspondences Through Work in Women's Studies." Working Paper #189. Wellesley College Center for Research on Women, 1988.

McKenna, George. "On Abortion: A Lincolnian Position." *Atlantic Monthly,* September 1995:51–67.

McKeown, Thomas. *The Modern Rise of Population.* New York: Academic Press, 1977.

McLanahan, Sara, and Dona Schwartz. "Life Without Father: What Happens to the Children?" *Contexts, 1,* 1, Spring 2002:35–44.

McLanahan, Sara, and Gary Sandefur. *Growing Up with a Single Parent: What Hurts, What Helps.* Cambridge, Mass.: Harvard University Press, 1994.

McLemore, S. Dale. *Racial and Ethnic Relations in America.* Boston: Allyn and Bacon, 1994.

McNeil, Donald G., Jr. "In Angola's Capital, Life Does Not Yet Imitate Art." *New York Times,* January 25, 1999.

McNeill, William H. "How the Potato Changed the World's History." *Social Research, 66,* 1, Spring 1999:67–83.

Mead, George Herbert. *Mind, Self and Society.* Chicago: University of Chicago Press, 1934.

Medlin, Richard G. "Home Schooling and the Question of Socialization." *Peabody Journal of Education, 75,* 1–2, 2000:107–123.

Meek, Anne. "On Creating 'Ganas': A Conversation with Jaime Escalante." *Educational Leadership, 46,* 5, February 1989:46–47.

Meltzer, Scott A. "Gender, Work, and Intimate Violence: Men's Occupational Spillover and Compensatory Violence." *Journal of Marriage and the Family, 64,* 2, November 2002:820–832.

Melucci, Alberto. *Nomads of the Present: Social Movements and Individual Needs in Contemporary Society.* Philadelphia: Temple University Press, 1989.

Menaghan, Elizabeth G., Lori Kowaleski-Jones, and Frank L. Mott. "The Intergenerational Costs of Parental Social Stressors: Academic and Social Difficulties in Early Adolescence for Children of Young Mothers." *Journal of Health and Social Behavior, 38,* March 1997:72–86.

Menzel, Peter. *Material World: A Global Family Portrait.* San Francisco: Sierra Club, 1994.

Merton, Robert K. *Social Theory and Social Structure.* Glencoe, Ill.: Free Press, 1949, Enlarged ed., 1968.

Merton, Robert K. *Social Theory and Social Structure,* enlarged ed. New York: Free Press, 1968.

Merton, Robert K. "The Social-Cultural Environment and Anomie." In *New Perspectives for Research on Juvenile Delinquency,* Helen L. Witmer and Ruth Kotinsky, eds. Washington, D.C.: U.S. Department of Health, Education, and Welfare, 1956:24–50.

Merwine, Maynard H. "How Africa Understands Female Circumcision." *New York Times,* November 24, 1993.

Messner, Michael A., Margaret Carlisle Duncan, and Cheryl Cooky. "Silence, Sports Bras, and Wrestling Porn." *Journal of Sport and Social Issues, 27,* 1, February 2003:38–51.

Mezentseva, E. *Russian Social Science Review, 42,* 4, July–August 2001:4–21.

Michael, Robert T., John H. Gagnon, Edward O. Laumann, and Gina Kolata. "How Many Sexual Partners Do Americans Have?" In *Exploring Social Life: Readings to Accompany Essentials of Sociology: A Down-to-Earth Approach, Fifth Edition,* James M. Henslin, ed. Boston: Allyn and Bacon, 2004:166–174.

Michels, Robert. *Political Parties.* Glencoe, Ill.: Free Press, 1949. First published in 1911.

"Microchips Under the Skin Offer ID, Raise Questions." *New York Times,* December 22, 2001.

Milbank, Dana. "Guarded by Greenbelts, Europe's Town Centers Thrive." *Wall Street Journal,* May 3, 1995:B1, B4.

Milbank, Dana. "Working Poor Fear Welfare Cutbacks Aimed at the Idle Will Inevitably Strike Them, Too." *Wall Street Journal,* August 9, 1995:A10.

Milgram, Stanley. "The Small World Problem." *Psychology Today, 1,* 1967:61–67.

Milgram, Stanley. "Some Conditions of Obedience and Disobedience to Authority." *Human Relations, 18,* February 1965:57–76.

Milgram, Stanley. "Behavioral Study of Obedience." *Journal of Abnormal and Social Psychology, 67,* 4, 1963:371–378.

Milkie, Melissa A. "Social World Approach to Cultural Studies." *Journal of Contemporary Ethnography, 23,* 3, October 1994:354–380.

Miller, Walter B. "Lower Class Culture as a Generating Milieu of Gang Delinquency." *Journal of Social Issues,* 14, 3, 1958:5–19.

Mills, C. Wright. *The Sociological Imagination.* New York: Oxford University Press, 1959.

Mills, C. Wright. *The Power Elite.* New York: Oxford University Press, 1956.

Mills, Karen M., and Thomas J. Palumbo. *A Statistical Portrait of Women in the United States: 1978.* U.S. Bureau of the Census, *Current Population Reports,* Series P-23, no. 100, 1980.

Minkler, Meredith, and Ann Robertson. "The Ideology of 'Age/Race Wars': Deconstructing a Social Problem." *Ageing and Society, 11,* 1, March 1991:1–22.

Mintz, Beth A., and Michael Schwartz. *The Power Structure of American Business.* Chicago: University of Chicago Press, 1985.

Mirola, William A. "Asking for Bread, Receiving a Stone: The Rise and Fall of Religious Ideologies in Chicago's Eight-Hour Movement." *Social Problems, 50,* 2, May 2003:273–293.

Mohawk, John C. "Indian Economic Development: An Evolving Concept of Sovereignty." *Buffalo Law Review, 39,* 2, Spring 1991:495–503.

Mol, Arthur P. *Globalization and Environmental Reform: The Ecological Modernization of the Global Economy.* Cambridge, Mass.: MIT Press, 2001.

Money, John, and Anke A. Ehrhardt. *Man and Woman, Boy and Girl.* Baltimore: Johns Hopkins University Press, 1972.

"Monkey Rescued From Being Put on Menu." Associated Press, July 16, 2004.

Montagu, M. F. Ashley, ed. *Race and IQ: Expanded Edition.* New York: Oxford University Press, 1999.

Montagu, M. F. Ashley. *The Concept of Race.* New York: Free Press, 1964.

Montagu, M. F. Ashley. *Introduction to Physical Anthropology,* 3rd ed. Springfield, Ill.: Thomas, 1960.

Morgan, Lewis Henry. *Ancient Society.* 1877.

Morris, Joan M., and Michael D. Grimes. "Moving Up from the Working Class." In *Down to Earth Sociology: Introductory Readings,* 13th ed., James M. Henslin, ed. New York: The Free Press, 2005: 365–376.

Mosca, Gaetano. *The Ruling Class.* New York: McGraw-Hill, 1939. First published in 1896.

Mosher, Steven W. "Too Many People? Not by a Long Shot." *Wall Street Journal,* February 10, 1997:A18.

Mosher, Steven W. "Why Are Baby Girls Being Killed in China?" *Wall Street Journal,* July 25, 1983:9.

Mosher, William D., Anjani Chandra, and Jo Jones. "Sexual Behavior and Selected Health Measures." *Advance Data from Vital and Health Statistics, 362,* September 15, 2005:1–56.

Mount, Ferdinand. *The Subversive Family: An Alternative History of Love and Marriage.* New York: Free Press, 1992.

Moynihan, Daniel Patrick. "Social Justice in the *Next* Century." *America,* September 14, 1991:132–137.

Munson, Martha L., and Paul D. Sutton. "Births, Marriages, Divorces, and Deaths: Provisional Data for November 2004." *National Vital Statistics Reports, 53,* 19, May 3, 2005.

Murdock, George Peter. *Social Structure.* New York: Macmillan, 1949.

Murray, Charles. "The Coming White Underclass." *Wall Street Journal,* October 29, 1993:A16.

Nabhan, Gary Paul. *Cultures in Habitat: On Nature, Culture, and Story.* New York: Counterpoint, 1998.

Nagourney, Eric. "Fertility: A Study Links Prayer and Pregnancy." *New York Times,* October 2, 2001.

Nakao, Keiko, and Judith Treas. "Occupational Prestige in the United States Revisited: Twenty-Five Years of Stability and Change." Paper presented at the annual meetings of the American Sociological Association, 1990. (As referenced in Kerbo, Harold R. Social Stratification and Inequality: *Class Conflict in Historical and Comparative Perspective,* 2nd ed. New York: McGraw-Hill, 1991:181.)

Nash, Gary B. *Red, White, and Black.* Englewood Cliffs, N.J.: Prentice Hall, 1974.

Nathan, John. *Sony: The Private Life.* New York: Houghton Mifflin, 1999.

National Center for Education Statistics. *Digest of Education Statistics.* Washington, D.C.: U.S. Government Printing Office, 1991.

National Institute of Child Health and Human Development. "Child Care and Mother–Child Interaction in the First 3 Years of Life." *Developmental Psychology, 35,* 6, November 1999:1399–1413.

National School Safety Center. School Associated Violent Deaths: Westlake Village, Calif., 2005.

National Women's Political Caucus. "Factsheet on Women's Political Progress." Washington, D.C., June 1998.

Nauta, André. "That They All May Be One: Can Denominationalism Die?" Paper presented at the annual meetings of the American Sociological Association, 1993.

Navarro, Mireya. "For New York's Black Latinos, a Growing Racial Awareness." *New York Times,* April 28, 2003.

Neely, Mark E., Jr. *The Fate of Liberty: Abraham Lincoln and Civil Liberties.* New York: Oxford University Press, 1992.

Neikirk, William, and Glen Elsasser. "Ruling Weakens Abortion Right." *Chicago Tribune,* June 30, 1992:1, 8.

Neugarten, Bernice L. "Personality and Aging." In *Handbook of the Psychology of Aging,* James E. Birren and K. Warren Schaie, eds. New York: Van Nostrand Reinhold, 1977:626–649.

Neugarten, Bernice L. "Middle Age and Aging." In *Growing Old in America,* Beth B. Hess, ed. New Brunswick, N.J.: Transaction Books, 1976:180–197.

Niebuhr, Gustav. "Studies Suggest Lower Count for Number of U.S. Muslims." *New York Times,* October 25, 2001.

Niebuhr, H. Richard. *The Social Sources of Denominationalism.* New York: Holt, 1929.

Nieves, Evelyn. "Lumber Company Approves U.S. Deal to Save Redwoods." *New York Times,* March 3, 1999.

Nisbett, Richard E. *The Geography of Thought: How Asians and Westerners Think Differently . . . and Why.* New York: The Free Press, 2003.

Nordland, Rod. "That Joke Is a Killer." *Newsweek,* May 19, 2003:10.

Nsamenang, A. Bame. *Human Development in Cultural Context: A Third World Perspective.* Newbury Park, Calif.: Sage, 1992.

Nussenbaum, Evelyn. "Video Game Makers Go Hollywood. Uh-Oh." *New York Times,* August 22, 2004.

O'Brien, John E. "Violence in Divorce-Prone Families." In *Violence in the Family,* Suzanne K. Steinmetz and Murray A. Straus, eds. New York: Dodd, Mead, 1975:65–75.

O'Brien, Timothy L. "Fed Assesses Citigroup Unit $70 Million in Loan Abuse." *New York Times,* May 28, 2004.

Offen, Karen. "Feminism and Sexual Difference in Historical Perspective." In *Theoretical Perspectives on Sexual Difference,* Deborah L. Rhode, ed. New Haven, Conn.: Yale University Press, 1990:13–20.

Ogburn, William F. *On Culture and Social Change: Selected Papers,* Otis Dudley Duncan, ed. Chicago: University of Chicago Press, 1964.

Ogburn, William F. "The Hypothesis of Cultural Lag." In *Theories of Society: Foundations of Modern Sociological Theory,* Vol. 2, Talcott Parsons, Edward Shils, Kaspar D. Naegele, and Jesse R. Pitts, eds. New York: Free Press, 1961:1270–1273.

Ogburn, William F. *Social Change, With Respect to Culture and Original Nature.* New York: Viking Press, 1938. First published in 1922.

Ogburn, William F. "The Family and its Functions." In *Recent Social Trends in the United States: Report of the President's Research Committee on Social Trends.* New York: McGraw-Hill, 1933:661–708.

O'Hare, William P. "A New Look at Poverty in America." *Population Bulletin, 51,* 2, September 1996a:1–47.

O'Hare, William P. "U.S. Poverty Myths Explored: Many Poor Work Year-Round, Few Still Poor After Five Years." *Population Today: News, Numbers, and Analysis, 24,* 10, October 1996b:1–2.

Oliver, Richard W. *The Biotech Age: The Business of Biotech and How to Profit From It.* New York: McGraw Hill, 2003.

Olmsted, Michael S., and A. Paul Hare. *The Small Group,* 2nd ed. New York: Random House, 1978.

O'Malley, Michael. "Ashcroft's Agenda: Civil Liberties Take a Back Seat to the Fight on Terrorism." *Orbis,* August, 2003.

"On History and Heritage: John K. Castle." *Penn Law Journal,* Fall 1999.

Ono, Hiroshi. "Who Goes to College? Features of Institutional Tracking in Japanese Higher Education." *American Journal of Education, 109,* 12, February 2001:161–195.

Ono, Yumiko. "By Dint of Promotion Japanese Entrepreneur Ignites a Soccer Frenzy." *Wall Street Journal,* September 17, 1993:A1, A6.

Orme, Nicholas. *Medieval Children.* New Haven, Conn.: Yale University Press, 2002.

Orwell, George. *1984.* New York: Harcourt Brace, 1949.

Osborne, Lawrence. "Got Silk." *New York Times Magazine,* June 15, 2002.

Ostling, Richard N. "Faith May Prevent Drug Abuse." *New York Times,* November 14, 2001.

Ouchi, William. "Decision-Making in Japanese Organizations." In *Down to Earth Sociology,* 7th ed., James M. Henslin, ed. New York: Free Press, 1993:503–507.

Ouchi, William. *Theory Z: How American Business Can Meet the Japanese Challenge.* Reading, Mass.: Addison-Wesley, 1981.

Padgett, Tim. "An Ivy Stepladder." *Time,* April 4, 2005.

Pagelow, Mildred Daley. "Adult Victims of Domestic Violence: Battered Women." *Journal of Interpersonal Violence, 7,* 1, March 1992:87–120.

Pager, Devah. "Blacks and Ex-Cons Need Not Apply." *Context, 2,* 3, Fall 2003:58–59.

Palen, John J. *The Urban World,* 7th ed. Boston: McGraw Hill, 2005.

Parfit, Michael, "Earth First!ers Wield a Mean Monkey Wrench." *Smithsonian, 21,* 1, April 1990:184–204.

Park, Robert Ezra. "Human Ecology." *American Journal of Sociology, 42,* 1, July 1936:1–15.

Park, Robert E., and Ernest W. Burgess. *Human Ecology.* Chicago: University of Chicago Press, 1921.

Parmesan, Camille, and Gary Yohe. "A Globally Coherent Fingerprint of Climate Change Impacts Across Natural Systems." *Nature,* January 2003:37–42.

Parsons, Talcott. "An Analytic Approach to the Theory of Social Stratification." *American Journal of Sociology, 45,* 1940: 841–862.

Partington, Donald H. "The Incidence of the Death Penalty for Rape in Virginia." *Washington and Lee Law Review, 22,* 1965:43–75.

Pascoe, C. J. "Multiple Masculinities? Teenage Boys Talk About Jocks and Gender." *American Behavioral Scientist, 46,* 10, June 2003:1423–1438.

Passell, Peter. "Race, Mortgages and Statistics." *New York Times,* May 10, 1996:D1, D4.

Patel, Pragna. "Third Wave Feminism and Black Women's Activism." In *Black British Feminism: A Reader,* Heidi Safia Mirza, ed. London: Routledge, 1997.

Pauken, Tom. Personal communication, January 10, 2003.

Pearlin, L. I., and Melvin L. Kohn. "Social Class, Occupation, and Parental Values: A Cross-National Study." *American Sociological Review, 31,* 1966:466–479.

Pedersen, R. P. "How We Got Here: It's Not How You Think." *Community College Week, 13,* 15, March 15, 2001:4–5.

Peña, Maria. "Patrullaje de voluntarios destaca urgencia de aprobar reforma." *EFE.* April 3, 2005.

Peters, Jeremy W., and Danny Hakim. "Ford's Lending Practices Challenged in a Lawsuit." *New York Times,* March 1, 2005.

Peterson, Iver. "1993 Deal for Indian Casino Is Called a Model to Avoid." *New York Times,* June 30, 2003.

Peterson, Janice. "Welfare Reform and Inequality: The TANF and UI Programs." *Journal of Economic Issues, 34,* 2, June 2000: 517–526.

Pfann, Gerard A., et al. "Business Success and Businesses' Beauty Capital." *Economics Letters, 67,* 2, May 2000:201–207.

Piaget, Jean. *The Construction of Reality in the Child.* New York: Basic Books, 1954.

Piaget, Jean. *The Psychology of Intelligence.* London: Routledge & Kegan Paul, 1950.

Pines, Maya. "The Civilizing of Genie." *Psychology Today, 15,* September 1981:28–34.

Piotrow, Phylis Tilson. *World Population Crisis: The United States' Response.* New York: Praeger, 1973.

Polsby, Nelson W. "Three Problems in the Analysis of Community Power." *American Sociological Review, 24,* 6, December 1959: 796–803.

Polumbaum, Judy. "China: Confucian Tradition Meets the Market Economy." *Ms.,* September–October 1992:12–13.

Pope, Justin. *"SAT Scores for the High School Class of 2004 Are Unchanged from a Year Ago."* Associated Press, September 1, 2004.

Pope, Liston. *Millhands and Preachers: A Study of Gastonia.* New Haven, Conn.: Yale University Press, 1942.

"Population Today." Washington, D.C.: Population Reference Bureau, *32,* 1, January–February, 2004.

"Population Today." Washington, D.C.: Population Reference Bureau, *34,* 1, January–February 2006.

"Population Today." Washington, D.C.: Population Reference Bureau, May/June 2002:7.

Portes, Alejandro, and Ruben G. Rumbaut. *Immigrant America.* Berkeley: University of California Press, 1990.

Powell, Lynda H., Leila Shahabi, and Carl E. Thoresen. "Religion and Spirituality: Linkages to Physical Health." *American Psychologist, 58,* 1, January 2003:36–52.

Prashad, Vijay. "Tolerance Arabia." *Colorlines Magazine, 5,* 1, Spring 2002:18–23.

Princiotta, Daniel, Stacey Bielick, and Chris Chapman. "1.1 Million Homeschooled Students in the United States in 2003." *Education Statistics Quarterly, 6,* 3, 2004:23–25.

Prystay, Cris, and Geoffrey A. Fowler. "They Shun Hard-Body Look, Preferring Pills, Teas and Gels." *Wall Street Journal,* October 9, 2003.

Purdum, Todd S. "NATO Strikes Deal to Accept Russia in a Partnership." *New York Times,* May 15, 2002.

Raghunathan, V. K. "Millions of Baby Girls Killed in India." *The Straits Times,* February 8, 2003.

Rainwater, Lee, and Timothy M. Smeeding. *Poor Kids in a Rich Country: America's Children in Comparative Perspective.* New York: Russell Sage, 2003.

Ramos, Jorge. "Project Minuteman Is Meaningless." *Oakland Tribune.* April 10, 2005.

Raney, Rebecca Fairley. "Study Warns of Risks in Internet Voting." *New York Times,* March 8, 1999.

Ray, J. J. "Authoritarianism Is a Dodo: Comment on Scheepers, Felling and Peters." *European Sociological Review, 7,* 1, May 1991: 73–75.

Reckless, Walter C. *The Crime Problem,* 5th ed. New York: Appleton, 1973.

Reed, Susan. "My Sister, My Clone." *Time,* February 19, 2001.

Reed, Susan, and Lorenzo Benet. "Ecowarrior Dave Foreman Will Do Whatever It Takes in His Fight to Save Mother Earth." *People Weekly, 33,* 15, April 16, 1990:113–116.

Regalado, Antonio. "Seoul Team Creates Custom Stem Cells from Cloned Embryos." *Wall Street Journal,* May 20, 2005.

Reibstein, Larry. "Managing Diversity." *Newsweek,* November 25, 1996:50.

Reich, Robert B. *Good for Business: Making Full Use of the Nation's Human Capital, The Environmental Scan.* Washington, D.C.: U.S. Department of Labor, March 1995.

Reiman, Jeffrey. *The Rich Get Richer and the Poor Get Prison: Ideology, Class, and Criminal Justice,* 7th ed. Boston: Allyn and Bacon, 2004.

Reiser, Christa. *Reflections on Anger: Women and Men in a Changing Society.* Westport, Conn.: Praeger Publishers, 1999.

Reitman, Valerie, and Oscar Suris. "In a Cultural U-Turn, Mazda's Creditors Put Ford behind the Wheel." *Wall Street Journal,* November 21, 1994:A1, A4.

Rennison, Callie Marie. "Intimate Partner Violence, 1993–2001." Washington, D.C.: Bureau of Justice Statistics, February 2003.

Renteln, Alison Dundes. "Sex Selection and Reproductive Freedom." *Women's Studies International Forum, 15,* 3, 1992:405–426.

Reskin, Barbara F. *The Realities of Affirmative Action in Employment.* Washington, D.C.: American Sociological Association, 1998.

Resnik, David B. "Financial Interests and Research Bias." *Perspectives on Science, 8,* 3, Fall 2000:255–283.

Reuters. "Fake Tiger Woods Gets 200-Years-To-Life in Prison." April 28, 2001.

Rich, Spencer. "Number of Elected Hispanic Officials Doubled in a Decade, Study Shows." *Washington Post,* September 19, 1986:A6.

Richardson, Stacey, and Marita P. McCabe. "Parental Divorce During Adolescence and Adjustment in Early Adulthood." *Adolescence, 36,* Fall 2001:467–489.

Ricks, Thomas E. "'New' Marines Illustrate Growing Gap Between Military and Society." *Wall Street Journal,* July 27, 1995:A1, A4.

Rideout, Victoria J., and Elizabeth A. Vandewater. "Zero to Six: Electronic Media in the Lives of Infants, Toddlers and Preschoolers." Kaiser Family Foundation, Fall 2003.

Rieker, Patricia P., Chloe E. Bird, Susan Bell, Jenny Ruducha, Rima E. Rudd, and S. M. Miller, "Violence and Women's Health: Toward a Society and Health Perspective." Unpublished paper, 1997.

Riley, Nancy E. "China's Population: New Trends and Challenges." *Population Bulletin, 59,* 2, June 2004:3–36.

Risen, James, David Johnston, and Neil A. Lewis. "Harsh C. I. A. Methods Cited in Top Qaeda Interrogations." *New York Times,* May 13, 2004.

Rist, Ray C. "Student Social Class and Teacher Expectations: The Self- Fulfilling Prophecy in Ghetto Education." *Harvard Educational Review, 40,* 3, August 1970:411–451.

Ritzer, George. "The McDonaldization of Society." In *Down to Earth Sociology: Introductory Readings,* 11th ed., James M. Henslin, ed. New York: The Free Press, 2001:459–471.

Ritzer, George. *The McDonaldization Thesis: Explorations and Extensions.* Thousand Oaks, Calif.: Sage Publications, 1998.

Ritzer, George. *The McDonaldization of Society: An Investigation into the Changing Character of Contemporary Life.* Thousand Oaks, Calif.: Pine Forge Press, 1993.

Robertson, Ian. *Sociology,* 3rd ed. New York: Worth, 1987.

Rodriguez, Richard. "Searching for Roots in a Changing Society." In *Down to Earth Sociology: Introductory Readings,* 8th ed., James M. Henslin, ed. New York: Free Press, 1995:486–491.

Rodriguez, Richard. "Mixed Blood." *Harper's Magazine, 283,* November 1991:47–56.

Rodriguez, Richard. "The Late Victorians: San Francisco, AIDS, and the Homosexual Stereotype." *Harper's Magazine,* October 1990:57–66.

Rodriguez, Richard. *Hunger of Memory: The Education of Richard Rodriguez.* Boston: Godine, 1982.

Rodriguez, Richard. "The Education of Richard Rodriguez." *Saturday Review,* February 8, 1975:147–149.

Roediger, David R. *Colored White: Transcending the Racial Past.* Berkeley: University of California Press, 2002.

Rogers, Joseph W. *Why Are You Not a Criminal?* Englewood Cliffs, N.J.: Prentice Hall, 1977.

Rogers, Stacy J., and Paul R. Amato. "Have Changes in Gender Relations Affected Marital Quality?" *Social Forces, 79,* December 2000:731–748.

Rosenfeld, Richard. "Crime Decline in Context." *Contexts, 1,* 1, Spring 2002:25–34.

Rosenthal, Elisabeth. "Harsh Chinese Reality Feeds a Black Market in Women." *New York Times,* June 25, 2001.

Rosenthal, Elisabeth. "China's Chic Waistline: Convex to Concave." *New York Times,* December 9, 1999.

Ross, Casey. "Jackpot Grandma Busy Eluding Moochers." *Boston Herald,* July 14, 2004:2.

Ross, Stephen L., and Margery Austin Turner. "Housing Discrimination in Metropolitan America: Explaining Changes Between 1989 and 2000." *Social Problems, 52,* 2, May 2005:152–180.

Rossi, Alice S. "Gender and Parenthood." *American Sociological Review, 49,* 1984:1–18.

Rossi, Alice S. "A Biosocial Perspective on Parenting." *Daedalus, 106,* 1977:1–31.

Roth, Louise Marie. "Selling Women Short: A Research Note on Gender Differences in Compensation on Wall Street." *Social Forces, 82,* 2, December 2003:783–802.

Rotstein, Arthur H. "Minuteman Volunteers May Have Played Prank." Associated Press, April 7, 2005.

Rubin, Zick. "The Love Research." In *Marriage and Family in a Changing Society,* 2nd ed., James M. Henslin, ed. New York: Free Press, 1985.

Rudner, Lawrence M. "The Scholastic Achievement of Home School Students." *ERIC/AE Digest,* September 1, 1999.

Ruggles, Patricia. "Short and Long Term Poverty in the United States: Measuring the American 'Underclass.'" Washington, D.C.: Urban Institute, June 1989.

Russell, Diana E. H. "Preliminary Report on Some Findings Relating to the Trauma and Long-Term Effects of Intrafamily Childhood Sexual Abuse." Unpublished paper.

"Russia: Expert Says Corruption in Education Costs $1 Billion a Year." *Asia Africa Intelligence Wire,* October 5, 2004.

Saenz, Rogelio. "Latinos and the Changing Face of America." Washington, D.C.: Population Reference Bureau, 2004:1–28.

Safran, William. "Pluralism and Multiculturalism in France: Post-Jacobin Transformations." *Political Science Quarterly, 118,* 3, Fall 2003:437–466.

Sahlins, Marshall D., and Elman R. Service. *Evolution and Culture.* Ann Arbor: University of Michigan Press, 1960.

Sales, Leila. "Facebook Is the Greatest Thing Since Marx." *Chicago Maroon,* May 4, 2004.

Salopek, Paul. "Shattered Sudan: Drilling for Oil, Hoping for Peace." *National Geographic, 203,* 2, February 2003:30–66.

Sampson, Robert J., Gregory D. Squires, and Min Zhou. *How Neighborhoods Matter: The Value of Investing at the Local Level.* Washington, D.C.: American Sociological Association, 2001.

Sampson, Robert J., Jeffrey D. Morenoff, and Felton Earls. "Beyond Social Capital: Spatial Dynamics of Collective Efficacy for Children." *American Sociological Review, 64,* October 1999:633–660.

Samuelson, Paul Anthony, and William D. Nordhaus. *Economics,* 18th ed. New York: McGraw Hill, 2005.

Sandefur, Gary D. "Children in Single-Parent Families: The Roles of Time and Money." *Focus, 17,* 1, Summer 1995:44–45.

Sapir, Edward. *Selected Writings of Edward Sapir in Language, Culture, and Personality,* David G. Mandelbaum, ed. Berkeley: University of California Press, 1949.

Savells, Jerry. "Social Change Among the Amish." In *Down to Earth Sociology: Introductory Readings,* 13th ed., James M. Henslin, ed. New York: The Free Press, 2005:510–519.

Sayer, Liana C., Philip N. Cohen, and Lynne M. Casper. "Women, Men, and Work." Washington, D.C.: Population Reference Bureau, 2004:1–31.

Sayres, William. "What Is a Family Anyway?" In *Marriage and Family in a Changing Society,* 4th ed., James M. Henslin, ed. New York: Free Press, 1992:23–30.

Scarr, Sandra, and Marlene Eisenberg. "Child Care Research: Issues, Perspectives, and Results." *Annual Review of Psychology, 44,* 1993:613–644.

Schackner, Bill. "How to Win New 'Friends' With a Click." *Pittsburgh Post-Gazette.* November 28, 2004.

Schaefer, Richard T. *Racial and Ethnic Groups,* 9th ed. Upper Saddle River, N.J.: Prentice Hall, 2004.

Schaefer, Richard T. *Sociology,* 3rd ed. New York: McGraw-Hill, 1989.

Schellenberg, James A. *Conflict Resolution: Theory, Research, and Practice.* Albany: New York University Press, 1996.

Schmiege, Cynthia J., Leslie N. Richards, and Anisa M. Zvonkovic. "Remarriage: For Love or Money?" *Journal of Divorce and Remarriage,* May–June 2001:123–141.

Schmitt, Eric. "How Army Sleuths Stalked the Adviser Who Led to Hussein." *New York Times,* December 20, 2003.

Schoenborn, Charlotte A. "Marital Status and Health: United States, 1999–2002." *Vital and Health Statistics, 351,* December 15, 2004:1–32.

Schottland, Charles I. *The Social Security Plan in the U.S.* New York: Appleton, 1963.

Scommegna, Paola. "Increased Cohabitation Changing Children's Family Settings." *Population Today, 30,* 7, October 2002:3, 6.

Scott, Janny. "White Flight, This Time Toward Harlem." *New York Times,* February 25, 2001.

Scott, Monster Kody. *Monster: The Autobiography of an L.A. Gang Member.* New York: Penguin Books, 1994.

Scully, Diana. "Negotiating to Do Surgery." In *Dominant Issues in Medical Sociology,* 3rd ed., Howard D. Schwartz, ed. New York: McGraw-Hill, 1994:146–152.

Scully, Diana, and Joseph Marolla. "'Riding the Bull at Gilley's': Convicted Rapists Describe the Rewards of Rape." In *Down to Earth Sociology: Introductory Readings,* 13th ed., James M. Henslin, ed. New York: The Free Press, 2005:48–62.

Scully, Diana, and Joseph Marolla. "Convicted Rapists' Vocabulary of Motive: Excuses and Justifications." *Social Problems, 31,* 5, June 1984:530–544.

Segal, Nancy L. *Entwined Lives: Twins and What They Tell Us about Human Behavior.* New York: Plume, 2000.

Sege, Irene. "Where Everybody Knows Your Name." *Boston Globe.* April 27, 2005.

Seltzer, Judith A. "Consequences of Marital Dissolution for Children." *Annual Review of Sociology, 20,* 1994:235–266.

Shane, Scott. "Through the Revolving Door, a Pot of Gold Still Awaits." *New York Times,* December 28, 2004.

Sharp, Deborah. "Miami's Language Gap Widens." *USA Today,* April 3, 1992:A1, A3.

Sharp, Lauriston. "Steel Axes for Stone-Age Australians." In *Down to Earth Sociology: Introductory Readings,* 8th ed., James M. Henslin, ed. New York: Free Press, 1995:453–462.

Sherif, Muzafer, and Carolyn Sherif. *Groups in Harmony and Tension.* New York: Harper & Row, 1953.

Sherman, Spencer. "The Hmong in America." *National Geographic,* October 1988:586–610.

Shibutani, Tamotsu. "On the Personification of Adversaries." In *Human Nature and Collective Behavior,* Tamotsu Shibutani, ed. Englewood Cliffs, N.J.: Prentice Hall, 1970.

Shields, Stephanie A. *Speaking from the Heart: Gender and the Social Meaning of Emotion.* New York: Cambridge University Press, 2002.

Shively, JoEllen. "Cowboys and Indians: Perceptions of Western Films Among American Indians and Anglos." *American Sociological Review, 57,* December 1992:725–734.

Shively, JoEllen. "Cultural Compensation: The Popularity of Westerns Among American Indians." Paper presented at the annual meetings of the American Sociological Association, 1991.

Sidel, Robin. "A Historian's Quest Links J. P. Morgan to Slave Ownership." *Wall Street Journal,* May 10, 2005.

"Sierra Leone: Female Circumcision Is a Vote Winner." African News Service, March 21, 2005.

Sills, David L. *The Volunteers.* Glencoe, Ill.: Free Press, 1957.

Silverman, Eric K. "Anthropology and Circumcision." *Annual Review of Anthropology, 33,* 2004:419–445.

Simmel, Georg. *The Sociology of Georg Simmel,* Kurt H. Wolff, ed. and trans. Glencoe, Ill.: Free Press, 1950. First published between 1902 and 1917.

Simon, Julian L. "The Nativists Are Wrong." *Wall Street Journal,* August 4, 1993:A10.

Simon, Julian L. *Theory of Population and Economic Growth.* New York: Blackwell, 1986.

Simon, Julian L. *The Ultimate Resource.* Princeton, N.J.: PrincetonR University Press, 1981.

Simons, Marlise. "Social Change and Amazon Indians." In *Exploring Social Life: Readings to Accompany Essentials of Sociology,* 5th ed., James M. Henslin, ed. Boston: Allyn and Bacon, 2004:158–165.

Simpson, George Eaton, and J. Milton Yinger. *Racial and Cultural Minorities: An Analysis of Prejudice and Discrimination,* 4th ed. New York: Harper & Row, 1972.

Skeels, H. M. *Adult Status of Children With Contrasting Early Life Experiences: A Follow-up Study.* Monograph of the Society for Research in Child Development, 31, 3, 1966.

Skeels, H. M., and H. B. Dye. "A Study of the Effects of Differential Stimulation on Mentally Retarded Children." *Proceedings and Addresses of the American Association on Mental Deficiency, 44,* 1939:114–136.

Skinner, Jonathan, James N. Weinstein, Scott M. Sporer, and John E. Wennberg. "Racial, Ethnic, and Geographic Disparities in Rates of Knee Arthroplasty Among Medicare Patients." *New England Journal of Medicine, 349,* 14, October 2, 2003:1350–1359.

Sklair, Leslie. *Globalization: Capitalism and Its Alternatives,* 3rd ed. New York: Oxford: University Press, 2001.

Smart, Barry. "On the Disorder of Things: Sociology, Postmodernity and the 'End of the Social.'" *Sociology, 24,* 3, August 1990:397–416.

Smedley, Brian D., Adrienne Y. Stith, and Alan R. Nelson eds. *Unequal Treatment: Confronting Racial and Ethnic Disparities in Health Care.* Washington, D.C.: The National Academies Press, 2003.

Smith, Beverly A. "An Incest Case in an Early 20th-Century Rural Community." *Deviant Behavior, 13,* 1992:127–153.

Smith, Christian, and Robert Faris. "Socioeconomic Inequality in the American Religious System: An Update and Assessment." *Journal for the Scientific Study of Religion, 44,* 1, 2005:95–104.

Smith, Craig S. "China Becomes Industrial Nations' Most Favored Dump." *Wall Street Journal,* October 9, 1995:B1.

Smith, Jackie, Charles Chatfield, and Ron Pagnucco. *Transnational Social Movements and Global Policy: Solidarity Beyond the State.* Syracuse, N.Y.: Syracuse University Press, 1997.

Smith John S. "Testimony Before Congress, March 14, 1865." Archives of the West, 1856–1868. Public Broadcasting Service online.

Smith, Simon C. "The Making of a Neo-Colony? Anglo-Kuwaiti Relations in the Era of Decolonization." *Middle Eastern Studies, 37,* 1, January 2001:159–173.

Smock, Pamela J., Wendy D. Manning, and Sanjiv Gupta. "The Effect of Marriage and Divorce on Women's Economic Well-Being." *American Sociological Review, 64,* December 1999: 794–812.

Snyder, Mark. "Self-Fulfilling Stereotypes." In *Down to Earth Sociology: Introductory Readings,* 7th ed., James M. Henslin, ed. New York: Free Press, 1993:153–160.

Solomon, Charlene Marmer. "Cracks in the Glass Ceiling." *Workforce, 79,* 9, September 2000:87–91.

Soss, Joe. "Lessons of Welfare: Policy Design, Political Learning, and Political Action." *American Political Science Review, 93,* 1999: 363–380.

Sourcebook of Criminal Justice Statistics. Washington, D.C.: U.S. Government Printing Office, published annually.

South, Scott J. "Sociodemographic Differentials in Mate Selection Preferences." *Journal of Marriage and the Family,* 53, November 1991:928–940.

Sowell, Thomas. *Inside American Education: The Decline, the Deception, the Dogmas.* New York: Free Press, 1993.

Spector, Malcolm, and John Kitsuse. *Constructing Social Problems.* Menlo Park, Calif.: Cummings, 1977.

Spencer, Jane. "Shirk Ethic: How to Face a Hard Day at the Office." *Wall Street Journal,* May 15, 2003:D1, D3.

Spengler, Oswald. *The Decline of the West,* 2 vols., Charles F. Atkinson, trans. New York: Knopf, 1926–1928. First published in 1919–1922.

Spickard, P. R. S. *Mixed Blood: Intermarriage and Ethnic Identity in Twentieth Century America.* Madison: University of Wisconsin Press, 1989.

Spitzer, Steven. "Toward a Marxian Theory of Deviance." *Social Problems, 22,* June 1975:608–619.

Spivak, Gayatri Chakravorty. "Feminism 2000: One Step Beyond." *Feminist Review, 64,* Spring 2000:113.

Sprecher, Susan, and Rachita Chandak. "Attitudes About Arranged Marriages and Dating Among Men and Women from India." *Free Inquiry in Creative Sociology, 20,* 1, May 1992:59–69.

Srole, Leo, et al. *Mental Health in the Metropolis: The Midtown Manhattan Study.* New York: New York University Press, 1978.

Stack, Carol B. *All Our Kin: Strategies for Survival in a Black Community.* New York: Harper, 1974.

Stampp, Kenneth M. *The Peculiar Institution: Slavery in the Ante-Bellum South.* New York: Vintage Books, 1956.

Stark, Rodney. *Sociology,* 3rd ed. Belmont, Calif.: Wadsworth, 1989.

Starna, William A., and Ralph Watkins. "Northern Iroquoian Slavery." *Ethnohistory, 38,* 1, Winter 1991:34–57.

"State of American Education: A 5-Year Report Card on American Education." U.S. Department of Education, February 22, 2000.

Statistical Abstract. See U.S. Bureau of the Census.

Stecklow, Steve. "SAT Scores Rise Strongly After Test Is Overhauled." *Wall Street Journal,* August 24, 1995:B1, B12.

Steele, Shelby, "Reparations Enshrine Victimhood, Dishonoring Our Ancestors." *Newsweek,* August 27, 2001:23.

Steinberg, Jacques. "Student Failure Causes States to Retool Testing Programs." *New York Times,* December 22, 2000.

Steinberg, Laurence, Stanford Dornbusch, and Bradford Brown. *Beyond the Classroom.* New York: Simon & Shuster, 1996.

Stevens, Mitchell L. *Kingdom of Children: Culture and Controversy in the Homeschooling Movement.* Princeton: Princeton University Press, 2001.

"Sticky Ticket: A New Jersey Mother Sues Her Son Over a Lottery Jackpot She Claims Belongs to Them Both." *People Weekly,* February 9, 1998:68.

Stinnett, Nicholas. "Strong Families." In *Marriage and Family in a Changing Society,* 4th ed., James M. Henslin, ed. New York: Free Press, 1992:496–507.

Stinson, Kandi M. *Women and Dieting Culture: Inside a Commercial Weight Loss Group.* New Brunswick, N.J.: Rutgers University Press, 2001.

Stipp, David. "Himalayan Tree Could Serve as Source of Anti-cancer Drug Taxol, Team Says." *Wall Street Journal,* April 20, 1992:B4.

Stockwell, John. "The Dark Side of U.S. Foreign Policy." *Zeta Magazine,* February 1989:36–48.

Stodgill, Ralph M. *Handbook of Leadership: A Survey of Theory and Research.* New York: Free Press, 1974.

Stolberg, Sheryl Gay. "Blacks Found on Short End of Heart Attack Procedure." *New York Times,* May 10, 2001.

Stone, Gregory P. "City Shoppers and Urban Identification: Observations on the Social Psychology of City Life." *American Journal of Sociology, 60,* November 1954:276–284.

Strategic Energy Policy: Challenges for the 21st Century. New York: Council on Foreign Relations, 2001.

Straus, Murray A. "Explaining Family Violence." In *Marriage and Family in a Changing Society,* 4th ed., James M. Henslin, ed. New York: Free Press, 1992:344–356.

Straus, Murray A., and Richard J. Gelles. "Violence in American Families: How Much Is There and Why Does It Occur?" In *Troubled Relationships,* Elam W. Nunnally, Catherine S. Chilman, and Fred M. Cox, eds. Newbury Park, Calif.: Sage, 1988:141–162.

Stryker, Sheldon. "Symbolic Interactionism: Themes and Variations." In *Social Psychology: Sociological Perspectives,* Morris Rosenberg and Ralph H. Turner, eds. New Brunswick, N.J.: Transaction Books, 1990.

"Study Suggests Lungs Damaged in Healthy Kids Exposed to High Levels of Air Pollution." *Canadian Press,* November 28, 2001.

Suizzo, Marie-Anne. "The Social-Emotional and Cultural Contexts of Cognitive Development: Neo-Piagetian Perspectives." *Child Development, 71,* 4, August 2000:846–849.

Sullivan, Andrew. "What's So Bad About Hate?" *New York Times Magazine,* September 26, 1999.

Sullivan, Andrew. "What We Look Up to Now." *New York Times,* November 15, 1998.

Sumner, William Graham. *Folkways: A Study in the Sociological Importance of Usages, Manners, Customs, Mores, and Morals.* New York: Ginn, 1906.

Sutherland, Edwin H. *White Collar Crime.* New York: Dryden Press, 1949.

Sutherland, Edwin H. *Principles of Criminology,* 4th ed. Philadelphia: Lippincott, 1947.

Sutherland, Edwin H. *Criminology.* Philadelphia: Lippincott, 1924.

Sutherland, Edwin H., Donald R. Cressey, and David F. Luckenbill. *Principles of Criminology,* 11th ed. Dix Hills, N.Y.: General Hall, 1992.

Sutton, Paul D., and T. J. Matthews. "Trends in Characteristics of Births by State: United States, 1990, 1995, and 2000–20002." *National Vital Statistics Reports, 52,* 19, May 10, 2004:1–150.

Suzuki, Bob H. "Asian-American Families." In *Marriage and Family in a Changing Society,* 2nd ed., James M. Henslin, ed. New York: Free Press, 1985:104–119.

Sweeney, Megan M. "Remarriage and the Nature of Divorce: Does It Matter Which Spouse Chose to Leave?" *Journal of Family Issues, 23*, 3, April 2002:410–440.

Sykes, Gresham M., and David Matza. "Techniques of Neutralization." In *Down to Earth Sociology: Introductory Readings,* 5th ed., James M. Henslin, ed. New York: Free Press, 1988:225–231. First published in 1957.

Szasz, Thomas S. *Cruel Compassion: Psychiatric Control of Society's Unwanted.* Syracuse: Syracuse University Press, 1998.

Szasz, Thomas S. "Mental Illness Is Still a Myth." In *Deviant Behavior 96/97,* Lawrence M. Salinger, ed. Guilford, Conn.: Dushkin, 1996:200–205.

Szasz, Thomas S. *The Myth of Mental Illness,* rev. ed. New York: Harper & Row, 1986.

Tach, Laura, and George Farkas. "Ability Grouping and Educational Stratification in the Early School Years." Unpublished paper, 2003.

Tafoya, Sonya M., Hans Johnson, and Laura E. Hill. "Who Chooses to Choose Two?" Washington, D.C.: Population Reference Bureau, 2005.

Taneja, V., S. Sriram, R. S. Beri, V. Sreenivas, R. Aggarwal, R. Kaur, and J. M. Puliyel. "'Not by Bread Alone': Impact of a Structured 90-Minute Play Session on Development of Children in an Orphanage." *Child Care, Health & Development, 28,* 1, 2002: 95–100.

Tavernise, Sabrina. "Gathering News in the New Russia Can Be Fatal." *New York Times,* April 16, 2002.

Taylor, Chris. "The Man Behind Lara Croft." *Time,* December 6, 1999:78.

Taylor, Howard F. "The Structure of a National Black Leadership Network: Preliminary Findings." Unpublished manuscript, 1992. As cited in Margaret L. Andersen and Howard F. Taylor, *Sociology: Understanding a Diverse Society.* Belmont, Calif.: Wadsworth, 2000.

Taylor, Monique M. *Harlem: Between Heaven and Hell.* Minneapolis: University of Minnesota Press, 2002.

Terhune, Chad. "Pepsi, Vowing Diversity Isn't Just Image Polish, Seeks Inclusive Culture." *Wall Street Journal,* April 19, 2005.

Thomas, Paulette. "Boston Fed Finds Racial Discrimination in Mortgage Lending Is Still Widespread." *Wall Street Journal,* October 9, 1992:A3.

Thomas, Paulette. "U.S. Examiners Will Scrutinize Banks with Poor Minority-Lending Histories." *Wall Street Journal,* October 22, 1991:A2.

Thomas, W. I., and Dorothy Swaine Thomas. *The Child in America: Behavior Problems and Programs.* New York: Alfred A. Knopf, 1928.

Thompson, Ginger. "Chasing Mexico's Dream into Squalor." *New York Times,* February 11, 2001.

Thompson, William. "Handling the Stigma of Handling the Dead." In *Life in Society: Readings to Accompany Sociology A Down-to-Earth Approach, Seventh Edition,* James M. Henslin, ed. Boston: Allyn and Bacon, 2005:70–82.

Thornton, Russell. *American Indian Holocaust and Survival: A Population History since 1492.* Norman: University of Oklahoma Press, 1987.

Thurow, Roger. "Farms Destroyed, Stricken Sudan Faces Food Crisis." *Wall Street Journal,* February 7, 2005.

Tilly, Charles. *Social Movements, 1768–2004.* Boulder, Colo.: Paradigm Publishers, 2004.

Timasheff, Nicholas S. War and Revolution. Joseph F. Scheuer, ed. New York: Sheed & Ward, 1965.

Tobias, Andrew. "The 'Don't Be Ridiculous' Law." *Wall Street Journal,* May 31, 1995:A14.

Toffler, Alvin. *The Third Wave.* New York: Morrow, 1980.

Tönnies, Ferdinand. *Community and Society (Gemeinschaft und Gesellschaft).* New Brunswick, N.J.: Transaction Books, 1988. First published in 1887.

Torres, Jose B., V. Scott H. Solberg, and Aaron H. Carlstrom. "The Myth of Sameness Among Latino Men and Their Machismo." *American Journal of Orthopsychiatry, 72,* 2, 2002: 163–181.

Toynbee, Arnold. *A Study of History,* D. C. Somervell, abridger and ed. New York: Oxford University Press, 1946.

"Transitions in World Population." *Population Bulletin, 59,* 1, March 2004:1–40.

Treiman, Donald J. *Occupational Prestige in Comparative Perspective.* New York: Academic Press, 1977.

Tresniowski, Alex. "Payday or Mayday?" *People Weekly,* May 17, 1999:128–131.

Trice, Harrison M., and Janice M. Beyer. "Cultural Leadership in Organization." *Organization Science, 2,* 2, May 1991:149–169.

Troeltsch, Ernst. *The Social Teachings of the Christian Churches.* New York: Macmillan, 1931.

"Tsunami Deaths Over 283,000." *News 24.com,* January 27, 2005.

Tumin, Melvin M. "Some Principles of Stratification: A Critical Analysis." *American Sociological Review, 18,* 1953:387–394.

Turner, Jonathan H. *The Structure of Sociological Theory.* Homewood, Ill.: Dorsey, 1978.

Tyler, Patrick E. "A New Life for NATO? But It's Sidelined for Now." *New York Times,* November 20, 2002.

Uchitelle, Louis. "How to Define Poverty? Let Us Count the Ways." *New York Times,* May 28, 2001.

Udry, J. Richard. "Biological Limits of Gender Construction." *American Sociological Review, 65,* June 2000:443–457.

Ullman, Edward, and Chauncey Harris. "The Nature of Cities." In *Urban Man and Society: A Reader in Urban Ecology,* Albert N. Cousins and Hans Nagpaul, eds. New York: Knopf, 1970: 91–100.

UNESCO Institute for Statistics. "World Illiteracy Rates." 2005.

United Nations. "World Urbanization Prospects: The 1999 Revision." New York: United Nations, 2000.

Urban Institute. *Assessing the New Federalism: Eight Years Later.* Washington, D.C.: Urban Institute, 2005.

U.S. Bureau of the Census. Current Population Survey, November 2004. May 26, 2005.

U.S. Bureau of the Census. *Statistical Abstract of the United States: The National Data Book.* Washington, D.C.: U.S. Government Printing Office. Published annually.

U.S. Department of Health and Human Services, Public Health Service. *Healthy People 2000.* Washington, D.C.: U.S. Government Printing Office, 1990.

Usdansky, Margaret L. "English a Problem for Half of Miami." *USA Today,* April 3, 1992:A1, A3, A30.

Useem, Michael. *The Inner Circle: Large Corporations and the Rise of Business Political Activity in the U.S. and U.K.* New York: Oxford University Press, 1984.

Van Hiel, Alain, Mario Pandelaere, and Bart Duriez. "The Impact of Need for Closure on Conservative Beliefs and Racism: Differential Mediation by Authoritarian Submission and Authoritarian Dominance." *Personality and Social Psychology Bulletin, 30,* 7, July 2004:824–837.

Varese, Federico. *The Russian Mafia: Private Protection in a New Market Economy.* Oxford: Oxford University Press, 2005.

Vartabedian, Ralph, and Scott Gold. "New Questions on Shuttle Tile Safety Raised." *Los Angeles Times,* February 27, 2003.

Veblen, Thorstein. *The Theory of the Leisure Class.* New York: Macmillan, 1912.

Vedantam, Shankar. "See No Bias." *Washington Post Magazine.* January 23, 2005.

Vega, William A. "Hispanic Families in the 1980s: A Decade of Research." *Journal of Marriage and the Family, 52,* November 1990: 1015–1024.

Von Hoffman, Nicholas. "Sociological Snoopers." *Transaction 7,* May 1970:4, 6.

Wagley, Charles, and Marvin Harris. *Minorities in the New World.* New York: Columbia University Press, 1958.

Wald, Matthew L. "Government Reversal Adds to Rift in South Carolina." *New York Times,* May 11, 2002.

Wald, Matthew L., and John Schwartz. "Alerts Were Lacking, NASA Shuttle Manager Says." *New York Times,* July 23, 2003.

Waldman, Amy. "Homes and Shops to Rise on Abandoned Harlem Properties." *New York Times,* December 27, 2000.

Waldrop, Deborah P., and Joseph A. Weber. "From Grandparent to Caregiver: The Stress and Satisfaction of Raising Grandchildren." *Families in Society: The Journal of Contemporary Human Services,* 2001:461–472.

Walker, Alice, and Pratibha Parmar. *Warrior Marks: Female Genital Mutilation and the Sexual Blinding of Women.* New York: Harcourt Brace, 1993.

Wallace, L. J. David, Alice D. Calhoun, Kenneth E. Powell, Joann O'Neil, and Stephen P. James. *Homicide and Suicide Among Native Americans, 1979–1992.* Atlanta, Ga.: National Center for Injury Prevention and Control, 1996.

Wallerstein, Immanuel. "Culture as the Ideological Battleground of the Modern World-System." In *Global Culture: Nationalism, Globalization, and Modernity,* Mike Featherstone, ed. London: Sage, 1990:31–55.

Wallerstein, Immanuel. *The Capitalist World-Economy.* New York: Cambridge University Press, 1979.

Wallerstein, Immanuel. *The Modern World System: Capitalist Agriculture and the Origins of the European World-Economy in the Sixteenth Century.* New York: Academic Press, 1974.

Wallerstein, Judith S., Sandra Blakeslee, and Julia M. Lewis. *The Unexpected Legacy of Divorce: A 25-Year Landmark Study.* Concord, N.H.: Hyperion Press, 2001.

Walter, Lynn. *Women's Rights: A Global View.* Westport, Conn.: Greenwood Press, 2001.

Walters, Alan. "Let More Earnings Go to Shareholders." *Wall Street Journal,* October 31, 1995:A23.

Wang, Hongyu, and Paul R. Amato. "Predictors of Divorce Adjustment: Stressors, Resources, and Definitions." *Journal of Marriage and the Family, 62,* 3, August 2000:655–668.

Watson, J. Mark. "Outlaw Motorcyclists." In *Society: Readings to Accompany Sociology: A Down-to-Earth Approach, Core Concepts,* James M. Henslin, ed. Boston: Allyn and Bacon, 2006:105–114. First published in 1980 in *Deviant Behavior, 2, 1.*

Watson, J. Mark. "Outlaw Motorcyclists." In *Down to Earth Sociology: Introductory Readings,* 5th ed., James M. Henslin, ed. New York: Free Press, 1988:203–213.

Watts, Jonathan. "Shanghai Eases China's One-Child Rule." *The Guardian,* April 14, 2004.

Wayne, Julie Holliday, Christine M. Riordan, and Kecia M. Thomas. "Is All Sexual Harassment Viewed the Same? Mock Juror Decisions in Same-and Cross-Gender Cases." *Journal of Applied Psychology, 86,* 2, April 2001:179–187.

Wayne, Leslie. "Foreigners Extract Trade-Offs From U.S. Contractors." *New York Times,* February 16, 2003.

Weber, Max. *Economy and Society.* Ephraim Fischoff, trans. New York: Bedminster Press, 1968. First published in 1922.

Weber, Max. *The Protestant Ethic and the Spirit of Capitalism.* New York: Scribner's, 1958. First published in 1904–1905.

Weber, Max. *The Theory of Social and Economic Organization,* A. M. Henderson and Talcott Parsons, trans. and ed. Glencoe, Ill.: Free Press, 1947. First published in 1913.

Weber, Max. *From Max Weber: Essays in Sociology.* Hans Gerth and C. Wright Mills, trans. and ed. New York: Oxford University Press, 1946.

Weeks, John R. *Population: An Introduction to Concepts and Issues,* 5th ed. Belmont, Calif.: Wadsworth, 1994.

Weiner, Tim. "A New Model Army Soldier Rolls Closer to Battle." *New York Times,* February 16, 2005.

Weiner, Tim. "Pentagon Envisioning a Costly Internet for War." *New York Times,* November 13, 2004.

Weiss, Rick. "Mature Human Embryos Cloned." *Washington Post,* February 12, 2004:A1.

Weitoft, Gunilla Ringback, Anders Hjern, Bengt Haglund, and Mans Rosen. "Mortality, Severe Morbidity, and Injury in Children Living with Single Parents in Sweden: A Population-Based Study." *Lancet, 361,* January 25, 2003:289–295.

Wessel, David. "As Populations Age, Fiscal Woes Deepen." *Wall Street Journal,* September 11, 1995:A1.

Wheaton, Blair, and Philippa Clarke. "Space Meets Time: Integrating Temporal and Contextual Influences on Mental Health in Early Adulthood." *American Sociological Review, 68,* 2003:680–706.

White, Jack E. "Forgive Us Our Sins." *Time,* July 3, 1995:29.

White, Joseph B., Stephen Power, and Timothy Aeppel. "Death Count Linked to Failures of Firestone Tires Rises to 203." *Wall Street Journal,* June 19, 2001:A4.

Whitehead, Barbara Dafoe, and David Popenoe. "The Marrying Kind: Which Men Marry and Why." Rutgers University: The

State of Our Unions: The Social Health of Marriage in America," 2004.

Whorf, Benjamin. *Language, Thought and Reality.* Cambridge, Mass.: MIT Press, 1956.

Wilford, John Noble. "In Maya Ruins, Scholars See Evidence of Urban Sprawl." *New York Times,* December 19, 2000.

Williams, Christine L. *Still a Man's World: Men Who Do Women's Work.* Berkeley: University of California Press, 1995.

Williams, Frank P., III, and Marilyn D. McShane. *Criminological Theory.* Upper Saddle River, N.J.: Prentice Hall, 2004.

Williams, Rhys H. "Constructing the Public Good: Social Movements and Cultural Resources." *Social Problems, 42,* 1, February 1995:124–144.

Williams, Robin M., Jr. *American Society: A Sociological Interpretation,* 2nd ed. New York: Knopf, 1965.

Willie, Charles Vert. "Caste, Class, and Family Life Experiences." *Research in Race and Ethnic Relations, 6,* 1991:65–84.

Willie, Charles Vert, and Richard J. Redlick. *A New Look at Black Families.* Walnut Creek, Calif.: AltaMira, 2003.

Wilson, James Q., and Richard J. Herrnstein. *Crime and Human Nature.* New York: Simon & Schuster, 1985.

Wilson, William Julius. *The Bridge Over the Racial Divide: Rising Inequality and Coalition Politics.* Berkeley: University of California Press, 2000.

Wilson, William Julius. *When Work Disappears: The World of the New Urban Poor.* Chicago: University of Chicago Press, 1996.

Wilson, William Julius. *The Truly Disadvantaged: The Inner City, the Underclass, and Public Policy.* Chicago: University of Chicago Press, 1987.

Wilson, William Julius. *The Declining Significance of Race: Blacks and Changing American Institutions.* Chicago: University of Chicago Press, 1978.

Wines, Michael. "Muckraking Governor Slain by Sniper on Moscow Street." *New York Times,* October 19, 2002.

Winslow, Ron. "More Doctors Are Adding On-Line Tools to Their Kits." *Wall Street Journal,* October 7, 1994:B4.

Wirth, Louis. "The Problem of Minority Groups." In *The Science of Man in the World Crisis,* Ralph Linton, ed. New York: Columbia University Press, 1945.

Wirth, Louis. "Urbanism as a Way of Life." *American Journal of Sociology, 44,* July 1938:1–24.

Wolfensohn, James D., and Kathryn S. Fuller. "Making Common Cause: Seeing the Forest for the Trees." *International Herald Tribune,* May 27, 1998:11.

Wolfinger, Nicholas H. "Family Structure Homogamy: The Effects of Parental Divorce on Partner Selection and Marital Stability." *Social Science Research, 32,* 2003:80–97.

Wood, Daniel B. "Latinos Redefine What It Means to Be Manly." *Christian Science Monitor, 93,* 161, July 16, 2001.

Wood, Scott Small. "The Price Professors Pay for Teaching at Public Universities." *Chronicle of Higher Education, 2001, 46,* 32, A18-A24.

Woodward, Kenneth L. "Heaven." *Newsweek, 113,* 13, March 27, 1989:52–55.

"The World of the Child 6 Billion." Population Reference Bureau, 2000.

Wright, Erik Olin. *Class.* London: Verso, 1985.

Wright, Lawrence. "Double Mystery." *New Yorker,* August 7, 1995: 45–62.

Wright, Lawrence. "One Drop of Blood." *New Yorker,* July 25, 1994:46–50, 52–55.

Wyatt, Edward. "City Plans to Let Company Run Some Public Schools in a First." *New York Times,* December 21, 2000.

Xie, Yu, and Kimberly A. Goyette. "A Demographic Portrait of Asian Americans." Washington, D.C.: Population Reference Bureau, 2004:1–32.

Yat-ming Sin, Leo, and Hon-ming Yau, Oliver. "Female Role Orientation and Consumption Values: Some Evidence from Mainland China." *Journal of International Consumer Marketing, 13,* 2, 2001:49–75.

Yellowbird, Michael, and C. Matthew Snipp. "American Indian Families." In *Minority Families in the United States: A Multicultural Perspective,* Ronald L. Taylor, ed. Englewood Cliffs, N.J.: Prentice Hall, 1994:179–201.

Yinger, J. Milton. *The Scientific Study of Religion.* New York: Macmillan, 1970.

Yinger, J. Milton. *Toward a Field Theory of Behavior: Personality and Social Structure.* New York: McGraw-Hill, 1965.

Zachary, G. Pascal. "Behind Stocks' Surge Is an Economy in Which Big U.S. Firms Thrive." *Wall Street Journal,* November 22, 1995:A1, A5.

Zald, Mayer N. "Looking Backward to Look Forward: Reflections on the Past and the Future of the Resource Mobilization Research Program." In *Frontiers in Social Movement Theory,* Aldon D. Morris and Carol McClurg Mueller, eds. New Haven, Conn.: Yale University Press, 1992:326–348.

Zald, Mayer N., and John D. McCarthy, eds. *Social Movements in an Organizational Society.* New Brunswick, N.J.: Transaction Books, 1987.

Zarakhovich, Yuri. "Closing the Door." *Time Atlantic, 157,* 8, February 26, 2001:25.

Zaslow, Jeffrey. "Will You Still Need Me When I'm . . . 84? More Couples Divorce After Decades." *Wall Street Journal,* June 17, 2003:D1.

Zellner, William W. *Countercultures: A Sociological Analysis.* New York: St. Martin's, 1995.

Zerubavel, Eviatar. *The Fine Line: Making Distinctions in Everyday Life.* New York: Free Press, 1991.

Zeune, Gary D. "Are You Teaching Your Employees to Steal?" *Business Credit, 103,* 4, April 2001:16.

Zielbauer, Paul. "Study Finds Pequot Businesses Lift Economy." *New York Times,* November 29, 2000.

Zogby America Post Election 11/3/04 to 11/5/04.

NAME INDEX

A

Addams, Jane, 9–10
Adler, Patricia, 73, 74
Adler, Peter, 73, 74
Adorno, Theodor, 230–31
Alger, Horatio, 217
Alston, Carol, 328
Amato, Paul, 345
Anderson, Elijah, 84
Appiah, Kwame Anthony, 224
Aron, Arthur, 329
Arquitt, George, 115, 116
Aries, Philippe, 77
Asch, Solomon, 132–33

B

Bacon, Kevin, 121
Banaji, Mahzarin, 228
Banks, Laurie, 13
Bates, Marston, 39
Becker, Howard S., 140
Becker, Selwyn, 131
Bleustein, Jeffrey, 197
Bell, Daniel, 305–306
Berger, Peter, 292
bin Laden, Osama, 14, 105
Blee, Kathleen, 228
Bleusein, Jeffrey, 197
Blumstein, Philip, 338
Bono, 190
Boyle, Lara Flynn, 102
Brajuha, Mario, 29
Bray, Michael, 370
Bronfenbrenner, Urie, 345
Brooks, David, 158
Buffet, Warren, 140
Bundy, Ted, 159
Burgess, Ernest, 9, 15, 404
Burkhart, Melvin, 142
Burns, Lucy, 264
Bush, George W., 102, 174, 175, 433
Butler, Robert, 281

C

Cage, Nicholas, 201
Calment, Jeanne Louise, 280
Calvin, John, 8, 372
Calvo, Marie Antonieta, 125
Capaci, Frank, 201
Capela, Stanley, 13
Castle, John, 198
Castro, Fidel, 44, 240
Chafetz, Janet, 259, 264
Chagnon, Napoleon, 139–40
Chain, David, 139–40, 433
Chambliss, William, 106–107, 147
Chaplin, Charlie, 93
Charlemagne, 178
Charles VII, King of France, 293
Cheadle, Jacob, 345
Cherlin, Andrew, 347
Clinton, Hillary, 276
Cloward, Richard, 148, 150
Coleman, James, 365
Collins, Randall, 354
Columbus, Christopher, 420
Comte, Auguste, 5, 6, 7, 9, 16
Cooley, Charles Horton, 14, 63–64, 66, 115
Copeland, Faye, 159
Corll, Dean, 158
Coser, Lewis, 18
Cowen, Emory, 230
Crick, Francis, 94
Croft, Lara, 72
Cumming, Elaine, 282

D

Dahmer, Jeffrey, 159
Darley, John, 130, 408
Darwin, Charles, 4, 6
d'Autriche, Elisabeth, 200
David, George, 197
Davis, Kingsley, 60, 175, 360–61
Day, Dorothy, 264
Degler, Jeffrey, 98

de Leon, Ponce, 278
Depp, Johnny, 204
De Salvo, Albert, 159
Dickerson, Tonda, 201
Doane, Ashley, 227
Dollard, John, 230
Domhoff, William, 197, 301
Dove, Adrian, 362
Du Bois, W. E. B., 10–11, 169, 249
Duneier, Mitchell, 84
Durkheim, Emile, 7–8, 9, 16, 94, 148, 163, 366–67, 371
Dutton, Donald, 329
Dye, H. B., 62

E

Eder, Donna, 70
Edgerton, Robert, 38, 141
Einstein, Albert, 7, 88
Ekman, Paul, 67, 69
Ellison, Lawrence, 197
Engels, Frederick, 173, 263
Escalante, Jaime, 365–66

F

Falcon, Pedro, 44
Farkas, George, 363
Faunce, William, 384–85
Ferraro, Kathleen, 348
Fiorina, Carleton, 271
Fischer, Edward, 329
Fisher, Sue, 268
Flanagan, William, 411
Flavel, John, 64
Ford family, 205
Ford, Henry, 422
Foreman, Dave, 435
Fox, Elaine, 115, 116
Fox, Vicente, 187
Francis of Assisi, St., 371
Franklin, Benjamin, 236
Freud, Sigmund, 7, 66–67, 161
Friedman, Dusty, 39

G

Gacy, John Wayne, 159
Galbraith, John Kenneth, 188
Gans, Herbert, 406–407
Garfinkel, Harold, 104
Gates, Bill, 128, 175, 196, 204
Genie (isolated child), 62, 64
Genovese, Catherine, 406, 408
Gilbert, Dennis, 202, 203
Gilder, Jeannette, 264
Goetting, Ann, 348
Goffman, Erving, 75, 100–101, 140–41
Gold, Ray, 200
Goldberg, Susan, 69, 70
Goldstein, Baruch, 370
Greehey, William, 197
Green, Leslie, 13
Greenwald, Anthony, 228
Guy, Scary, 163

H

Hall, Edward, 97–98
Harlow, Harry, 63
Harlow, Margaret, 63
Harrington, Michael, 188
Harris, Chauncey, 405
Harris, Marvin, 263
Hart, Charles, 276–77
Hart, Johnny, 211
Hartley, Eugene, 228
Hawking, Stephen, 88
Hawthorne, Nathaniel, 87
Hayakawa, S. I., 240
Hellinger, Daniel, 197
Henley, Elmer Wayne, 158
Henry, William, 282
Hetherington, Mavis, 345
Higginbotham, Elizabeth, 210
Hill, Paul, 370
Hill, Zettie Mae, 207
Hipler, Fritz, 231
Hirschi, Travis, 145
Hitler, Adolf, 61, 105, 133, 222, 230, 232, 294, 296, 394, 419
Hoan, Nguyen Thi, 262
Hochschild, Arlie, 327–28
Hoffer, Thomas, 365

Holbein, Hans, 417
Horowitz, Ruth, 144
Howells, Lloyd, 131
Hoyt, Homer, 404
Huggins, Martha, 181
Huizenga, Wayne, 198
Humphreys, Laud, 29–30
Hussein, Saddam, 14, 119, 178, 296

I

Irani, Ray, 197
Isabelle (isolated child), 59, 60
Iutcovich, Joyce Miller, 13

J

Jackson, Jesse, 242
Jaggar, Alison, 276
James, LeBron, 204
Janis, Irving, 135
Jankowiak, William, 329
Jankowski, Martin Sanchez, 150
Jarrell, John, 201
Jarrell, Sandy, 201
Jefferson, Thomas, 295
Jerrome, Dorothy, 283
Jesus, 369, 371, 377
Joan of Arc, 293, 294
Johns, Charlie, 326
Johns, Eunice, 326
Johnson, Benton, 373
Jones, Robert Trent, 409
Judd, Dennis, 197

K

Kahl, Joseph, 202, 203
Kanter, Rosabeth Moss, 126
Karatz, Bruce, 197
Karp, David, 408, 409
Keibler, Stacy, 114
Kelly, Julie, 167
Kelly, Michael, 167
Kelly, Patti, 167–68
Kelly, Rick, 167–68
Kennedy, John F., 198, 251
Kennedy, Rose, 198
Keyes, Alan, 243
King, Martin Luther, Jr., 242, 369

Kingston, Maxine, 39
Kleinfeld, Judith, 121
Klinebiel, Michael, 201
Klinebiel, Phyllis, 201
Kody, Monster. See Scott, Kody.
Kohn, Melvin, 71, 73, 333
Kovacevich, Robert, 197
Kraybill, Donald, 96
Kutcher, Ashton, 282

L

Lamont, Blanche, 354
Landes, Judah, 230
Latane, Bibb, 130, 408
Lauer, Jeanette, 349
Lauer, Robert, 349
Lee, Alfred, 428
Lee, Elizabeth, 428
Lenin, Vladimir Ilyich, 179
Lenski, Gerhard, 177, 200
Lerner, Gerda, 169, 263
Letterman, David, 194
Lewis, Michael, 69, 70
Lewis, Oscar, 188
Liebow, Elliot, 84
Lincoln, Abraham, 175, 306
Linton, Ralph, 37
Lippitt, Ronald, 131–32
Liu, Lucy, 204
Locke, Gary, 247
Locke, Harvey, 16
Lopez, George, 100
Lopez, Jennifer, 204
Luther, Martin, 374

M

Mackey, Daniel, 100
Mackey, Jennifer, 98, 100
Mahashury, 171
Maher, Sarah, 235
Malthus, Thomas, 384, 386
Maris, Roger, 408
Martineau, Harriet, 9
Marx, Karl, 7, 8, 18, 173, 174, 176–77, 179, 197, 202, 217, 372, 416, 419, 420
Mary, mother of Jesus, 371
Massey, Douglas, 44, 245
Matza, David, 146

McAuliffe, Christa, 415
McCarthy, John, 427
McGwire, Mark, 408
McIntosh, Peggy, 238
McKinley, William, 186
Mead, George Herbert, 9, 15, 64–65, 66
Mendelssohn, Felix, 100
Merton, Robert King, 16–17, 117, 148, 363
Michaelangelo, 371
Michels, Robert, 117
Milgram, Stanley, 119, 121, 133–34, 135
Milkie, Melissa, 70
Mills, C. Wright, 19–20, 197, 301, 412
Ming, Yao, 223
Minkler, Meredith, 286
Mitchell, John, 168
Montagu, Ashley, 223
Moore, Blanche Taylor, 159
Moore, Demi, 282
Moore, Wilbert, 175, 360–61
Morgan, Lewis, 419
Morita, Akio, 128
Mosca, Gaetano, 176
Moseley-Braun, Carol, 274
Mosher, Steven, 394
Moyers, Bill, 231
Moynihan, Daniel, 215
Mulleta, Getu, 167
Mulleta, Zenebu, 167
Munimah, 278
Mussolini, Benito, 230, 419

N

Nader, Ralph, 433,
Nation, Carrie, 424
Niebuhr, Richard, 378

O

Obama, Barack, 243
Ogburn, William, 15, 54–55, 419, 420–21
Ohlin, Lloyd, 148, 150
Orwell, George, 291
Ouchi, William, 128

P

Park, Robert, 9, 404
Parker, Alisha, 151
Parker, Brant, 211
Parks, Rosa, 242
Parsons, Talcott, 12, 360–61
Partington, Donald, 158–59
Pelosi, Nancy, 275
Perdue, Frank, 319
Perot, Ross, 297
Piaget, Jean, 65–66
Pontiac, 248
Pope Leo III, 178
Pope, Liston, 373
Portes, Alejandro, 249–50
Powell, Colin, 174, 175
Powell, Linda, 368
Puente, Dorothea Montalvo, 159

R

Rader, Dennis, 159
Ram, Arun Bharat, 330
Ram, Manju, 330
Reagan, Ronald, 174, 175
Reckless, Walter, 145
Reskin, Barbara, 251
Rich, Lucky, 25
Ridgway, Gary, 159
Riis, Jacob, 173
Rist, Ray, 362–63
Ritzer, George, 125
Robertson, Ann, 286
Robertson Ian, 46–47, 179
Robertson, Pat, 377
Rockne, Knute, 86
Rodriguez, Richard, 74
Romanach, Leopoldo, 17
Roosevelt, Franklin Delano, 124, 135, 246, 284
Roosevelt, Theodore, 247, 258, 296–97
Rossi, Alice, 258
Rumbaut, Ruben, 249–50
Russell, Diana, 349

S

Salk, Jonas, 124
Samuelson, Paul, 195

Sanders, Howard, 403
Sanderson, Mary, 403
Sapir, Edward, 45–46
Sayres, William, 324
Schaet, Donald, 230
Schuller, Robert, 377
Schwartz, Pepper, 338
Schwarzenegger, Arnold, 174
Scott, Kody, 113–14, 117, 134
Scully, Diana, 268
Seinfeld, Jerry, 198
Shakespeare, William, 88, 89
Shelton, Robert, 76
Shepard, Matthew, 161
Sherif, Carolyn, 231
Sherif, Muzafer, 231
Shibutani, Tamotsu, 302
Shipman, Harold, 159
Shively, JoEllen, 51
Simmel, Georg, 129
Simon, Julian, 393
Simpson, George Eaton, 234
Singh, Thaman, 391
Skeels, H. M., 62
Small, Albion, 9
Snyder, Mark, 98–99
Sowell, Thomas, 364
Spencer, Herbert, 6–7, 16
Spengler, Oswald, 419
Stalin, Joseph, 356
Starr, Ellen G., 10
Steele, Shelby, 246
Stewart, Martha, 152
Stinnet, Nicholas, 349
Stohr, Oskar, 61
Straus, Murray, 347
Summers, Larry, 266
Sumner, William, 37
Sutherland, Edwin, 144, 150
Suzuki, Bob, 336
Sykes, Gresham, 146
Szasz, Thomas, 161–62

T

Taft, Robert, 297
Takewell, Terry, 207
Timasheff, Nicholas, 302, 304
Thomas, Dorothy S., 105, 223
Thomas, William I., 14, 105, 223

Timasheff, Nicholas, 302
Tito, Marshall, 233
Toennies, Ferdinand, 94, 96
Townsend, Francis, 284
Toynbee, Arnold, 419
Troeltsch, Ernst, 373
Trotsky, Leon, 179
Troyer, Verne, 223
Trudeau, Gary, 327
Trump, Donald, 140, 203
Tumin, Melvin, 175–76

U

Ullman, Edward, 405
Useem, Michael, 316

V

Vanderbilt, Cornelius, 173
Vanderbilt, Gladys, 173
Veblen, Thorstein, 305

W

Wallerstein, Immanuel, 186
Wallerstein, Judith, 344
Watson, James, 94
Watson, Mark, 147
Wayne, John, 51
Weber, Lynn, 210
Weber, Max, 8, 9, 10, 121, 123, 173,
        174–75, 202, 204, 217, 292,
        372, 416, 417
Welch, Jack, 140
White, Ralph, 131–32
Whorf, Benjamin, 45–46
Wilder, L. Douglas, 243
Williams, Christine, 272
Williams, Robin, 50
Williams, Serena, 174, 428
Williams, Venus, 174
Williams, Wayne, 159
Wilson, William Julius, 243–44, 409

Winfrey, Oprah, 194
Wirth, Louis, 226, 406
Woods, Tiger, 223, 224, 428
Wright, Erik, 202
Wuornos, Aileen, 159
Wurabuti, 277

Y

Yao, Ming, 223
Yinger, J. Milton, 234
Yoels, William, 408
Yufe, Jack, 61

Z

Zald, Mayer, 425, 427
Zerubavel, Eviatar, 46

SUBJECT INDEX

A

AARP (American Association of Retired Persons), 282
Abkhazians, 277
Abolitionists, 9
Aborigines, 420
Abortion, 394, 429–30
Abu Ghraib prison, 302, 303
Achieved status, 87, 171
Acid rain, 430
Activity theory, 283
Adolescence, as a social invention, 78
Adultolescents, 79, 334
Advertising, 262, 282
Affirmative action, 251, 264
Africa
    ethnic conflicts in, 418
    famines in, 387–88
    female circumcision in, 274–75
    fertility in, 393
    and global stratification, 186
    slavery in today, 169–70
African Americans. *See also* Slavery.
    and civil rights, 242
    education of, 240, 241
    enslavement of, 169, 224, 240
    families of, 334–35
    and health care, 229–30
    home ownership of, 241
    income of, 241, 242
    and politics, 242–43
    poverty of, 213, 214, 241, 243
    in prison, 154
    segregation of, 234, 242
    and self-terms, 45, 234
    social class of, 209, 242
    social mobility of, 209
    syphilis experiment and, 221
    voting by, 240, 297–98
    and W. E. B. Du Bois, 10–11
Age. *See also* Adultolescents; Children; Elderly.
    and marriage, 143
    meaning of, 281
    poverty and, 214, 286
    of prisoners, 155

Age cohorts, 282
Ageism, 281
Agents of socialization, 69–75, 264–67
Aggregate, 114, 116
Aging
    as a disease, 52–53
    as part of life course, 79–80
Agricultural societies, 92, 305
Al-Qaeda, 303, 420, 426
Alcoholics Anonymous, 75
Alienation
    in bureaucracies, 126
    in the city, 406–408
    defined, 406
    resisting, 126
    and voting, 297, 299
American Airlines, 319
American Civil Liberties Union (ACLU), 306
American Dairy Association, 319
American Revolution, 5, 426
American Sociological Association, 29, 258, 266, 435
American Sociological Society, 10
"Americanization" of immigrants, 354
Amish (the), 96, 119, 374
Amsterdam, 255
Anarchy, 300
Animal rights movement, 426
Anomie, 148, 201, 231
Anti-Malthusians, 385–88
Anti-Semitism, 230, 231. *See also* Jews; Nazis.
Anticipatory socialization, 75
Ants, eating of, 39
Apartheid, 226, 234
Apathy, and voting, 297, 299
Applied sociology, 12–14
Arabs
    and culture, 35–36
    greetings among, 68
    image of, 118
    torture of, 118
Armenians, 227
Arranged marriages, 330
Aryan Nations, 228
Aryans, 222, 394
Ascribed status, 87, 171

Asian Americans
    as artificial category, 246
    assimilation of, 247
    bias toward, 363
    discrimination against, 246
    and education, 241, 247
    family life of, 247, 336
    home ownership of, 241
    income of, 241
    and internment camps, 233, 246
    politics and, 247
    poverty among, 241, 247
    stereotypes of, 247
    success of, 247
    terms for, 45
    unemployment of, 241
    voting by, 299
Assimilation, 127, 220, 233, 234, 247
Atlanta Union Mission, 4
Atlanta University, 9
Attractiveness. *See* Beauty.
Authoritarian leaders, 131–32, 230
Authoritarian personality, 230–31
Authority
    in the family, 325
    transfer of, 294
    types of, 292–94
Automobile (the), and suburbanization, 403
Automobile industry, as example of social class, 205–206
Aveyron, wild boy of, 60
Axes, 420
Aztecs, 295, 367, 369

B

Back stages, 100
Background assumptions, 37, 104
Baghdad, 14
Bankers, 229
Baptists, 206, 374, 375, 378
Barbie dolls, 314
Baseball, 64, 65
Basic (or pure) sociology, 12
Battering. *See* Spouse abuse.
Beauty
    changing ideas of, 262

Beauty (*continued*)
  culture and, 40, 257
  and income, 99, 103
  internalizing norms of, 102–103
  stereotypes of, 98–99, 102–103
Belgium, 186
Belonging, sense of, 115, 117, 120, 145, 201, 223, 227
Berdache, 324
Bias
  and criminal justice system, 152–54
  in death penalty, 157–60
  and IQ testing, 361–62
  in research, 25, 26–27
"Big Brother," 291, 306, 318, 422
Bikers, 147
Bilingualism, 44
Bioengineering, 94, 387
Biology. *See* Nature vs. nurture.
Biotech society, 91, 93–94, 95, 308
Birth control, 96, 358, 392
Birth defects, 124
Birth rates, 16, 250, 385, 386, 393, 394, 396, 417
Births to single women, 214, 215, 334, 340
Bison, 53
Bloods (the), 113–14, 117
Bloomingdale, 151
Blue-bloods, the, 203
Blue-collar jobs, 198, 203, 308
"Boat people," 240
"Body messages," 101, 102–103
Boeing Satellite, 152
"Boomerang children," 334
Bonded laborers, 171, 261, 278
Boot camp, 75, 76
Borden Chemicals, 431
"Born again," 371
Bosnia, 223, 233, 393, 418
Botox injections, 103, 282
Bourgeoisie, 7, 18, 173, 175, 177, 202
Bratz dolls, 314
Brazil
  environmental movement in, 435
  homeless children in, 181
  and offense at gesture, 40
  race in, 225
Bride selling, 262
British Museum, 74
Buchenwald concentration camp, 222
Bull Moose Party, 296
Bullfighting, 38
Bureau of Indian Affairs, 249

Bureaucracies, 121–26
  alienation in, 126
  defined, 121, 123
  perpetuation of, 123–24
  and rationalization of society, 124–26
  red tape in, 124–25
Burial, as a family function, 17
Business
  computers in, 424
  global, 189, 319

C

Calvinists, 8, 371, 373
Cambodia, 4, 60, 184–85
Cameras, security, 178
Cancer, 13, 93, 268, 423, 434
Capital punishment. *See* Death penalty.
Capitalism. *See also* Globalization of capitalism.
  "boom and bust" cycles of, 189
  characteristics of, 313
  in China, 315
  and class conflict, 7, 18, 176
  corporate, 316
  defined, 313
  ideology of, 315
  early stages of, 18, 176, 309
  and religion, 8, 371–72
  Russia's transition to, 315, 356–57
  social class and, 173
  and U.S. political parties, 296
Capitalists and capitalist class, 153, 202–204
Car-hopping, 52
Carcasonne, France, 397
Casey v. Planned Parenthood, 429
Casinos, 249
Caste
  defined, 171
  and gender, 172
  in India, 171–72, 261, 330, 372
  marriage and, 172, 330
  and religion, 171–72, 371
  in the United States, 171–72
Category, defined, 114, 116
CBS Records, 128
Cedars-Sinai Medical Center, 267
Celebration, Florida, 409
Centers for Disease Control, 13
CEOs (chief executive officers), 196–97, 271, 272, 342
Challenger space shuttle, 415
Charisma, 293, 294, 374

Charismatic authority, 293, 294, 374
Child labor, 10, 308, 309
"Child penalty," 270
Childbirth, global, 393
Childhood
  and industrialization, 78
  in the Middle Ages, 77–78
  and poverty, 213, 214–15
Children. *See also* Childhood.
  abuse of, 347–48
  books for, 265
  of divorce, 15–16, 344–45
  as economic assets, 390–91
  feral, 60
  institutionalized, 60, 62
  isolated, 59, 60
  in Least Industrialized Nations, 78, 197, 309, 390–91
  of one-parent families, 337, 345
  and poverty, 213, 214–15
  rearing of, 77–78, 332–34
  and social class, 71, 73, 332–34
  socialization of, 59–75, 332–34
  views of, 77–78
  starvation of, 388
China
  abortion in, 394–95
  advertising in, 103
  beauty in, 1, 262
  bride selling in, 262
  education in, 357
  female infanticide in, 395
  and food customs, 39
  foot binding in, 263
  and G-8, 418
  and missile technology, 152
  Naxi (the), 325
  and nuclear weapons, 152
  "one couple, one child," 262, 394–96
  and thinness, 103
  urban renewal in, 411
Chinese Exclusion Act of 1882, 246
Christian Solidarity International, 170
Church, 367, 374
Cinco de Mayo, 240
Circumcision
  of females, 38, 274
  medical accident during, 258
Cities. *See also* Urbanization.
  alienation in, 406–408
  community in, 406–408
  defined, 397
  and deindustrialization, 410–11
  development of, 397–401

and disinvestment, 410
enterprise zones in, 411
as gated fortresses, 409
gentrification of, 402–403
and globalization of capitalism, 407–408
life in, 406–408
Medieval, 397
models of growth of, 404–406
revitalization, essentials for, 411
social policies for, 411
Citizenship, 295–96, 420
City states, 295
Civil rights, 242, 306–307
Civil Rights Act of 1964, 242
Civil Rights Act of 1968, 242
Class. *See* Social class.
Class conflict, 7, 18, 176
Class consciousness, 173, 176–77, 179
Cleveland Cavaliers, 204
Cliques, 119
Cloning, 95
Clothing, as symbol, 49, 80, 97, 147
Coalitions, 129
Cohabitation, 339, 340, 341, 350
Cold War, 10, 124, 132, 315
College professors, 199, 200
Colombia
    childhood in, 15
    and food customs, 39
    tribal peoples in, 434
    urbanization in, 397, 398–99
Colonialism, 186, 188, 233
Color line, 224, 249, 331
Columbia space shuttle, 135
Common sense
    as everyday theory, 14
    and function of language, 45
    race and, 225
    sociology and, 21–22
    and views of children, 78
Communism, 7, 179, 356
Communist Party, 179, 315, 356, 379, 426
Community colleges, 355
Community, sense of
    among the Amish, 96
    in the city, 406–408
    in gangs, 114, 147
    in Harlem, 403
    and long life, 277, 368
    in villages, 94
Compartmentalization, 233

Computers
    medicine and, 423
    social change and, 422–24
    and social relationships, 106, 107, 118
Concentration camps, 222
Concentric zone model, 404, 405
Conflict perspective (theory)
    applications of, 18, 177
    criminal justice system, 152–53
    defined, 18
    on divorce, 18
    on education, 361–62
    on elderly, 284–87
    on global birth control, 392
    on global stratification, 176–77
    and macro level of analysis, 18–19
    of marriage, 327–29
    origin of, 7
    overview of, 19
    of poverty, 216
    of prejudice, 231–32
    of race-ethnicity, 232
    of religion, 372
    on reproduction, 391
    on social stratification, 173–74, 176–77, 202
    on U.S. political system, 301–302
    on welfare, 216
Conformity, 131–35
Congo, 186, 369, 393
Conscientious objection, 96
Consensus, 96, 128, 131
Conspicuous consumption, 305
Continuity theory, 284
Control groups, 28, 62, 221, 368
Control theory, 145–46
Convergence theory, 315–16
Coors Brewery, 127, 319
Coping devices, 162
Coral Gables Board of Realtors, 44
Coronary bypass surgery, 229, 267
Corporate capitalism, 316
Corporate crime, 150–51
Corporate culture, 126–27
Corporate welfare, 431
Corporations. *See also* Multinational corporations.
    culture of, 126–27
    and day care, 342
    defined, 316
    gender inequality in, 258–59
    in Japan, 128–29
Counterculture, defined, 47, 48
Credential societies, 354

Crime. *See also* Deviance; Prisoners.
    corporate, 150–51, 152, 153
    decline in, 156
    defined, 140
    gender and, 157
    and global domination, 189–90
    and recidivists, 156–57
    social class and, 149–51
    street, 143
    and technology, 160
    white-collar, 150–51, 163
Criminal justice system, 152–61
Crips (the), 113–14, 117
Crisis, a journal, 10
Crusades, the, 370
Cuddling, 63
Cults, 373–74
Cultural diffusion, 55, 420–21
Cultural goals, 148–49
Cultural lag, 54–55, 421
Cultural leveling, 55
Cultural relativism, 38–39
Culture, 35–55
    and beauty, 40
    corporate, 126–27
    crisis in, 419, 425
    defined, 35, 87
    and ethnocentrism, 38–40, 247, 257, 275
    germs and, 36, 105
    gestures and, 41–42
    ideal, 54
    language and, 42–46
    and marketing, 319
    material, 35, 55
    nonmaterial, 35, 36–37, 39–47, 54–55, 421
    and nonverbal interaction, 19, 40, 46, 97–98, 99
    perception and, 45–46, 68
    and perspective on life, 36
    real, 54
    symbolic, 35, 36–37, 39–47, 54–55, 421
    and values, 50–54
Culture clash, 142–43
Culture of poverty, 188, 215
Culture shock, 37, 38
Culture wars, 53

D

Dalit (the), 171, 188, 234
Date rape, 273

Dating. *See* Mate selection.
Day care
    as agent of socialization, 73, 332
    and corporations, 342
    quality of, 332
    schools as, 355
Death penalty
    bias in, 157–60
    photo of, 292
    and propaganda, 427
    by state, 157, 292
Death rates, 393
Death row, 158–60
Deferred gratification, 337
Definition of the situation, 105, 141
Degradation ceremonies, 75
Dehumanization, 302–304
Deindustrialization, 410–11
Delinquency. *See* Juvenile delinquency.
Democracy
    and citizenship, 295
    information control in, 178
    origin of, 295
    as a value, 50
Democratic façade, 197
Democratic leaders, 131–32
Democratic Republic of the Congo,
    369
Democratic socialism, 315
Democrats and Democratic Party,
    26–27, 207, 296, 299, 428
Demographic variables (the), 392–93
Demography. *See* Population.
Denmark, 338
Department of Homeland Security, 306,
    307
Dependency ratio 285
Depression, economic, 118, 210, 221,
    284
Descent, reckoning, 325
Desexualization, 105–106
Deviance, 139–63. *See also* Crime;
    Prisoners.
    and cultural goals, 148–49
    functions of, 148
    and institutionalized means, 148–49
    medicalization of, 161–62
    neutralization of, 146–47
    reactions to, 154–63
    relativity of, 142–43
    and social class, 106–107, 147,
        149–53
    sociological perspective on, 140
    theoretical perspectives on, 144–53

Dictatorships
    information control in, 178
    and seizure of power, 296
Differential association, 144, 145, 148
Diffusion
    of cultural items, 55, 420–21
    of responsibility, 130, 408
Digitized money, 424
Dinkas, 170
"Dirty work"
    and dehumanization, 302, 303
    and Holocaust, 118
Disabilities. *See* People with disabilities.
Discrimination
    against W. E. B. Du Bois, 10
    defined, 227
    in health care, 229–30, 267–68
    individualistic, 229–30
    institutional, 229–30
    in loans, 229
    names as basis for, 244, 271
    personal social networks and, 122
    and sense of ethnicity, 227
    unintended, 122
Disengagement theory, 282–83
Disfigurement, 88
Disinvestment, 410
Distance learning, 423
Diversity. *See* Social diversity.
Diversity training, 127
Divine right of kings, 177–78
Division of labor, 91, 92, 94, 121, 305,
    400, 417, 427
Divorce
    among the Amish, 96
    chances of, 344
    changed meaning of, 15–16
    children of, 15–16, 344–45
    conflict perspective on, 18
    ex-spouses, 346
    functionalist perspective on, 16–18
    grandchildren of, 345
    measurement of, 343
    rate of, 15
    risk factors in, 344
    and social class, 206
    symbolic interactionist perspective on,
        15–16
DNA, 94, 95, 157, 159, 287
Documents, in research, 28
Dogs, as food, 39
Dolls, 70, 258, 314
Dolphins, 433, 435
Dominant group, defined, 226

Double standard
    of in-groups and out-groups, 117
    sexual behavior and, 341
Downsizing, 309
Dramaturgical analysis. *See* Dramaturgy.
Dramaturgy, 100–103
Drape sheet, 105
Dresden, Germany, 389
Drugs and drug use, 139, 146, 150,
    152, 157, 161, 207, 216, 259, 367,
    378
Dump people of Phnom Penh,
    Cambodia, 184–85
Dupont Circle, 83–84
Dyads, 129
Dysfunctions, 16, 17, 19, 118, 124,
    126, 231, 326, 367, 369, 408

E

Earnings. *See* Income.
Ecclesia, 374
Economic colonies, 186
Economic depression, 118, 210, 221,
    284
Economy, 305–319
Ecosabotage, 433
Ecstasy (the drug), 146
Edge cities, 402
Education, 354–66. *See also* Schools.
    and affirmative action for men, 265
    as agent to "Americanize," 74, 236,
        237, 354, 360
    of the Amish, 96
    and Asian Americans, 241
    in China, 357
    community colleges, 355
    computers in, 422–23
    conflict perspective of, 361–62
    distance learning, 423
    and earnings, 269–70
    in Egypt, 357–58
    functional analysis of, 358–61
    and gender, 265–70
    global perspective on, 354
    grade inflation in, 364–65
    in Great Britain, 179
    home schooling, 353, 359
    and industrialization, 354
    in Japan, 354–56
    kindergarten, 362–63
    and length of school year, 55
    and poverty, 214
    prep schools, 206

problems in, 363–66
and race-ethnicity, 241
and reproduction of social structure, 361–62
in Russia, 356–57
and social class, 206, 361
and social integration, 358–59, 360
symbolic interactionist perspective of, 362–63
teacher expectations, 362–63
and transmission of values, 358
and voting, 297, 298
Ego (the), 65
Egypt, 357–58
Elderly
in advertising, 382
care of, 342
life course and, 79–80
and poverty, 214, 286
theoretical perspectives on, 282–83
Elections. *See* Politics.
Electrolux, 319
Electronic church, 377
Electronic communities, 121
Elite. *See also* Power elite.
in Least Industrialized Nations, 189
and maintenance of power, 177–78
E-mail, 43, 121, 178, 422
Emoticons, 43
Emotions
expressing, 67–68
gender and, 67–68
and gestures, 41–42
as social control, 69
socialization into, 67–69
Empty nest, 334
Endogamy, 171, 324–25
Energy shortages, 432
"English only," 239–40
Enterprise zones, 411
Entertainers, social class of, 204
Environment, 430–36
fossil fuels and, 430, 431
and globalization of capitalism, 430
or heredity, 143, 256–61
and industrialization, 430–33
injustice and, 432
multinational corporations and, 432
rain forests and, 433, 434
and technology, 435–36
as a value, 53
Environmental injustice, 432
Environmental movement, 433
Environmental sociology, 435–36

Equality
and gender, 71
ideology of, 197
and social networks, 122
as a value, 50, 52
Ethics, in social research, 29–30
Ethiopia, 167
Ethnic cleansing, 223, 233
Ethnic conflicts, 418
Ethnic maps, 228
Ethnic work, 227, 240, 335
Ethnicity. *See* Race-Ethnicity.
Ethnocentrism
authoritarian personality and, 230–31
and beauty, 40
and cultural relativism, 37
defined, 37
murder and, 434
and race-ethnicity, 223
Ethnomethodology, 103–105
Eton, 179
European Americans, 235–37, 248
European Union, 318, 394
Everyday life
and looking-glass self, 63–64
presentation of self in, 98–105
and stereotypes, 99
symbols in, 15
"Excess of definitions," 144
Executions. *See* Death penalty.
Exercising, 102–103
Experimental groups, 28, 62
Experiments
on authority, 133–34
diagram of, 28
explanation of, 28–29
on group size and attitudes, 130–31
with institutionalized children, 60, 62
on leadership, 131–32
on love, 329, 330
on monkeys, 63
on peer pressure, 132–33
on syphilitics, 221
Expressive leaders, 131
Extinction of species, 53, 433
Exxon Corp., 431

F

Face-to-face interaction. *See* Interaction.
Face-saving behavior, 101
False consciousness, 173
Family and Families. *See also* Marriage.

as agent of socialization, 69–70, 71, 72, 144
among the Amish, 96
authority in, 325
blended, 338
characteristics of, 324–25
dark side of, 342–49
defined, 324
of delinquents, 144
extended, 324
functionalist perspective on, 17–18, 72, 326
of gays, 338
incest in, 326
incest taboo and, 325
in Least Industrialized Nations, 167, 383, 388, 390–91
life cycle of, 329
mothers working, 211, 333
nuclear, 324
of orientation, 324
of procreation, 324
and race-ethnicity, 334–37
rural, 390
and social class, 71, 73, 206, 334–37
symbolic interactionist perspective on, 15–16
without children, 337–38
Farms, 181, 205
Fascism, 426
Fatherhood, serial, 346
FBI (Federal Bureau of Investigation), 159, 245, 273, 303, 306
Federal empowerment zones, 411
Federal Trade Commission, 153
Female circumcision, 274–75
Female infanticide, 262, 395
Females. *See* Gender.
Feminism, and Feminists
conflict theory and, 18
and Freud, 67
on sexual harassment, 272
studies of social mobility, critiques by, 210
three waves of, 264–65
view of reproduction of, 391
and violence, 273–74, 275
Femininity, *See* Gender.
Feminization of poverty, 214
Feral children, 60
Fertility, 392–93
Feudal society, 92, 416
Fictive kinship, 334
Fieldwork. *See* Participant observation.

Firebombing, 389
Firestone, 151
First impressions, 97
First World. *See* Most Industrialized
 Nations.
Flava dolls, 314
Folkways, 46–47, 142
Food customs, 39
Foot binding, 263
Football, as example of social structure,
 86
Ford Motor Company, 129, 151,
 205–206, 316
Foreign Miner's Act of 1850, 246
Fossil fuels, 430–31
Free speech, 118, 296
Freedom, as a value, 50
French Revolution, 5, 6, 426
Friendship, 94, 115, 120, 129, 283, 407,
 416
Front stages, 100
Frustration, and prejudice, 230
Functional illiteracy, 205, 364–65
Functionalism. *See* Functionalist
 perspective.
Functionalist perspective
 defined, 16
 on deviance, 148–52
 on divorce, 17–18
 on education, 358–61
 on elderly, 282–84
 on gangs, 150
 on governance, 300–301
 on in-groups and out-groups, 118
 and macro level analysis, 18–19
 on marriage and family, 17–18, 326
 overview of, 16
 on prejudice, 231
 on religion, 367–69
 on social stratification, 175–76
Functions. *See also* Functionalist
 perspective.
 defined, 16
 of education, 358–61
 the family and, 16–18, 326
 stratification and, 175–76
Fundamentalist revival,
Furman v. Georgia, 159
Future
 of social class relations, 173
 of elder care, 278
 fears of, 210–11
 of gender relations, 275–76
 of intergenerational relations,
  284–85

life span in, 287
 of marriage and family, 350
 race-ethnic relations in, 249–50
 of religion, 379
 of technological impact, 287
 of war, 425

G

G-7, 418
G-8, 190, 418, 420, 433
Gambling, 150, 249
Games, 64
Gangs
 motorcycle, 47, 50, 147
 urban, 113–14, 115, 145, 147,
  150
Garbage dumps, 181, 184–85, 397,
 398–99
Gatekeeping, 360–61, 427
Gemeinschaft, 94, 96, 390, 416
Gender and gender roles. *See also*
 Masculinity; Men; Nature vs.
 nurture; Women.
 among the Amish, 96
 and caste, 172
 as a core value, 53
 crime and, 152
 and death penalty, 158
 defined, 256
 and education, 179, 265–67
 equality of, 276, 347, 417, 420–21
 and ethnocentrism, 257
 expressing emotions and, 67–68
 and family, 69–70
 future of, 275–76
 and health care, 267–68
 housework and, 327–29
 and illiteracy, 172
 in India, 260–61
 and industrialization, 17–18
 and mass media, 70–71
 and pay gap, 268–71
 and peers, 70
 power and, 327–29
 preference for sons, 262, 395
 social stratification and, 168, 172–73,
  179, 210, 256
 socialization into, 69–71, 260
 sports and, 67
 stereotypes of, 70–71
 and strength, 274, 335
 toys and, 69–70
 and video games, 72
 and violence, 272–74

and voting, 299
 and work, 258–59, 268–71
Gender age, 282, 326
Gender gap
 in math and science, 266
 in pay, 22, 23, 268–71
 in voting, 299
Gender tracking, 265
Generalizability, 121, 336
Generalized other, 64, 65
Genocide, 222, 232, 248
Genomes. *See* Human genome system.
Gentrification, 402–403
Georgia Pacific, 431, 433
Germany, 182, 221, 231, 232, 278, 294,
 296, 389, 394, 418, 419, 425, 433
Germs and culture, 36, 105
Gesellschaft, 94, 96, 416
Gestapo, 296
Gestures
 and culture, 40–42
 emotions and, 41–42
 offensive, 40–41
 written, 43
Ghana, 10
Gillette, 189
"Giving the finger," 40, 46
Glass ceiling, 271–72
Glass escalator, 272
Global Positioning System, 425
Global stratification. *See* Social
 stratification.
Global village, 54–55, 304, 308, 319,
 405
Globalization of capitalism
 and automobiles, 129
 children's toys and, 314
 and cultural leveling, 55
 defined, 185
 effects on U.S. cities, 310–11, 410–11
 and environmental decay, 430
 and jobs, 309
 New World Order and, 317–18
 and Western culture, 319
Goal displacement, 123–24
"Good old boys," 122
Grade inflation, 364–65
Graduate school, 265–66
Grandparents
 and divorce, 345
 in Native American families, 336
 as parents, 342
Graying of America, 278–80
Graying of the globe, 278, 279
Great Depression, 210, 221, 284

Green parties, 433
Greenhouse effect, 432
Greenpeace, 433
Group dynamics, 129–35
    authority, 153–54
    conformity, 132–34
    group size, 129–31
    groupthink, 135
    leadership, 131–32
    peer pressure, 132–33
Groups, 113–35
    defined, 89, 114
    electronic, 121
    in-groups, 37, 117, 118, 122, 230
    networks, 119, 120, 121, 122, 203,
        308, 326
    out-groups, 37, 117, 118, 122,
    primary, 115, 116
    reference, 118–19, 122, 209, 264
    secondary, 115, 116
Groupthink, 135
Gulf Wars, 55, 180
Gynecological examinations, 105–106
Gypsies, 40, 134, 222

H

Handicaps, 88, 360
Hanibal High School, 106
Harlem, 403
Harvard University, 266, 365
Hate crimes, 153, 160–61
Hazardous waste sites, 430, 431
Health. *See also* Health care.
    and elderly, 286
    lifestyles and, 207, 367, 368
    and religion, 367, 368, 378
    and social class, 194, 197, 198, 202,
        204, 207, 243, 260
Health care
    discrimination in, 207, 208, 229–30,
        267–68
    gender and, 267–68
    and race-ethnicity, 229–30
Heart surgery, 267–68
Height
    and ethnic groups, 35
    and earnings, 270
    gestures to indicate, 41
Hells Angels, 50
Heredity, or environment, 60–61,
    256–61
Hidden curriculum, 361
Hitler Youth, 61
Hmong, 143

Holocaust, 117–18, 134, 222, 232
Holy Roman Empire, 178
Home ownership, 241
Home schooling, 353, 359
Homeland Security, 178, 306
Homeless (the)
    in Brazil, 181
    in India, 181
    in Japan, 179
    mental illness of, 162
    participant observation of, 3–4, 83,
        193, 208, 211
    shelters for, 3–4, 193
    and technology, 205, 211
    as underclass, 205
"Homies," 114
Homosexuals
    and culture war, 53
    hate crimes against, 161
    marriage of, 53
    and Nazis, 134, 222
    political power of, 153
    sexual harassment of, 272
Hong Kong, 393
"Honor killings," 273
Hopi Native Americans, 45, 46
Horatio Alger myth, 217
Horticultural societies, 91, 262, 305,
    416
Housework, 327–29
Hughes Electronics, 152
Hull-House, 10
Human ecology, 404
Human genome system, 91, 94, 124,
    223, 308, 416
Humanitarianism, 50
Hunting and gathering societies, 89, 91,
    177, 262, 276, 305, 357, 416, 434
Hurricane Katrina, 126
Hutus, 223, 232
Hygiene, and culture, 36, 106
Hypothesis
    defined, 20
    of political radicalism, 200
Hysterectomies, 268

I

"I" (the), 65
Id (the), 67
Ideal culture, 54
Ideal types, 417
Identity
    as anchor in life, 201
    and deviance, 147

and gender, 70
    initiation rites and, 78
    marines and, 76
    of minority groups, 227
    national, 360
    primary groups as source of, 115
    and race-ethnicity, 224, 226, 227,
        234, 246, 249
    and religion, 371, 374, 376, 378
    and social class, 173
Identity theft, 422
Ideology
    of capitalism, 315
    defined, 169
    and the elite, 176, 177–78, 197
    of equality, 217
    and racism, 169
    and slavery, 169
    social classes and, 176
    of socialism, 179, 314
    and success, 217
Ifaluk, 68–69
Illegitimate opportunity structures,
    149–52
Illiteracy
    functional, 205, 364–65
    and gender, 172
    in Least Industrialized Nations, 168,
        181, 358
    and technology, 211
Imitation, 64
Immigrants
    "Americanization" of, 236, 237, 354,
        360
    and changing racial-ethnic mix,
        249–50
    country of origin of, 394
    and culture clash, 74, 142–43
    debate about, 249–50, 393
    as demographic variable, 393
    and depression, economic, 118
    discrimination against,
    and education, 74, 360
    Hull-House and, 10
    illegal, 394
    and invasion-succession cycle, 404
    language of, 44, 74, 250, 355
    neighborhoods of, 407
    as outgroup, 118
    push and pull factors of, 393
    socialization of, 74, 354
Immigration. *See* Immigrants.
Immigration and Naturalization Service
    (INS), 235
Implicit Association Test, 228

Impression management, 100–103
Incas, 295
Incest, 347, 349
Incest taboo, 325, 326
Income
    and beauty, 99, 103
    defined, 194
    distribution of, 195–96, 296, 299,
        312
    and education, 241
    in global perspective, 182–83, 197
    and inflation, 312
    race-ethnicity and, 241
India
    arranged marriages in, 330
    bonded laborers in, 171, 261, 278
    British rule of, 226
    child labor in, 171, 308, 309
    children, reasons for having many,
        383, 388, 390–91
    female infanticide in, 395
    gender in, 171, 258–59, 278
    love in, 330
    photo of deviant in, 140
    religion in, 171, 188
    tsunami deaths in, 389
    work in 258–59, 309
Individualism, 50
Indonesia, 389
Industrial Revolution, 92, 186
    and adolescence, 78
    due to Protestantism, 8, 371–72, 416
    and social upheaval, 92
Industrial society
    and conspicuous consumption, 305
    development of, 92–93
    social institutions in, 90
Industrialization
    and children, views of, 77–78
    education and, 354
    and elderly, 278
    and family functions, 17
    gender roles and, 17–18
    global stratification and, 186–88,
        430–33
    population growth and, 388–96
    and transformation of society, 305,
        308
Industrializing Nations
    education in, 357–58
    environmental problems in, 430–33
    and global stratification, 186–88,
        430–33
    map of, 182–83
Inequality. *See* Social inequality.

Infanticide, 262, 394, 395
Inflation, and paychecks, 312
Information society
    control of, 178
    development of, 93
    overview of, 305–306
    social institutions in, 90
In-groups, 117–18
Inheritance, 325
Initiation rites, 78
Inner circle
    of a corporation, 127
    and groupthink, 135
    and law of oligarchy, 115–17
    of secondary groups, 115, 116
Inner city
    as center of despair, 243, 409
    gentrification of, 403
    and poverty, 205, 213, 243, 244
    schools in, 361, 366
    and technology, 243
Inner controls, 145–46
Inquisition, 370
Instincts, 4
Institutionalized means (for achieving
    cultural goals), 148–49
Instrumental leaders, 131
Intelligent design, 379
Interaction
    face-to-face, 15, 19, 21, 22, 31, 43,
        97, 106, 115, 362
    on the Internet, 106
    nonverbal, 19
Interlocking directorates, 316
Internal colonialism, 233–34
Internet, social interaction on, 106, 107
Internment camps, 233, 246
Interviewing
    of abused women, 26
    as a research method, 22–26
Intimacy, 115, 129–30, 131, 330, 341,
    408
Invasion-succession cycle, 404–405
Inventions, 420. *See also* Social
    inventions.
"Invisible knapsack," 238
IQ testing, 361–62
Iraq, 14, 142, 273, 296, 303, 400, 425
Iron law of oligarchy, 115, 116
Iroquois Federation, 249
Iroquois Native Americans, 247, 249,
    295
Islam. *See* Muslims.
Israel, 226, 227, 304
Israelites, 168

It Could Happen to You, 201
Italy, 41, 426
Ivory Coast, 169

J
Japan
    corporations in, 128–29
    education in, 354–56
    in global stratification, 188
    and perception, 68
    and technology, 211
Jews
    discrimination among, 227, 376
    as ethnic group, 223–24, 226
    hate crimes against, 160–61
    and identity, 223
    Nazis and, 61, 117–18, 134, 222, 232
    religious symbols of, 371
    in Russia, 233
    and terrorism, 370
Jim Crow laws, 240
Job loss, to Least Industrialized Nations,
    19, 26, 187, 189, 301, 308–309
Juvenile delinquency
    families of, 144, 344
    historical origin of, 160
    neutralization techniques of, 146–47
    and social class, 106–107

K
Kayapo, 434
Kennedy Space Center, 415
Khmer Rouge, 60
Killings. *See* Murder.
Kosovo, 170, 233, 418
Ku Klux Klan, 118, 228, 230
Kuwait, 186, 393
Kwanzaa, 335

L
Labeling theory, 146–47
Labels. *See* Symbols.
Laissez-faire leaders, 131, 132
Language
    of the Amish, 96
    and becoming human, 60, 63, 65
    culture and, 42–46
    defined, 42
    diversity of in U.S., 237, 239, 240
    and education, 73
    function of, 42–46
    and the mind, 45–46
    perception and, 45–46

and race, 45
and social class, 179
time and, 42–43
Latent functions. *See* Functions.
Latinos, 237–40
and car-hopping, 52
country of origin of, 239
discrimination against, 235
divisions among, 240
and education, 241
and family, 335–36
hate crimes against, 161
home ownership of, 241
income of, 241
in politics, 240
poverty and, 241
and prison, 155, 160
Spanish language and, 239–40
terms for, 45
unemployment of, 241
voting by, 297, 298
Law, as means of oppression, 153
Leaders and leadership
charismatic, 293–94, 374
defined, 131
and politics, 300–302
styles of, 131–32
types of, 131
view of followers, 116
Least Industrialized Nations
child labor in, 308, 309
children in, 78, 309, 390–91
education in, 357–58
environmental problems in, 432–33
family in, 167, 383, 388, 390–91
and global stratification, 181–86
map of, 182–83
population growth in, 388–91
poverty in, 181, 184–86
Legal system. *See* Law.
Leisure
in hunting and gathering societies, 91
and happiness in marriage, 349
and industrialization, 78, 357
as a value, 52
and views of children, 78
Liaison Agency Network, 170
Libraries, 92, 306, 359, 408, 424
Life course, 77–80
Life expectancy, 278
Life span, 287
Lifestyles
effects on ideas, orientations, 176
and environment, 434

and ideas, 176
and social class, 194, 197, 198, 202, 204, 207, 243, 260
and health, 207, 367, 368
Liposuction, 103
Loans, 229
Lobbyists, 299–300
Looking-glass self, 63–64
Lottery winners, 201
Love
defined, 329
and mate selection, 329–30
as a value, 51
Loyalty, 61, 117, 128, 135, 147, 178, 291, 355, 358, 422
Lutherans, 374, 375, 377
Lynchings, 10, 245

M

Machismo, 335, 336, 390
Macro level of analysis. *See* Macrosociology.
Macrosociology, 18–19, 84–96, 97, 106–107
Macy's, 151
Mafia
and killings, 144–45
Russian, 179–80
Mainstreaming, 360
Males. *See* Gender.
Malthus theorem, 384
Manhood, and initiation rites, 78
Manifest functions. *See* Functions.
Manliness, and violence, 144–45
Maquiladoras, 187–88
March of Dimes, National Foundation for, 123–24
Marginal working class, 153
Mara Salvatrucha gang, 145
Marietta College, 273
Marines, U.S., 76
Marital roles, changes in, 14, 15
Marriage. *See also* Divorce; Family; Mate selection.
abuse in, 326, 347–49
age at, 143, 326
among the Amish, 96
arranged, 330
changed meaning of, 14, 15
commitment in, 340
conflict perspective on, 327–29
defined, 324
functionalist perspective on, 17–18, 326

future of, 350
among the Hmong, 143
of homosexuals, 338
incest in, 349
and inheritance, 325
interracial, 331
and intimacy, 15, 129, 330, 341
among Iraqis, 142
lesbian, 338
and personality, 15
polyandry, 324
polygyny, 50, 324
postponement of, 339
remarriage, 346–47
as a social anchor, 154
social channels of, 331
and social class, 206
success in, 349
symbolic interactionist perspective on, 15–16, 329, 349
Marxism
and Marx, 7
and W. E. B. Du Bois, 10
Masculinity. *See* Gender.
Mass media
and body images, 102–103
characteristics of, 90
in China, 103, 262
and elderly, 281, 182
gender and, 70–73, 274
pornography in, 107
and prejudice, 231
and propaganda, 231, 426–27
and slavery, publicizing of, 170
as a social institution, 90
stereotypes and, 70–71
and Westerns, 51
Massachusetts, 338
Master status
defined, 88, 141
disability as, 88
gender as, 256
of a minority group, 227
Mate selection. *See also* Incest taboo; Marriage.
the color line and, 331
as cultural theme, 324–25
and love, 330, 331
minority groups and, 226
and social class, 331
Math, and gender, 270
Mattel Toys, 314
Mauritania, 169
Mazda Corporation, 129
McDonaldization of society, 125

McDonald's
  and cultural leveling, 55
  minimum wage at, 194
  and rationalization of society, 124
"Me" (the), 65
Means of production, 7, 18, 152,
    173–74, 175, 177, 194, 202, 313,
    315, 416
Mechanical solidarity, 94, 95
Medellin, Colombia, 398–99
Media. *See* Mass media.
Medical accident, 260
Medical care, two-tier system of,
    207–208
Medicalization of deviance, 161–62
Medicare, 284, 286
Medicine. *See also* Health; Mental
    illness.
  characteristics of, 90, 207–208
  and computers, 423
  discrimination in, 207–208, 268
  exportation of western forms, 417
  telemedicine, 423
"Melting pot," 227
Men, stereotypes of. *See also* Gender.
Mental hospitals, 163, 208
Mental illness
  and the homeless, 162, 208
  as medicalization of deviance,
    161–62
  and social class, 207–208
  treatment of, 208
Mental retardation, 62
Mentors, 271
Meritocracy, 176
Mexico
  childbearing in, 392
  discrimination in, 227
  gestures in, 41–42
  immigration from, 393, 394
  maquiladoras in, 187–88
  marketing in, 319
  megalopolis in, 401
  pollution in, 432
  population growth of, 383, 392
  slavery in, 169
  war with U.S., 226
  Zapotec Indians of, 141
Miami, 44
Mickey Mouse, 54
Micro level of analysis. *See*
    Microsociology.
Microcase, 22
Microsociology, 84–85, 97–107,
    107–108

Microsoft Corporation,
Middle age, 79, 282
Middle ages
  and childhood, 77–78
  and monarchies, 372
Middle class. *See* Social class.
Migrant paths, 393
Military, characteristics of, 90
Mind, socialization into, 63–65
Minimum wage, 187, 194
Minorities. *See* specific groups.
Minority group
  defined, 226
  location of, 237
  and mate selection, 226
  origins of, 226–27, 261–62
Minutemen, 239
Miss Rivers' Lodge, 221
Modern Times, 93
Modernization, 417
Mohawk Native Americans, 48
Monarchies, 177–78, 295
Money, digitized, 424
Monkeys
  eating of, 39
  experiments with, 63
Moral holidays, 46
Moral imperative, 38
Morality, inability of science to
    determine, 143, 379
Morehouse College, 242
Mores, 46–47, 142
Mormons, 50, 53
Morocco, 35
Mortality, 368, 393, 396
Mortgages, 229
Most Industrialized Nations
  colonialism by, 186, 188, 233–34
  education in, 354–55, 357
  environmental problems in, 430–32
  and global stratification, 177–78,
    180, 392
  and multinational corporations, 189
  population growth in, 386, 388–89
Mothers
  single, 213, 214, 215, 332, 333, 334,
    337, 340
  working, 73, 333
Motorcyclists, 47, 50, 147
Multiculturalism, 234, 251
Multinational corporations
  and energy shortage, 432
  global stratification and, 189,
    316–17
Multiple-nuclei model, 405

Murder
  and ethnocentrism, 434
  and gender, 273–74
  of homeless children in Brazil,
    181
  and honor, 144–45, 273
  by Mafia, 144–45
  manliness and, 70
  serial, 158–59
  of women, 273
Muslims
  and al-Qaeda, 426
  and female circumcision, 274
  religious symbols of, 371
  Serbs and, 222, 233
  as victims of hate crimes, 161
Myths
  Horatio Alger as, 217
  about the poor, 213
  of race, 222–23

N

9/11, 102, 135, 303, 304, 306, 370
NAACP (National Association for the
    Advancement of Colored People),
    10, 45, 242, 245, 424
NAFTA (North American Free Trade
    Agreement), 317
Names, as basis for discrimination, 244,
    271
Nannies, 332
National Crime Victimization Survey,
    273
National elites, 189, 318, 394
National Islamic Front, 170
National Women's Party, 264
Native Americans
  and casinos, 249
  diversity among, 247
  and education, 241
  and European diseases, 232, 248
  and families, 336
  grandparents and, 336
  and pan-Indianism, 249
  poverty of, 241
  self-determination of, 249
  and separatism, 249
  slaughter of, 232, 248
  and subculture, 48
  suicide and, 248
  terms for, 45
  treaties with, 248
  unemployment of, 241
  and Westerns, 51

NATO (North Atlantic Treaty Organization), 124, 318
Natural disasters, 108–109
Naturalization Act of 1790, 235
Nature vs. nurture
    and gender, 256–61
    sociobiology, 143
    and twins, 60, 61, 231
Naxi, of China, 325
Nazis, 61, 117–18, 134, 222, 230, 231, 232, 296
Neighborhood, as agent of socialization, 73, 144
Neocolonialism, 188
Neo-Nazis, 118
Network analysis, 14
Networking, 122
Networks. *See* Social networks.
Neutralization, techniques of, 146–47
New girl network, 122
New Malthusians, 383–88
New Orleans, 193
New technology. *See* Technology.
New World Order, 222, 290, 317–18, 426
New York City Health Department, 13
Nobel Peace Prize, 10
Nobility, 177, 199, 417
Nomads, 89, 91, 168, 434
Nonmaterial culture, 35, 36–37, 39–47, 54–55, 421
Nonsexuality, 105, 106
Nonverbal interaction
    cultural determinants of, 41–42
    defined, 19
Norms
    defined, 46
    as essential to social order, 141–42
    hidden 136
    ideal vs. real, 141
    internalizing dominant, 228
    of noninvolvement, 408
    sexual behavior and, 141
Nuclear family, 324, 325, 326, 336, 337, 417
Nuclear power, 435
Nuclear weapons, 128, 135, 152, 186, 304, 418, 420, 434
Nudity, 46
Nuremberg war trials, 222, 231

O

Obesity, 102, 141
Occupations, prestige of, 197–99

Oil, 170, 186, 188
Oil-rich nations, 183, 188, 393
Oligarchies, 115, 117, 296
Omerta, 144
"One couple-one child" policy, 262, 394–96
One-parent families, 213, 214, 215, 332, 333, 334, 337, 340
Onondaga, 247, 249
Operational definitions, 20–21
Opportunity structures, 149–50
Ordnung, 96
Organic solidarity, 94, 95
Orphanages, 60, 62
Outer controls, 145–46
Out-groups, 117–18

P

Pacific Bell, 249
Pacific Lumber Company, 433
Palestinians, 304, 370
Pan-Indianism, 249
Parenthood, meanings of, 15–16
Parker Pen, 319
Participant observation
    of families, 328
    of the homeless, 3–4, 83, 193, 208, 211
    of motorcycle gangs, 147
    as a research method, 28
    of streetcorner men, 83–84
    of urban gangs, 150
Parris Island, 76
Passenger pigeons, 53
Pastoral societies, 91, 262, 305, 416
Patriarchy, 262–63, 325
Patriotism, and schools, 358
Pay gap, gender, 22, 23, 268–71
Peace movement, 10
Pearl Harbor, 135, 246
Peer groups. *See also* Friendship.
    and gender, 70
    socialization and, 70, 73, 75
    and success in education, 365
Peer pressure, 132–33
Pelvic examinations, 105–106
Pensions, 281, 282, 284, 395
Pentagon, 102, 304, 425
People with disabilities
    discrimination against, 227
    mainstreaming of, 360
    and master status, 87, 88
    as victims of hate crimes, 161
    as victims of Nazis, 134, 222

Pequot Native Americans, 249
Perception
    and culture, 68
    language and, 45–46
    and mass media, 282
    stereotypes and, 70, 71, 72
Personal identity kit, 75
Personal Responsibility and Work Opportunity Reconciliation Act, 216
Personal space. *See* space.
Personality
    and crime, 143
    development of, 61, 66–67, 79
    disorders of, 143, 161
    and marriage, 15
Petty bourgeoisie, 202
PGP (Pretty Good Privacy), 178
Phnom Penh, 184–85
Photo essays
    dump people of Phnom Penh, Cambodia, 184–85
    gender, 260–61
    small towns, 310–11
    subcultures, 48–49
    tornado, 108–109
    urbanization, 390–99
Physical fitness, as a value, 52
Pieta, 371
Pinatas, 54
Plagiarism, 29, 90
Plastic surgery, 103, 282
Play, children's, 64, 69–70,
Plesey v. Ferguson, 240
Plow (the), 91, 92, 305, 397
Pluralism, 234, 300
Pokot tribe, 141
Political action committees (PACs), 296, 300
Political parties
    inner circle of, 115, 117
    in U.S., 296–97
Political radicals, 200
Politics
    characteristics of, 90
    conflict perspective on, 301–302
    elections, 115, 179, 264, 274, 296–97, 433
    and race-ethnicity, 297–98
    social class and, 206–207
    and status inconsistency, 200
    women in, 274–75
Polygyny, 50, 324
Poor (the). *See* Poverty; Social class.
Population, 384–386
    debate about overpopulation, 384–87

Population (*continued*)
  demographic transition, 385–86
  demographic variables, 392–93
  exponential growth curve, 384–85
  forecasting of, 394–96
  and global birth control, 386
  growth of, 388–96
  Malthus theorem, 384
  starvation and, 387–88
  and the tsunami, 389
  zero population growth, 396
Population momentum, 386
Population pyramids, 391–92
Population shrinkage, 387
Population transfer, 233
Pornography, 13, 107
Positivism, 6
Postindustrial society. *See* Information
  society.
Potato (the), 384
Poverty. *See also* Poverty line; Social class.
  and age, 214, 285, 286
  births to single women in, 214, 215,
    334
  and childhood, 215
  children and, 213, 214–15
  conflict analysis of, 216
  culture of, 188, 215
  cycle of, 213, 215
  dynamics of, 215–16
  and education, 214, 365
  of the elderly, 214, 285, 286
  and families, 337
  feminization of, 214
  in Latin America, 181, 197
  in Least Industrialized Nations, 383,
    393, 418, 424, 433
  myths about, 213
  and race-ethnicity, 11, 212–14, 241,
    242, 243, 247, 248, 253, 334
  reasons for, 186–88, 215, 216–17
  in rural areas, 11, 213
  and social structure, 216–17, 315
  in the South, 11, 212
Poverty line, 211–12
Power
  and authority, 291, 292
  gender and, 327–29
  and inequality, 197
  maintenance of, 177–78
  social class and, 174, 197
Power elite
  control of workers, 232
  and criminal justice system, 152–55

defined, 12, 197
  and national decisions, 197, 301
  in U.S. political system, 197, 301
Prayer, 368
Prejudice
  defined, 228
  and frustration, 230
  theories of, 230–32
Prep schools, 206
Preschoolers, 333
Preschools, 206
Prestige
  as determinant of social class, 174,
    197–200
  display of, 199–200
  of occupations, 197–99
Primary groups, 115, 116
  defined, 115
  and sense of self, 115
Prisoners
  abuse of, 302, 303, 394, 429–30
  characteristics of, 155
  execution of, 157–60
  numbers of, 154
  rape of, 273
  in San Salvador, 145
Prisons. *See* Prisoners.
Prochoice, 429–30
Profiteering, 140
Profits, 150–51, 186, 189, 202, 271,
    313, 314, 315, 317, 318
Progress
  in cultural evolution, 419
  as a value, 50
Prohibition, 424
Proletariat, 7, 18, 173, 175, 190, 202
Prolife, 429–30
Propaganda, 426–27, 428
Property, 174, 194
Proposition 209, 251
Prostitution, 38, 150, 255, 262, 397
Protestant ethic, 8, 305, 372
Protestants, and origin of capitalism, 8,
    371–72
Psychoanalysis, 66
Psychologists, 143

Q

Quakers, 374
Questions, in survey research, 25–26
Queuing behavior, 35–36

R

Race-ethnicity, 221–51
  and caste, 172
  conflict perspective on, 232
  controversy over terms for, 234
  and death penalty, 158–60
  defined, 223
  in early U.S., 10–11
  education and, 241
  and families, 334–36
  future mix, 249–51
  and hate crimes, 161
  health care and, 229–30
  and home ownership, 241
  identity and, 224, 226, 227, 234,
    246, 249
  and income, 241
  lending, discrimination in, 229
  myth of pure races, 222–23
  plasticity of, 249
  and poverty, 212–14, 215, 241
  of prisoners, 155
  religion and, 376
  terms for, 45, 225, 234, 237
  unemployment and, 241
  in U.S. census, 224
  and voting, 297, 298, 299
Racial-caste system, 172
Racism
  defined, 227
  in earlier U.S., 10, 247
  in everyday life, 209, 238, 244–45,
  ideology and, 169
  learning, 228
  and slavery, 168–69
  as a value, 50, 52
Rain forests, 433, 434
Rape
  cultural perspectives on, 142–43
  and death penalty, 159
  executions for, 158–59
  in prison, 273
  of slaves, 169, 170
  in U.S., 273
Rapport, 26
Rational-legal authority, 293–94
Rationalization of society, 124, 125
Real culture, 54
Reality
  multiple, 188, 427
  social construction of, 104–106,
    277–78
Reasoning, development of, 65–66
Recidivism, 156–57

Red tape, 124
Redwoods, 433
Reference groups, 118–19, 122, 209, 264
Reform. *See* Social reform.
Reform Party, 297
Reformation (the), 372–73, 416
Relationships. *See* Social relationships.
Religion
　as agent of socialization, 73
　and capitalism, 8, 371–72
　and caste, 171–72, 372
　characteristics of, 90
　conflict perspective on, 372
　defined, 366–67
　electronic church, 377
　and fatalism, 188
　functional analysis of, 367–69
　fundamentalist revival in, 377
　future of, 379
　and health, 368
　and origin of capitalism, 372–73
　and race-ethnicity, 376
　rituals in, 371
　secularization of, 377–79
　and slavery, 372, 374
　social class and, 375–76
　and status inconsistency, 376
　symbolic interactionist perspective on,
　　369–71
　and terrorism, 306, 369, 370
　as a value, 50–51
Religious experience, 371
Relocation camps, 233
Remarriage, 346–47
Reparations for slavery, 244–45
Replication, need of, 30–31, 121
Reproduction
　conflict perspective on, 391
　symbolic interactionist perspective on,
　　390
Republicans and Republican Party,
　　26–27, 207, 296, 299, 428
Research, social
　bias in, 25, 26–27, 119, 121, 132
　ethics in, 29–30
　and hypothesis, 20
　methods of, 22–29
　model of, 20–22
　and operational definitions, 20–21
　overview of, 20–31
　rapport in, 26
　and reliability, 21
　replication of, 30–31
　sampling in, 24–25

　surveys in, 22–26
　and theory, 19–20
　topics of, 20
　and validity, 21
　values in, 30–31
　variables in, 20
Reservations, 233, 248, 249
Reserve labor force, 231
Resistance, strategies of, 328
Resocialization, 75–77
Retirement, 282, 283, 284
Reverse discrimination, 251
Revolution
　American, 50, 295, 426
　Cuban, 44, 240, 426
　French, 5, 6, 426
　Industrial, 5
　Russian, 179, 356, 426
　Social, 89–94, 416
　of workers, 7, 173, 176–77
Rich (the). *See* Social class.
Riots, 370, 410
Ritual pollution, 170
Rivalries, 117, 232, 401, 411, 418
Roe v. Wade, 429
Role conflict, 100–101
Role, defined, 89
Role expectations, 86
Role performance, 100
Role strain, 101
Role-taking, 64–65
Roman Catholicism
　charismatic leaders in, 294
　origin of capitalism and, 8, 178,
　　372–73
　and propaganda, 426
　and schools, 365
　social class and, 375
Romantic love, 329–30
"Roughnecks" (the), 106–107, 147
Routinization of charisma, 294
Ruckus Society, 433
Ruling class. *See* Power elite.
Rural rebound, 404
Russia, 315, 318, 356–57, 379, 418,
　　432
Rwanda, 183, 223, 232–33, 418

S

"Saints" (the), 106–107, 147
Sampling, 24–25
Sanctions
　defined, 46
　negative and positive, 46, 142

"Sandwich generation," 342
Sapir-Whorf hypothesis, 45–46
SAT tests, 355–56, 364
Saudi Arabia, 143, 182, 188
Scapegoats, 230, 231
Schools. *See also* Education.
　and affirmative action, 251, 264
　as agent of socialization, 73–75
　of the capitalist class, 204, 206
　funding of, 362
　and gatekeeping, 360–61
　and gender, 265–70
　in inner city, 365–66
　patriotism and, 358
　Roman Catholic, 365
　student culture of, 365
　violence in, 22, 23, 365
Science
　characteristics of, 90
　defined, 5
　gender and, 270
　and inability to determine morality,
　　143, 379
　and theory, 5
　as a value, 50
　versus tradition, 5–6
Scientific creationism, 379
Scientific method, 5
Sea Shepherds, 433
Searchers (The), 51
Sears, 150–51
"Second shift" (the), 327–28
Second World. *See* Industrializing
　　Nations.
Secondary analysis, 28
Secondary groups, 115, 116
Sector model, 404
Sects, 374
Security, lifetime, 128
Segregation, 226, 233, 234,
　　240–42
Selective perception, 232
Self
　development of, 63–64, 80, 145
　emotions and, 67–69
　presentation of in everyday life,
　　98–103
　and primary groups, 114, 115
Self-control, 71, 145
Self-fulfilling prophecies
　corporate culture and, 126
　of marriage, 349
　and prejudice, 232
　of teacher expectations, 362–63

Self-fulfilling stereotypes, 98–99
Self-fulfillment, as a value, 52
"Set" (the), 113–14
Sex, defined, 256
Sexism
    in medicine, 268
    and profits, 127
    in sociology, 9
    as a value contradiction, 52
Sexual attraction, and love, 330
Sexual behavior, 141
Sexual harassment, 272
Sexual revolution, 341
Shell Oil Co., 431
Shopping, 29, 93, 125, 404, 406, 408
"Showcasing," 127
Significant others, 64
Sing Sing Prison, 292
Single mothers
    births to, 214, 215, 334, 340
    and childrearing, 332, 333
    and poverty, 213, 337
Single-parent families, 337
Singles, the, 407
Sinkyone Native Americans, 433
Slavery. *See also* Bonded laborers.
    and abolitionists, 9
    causes of, 168–69
    and census, 224
    defined, 168
    and gender, 169
    origin of, 168–69
    and racial classifications, 169, 224
    racism and, 168–69
    and religion, 372, 374
    reparations for, 244–45
    today, 169–70
Slums, 150, 176, 181, 406
Small world phenomenon, 119, 121
Social activism. *See* Social reform.
Social change
    the Amish and, 96
    computers and, 422–24
    and cultural lag, 54–55, 421
    dialectical model of, 419–20
    and medicine, 423–24
    origin of capitalism in, 8, 372–73
    and origin of sociology, 6
    processes of, 419–21
    and religion, 8, 372–73
    from social movements, 424–30
    and technology, 417, 419–24
Social class. *See also* Homeless; Poverty;
    Social mobility; Social stratification.
    of African Americans, 242

in automobile industry, 205–206
and capitalism, 173
childrearing and, 71, 73, 332–34
and college attendance, 361
conflict analysis of, 173–74, 176–77, 202
consciousness of, 173
consequences of, 206–208
contradictory locations in, 201
in criminal justice system, 147, 152–53
and death penalty, 158
defined, 87, 172, 194
and delinquency, 106–107
determinants of, 173–75, 200–206
and deviance, 106–107, 147, 149–53
and education, 203–206, 361
of entertainers, 204
false class consciousness, 173
and family, 71, 73, 206, 334–37
functionalist analysis of, 175–76
gender and, 168, 172–73, 179, 210, 256
health and, 207–208
and ideology, 176
and interaction styles, 147
language as marker of, 179
and lifestyles, 194, 197, 198, 202, 204, 207, 243, 260
and marriage, 206
models of, 200–206
politics and, 206–207
and power, 174
prestige and, 197–200
and religion, 206, 375–76
and social mobility, 172, 208–210
status inconsistency and, 200
and status symbols, 199–200
super-rich, 194, 198
and testosterone, 258, 259
underclass, 203, 205–206, 211
versus race, 243–44
working, 126, 153, 205
Social class ladder, 203
Social construction of reality, 104–106, 277–78
Social control
    by emotions, 69
    and norms, 141–42
Social Darwinism, 6–7
Social diversity
    and contradictory standards, 118–19
    in the corporation, 127
    and in-group loyalty, 37, 117–18
Social groups. *See* Groups.

Social inequality. *See also* Gender;
    Poverty; Power; Race and ethnicity;
    Social class.
    and cyberspace, 424
    origin of, 92
    and social networks, 122
Social institutions
    defined, 89
    depicted, 90
Social integration
    and education, 358–60
    and suicide, 7–8
Social interaction
    defined, 19, 85
    on the Internet, 106, 107, 120
    and leadership, 131
    nonverbal, 19, 98–99
    and numbers, 129–31
    and social class, 107, 147
Social inventions
    adolescence, 78
    bureaucracies, 121–26
    capitalism, 312–13, 372–73, 416
    citizenship, 295–96
    corporation, 126–27, 316–17
    democracy, 295–96
    socialism, 314–16
Social location
    and behavior, 87
    defined, 4
    and deviance, 152
    life course and, 77
    and social class, 85, 87, 173
Social mirror, 64, 69
Social mobility
    of African Americans, 209
    defined, 172
    types of, 208
    women and, 210
Social movements
    abortion as, 429–30
    institutionalization of, 429
    propaganda and, 426–27, 428
    resource mobilization and, 427
    stages of, 427, 429
    types of, 424–26
Social networks, 119, 120, 121, 122, 203, 308, 326
Social order (the), 5, 6, 90, 142, 148, 153, 367, 372, 419, 426
Social organization
    of dump people, 184–85
    reestablishing after a natural disaster, 108–109
Social reform, and sociology, 6, 9–13, 31

Social Register, 203
Social relationships
    cloning and, 95
    and the computer, 106
Social research. *See* Research, social.
Social Security, 278, 284, 285
Social solidarity
    mechanical, 94, 95
    organic, 94, 95
Social status, 87, 200
Social stratification, 167–90, 193–217.
        See also Caste; Social Class; Poverty;
        Slavery.
    conflict perspective on, 176–77
    and cyberspace, 189–90
    defined, 168
    functionalist perspective on, 175–76
    and gender, 168, 172–73, 179, 210,
        256
    on a global level, 180–90, 392, 419,
        424, 426
    in Great Britain, 179
    maintenance of, 177–78
    and oil, 183, 188, 418
    regional shift in, 401
    in Russia, 179–80
    underclass in, 203, 205–206, 211
    universality of, 175–77
Social structure. *See also* Social class;
        Social institutions; Social mobility.
    and behavior, 85–87
    defined, 85
    gender as, 256
    reproduction of, in education,
        361–62
Socialism, 314–16
Socialization, 59–80. *See also* Nature vs.
    nurture.
    agents of, 71–75
    anticipatory, 75
    through children's books, 264, 265
    defined, 63
    into emotions, 67–69
    and freedom, 80
    into gender, 69–71, 72
    into human nature, 60–62
    of immigrants, 74, 360
    and the life course, 77–80
    mass media and, 70–71
    and the mind, 63–64
    personality and, 66–67
    and reasoning, 63–64, 65–66
    and the self, 63–66
    self-control and, 69
    and video games, 71

Society
    defined, 4, 89
    historical transformations of, 89–94
    rationalization of, 124, 125
    types of, 89–94
Society for Applied Sociology, 12
Sociobiology, 143
Sociological imagination, 4, 378. *See also*
        Sociological perspective.
Sociological perspective, 31, 37, 140,
        144, 231. *See also* Theory.
    defined, 4–5
    and suicide, 7–8
Sociology. *See also* Research, social.
    applied, 12–14
    basic (or pure), 12
    central principle of, 67
    and common sense, 21–22
    defined, 6
    environmental, 435–36
    and inability to determine morality,
        143, 379
    macro level of, 85–96
    majoring in, 439–440
    micro level of, 85–86, 97–107
    origins of, 5–8
    and reform of society, 6, 9–13, 31
    self-discovery and, 5–6
    sexism in, 9
    value-free, 30, 32
Solidarity. *See* Social solidarity.
Souls of Black Folk (The), 11
South (the)
    and economic-power shift, 401
    lynching in, 10, 245
    and poverty, 11, 212
    segregation in, 234, 242
Southern Baptist Convention, 374
Space, use of personal, 97–98
Space weapons, 425
Spanish (language), 44, 239–40
Special-interest groups, 300
Speech. *See* Language.
Spirit of capitalism, 8, 372–73
Split labor market, 87, 232
Sports, and socialization, 64–65, 67, 70
Spouse abuse
    overview of, 347–48
    as research example, 20–29
Standards. *See* Norms.
Star wars, 425
Staring, and culture, 35
Starvation, 387–88
Statistical Package for the Social Sciences,
    22

Statistics, misuse of, 344, 349
Statue of Liberty, 246
Status, 87. *See also* Social status.
Status inconsistency, 88, 200, 201, 376
Status set, 87
Status symbols, 87–88, 199–200
Steam engine, 91, 92, 110, 305, 416
Steel, iron workers, high-rise, 48
Stereotypes
    of Asian Americans, 246
    of elderly, 281–82
    in everyday life, 97, 98–99
    and first impressions, 97, 98–99
    and gender, 70, 71–72, 260, 271, 272,
        275–76
    from mass media, 98, 282
    self-fulfilling, 98–99
Stigma, 87–88
St. Louis, Missouri, 400–401
Stockholder's revolt, 316
Strain theory, 148–49
Stratification. *See* Social stratification.
Street crime, 149–50, 154–56, 163
Streetcorner men
    participant observation of, 83–84
    and social structure, 85
Strength, as a value, 274, 335
Structure. *See* Social structure.
Students. *See* Education; Schools.
Subculture
    defined, 47
    photo essay on, 48–49
Suburbanization, 403, 408–410
Sudan, 39, 169, 170, 278
Suffragists, 264
Suicide, 7–8, 22, 23
Suicide terrorism, 304, 370
Sumo wrestling, 67
Superego (the), 66
Super-rich, 203
Surveys, 22–26
Sustainable environment, 430
Symbolic culture, 35, 36–37, 39–47,
        54–55, 421
Symbolic interactionist perspective
    development of, 9, 14–16
    on deviance, 144–48
    on divorce, 15–16
    on education, 362–63
    on the elderly, 281–82
    on the homeless, 3–4, 83, 193, 208,
        211
    on marriage, 15–16, 329, 349
    and micro level of analysis, 18–19
    overview of, 14–16

Symbolic interactionist perspective
  (*continued*)
    on population growth, 383, 390
    on prejudice, 232
    on religion, 369–71
    on reproduction, 390
    on statistics, 349
Symbols. *See also* Status symbols.
    defined, 39
    and divorce rate, 15–16
    in everyday life, 15
    the mind and, 63–66
    religious, 369–71
    and social class, 200
Syphilis experiment, 221

T

Tables, how to read, 23
Taboo, 47
Tact, 101
Taking the role of the other, 64
"Talk lines," 131
Tasmanians, 55
Tattooing, 25, 49, 118
Teamwork, 101, 106, 111, 128
"Tearooms," 29, 30, 32
Technology
    and crime, 160
    cultural leveling and, 55
    defined, 54, 421
    and the environment, 435–36
    gender and, 54
    and global stratification, 54–55, 166,
        189–90, 424
    and information control, 178
    to maintain stratification, 178,
        189–90
    medicine and, 423
    and missile delivery system in China,
        152
    effects on nonmaterial culture, 54
    Ogburn's theory of social change,
        420–21
    and robots, 211
    and social stratification, 210–211
    sociological significance of, 54
    and voting, 295
Telemedicine, 423
Televangelists, 377
Television, 70–71, 149, 159, 170, 231,
    282, 421
Tenure, 128, 309

Terrorism
    9/11, 102, 135, 303, 34, 306
    defined, 303
    and religion, 306, 369, 370
Testosterone, 258, 259, 270
Theory, defined, 14. *See also* Conflict
    theory; Functionalist perspective;
    Symbolic interactionism.
Thinness, as a value, 102–103
Third World. *See* Least Industrialized
    Nations.
Thomas theorem, 105
"Three strikes" laws, 155–56
Time, and language, 42–44
Tiwi, 276–77
Tomb Raider, 72
Tornado, 108–109
Torture, 118, 135, 158, 181, 303, 369
Total institution, 75–77
Totalitarianism, 296
Townsend Plan, 284
Toys, 62, 69–70, 109, 360, 362–63
Tracking, in education, 360, 362–63
Trade agreements, 187, 318
Tradition (versus science), 5–6
Traditional authority, 293
Trail of Tears, 248
Transitional adulthood, 79
Transportation Security Administration,
    306, 307
Triads, 129
"Tricks of the trade," 428
tsunami, the, 389
Tunisia, 255
Tuskegee University, 221
Tutsis, 223, 232, 418
Twins, and environment or heredity, 60,
    61, 231

U

Underclass, 203, 205–206, 211. *See also*
    Homeless; Social class.
Unemployment, 19, 51, 153, 216, 230,
    231, 241, 243, 248, 316, 390
United Fruit Company, 189
University of Berlin, 10
University of Bordeaux, 7
University of California at Berkeley, 9,
    75
University of Chicago, 9, 404
University, as example of bureaucracy,
    123

University of Kansas, 9
University of Michigan, 63, 251, 330
University of Minnesota, 61
Unobtrusive measures in research, 29
Untouchables, 171, 172, 234
Urban renewal, 407, 411
Urbanization, 397–411. *See also* Cities.
    cities, development of, 397–404
    defined, 400
    and family functions, 17
    in Least Industrialized Nations, 187,
        397
    process of, 400
    social policy and, 408–411
    in U.S., 401–404
U.S. Cavalry, 248
U.S. Public Health Service, 221, 223
U.S. Secret Service, 102
U.S. Senate, 117, 243, 274, 276, 300,
    430
U.S. State Department, 10
USA Today, 125
Utah, 50

V

Vaginal examinations, 105–106
Validity, defined, 21
Value clusters, 52
Value contradictions, 52
Values
    of the Amish, 96
    as blinders, 53–54
    and the body,
    changes in, 52–53
    concerning children,
    Confucian, 336
    core, 46, 50, 52, 53, 358
    and culture, 50–54
    defined, 30, 46
    and education, 50, 206
    emerging, 52–53
    hidden, 126
    ideal, 54
    real, 54
    self-fulfilling, 126
    in social research, 30–31
    transmission of, 358
    in U.S., 50–53
Variables
    defined, 20
    dependent, 28
    independent, 28

Veterans of Foreign Wars (VFW), 115, 116
Victoria's Secret, 103
Video games, 70, 71–72
Vietnam
    capitalism in, 315
    war in, 135, 259
Vietnam veterans, 260–61
Violence
    among the Amish, 96
    gendered, 272–74
    in inner city, 410, 411
    and manliness, 70, 347
    religion and, 370
    in schools, 22, 23, 365
    and the state, 157, 292
    in virtual reality, 107
    against women, 263, 264, 272–74
Voluntary associations, 115
Voting
    apathy and, 297, 299
    education and, 297, 298
    gender gap in, 299
    and income, 22, 23, 268–71, 298
    race-ethnicity and, 297, 298
    and social integration, 297
    women and, 299
Voting Rights Act of 1965, 242

W

Walkman, 128
War
    computers in, 425
    conscientious objection, 96
    defined, 302
    and dehumanization, 302–303

essential conditions for, 302
    in the future, 425
    and global stratification, 392
    in space, 425
    in Vietnam, 135, 259
WASPs, 235, 236, 237
Wealth, 194
Wealthy (the). *See* Social class.
Webster v. Reproductive Services, 429
Weight, 102–103
Welfare, corporate, 430, 431
Welfare reform, 216
Westerns, 51
Whales, 434, 435
White-collar crime, 15–51, 163
White-collar jobs, 198, 205, 209, 210, 243, 308, 408
White ethnics, 235
White privilege, 238
Widowhood, 282, 334
Wilberforce University, 10
Witches, 369
Women. *See also* Gender.
    and crime, 152
    on death row, 160
    discrimination against, 227, 234, 245, 263, 264, 268
    double bind of, 245
    and height, 270
    in the KKK, 228
    as a minority group, 261–62
    in politics, 274–76
    poverty and, 214, 215
    and social mobility, 210
    traditional roles, 9
    violence against, 272–74
    and work, 260, 264, 268–72

Women suffrage, 10
Women's Christian Temperance Union, 425
Women's Medical College of Philadelphia, 9
Work
    and gender, 258–59, 260, 264, 268–72
    revolutionary change in, 308
Workers. *See* Working class.
Working class
    alienation of, 126
    characteristics of, 205
    class conflict and, 7
    and criminal justice system, 149–51
    defined, 153, 205
Working poor (the), 205
Workplace. *See also* Corporation.
    as agent of socialization, 75
    diversity, 127
    gender inequality in, 127
World Bank, 433
World system theory, 186–88, 417
World Trade Center, 12
World Trade Organization, 318
Wounded Knee, 248

Y

Yanomamo Indians, 4–5, 139–40
Youthfulness, as a value, 52

Z

Zapotec Indians, 141
Zero population growth, 396

PHOTO CREDITS

Chapter 1 p. 3: © Larry Downing/Woodfin Camp & Associates; **p. 4**: © Brant Ward/San Francisco Chronicle; **p. 5**: © Gianni Dagli Orti/CORBIS; **p. 6**, left: Mary Evans Picture Library; right: © Huton-Deutsch Collection/CORBIS; **p. 7**, left: North Wind Picture Archives; right: © Bettmann/CORBIS; **p. 8**: The Granger Collection, New York; **p. 9**: The Granger Collection, New York; **p. 10**, top: North Wind Picture Archives; **p. 10**, bottom: The New York Public Library/Art Resource, NY; **p. 11**: Culver Pictures; **p. 12**: Photo by Yaroslava Mills; **p. 14**: AP/Wide World Photos; **p. 17**: © Christie's Images/SuperStock; **p. 25**: © Torsten Blackwood/AFP/ Getty Images; **p. 26**: © William Whitehurst/CORBIS; **p. 27**: © EPA/Barbara Walton/Landov.

Chapter 2 p. 35: © Mian Khursheed/Reuters/Landov; **p. 38**: © Bob Krist/CORBIS; **p. 39**: © Pierre Vauthey/CORBIS; **p. 40**, top, left to right: © Julia Waterlow/Eye Ubiquitous/CORBIS; © Bill Bachmann/The Image Works; center, left to right: © SuperStock; © LindsayHebberd/Woodfin Camp & Associates; © Ben Mangor/SuperStock; bottom, left to right: © Jim Henslin; © Art Wolfe, www.artwolfe.com; © Ellen Senisi/The Image Works; **p. 41** (dog and boy): © 2001 PhotoDisc, Inc.; **p. 42**: © Jim Henslin; **p. 44**: © Jeff Greenberg/PhotoEdit, Inc.; **p. 46**: © David Gray/Reuters/Landov; **p. 48**: © Catherine Lerov/Sipa Press; **p. 49**, top, left to right: © Jeff Greenberg/Index Stock Imagery; © Andres Stapff/Reuters Limited; Jeff Greenberg/PhotoEdit, Inc.; middle, left to right: CORBIS Royalty-Free; Ken Cavanagh/Photo Researchers, Inc.; bottom, left to right: Vandystadt/Photo Researchers, Inc.; Patricia McDonough/Getty Images; AP/Wide World Photos; **p. 51**: © Photofest; **p. 52**: © A. Ramey/PhotoEdit, Inc.; **p. 53**: © Clarke Historical Museum, Eureka, California; **p. 54**: © Caroline Von Tuempling/SuperStock.

Chapter 3 p. 59: © Julie Denesha/Panos; **p. 60**: © Jim Henslin; **p. 61**: © Polaris Images; **p. 63**: © Harlow Primate Laboratory/University of Wisconsin; **p. 64**: © Myrleen Ferguson Cate/PhotoEdit, Inc.; **p. 65**: Ariel Skelley/CORBIS; **p. 67**: Reuters/Carlos Cortes IV/Landov; **p. 68**: © Tim Watson; **p. 72**, left: Picture Desk, Inc./Kobal Collection; **p. 72**, right: Courtesy © Eidos Interactive; **p. 74**: © Stockbyte/Getty Images; **p. 76**: © Scott Olson/Getty Images; **p. 77**: © The Bridgeman Art Library/Getty Images; **p. 78**: © Michael MacIntyre/The Hutchison Library.

Chapter 4 p. 83: Photo by Jenifer Forkner; **p. 84**: © Patrick Forestier/CORBIS Sygma; **p. 88**: © Miguel Riopa/Agence France Press/Getty Images; **p. 91**: © Thomas Kelly/Aurora; **p. 93**: © The Museum of Modern Art/Film Stills Archive; **p. 95**: © Stockbyte/Getty Images; **p. 96**: AP/Wide World Photos; **p. 97**, left: © Dominic Arizona Bonuccelli/Photographersdirect.com; **p. 97**, right: Miyuki Ryoko/Agence France Press/Getty Images; **p. 98**, left: Voisin/Photo Researchers, Inc.; **p. 98**, right: Michael Newman/PhotoEdit, Inc.; **p. 99**, left: AP/Wide World Photos; **p. 99**, right: © Franz Lanting/Minden Pictures; **p. 100**: Richard Cartwright/ABC, Inc. Photography; **p. 102**, left: © Gregg Deguire/WireImage.com; **p. 102**, right: © Robert Daly/Stone/Getty Images; **p. 104**: © Heidi Levine/Sipa Press; **p. 107**: CORBIS Royalty Free; **p. 108, 109**: © Jim Henslin.

Chapter 5 p. 113: © Greg English/CORBIS Sygma; **p. 114**: © John Barrett/Globe Photos, Inc.; **p. 116** (clockwise from upper left): AP/Wide World Photos; © Rudi Von Briel/PhotoEdit, Inc.; © Barbara Maurer/Stone/Getty Images; © Matt Henry/Stone/Getty Images; © Erin Moroney Labelle/The Image Works; © Art Vandalay/PhotoDisc/Getty Images; **p. 118**: AP/Wide World Photos; **p. 119**: © Tom Carter/PhotoEdit, Inc.; **p. 120**: © Jonathan Nourok/PhotoEdit, Inc.; **p. 122**: Photo Courtesy of Emily Mahon/Eastern Sociological Society; **p. 124**, left: Bettmann/CORBIS; **p. 124**, right: March of Dimes Birth Defects Foundation; **p. 125**: © Earl & Nazima Kowall/CORBIS; **p. 126**: © Reuters/David J. Phillip/Landov; **p. 127**: Jon Feingersh/Getty Images; **p. 129**: © Michael Wolf/Visum/CORBIS SABA; **p. 134**: © 1965 by Stanley Milgram. From the film *Obedience*, distributed by Pennsylvania State University, Audio Visual Services.

Chapter 6 p. 139: © Victor Englebert; **p. 140**: © Jim Henslin; **p. 142**: © Mark Mirko/The Palm Beach Post; **p. 143**: © Frans Lemmens/CORBIS Zefa Collection; **p. 145**: © Christian Poveda/CORBIS; **p. 146**: © Boris Kudriavov/R.P.G./Sygma/CORBIS; **p. 150**: © A. Ramey/PhotoEdit, Inc.; **p. 151**: © McClatchy-Tribune Information Services. All rights reserved. Reprinted with permission; **p. 152**: © Frank Franklin II/AP Wide World Photos; **p. 156**: Mark Richards/PhotoEdit, Inc.; **p. 159**: © Bettmann/CORBIS; **p. 163**: AP/Wide World Photos.

Chapter 7 p. 167: © Peter Menzel/www.menzelphoto.com; **p. 168**: CORBIS; **p. 170**: © Alain Morvan; **p. 171**: © C. S. I./Gamma Press; **p. 172**: © Jim Henslin; **p. 173**, left: Photo by Jacob Riis/© Bettmann/CORBIS; **p. 173**, right: © Bettmann/CORBIS; **p. 174**, left: CIACCIA/SIPA Press; **p. 174**, right: © Chip East/CORBIS/Reuters America LLC; **p. 176**: The

© Bernard Boutrit/Woodfin Camp & Associates; **p. 407:** © Rudi Von Briel/PhotoEdit, Inc.; **p. 409:** © Myrleen Ferguson/PhotoEdit, Inc.; **p. 410:** © Kirk Condyles/New York Times Agency; **p. 411:** © AFP/Getty Images.

Chapter 15 p. 415: NASA; **p. 416:** Roger-Viollet; **p. 417:** Hans Holbein the Younger, The French Ambassadors of King Henry II at the court of the English King Henry VIII. 1533. Oil on canvas. National Gallery, London, Great Britain. Photo © Erich Lessing/Art Resource, NY; **p. 418:** © Transit Leipzig/Sovfoto; **p. 421:** © Kevin Schafer/Stone/Getty Images; **p. 422,** left: © Keystone Features/Getty Images; **p. 422,** right: AP/Wide World Photos; **pp. 423, 424:** AP/Wide World Photos; **p. 427:** © Jim Henslin; **p. 429:** © Jose Traver/Gamma-Liaison/Getty Images; **p. 434:** © Claudine Laabs/Photo Researchers, Inc.; **p. 435:** © Reuters/Bruno Domingos/Landov.

FOLDOUT PHOTO CREDITS

1900: The New York Public Library/Art Resource; **Late 1900s:** Catherine Ledner/Stove/Getty Images; **2000:** (top) U. S. Bureau of the Census, (bottom) David Young-Wolff/Stone/Getty Images; **2006:** PunchStock